J. BURKE SEVERS

GENERAL EDITOR

A Manual of the Writings in Middle English

1050–1500

J. BURKE SEVERS

GENERAL EDITOR

A Manual of the Writings in Middle English

1050-1500

By Members of the Middle English Group of the
Modern Language Association
of America

Based upon
A Manual of the Writings in Middle English 1050–1400
by John Edwin Wells, New Haven, 1916,
and Supplements 1–9, 1919–1951

The Connecticut Academy of Arts and Sciences

New Haven, Connecticut

MDCCCCLXVII

Fascicule 1

I. ROMANCES

by

Mortimer J. Donovan Charles W. Dunn Lillian Herlands Hornstein
R. M. Lumiansky Helaine Newstead H. M. Smyser

PREFACE

This manual of Middle English literature is a collaborative project of the Middle English Group of the Modern Language Association of America. It is a rewriting and expansion of John Edwin Wells's *A Manual of the Writings in Middle English 1050–1400*, New Haven, 1916, and its nine supplements, 1919–51, which dealt with the scholarship and criticism through 1945. The present manual is an expansion in that it embraces the literature of the fifteenth century as well as the three and a half earlier centuries—all the writings of the period 1050–1500; it is an expansion also in that it deals with the scholarship and criticism down to the present. It is a rewriting in that the Commentary on the literature and on the scholarship and criticism is a fresh summary and evaluation, seeking to present proportionately and authoritatively the findings of scholars and critics to date.

The work falls into two parts. For each piece of literature there is a Commentary presenting briefly what is known of its manuscripts, date, dialect, source, form, extent, and content, plus a summary of scholarly and critical views concerning it. For each piece there is also a Bibliography listing its manuscripts and, analytically, the scholarly and critical studies of it. Each piece is given an identifying number to facilitate reference from the Commentary to the Bibliography.

The Bibliography is intended to be complete for all serious studies down through 1955 and to include all important studies from 1955 to the present (that is, date of going to press). All references in Wells and his nine supplements are repeated here, except erroneous, worthless, or irrelevant items. For instance, we have included only those reviews which are really critical or themselves make a significant contribution; we have excluded papers read at scholarly meetings but not thereafter published; and we have excluded research in progress and unpublished doctoral dissertations (with a few important exceptions). Also, since our manual is devoted to the writings in Middle English, we have found it necessary, in dealing with non-English medieval literature, to include only selected, most important items; but we have sought to include references which will put the student in full touch with the Latin and French literature, such as items containing bibliography and editions and studies of foreign sources significant for the relations of the sources to the Middle English works.

The Bibliography is analytical. That is, the references for any given piece of literature are arranged in topical divisions under such headings as MSS, Editions, Selections, Modernizations and Abstracts, Textual Matters, Language, Versification, Date, Authorship, Sources and Literary Relations, Other Scholarly Problems, Literary Criticism, General References, and Bibliography. The number and nature of the topical divisions for any given piece of literature will of course depend upon the fullness and variety of the scholarly and critical studies devoted to it. In each ultimate division, the items are arranged chronologically, except for occasional obvious departures for convenience. Usually each reference begins on a new line; occasionally a few related items are paragraphed together as a subdivision. General References and Bibliography are usually put together without heading at the end.

When it is completed, the manual, as has been said, will deal with all the writings in Middle English from 1050 to 1500. The present fascicule deals with the Romances. As the remaining sections of the work are completed, they will be published in separate fascicules, in the order in which the editors complete them. The chapter divisions of the work will follow approximately those in Wells's *Manual*, according to types, subject-matter, and authors. Fifteenth-century writing will be included in the chapters dealing with earlier pieces of the same type or subject-matter. Accordingly, fifteenth-century Romances which were not treated in Wells's *Manual* will be found in the present fascicule along with all the other Romances. But just as Rolle, Wyclyf, the *Pearl* poet, Gower, and Chaucer will be given separate treatment, with all their works being dealt with in one place, so separate treatment will be accorded the later authors, Lydgate, Hoccleve, Malory, Caxton, and the Middle Scots writers James I, Henryson, Dunbar, and Douglas. It is hoped that cross references and the Index will readily lead the user of the manual to the treatment of any work in which he is interested.

Though it is intended that the full, primary treatment of each piece of literature will occur in one chapter of the manual according to the principles outlined above, cross references will occur in other appropriate chapters, occasionally with secondary consideration of the piece as it is related to the other pieces in the chapter. Thus, though the Ballad will be dealt with in a later fascicule, certain ballad versions of the Romances are considered in this fascicule for their connection with the Romance materials; and though Caxton will be dealt with primarily in a later fascicule, his translation of the *Fierabras* is in this fascicule put into proper relation to the other Romances of the Firumbras Group; etc. The extent and fullness of such secondary treatment will of course in each instance depend upon each editor's judgment of its contribution to an adequate treatment of his section.

Appreciation for some of the basic work on fifteenth-century bibliography should be expressed to the late Professor Mary MacDonald Long. She for many years had been collecting cards for an extension of Wells's work; and when in 1955 the Middle English Group of the Modern Language Association undertook the project, she generously turned over all her files to the general editor, who in turn distributed their contents to the editors of the various chapters. Though her notes have had only slight relevance to the bibliography in the present fascicule, in varying degree they have formed a helpful nucleus for the work of a number of the editors on the project.

A volunteer searching committee headed and recruited by Kenneth G. Wilson was of some aid to some of the editors. My successive graduate assistants—Jasper J. Collura, Douglas A. Burger, and Peter G. Beidler— and my able secretary, Elizabeth J. Salay, were of considerable help in preparing the copy for the printer. My colleague, Professor Albert E. Hartung, assisted with the proofreading. I am indebted also to Lehigh University and to the Lehigh Institute of Research for released time and financial support which aided me in performing my editorial duties. Finally, the Middle English Group is deeply grateful to the Connecticut Academy of Arts and Sciences for undertaking the publication of this revised *Manual*, as it had undertaken the publication of the original.

February 16, 1966   J. Burke Severs
                                                     General Editor

CONTENTS

I. ROMANCES

GENERAL

by

Helaine Newstead

Because of the volume and diversity of Middle English romances, the genre is difficult to define, but the recent studies of D. Everett, G. Kane, and A. C. Baugh have clarified the essential characteristics. The medieval romance is a narrative about knightly prowess and adventure, in verse or in prose, intended primarily for the entertainment of a listening audience. Didactic elements, to be sure, appear in some romances, but they are subordinate to the aim of entertainment. Although the romancers draw upon an extremely broad range of subjects, the story is presented, even for bourgeois audiences, in terms of chivalric life, heightened and idealized according to the varying imaginative powers of the individual authors, whether pedestrian, crude, or genuinely sensitive to poetic values. The effort to idealize chivalry produces simplified characters, either heroes or villains, without psychological subtleties, and the happy ending is customary. Innocence is vindicated, virtue rewarded, and wickedness punished or cast out by repentance. The romancers stress the lavishness and splendor of feasts and other public ceremonies, often with a prolixity irritating to the modern reader, and describe in similar detail the paraphernalia of courtly life. Since the romances, like other kinds of medieval narrative, show little concern with historical accuracy in the modern sense, they regularly interpret ancient or exotic stories in terms of the contemporary and the familiar. Another marked characteristic is the conspicuous presence of the supernatural, once regarded as an indication of medieval naiveté but now recognized rather as a larger acceptance on the part of the medieval public of strange and unusual phenomena not explicable by reason or experience.

The English romances that have been preserved appear relatively late in the history of the genre, a few after the middle of the thirteenth century, the rest in the fourteenth and fifteenth centuries. Most of them are based upon French originals composed after the continental romances had begun to deteriorate in artistic quality if not in number. The Middle English romances adhere faithfully to their French models; many an English author seems to have worked with the French text before him. Others adapt more freely, or reproduce the sources from memory. Yet the conventional stylistic devices—the rime tags, the padding, the literary formulas—which Chaucer brilliantly parodies in *Sir Thopas*, owe much, as Baugh has shown, to the practice of oral recitation, when the author or the minstrel, reciting his text in public from memory, had no opportunity to revise what was once uttered and so had to improvise from a convenient stock of phrases. These stereotyped formulas were also used, according to Mrs. L. H. Loomis's study of the Auchinleck MS, by literary hacks who worked from written texts as translators and versifiers in manuscript shops. In general, the English romances are less sophisticated and less polished than the French, possibly in response to the audiences that they were intended to reach in fourteenth and fifteenth century England, and possibly because their authors were writers of modest literary abilities.

The English romances appear in a variety of forms. The four-stress couplet, an English adaptation of the French octosyllabic couplet, is common; and many romances are composed in tail-rime stanzas, either short or long, a meter with advantages for public recitation though not for smooth narration. An important group of romances, usually of West Midland, Northern, or Scottish origin, are written in alliterative meter—a four-beat line with at least three alliterating words—sometimes worked into elaborate stanzas combined with rime. Prose becomes a medium for romances after 1400.

The literary quality of the English romances varies as strikingly as the other features, and it is difficult to discern any consistent trend towards improvement or degeneration. The individual author always determines the result. The undistinguished and incompetent romances produced during the fifteenth century, for example, hardly suggest even the possibility of an achievement like Malory's masterpiece. Similarly, in any period *Sir Gawain and the Green Knight* would be a unique triumph, and its distinction can be explained only by the author's own genius. The English romances, in fact, illustrate not only the wide range of technical and artistic ability displayed by the miscellaneous authors, versifiers, or minstrels who contributed the extant texts, but also the diversity of literary taste to be expected in a span of three centuries marked by profound linguistic and social changes.

The Romances Listed According to Probable Chronology and Dialect of Original Composition

1225–1300

King Horn: ca. 1225, Southwestern or South Midland.

Floris and Blauncheflur: ca. 1250, Southeast Midland.

Arthour and Merlin: ca. 1250–1300, Kent.

Havelok: ca. 1280–1300, Northeast Midland.

Sir Tristrem: late 13th century, Southeast Midland? Northern?

Amis and Amiloun: near end of 13th century, East Midland.

Guy of Warwick: ca. 1300, Warwickshire.

Bevis of Hampton: ca. 1300, Southampton.

1300–1350

Richard Coer de Lyon: soon after 1300, mixed Midland of London area (Cambridgeshire? Kent?).

The Lyfe of Alisaunder: beginning of 14th century, London.

Lai le Freine: beginning of 14th century, Southeastern or possibly Westminster-Middlesex.

Sir Orfeo: beginning of 14th century, Southeastern or possibly Westminster-Middlesex.

Sir Isumbras: early 14th century, East Midland.

The King of Tars: early 14th century, London.

The Seege of Troye: ca. 1300–25, Northwest Midland.

Horn Child: ca. 1320, Yorkshire.

Sir Degare: before 1325, probably Southwest Midland.

Sir Perceval of Galles: ca. 1300–40, Northern.

Ywain and Gawain: ca. 1300–50, Northern.

Sir Landeval: ca. 1300–50, Southern.

Otuel a Knight: before 1330–40, East Midland.

Otuel and Roland: before 1330–40, East Midland.

Roland and Vernagu: before 1330–40, East Midland.

Libeaus Desconus: ca. 1325–50, Southern.

Sir Eglamour of Artois: ca. 1350, Northern or North Midland.

Joseph of Arimathie: ca. 1350, West or Southwest Midland.

Octavian: ca. 1350, two versions Northern and Southeastern.

1350–1400

The Alliterative Alexander Fragments A, B: ca. 1340–70, region of Gloucester-shire.

William of Palerne: ca. 1350–61, Southwest Midland.

Morte Arthure, alliterative: ca. 1360, Northwest Midland.

Gamelyn: ca. 1350–70, Northeast Midland.

Arthur: ca. 1350–1400, Southern.

Chevalere Assigne: ca. 1350–1400, East Midland.

Gest Historiale of the Destruction of Troy: ca. 1350–1400, Northwest Midland.

Athelston: ca. 1355–80, East Midland.

The Awntyrs off Arthure at the Terne Wathelyne: after 1375, Northern.

Apollonius of Tyre: ca. 1376–81, Southwest Midland.

The Fillingham Firumbras: ca. 1375–1400?, East Midland.

Sir Gawain and the Green Knight: ca. 1375–1400, Northwest Midland.

Titus and Vespasian, couplet version: 1375–1400, London or its environs.

The Ashmole Sir Firumbras: ca. 1380, Southwestern.

Chaucer's tales.

Gower's tales.

Siege of Jerusalem, alliterative version, originally quatrains: 1390–1400, Northwest Midland.

Le Bone Florence of Rome: late 14th century, North Midland.

Sir Cleges: late 14th century, North Midland.

Ipomadon, tail rime: late 14th century, North Midland-Lancashire.

Sir Degrevant: late 14th century, North or Northeast Midland.

Sir Triamour: late 14th century, North or Northeast Midland.

Sir Amadace: late 14th century, Northwest Midland.

Generides: late 14th century, Midland.

The Knight of Curtesy and the Fair Lady of Faguell: late 14th century, London or its southern environs.

Roberd of Cisyle: late 14th century, Southeast Midland.

Sir Launfal: later 14th century, Southeastern.

The Sege of Melayne: ca. 1400 or somewhat earlier, Northern.

Duke Roland and Sir Otuel of Spain: ca. 1400 or somewhat earlier, Northern.

Emare: ca. 1400, Northeastern.

Sir Gowther: ca. 1400, Northeast Midland.

The Earl of Toulous: ca. 1400, Northeast Midland.

Le Morte Arthur, stanzaic: ca. 1400, Northwest Midland.

The Sowdon of Babylon: ca. 1400, East Midland.

The Song of Roland: ca. 1400, East Midland.

The Laud Troy-Book: ca. 1400, East Midland.

Sir Torrent of Portyngale: ca. 1400, East Midland.

Syre Gawene and the Carle of Carelyle: ca. 1400, near Shropshire.

1400–1500

Lydgate's *Troy-Book:* 1410.

Lydgate's *Siege of Thebes:* 1420–22.

Lovelich's *History of the Holy Grail:* ca. 1420, Southern or South Midland.

The Lyfe of Ipomydon, couplets: before 1425, East Midland.

Lovelich's *Merlin:* ca. 1425, Southern or South Midland.

The Avowynge of King Arthur: ca. 1425, Northern.

King Ponthus: ca. 1400–50, London?

The Prose Alexander: 1400–50, Northern.

The Prose Siege of Troy: 1425–50, Southern.

The Alexander Buik: 1438, Scottish.

Amoryus and Cleopes: 1448–49, Norfolk.

The Alliterative Alexander Fragment C: ca. 1450, Northumbrian.

Eger and Grime: ca. 1450, Northern.

The Prose Siege of Thebes: ca. 1450, Southern.

The Weddynge of Sir Gawen and Dame Ragnell: ca. 1450, East Midland.

The Prose Merlin: ca. 1450.

Ipomedon, prose: ca. 1460, mixed dialect.

Malory's *The Book of Arthur and His Knights* (*Le Morte Darthur*): 1469–70, North Midland.

The Jeaste of Syr Gawayne: ca. 1450–1500, Southern or South Midland.

The Taill of Rauf Coilyear: ca. 1465–1500, Scottish.

Caxton's *The Recuyell of the Historyes of Troye:* 1469–76?, London.

Caxton's *History of Jason:* 1476–78, London.

Caxton's *Godefroy of Boloyne:* 1481, London.

Caxton's *Charles the Grete:* 1485, London.

Caxton's *Paris and Vienne:* 1485, London.

Caxton's *Blanchardyn and Eglantine:* 1489–91, London.

Caxton's *The Foure Sonnes of Aymon:* 1489–91, London.

Caxton's *Eneydos:* 1490, London.

The Cambridge Alexander-Cassamus Fragment: 15th century.

Partonope of Blois, couplet version: 15th century, Southern.

Gilbert Hay's *Buik of King Alexander:* 15th century, Scottish.

Lancelot of the Laik: late 15th century, Scottish.

Roswall and Lillian: late 15th century, Scottish.

The Dublin Alexander Epitome: late 15th century.

Golagrus and Gawain: not long before 1500, Scottish.

The Grene Knight: ca. 1500, South Midland.

The Turke and Gowin: ca. 1500, North or Northwest Midland.

The Squyr of Lowe Degre: ca. 1500, East Midland.

Melusine: ca. 1500.

The Romauns of Partenay: ca. 1500, Northeast Midland.

The Three Kings' Sons: ca. 1500.

Two Scottish Troy Fragments: probably 15th century, Scottish.

After 1500

Clariodus: 16th or 15th century, Scottish.

Valentine and Orson: ca. 1502.

R. Copland's *Helyas, Knight of the Swan:* 1504.

De Worde's edition of the prose *Lyfe of Joseph:* 1511?

Pynson's edition of *De Sancto Joseph:* 1516.

Pynson's edition of *Here Begynneth the Lyfe of Joseph:* 1520.

Pynson's edition of *A Praysing to Joseph:* 1520.

De Worde's edition of the prose *William of Palerne* (frag): 1520–29.

The Carle off Carlile: ca. 1500–50, Lancashire.

Lord Berners' *The Boke of Duke Huon of Burdeux:* ca. 1530.

Lord Berners' *Arthur of Little Britain:* before 1533.

1. ROMANCES DERIVED FROM ENGLISH LEGENDS

by

Charles W. Dunn

The Celtic Arthur, the Continental Charlemagne, and other alien figures tend to usurp the place of native English heroes in the literature composed in England after the Norman Conquest. Some indigenous folktales and legends, however, were recorded in Latin chronicles for the sake of scholars or were transformed into Anglo-Norman romances for the entertainment of courtiers and into Middle English romances for the common people. Generally, these English romances seem to have been derived from Anglo-Norman models, but their ultimate sources may very well have been current in some form in pre-Norman England.

The earliest extant romance of this type is *King Horn*, ca. 1225, which is preceded by an Anglo-Norman romance dated ca. 1170–80; and the substance of *Havelok*, ca. 1280–1300, is recorded earlier by an Anglo-Norman chronicler ca. 1135–40. The English *Bevis of Hampton* and *Guy of Warwick* were translated ca. 1300 from Anglo-Norman romances which had been composed at an earlier period, ca. 1200 and ca. 1232–42, probably in order to embellish local family traditions.

The later romances *Gamelyn*, ca. 1350–70, and *Athelston*, ca. 1355–80, have no Anglo-Norman counterparts. The first is an English tale of outlawry which seems to have been adapted from a universal folktale at an undeterminable period; the second, though set in pre-Norman England, is a pseudo-historical romance.

William of Palerne, a translation of a French romance, is included in the present section only for editorial convenience. It used to be described as Germanic in origin, but its subject is neither specifically English nor generally Germanic. *Richard Coer de Lyon*, on the other hand, which is dealt with later under Romances on Historical Themes, might appro-

priately have been included here except for the fact that its hero belongs
to the post-Conquest period.

Many romances derived from English legends have been lost. The author
of the *Laud Troy Book* (ca. 1400) mentions a long list of heroes whose
tales are recited at banquets and whose deeds are recalled "in many a
fair romance." Among these are Bevis, Guy, Havelok, Horn, and Wade.
Yet nothing concerning Wade, a continental Germanic leader, has survived in Middle English except for casual allusions of this sort. The lost
English tale of Waldef survives in an Anglo-Norman translation, and the
lost tale of Hereward survives in a Latin translation. But the medieval
English minstrel undoubtedly possessed a much larger repertoire of native
romances than the entire inventory of known examples or reconstructed
survivals would suggest.

The story of Horn appears in a group of four loosely related versions:
the Anglo-Norman romance of *Horn et Rimenild*, composed by Mestre
Thomas ca. 1170–80; the Middle English *King Horn*, composed ca. 1225;
Horn Child, composed ca. 1320; and the *Ballad of Hind Horn*, which may
have been introduced into folk tradition as early as the fourteenth century.
Scholars used to posit a number of lost intermediaries connecting the four,
but the present tendency is to view each as an adaptation of its immediate
predecessor.

The Horn story was also revived when ca. 1390 the Anglo-Norman
Horn et Rimenild was transformed into the French prose romance *Ponthus
et la belle Sidoine*. This romance was in turn translated into the Middle
English prose *King Ponthus* ca. 1400–50 and was disseminated in other
European vernaculars.

KING HORN [1]. Extant manuscripts, differing in minor particulars, may be derived from a Middle English original composed ca.
1225, probably in Southwestern or South Midland dialect. The Cambridge University MS contains 1530 lines; Bodleian (Laud), 1569 lines;
and Harley, 1546 lines. The pattern of the meter has been much debated; many lines resemble Old English half-lines but lack systematic
alliteration; stresses vary between two, three, and four beats; but the
rime scheme seems to be modeled upon the octosyllabic couplet popular
in Anglo-Norman romances.

(Harley MS.) Horn's father Allof, king of the island of Sudene (stress on second syllable), is killed by Saracen pirates. Fearing Horn's vengeance, they set the boy adrift with his young companions, including the faithful Athulf and the wicked Fikenild. They land in Westnesse and are received by King Aylmer. Rymenild, the king's daughter, falls in love with Horn and persuades her father to knight him. Horn undertakes to prove his worth before he will marry her and soon distinguishes himself by killing a band of Saracen pirates. Rymenild dreams that a fish has broken her net; Horn correctly predicts that some ill-wisher will destroy their happiness. Fikenild tells the king that Horn has seduced Rymenild and intends to destroy the king. The latter believes the libel when he discovers Horn in the arms of his daughter, and he therefore exiles him. Horn sets sail and reaches Ireland.

Adopting the name of Godmod, he serves as a knight under King Thurston. He avenges his own father's death by killing an invading giant, whom he discovers to be the same Saracen who had killed Allof in Sudene. He remains in Thurston's court for seven years but does not accept the daughter whom the king offers to him in marriage.

Rymenild is promised to King Mody of Reynis and therefore sends a messenger to find Horn. The messenger delivers the news but is drowned before he can bring her the information that Horn will return. Horn lands in Westnesse with a bodyguard, disguises himself as a beggar, and forces his way into the castle. He makes himself known to Rymenild by making puns about the drinking horn, by alluding to a fishing net which has been set for seven years, and by dropping into her goblet a ring which she had given him. He slays Mody, denounces Fikenild's treachery, and then sets off with Athulf to regain Sudene. He reaches the island in five days, regains his heritage, and restores his mother. Meanwhile, Fikenild builds a castle and attempts to force Rymenild into marrying him. Horn, recalled by a warning dream, gains entry into the castle disguised as a harper and slays Fikenild. Horn appoints Arnoldyn (cousin of the faithful Athulf) to succeed Aylmer as King of Westnesse; he makes Rymenild's trusty steward King of Reynis in place of Mody; and he gives Athulf in marriage to King Thurston's daughter in Ireland. He and Rymenild reign in Sudene.

The plot of *King Horn* closely follows that of Mestre Thomas' Anglo-Norman romance *Horn et Rimenild* (composed ca. 1170–80 in 5250 alexandrines rimed in tirades). No source common to the two works has been discovered. Though the setting, like that of *Havelok*, seems to reflect the period of Viking raids in Britain, attempts to identify Horn with some specific figure such as the Danish leader Horm (who settled in Ireland in 851) have found little support. Unlike Gaimar and the author of the Middle English *Havelok*, Thomas and the author of *King Horn* are not concerned with historical and geographical details. The name Reynis (also appearing as Reynes and Reny) in the English romance has been interpreted as equivalent to Rennes, and on this slight basis a Breton or common Celtic origin for the story has been proposed; but Reynis might as well be Rheims, and even more probably it represents an English redactor's misinterpretation of the name Fenenie which appears in the Anglo-Norman *Horn*.

The prologue to the twelfth-century Anglo-Norman romance *Waldef* (unpublished) refers to a romance of "Aelof the good king" as being much loved in England. This may be the Aalof referred to as Horn's father in Thomas's *Horn* and in *King Horn* (Harley MS only, lines 4, 33, 73; otherwise named Murry, lines 873, 1345, and in other manuscripts). The romance of Aelof has not survived, however, and, even if it had, its contents would probably not provide conclusive information as to the ultimate source, the date of origin, or the provenance of the existing Horn stories. Basically, the plot of *Horn* is very similar to that of *Bevis of Hampton* and other expulsion-and-return tales of the Apollonius type. Consequently M. K. Pope's argument that the germ of the romance was a simple English love story or folktale seems more convincing than the more specific identifications suggested earlier by Deutschbein and others.

Whatever its source, *King Horn* is artistically most successful. The well-knit plot is managed with an exemplary economy seldom displayed by English romances. The love story possesses a rare charm. The anxious dreams of Rymenild and of Horn are psychologically convincing and dramatically apt. The primitive and intuitive sense of psychology which pervades the romance may not be the subtle brand developed by Chrétien de Troyes, but it matches the comparable achievement of the Norse sagas and foreshadows the best tradition of the English ballads.

HORN CHILD [2] is composed in twelve-line tail-rime stanzas, $a^4a^4b^3$ $a^4a^4b^3$ $c^4c^4b^3$ $d^4d^4b^3$, with many irregularities. The unique manuscript (Advocates, ca. 1330), containing 1136 lines, lacks a leaf after line 783 (probably consisting of four 44-line columns) and breaks off in the midst of a stanza at a point obviously near the end of the poem. This revision of the King Horn story was composed ca. 1320, evidently by someone well acquainted with Yorkshire; the dialect has been affected by redactors who prepared the Advocates MS in a London bookshop.

Horn Child is the son of Hatheolf, who rules all England north of the Humber. Among his eight comrades are the trustworthy Arlaund, Wiard, and Hatherof, and the false Wikard and Wikel. When Horn's father is slain by Irish invaders led by King Malkan, Arlaund brings the boy to the protection of King Houlac in the south of England. Houlac's daughter Rimnild falls in love with him. Wikard and Wikel accuse Horn before the king of seducing Rimnild. The king beats his daughter; she persuades Horn to flee, promises to wait for him for seven years, and gives him a ring to serve as a token of her fidelity.

Horn, taking the name of Godebounde, serves the King of Snowdon in Wales and King Finlak of Youghal in Ireland. (Hiatus in the manuscript.) He kills Finlak's adversary King Malkan and thus avenges his own father's death. Finlak's daughter falls in love with Horn, but he returns to England, recalled by Rimnild's magic ring, just as his lady-love is about to be given in marriage to an unwanted suitor named Moging. Attending the banquet disguised as a beggar, Horn reveals himself to her by putting her ring in the goblet with which she serves him. Hatherof describes the heraldic devices which Horn's enemies are to wear in tournament, and Horn is thus able to identify and overthrow his rival, to kill the treacherous Wikard, and to blind Wikel. He marries Rimnild and returns to conquer his own land in the north. (Conclusion missing in the manuscript.)

The romance seems to be the product of an unsuccessful attempt to revitalize some earlier version of *King Horn*. The reference to "Staynes More" (line 175) has been interpreted as an indication that the romance arose from traditions connected with the battle of Stainmoor (954 A.D.), but this is merely one of a group of Yorkshire place-names which the romancer introduces for the sake of realism. In referring to Horn's kingdom north of the Humber, he mentions not only the more obvious names Humberside, Northhumberland, Westmorland, and York, but also the less familiar: Allerton Moor in the West Riding of Yorkshire, and Blakey (earlier Blakehou) Moor, Cleveland, Pickering, "Seyn Sibeles Kirke" (apparently near Cleveland; unidentified), Stainmore, and Tees-side in the North Riding.

Horn Child when complete must have been approximately the same length as *King Horn*, but artistically it is much less effective. Incidents of battle are disproportionately numerous; Rimnild's forthright love for Horn is insensitively protrayed; the motif of the lovers' dreams is misunderstood; and the versification represents the tail-rime at its worst, as Chaucer realized when he referred to *Horn Child* in his parody of *Sir Thopas*.

BALLAD OF HIND HORN [3]. The Horn material passed at an unknown date into ballad form. The earliest of the nine versions published by Child was only recorded at the beginning of the nineteenth century, but the age of the folk tradition may well reach back to the fourteenth century. Versions published by Child and others differ from one another; but all, in characteristic ballad style, have reduced the original narrative to a dramatic minimum. Horn returns (after seven years) to his lady-love, reveals his identity by producing her ring, and claims her as his bride. Because of a slight preponderance of resemblances, *Horn Child* rather than

King Horn is thought to have provided the source for the ballad. That the ballad is still current in the folk repertoire is a tribute to the universal charm inherent in the original plot. See also under Ballads.

KING PONTHUS [4]. The Anglo-Norman *Horn et Rimenild* (ca. 1170–80) was transformed into a pedagogic romance, *Ponthus et la belle Sidoine*, composed in French prose ca. 1390 by an unidentified author living in Brittany. He was probably Geoffrey IV de La Tour Landry (not, as used to be assumed, Ponthus de La Tour Landry). This new romance was in turn translated into English prose ca. 1400–50 at least once or possibly twice; the manuscript version differs considerably in phraseology from the version printed by de Worde.

The French adaptation was designed to exemplify the rules of behavior proper to a gentleman. The plot follows that of *Horn et Rimenild* closely, with a few additions borrowed from Chrétien de Troyes and other romancers; but the setting is entirely changed, the tone is sententious, and the primitive power of the original has disappeared. Ponthus (Horn) belongs to Galicia, and Sidoine (Rimenild) to Brittany, and England is the scene of the hero's foreign exile.

In this form the Horn story (see p. 18 above) reached an international audience otherwise denied to it. Eleanor of Tyrol, daughter of James I of Scotland, translated the French *Ponthus* into German ca. 1448; a Dutch version was printed in 1601; and the material was adapted in the Icelandic *Pontus-rimur* in the sixteenth century.

HAVELOK [5]. The Middle English romance, composed ca. 1280–1300, complete in the Bodleian MS except for lines 1445–1624, contains 3001 lines in four-stress couplets. Cambridge University fragments supply variants of lines 174–83, 341–64, and 537–49, and eleven additional lines not in Bodleian. The language of the original Middle English romance probably was the dialect of Lincolnshire (Northeast Midland), which scribes of the extant manuscripts have altered.

When King Ethelwold of England dies, he leaves his daughter Goldborough as ward of Godrich, Earl of Cornwall. At the same time King Birkabeyn of Denmark leaves his son Havelok as ward of Earl Godard. Godard, wishing to seize the throne of Denmark, gives Havelok over to a fisherman named Grim to be killed. When Grim sees a miraculous light issuing from Havelok's mouth and a royal mark on his shoulder, he realizes that the child is destined to become king and therefore flees with him to England.

Grim and his family settle at the mouth of the Humber and thus found Grimsby. Havelok grows exceptionally strong and becomes a scullion in Godrich's castle at Lincoln. Godrich, who had promised Goldborough's father that he would give her in marriage to the strongest man in the kingdom, attempts to remove her claim to the throne by marrying her to the scullion. The couple go to Grim's house to live. Goldborough sees Havelok's light and mark; an angel assures her of her husband's royalty; and Havelok dreams that he will become a great king.

Grim escorts Havelok and Goldborough back to Denmark, where Earl Ubbe also perceives Havelok's light and mark and therefore dubs him knight. Havelok defeats Godard, becomes King of Denmark, returns to England, defeats Godrich, and becomes King of England.

A very similar story is incorporated by Gaimar in his Anglo-Norman *Estoire des Engles* (written in octosyllabic couplets ca. 1135–40; lines 47–818). According to his version, Argentille, daughter of the Danish King Adelbrit of Norfolk, is forced into marriage with Haveloc, son of King Gunter of Denmark, by her evil uncle Edelsie, the Danish King of Lincoln and Lindsey; Haveloc defeats Edelsie and reigns as king for twenty years. Gaimar presents Haveloc as a local, interim ruler of the disorderly period ca. 500 A.D. following the defeat of Arthur. Presumably he learned the legend in Lincolnshire when his patroness's husband went north to serve the Earl of Lincoln, was unable to ascertain its chronological basis, but decided to insert it in his work because of its possible historical value.

An anonymous poet ca. 1200 turned Gaimar's legend into a *Lai d'Haveloc* (Anglo-Norman, 1106 lines, octosyllabic couplets), written in imitation of Marie de France's Breton lays.

Attempts have been made to find the origin of the Havelok story in the career of Anlaf Cuaran Sihtricson, who became the Danish King of York in 941. His Irish identifying name Cuaran ("sandal") is an alternate name given to Haveloc by Gaimar. (The author of the *Lai* invents an explanation for Haveloc's extraneous name by claiming that in Breton it means "scullion"; the Middle English romancer omits it altogether.) Anlaf's first name has been equated with the name Havelok on the grounds that the Welsh chronicles render the English name Anlaf (Norse Olaf) by a native Welsh name Abloyc. The three names, Havelok, Anlaf, and Abloyc, have, however, no etymological connection with one another, so that the transformation of Anlaf into Havelok could only have arisen from an inexact folk-etymology.

The apparent historicity of the setting of the Middle English romance is equally inconclusive. It is true that Danes settled in Lincolnshire, that the Scandinavian place-name Grimsby means "Grim's settlement," and also that the Danish Canute became, like Havelok, king of both Denmark (1017) and England (1019). But the romancer is merely a successful fabricator and is entirely indifferent to consistency. Birkabeyn, Havelok's father (Gunter in Gaimar), has a Norse name (meaning "wearer of birch-bark leggings"), but its only historical connection is with Sverre Birkibeinn who was proclaimed King of Norway by outlaws in 1184. Thus most scholars now argue that the Havelok story is basically a folktale variant of the wide-spread expulsion-and-return formula and that any historical features in Gaimar's version, the *Lai*, or the romance are later additions rather than survivals of a genuine historic tradition.

As with *Bevis of Hampton* and *Guy of Warwick*, local traditions have sustained the popularity of the Havelok story. The official town-seal of the fishing-port of Grimsby (dated ca. 1272–1307) shows three figures labeled Gryem, Habloc, and Goldeburgh; and folk tradition even now attributes the town's foundation to Grim the fisherman. Chroniclers accepted and amplified the story. Langtoft alludes to Havelok (whom he places in the reign of Alfred). Robert Manning apparently did not know of Gaimar's account or of the *Lai*, but he remarks in his *Story of England* (1338) that the common people still tell in English how Havelok won the land; and a later anonymous interpolator in the Lambeth MS of Manning's *Story* provides an 82-line summary of the plot. Raouf de Boun's *Petit Brut* (1310, unpublished), the anonymous *Brut* and its Middle English translation, Grey's *Scala chronica* (1335), and the *Eulogium historiarum* (ca. 1400) all recount some form of the legend, and Knighton cites Havelok's kingship as a precedent for Canute's.

In contradistinction to its antiquarian interest, the literary appeal of the romance was evidently limited. No Continental adaptations were made, as with the less plebeian romances such as *Bevis*, and no black-letter prints or prose redactions appeared in England after the introduction of printing. Unlike Gaimar and the author of the *Lai*, the English romancer aimed not at a courtly or learned audience but at the common people. Havelok is a folk-hero in the most literal sense. Though Horn, with whom he is often compared, may disguise himself as a beggar, Havelok does not masquerade when he serves as a scullion; and the romancer portrays his hero's experiences with the gusto of one who himself relishes life in the kitchen and the fish-market. Consequently, whatever its social limitations, Havelok remains one of the freshest, most timeless, and most appealing of the early Middle English romances.

BEVIS OF HAMPTON [6]. Translated from an Anglo-Norman romance ca. 1300, probably in the dialect of Southampton. The earliest extant Middle English version (Auchinleck), ca. 1330, consists of lines 1–474, in tail-rime stanzas generally riming $a^4a^4b^2c^4c^4b^2$, and lines 475–4620, in octosyllabic couplets. Two variants (Egerton and Naples) have revised the meter; two others (Chetham and Pynson) have eliminated short lines. All extant versions vary freely in wording and even in incidents.

Late in life, Guy, Earl of Southampton, marries the King of Scotland's evil daughter. Bevis is born to them. His mother's lover, Devoun of Germany, slays Guy; but Saber, a faithful steward, protects the child. Bevis is taken from England by pirates and given to the Saracen King of Armenia. Josian, the king's daughter, falls in love with Bevis and promises for his sake to become Christian. She presents him with an invaluable war-horse named Arundel. Bevis is imprisoned on a false charge of having seduced her. Josian is forced into marriage with King Yvor of Mombrant but preserves her virginity by a charm.

After seven years Bevis escapes from prison. Disguised as a palmer, he rescues Josian from the King of Mombrant and subdues the giant Ascopart to his service. Bevis, Josian, and Ascopart flee as far as Cologne. Josian is baptized; Bevis frees the city from a dragon. Bevis hastens back to England, landing at the Isle of Wight, to assist the faithful Saber against Devoun, who has usurped the title of Earl of Southampton; but he has to return to Cologne to rescue Josian because she has killed a knight who had forced her into marriage. Bevis then returns with Josian and Ascopart to Wight. Here, with the help of Saber, he avenges his father's death by destroying Devoun. His evil mother dies. He is recognized as the legitimate successor to Southampton, marries Josian, and builds Arundel Castle.

When his horse Arundel kills the son of King Edgar of England, Bevis must once more leave his native country. On the way to the land of Mombrant, while Bevis is absent, Josian gives birth to twin sons, and Ascopart treacherously abducts her. Saber rescues her and kills Ascopart. Then for seven years Saber and Josian, disguised as palmers, wander in search of Bevis. When the family is reunited, one of the twin sons, Guy, becomes King of Armenia. Bevis kills Yvor and himself becomes King of Mombrant. For the last time Bevis returns to England, on this occasion to support Saber's son against the usurpation of King Edgar. Miles, Bevis's other twin son, becomes heir to the throne of England by marriage with Edgar's daughter, and Saber is appointed Earl of Southampton. Bevis retires to Mombrant, where he and Josian die in sanctity.

The plot of the Anglo-Norman original (and hence of the Middle English romance) is unhistorical. There is no apparent connection between the

Edgar of the romance and the English King Edgar (who ruled 944–75); nor is there any evidence of the existence of a pre-Conquest ruler of Hampton (i. e., Southampton, Old English Hammtun) such as Bevis. Perhaps it was manufactured to supply a tradition complimentary to William Earl of Sussex (1154–76), who was granted the honor of Arundel.

Scholars used to maintain that Bevis must have been originally a Continental rather than an English hero and that his story had been adapted from a legend associated perhaps with Hamlet or some other European or even Oriental prototype. The central theme of the romance, however, is the familiar one of a princess's love for an exiled hero. Well known examples such as the story of Apollonius (see [95] below) or Chrétien de Troyes's *Cligès* could have supplied ideas for the plot to an Anglo-Norman romancer intent upon glorifying the past of Southampton and Arundel, and tales of the Crusaders could have suggested the background for the hero's far-flung travels.

The proliferation of the romance can be explained in the following sequences. From various versions, the original Anglo-Norman romance of ca. 1200 was converted into a Continental French romance at the beginning of the thirteenth century, was translated ca. 1250–75 into Welsh prose, was turned into the lost original of the surviving Middle English variants of the romance ca. 1300, and was translated into Norse prose in the fourteenth century. Some version of the Middle English romance was turned into Irish prose of the fifteenth century.

The Continental French romance meanwhile traveled independently. It was turned into French prose in the fifteenth century, into a Dutch prose version printed in 1502, and into a series of Italian versions, including one composed in verse of the thirteenth century and a later one in prose appearing in *I reali de Francia* (1491). A Yiddish poetic version, derived from Italian and frequently reprinted, was composed in 1501, and this eventually served as the source for a Rumanian translation (1881); and a Russian version of the Italian appeared at least as early as the sixteenth century.

The Anglo-Norman romancer shows his familiarity with the English setting. The hero bears a name (Boefs or Boves) actually used by Anglo-Normans; Haumtone (Southampton) was in fact a strategic center; Arundel was already famous in the twelfth century for its castle. The Middle English romancer adapted his source more fully to an English audience by the introduction of new inventions, amounting in all to some 850 lines. A passage of some 300 new lines is devoted to Bevis's fight with the dragon of Cologne, which was greater, we are told, than any contest waged by Lancelot, Guy of Warwick, or Wade. Bevis, who invokes St. George, is obviously intended to rival his patron as a dragon-slayer. Another new scene of some 250 lines vividly depicts Bevis's struggle against the Londoners. The local place-names (including Bow, Cheapside, Leadenhall, London Gate, London Stone, Tower Street, Westminster, the Thames, and Putney) are introduced accurately and effectively. The adaptation has also in general inflated the style of the original and enlarged the element of fantasy.

English folk tradition willingly accepted and amplified the contents of the English romance. Figures of Bevis and Ascopart used to be displayed on the Bar Gate at Southampton, and the town's Arundel Gate still recalls the romance by its name. In Robert Manning's *Story of England* (1338) Bevis of Hamptone is anachronistically introduced as the name of an Arthurian knight. And, from the time of the introduction of printing, popular audiences consistently demanded copies of the romance either in verse or in prose, until in the nineteenth century the story sank to the level of a children's tale.

Though by modern standards unduly protracted, the romance retains the vigor, movement, and occasional humor of its source. Its richness of incident is unmatched by the earlier and more restrained native English romances such as *King Horn*. Love plays an interesting, even if unsophisticated, role. The chastity and fidelity of the hero and the heroine are recurrently tested and dramatically vindicated. The romancer's concept of heroism is attractively colored by the popular idea of the Crusader. Bevis is a pious Christian champion and a dauntless wayfarer; Josian is a fit heroine because she desires to be baptized; the infidels are all automatically villainous. Thus the romance offered its English readers and listeners an account of the birth, life, and death of a fictitious hero whose actuality the credulous could accept and whose excellence even the incredulous could admire.

GUY OF WARWICK [7]. The Middle English versions of *Guy of Warwick* are ultimately derived from an Anglo-Norman romance composed ca. 1232–42. An early translation (probably in octosyllabic couplets like the original) may have been made ca. 1300 in Warwickshire. Later surviving variants differ in date, in completeness, in wording, and in meter. The earliest extant version (Advocates, ca. 1330, beginning and conclusion missing—also called the Auchinleck MS) was probably produced in a London bookshop by redactors of differing dialects; the materials have been rearranged as three separate romances—I. Guy before marriage, II. Guy after marriage, and III. Guy's son Reinbrun.

The first section of the Advocates tripartite version consists of lines 1–6898 (equivalent to the published Anglo-Norman version lines 96–7408) composed in octosyllabic couplets. The second section consists of lines 6899–10479 (equivalent to the Anglo-Norman lines 7409–11656) written in 299 twelve-line stanzas, riming generally $a^4a^4b^3a^4a^4b^3c^4c^4b^3d^4d^4b^3$. The third section consists of lines 10480–12000 (equivalent to the Anglo-Norman lines 11657–12888) written in 127 stanzas like those in the second section and is supplied with a separate title. Although the change of meter between the first and second sections may have been deliberately introduced to distinguish one from the other, it is similar to the abrupt change which occurs in the midst of the Advocates version of *Bevis of Hampton* (see [6] above).

All other surviving versions are written entirely in couplets. Caius, which contains a consecutive rendering of only the first two parts, runs to approximately 11,000 lines. Sloane, a fragment, contains only 216 lines. Both of these manuscripts, though later in date than Advocates, preserve the language of about the same date as Advocates. The Cambridge University MS preserves a revised version written ca. 1425–75, containing 11,976 lines (equivalent to the entire Anglo-Norman romance, lines 1–12926).

The British Museum Additional MS contains a fragment (ca. 1325–50) of some 500 lines apparently related to the prints published by Pynson (ca. 1500), de Worde (ca. 1500), and Copland (ca. 1560, complete in 7976 lines).

The precise relationship of the different Middle English versions has not been conclusively established, but they all retain the substance of the Anglo-Norman original, and none contains independent inventions such as are found in the Middle English *Bevis of Hampton*.

(Advocates I. Guy before marriage.) Rohaut, the Earl of Warwick, Oxford, and Buckingham, has a daughter Felice, whom Guy, son of Syward of Wallingford, loves. Since she scorns him, he journeys overseas to gain her favor by winning fame in tournaments. His success attracts the love of a French princess, but Guy returns to Felice, who sends him abroad again for further testing. He distinguishes himself in battle, first before the Emperor of Germany and then before the Emperor of Constantinople. The latter attempts to reward him by offering him his own daughter in marriage, but Guy still remembers Felice. He befriends Tirri of Gormoise (Worms), helping him to recover a lost lady-love. After seven years of adventures, he returns to England, slays a dragon in Northumberland, and marries Felice.

(Advocates II. Guy after marriage.) After fifty (erroneous manuscript reading "fifteen" later corrected) days of married life, Guy leaves his wife, who is now pregnant, and sets out on a pilgrimage in order to atone for his earlier life of fighting. In Alexandria he saves a friend by killing the giant Amoraunt. He again aids his friend Tirri, this time rescuing him from false accusations by championing him in a duel. He returns to England, disguised as a palmer, and saves King Athelstan from King Anlaf and his invading Danes by defeating their champion, the African giant Colbrond. On his death-bed, Guy reveals his identity to Felice by sending her a ring; she buries him in his hermitage and joins him in death soon afterwards. Tirri translates Guy's remains to an abbey in Lorraine.

(Advocates III, Guy's son Reinbrun.) Reinbrun, who is born after his father's renunciation of married life, is stolen from Wallingford by pirates at the age of seven. He is reared by the daughter of King Argus of Africa. Heraud, Guy's faithful steward, searches for Reinbrun and eventually finds him, after unwittingly duelling with him. The two set out for England. Reinbrun frees Amis, a knight who had been imprisoned for aiding Guy. Reinbrun unwittingly duels with Heraud's son, who has also been searching for the missing heir. Reinbrun, Heraud, and Heraud's son reach home safely.

The historical basis for the Anglo-Norman original seems to be very slight. The romance, apparently inspired by the same kind of antiquarianism underlying *Bevis of Hampton*, may have been composed by a poet connected with the Augustinian abbey of Osney in order to provide the houses of Warwick and Wallingford with an heroic ancestor. The name of the hero, Guy (from Wig?), was perhaps chosen because of the fame of Wigod of Wallingford, a cupbearer of Edward the Confessor.

The main details of the plot concerning a dragon-slaying, giant-killing knight who travels in the steps of the Crusaders and ignores the advances of infidel maidens is strikingly reminiscent of the Anglo-Norman *Bevis of Hampton*. Guy's conversion to the life of a hermit may ultimately be derived from the French pietistic legends attached to St. Alexis and to Guillaume d'Orange. Guy's fight with Colbrond may have been adapted from some English tradition of the Viking invasions, though no similar historical encounter occurred at Winchester, where the romancer places the event.

From the time that the Anglo-Norman romance was first turned into Middle English ca. 1300 until the nineteenth century, the story of Guy of Warwick has continued to appeal to English audiences even more strongly than that of Bevis of Hampton, although its success on the Continent has been much more limited. An English version was transformed into an Irish prose romance in the fifteenth century, and the English story also provided the chief source of the popular Catalan romance *Tirant lo Blanch* (Valencia 1490), which was in turn translated into Castilian, Italian, and French. Meanwhile, the Anglo-Norman romance circulated in France and was converted ca. 1450 into a French prose romance, which was published in printed form at least as early as 1525.

An English or French version of the episodes concerning the friendship of Guy and Tirri was introduced into the Latin *Gesta Romanorum* (chap. 172), and this chapter was translated into German prose as *Gydo und Thyrus* in the fifteenth century and was transformed into a French mystère by Louvet (Paris 1537).

In England the material of the romance was disseminated in a variety of ways. A separate stanzaic poem on GUY AND COLBROND [8] which survives in the Percy Folio MS (ca. 1600) may represent a late survival of the lost *Lay of Colbrond* (*Canticum Colbrondi*) referred to in a Winchester record of 1338; the episode of Guy's single combat has been abstracted from the romance. The Guy tradition also gave rise indirectly to the *Speculum Guy* (see under Homilies).

A certain Gerard of Cornwall at an unknown date wrote in Latin prose an account of the battle between Guy and Colbrond; and a long line of historians, including Knighton, Rudborne, Hardyng, Rous, Fabyan, Grafton, Holinshed, Stow, and Dugdale accepted the legend as an actual event occurring in the reign of Athelstan (the hero of Brunanburgh, 937). Lydgate (ca. 1449) turned Gerard's account into a poem of 74 eight-line stanzas (see under Lydgate).

When the popularity of metrical romances waned, various adaptations of the tradition appeared. *The Plesante Songe of Guy* (a stall-ballad, licensed 1592) added a popular motif concerning Guy and the Dun Cow. Rowlands (ca. 1608) published *The Famous History of Guy* in verse, an excerpt from which, as *Guy and Amaraunt*, appears in the Percy Folio MS; Lane wrote a *Corrected History of Sir Gwy* (1617, 1621, extant in manuscript, unpublished); Dekker and Day turned the story into a play (1618); and Shurley published *The Renowned History of Guy* (1681) as a prose chapbook. G. L., combining Rowlands and Shurley, wrote *The Noble and Renowned History of Guy* (1706), which has been frequently adapted in guide-books and children's stories.

Local traditions have also assisted in perpetuating the memory of Guy. Guy's sword, armor, and statue are still displayed at Warwick Castle, and his alleged hermitage can be seen at Guyscliffe near Warwick.

The Middle English *Guy of Warwick* does not deserve to have excelled the superior and more original *Bevis of Hampton* in popularity. Its incidents are unduly repetitive and prolix; the Middle English adapters show no inventiveness or critical sense; and the metrical inconsistency of the Advocates version is scarcely effective. Appropriately, Chaucer in the tale of *Sir Thopas* parodies *Guy* more completely than any other romance. The extent of its appeal is presumably dependent more upon the fame of Warwick Castle than upon its literary merit.

GAMELYN [9] was composed ca. 1350–70 in the Northeast Midlands (perhaps in Nottinghamshire); it survives in twenty-five manuscripts (and a late transcript) of the *Canterbury Tales*. It contains 902 long lines, riming in couplets; the lines consist of two halves, the first usually carrying three or four stresses, and the second usually three.

Sir Johan of Boundys before death divides his property equally between his three sons, Johan, Ote, and Gamelyn. As soon as their father dies, the eldest son (Johan) appropriates the share of the youngest (Gamelyn). As he grows up, Gamelyn becomes extremely strong and is able to intimidate Johan into promising restitution. After winning a wrestling match, he returns with his friends to his brother's house and finds that Johan has locked him out. He breaks in, throws the porter down the well, and with his companions consumes the household wine, which he feels belongs rightfully to him. When they leave, Johan tricks Gamelyn into allowing himself to be bound, and then he entertains his own friends. His guests, who are all members of the religious orders, mock Gamelyn. Adam, the household spenser (dispenser), sets him free. Gamelyn breaks Johan's back and, with Adam's assistance, punishes the guests.

To escape reprisal, Gamelyn and Adam take refuge in a forest, where they join a band of outlaws. Eventually, Gamelyn becomes king of the outlaws but robs no one except members of religious orders. Johan is appointed as a sheriff and proclaims Gamelyn outlawed ("cries him wolf's head"). Ote offers himself as bail for his younger brother. On the day set for the inquest, since Gamelyn has not appeared, Ote is condemned to death by Johan in collusion with the twelve jurors, whom he has bribed. Gamelyn arrives just in time, seizes control of the court, and sentences Johan and the jurors to be hung. The King makes Ote a justice, and appoints Gamelyn as "chief justice of his free forest." Gamelyn takes possession of his inheritance, marries, and lives happily.

The plot has no specifically identified source but closely resembles the typical folktale of the persecuted youngest son. The composition seems to be of native English origin and presumably stems from the same tradition which gave rise to the Robin Hood ballads (already current in 1377) and perhaps even to the earlier legend of Fulk Fitzwarin (recorded only in Anglo-Norman; twelfth century). No place-names are mentioned, apart from the unidentified Boundys; and the few personal names which appear give no clue as to the place of composition. The name Gamelyn (riming with "wȳn") is Norse in origin but was common in England. The ballad of Robin and Gandelyn (Child no. 115) seems to contain the same name but shows no other connection with the romance.

In tone the romance is reminiscent of *Havelok* (see [5] above) in that it is plainly addressed to the common people, but the author is much more concerned with reality than his predecessor had been. He has an unusually detailed knowledge of the terminology and customs of fourteenth-century law, and his romance presents a crude but convincing demonstration of the clash between false legality and true justice. He is contemptuous of uncharitable members of the monastic and mendicant orders; specifically, he mentions abbots, monks, priors, friars, grey friars, and canons. The clergy, on the other hand, escape his indignation. His critical attitudes thus reflect the revolutionary spirit typical of his age.

The romance survives because it was included among the manuscripts of the *Canterbury Tales*. In an attempt to supply a portion of the tales left unfinished by Chaucer, some scribes entitled it the Cook's Tale. If, as has been suggested, Chaucer himself intended to rewrite the tale of Gamelyn, he might more appropriately have assigned it to the Yeoman as a lover of outdoor life or to the Franklin as a rural magistrate.

The plot was reworked as a later ballad, *Robin Hood Newly Revived* (Child no. 128). Lodge, who must have had access to a manuscript version of *Gamelyn*, expanded it into the first part of his *Rosalynde* (1590) and thus provided Shakespeare with the outline of *As You Like It*.

Despite the good intentions of the author, the spirit of the narrative is sometimes brutal and callous; the refinement of romantic love is unfortunately absent; and the repeated summons of the minstrel to listen to his tale disturbs its dramatic pace. Yet the romance has redeeming features. The atmosphere of the outlaws' forest life is delightfully refreshing. The author's wry humor can sometimes be startlingly effective, as when he remarks that the villains are hung up, "to swing with the ropes and to dry with the wind." And the touches of psychological realism are occasionally worthy of *As You Like It*, as when the unwilling outlaw, Adam, ruefully complains: "Now I see it is merry to be a spenser; that I would sooner bear keys than walk in this wild wood to tear my clothes."

ATHELSTON [10]. Composed ca. 1355–80. Survives in only one manuscript, written ca. 1420 in the East Midland dialect. 812 lines, in 75 stanzas consisting of four-stress couplets linked by a recurrent three-stress tail-rime. Dominant pattern, occurring in 53 stanzas, is $a^4a^4b^3\ c^4c^4b^3\ d^4d^4b^3\ e^4e^4b^3$; others vary.

Four messengers, Athelston, Wymound, Egeland, and Alryke, meet by chance and become sworn brothers. On becoming king of England, Athelston appoints Wymound as Earl of Dover, Egeland as Earl of Stone, and Alryke as Archbishop of Canterbury, and gives his sister Edyff in marriage to Egeland. The envious Wymound falsely accuses Egeland and Edyff of treason; Athelston imprisons them and their two sons and, in rage, kills his own wife's unborn child by kicking her. When Alryke pleads before Athelston for a fair trial for Egeland, he is threatened with banishment. By a counterthreat of excommunication he forces Athelston to free Egeland and his family, and he then demonstrates their innocence by submitting them to the ordeal of fire. During the ordeal, Egeland's wife gives birth to a third son, the future St. Edmund, whom she presents to her brother Athelston as a substitute heir to the throne. The king absolves himself of his own guilt by naming Wymound as the false accuser. Wymound undertakes the ordeal of fire, fails, and is executed.

The plot is unhistorical. The hero may vaguely reflect the actual King Athelstan (ruled 925–40), whose victory at Brunanburh was celebrated in Old English and whose name became associated with various English legends including that of *Guy of Warwick* (see [7] above). The romancer shows his indifference to this connection, however, when he claims that Athelston became uncle of St. Edmund (King of East Anglia), who died in 870, long before King Athelstan came to the throne.

No source is known for the romance, and there is no trace of any earlier version, either in Middle English or in Anglo-Norman. In its central motifs of sworn brotherhood, false accusation, and trial by ordeal, it may have borrowed something from the earlier Anglo-Norman or Middle English *Amis and Amiloun* (see [112] below), but these are all commonplaces of medieval narrative. The details of the ordeal—a custom no longer practiced

3

in fourteenth-century England—may have been suggested by the widespread legend of Queen Emma, the mother of Edward the Confessor (ruled 1043–66). She was reputed to have saved herself from an accusation of adultery by walking on nine red-hot ploughshares. The conflict between Athelston and the archbishop probably reflects a memory of the feud between Henry II and Becket in the twelfth century, but the threat of excommunication was an ecclesiastical weapon widely used in the fourteenth century.

Some ecclesiast either at Bury St. Edmunds (in Suffolk) or at Westminster may have shaped the composition. The author's attitude seems religious rather than courtly or popular; his sympathy lies with the archbishop and not with either Wymound the courtier or even Athelston, the nominal hero. The prominence of St. Edmund in the romance may be explained by the contemporary antiquarian enthusiasm for this royal exemplar, who was chosen as a patron by Richard II (see the Wilton Diptych).

The unusually specific topographical references to Westminster, London, and the Dover road reflect the romancer's familiarity with the London-Canterbury area. Linguistic evidence as to the romance's place of composition is inconclusive, however, for conflicting dialect traits in the manuscript suggest a difference between the dialect of the scribe and that of the original composer.

The literary qualities of the romance vary in effectiveness. The plot is dramatic, the narrative swift, and the elements of the marvellous well maintained. The characterization of Athelston, however, is awkwardly unheroic. The plot precludes the hero from showing either the primitive virtue of a Havelok or the exquisite chivalry of a Gawain; but his gullibility and his violence might have been rendered less extreme. The tail-rime stanzas are generally attractive, but their empty tags and phrases deserve the parody which Chaucer accorded the genre in *Sir Thopas*.

WILLIAM OF PALERNE [11]. Translated ca. 1350–61 from the French romance *Guillaume de Palerne*, probably in dialect of Gloucestershire (Southwest Midlands). The only surviving manuscript (ca. 1360–75) has been affected by the dialect of East Midland scribes. 5540 lines survive, composed in alliterative verse. As many as three folios may be missing at the beginning, each containing 72 lines, corresponding to *Guillaume* lines 1–186; and f. 10

is missing, corresponding to *Guillaume* lines 693–837. The translator mentions that his first name is William and that his patron is Humphrey de Bohun, Earl of Hereford and Essex.

[(Lost beginning supplied by French romance.) In Palerne (Palermo) the brother of the King of Sicily, Apulia, and Calabria plots against William, the King's son. To rescue him from danger, a werwolf carries the child away to a secluded rural area near Rome.] A kind-hearted cow-herd finds William and adopts him. The werwolf departs contented. He is actually a prince, Alphouns son of the King of Spain, but has been changed magically into wolf's form by his step-mother. William grows up to be a handsome youth. The Emperor of Rome discovers him and entrusts him to the care of his daughter Melior. Melior and the foundling fall in love. William is knighted and proves his worth by defeating the Saxons who have attacked Rome.

When Melior is promised in marriage to a Greek prince, she and William, on the advice of her confidante Alisaundrine, flee from Rome dressed in bearskins. The helpful werwolf reappears, misleads the pursuers, provides the fugitives with deerskins as a change of disguise, and leads them to Sicily. Here William, though unaware of his own identity, saves his patrimony. His father, the King of Sicily, has died. Braundinis, the son of the Queen of Spain (who had bewitched Alphouns), has claimed William's sister, Florence, in marriage. The Queen of Sicily (William's mother) has refused consent and has consequently been besieged by the Spanish army. William leads the Palermitans in victory against the aggressors. The Queen of Spain is forced to disenchant Alphouns, and he is then able to identify William as the lost heir to the throne of Sicily. William marries Melior; Alphouns marries William's sister; and Melior's faithful Alisaundrine is given in marriage to Braundinis, the disappointed suitor. William at once becomes king and later, after the death of Melior's father, becomes Emperor of Rome. William and Melior have two sons who succeed their father.

The Old French original of this romance was written ca. 1194–97 for Yolande of Hainaut, Countess of St. Pol. The author shows an exceptional knowledge of the Norman Kingdom of the Two Sicilies (Sicily, Apulia, and Calabria) and its capital, Palermo. He may have acquired familiarity with the setting either at first hand or through contact with Yolande's crusading husband Hugh of St. Pol, her brother Baldwin of Hainaut and Flanders, and her nephew Baldwin, who became Emperor of Constantinople in 1204. The events find partial parallels in the history of Sicily. The siege of Palermo is reminiscent of the deposition (1194) of King William III of Sicily, when Henry VI surrounded the forces of the Queen Regent in Palermo Palace and slaughtered the game in the Royal Park in order to feed his troops.

The plot is based on the expulsion-and-return formula, with the peculiar modification that the rescuing animal is a man transformed—a motif

3*

introduced here possibly under the influence of Marie de France's *Bisclavret*. The main plot may have been derived from a local Norman-Sicilian legend or adapted from some folktale.

The Old French romance was translated into French prose by Pierre Durand (printed ca. 1552 and again later). The Middle English romance was turned into an English prose romance (printed by de Worde ca. 1520–29); and this prose version was in turn translated into Irish prose (with added poems) ca. 1520/29–1600.

Nothing is known about the William who names himself (line 5521) as the author of the Middle English romance. It has been assumed that he lived in Gloucester because of his dialect and also because of the reference which he makes to the town (line 166): "Preieth for Humfray de Bowne, the King Edwardes newe at Glouseter that ligges." This has been interpreted to mean: "Pray for Humphrey, King Edward's nephew, who resides at Gloucester." From this interpretation the inference has been drawn that the poet was writing at or near Gloucester while his patron was living there. In the context, however, the poet must mean: "Pray for Humphrey, nephew of the King Edward who lies buried in Gloucester." The poet's allusion to the famous tomb of Edward II (died 1327) in Gloucester Cathedral would be self-evident to contemporaries, and it would serve to distinguish this king from the reigning monarch, Edward III, and also from Edward I, Humphrey's grandfather, the "good King" referred to elsewhere (line 5531) in the poem.

Moreover, Humphrey owned no residence in the town of Gloucester and only two manors in the shire, while he held many other properties in England, extending from Herefordshire in the west to Essex in the east; and he seems to have spent most of his time in Pleshey Castle (Essex), where he died.

Humphrey may have obtained a copy of the original romance in France, for he served there on at least three occasions (1340, 1346, 1359); but with such scant information, the dating of the translation is as inconclusive as is the localization of the translator's place of origin. The latest possible date, however, is 1361, the year of Humphrey's death; and this establishes the composition as a pioneering work in the alliterative revival.

The translator handles his materials freely and confidently. He makes omissions, additions, and rearrangements to suit a popular English audience.

He abandons many of the geographical details which would be unfamiliar and compensates by amplifying the allusions to nature. He introduces a light-hearted incident (lines 2753–58) apparently copied from *Melion* (lines 241–44), a thirteenth-century French lay. He reduces but does not completely eliminate the extended monologues and debates concerning love; and in general he reduces the mannered style of the original to a more colloquial and realistic level. As a result, his primitive wonder-tale with its overtones of courtly sensibility is a worthy forerunner of *Sir Gawain and the Green Knight.*

2. ARTHURIAN LEGENDS

by

Helaine Newstead

Medieval Arthurian literature is remarkable for its prolonged and extensive vogue as well as for its protean forms. The Arthurian legends appear in almost every European language, and as chronicle, pseudo-history, romance, epic, saga, ballad, and folktale. It is probable that the legendary Arthur originated in a historical figure celebrated in Britain in the sixth century for his exploits in repelling the Saxon invaders. Although his identity cannot be established with any certainty, he seems to have been a military leader whose memory was cherished by the Celtic population after their defeat. A Welsh poem dated about 600 alludes to his fame in battle, as do other early sources of Welsh origin. By 1100 in Wales he had become the hero of fabulous adventures, the chieftain of a band of warriors endowed with supernatural attributes, including not only the familiar Kay and Bedivere but also many others derived from Welsh myth. In a story extant in several versions, he leads a raid with these companions upon an Otherworld fortress to carry off magical talismans.

The Cornish and the Bretons, closely related to the Welsh in language and culture, also contributed to the spread of Arthur's fame. Both groups, according to Continental sources, believed so passionately in the survival of Arthur that they would tolerate no expression of doubt. Cornish tradition, known to Geoffrey of Monmouth, located Arthur's birth and death in Cornwall; the Welsh knew of Kelliwic as the site of one of Arthur's courts; and many place names testify to his popularity in Cornwall.

The Bretons, however, played the major role in the diffusion of the insular Arthurian tradition on the Continent in the twelfth century. The Bretons were bilingual, fluent in both French and their native Celtic language. Many earned a living as professional entertainers at the courts of French or Breton nobles because of their cultivated gifts as reciters of tales. As a result, although no written records of their work survive despite frequent allusion to it, the Arthurian legends appear wherever French was known, over a wide territory embracing England, France, Provence, Italy, Sicily, and even the Latin kingdoms of Asia Minor. The most dramatic example of the early dissemination of Arthurian story is the sculptured archivolt of Modena cathedral in northern Italy, dated in the first decade of the twelfth century, which depicts a scene from the abduction of Guinevere, with names inscribed over the figures that are intermediate between the Welsh forms and the later French versions. The sculptors must have received the story and the names from a French-speaking Breton; otherwise the Breton forms of the names are unaccountable.

About 1136 the Latin prose *Historia regum Britanniae* of Geoffrey of Monmouth brought the prestige of the learned tradition to the story of Arthur's conquests. The Saxon wars are followed by a series of victories on the Continent that would have extended Arthur's empire even to Rome if they had not been interrupted by Modred's treason at home. The pseudo-history of Britain spread Arthur's renown among clerical and learned circles, and in 1155 it was translated into French by the Norman poet Wace for a courtly audience, possibly feminine, interested in manners, dress, and exemplary behavior. Although some of Geoffrey's contemporaries suspected the largely fictitious nature of his work despite the plausible sobriety of his style, the *Historia* was nevertheless accepted by most chroniclers and historians until the sixteenth century as the standard authority for the early history of Britain.

Arthur's prestige on the Continent, propagated by the Bretons, attracted stories of diverse origins. It was not Geoffrey or his followers, but the French romancers, who developed the legends of Lancelot, Tristram, Gawain, and the Grail. In the second half of the twelfth century romances on Arthurian themes began to appear in French, exploiting the richly imaginative resources of the Breton repertory of tales. In these romances, Arthur, no longer the protagonist, recedes into the background to become the center of a splendid court serving as a norm for chivalric conduct. The hero is usually an unproved knight who sets out on a series of hazardous adventures to test his valor, his devotion to chivalric values, or his solution of problems arising from conflicting ethical obligations. His success is rewarded by an appropriate ceremony on his return to Arthur's court.

The combination of such moral themes with the fantastic enchantments and marvels of the Matter of Britain resulted in the prodigious vogue of these romances among the French aristocracy. Sophisticated poets like Chrétien de Troyes or Thomas of Britain manifested an interest in psychological analysis, and brought clarity and refinement to the sometimes crude narratives inherited from their predecessors.

In the thirteenth century the development of Arthurian romances is distinguished by a vast expansion of material, the use of prose rather than verse, and a tendency to combine separate narratives. One powerful impulse towards this kind of synthesis was the progessive Christianization of the Grail legends during the early thirteenth century and the resulting adaptation of stories about Lancelot, Perceval, Arthur, and other figures to the quest of the Grail. The so-called Vulgate cycle of prose romances is the most impressive of these achievements not only for its own merits but because of its importance as a major source for Malory's work.

The English romances appear late in the history of Arthurian literature, from the second half of the thirteenth century on. Since the material is heterogeneous, it seems best to retain Wells's classification by subject: I. The Whole Life of Arthur; II. Merlin and the Youth of Arthur; III. Lancelot and the Last Years of Arthur; IV. Gawain; V. Perceval; VI. The Holy Grail; VII. Tristram. Added is VIII. Arthur of Little Britain. Malory will be considered in a separate chapter.

I. The Whole Life of Arthur

The whole life of Arthur is related in Middle English in Layamon's *Brut*; a short poem *Arthur* interpolated in the Latin chronicle belonging to the Marquis of Bath; the alliterative *Morte Arthure*; and the ballad, *The Legend of King Arthur*. The whole life of Arthur also appears in certain chronicles and, of course, in Malory's *Morte Darthur*, which are discussed in subsequent chapters.

The early traditions [12] about Arthur are recorded in works of Welsh provenance. Possibly the earliest reference occurs in the Welsh elegy, *The Gododdin*, composed about 600, in which a slain hero is compared to Arthur, the greatest of warriors. The Welsh priest Nennius in the *Historia Brittonum*, a Latin chronicle composed about 800, lists Arthur's twelve victories against the Saxons and refers to local legends attached to his name. Another Latin chronicle of Welsh origin, the *Annales Cambriae* (ca. 995) mentions Arthur's victory at the battle of Badon (located probably in the south of England) and also the battle of Camlann, in which Arthur and Modred fell.

In early Welsh literature Arthur appears as a hero of fabulous adventure. *The Spoils of Annwn*, a Welsh poem of the tenth century, relates Arthur's disastrous expedition to raid the fortress of Annwn, the Celtic Otherworld, in a attempt to capture magical talismans. The Welsh prose romance *Culhwch and Olwen* (ca. 1100) includes a euhemerized version of Arthur's expedition to Annwn and presents him as the leader of a host of personages with fantastic supernatural powers.

An important document in stone illustrates the early diffusion of Arthurian tales to the continent by the Bretons. The sculptured archivolt of Modena cathedral, dated in the first decade of the twelfth century, depicts a version of the abduction of Guenevere that must have been transmitted to the sculptors by a French-speaking Breton since the names over the figures are transitional in form between the Welsh originals and the names current later in French romances.

The whole life of Arthur as it has become familiar in later works was first outlined by Geoffrey of Monmouth [13] in his *Historia regum Britanniae*, composed in Latin prose about 1136. Geoffrey intended his book to provide an account of early British history that could stand comparison with existing histories of the Normans, the French, and the Saxons. He knew Nennius and other Latin historical sources available to a trained ecclesiastic, as well as a list of Welsh genealogies. But no trace has ever been found of the ancient book in the British tongue that he claimed to be translating, and most of his history is the product of his own imagination elaborating the slight material in his known sources. The result is so plausible that the *Historia* remained the standard source for early British history as late as the sixteenth century, despite the skeptical views of its authenticity expressed by some of Geoffrey's contemporaries.

Geoffrey links the British past with the ancient glories of Troy and Rome by describing the foundation of the kingdom of Britain by Brutus, a direct descendant of Aeneas. The career of Arthur is the central section of the history and its climax. The story begins with the love of Uther for Ygerne, and the begetting of Arthur with Merlin's magical aid. Although Merlin plays an important role in the hero's

youth, the emphasis is directed toward the glorification of Arthur's military achievements. After the conquest of the Saxons and other peoples on the Continent, Arthur refuses a demand for tribute from Lucius Hiberus, Emperor of Rome, and
engages in a war with him. He and his allies defeat the enemy in battle and would
have conquered Rome itself if Modred had not treacherously usurped his throne
and seized his queen during his absence. The queen takes refuge in a convent,
Modred is slain in battle, and Arthur, mortally wounded, is borne to Avalon.
After Arthur's downfall, Geoffrey recounts the decline of the empire built by Arthur
until its extinction in the seventh century.

Arthur, as Tatlock has shown, is imagined as a twelfth-century monarch,
surrounded by a court of vassal kings and nobles from all parts of Europe.
By developing the imperial theme and insisting upon the independence of
Britain, Geoffrey evidently intended to support the political policies of the
Anglo-Norman kings of his own day.

In 1155 the *Historia* was translated into French verse with the title
Le roman de Brut by the Norman poet Wace [14] and adapted to the taste
of a courtly audience. Wace used not only the Vulgate or standard text
of Geoffrey but also the Variant version. He follows his source faithfully,
expanding it chiefly with descriptive detail. Wace seems to have been a
sober discriminating antiquarian. He is the first to mention the tradition
of the Round Table constructed at Arthur's command to avoid disputes
over precedence, and he reports the Breton belief in Arthur's survival in
Avalon. His repeated references to the Breton tellers of Arthurian tales
are reliable testimony of their activities. Wace's *Brut*, in its turn, influenced
later writers, especially in England, until about the middle of the fourteenth
century. Unquestionably the most significant result of this influence is
the first poem in English to celebrate the deeds of Arthur, Layamon's *Brut*.

Layamon's *Brut* as a whole will be discussed with the other chronicles
and its bibliography will be found there; only the treatment of the Arthurian
material will be considered here. Layamon's poem is an expanded paraphrase of Wace in English alliterative verse, dated, according to Tatlock's
evidence, in the last decade of the twelfth century or shortly thereafter.
Almost a third of the entire work is devoted to the story of Arthur.

Through the aid of Merlin's magic, Uther begets Arthur upon Ygaerne, wife
of Gorlois of Cornwall. Gorlois is slain, and Uther marries Ygaerne. When Arthur
is born, fays bestow on him the gifts of riches, long life, and princely virtues. Uther
wars in defense of his kingdom and dies by poison.
Arthur is summoned from Brittany, and at the age of fifteen becomes king. He
wars against the rebels and the Scots, Picts, and Saxons; with French allies, he

crushes them. While he is subduing Orkney and Galloway, Man and Norway, the pagans treacherously invade the south. Arthur defeats the heathen at Bath and slays their chieftain Childric. Then he conquers Scotland, whose miserable people he spares. Returning to York, he re-establishes the churches, restores land to those bereft, and distributes parts of the realm to Urien, Angel, and Loth, the husband of Arthur's sister, whose sons are Walwain and Modred. In Cornwall he weds Wenhaver. After a bloody battle among Arthur's vassals over precedence at a royal feast, a wonderful table is made for him which can be carried from place to place and which will provide equality of seating for all his knights, high and low. Arthur makes Loth King of Norway, and receives the subjection of Denmark. After the conquest of Flanders, Boulogne, and France, he establishes at Caerleon on Usk a splendid court. At a great feast, twelve ambassadors from Rome demand tribute from Arthur and his subjection to the emperor Luces. Arthur declares war. Wenhaver is left with the realm in care of Modred. After slaying the giant of Mount Saint Michael, who has caused the death of Howel's daughter, Arthur advances toward Rome. As Arthur's ambassador, Walwain utters a noble defiance of the emperor and valiantly repulses his pursuers. Arthur gradually subdues his enemies, and the emperor is slain. Just as the king is about to enter Rome, he has a dream, which is later verified, that Modred has seized Wenhaver and the realm. With the loyal Walwain, Arthur returns, intending to slay Modred and burn the queen. Although Walwain wins a landing for the king, he is slain in the battle. Arthur laments his loss. Modred is driven to Winchester, where he is besieged. He steals away to Cornwall. After capturing Winchester, Arthur pursues Modred. Wenhaver takes the veil at Caerleon. At Camelford on the Tambre the hostile armies engage in battle. Modred and all his knights are slain. The wounded king and two of his knights are the only survivors on his side. Arthur gives his realm to Constantine, son of Cador. He announces that he will go to Avalon, where Argante, queen of the fays, will heal his wounds; afterwards, he will return and dwell with joy among the Britons. He is borne away in a boat containing two queens, and the Britons believe that he still dwells in Avalon with the fairest of fays and that he will some day return.

Although Layamon's source was French, he recreates the story in the vigorous epic manner, language, and style characteristic of native English verse. His medium, however, is not the classical meter of Old English poetry but rather the looser alliterative line current in the eleventh and twelfth centuries. Two other features of his style, rime and elaborated similes, may perhaps be due to the influence of Wace. Layamon's dramatic imagination transforms his material into a fresh and original narrative that reflects little of the courtly refinement of its source. Most of his expansions introduce concrete detail, direct address, and specific localizations lacking in Wace. Layamon is less intellectual than his model, but more passionate and emotionally identified with his hero Arthur. Arthur's role, for example, is magnified as Merlin's is minimized in the earlier episodes.

In addition to this kind of expansion, Layamon introduces traditions of Breton origin which, according to Loomis, he may have heard or read in French. One of these is the charming story of the three gifts bestowed by fays upon Arthur at his birth. Another is the account of the violent brawl over precedence that caused the establishment of the Round Table, which differs from Wace's version and agrees rather with Breton traditions of a similar magical table that is portable yet indefinitely expandable. A third is the story of Arthur's passing—his departure in a boat accompanied by two queens to Avalon to be healed of his wounds by Argante, and the prophecy of his survival and expected return to his people.

A distinctive trait of Layamon, pointed out by Tatlock and Loomis, is his explicit delight in slaughter and harsh punishment. He describes with gusto scenes of physical mutilation, bloodshed, and violence. Layamon's imaginative transformation of Wace's restrained, sober, and idealized narrative is most clearly revealed in such scenes. More significant perhaps is the fact that Layamon's poem is the first of many to adopt Arthur as an English hero, regardless of the historical tradition that he was the foe of the poet's ancestors.

ARTHUR [15]. Interpolated in an incomplete Latin chronicle in the Marquis of Bath's MS (ca. 1425) is a brief account in English of Arthur's life, composed probably in the second half of the fourteenth century, in 642 rimed four-stress couplets in the Southern dialect. It summarizes a version, perhaps Wace's, of Arthur's begetting and birth, his coronation, the establishment of the Round Table, his conquest of the Romans, the treachery and death of Modred, and the transportation of Arthur to Avalon, here identified with Glastonbury, and his burial there. This bare account is embellished with tedious lists and enumerations, pedestrian explanations of the name Pendragon, the difference between Great and Little Britain, and the like. The author, as Wells observed, "had little imagination, no sense of proportion, no poetical power."

MORTE ARTHURE [16]. This poem, a masterpiece of the alliterative revival, is preserved in a single manuscript, Lincoln Cathedral 91, written in the hand of Robert de Thornton about 1440. It treats the subject of Arthur's triumphs and ultimate downfall in 4346 alliterative long lines. The date of composition, according to O'Loughlin, is about 1360. Its authorship has been much disputed, but the evidence fails to support the conjecture that Huchown was the author or that it was the work of a Scot. The problem is further complicated by the linguistic confusion of the sole text. The original dialect seems to have been Northwest Midland, modified by a Southern scribe and later by the Yorkshire forms of Robert de Thornton. The text, moreover, was apparently reproduced from memory, as a comparison with the Winchester MS of Malory shows in those portions which he derived from the alliterative *Morte Arthure*.

Although the poem has usually been classified as an epic, Matthews has recently argued that it is constructed as a medieval tragedy of fortune, recounting the triumphant rise of Arthur and his sudden, catastrophic downfall. Both views, however, are compatible. The poem, after an account of Arthur's early conquests, centers on the Roman war. After rejecting the demands for tribute from the Roman emperor Lucius, Arthur and his vassals win a series of victories on the continent that reach a climax after the promised submission of the Romans. That night he dreams of Fortune's wheel and the Nine Worthies, a dream which is interpreted for him as a prophecy of his fall. This ominous experience is immediately followed by the news of Modred's treason and the disastrous sequence of events leading to Arthur's death. The framework, the rise and sudden fall of a noble king, indeed agrees with the concept of the medieval tragedy of fortune, but the poem is undeniably epic in its breadth and heroic scale. Arthur is magnified so that he dominates the action, and the story is presented with a constant awareness of its grandeur in a succession of brilliantly dramatic scenes. Among the notable passages are the accounts of Arthur's two dreams (the dragon and the bear, and the wheel of Fortune and the Nine Worthies), the fight with the giant of Mont St. Michel, the battle with the Roman emperor, the sea battle, and the moving scene in which Arthur discovers Gawain's body and his threnody for the slain hero. The epic tone is maintained throughout, even at the close. Instead of the familiar voyage to Avalon with its supernatural overtones, the poem ends with the description of Arthur's death and burial at Glastonbury, with all the solemn ceremony befitting a national hero.

The poet's principal source seems to have been a version of Wace, but he also drew liberally upon the Alexander legends, especially *Les voeux du paon* and *Li fuerres de Gadres*, as well as other sources, all of which he handled freely. The poet was also inspired by the military campaigns of Edward III, especially the sea battle of Winchelsea, known as *Les Espagnols sur mer*. Whether the poem is tragedy or epic, or a blend of both, it remains one of the most powerful and original treatments of the Arthurian tradition derived from Wace and Geoffrey of Monmouth.

THE LEGEND OF KING ÁRTHUR [17] is a ballad summary in 100 verses in the Percy Folio MS (ca. 1650). Arthur himself recounts his history, from his begetting to his last battle after the treason of Modred. As Ackerman suggests, this version sounds like a late fifteenth century speech in a play or a pageant.

II. Merlin and the Youth of Arthur

The accounts of Arthur's youth also include the story of Merlin, who plays a part in the events leading to Arthur's coronation and his subsequent attempts to consolidate his kingdom and extend his rule. The Welsh counterpart of Merlin is Myrddin, noted as a bard, seer, and magician. He is also depicted as a "wild man of the woods," who has lapsed into madness for various reasons and dwells in the forest. Such Welsh traditions underlie Geoffrey of Monmouth's treatment of Merlin. His lost *Prophetiae Merlini*, composed before 1135, but incorporated in the *Historia regum Britanniae*, presents Merlin as a prophet of British supremacy over the Saxons. In the *Historia* Geoffrey attaches to Merlin Nennius's tale of the prodigious Ambrosius, who as a child proved his superiority to Vortigern's magicians by revealing the presence of the fighting dragons beneath the foundation of Vortigern's tower as the true reason for its repeated collapse. Later in the reigns of Vortigern's successors, Merlin continues to prophesy and advise. The magical arts of Merlin help to bring about the begetting of Arthur by Uther upon Ygerne and the death of her husband Gorlois. The *Vita Merlini*, a Latin poem composed by Geoffrey of Monmouth between 1148 and 1151, includes stories probably derived from Welsh tradition about Merlin's madness and his life in the forest, but although this treatment was responsible for the later distinction between Merlin Silvester or Celidonius and Merlin Ambrosius, it was far less influential than the *Historia*. The accounts of Merlin in the chronicles (see under Chronicles) depend, of course, upon the *Historia* or Wace's *Brut*.

At the end of the twelfth century or the beginning of the thirteenth, the story of Merlin appears in French romances. About 1200 Robert de Boron composed his *Merlin*, intended as a continuation of *Joseph d'Arimathie*. Although only 502 verses of this work survive, its substance is preserved in French prose. The *Merlin* was designed to continue the narrative begun in the *Joseph*, which dealt with the early history of the Grail in apostolic times. The story of Merlin is set in Britain in the period of Arthur and his immediate ancestors. Robert's plan may also have included a *Perceval* and a *Mort Artu*, which were to have followed the *Merlin*. The prose redaction of Robert's *Merlin* has been transmitted in two versions. One is incorporated in the Vulgate *Merlin* and adapted to the structure of the vast Vulgate compilation. The other, generally considered closer to Robert's original, forms the introduction to *La suite de Merlin*. In both later versions long sequels have been added to the original narrative of Robert. From the prose redactions of Robert's poem and its continuations are derived the English versions of the story: the verse *Arthour and Merlin*; Henry Lovelich's verse *Merlin*; the English prose *Merlin*; and the corresponding section of Malory (see under Malory).

ARTHOUR AND MERLIN [18] survives in two versions. The earlier and better is preserved in the Auchinleck MS (Advocates 19.2.1, ca. 1330). It consists of 9938 lines in four-stress couplets composed in the dialect of Kent probably between 1250 and 1300. Four manuscripts of the fifteenth century or later represent a variant version extant in briefer forms but in the same meter. All four seem to be derived from a common original. Lincoln's Inn 150 (before 1425) contains 2492 verses: Douce 236 (Bodleian 21880, late fifteenth century), 1278 verses; Percy Folio MS (ca. 1650), 2378 verses; Harley 6223 (late fifteenth century), 62 verses. All four deal only with the early incidents of the story, ending before the coronation of Uter.

The Auchinleck MS relates the story from the death of Constans to the betrothal of Arthur and Guenevere and the subsequent defeat of Rion. The author seems to have followed a source that includes two recognizable stages in the development of the Merlin story. The first part, culminating in the coronation of Arthur (vs. 3133), represents an expanded redaction of the chronicle story earlier than the version of Robert de Boron; the remainder follows the Vulgate sequel. The poem is essentially a skilfully abridged translation.

Constaunce, King of England, had three sons, Constaunt or Constantine, Aurelis Brosias, and Uter Pendragon. At his death the eldest son becomes king, although he has been a monk. Fortiger, the steward, vows to aid the children. Constaunt, the new king, called King Moyne by his dissatisfied subjects, fails to defend them against the Danes and Saxons. When the barons learn that Fortiger would accept the throne were the king dead, they murder Constaunt. Fortiger expels the Danes. Aurelis and Uter escape. Fortiger executes the murderers, and in the civil war that follows, he obtains the aid of the Saxon Angys. After the defeat of the rebels, he weds Angys' daughter. Later, fearful of Aurelis and Uter, he attempts to build a great castle at Salisbury. Each night the work of the day is destroyed. Ten wise clerks advise him that the blood of a child not of man's begetting must be smeared on the work. Fortiger sends to seek the child. The devils in hell plan to beget a child that shall do as much harm as Christ did good. The devil destroys the family of a girl, begets on her a boy, and makes her a woman of the town. The pious girl is brought to judgment; but her confessor, the hermit Blasi, postpones the decision until the child is two and a half years old. Blasi christens the boy Merlin, who at once speaks in defence of his mother. He is good, not evil, and exhibits wonderful sagacity. He makes his mother a nun. Blasi is to write down what he reveals and what he shall perform as master of four kings.
   At the age of five he is brought before Fortiger. He explains that a white dragon and a red fight every night beneath the foundations of the castle. The dragons are dug up; they fight, and the white dragon destroys the red one and flees. Merlin confounds the sages by interpreting the omen. The white dragon is the rightful heir who shall drive out Fortiger. Merlin disappears. Aurelis and Uter defeat Fortiger, burn him and the castle, and with Merlin's aid, slay Angys. Uter becomes king, and destroys the Danes who slew Aurelis. Counseled by Merlin, Uter conquers much of France. He founds the Round Table at which may sit only the noblest, wisest, most courteous, and valiant, and he establishes a code of conduct that binds the knights. With Merlin's aid Uter begets Arthur on Ygerne and weds her after her husband's death. Merlin gives Arthur at his birth to Antour, who brings him up as his own child with his son Kay. After the death of Uter, Arthur proves his rights to the throne by pulling out of a stone a sword, Estalibore. When Merlin reveals his true parentage, Arthur is crowned. Arthur overcomes those kings who refuse to accept his rule, and Merlin aids him in the five years of civil strife and invasion. Merlin also helps him against King Rion, the enemy of King Leodegan of Carohaise, and Arthur wins the love of Gvenour, Leodegan's daughter. After a long series of contests in which pagans and rebels are subdued, Arthur defeats Rion and is betrothed to Gvenour. The victors rejoice at Carohaise.

The most notable merits of the poem are its clearly presented narrative and its smooth, competent handling of the couplets. If the succession of battles after Arthur's coronation seems monotonous to the modern reader, the listening audience might have responded otherwise. A more than mechanical approach to the material is implied by the numerous lyrics about spring and the descriptions of nature which, though conventional, are nevertheless refreshing. They may be the poet's own additions. According to Kölbing and Smithers, similar passages in *Kyng Alisaunder* and *Richard Coer de Lyon*, together with other evidence, suggest common authorship. *Arthour and Merlin* may not be a major poem, but the author's technical skill and clear sense of narrative are not negligible literary virtues.

THE PROSE MERLIN [19]. The Vulgate version of the *Merlin* was turned into English prose about 1450, and is preserved in a manuscript in the Cambridge University Library written in the late fifteenth century. A fragment of another manuscript in the Bodleian Library was noted by Kölbing. The *Prose Merlin* is a faithful translation of the Vulgate story, though not without errors, beginning with the council of the devils in hell and the begetting, birth, and marvelous *enfances* of Merlin. The narrative includes the events related in *Arthour and Merlin* but continues with the account of Arthur's marriage, the Round Table, the wars with the Saxons and on the Continent, the war with Rome, the enchantment of Merlin by Nimiane, and it ends with the birth of Lancelot, son of Ban of Benoyk. The *Prose Merlin* is important chiefly because it is an Arthurian text written in English prose shortly before Malory.

LOVELICH'S MERLIN [20]. Another translation of the French Vulgate *Merlin* was attempted by Henry Lovelich, a member of the London Company of Skinners. As a compliment to a fellow-member and friend, Harry Barton, twice Lord Mayor of London, Lovelich undertook to translate the *Holy Grail* and the *Merlin*. The results are preserved in a single manuscript, Corpus Christi College Cambridge 80, dated possibly as early as 1425. Although the *Merlin* runs to 27,852 lines, it represents only the first half of the French source, which was close to that of the *Prose Merlin*. Although his literary models were the romances produced by translators employed in London manuscript shops, Lovelich seems to have been an amateur in every sense of the word, who devoted his leisure to this task. He had no talent for writing and no ear for verse, but he deserves some attention because he was evidently a man of substance who respected poetry and considered it a worthy offering to an admired friend.

4

III. Lancelot and the Last Years of Arthur

The story of Lancelot is represented in English by five late works: the stanzaic *Morte Arthur*, Malory's *Morte Darthur*, the Scottish *Lancelot of the Laik*, and two imperfectly preserved ballads in the Percy Folio MS. Although Lancelot is not mentioned by Geoffrey or Wace, legends circulated about him in the twelfth century. He is listed high among Arthur's knights in Chrétien's *Erec* and *Cligès*, and he is the hero of the same poet's *Conte de la charrette*, depicted in his most celebrated role as the lover of Guenevere and her champion and rescuer. Other traditions appear in the *Lanzelet* of Ulrich von Zatzikhoven, a Swiss priest who translated about 1194 into German an Anglo-Norman romance composed about 1180. This source was biographical in structure, beginning with Lancelot's birth and his fosterage in the palace of a water fay and continuing with a series of amorous adventures and hazardous exploits that culminate in his marriage. Although he acts as champion of Arthur's queen in a duel, there is no hint of the famous love affair that is the substance of Chrétien's romance. As Cross, Webster, Loomis, and others have shown, Irish, Welsh, and Breton traditions contributed to the formation of the early Lancelot legend.

The most influential version of the story is the great Vulgate *Prose Lancelot*, composed between 1215 and 1230, which includes the *enfances* of Lancelot and the *Charrette* material together with many other episodes. The *Prose Lancelot* is the first part of a trilogy, which continues with the *Queste del Saint Graal* and concludes with the *Mort Artu*. Lancelot is presented in this work as the most valiant of Arthur's knights, the embodiment of earthly chivalry; in the *Queste*, although his quest ends in failure, he is the father of Galaad, the knight destined to achieve the Grail quest because he is the only one wholly dedicated to the Cistercian concept of chastity; and in the *Mort Artu*, Lancelot plays a noble but tragic role in the final catastrophe that leads to the extinction of Arthur's realm.

LANCELOT OF THE LAIK [21]. This Scottish romance, preserved in a single manuscript (Cambridge University Library, Kk. 1.5, of the late fifteenth century), not only attempts to imitate Chaucer's dream vision technique but also includes a lengthy passage on the duties of a king that seems to be directed to the reigning monarch in Scotland. The poem has slight claim to literary merit or originality. It is a paraphrase of the first part of the Vulgate *Lancelot* in 3346 lines of rough five-stress couplets, marked by the incompetence that the poet freely admits.

The prologue of 334 lines, apparently the poet's own contribution, relates how, overcome by love, he falls asleep and dreams that a bird sent by the God of Love advises him to write a treatise for his lady. He decides to translate part of a French story about Lancelot, Arthur, and King Galiot, despite his imperfect knowledge of French. The first book is a somewhat confused account of the war between Arthur and Galiot, arising from Arthur's refusal to yield to Galiot's demand for submission. Lancelot, though a prisoner of the Lady of Melyhalt, is permitted to fight for Arthur disguised in red armor, and he performs such prodigious deeds inspired by the presence of the queen that Galiot decides to declare a truce. The second book begins at this point: a wise clerk Amyntas rebukes Arthur for his failure to observe the proper duties of a king. After Arthur confesses to a priest, the announcement of the truce is interpreted by Amyntas as a reward for Arthur's penitence. The king listens to further instruction from the wise clerk on the political responsibilities of a ruler and puts them into practice during the year's truce. The third book resumes the narrative, as Lancelot in the disguise of a black knight performs brilliantly in response to the message of the queen to do his best. At this point the single copy of the romance breaks off.

Skeat suggested that the extended political discourse in the second book, which greatly elaborates a mere hint in the French source, was intended as advice to a contemporary king of Scotland, probably James III (1460–88), who, like Arthur, trusted astrologers. This suggestion of Skeat's was later convincingly developed by Vogel, who explained the underlying political theory. Because of this lengthy passage in the second book, the poem is thought to have been composed between 1482 and 1500. The weakness of the poem, as Ackerman observes, is due to the unsuccessful attempt to combine politics with the love story of Lancelot and Guenevere.

SIR LANCELOT DU LAKE [22]. This is a ballad in 124 verses in the Percy Folio MS, relating Lancelot's victory over Sir Tarquin in single combat.

LE MORTE ARTHUR [23]. The so-called stanzaic *Morte Arthur* is an impressive literary achievement, important not only for its own sake but also for its influence upon Malory. It consists of 3969 four-stress lines arranged in eight-line stanzas usually riming abababab. The romance, preserved in a single manuscript, Harley 2252, was probably composed about 1400 in the Northwest Midlands.

4*

The story, derived from a version of the French prose *Mort Artu* not identical with that which has come down to us, recounts Lancelot's experience with the hapless Maid of Astolat, his championship of the queen against a false accusation of poisoning a knight, the betrayal of the lovers by Agravain, and the fateful sequence of events leading to the death of Arthur.

At the tournament of Winchester Lancelot, fighting incognito, is wounded. Tended in the castle of Ascolot by the lord's daughter, who cherishes a hopeless passion for him, he leaves his armor with her as a keepsake in order to comfort her. Later when Gawain visits Ascolot, the maid shows him the armor as proof that she is Lancelot's love. Gawain innocently reveals this story in the presence of Arthur and the queen. When she reproaches Lancelot for his apparent perfidy on his return to court, he departs in sorrow and anger. At this point the queen is falsely accused of poisoning a Scottish knight and is condemned to death unless a champion can be found to defend her against the slain knight's kin. One day a barge bearing the dead maid of Ascolot floats down to Arthur's palace. A letter in her purse attributes her death to Lancelot's refusal of her love, and Gawain explains his mistake to Guenevere. Lancelot returns to defend the queen, defeats her accuser, and becomes reconciled to her.

Agravain, one of Gawain's brothers, betrays the lovers to Arthur but is slain by Lancelot. When the queen is condemned to be burned at the stake, Lancelot carries her away to safety but in doing so slays Gawain's brothers. Vowing vengeance, Gawain joins Arthur in besieging the lovers in Joyous Garde, Lancelot's stronghold. Although after papal intervention Lancelot restores the queen to Arthur and retires to Brittany, Arthur and Gawain pursue him there, rejecting his offers of peace. Gawain is severely wounded by Lancelot in battle. Meanwhile Modred seizes Arthur's kingdom and seeks to wed the queen, who flees to the Tower of London. When Arthur lands at Dover, Gawain is slain. Modred is forced to retreat to Cornwall, where the last great battle takes place. All on both sides die except Arthur, Sir Bedivere, Sir Lucan, and Modred. In single combat Arthur and Modred mortally wound each other. After two vain attempts to save Excalibur, Bedivere finally obeys Arthur's command to hurl the sword into the sea, where a hand rises to receive it. A rich ship filled with fair ladies bears Arthur to Avalon. Bedivere later finds Arthur's tomb in a chapel, and, taking orders, remains to watch over his lord's grave. The queen takes the veil at Amesbury. Lancelot, arriving with an army to aid the king, learns that he is too late. In a final interview, the queen bids him farewell, affirming her religious vows. He becomes a hermit-priest, dwelling with the other guardians of Arthur's grave, until his death seven years later. Visions reveal his salvation, and he is buried, as he wished, in Joyous Garde. The queen is buried beside Arthur at the site of Glastonbury Abbey.

The romance is notable less for stylistic brilliance than for its sure grasp of narrative values. Although the typical mannerisms of the minstrel style are evident, they never impede the skilful and concise management of the action. The Middle English poet must have understood the powerful effect of inevitability that characterizes the design of the French *Mort Artu*, for he creates in his own way the same impression through concentration upon the chain of events linked by cause and effect that leads inexorably to the destruction of Arthur's realm. No digressions mar the steady progress of the story or disturb its well-proportioned structure. The moving quality inherent in the story is conveyed by the simple and straightforward narration itself. Malory's response to the poet's clarity and logic is revealed in its influence upon his account of Lancelot's farewell to the queen, the last battle, and the passing of Arthur.

KING ARTHUR'S DEATH [24] is a ballad version in 155 verses of the last battle, summarizing the story in a form similar to that in the stanzaic *Morte Arthur*. In the Percy Folio MS, in which it is recorded, it is mistakenly combined with the *Legend of King Arthur* (see above).

IV. Gawain

Gawain is closely associated with Arthur in the earliest texts as a kinsman and a member of the royal household. Geoffrey of Monmouth and Wace assign him a prominent role in Arthur's Roman war and celebrate his prowess. Chrétien de Troyes lists him first among the Arthurian knights, and although Gawain is not actually the hero of any of Chrétien's romances, he sets the standards for the other knights, whose character and achievements are measured against his. His fame was widespread early in the twelfth century: in Padua a man born about 1121 was named for him, and in 1125 William of Malmesbury commented on his pre-eminence and described his tomb. Still earlier, on the Modena sculpture, he is depicted as Galvaginus (an archaic form of his name), who is a prominent ally of Arthur in the attempted rescue of Guenevere.

This noble concept of Gawain as the paragon of Arthurian chivalry predominates in the Middle English romances. Although Gawain's character was blackened as a result of ecclesiastical influence upon the French prose romances and he was contrasted unfavorably with more pious heroes, his glorious reputation remained undiminished in England, except in the stanzaic *Morte Arthur* and Malory.

The English Gawain romances are *Sir Gawain and the Green Knight, The Grene Knight, The Turke and Gowin, Syre Gawene and the Carle of Carelyle,*

The Awntyrs off Arthure, Golagrus and Gawain, The Avowynge of Arthur, Ywain and Gawain, The Weddynge of Sir Gawen and Dame Ragnell, The Jeaste of Syr Gawayne, King Arthur and King Cornwall, and *Libeaus Desconus*. No other Arthurian knight is the hero of so large a group of English poems. As Jessie Weston argued from certain parallels in the First Continuation of Chrétien's *Perceval*, these English poems perhaps may be the survivors of a large body of tales about Gawain which are now lost.

SIR GAWAIN AND THE GREEN KNIGHT [25] is not only the best of these romances but also one of the acknowledged gems of Middle English literature. It is preserved in a single manuscript, Cotton Nero A.x, which also contains *Pearl, Purity*, and *Patience*. The four works are generally attributed, on the basis of internal evidence, to one author, whose identity still remains unknown despite ingenious efforts to discover it. The dialect is Northwest Midland, and the date seems to be the last quarter of the fourteenth century, probably toward the end. The poem consists of 2530 lines arranged in stanzas of unrimed alliterative lines followed by a "bob and wheel" of five short rimed lines. The unrimed lines vary in number from 12 to 38 in a stanza.

After a brief historical introduction, the story opens with a description of the festivities at Arthur's court in Camelot during the Christmas season. On New Year's day a great feast is prepared, but Arthur refuses to be served until a marvel occurs. As he waits, a huge knight clad all in green and mounted on a green steed rides into the hall, bearing a mighty axe and a holly bough. He challenges any knight to a game: the knight shall deal him a blow with the axe and receive from the Green Knight a blow in return a year later. The challenger laughs loudly at the astonished silence of the court. Stung to anger, Arthur himself seizes the axe, but Gawain asks for the adventure. Swearing to observe the conditions set by the challenger, he strikes off the green head with a single blow. The Green Knight picks up his head, mounts his horse, and reminding Gawain to keep his appointment at the Green Chapel a year hence, rides swiftly out of the hall.

The year passes, and after All Saints' Day, Gawain leaves the sorrowing court and sets out on his journey. Beset with perils and hardship, he searches fruitlessly for the Green Chapel. In response to his prayers in a desolate wilderness on Christmas Eve, he finds shelter in a splendid castle near the forest in which he had been wandering. The lord gives him a hearty welcome and entertains him lavishly. When Gawain wishes to resume his quest on St. John's Day, the host persuades him to remain three days longer until New Year's morning, since the Green Chapel is near by. For the entertainment of Gawain during the interval, the lord proposes a game: each evening host and guest shall exchange whatever they have gained during the day. On the first day, while the host is hunting deer in the forest, his fair wife visits Gawain in his chamber and wakens him. Although he resists her amorous advances, he courteously accepts a kiss from her. This he exchanges for the spoils of the chase — on this occasion, a deer. On the second day, the host hunts a dangerous boar, and the lady, using a more direct approach, wins two kisses from Gawain. Again, the exchange is effected. But on the third day, when the host hunts a wily fox, the lady not only insists upon three kisses but offers him rich love-tokens, which he rejects firmly without offending her. Finally, referring to Gawain's ordeal the next day, she proffers a green girdle, which, she declares, will protect his life though he must conceal the gift for her sake. Gawain hesitantly accepts it, and when the host offers him the fox's skin, he presents only the three kisses in return.

In the wintry cold next morning he rides over the hills to the Green Chapel, a cave in a green mound. He recognizes his destination when he hears the grim sound of the whetstone sharpening an axe. The Green Knight appears, and Gawain prepares to receive the blow. As the axe descends, he flinches involuntarily and the Green Knight turns the blade aside. After another feint with the weapon, the Green Knight at the third attempt wounds him slightly in the neck. As Gawain springs up ready to defend himself, the Green Knight cheerfully explains that he is none other than the host, who had planned the temptations in his castle and who knew all about Gawain's conduct. The slight wound punishes Gawain's single lapse from complete fidelity to his troth—his concealment of the green girdle. The host invites Gawain to return to his castle, but the hero, overcome by bitter shame, declines. The host identifies himself as Sir Bercilak de Hautdesert and explains that the whole scheme was devised by Morgan le Fay to test the knights of the Round Table and to alarm Guenevere. Gawain vows to wear the green lace always to remind him of his humiliating experience. After his return to Arthur's court he relates his adventure to the lords and ladies, who decide to wear a similar green baldric in honor of Gawain's loyalty. It becomes a mark of honor ever afterwards.

The principal theme of the plot is the Challenge or Beheading Game, which is combined with a second theme, the Temptation. The earliest extant version of the Beheading Game appears in two variant forms in *Bricriu's Feast*, a composite Irish saga of the eighth century preserved in a manuscript written before 1106. In this saga the beheading game is used by a shape-shifting magician to test Cuchulainn and his rivals for the championship of Ulster. Cuchulainn wins the championship because he is the only one who keeps his promise to submit to the challenger's axe. As Kittredge pointed out, the French analogues to the Beheading Game show that this Irish tale, with inevitable modifications adapted to the courtly milieu, was absorbed into French Arthurian romances. The closest of these is an episode in the *Livre de Caradoc* in the First Continuation of Chrétien's *Perceval* or *Conte du Graal*, where the Beheading Game is attached to Caradoc. None of the analogoues, however, preserves so many details derived from the Irish saga as *Gawain and the Green Knight*. A striking illustration is the name of the Green Knight, Bercilak, which can be best explained as a French adaptation of the Irish word *bachlach* (a trisyllabic form in Irish meaning "churl"), a common noun repeatedly used to designate the challenger. The resemblances between *Gawain and the Green Knight* and the French analogues suggest a common source ultimately derived from the Irish.

Perhaps attracted to this story of testing by decapitation was another kind of test, the series of attempts by the lady to seduce Gawain. Here again, French analogues to the Temptation, attached to Lancelot and other Arthurian heroes, suggest a common source. A Welsh analogue in the mabinogi of *Pwyll*, dated probably in the eleventh century, indicates that Celtic tradition may have provided this theme as well as the Beheading Game. The Exchange of Winnings, which links the two together in *Gawain and the Green Knight*, however, is not Celtic nor is it found elsewhere in Arthurian fiction. The English poet himself may have introduced it although, as Hulbert showed, he did not invent it.

The structure of *Gawain and the Green Knight* is remarkably unified and balanced. The single adventure of the Beheading Game is the framework of the plot, and the originally independent Temptation story is so skilfully integrated with it that the hero's resistance to the lady's advances affects the final outcome of the Beheading Game. The action spans a year, but no extraneous episodes impede the progress of the narrative, and each developed incident fits into the poet's design.

The imaginative power that distinguishes *Gawain and the Green Knight* is due partly to the poet's sense of the dramatic, especially his understanding of suspense, and partly to his mastery of an extraordinary range of descriptive effects, so precise and so vividly realized that the poem, however fantastic the subject matter, seems rooted in the actual life of its time, although the events are carefully placed in the past. Both indoor and outdoor scenes contribute to this effect of solidity. The courts held at Camelot and at Bercilak's castle are no conventional, perfunctory descriptions, but rather each is varied in detail to fit the particular occasion and the emotional tone suitable for the stage reached in the narrative. The outdoor scenes depicting Gawain's perilous, lonely journey in the harsh northern winter are evidently intended to contrast with the warmth, companionship, and cheer that characterize the courtly revels. In a different way the poet deliberately contrasts the three distinctive hunting scenes with the corresponding but subtly varied temptation scenes occurring simultaneously in Gawain's bedchamber in the castle. The poet's delight in the aristocratic world about him appears in the architectural details about Bercilak's castle and in the technically expert account of the procedures in hunting the deer, the boar, and the fox, as well as in the famous passage on the seasonal cycles.

The emotional range of the poem also contributes to the effect of richness. On the surface, the poem is a sophisticated comedy of manners, expressed most effectively in the brilliant scenes of conversation between the seductive lady and the reluctant Gawain, a dialogue testing the knight's courtesy. There is also a more profound undercurrent—the testing of Gawain's character in the essential quality of chivalric honor, his fidelity to his troth. He passes the test in the Beheading Game easily enough because the danger is obvious. The more subtle seduction of the lady is concealed beneath the appearance of sexual temptation, but its real purpose is to make the hero, as the Green Knight puts it, "fail a little," in order to satisfy the more powerful urge to live. In view of Gawain's savage rage against himself, the significance of the lapse can hardly be denied. It is perhaps Gawain's eventual triumph that, of all the Arthurian court to whom he tells his adventure on his return, he is the only one to realize fully the meaning of his experience. He will wear the green girdle to remind him of his failure; the ladies and knights vow to wear a similar token for Gawain's sake, and it becomes a signal honor. Both interpretations are true. Perhaps Arthur's court, somewhat too engrossed in revelry and pleasure, needed the reminder from the world of Morgan le Fay.

THE GRENE KNIGHT [26] is a poem of 516 lines of tail-rime stanzas preserved in the Percy Folio MS. Composed in the South Midland dialect about 1500, it appears to be a condensed version of *Sir Gawain and the Green Knight* with none of the literary distinction that marks its model.

The Green Knight, we learn in advance, is Sir Bredbeddle of the West Country, whose wife, as he knows, loves Sir Gawain, though she has never seen him. For her sake her witch-mother transforms Sir Bredbeddle and sends him to Arthur's court at Carlisle to fetch Sir Gawain and to test him. A porter, after conversation with the Green Knight, announces his arrival to the assembled court. The Green Knight addresses them courteously, and when Kay first offers to claim the challenge, the king intervenes so that Gawain may accept it. The blow is postponed until after the feast, which the Green Knight shares. Later, as Gawain reaches the castle, the author explains that it is the Green Knight's home. The lady tempts Gawain only once, giving him three kisses and a white "lace." On the same day, the Green Knight hunts does, boars, and foxes. After the exchange, Gawain finds his way to the chapel alone, and hears the sound of a horn from a mountain as he approaches. The Green Knight strikes one blow, wounding Gawain slightly, and explains that the concealment of the "lace" means the loss of Gawain's three virtues: truth, gentleness, and courtesy. Gawain will be forgiven if he agrees to take the Green Knight to Arthur's court. Both knights return to the court, where they are joyfully welcomed. The author explains that the white "lace" was adopted as insignia by the Knights of the Bath, a custom established by Arthur at Gawain's request.

The explanatory habits of the author, of course, obliterate the wonder and suspense of *Gawain and the Green Knight*. Although such additional details as the parley with Arthur's porter and the behavior of Sir Kay are commonplaces, the localizations may be of more than passing interest. As Ackerman notes, the Green Knight's home is supposed to be Castle Hutton in the West Country, possibly Hutton Manor, Somersetshire, and Arthur's court is located not only at Carlisle but also at an otherwise unknown Castle Flatting in Delamere Forest, Cheshire. The allusion to the Order of the Bath may reflect the fact that in the fifteenth century new members were expected to wear a white silk shoulderknot until their first notable feat of arms.

THE TURKE AND GOWIN [27], a tail-rime poem in the Percy Folio MS, was composed about 1500 in the North or Northwest Midland dialect. About half of the text is lost as a result of mutilation of the pages on which it was recorded in the Percy Folio. Only 335 verses remain.

As Arthur sits at table, a strange man enters, not tall but broad and shaped like a Turk. He asks for an exchange of buffets. Kay derides him, offering to beat him down, but is rebuked by Gawain for discourtesy. Gawain gives the Turk a blow, but the return must be delivered elsewhere. Gawain rides northward with the Turk for two days. When he complains of hunger, the Turk leads him into a hill, where they encounter terrifying storms. They enter a castle which is mysteriously supplied with abundant food. At first the Turk forbids Gawain to touch any of it but eventually serves him lavishly. They sail over the sea to the castle of the King of Man and his band of giants. The Turk promises to help Gawain in any perilous encounter. The King of Man taunts Gawain about Arthur and his knights and the clergy as well. Gawain plays tennis with a troop of nine giants and a huge ball of brass; he is helped by the Turk. Other tests of strength follow. When a giant lifts a huge brazier, Gawain's "boy," the Turk, seizes it and swings it in the air. The king attempts to plunge Gawain into a caldron of molten lead presided over by a fierce giant. The Turk, clad in an invisible garment, throws the giant in first and then the king. Apparently after the Turk gives Gawain the return buffet, he brings a golden basin and asks Gawain to strike off his head. Gawain reluctantly does so. In place of the Turk, a stalwart knight arises,—Sir Gromer,— who sings a *Te deum* in gratitude for his release from enchantment. They liberate the captives and return to court, where Arthur makes Sir Gromer the King of Man.

Two plots are combined in this romance: the challenge story and the series of adventures among the giants. The beheading here takes place at the end rather than at the beginning, and it releases the challenger from an apparently disfiguring enchantment. This version of the challenge is combined with a different story of grotesque contests of strength between the hero and the king of a supernatural realm. Some of these exploits resemble those recounted in the twelfth-century *Pèlerinage de Charlemagne*. In this series of incidents the Turk's role as the helpful attendant of the hero finds no counterpart in the various versions of the challenge story, though a supernatural helper is conspicuous in the other plot. Since the *Pèlerinage de Charlemagne* is too remote to be the source, and since similar episodes are scattered in other Arthurian romances and tales, it is likely that these analogues, both Carolingian and Arthurian, derive ultimately from a story about the visit of a king to a rival monarch's domain in the Otherworld, a story attached quite early to both Charlemagne and Arthur. The second plot seems to have exercised a decisive influence upon the challenge story in *The Turk and Gowin* in the changed nature of the challenger from an eerie shape-shifter with a replaceable head to a bespelled knight who serves the hero as a helpful servant.

SYRE GAWENE AND THE CARLE OF CARELYLE [28] is the title usually assigned to the poem preserved in the Porkington MS, but the story is also extant in a later version in the Percy Folio MS (see below). The Porkington version consists of 660 verses in twelve-line tail-rime stanzas aabccbddbeeb, composed near Shropshire about 1400. As Miss Kurvinen's comparison shows, the two texts are derivatives of an earlier tail-rime poem, now lost. Neither extant version reproduces the original exactly or completely, but since they complement each other, the full story can be reconstructed by a comparative study of the two texts.

Accompanied by a great troop of knights, Arthur goes hunting. Gawain, Kay, and Bishop Baldwin seek shelter for the night in the castle of the fearsome giant the Carle of Carlisle. When they enter the hall, a bull, a boar, a lion, and a bear lying near the fire spring to attack them, but the Carl quiets his pets. When Gawain kneels courteously, his host, who is only a carl, bids him rise. The knights drink from a huge, nine-gallon cup of wine. During the entertainment, the guests one by one leave the hall to tend their horses. Finding the Carl's foal near his horse, Baldwin drives it away. The Carl gives him a buffet. Kay experiences the same treatment. When Gawain goes out, he finds the foal soaked with rain. He leads it into the stable, covering it with his green mantle. The Carl thanks him for his courtesy. At table, Kay greatly admires the beautiful lady of the castle, but the host reads his thoughts and rebukes him. At the Carl's bidding, Gawain aims a spear-thrust full at his face. The Carl lowers his head, and the spear shatters against a wall. When Gawain falls in love with the Carl's wife, the giant advises him to forget her. Then the Carl's lovely daughter joins the company, playing the harp and singing of love and Arthur's feats. Afterwards the Carl places Gawain in bed with his wife, bidding him kiss her. When he is tempted to do more, the Carl interrupts him. Then the Carl brings his daughter to Gawain as a companion for the night.

Next day, at the host's insistence Gawain reluctantly beheads him. A knight of normal shape appears, who thanks Gawain for liberating him from an enchantment destined to endure until a knight of the Round Table should behead him. Twenty years earlier the Carl had made a vow, which he had strictly fulfilled, to slay those visitors to his castle who refused to obey him. He exhibits the bones of those he had slain. Gawain alone succeeded in passing the test. He promises to reform his ways and offers masses for his victims. The three knights, with the Carl's daughter, return to Arthur's court. Arthur accepts the Carl's invitation to dinner the next day and makes the Carl a knight of the Round Table and lord of the country about Carlisle. Gawain marries the daughter. The Carl builds a rich abbey at Carlisle, which becomes a bishop's seat.

The Porkington text lacks the crucial incident of the beheading, which is preserved in the later version. The omission may be due, as Miss Kurvinen suggests, to the loss of a folio from the scribe's manuscript.

Though the plot is obviously related to the Temptation and Beheading themes in *Gawain and the Green Knight*, and the Transformation by Decapitation in the *Turk and Gowin*, the differences are more striking than the resemblances. Other analogues in *Le chevalier à l'épee* and *Hunbaut* show that the correspondences are due not to direct borrowing but rather to a common underlying tradition. According to Kittredge, *The Carle of Carelyle* combines a variant of the Temptation theme known as the Giant's Daughter with the Beheading Game or Champion's Bargain in *Bricriu's Feast*. The minstrel who composed the unsophisticated, crude *Carle of Carelyle* was evidently intent upon demonstrating Gawain's supremacy as a model of chivalry in the series of tests imposed by the Carl. In his own way he adapted the traditional materials to his purpose with the simple taste of his audience in mind.

THE CARLE OFF CARLILE [29] is the title given to the Percy Folio version, composed probably in Lancashire in the first half of the sixteenth century. Although in its present form it is a poem of 500 lines in couplets, Miss Kurvinen's detailed comparison shows that it was probably derived from the same tail-rime poem, now lost, that was the source of the earlier text in the Porkington MS. Although the earlier version in general seems to be closer to the lost original, the Percy Folio text preserves the beheading incident and the Carl's release from enchantment, which are missing in the Porkington MS.

THE AWNTYRS OFF ARTHURE AT THE TERNE WATHELYNE [30] was composed probably in the North of England near Carlisle after 1375. It is preserved in four manuscripts of the fifteenth century: Lincoln Cathedral 91 (Thornton, ca. 1440); Lambeth Palace 491. B (before 1450); Bodleian 21898 (Douce 324, late 15 century); Ireland Blackburn (ca. 1450). It consists of 715 alliterative verses arranged in thirteen-line stanzas, riming abababababcdddc. Each stanza is made up of nine long alliterative lines and four short lines. A striking feature of the verse is iteration, the repetition of an important word or phrase in two consecutive lines in order to link two stanzas together or to bind the "wheel" to the rest of the stanza. The alliteration and the repetition are more regular in the first part than in the second part of the poem.

From Carlisle Arthur goes out hunting at Tarn Wadling. Accompanied by Gawain, Guenevere rides out and rests under a laurel. During a sudden, violent storm, a terrifying apparition rises from the lake—the ghost of Guenevere's mother. The spirit warns Guenevere of the consequences of sin, prophesies the downfall of Arthur and the Round Table, and appeals to her daughter for thirty masses to be said for the salvation of her soul. The ghost vanishes, the storm subsides, and when the king and his company return, they are informed of the wondrous occurrence. When Arthur and his court are at table, a gorgeously attired lady leads into the hall Sir Galeron of Galloway, a Scottish knight who challenges one of Arthur's knights to combat to correct an injustice. Gawain undertakes the duel, but just as he is about to win the victory, the distraught lady appeals to the queen to ask Arthur to intervene. Geleron yields his claim, acknowledging Gawain's superiority. By Arthur's decree Galeron becomes a knight of the Round Table and marries the lady.

The first episode of the poem is based upon the *Trental of St. Gregory*, a story known elsewhere in Middle English. It is combined with an unrelated incident fairly common in Arthurian romance. The first episode is obviously didactic in purpose, perhaps intended for the moral instruction of rulers. The second incident exalts the valor of Gawain, who is the invincible champion of Arthur's court, as he is in most Middle English romances.

Despite the weakness of structure, the poem displays not only considerable skill in the management of a complicated verse form but also a gift for colorful and dramatic scenes expressed most vividly in the apparition of the ghost, the hunting scenes, which may have been influenced by *Sir Gawain and the Green Knight*, and the description of Sir Galeron and his lady.

GOLAGRUS AND GAWAIN [31], a poem in Middle Scots composed not long before 1500, is extant only in the Chepman and Myllar text printed in Edinburgh in 1508 and preserved in the National Library of Scotland. It consists of 105 stanzas of thirteen alliterative lines riming ababababcdddc. In each stanza there are nine alliterative long lines followed by a wheel of four lines. Two separate episodes in the First Continuation of Chrétien's *Perceval* or *Conte du Graal*, in a very free adaptation, provide the substance of the story (vss. 1–234, 235–1362).

On the way to the Holy Land, Arthur and his host need food and shelter. Kay at his own request seeks supplies in a castle. His churlish behavior earns him a beating. When Gawain undertakes the mission, his courtesy wins a warm welcome from the lord of the castle, and Arthur and his host are entertained there for four days. As Arthur continues his journey, he reaches a rich castle whose owners have never acknowledged an overlord. He vows that on his return he will exact homage from its lord Golagrus. On the way he sends Gawain, Lancelot, and Ywain as emissaries to demand submission, but Golagrus refuses. A siege, with many duels, follows. Golagrus is finally overcome by Gawain, but despite the victor's plea to preserve his life by yielding, he refuses. At last, Golagrus proposes that Gawain accompany him to the castle as if defeated. To save so noble a knight, Gawain pretends to be vanquished, to the dismay of Arthur's retainers. In the castle, Golagrus informs his knights of Gawain's generosity, and all gladly submit to the true victor. They accompany Gawain to Arthur's camp, and Golagrus yields homage to the king. After a feast of nine days, Arthur liberates Golagrus from allegiance and departs.

The poem, of course, glorifies Gawain, and its treatment of the story is vigorous and picturesque. Like other poets in the alliterative tradition, the author seems to prefer scenes of combat and battle. The love interest, which is prominent in the French source, the episode of the Riche Soudoier and the siege of Chastel Orguellous, is absent from *Golagrus and Gawain*. In the French romance, for example, it is the *amie* of the Riche Soudoier who demands that he remain unvanquished, and Gawain pretends to be defeated in order to satisfy her. In *Golagrus and Gawain*, the hero's generous action is prompted by his chivalrous nature alone.

As Wells has noted, the poem is distinguished by the use of a character, Sir Spinogras, who interprets the history, motives, and conduct of Golagrus, a literary device that tightens the narrative. The poet not only knows how to present his story effectively but he also handles the intricate verse form with unusual skill.

THE AVOWYNGE OF KING ARTHUR, SIR GAWAN, SIR KAYE, AND SIR BAWDEWYN OF BRETAN [32] is preserved only in the Ireland Blackburn MS, in the same hand as the *Awntyrs*. It seems to have been composed in the North about 1425 and copied by a West Midland scribe. It consists of 72 tail-rime stanzas of sixteen lines each, riming aaabcccbddddbeeeb. Alliteration, though not regularly used, is a marked feature, and some stanzas are linked by iteration.

The story is a skilful composite, its principal theme the accomplishment of vows made by Arthur and his three companions after their encounter with a ferocious boar in Inglewood Forest, a district familiar in other Arthurian romances in English. Arthur vows to kill the boar alone before morning. By command of the king, Gawain vows to watch all night at Tarn Wadling; Kay, to ride the forest till day, and to slay any who would restrain him; Baldwin, never to be jealous of his wife or any fair woman, never to refuse food to any man, and not to fear any threat of death. Arthur succeeds in slaying the boar, cuts him up, and offers thanks to the Virgin. Kay attempts to rescue a maiden from Sir Menealfe of the Mountain but is himself captured. He will be released if Gawain runs a course with Sir Menealfe. At the Tarn, Gawain runs the course and frees Kay; and when he runs another, the maiden is liberated. Gawain sends the maiden and Menealfe first to the queen, who then gives them to Arthur. Menealfe is admitted to the Round Table. At Kay's urging the king sends Kay and five other knights to test Baldwin. Baldwin overthrows all of them. He is equally successful in meeting the test of hospitality set by the king. Similarly, a third test proves Baldwin's faith in his wife. At Arthur's suggestion, Baldwin relates three incidents of his experience in a besieged castle that led him to his triple vow.

The framework of the story is the series of vows that may have been suggested by the knightly custom recorded in such poems as *Les voeux du paon*. All the vows except Baldwin's are connected with the circumstances of the hunt and its wild forest setting. Baldwin's three vows, so different in context, not only set him apart from the other Arthurian knights but make him actually the central figure in the story. These unusual vows, his success in meeting Arthur's testing of them, and the final explanation for his convictions contribute to the characterization of Baldwin as a knight whose experience with human nature has disillusioned him. The anecdote explaining his refusal to be jealous of any woman is a cynical antifeminist fabliau. The characterization of Arthur in this romance is also unusual: he is a sportsman, fond of conviviality and practical jokes, rather than the majestic king of Britain. The poem is popular in tone, but well constructed. The author fits his diverse elements into the framework of the vows, and skilfully presents them so that Baldwin's experiences form the climax of the narrative.

YWAIN AND GAWAIN [33], composed in the Northern dialect probably between 1300 and 1350 and preserved in a single manuscript (Cotton Galba E. ix of the early fifteenth century), is the only extant version in Middle English of any of the romances by Chrétien de Troyes. It is a condensation, freely handled, in four-stress couplets, of Chrétien's *Yvain*. The English poet reduces the 6800 lines of the French source to about 4000 by omitting many of Chrétien's reflective comments and his descriptions of the characters' emotional conflicts. He also uses English colloquial expressions and proverbs instead of the elevated literary conventions of Chrétien, as Whiting has shown. The result is a smoothly flowing, straightforward narrative that does justice to the excellent tale though without the delicate irony that distinguishes Chrétien's treatment.

To his fellow-guards at the door of Arthur's bedchamber Colgrevance relates some of his adventures. Taunted by Kay and urged by the queen, who has joined them, he tells of meeting a hideous churl in a wood, who directed him to a well in the forest, where he was to pour water in a golden basin and cast it upon a stone. A sudden storm breaks after he has done so, and a strange knight appears, overthrows him in a joust, and bears away his horse. This humiliating experience arouses the interest of Arthur, who vows to seek the adventure, but Ywain secretly precedes him. He vanquishes the knight, wounding him mortally, and pursues him to his castle. Ywain is caught between two portcullises. A damsel, Lunet, whom he had treated well at Arthur's court on an earlier occasion, befriends him, giving him a ring that keeps him invisible. Ywain falls in love with the lovely widow of the slain guardian of the castle. Lunet with amazing skill eventually persuades her to forgive Ywain and to marry him. He succeeds her late husband as guardian of the spring, and when Arthur attempts the adventure, Ywain assumes the defence. He overthrows Kay, reveals his identity, and entertains Arthur, Gawain, and the others at his castle.

Urged by Gawain, Ywain leaves his wife Alundyne to seek glory on condition that if he fails to return within the year, he will lose her. He forgets, and when Lunet denounces his lapse in the presence of Arthur's court, he goes mad with grief.

After a period of wandering naked and crazed with sorrow, he is cured by a maiden who applies a magic ointment. He defends her mistress's castle; rescues a lion, who becomes his faithful attendant; preserves Lunet from burning for treason, and performs a number of other notable feats. Finally, Ywain and Gawain fight incognito, and just as they are about to break off, they discover each other's identity and are reconciled. Ywain returns to the fountain and raises the storm. Since Alundyne has no defender, Lunet cleverly persuades her to make peace between the Knight of the Lion and his wife. Thus Alundyne and Ywain are reunited, and Lunet lives happily with them thereafter.

The romance is generally acknowledged to be one of the most successful in Middle English. The poet achieves fluency with his use of the short couplet, and the concentration on action results in a direct, well-controlled sequence of adventures which emphasizes chivalric conduct rather than courtly love.

THE WEDDYNGE OF SIR GAWEN AND DAME RAGNELL [34], composed in the East Midlands about 1450, is preserved in one manuscript, Bodleian 11951 (Rawlinson C. 86) of the early sixteenth century. It consists of 852 lines in tail-rime aabccb; one leaf is missing in the manuscript.

The story is a mediocre version of the widespread legend of the loathly lady and her transformation, which appears in six English forms as well as in other vernaculars such as Irish, French, Old Norse, as Maynadier has shown. The most familiar version, of course, is Chaucer's *Wife of Bath's Tale*.

The Weddynge of Sir Gawen relates that Arthur, hunting in Inglewood Forest, leaves his retinue to pursue a great hart. As he stands by the slain deer, a stalwart knight, Sir Gromer Somer Joure, appears, who threatens to kill him for giving his lands to Gawain. Arthur pleads the shame of slaying an unarmed knight and promises amends. Sir Gromer spares him on condition that he appear a year later, alone, in the same garb, prepared to tell what it is that women love best. Although he has promised to keep the matter secret, the king reveals his plight to Gawain. Independently they travel far and wide, seeking the answer and keeping a record of the replies. On their return a month before the year's end they find that their books of answers are useless. Urged by Gawain, Arthur goes to the forest. There he meets the hideous Dame Ragnell, who promises her aid if Gawain will marry her. Although the king is horrified at the prospect, Gawain agrees to marry the hag in order to save his lord. Dame Ragnell tells Arthur that women love sovereignty most. After trying other solutions, the king offers the answer proposed by Dame Ragnell. Sir Gromer curses his sister for betraying the secret and permits Arthur to go free. At the lady's insistence Gawain weds her openly in church. Afterwards at the wedding feast she gorges herself, to the dismay of Gawain's friends. Later, in bed with her bridegroom, she pleads for at least a kiss, and when he courteously complies, she becomes young and lovely. She then asks her delighted husband whether he would have her fair either by day or by night. Gawain bids her choose.

Given the sovereignty, she promises to be always fair, explaining that her step-mother had enchanted her until she married the best of knights and obtained sovereignty over him. The court rejoices at the outcome, and the king and Sir Gromer become reconciled. Dame Ragnell bears a son Gyngolyn, and though Gawain was wedded often, his five years of marriage with Ragnell before her death were the most blissful of all.

THE MARRIAGE OF SIR GAWAINE [35] is an incomplete ballad version of the story preserved in the Percy Folio MS but composed probably in the fifteenth century. See also under Ballads.

King Arthur holds court at Carlisle at Christmas. At Tarn Wadling he encounters a belligerent baron who demands in a year's time the answer to the question, "What do women desire most?" The king confides the story to Gawain. At the appointed time he meets on the way to Tarn Wadling an ugly hag clad in scarlet who promises to help him. Arthur offers her marriage with Gawain. The baron refuses all the answers that Arthur has collected except that of the hag, whose answer is that women wish to have their will. Cursing the hag, his sister, he swears revenge. The loathly lady marries Gawain, telling him to choose whether to have her fair by day or by night. When he asks her to decide, she announces that she will be fair at all times because he has released her from the enchantment of her stepmother. All rejoice, even Sir Kay, who had scorned the hideous bride.

The two versions are obviously related, but not so closely that one can be said to be the source of the other. These and other analogues are ultimately derived from an Irish tradition, represented in the *Adventures of the Sons of Eochaid Mugmedon*, that relates the encounter of a king or destined king with a loathly hag, who demands that he kiss her or lie with her. When he does so, she is transformed into a radiantly beautiful damsel, the Sovereignty of Erin or Eriu, who had tested in this way his fitness for the kingship of Ireland. Underlying this saga tradition of early date may be a still earlier fertility myth of the union of the goddess Eriu with the sun god Lug. In any event, the tale of the loathly damsel and her transformation was absorbed into the legend of Gawain, and other motifs, such as the question test that determines the hero's survival and the choice of beauty by day or night, were introduced. Another modification was the change from political to domestic sovereignty. In these two English versions the functions of the original hero are divided between Arthur and Gawain: Arthur must find the answer to the question or lose his life, and Gawain, because of loyalty to his king, must marry the loathsome hag. This modification seems to be due to the English tendency to exalt the courtesy and fidelity of Gawain.

THE JEASTE OF SYR GAWAYNE [36], preserved in a single manuscript, Bodleian 21835 (Douce 261), consists of 541 verses of tail-rime
stanzas, aabccb, composed in the South or South Midland during the
second half of the fifteenth century. The opening lines of the poem are
missing.

Gawain, enjoying the love of a lady whom he has found in a pavilion, is interrupted by her father, who angrily challenges him. Gawain offers amends but
nevertheless is forced to fight. After the overthrow of the father, the lady's two
brothers, in turn, engage Gawain in combat and are likewise defeated. The third
brother, Sir Brandles, a powerful, splendidly attired knight, fights Sir Gawain so
valiantly that neither wins the victory. They part, agreeing to resume the duel
when they next meet. The brother beats his sister severely and cares for his wounded
father and brothers. The lady wanders off to the woods, never to be seen again.
To the joy of the court, the meeting between Gawain and Brandles never occurs.

The story is derived from two episodes in the First Continuation of
Chrétien's *Perceval* or *Conte du Graal*. The first recounts the seduction of the
damsel; the second, Gawain's combat with Brandelis, resumed much later
in the action. The renewed duel ends only when the sister of Brandelis
pleads with them for peace and presents her son Ginglain, whom she has
borne meanwhile to Gawain. As Ackerman suggests, the emphasis in the
English version upon the dismissal of the lady and the explicit statement
that Gawain and Brandles never met afterwards may indicate the poet's
conscious effort to compose a short, wellrounded romance.

KING ARTHUR AND KING CORNWALL [37] is a ballad in the
Percy Folio extant in the mutilated part of the manuscript. The original
must have been about twice as long as the 301 lines of the eight fragments
in the text. Although it is difficult to reconstruct the story from this damaged
version, its outlines can be discerned.

Arthur, here the King of Little Britain, boasts of his Round Table to his cousin
Gawain. The queen observes that she knows of one much richer and more splendid,
contained in a palace worth all of Little Britain, but she refuses to reveal its location.
Arthur vows to seek it with his companions Gawain, Tristram, Sir Bredbeddle, and
Sir Murramiles. Assuming the guise of palmers, they travel in many a strange
region, reaching at last the palace of King Cornwall, whose porter is clad in gold.
The porter introduces them, and King Cornwall boasts that during his sojourn
in Little Britain he had begotten a daughter upon Arthur's wife, an accomplishment which Arthur could not equal. He also boasts to the visitors of a miraculous
horse, a sword, and a horn, as well as a seven-headed, fire-breathing fiend who
serves him. As Arthur lies in bed, the fiend, concealed in the bedchamber, reports
on the boasts of Arthur's knights. Arthur vows to kill Cornwall, Gawain to take

5*

Cornwall's daughter, Tristram to carry off the horn, Murramiles the steed, and Bredbeddle the sword. Bredbeddle, with the aid of a small book of Evangiles, subdues the fiend and obtains his services in carrying out the boasts concerning the three magical objects. With the sword Arthur decapitates Cornwall.

The plot in its general outlines resembles *Le pèlerinage de Charlemagne*, but not so closely that one can assume direct dependence. As in the *Turke and Gowin*, Arthurian and Celtic analogues make it clear that the story of a king's visit to a rival monarch with supernatural attributes was attached to Arthur as well as to Charlemagne. The English ballad seems to be a combination of motifs already traditionally linked to Arthur. Even the pilgrimage theme appears in such an Arthurian work as *Golagrus and Gawain* in combination with Arthur's visit to the court of a powerful king of extraordinary wealth.

LIBEAUS DESCONUS [38] is the story of Gawain's son Guinglain (English Gingelein), "The Fair Unknown." Its popularity in England, perhaps due to the intense interest in Gawain, is indicated by the six manuscripts that preserve it, in contrast to the single manuscript of the French version, *Le bel inconnu* by Renaut de Beaujeu (ca. 1190). The English poem may have been composed by Thomas Chestre, the author of *Sir Launfal* and *Octavian*, which appear together with *Libeaus Desconus* in Cotton Caligula A. ii and which are likewise written in the Southern dialect and dated in the same period, the second quarter or the middle of the fourteenth century. The manuscripts of *Libeaus Desconus*, however, were all written in the fifteenth century; in addition to the Cotton text, the romance is found in the following: Bodleian 6922 (Ashmole MS 61, late fifteenth century), Percy Folio (ca. 1650), Lambeth MS 306 (late fifteenth century), Lincoln's Inn 150 (before 1425), and Naples, Royal Library XIII, B 29 (1457). In Kaluza's edition, which is a composite of the several texts, there are 186 tail-rime stanzas, usually aabaabccbddb, though with some metrical variations.

Gingelein, the bastard son of Gawain, is brought up in seclusion by his mother. One day, while hunting, he dons the armor of a knight whom he finds dead, and goes to Arthur at Glastonbury demanding knighthood. Since he does not know his own name, he is knighted as Libeaus Desconus. Gawain trains him, and Arthur reluctantly grants his request for the first adventure that may occur. A maiden, Elene, and her dwarf companion appeal to Arthur for a knight to deliver the imprisoned lady of Sinadoune. Contemptuously they accept the novice as the champion. Mocking him, the damsel rides forth to encounter William Salebraunche. Libeaus overcomes him and sends him to Arthur. Elene apologizes for her doubts of his prowess. Then he defeats and sends to Arthur several nephews of William who seek to avenge their uncle. Next he rescues a maid from two giants, one red, one black, whose heads he dispatches to Arthur, but declines an offer to marry her. He matches Elene for beauty against the lady of Sir Giffroun and, losing the judgment, challenges and defeats the knight. The prize, a gerfalcon. is sent to Arthur. Libeaus overcomes Sir Otes de Lile and twelve companions, all of whom he sends to the king. Arthur elects Libeaus to the Round Table.

After many more adventures in Ireland and Wales that are not recounted, the hero slays a giant who besieges the fair lady of the Isle d'Or. Through her magic arts he forgets in the enjoyment of her love all his honor and his quest for a whole year. At last, when Elene makes him realize his neglected duties, he sets out once more. At Sinadoune, Libeaus overcomes the steward, Sir Lambard. The lady is imprisoned by two brothers, the magicians Maboun and Irain, who seek to force her to wed Maboun. Libeaus enters the magic hall; the music ceases suddenly, the lights are quenched, the building shudders and quakes. He slays Maboun; Irain, wounded, vanishes. A serpent with a woman's face enfolds him. As she kisses him, she is transformed into a lovely lady. She was thus bespelled until she should kiss Gawain or one of his kin. She becomes the bride of Libeaus Desconus.

In addition to *Le bel inconnu*, the other analogues to *Libeaus Desconus* are the Middle High German *Wigalois* (ca. 1210) and the Italian *Carduino* (ca. 1375). Although the French poem is the closest of these, it is not the immediate source. Not only is it three times as long as the English romance, but there are also wide differences in the order of the incidents and in the forms of names. Both *Le bel inconnu* and *Libeaus Desconus* are probably independent versions of an earlier French source, perhaps, as Loomis suggests, an Anglo-Norman work.

The plot itself blends the story of the Fier Baiser with the well-known motif of a woman transformed into a serpent. In the Irish source of the Fier Baiser the hero, like Libeaus, wins a bride as well as a kingdom after destroying the enchantments. The account of Libeaus' *enfances* resembles, too, similar stories attached to Perceval and other Arthurian heroes. Among other themes familiar in Arthurian romance is the sparrow-hawk adventure, related to Chrétien's *Erec* but not derived from it. Loomis has shown that the uncanny adventures at Sinadoune, the *cité gaste*, drew upon a Breton legend about the ruined Roman fort at Segontium near Caernarvon.

The principal interest of *Libeaus Desconus* lies in its relationships to other forms of the story. Although the English romance is clearly, even briskly, narrated, it displays few literary merits and little imagination. It is not surprising that a sophisticated poet like Chaucer should have found in its pedestrian treatment of romantic adventure the inspiration for some of the most brilliant moments of parody in *Sir Thopas*.

V. Perceval

The legend of Perceval, though important in Arthurian literature, appears in English only in the tail-rime romance *Sir Perceval of Galles* and in Malory. Perceval is the principal hero of the last romance composed about 1180 by Chrétien de Troyes, *Le conte du Graal*. Left unfinished apparently because of the poet's death, this work was vastly expanded not only by two separate prologues, but by four continuations. Although Gawain is the hero of the First Continuation, Perceval's adventures form the center of interest in the Second Continuation, and in those of Manessier and Gerbert; he also figures prominently in the French prose *Didot Perceval*, *Perlesvaus*, and the Vulgate *Queste*. In German the legend is represented, of course, by the masterpiece of Wolfram von Eschenbach, *Parzival*, dated between 1200 and 1212. The Welsh prose *Peredur* is also an important text that seems to have been derived, as Foster shows, from a French source accessible to Chrétien; the hero is identified by the Welsh author with the historical figure Peredur.

All of these texts associate Perceval with the Grail legends, but although this aspect is of major significance, the actual legend of Perceval deals rather with his early experiences, his *enfances*. The Italian *Carduino*, for this reason, must also be considered an analogue of the Perceval story. The ultimate origin of the *enfances* of Perceval is to be found in the Irish sagas recounting the early exploits of the two major Irish heroes, Cuchulainn and Finn, especially the latter.

SIR PERCEVAL OF GALLES [39], in Lincoln Cathedral MS 91 (Thornton, ca. 1440), was composed between 1300 and 1340 in the Northern dialect, though with an admixture of Midland forms. It consists of 2286 verses in sixteen-line tail-rime stanzas, aaabcccbdddbeeeb. Most of the stanzas are linked together, as in the *Awntyrs off Arthure* found in the same manuscript and in the *Avowynge of Arthur*, by repetition in the first line of a key word in the final line of the preceding stanza.

Perceval, father of the hero and husband of Arthur's sister, soon after his son's birth is slain in combat by the Red Knight. The mother rears the child in the woods so that he is ignorant of men and of all knightly customs. He becomes expert with the dart. One day, after his mother has instructed him about God, he sets out to seek Him. Meeting Ywain, Gawain, and Kay, he asks which one of them is God. Although Kay is rude, Gawain replies courteously that they are knights of Arthur's court. The boy desires to be knighted. On his way back to his mother, he captures and rides a wild mare. Next day he sets out for Arthur's court on his unconventional mount. He rests at a hall without seeking permission, takes a ring from the finger of a sleeping lady, and leaves in exchange the one that his mother had given him as a recognition token. At Arthur's court he demands knighthood, and the king notes the striking resemblance between the uncouth boy and his lamented brother-in-law. The Red Knight suddenly enters, drinks a cup of wine, and carries off the goblet. The king expresses his sorrow because the Red Knight has stolen his goblets for five successive years. Perceval sets out after the thief with Arthur's promise to grant him knighthood if he can recapture the stolen vessel. Perceval slays the Red Knight with his dart and on foot seizes his horse. Unable to remove the knight's armor, he tries to burn him out of it. Gawain comes to his assistance and attires him in the armor. Sending the stolen cup back to Arthur, the youth goes forth to seek adventures. He slays the witch mother of the Red Knight and casts her into the fire that is consuming her son's corpse. He encounters an old knight and his nine sons who entertain him with lavish hospitality after learning that he has slain their enemy, the Red Knight.

Informed by a messenger sent from Maydenlande to Arthur's court that the lady Lufamour is besieged by a sultan who seeks her hand and lands, Perceval sets forth to rescue her with the aid of three of his host's sons. When the messenger reaches Arthur, the king and three of his knights go to the assistance of Perceval. The youth penetrates by valorous fighting the defenses of the beleaguered castle and is welcomed by Lufamour. Next day he slays many Saracens and engages in battle incognito against Arthur, Gawain, Ywain, and Kay. In the duel with Gawain, which neither wins, they recognize each other. Perceval is knighted, and after vanquishing the sultan, he weds Lufamour.

After a year with his bride, he seeks his mother. On the way he discovers bound to a tree the lady with whom he had left his mother's ring. The lady's ring, which he had taken with him, had magical protective properties, and the exchange had led her lover, the Black Knight, to judge her faithless. Perceval defeats the Black Knight and exonerates the unfortunate lady. His mother's ring, meanwhile, had been given to a giant brother of the sultan. He slays the giant, and the ring flies out of the treasure chest to its true owner. The porter explains that the giant had offered the ring to Perceval's mother, who identified it and assumed that her son was dead. Mad with grief, she tore off her garments and roamed wild in the woods. The hero vows never to wear armor again until he rescues her. Wearing goat-skins, he searches for her and eventually discovers her by a well near their forest home. She recognizes him, and after her complete recovery, he takes her home to his bride. Perceval is said to have won later many victories in the Holy Land, where he was eventually slain.

Although *Sir Perceval* is an important text for the study of the Grail legends and their origins, the Grail itself does not appear in the poem. The early adventures of Perceval—that is, to the slaying of the Red Knight—

correspond to the *enfances* of the hero in Chrétien's *Conte du Graal*, Wolfram's *Parzival*, the Welsh *Peredur*, and the Italian *Carduino*. The exact source of the English poem is unknown, but it could hardly have been Chrétien's romance. Unlike Chrétien's Perceval but like Carduino, for example, Sir Perceval is reunited with his mother after his exploits. Strucks's study, in fact, shows that *Sir Perceval*, *Parzival*, and *Carduino* are based upon quite different sources from those used by Chrétien.

The Irish sagas about the boyhood deeds of Finn and Cuchulainn contributed to the early development of the story preserved in *Sir Perceval* and its analogues. Such features as Perceval's secluded childhood in the forest under his mother's tutelage and his skill as a hunter with darts are indebted to the Finn saga. A striking parallel is the vengeance quest of the two heroes: like Finn, Perceval avenges the death of his father by slaying unwittingly the hereditary foe of his kin, the Red Knight.

Sir Perceval is an unsophisticated romance that stresses action and marvels. The best scenes, as Wells and Ackerman have noted, are those in which the poet indulges his taste for the grotesque, as in the simple Perceval's questioning of his mother and the Arthurian knights about God, the burning of the Red Knight and the witch, and the duel with the giant. Though crude, the romance is vigorously narrated.

VI. The Holy Grail

The mysterious vessel known as the Grail, although not mentioned in *Sir Perceval*, appears in Chrétien's *Conte du Graal*, the earliest extant Grail text, composed about 1180. The word Grail is derived from the Old French *graal*, a rare term for a large serving platter. The word is so understood in Chrétien's romance, where the *graal* is described as a large jeweled platter carried by a maiden through the castle hall during a feast. But since the Old French word is uncommon, it was variously misinterpreted in other romances as a chalice, a cup, and even a stone.

Since the Grail romances are part of the Arthurian legend, the sources of the Grail itself are to be sought in that body of Celtic tradition that furnished the substance for much else in Arthurian fiction. Irish and Welsh traditions abound in stories about miraculous, food-providing vessels of diverse forms and powers. These Celtic vessels are drinking horns, platters, or cups, and although they are all vessels of plenty, some also have the power to discriminate between truth and falsehood, to select destined kings, and to preserve youth. They are to be found in the Otherworld among the treasures of the Celtic gods. The Grail seems to have absorbed these attributes, sometimes singly, sometimes in combination.

When this composite tradition reached the French romancers of the twelfth century, it was natural to associate a vessel described as the source of miraculous, mysterious effects of bliss with the divine Christian miracle and mystery, the ceremony of the eucharist. The process of Christianization had already begun when Chrétien wrote; although his Grail scenes in the castle hall can hardly be interpreted as a description of a Christian sacrament, there is an isolated later reference to the Grail as the container of a single mass wafer that had life-sustaining powers. The eucharistic suggestions of the vessel were developed in later romances. The *graal* became the *saint graal*, and because the word itself was uncommon, it was identified with the chalice of the mass or a ciborium. The *saint graal* was also misinterpreted as the *sang real* and linked with the blood of Christ.

In Robert de Boron's *Joseph d'Arimathie* (before 1191), the Grail is equated with the vessel of the Last Supper, in which Joseph preserved the blood of the Savior, and the sacred vessel is destined to be brought to the far west, presumably to play a part in evangelizing Britain. Robert also planned a continuation, *Merlin*, to bridge the chronological gap to the time of Arthur (see above, Merlin). The prose version of Robert's *Merlin*, the *Didot Perceval*, and the *Mort Artu* section that follows it represent an attempt to synthesize these diverse stories. The great Vulgate prose cycle is a more ambitious and successful effort (see above, Lancelot). The trilogy of the *Lancelot—Queste del Saint Graal—Mort Artu* was expanded by the *Estoire del Saint Graal*, a "prologue" dealing with the Joseph legend and the early history of the Grail. Still later a prose version of Robert's *Merlin* and its sequel were added.

Malory's retelling of the Vulgate *Queste* is the only English version of that important text (see under Malory). The other English versions dealing with the Grail are concerned with the early history of the vessel: the alliterative *Joseph of Arimathie*, Henry Lovelich's incomplete translation of the French *Estoire*, and three late versions of the Joseph legend extant only in printed form.

JOSEPH OF ARIMATHIE [40], in the Vernon MS (dated ca. 1390) in the Bodleian Library, is probably the earliest extant alliterative poem, composed in the mid-fourteenth century in the West or Southwest Midland dialect. It is a fragment of 709 lines, defective at the beginning, relating in condensed form the experiences of Joseph in the *Estoire* from his release from prison to his departure from Sarras.

The fragment begins with Joseph's statement that his forty-two years of imprisonment seemed only three nights. He, Vespasian, and fifty others are baptized. The Jews are punished. Directed by a voice, Joseph, his wife, and son Josaphe, and the fifty others, go to Sarras, bearing the dish containing Christ's blood in a box that they make for it. Joseph tries to convert Evalak, King of Sarras, explaining the doctrine of the Trinity. The king treats him well but doubts the doctrine. The next night he is converted by two visions: one of the Trinity as three stems of a single tree trunk that merge into one, and the second a vision of the spotless Incarnation. Josaphe, Joseph's son, also has a vision of the Crucifixion upon gazing into the box containing the Grail, and later a vision of Christ with the Lance, the Nails, and the Grail. Josaphe is consecrated bishop by Christ. In Evalak's palace a clerk appointed by the king to dispute with Joseph and Josaphe is stricken dumb and blind. The heathen idols are destroyed.

Tholomer, King of Babylon, invades Evalak's realm. Joseph reveals Evalak's early history, and Josaphe gives him a shield with a red cross, advising him to pray to Christ if he is in distress. At first successful, Evalak is nevertheless captured later. Praying as Josaphe had directed, he is rescued by an angel in the form of a White Knight who slays Tholomer and aids Evalak to win the victory. Meanwhile, Joseph discovers that Evalak's queen is a Christian, converted by the miraculous healing of her mother. On their return, Evalak and his brother-in-law Seraphe are baptized as Mordreins and Naciens. Josaphe baptizes more than five thousand others, and goes forth with Naciens on a missionary journey, leaving the Grail at Sarras in charge of two of Joseph's company.

The poem is more than a mechanical condensation of the very long section of the *Estoire* that is its source. The poet has retold the story in his own terms and in his own idiom, reducing the scale to the dimensions of the adventures at Sarras. The simplified treatment of the narrative consistently sustains the atmosphere of pious legend; even the generally admired battle scenes (vss. 489–614) are handled so that they are subordinated to the major themes of miracle and conversion.

THE HISTORY OF THE HOLY GRAIL [41], by Henry Lovelich, is preserved in the same manuscript as his verse *Merlin* (see above, MERLIN [20]), Corpus Christi Cambridge 80. The opening of the poem is lost, but 11,892 short couplets remain. His dialect is Southern or South Midland. Lovelich's *History* is a close translation of the French *Estoire del Saint Graal*.

The text begins with Evalak's preparations to resist Tholomer, continues with the incidents related in *Joseph of Arimathie*, and goes on with the story of Joseph, Naciens, Mordreins, and their children, up to the life of King Launcelot, grandfather of Launcelot de Lake. Lovelich followed this translation with his *Merlin* (see above).

THE PROSE LYFE OF JOSEPH, DE SANCTO JOSEPH, HERE BEGYNNETH, A PRAYSING [42]. Three later versions of the Joseph legend survive only in printed form: the prose *Lyfe of Joseph of Armathy*, printed by Wynkyn de Worde; the prose *De Sancto Joseph Ab arimathia* printed by Pynson in 1516; and the legend *Here begynneth the lyfe of Joseph of Arimathia* with *A Praysing to Joseph* (in 456 verses), printed by Pynson in 1520. These three versions, as Skeat showed, are based on the *Nova legenda Angliae* of Capgrave, who died in 1464. It is possible that the popularity of the legend of Joseph and its fictitious association with the evangelization of Britain owed something to the acceptance of the legend by the monks of Glastonbury at the end of the fourteenth century. Although they accepted the story of Joseph's mission to Britain, the Grail was entirely omitted and replaced by two cruets, which contained the blood and the sweat of Christ. The 1520 verse biography of Joseph printed by Pynson explicitly urges pilgrimages to St. Joseph's shrine at Glastonbury.

VII. Tristram

Although the story of Tristram or Tristan is sparsely represented in Middle English only by the late thirteenth-century *Sir Tristrem* and Malory's treatment of the Prose *Tristan*, earlier and superior forms of the legend were known in England in Anglo-Norman versions of the romance as well as in the series of illustrative tiles in Chertsey Abbey.

The most important of the full-scale Tristan romances is the twelfth-century Anglo-Norman version by Thomas of Britain, preserved in French only in fragments dealing with the final episodes. Fortunately, however, the entire romance can be reconstructed from the Old Norse translation made by Brother Robert in 1226 at the command of the King of Norway; despite some serious omissions, this Norse prose translation is our most valuable source for the earlier episodes of Thomas's romance. Gottfried von Strassburg's Middle High German *Tristan*, one of the great master-pieces of medieval literature, is derived largely from Thomas, although the German work is also incomplete, ending just before the marriage of Tristan to Isolt of the White Hands.

Another less courtly version of the story is preserved in the German poem of Eilhart von Oberge, which likewise survives only in fragments and must be reconstructed from translations. An Anglo-Norman poem by Béroul, extant also in fragments, is closer to Eilhart's version than to Thomas's in spirit and substance.

The legend circulated in shorter forms as well. Marie de France's Anglo-Norman *Chevrefoil* recounts a brief incident: the banished Tristan carves a message on a hazel wand and places it on the forest path that Isolt must travel. Her recognition of it leads to a brief, clandestine meeting of the lovers before they part again. Two short poems based on the assumed madness of Tristan, the Berne *Folie Tristan* and the Oxford *Folie Tristan* preserve valuable evidence of the lost contents of the longer romances. In both, Tristan, disguised as a madman, relates his adventures in order to reveal his identity to Isolt. The Oxford *Folie* is derived from Thomas's romance, and the Berne *Folie* from that represented by Eilhart and Béroul. Other poems dealing with individual episodes indicate the widespread popularity of the story.

The Tristan legend is a composite of many elements. The nucleus was a tradition that developed about the Pictish king Drust son of Talorc (ca. 780) and his deliverance of a foreign land from a forced human tribute. A version of this story, including the rescue of the intended victim, a princess who confounds the false claimants of the victory by identifying the hero, is preserved in an Irish text of the tenth century. Another Irish source, the elopement of Diarmaid and Grainne, a part of the Finn cycle, contributed the pattern of the love story, especially the magic compulsion that binds the lovers, the flight to the forest, and the pursuit of the husband. The Welsh seem to have blended the originally independent Pictish tradition with this Irish material, since in Welsh sources the triangular relationship of Tristan, Esyllt, and King March is well known. The Welsh not only introduced into the story King Mark, a legendary monarch of Cornwall, but also linked all these personages with Arthur. The influence of the Bretons is evident in various localizations in Brittany and in the in-

troductory episodes about the love of Tristan's parents and the concluding
episodes about Isolt of the White Hands. In the course of oral transmission,
other elements from folktales and Oriental fabliaux were included among
the episodes. All these diverse elements were combined into a narrative
of extraordinary dramatic power, but it remained for Thomas and Gottfried to transform the legend into a literary masterpiece.

SIR TRISTREM [43], the only Middle English version of the story
except for Malory, is preserved in the Auchinleck MS (Advocates 19.2.1,
about 1330). The romance consists of 3344 verses in stanzas of eleven lines,
abababcbc; all the lines in each stanza have three stresses except the
ninth, which has only two syllables. The date is probably late thirteenth
century, but the place of origin is difficult to determine because of the
mixed linguistic forms in the manuscript. Kölbing considered the original
language Northern, modified by a Southern scribe; but more recently
Vogel has proposed that the poet's basic dialect was Southeast Midland.
Since the time of Sir Walter Scott, the five allusions in the poem to "Tomas"
as the narrator have prompted speculations about the authorship. The
identification with Thomas of Ercildoun or Thomas of Kendale rests on
shaky evidence, and the references could just as reasonably be allusions to
the French author. Kölbing's plausible supposition that the poet was a
minstrel who reproduced the romance from memory would explain his
confusion of the true author of the French source with a more familiar
English figure. *Sir Tristrem* faithfully follows the French romance of Thomas,
though only the skeleton of the story is presented. Yet this version includes
all the incidents except the conclusion and thus affords additional evidence
of the content of the lost portions.

Rouland Riis of Ermonie begets a child on Blauncheflour, sister of King Mark
of England. Duke Morgan treacherously slays Rouland and seizes his lands. Blauncheflour bears a son, who is named Tristrem. After bequeathing him a ring received from Mark and entrusting him to the care of the faithful Rohand, the
mother dies. Rohand rears the child as his own, educating him in music, sports,
and hunting as well as in books. At fifteen, Tristrem wins a chess game against
a sea captain from Norway. He is abducted by the seamen and deposited with
his winnings on a strange shore, that turns out to be England. On the way to
Mark's court he teaches hunters the proper way to brittle deer. At the court,
where he is well received, he displays his skill in music. Meanwhile, Rohand,
searching for Tristrem, arrives at Mark's court and reveals the youth's parentage
and early history. Mark knights his nephew, who sets out to avenge his father's

death. He slays Morgan, and gives Almain and Ermonie to Rohand and his sons to rule for him.

On his return to England, he finds everyone grief-stricken because the Irish king Moraunt has demanded his cusomary tribute of a hundred youths. In a battle with Moraunt on an island, Tristrem slays the foe, leaving a sword splinter in his skull. The wound which Moraunt had dealt Tristrem will not heal. After languishing thus for three years, he sets forth in a ship and lands in Ireland. As Tramtris, a minstrel, he plays the harp so charmingly that he attracts the attention of the Irish queen Ysonde, the sister of Moraunt. She heals his wound, and during his convalescence he teaches her fair daughter, also named Ysonde, to play the harp and to sing. After a year, he returns to his uncle and tells him of the princess Ysonde. Jealous barons, fearful that Tristrem seeks to prevent Mark's marriage in order to succeed him as king, demand that Tristrem risk the danger of a visit to Ireland to obtain the princess as a bride for the king. In the guise of a merchant Tristrem wins her by delivering her from a dragon to which she was to be sacrificed. Ysonde recognizes Moraunt's slayer by his broken sword and the matching fragment retrieved from his victim. She and her mother plan to kill him, but he persuades them to spare his life.

By mistake, Tristrem and Ysonde drink a magic love potion prepared by her mother for Mark and his bride. Thereafter Tristrem and Ysonde are unable to resist its power. Mark weds the princess, but she substitutes her maid Brengwain for herself on the wedding night and later plans her murder to conceal the secret. Brengwain saves herself and returns to her repentant mistress. Tristrem next rescues the queen from a minstrel who has won her from the king by a ruse. When Meriadok reports the love of Tristrem and Ysonde, the king seeks to determine the truth. Craftily he arranges to overhear the interview of the lovers, but they detect his presence and succeed in deceiving him. When they are at last discovered, Ysonde offers to undergo an ordeal by oath. Swearing an ambiguous oath that states the literal but incomplete truth, she evades punishment. Eventually, however, Mark banishes the lovers when he is finally convinced of their relationship. They live happily in the forest for about a year. One day, Mark comes upon them asleep with a naked sword between them. Persuaded now that he was mistaken, he summons them back to court. But soon again Tristrem is driven into exile, though Mark forgives the queen.

Tristrem weds Ysonde of the White Hand, daughter of the Duke of Brittany, because of her name, but sight of the queen's ring, given to him as a token, reminds him of her love and he refuses to consummate the marriage. He defeats a giant, with whose aid he constructs a hall adorned with images of the chief persons in Tristrem's story. Ganhardin, his brother-in-law, reproaches him for neglecting his wife. Sight of the images satisfies Ganhardin and causes him to fall in love with Brengwain. They set off for England to get Brengwain for Ganhardin. After further adventures and a brief meeting with Ysonde and her attendant, the knights flee. After Ganhardin returns to Brittany, Tristrem, fighting in behalf of a knight of his own name, is struck by an arrow in his old wound.

The text of *Sir Tristrem* ends at this point. The conclusion was evidently lost when the following leaf was cut from the manuscript. The complicated and difficult stanza chosen by the author seems to have preoccupied his attention so that he sacrificed the story to the demands of meter and rime. The treatment of the narrative is perfunctory, the expression is undistinguished and clogged with rime tags, and the jerky meter must have been as distracting to the medieval listener as it is to the modern reader. The effort to conform to the conventions of minstrel technique, which accounts for the drastic condensation of the story and the elimination of the debates and soliloquies characteristic of the original, is easier to understand than the lack of response to the dramatic qualities of the narrative. *Sir Tristrem* is unfortunately a much coarsened version of its subtle and moving original, significant chiefly because it preserves, however inadequately, the lost episodes of its source.

VIII. Arthur of Little Britain

ARTHUR OF LITTLE BRITAIN [44] is a prose translation by Sir John Bourchier, Lord Berners, of a fourteenth-century French romance, *Artus de la Petite Bretagne.* The English version was printed about 1555, long after Berner's death in 1533. It indicates the continuing taste for Arthurian marvels and adventure even in the mid-sixteenth century. The French source was prized as well on the Continent in the fifteenth century. An illuminated manuscript of the fifteenth century, now in the New York Public Library, was once part of the great library of Jacques d'Armagnac, Duke of Nemours. Another discriminating collector of the same period, Louis de Bruges, also owned a copy.

As Loomis has shown, the hero's exploit in ending the enchantments of Porte Noire and winning a bride preserves a number of early features traceable to the Celtic sources of such familiar Arthurian motifs as the Perilous Bed, the revolving castle, and an attacking giant bearing an axe and clad as a herdsman.

Although Lord Berners in the preface to his translation announced that his purpose was to keep alive "the chivalrous feats and martial prowesses of the victorious knights of times past," it was clearly the story itself that captivated his imagination and enabled him to achieve, as C. S. Lewis observes, "that admirable blend of fantasy in large things with homely and realistic detail in small ones, which produces such whimsically convincing effects." Although the accumulation of marvels and wonders may seem cloying, the stylistic excellence of the translation conveys the charm of the lengthy romance so effectively that it holds the modern reader as well as those who cherished it in earlier times.

3. CHARLEMAGNE LEGENDS

by

H. M. Smyser

In the poetry of medieval Europe no figure except King Arthur looms larger than the Emperor Charlemagne (742–814). Though Germanic by descent and speech, Charlemagne became the predominant national hero of the French. Associated with him in intimate or remote fashion and with his twelve peers and other vassals both loyal and rebellious are some fifty-six *chansons de geste*; William of Orange, his only rival in that epic genre, is celebrated, with his followers, in only twenty-four *chansons*, and this numerical imbalance does not half tell the story of Charlemagne's preëminence in poetic fame.

Viewed in the large, the cycle of Charlemagne differs from the similarly great cycle of Arthur perhaps most importantly in being more commonly and lastingly infused with the spirit of patriotism. Though Arthur was successively a figure of British, Anglo-Norman, and English national feeling, he and his court came to represent cosmopolitan Christian chivalry. It is not odd that Chrétien de Troyes should treat of Arthurian themes, and the Grail story is as much at home in Germany as Wales. The Charlemagne legends, on the other hand, lost an essential element of patriotic appeal when exported. Such cosmopolitanism as they gained in the late Middle Ages they gained at the cost of the spirit which had animated them at the beginning. The earlier Charlemagne romances outside France consist of translations, adaptations, and compendia.

Even as such the English Charlemagne romances are in the main undistinguished, to say the least. The best of the lot, the ebullient *Taill of Rauf Coilyear*, is only nominally a Charlemagne romance. All come from the fourteenth century or later. A recurrent stress on religion suggests clerical authorship of some of them, and they seem to have been addressed to a popular rather than stylish audience.

Of the *chansons de geste* one of the most favored outside France was the *Fierabras*, a *chanson* of which the plot is so lively that it can survive even mediocre handling. Barbour tells us that Robert the Bruce read the romance of Ferumbras to his men on the shores of Loch Lomond, and, though no such early version is known to survive, we have four versions in English, respectively, the *Sowdon* (Sultan) *of Babylon*, the Ashmole *Sir Firumbras*, the fragmentary Fillingham *Firumbras*, and Caxton's prose *Charles the Grete*.

A number of English romances are based upon or associated with the French *chanson* of *Otinel* and are known as the Otuel Group. These consist of the Auchinleck *Roland and Vernagu*, the Fillingham *Otuel and Roland*, the Auchinleck *Otuel a Knight*, the *Sege of Melayne*, and finally *Duke Roland and Sir Otuel of Spain*.

In addition there are several detached romances: the fragmentary *Song of Roland*; the aforementioned *Taill of Rauf Coilyear*; a second prose translation by Caxton, *The Right Goodly Historie of the Foure Sonnes of Aymon*; and a prose translation by Sir John Bourchier, Lord Berners, entitled *The Boke of Duke Huon of Burdeux*.

Finally, and to be considered only in this place, is a lost English romance which, toward the end of the thirteenth century, was translated into Old Norwegian prose for incorporation in the Karlamagnus saga. This work, known as *OLIVE AND LANDRES [45], has as closest analogue the *chanson Doon de la Roche*. The story is that of a falsely accused queen, Olive, the daughter of Pepin, who is cast into a dungeon. Her son, Landres, is driven from the court, but after various adventures he secures the help of his uncle, Charlemagne, and effects his mother's rescue and vindication. The translation seems close enough to have preserved certain clichés and rime-tags commonly found in Middle English romances. The lost poem was among the very earliest of romances in English and was much older than the surviving English Charlemagne romances. Like the *Taill of Rauf Coilyear*, its connection with the Charlemagne cycle was very slight.

I. The Firumbras Group

In the *Chronique rimée* of Philippe Mouskés, written about 1243, we have a brief summary of a lost twelfth-century *chanson de geste* which we call the

6

Balan. This describes the seizure and sack of Rome by the Saracens under Balan and its recapture by Charlemagne after Oliver has overcome the Saracen champion Fierabras in single combat.

The combat between Oliver and Fierabras was detached from the *Balan* and made the beginning of a *chanson* called the *Fierabras*, of about 1170, which runs to 6219 alexandrines. This poem is a fabrication of many stock episodes and motives, though, as said above, of a liveliness exceptional among its kind. It is set not at Rome but in Spain. A purpose of the poet was to explain how the relics of the Passion came to be located in France. Of the *Fierabras* we have seven complete manuscripts and three fragments, besides prose redactions and translations into various languages. Alone among the four English versions, the *Sowdon of Babylon* is derived from the *Fierabras* in rather special fashion, as follows:

Being a product of the truncation of the *Balan*, the *Fierabras* has an abrupt beginning. A poet who knew the *Balan* constructed a prefatory poem to *Fierabras*, known as the *Destruction de Rome*. This prefatory poem survives in a Hanover MS, where it is followed by a copy of *Fierabras* which has in no way been adapted to form a consistent whole with it. Alongside this we have, in a manuscript that became generally known only in the 1930's (British Museum Egerton 3028), an Anglo-Norman radical redaction and abridgement (by about one-third) of the Hanover *Destruction de Rome* and following it a similar radical redaction and abridgement (by about two-thirds) of the *Fierabras*. (For something of the stemmatic history of the latter abridgement, see the description of the Ashmole *Firumbras*, below.) The two parts of Egerton show some traits of unity and are obviously ultimately the work of the same hand. This Anglo-French poem is closely allied to the *Sowdon of Babylon*; the two have many lines and details in common, and they show a similar re-ordering of various minor episodes, as against the other versions. Yet the *Sowdon* is not a translation of the Egerton; the two poems closely follow a common lost original.

THE SOWDON OF BABYLON [46]. East Midland; composed ca. 1400 or perhaps somewhat later—at any rate, some time after the *Canterbury Tales* were being read (see below) and before 1450, the estimated date of the manuscript; 3274 lines predominantly four-stress and riming ordinarily abab. Numbers of verses, sometimes in considerable passages, contain but three stresses; when these verses occur as b lines they make the stanzas approach the regular "ballad stanza."

At the beginning of the English poem, Laban (the Balan of Mouskés), the Sowdon of Babylon, is at his capital of Aigremore in Spain, whence he sails with his son Ferumbras and his daughter Floripas to besiege Rome. His army ravages the Roman countryside and by the ruse of counterfeited arms gains admission to the first ward. The Pope sends to Charlemagne for aid. There follow further attacks upon the city; in one of these the Pope himself is overcome by Ferumbras, who scornfully spares him when he sees his tonsure: "Go home and kepe thy qwer!" Charles prepares to come to the rescue, sending Guy of Burgundy ahead with a force. Before Guy arrives, however, Rome has fallen. The Saracens seize the relics of St. Peter's, plunder and burn the city, and return to Aigremore, where they spend three months in heathen rites and revelry. Guy awaits Charlemagne, and the combined Christian forces sail to Aigremore. They lay waste the country-side. Ferumbras issues with a great host and there is a prolonged battle. After-wards, Charles praises his old knights and counsels the young to take example from them.

Here the *Destruction* part of the *Sowdon* comes to an end. There follows a passage of 111 lines (939–1050) not found in the French versions. This passage opens with a Saracen prayer for victory addressed to "Thow rede Marȝ Armypotente," con-tinues with a conventional invocation to Spring, and then gives a description of the Sowdon's army: it is composed of warriors from India Major, Assye, Ascoloyne, Venys, etc., etc., some blue, some yellow, and some "blake as More." After these have drunk the blood of wild beasts "as is here use to egre here mode," the Sowdon orders a sacrifice to his gods. There are further rites, and Ferumbras is given com-mand of an assortment of tribes to lead on the morrow.

The *Fierabras* part of the *Sowdon* begins with Ferumbras' leading this host forth. Hiding it in a woods, he advances and challenges Roland, Oliver, and four other peers to fight him alone. Roland bids Charles depend for a champion on his old knights whom he has so praised. Oliver finally undertakes the duel. The fight lasts all day but at length Ferumbras is wounded and overcome. He asks for baptism.

In a melee, Roland and Oliver are taken captive and brought before the Sow-don, who has them thrown into a dungeon. Some days later, Floripas, while gather-ing flowers in her garden "in morne colde," hears the prisoners lamenting and resolves to help them. (This scene, suggestive of the *Knight's Tale*, is also found in Egerton.) When her duenna refuses to cooperate, Floripas calls her to the win-dow to see the porpoises play and pushes her out. She goes to the prison, dashes the warden's brains out with his own key-clog, and takes the prisoners to her chamber. Meanwhile Charles has sent Guy of Burgundy and the rest of the peers to demand the release of Roland and Oliver; Laban orders them to be seized and Floripas manages to get them also into her chamber. She becomes affianced to Guy, whom she has long loved. The peers rush upon Laban at supper and void the castle of him and his followers.

The Sowdon assails the castle but fails to take it. Floripas has a magic girdle which is a talisman against hunger; the Sowdon sends a thief to steal it. The French sally forth and seize supplies of food. A renewed assault on the castle comes to nought when Floripas has the Sowdon's treasure thrown over the walls to distract the assailants. Richard of Normandy is sent to Charles for help. There are more sallies and a rescue of Guy from under Saracen gallows. Richard reaches Charles just as the latter has been persuaded by the traitorous Ganelon that the peers are dead. The Emperor vows vengeance on Ganelon and sets out for Aigremore with his army and with Ferumbras. The peers sally forth to meet their relief and Laban is overcome. Floripas welcomes Charlemagne and gives him the relics. At Ferumbras' request Laban is offered baptism, but he spits into the holy font and is forthwith beheaded. Floripas is baptized and married to Guy. Charles gives Spain to Guy and Ferumbras to divide; he returns to Paris, whence he distributes the relics to various shrines and where he orders Ganelon to be drawn and hanged.

As noted above, the *Sowdon* is a translation of the original of Egerton and this original was a radical abridgement and adaptation of the materials of the Hanover *Destruction de Rome* and the *Fierabras*. The Englishman's hand is evident in the interpolated passage between the *Destruction* part and the *Fierabras* part, where the invocation to Spring, besides having a freshness not usual in the poem nor, in fact, in most translations, seems to echo the opening and lines 356–59 of Passus XI of the B-Text of *Piers Plowman* and perhaps *Troilus and Criseyde* I, 156–58. The opening of the Prayer to Mars recalls the *Knight's Tale* (I, 1982) and the opening of *Anelida and Arcite*. Elsewhere in the *Sowdon*, in lines 41–49, which are not paralleled in Egerton, are several phrases reminiscent of the General Prologue of the *Canterbury Tales* (lines 1, 10, 11, 97, and 98). The hand of the translator may also be evident in a more copious display of "learning" of things Saracen—ritualistic and ethnological—in the body of the English poem as well as in the interpolation. Somewhat more conspicuous, too, in the *Sowdon* than in Egerton is the vein of gay if often slapstick comedy, as when (twice) a Saracen's imprecations are cut short by an arrow or (again twice) a Saracen is bisected by a portcullis.

THE ASHMOLE SIR FIRUMBRAS [47]. Southwestern; ca. 1380. This, unlike the loose and very much curtailed *Fierabras* offered by the latter part of the *Sowdon* (lines 979 ff.), is a full and close translation. The beginning, a leaf after line 4775 a, and the end are missing and must be supplied by respectively 37, 62, and 214 lines from the Old French. The Ashmole poem, though not so lively as the *Sowdon*, is metrically more finished, and its narrative is less erratic as well as more leisurely. It is also more leisurely—perhaps one should say prolix—than its French original, though it is often lively and entertaining, as, for example, in the baptismal scenes at the end. An adequate notion of the basic plot is conveyed by the outline of the *Fierabras* part of the *Sowdon*, above.

The manuscript, Ashmole 33 of the Bodleian, is of considerable interest. It is in one hand throughout and is an autograph, like the *Ormulum*, the *Aȝenbite of Inwyt*, the Peterhouse *Equatorie of the Planetis* (perhaps to be ascribed to Chaucer), and few if any other important Middle English manuscripts. It is bound in a triple envelope of parchment consisting of two documents of minor importance concerning the diocese of Exeter; the outer is dated 1357, the inner (folded double, hence the triple envelope) is dated 1377. On the back of the inner cover is an original draft, in the same hand as the manuscript proper, of lines 331–759 of the *Firumbras*, and elsewhere on the covers an original draft also of some thirty scattered other lines. Nothing in the text clashes with the evidence of the covers that the Ashmole *Firumbras* is to be dated toward the end of the fourteenth century and that it originated in the neighborhood of Exeter. '

The poem is characterized by a change of meter beginning with line 3411. Down to that point, the lines are septenary couplets with interlocking internal rimes that might be written as ballad measure. Konick calls this part of *Firumbras* Ash. I. The remainder (lines 3411 to end, Ash. II) is in tail-rime stanzas aabccb, the couplets being four-stress, the b lines, three.

Among extant versions of *Fierabras* and translations of it, Konick distinguishes two traditions, and he equates the shift of meter after line 3410 of Ashmole *Firumbras* with a shift of source from one to the other of these traditions. The first tradition he calls the Abbreviating or non-Vulgate; the second the Vulgate, represented in the printed edition and in several manuscripts. The lost parent version of the Abbreviating tradition, though itself probably not very dissimilar to other Vulgate manuscripts, gave rise to a long development of versions (in French, Provençal, Latin, Irish, etc.) "characterized not only by their common omissions, but also by great independence in invention of names, renderings of the original source, and even by additions" (*The Authorship*, p. 34). High on the stemma of Abbreviating texts is the source of Ash. I. (At the top of this stemma and derived from the Vulgate parent of the Abbreviating texts, is the source of Caxton's version; at the bottom, and heir to the greatest number of omissions and other alterations, is the common source of the *Sowdon* and Egerton.) Ash. II derives from the Vulgate tradition (as does, independently of it, the Fillingham *Firumbras*).

Unlike Ash. I, with its evidences of a first draft, Ash. II seems to have been written "straight off," and Konick thinks that it is little more than a copy of an earlier English translation. There are stylistic differences between the two parts; Ash. I is a freer translation; its author seems to have had greater interest in warfare and the out-of-doors, and it is less careful in preserving religious detail, for example, than Ash. II. The shift of source might be due to defectiveness of either or both of the source manuscripts or to the author's having learned of the presumably English source of Ash. II only when he reached line 3411.

THE FILLINGHAM FIRUMBRAS [48], 1375–1400 (?), is the first item of the Fillingham MS (1475–1500), which disappeared for over a hundred years after it was described by George Ellis. Rediscovered in 1907, it was acquired by the British Museum, where it is now catalogued as Additional 37492. It contains also the *Otuel and Roland* discussed below as part of The Otuel Group.

The Fillingham *Firumbras* is a fragment. It begins at that point in the story of Fierabras at which the peers sally from Floripas' bower to attack the Sowdon at supper. The remaining story of Fierabras, slightly more than half, is told in 921 couplets, of which each verse has usually three stresses before and three after a caesural pause. There is no alliteration. The confused dialect seems basically East Midland, with suggestion of London influence. The text is neatly written but is obviously based on a damaged original which had evidently also been deliberately abridged. The editor, M. I. O'Sullivan, suggests that the lost original was a jongleur's manuscript which became worn, torn, and thumbmarked; the text which we have "is unquestionably a jongleur's version" (p. xxiv). Like Ash. II (Ashmole *Firumbras* lines 3411–end), but independently of it, the Fillingham *Firumbras* stems from the Vulgate, rather than Abbreviating, *Fierabras* tradition.

CAXTON'S CHARLES THE GRETE [49], of 1485, is a very close, even slavish, translation of a French prose work by a Swiss, Jean Bagnyon, published in 1478 and entitled *Fierabras*, though actually it is a "whole life" of Charlemagne, in three Books, of which only the second has to do with Fierabras. This second Book, however, which comes to 163 pages in the EETS edition, is more than twice the length of the other two Books taken together. In Bagnyon's prologues and epilogue, as preserved in Caxton, we are told that the "Myrrour Hystoryal" (of Vincent of Beauvais) is a chief source of the first and third Books (it is actually the sole source) and that the source of the second Book (*Fierabras*) is "an olde romaunce in Frensshe."

The first Book deals with the kings of France from Francus, a companion of Aeneas, down to Charlemagne, whose person and customs are described, as well as his journey to Constantinople, whence he returned with the relics of the Passion. Some of this material came to Vincent from two twelfth-century Latin texts, the *Descriptio qualiter Karolus Magnus* (etc.) and the *Pseudo-Turpin*, both of which are described below in connection with *Charlemagne and Roland*. The third Book tells of Charlemagne's conquest of Spain, the duel between Roland and Ferragus, the battle of Roncesvalles, and finally the death of Charlemagne himself, and is simply the bulk of the *Pseudo-Turpin* as appropriated by Vincent.

In the prologue to his second Book, Bagnyon says (as translated with characteristic closeness by Caxton): "I ne entende but onely to reduce thauncyent ryme in to prose . . . wythoute to adiouste ony thynge that I haue not founde in the book competent, & in lyke wyse as I shal fynde I shal reduce." The version which he thus faithfully reduced to prose stood, as we have seen, midway between the Vulgate *Fierabras* as found in the modern published version and the source of Ash. I. (See also under Caxton.)

II. The Otinel (Otuel) Group

Like *Fierabras*, the slightly younger French romance of *Otinel* [50] tells the story of a Saracen (Otinel or Otuel) who accepts baptism and fights in defense of his adopted faith. It runs to 2133 decasyllabic lines in the printed version, which is based on the sole Central French MS, with variants from the Anglo-Norman MS. There are also two brief fragments and six translations: three in English, two in Welsh, and one in Icelandic. All translations are closer to the Anglo-Norman than to the French text.

The poems of the Otuel Group consist of *Roland and Vernagu*, *Otuel and Roland*, *Otuel a Knight*, *The Sege of Melayne*, and *Duke Roland and Sir Otuel of Spain*. By way of explaining the relationships among the first three of these romances, it will be well to describe briefly (1) the reconstructed cyclic romance *Charlemagne and Roland*; and (2) Laura Hibbard Loomis' theory of the Auchinleck Bookshop.

1. *CHARLEMAGNE AND ROLAND [51] is the name given to a composite Middle English tail-rime romance which has come down to us broken in two, the one fragment, *Roland and Vernagu*, being preserved in the Auchinleck MS (1330–40), the remaining and larger portion, *Otuel and Roland*, being preserved in the Fillingham MS (1475–1500). *Roland and Vernagu (RV)* first tells briefly of Charlemagne's journey to Constantinople and his return with relics of the Passion; it then continues with his conquest of Spain as set forth in the enormously popular twelfth-century Latin prose *Chronicle of the Pseudo-Turpin* (ca. 1140), down to and including the episode of the slaying of the Saracen giant Vernagu by Roland. Here it breaks off with the statement that news of Vernagu's death comes to the ears of the Saracen Otuel, a figure unknown to the *Pseudo-Turpin*. The *Otuel and Roland (OR)* of the Fillingham MS gives first a version of the romance of Otuel and then returns to and concludes the *Pseudo-Turpin* account of Charlemagne's victories in Spain, which ends with Roland's death at Roncesvalles and Charlemagne's vengeance therefor.

The immediate source of all these materials except the *Otuel* is an Old French prose work known as the *Estoire de Charlemagne*, or *Redacted Johannis Turpin*, which dates from 1206 and survives in eighteen manuscripts. This is a French translation of the *Pseudo-Turpin* redacted to include in the first chapter a précis of the *Descriptio qualiter Karolus Magnus clavum et coronam Domini a Constantinopoli Aquis Grani detulerit*, an ecclesiastical version of the story which also lies behind the *Pèlerinage de Charlemagne*. Thus *CR may be defined as a tail-rime English translation of the *Estoire de Charlemagne* into which has been inserted a tail-rime translation of *Otuel*. A more detailed account may be got by joining together the plot summaries of *RV* and *OR* below. Against the background of the *Estoire*, however, it is clear that some loss, repetition, and transposition of episodes have come about. A four-stanza "table of contents" of *CR with which *OR* begins once stood at the head of *RV* in the Auchinleck MS, as is attested by certain matching letters on the stub of an excised leaf in that pillaged volume (see Spec 21.279). This table of contents throws further light on the disarrangement and loss of *Estoire* episodes. It also lists the story of the "caytyf Emoun" of "Mount Awbane" as preceding the *Otuel*—surprisingly, for there is nowhere else evidence that any version of the *Foure Sonnes of Aymon* ever appeared in English before Caxton.

2. THE AUCHINLECK MS AND THE LOOMIS BOOKSHOP THEORY [52].

Forty-four articles, in six hands, of an original fifty-six or more survive in the invaluable Middle English poetic miscellany known as the Auchinleck MS (1330–40). Arguing from the plainness of the book and especially from certain relationships among its articles, Laura Hibbard Loomis concludes that it is the product of a London commercial scriptorium, in which a group of translators and scribes, or translator-scribes, worked under the direction of a master-craftsman or general editor. Thus we find the materials of the Old French *Gui de Warewic* used to make three romances in the Auchinleck: (1) a couplet *Guy*, narrating the hero's adventures down to his killing of the Northumberland dragon; (2) a stanzaic *Guy*, celebrating his subsequent exploits but omitting the embedded story of his son Reinbrun; and (3) a stanzaic *Reinbrun*, a wholly novel entity composed of the aforementioned matters thriftily omitted from the stanzaic *Guy* (see [7] above). A very large number of verbal parallels, some quite extensive, between various poems of the Auchinleck MS, pointed out by Mrs. Loomis in her original article on the Auchinleck MS and a possible London bookshop, and subsequently augmented by herself and others (see Bibliography), seem hard to explain except as due to collaboration within one shop. Walpole was able to identify, on the basis of unique errors and forms of place-names, the precise manuscript of the *Estoire de Charlemagne* used by the compiler-translator of *CR. At the time that the Auchinleck MS was composed, this manuscript was a part of an Old French miscellany known as the Edwardes MS, of which another part was the manuscript of *Gui de Warewic* previously described by Mrs. Loomis as "close to" the source of the Auchinleck Guy poems. The Edwardes MS, certainly used for *CR and thus by implication once a property of the Bookshop, also contained other French poems of which translations appear in the Auchinleck MS, though these, like the Edwardes *Gui de Warewic*, have not yet been finally scrutinized for evidence of direct filiation.

The theory also has a special bearing on *Charlemagne and Roland*. The first part of *CR, that is, *Roland and Vernagu*, appears in the Auchinleck MS as the thirty-first article and ends with link-lines introducing the *Otuel*. Why the rest of *CR was not copied into the Auchinleck MS is not known. But following *RV*, as article thirty-two, is a couplet *Otuel*, entitled *Otuel a Knight*. Between this couplet *Otuel* and the tail-rime *Otuel* of *CR in the Fillingham MS there are about thirty extensive line-parallels (see O'Sullivan). Neither poem seems to be derived from the other—certainly the circumstantial Fillingham *Otuel* is not derived from *Otuel a Knight*. O'Sullivan thinks that both poems are derived from a lost English *Otuel, presumably in couplets. In any event, we here have duplication of materials associated with the Auchinleck MS not unlike the duplication of Guy of Warwick poems.

ROLAND AND VERNAGU [53]. Before 1330–40; 880 verses in tail-rime stanzas aabccbddbeeb, the couplets being chiefly four-stress lines, the tail-lines three; East Midland, with some Southwestern traces (but cf. Bibliography). Forty-four lines have been lost at the beginning; as noted above at the opening of this section on the Otuel Group, these were the bulk of a four-stanza (forty-eight-line) table of contents of *CR.

The contents of *RV* have been described above in terms of their ultimate Latin sources. These are ecclesiastical, tendentious, and episodic almost to the point of being anecdotal, and their material gains nothing from being retold in doggerel. The focus of the *Descriptio* is on the relics of the Passion and on the miracles that attest their genuineness, to the point that the English versifier quite forgets to mention Charlemagne's battles against Ebrahim on account of which the relics were given up by the grateful Emperor of Constantinople. Charlemagne's conquest of Spain, as in the *Pseudo-Turpin*, is a triumphal procession in which scores of cities are taken, with or without the agency of miracles. There are also miracles of purely moral interest, as when a false executor who has appropriated money left to poor clergy is swept away by devils; and there is a description of Charlemagne's person and customs (see also *OR*, below). The final and longest episode is Roland's duel with the giant Vernagu (Ferragus), "the earliest complete example" of such a Christian-Saracen duel (Meredith Jones, Spec 17.222). On their second day of fighting, Roland graciously adjourns the combat to permit the giant to sleep and puts a great stone under his head to relieve his snoring. Charmed with this act, Vernagu inquires of the faith that prompted it and Roland explains to him the mysteries of the Trinity, the Incarnation, the Virgin Birth, etc. The giant declares that, having mastered these points, he is ready to go on with the fight to prove which religion is the better. Roland slays him. *RV* ends with the statement that the Saracen Otuel hears of Vernagu's fate.

OTUEL AND ROLAND [54], East Midland, gives the story of Otuel in about 1700 lines and then resumes and concludes the *Estoire de Charlemagne* in some 1100 additional lines. The *Otuel* preserves more details of the original than do either of the other two English translations of *Otinel*. It is in tail-rime stanzas aabaabccbddb—a slightly more exacting form than that used in *Roland and Vernagu*; the resumed and concluded *Estoire de Charlemagne* is in the *RV* stanza (aabccbddbeeb). In both parts the lines are generally four-stress, except for tail-lines, which are three-stress. *OR* has been badly messed up in transmission; parts of many stanzas have been lost and many lines and rimes have been garbled. In addition the Fillingham MS has suffered loss of leaves. Episodes are introduced by "Here bygynnyth" stanzas, usually of six lines; no such stanzas appear in *RV*. As originally a part of **CR*, *OR* is to be dated before ca. 1330–40; the Fillingham MS (Additional 37492) is dated 1475–1500.

After four "table of content" stanzas copied from the beginning of **CR*, we learn how Sir Otuel arrives before Charlemagne's court at St. Denis with an insulting ultimatum from Garcy. Roland undertakes the duel; he is armed by Charlemagne's daughter Belisent. The combat is elaborately described. At length the Holy Ghost in the form of a Dove alights on Otuel's helmet; Otuel cries recreant and is christened and offered the hand of Belisent.

Charles gathers a great host and sets out to invade Lombardy and overcome Garcy at his capital, Utaly. Roland, Oliver, and Ogier go out looking for adventure; they slay three Saracen kings and capture a fourth, Clarel, but they are set upon by thousands. Clarel is freed; he now captures Ogier and sends him to his sweetheart, Enfamy, for safekeeping. Otuel comes to the rescue of Roland and Oliver; the Saracens are routed. Clarel and Otuel fight a long duel and Clarel is killed. Charlemagne moves his forces up and a general battle begins. Ogier escapes from Enfamy's jailers and rejoins his fellows. Garcy's forces are crushed and Garcy is taken to Paris and baptized by Archbishop Turpin. (End of *Otuel*).

(The *Estoire de Charlemagne* is resumed.) Not long after, Ebrahim brings a power to Cordova and Charles attacks him. The Saracens blow horns to affright the Christians' horses, but on the second day the Christians blindfold their horses and stop their ears with wax. The Saracens are routed; Charles kills Ebrahim. The next enemy is the King of Navarre. Charles prays for a sign as to which of his men will be killed in the battle and such show a red cross on their shoulders. He leaves these men in a chapel and wins a bloodless victory, but, alas, he finds the stigmatized men dead on his return. He now divides Navarre and other lands among his followers and makes Compostela the archiepiscopal see of Spain and Galicia. There follows a description of Charles' person and customs (this has appeared verbatim in *RV*, where it is out of its true *Estoire* order.)

Charles is at Pamplona when "Mansure" and "Belgians" affect willingness to become Christian. Ganelon is sent as envoy and accepts a bribe. There follows the ambush at Roncesvalles in the flat and insipid tradition of the *Pseudo-Turpin*, with some battle episodes of a stereotyped sort added by the English versifier. In this tradition Turpin is not on the battlefield and at the end of the battle he is saying Mass in "Charlys chapyll" when he sees devils carrying Mansure to hell and angels carrying Roland to heaven. Charles returns to avenge Roland and on a day prolonged to three defeats the Saracen host. The poem closes with the punishment of Ganelon.

OTUEL A KNIGHT [55]. East Midland; 1738 lines in couplets of four-stress lines or three-stress lines seemingly at random. The poem's presence in the Auchinleck MS gives it a date before 1330–40. Eight lines are lost following line 120 and the poem breaks off with the submission of Garcy before Charlemagne, the remaining lines, probably few, having been on a lost folio. For the presence of this *Otuel* immediately following *RV* in the Auchinleck MS, see above.

The outline of the Otuel part of *OR* above describes the plot of *Otuel a Knight*. Extensive and striking as are the verbal parallels between these two *Otuels*, the author of the latter has dealt freely with his source: many particulars of the Otinel story which survive in *OR* are omitted in *Otuel a Knight*—even, for example, the name of Garcy's capital. There are also idiosyncrasies in the treatment of episodes. The poem begins with a 54-line introduction describing Charlemagne and Garcy which is not found in the Otinel-Otuel tradition proper, and it has an exceptionally circumstantial account of Ogier's escape from Enfamy's prison. Lines 909–58 may serve as a convenient example of the banality all too frequently found in most of the English Charlemagne romances.

THE SEGE OF MELAYNE [56]. Northern; about 1400 or somewhat earlier; preserved, like *Duke Roland and Sir Otuel*, in the mid-fifteenth-century MS Additional 31042. A gap, probably of a single leaf, occurs after line 1365; the poem breaks off at line 1602, in the midst of what appears to be the final and climactic battle. In tail-rime stanzas of the form aabccbddbeeb. Irregular alliteration is quite conspicuous at times.

The Saracen Arabas conquers Lombardy and drives Sir Alantyne, Lord of Milan, out of his city. In a dream, an angel bids Alantyne to seek help from Charles; in a dream, an angel shows Charles the destruction that has befallen Milan and bids him to help Alantyne. When Alantyne arrives before Charles, Bishop Turpin supports his appeal, but Ganelon persuades Charles that, instead of going himself to the relief of Milan, he should send Roland. The expedition under Roland proves as ill-starred as his stepfather could have wished. Vast numbers of Christians, including Alantyne, are killed. Roland, Oliver, Gawter, and Guy of Burgundy are taken prisoner but regain their freedom when the Saracens are blinded in a blasphemous attempt to set fire to a cross. They kill Arabas and return to France, the sole survivors.

Turpin now steps very much to the force. He raises an army of 100,000 "priests with shaven crown." Under the influence of Ganelon, Charles refuses to resume the war; Turpin excommunicates him and besieges him in Paris. Charles submits and collects forces.

The Saracens have in the meantime crowned Garcy sultan. When the French reach the scene of their former disaster, Turpin says a Mass for which God miraculously supplies the wine and bread. In a melee, Turpin is wounded but he and his clergy drive the sultan into Milan. Turpin refuses to show Charles his wound or to eat or drink while Milan remains untaken. The next day he is again wounded, this time in the side with a spear. The battle rages back and forth. At length the Saracens are put to flight. Charles weeps for Turpin, who still will not let his wounds be dressed and who continues his fast, now three days old. The French ready their engines to attack the walls of Milan. Here the poem breaks off.

No French source is known, but that one existed is in itself probable and is also the implication not so much of several references to "the Cronekill" as of persistent use of the pronoun "our"—"our knights," "our worthy men," "our rearguard," "our Bretons," and the like. Gaston Paris and Gautier suggested that the *Sege of Melayne* forms a kind of introduction to *Otuel* in the same way as the *Destruction de Rome* is introductory to *Fierabras*, and the *Sege* has ever since been placed in the Otuel Group. This classification is here held to with some misgivings. The *Sege* never names Otuel and we do not known how its story ended. No version of *Otuel* has been adapted to accommodate it to the *Sege* as a prologue. But the fact remains that the villain of the *Sege* is Garcy and the scene is Lombardy; and in fabricating his stock romance, the author of the *Sege* drew as heavily on the *Otuel* as on any other romance, even *Fierabras* or the *Chanson de Roland*. Furthermore, it may not be insignificant that the tail-rime *Sege* precedes the tail-rime *Duke Roland and Sir Otuel* in MS Additional 31042. As an independent, "detached" romance, the *Sege* would have ended with either the death or the baptism of Garcy. On the whole it seems less likely that it ended with any such flat contradiction of a poem well known to the author and many of his contemporaries than that it ended with the escape of

Garcy from Milan to Attaly, from which capital he sends his challenge to Charlemagne at the opening of *Otuel*.

Though the *Sege* is thus taken as a chronological preface to *Otuel*, it does not otherwise stand to the *Otuel* as the *Destruction* stands to *Fierabras*. The purpose of the *Destruction* is to introduce *Fierabras* by explaining the circumstances of its opening. Nothing in the *Otuel* calls for explanation, and the *Sege* obviously has its own purpose: to glorify Bishop Turpin, though unlike its ecclesiastical counterparts *RV* and the latter portion of *OR* it does not happen to use materials of the *Pseudo-Turpin Chronicle*. His ridiculous clericalism apart, the author is no mean versifier.

DUKE ROLAND AND SIR OTUEL OF SPAIN [57]. Northern; about 1400 or somewhat earlier. It is in the most difficult of tail-rime stanzas: aabaabccbccb; in stresses its lines are like those of *RV-OR* and the *Sege*, each third line being of three stresses and the rest of four. The author is a competent versifier, with some tendency to use irregular alliteration. Its 1596 lines, in MS Additional 31042, follow the *Sege of Melayne* after an interval of two pages containing a Latin prayer and hymn. The poem follows the story of Otuel faithfully as regards outline but omits many details; the translation is decidedly free throughout and increasingly so toward the end, where 500 lines of the original are represented by only about 200. The scene of the arming of Otuel by Charlemagne's daughter Belisent (lines 391–432) is one of the best in the poem, as it is one of the best also in the original *Otinel* (lines 341–87). It may be used as a fair point of comparison among the three English *Otuels*. In the present poem, barring a ludicrous mistranslation in line 424, it presents a simplification of the original but a simplification with considerable charm; in *OR* (lines 339–401) it has little simplification and no charm; and it is omitted altogether from *Otuel a Knight*.

III. Detached Romances

*OLIVE AND LANDRES—see above [45].

THE SONG OF ROLAND [58]. East Midland; ca. 1400; a fragment of 1049 lines preserved in Lansdown MS 388, of 1475–1500. The beginning and end are lacking, as are lines here and there in the manuscript. The

lines are four-stress and rimed in couplets; the rimes are very often imperfect, however, and numbers of "couplets" do not rime at all. Irregular
alliteration. About one-fourth as long as the Oxford *Chanson de Roland*,
the fragment covers roughly a fourth of the story of the *Chanson*, beginning
with the return of Ganelon from his embassy to Saragossa and ending
at that moment in the battle of Roncesvalles when Roland finally decides
to summon help (Oxford *Roland*, lines 669–1705).

Ganelon brings wine and a troop of Saracen maidens from Saragossa as presents
from the sultan, whom he represents as ready to come to France for baptism.
Charles joyfully starts home. That night his men drink the wine and lie with the
damsels. Charles dreams of treachery. At the Gates of Spain Ganelon suggests
that Roland lead the rearguard; Charles denounces Ganelon for constantly schem-
ing against Roland's life. Roland defiantly accepts the post of danger; the douzepers
and other knights join him. Ganelon leads the van of the army as it starts again
toward France.
The Saracens prepare for battle. Amaris asks leave to go ahead and seek out
Roland; he hastens forth with 40,000. Roland warns his men to be alert: Ganelon
may have betrayed them. He sends Gauter out with 10,000 to reconnoitre. There
is a fearful battle; Gauter's host is killed and he is sorely wounded but returns to
warn Roland that they have been betrayed. Meanwhile, Charles is alarmed at the
long absence of his knights and tells of his dreams; his barons accuse Ganelon of
treason. Ganelon insists that Roland is merely hunting. The king is anxious but
goes on to Cardoile. Some of Roland's knights urge him to blow for succor. Amaris
tells the Sultan how he has slain all the French but one; he is now given eleven
kings and 100,000 men. Oliver and all the other French barons urge Roland to
blow his horn, but he rebukes them. Day breaks; Turpin says Mass; the battle is
joined. In a series of duels each Saracen king is slain by a douzeper; great is the
slaughter; by nightfall the Saracens are all killed. The main body of Saracens now
appears. In France, there is a great, dark storm during the battle and a red cloud
mirrors the deaths of so many brave men. Roland, Oliver, and the other peers
perform prodigies of valor. Roland bids his men rest and proposes to send a messenger to Charlemagne for help. Oliver angrily tells him to "let be all siche sawes."
Here the poem breaks off.

Though it makes some use of the *Pseudo-Turpin*, the *Song of Roland* is
basically a translation of the *Chanson de Roland*. The version of the *Chanson*
used is not among those known. In some particulars the *Song* agrees with
the Oxford *Roland* as against the other, inferior versions; in some, with
the other versions as against the Oxford. Some episodes in the *Song*, such
as the wounding and defeat of Gauter (lines 331–56), are not found elsewhere except in interpolated passages common to only three rimed versions
(C, V 7, and P). We are thus confronted not by descent from a lost original
of both Oxford and the rimed versions (see Mortier's *stemma*, I, [ix]), but
by conflation. Either the English poet made a conflate version of the

Chanson or, what is vastly more probable, he had a conflate version as source. The episode of the women and wine at the beginning of the fragment is drawn from the *Pseudo-Turpin*, where the disaster of Roncesvalles is thus explicitly made a punishment for sin. Wichmann, who felt, with some reason, that the author of the *Song* was a cleric, viewed this borrowing as having been made by him for the purpose of giving a moral basis for the disaster. But whoever borrowed the episode left the moral behind in the *Pseudo-Turpin*; the cause of the disaster in the *Song* is solely the treason of Ganelon, as it is in the *Chanson*. It is possible, too, that the *Turpin* has had further influence, as, for example, in the stress on greed as Ganelon's motive, or the hint that Charles is to learn of the disaster by word of mouth.

The translation is very free in the description of battle-deeds. It is not wholly lacking in movement, but the *desmesure* of the hero of the *Chanson* is barely recognizable in Roland's refusals to summon help; and the dramatic climax of the *Chanson* is sadly mishandled: when Charlemagne expresses alarm at the absence of the rearguard, Ganelon assures him that Roland is merely hunting, though there has been (and is to be) no blast on a hunting horn; and Roland disdains to blow for help but finally decides to send a messenger. Lines 226–27 and especially 393–97 may reflect the attitude toward Charlemagne and his court of late romancers.

THE TAILL OF RAUF COILYEAR [59], or Ralph the Charcoal-Burner. Listed in the index of the Asloan MS (ca. 1515) but found first in a printed edition by Robert Lekpreuik of St. Andrews, 1572; last third of the fifteenth century (?); Scottish; 975 lines in the Gawain-school stanza, ababababcdddc, the first nine lines of each stanza being of four stresses each and alliterative, the remainder of two stresses. The poem is almost certainly of insular origin and its connection with the Charlemagne cycle is external. In it, Roland, far from being headstrong and even insubordinate, is described as above all one who never acts without the Emperor's consent, and he bears himself toward the irascible Rauf with amused tolerance; Charlemagne, good-natured and approachable, is neither the austere patriarch of the *Chanson de Roland* nor the willful tyrant of the late romances. "Paris" is surrounded by "myrk montanis," and at the beginning we hear of "fellis wyde," the "rude mure," and a fierce blizzard blown from the east.

In this blizzard, on Christmas Eve, Charlemagne is separated from his retinue and given a night's lodging by Rauf, who, not recognizing his royal guest, treats him with rough-handed—in fact, violent—familiarity. Charlemagne takes all in good part; he describes himself as a courtier and servant of the queen and promises his host that if he will bring a load of coals to court he shall be guaranteed an excellent market for them.

After the departure of his guest in the morning, Rauf loads his horse and sets out for Paris. On the way he encounters Roland, whom Charlemagne has sent out to look for him. The rude collier quarrels with the knight and challenges him to fight a duel on the following day. They proceed by separate ways to Paris. At the court, Rauf is alarmed to recognize his late guest, but the Emperor knights him and bids him win his spurs. The next day, Rauf sets out to meet Roland. He encounters instead a Saracen, Magog, who has come from the Chan of Tartary with an ultimatum for Charlemagne. Both spears are shivered; both steeds slain; the warriors fight afoot at desperate length. Finally, Roland arrives and ends the duel by bribing Magog to renounce Mahound in return for the hand of Lady Jane of Anjou. The trio proceed to the court, where they are welcomed with rejoicing; Rauf is made marshal of France.

The poem offers us a version of the widespread folktale known as the "King in disguise," to which is added a sequel, Rauf's winning of his spurs. Numerous details, especially in the description of Rauf's household and his entertainment of his royal guest, show a close relationship with an English lay of somewhat earlier date, John the Reeve, in which John, after entertaining Edward Longshanks, is summoned to court and knighted. The Scottish poet seems to have had at hand also a second version of the "King in disguise," for which warrant is to be found on the Continent: a collier entertains his sovereign, who induces him to bring a load of coals to court on guarantee of a good market; in this fashion he is rewarded for his hospitality. The two versions (John the Reeve's and the Continental) are skilfully combined. Rauf sets out with his load of coals and on the way encounters Roland, who has been sent out, like the messenger in John the Reeve, to fetch him to the court. Rauf's bickerings with Roland lay the groundwork for the sequel of Rauf's winning of his spurs. The sources of the sequel are more formally literary. In Rauf's combat with Magog, the poet has constructed, in the broadly comic vein of his whole piece, a burlesque of the stereotyped combat of the *chanson de geste*. Such details in this scene as are not wholly commonplace point to the "titular" combats of *Otinel* and *Fierabras*, as might be expected from the popularity of these romances in Great Britain (HSNPL 15.135).

The poem is unflaggingly high-spirited throughout—from Rauf's churlish but ready proffer of hospitality at the beginning, to his unbounded delight in fighting a real Saracen at the end.

The Right Pleasaunt and Goodly Historie of THE FOURE SONNES OF AYMON [60] is the title of Caxton's minutely close translation, made about 1489, of the French prose *Quatre fils Aymon*, often called *Renaud de Montauban*. The EETS text of Caxton runs to 592 pages. Caxton seems to have used an edition printed at Lyons about 1480, of which an exemplar is to be found in the British Museum. The French prose version in its turn is based upon a *chanson*, *Renaud de Montauban*, of about 18,000 lines, which originated about the beginning of the thirteenth century; the prose version is much inferior to the *chanson* but follows its matter fairly closely. These versions have been endlessly adapted, translated, and imitated all over Europe. The chief characters, along with Charlemagne, Roland, Ogier, and other peers, are Renaud and his three brothers, their father Aymon, their cousin the magician Maugis, and Renaud's marvelous horse, Bayard, who can cover thirty feet at a stride. The mainstay of the plot is a long siege by Charlemagne of the rebellious brothers in their castle of Montauban, but the action ranges from the north to the south of France and back again, and toward the end, Renaud goes as a pilgrim to Jerusalem, where he drops his disguise long enough to free the city from Saracen occupation. He is finally "martyred," again in disguise, while assisting as a laborer at the building of St. Peter's in Cologne. Charlemagne is presented as cruel and unjust. Aymon himself remains faithful to Charlemagne, except for fleeting episodes of assistance to his sons. Maugis uses his magic only rarely and finally forswears it forever, praying God and the saints for power to keep his resolve. Bayard falls into Charlemagne's clutches but escapes to the forest of Arden, where folk say that he is still alive.

For an allusion to the *Four Sons* in **Charlemagne and Roland*, see [51] above. See also under Caxton.

THE BOKE OF DUKE HUON OF BURDEUX [61] was translated by Sir John Bourchier, Lord Berners, probably about 1530, and published, probably by Wynkyn de Worde, about 1534. It is from first to last an extremely faithful translation of a French prose version of 1455, first printed in 1513 in an edition of which a copy survives in the British

Museum. The romance falls into two Parts. The first Part (269 pages in the EETS edition) follows an original thirteenth-century *chanson*, of about 10,000 lines.

The young Huon, as a consequence of feuds at court, is deprived of his lands by the wrathful Charlemagne and ordered to fetch from Babylon the beard and four teeth of the mighty Admiral Gaudyse. On the way he encounters and wins the favor of Oberon, the king of the fairies, a dwarf in stature but of angelic visage and high moral principles. After many adventures, Huon arrives at Babylon and, with the help of Oberon, obtains the trophies; he also obtains the Admiral's daughter Esclaramonde, who has fallen in love with him and befriended him. On the way to France the two lovers are separated and re-united; Huon's brother, who has usurped the dukedom of Bordeaux, imprisons the pair, and Charlemagne comes to Bordeaux demanding Huon's life. But again Oberon "wishes" himself present and sets all to rights, before returning to Fairyland with the injunction that Huon follow him thither after four years.

The second Part (pp. 273–782 in the EETS edition) contains three sequels from a thirteenth-century expanded verse *Huon* of 30,000 lines and concludes with a fourth sequel from a lost source of the fourteenth century. These sequels narrate respectively: (1) the besieging of Huon and Esclaramonde at Bordeaux by the Emperor of Almayn and a second journey to the East by Huon; (2) the winning of Clariet, daughter of Huon and Esclaramonde, by Florent, prince of Aragon, in competition with felonious and powerful rivals but with timely help from Huon, who by now has come to the throne of Fairyland on the death of Oberon; (3) the adventures of Ide, daughter of Florent and Clariet, who, disguised as a man, becomes constable of Rome and marries the Emperor's daughter, Olive, but is changed to a man by divine interposition and begets a son, Croissant; and (4) the adventures of Croissant.

Huon's second journey to the East, in the first, or Esclaramonde, sequel, offers the more dazzling series of episodes involving oriental magic and splendor—jewels, rings, armor, and swords of supernatural power; an island of adamant that attracts ships fatally by their metal nails; apples of youth; and the like. We hear Cain cursing and lamenting from within an iron tun, and see Judas riding forever on the whirlpool of the gulf of Hell. Down through this sequel, far more than Maugis in the *Foure Sonnes*, Oberon is ever at hand in times of need. The later appearance of this figure, albeit considerably metamorphosed, in Shakespeare and elsewhere in English and other literatures lends it, of course, especial interest.

7*

Only the first Part of the romance can be said to belong to the Charlemagne cycle; Charlemagne's death is alluded to in the first sequel. The whole romance, and especially Part II, is a hodgepodge of characters and events from many sources: King Arthur disputes Huon's claim to the throne of Fairyland; Merlin is mentioned as the son of Ogier the Dane, and Julius Caesar as the father of Oberon; there are borrowings from the Alexander stories; and so forth.

4. Legends of Godfrey of Bouillon

by

R. M. Lumiansky

The career, both actual and legendary, of Godfrey of Bouillon (1060?–1100) includes a series of favorable circumstances difficult to match from either history or legend. Both his parents claimed descent from Charlemagne. Though a second son, he inherited from an uncle the Duchy of Lower Lorraine in 1076. In 1099 he became King of Jerusalem, and thus famous throughout Christendom, chiefly because no other one of the leaders of the First Crusade desired this position. Within 75 years after his death, the miraculous legend of the Swan-Knight was attached to his ancestry. And later he was named one of the Nine Worthies.

The question of the ultimate myth from which grew legends of swan-knights, swan-maidens, and swan-children is much debated. More to our point is the fact that in the latter half of the twelfth century in France a cycle of poetic romances, known as *Le Chevalier au Cygne*, was developed and attached to Godfrey of Bouillon. This cycle has five main parts: (a) *Chanson d'Antioche*, (b) *Chanson de Jérusalem*, (c) *Les chétifs*, (d) *Hélias*, and (e) *Les enfances de Godefroy de Bouillon*. Whatever the chronology of composition for these parts, the cycle covers events from the birth of Godfrey's ancestor, the Swan-Knight, through the capture of Jerusalem by Godfrey. Clearly, the chief motivation for the cycle was to add supernatural ancestry to the military and religious glory of Godfrey.

CHEVALERE ASSIGNE [62]. Second half of the fourteenth century. 370 alliterative long lines. East Midland; perhaps a copy of a Northwest original. Perhaps an epitome of the first 1083 lines of a French poem in the British Museum MS Royal 15. E. vi; or perhaps from the same source as the Latin version in the Bodleian MS Rawlinson Misc 358 (where the hero's name, as in *Chevalere Assigne*, is "Enyas" not "Helyas").

King Oriens of Lyon is sad because he has no heir. One day he weeps at the sight of a peasant woman fortunate enough to have twins. His queen, Beatrice, wrongly says that twins are not possible because each child must have a separate father. That night conception occurs for the king and queen, and in time, as punishment for the queen's erroneous statement, six sons and a daughter are simultaneously born, each with a silver chain about its neck. Matabryne, Oriens' evil mother, plans to destroy the children, and will allow no one else to be present until the birth is over. Then she summons her man Markus and orders him to drown the new-born children. When he removes the children, she replaces them with whelps, shows Oriens the whelps, and tells him that Beatrice must consequently be burned. The king refuses, but puts Beatrice under Matabryne's control. For the next eleven years the queen suffers in prison.

Pity causes Markus to leave the children in a forest rather than drown them. A hermit finds them and God sends a hind to suckle them. The hermit rears the children, but the wicked forester Malkedras sees them and reports their presence to Matabryne. She puts out Markus' eyes for deceiving her and sends Malkedras to kill them and bring her the silver chains. He finds six children—the hermit and one child are in the forest—and cuts off their chains. At once the six change to swans and fly to the nearby river. Malkedras takes the chains to Matabryne, who summons a smith to make them into a cup. When he breaks the first chain it grows, so that half of it is sufficient to make the cup. His wife advises him to keep the other five chains. He does so, giving Matabryne only the cup and the other half-chain; the latter she returns to him as pay.

Next, Matabryne tells Oriens he must burn Beatrice. He reluctantly agrees. But the night before the burning an angel comes to the hermit to tell him that the swans on the river are Beatrice's children, and that the one remaining child is to be called Enyas and taken to the court to defend his mother. The hermit explains matters to the boy, and they go to the court. An angel is ever on the boy's right shoulder as counsellor.

The boy accosts Oriens in the field where the burning is to occur; he tells him that Matabryne is in league with the devil, and he offers to fight for Beatrice. Matabryne angrily tears at Enyas' hair, and orders Malkedras to fight against the boy. An abbot christens Enyas and all the nearby bells ring themselves throughout the fight to show Christ's pleasure. Oriens makes Enyas a knight and gives him horse, armor, and weapons. Another knight explains to Enyas the uses of these items and the methods of single combat. In the fight, Enyas' horse Ferraunce blinds Malekdras' horse. Enyas with miraculous aid from an adder and a fire, both coming from the Cross on his shield, blinds Malkedras. Then Enyas, Chevalere Assigne, kills his opponent, and thanks God for the victory. Matabryne is burned at the stake; Beatrice is released; and Enyas tells the whole story to Oriens. The goldsmith produces the five chains, which are returned to five of the six swans, who become human again. The sixth remains a swan and grieves piteously. God's help brought about the restoration of the five.

Though this piece closely follows events usual in the cycle, though Enyas is called "Chevalere Assigne" (lines 333 and 369), and though one of the restored children is named "Godyfere" (line 367), the writer gives no evidence of intending to connect this poem with Godfrey of Bouillon. In fact, the usual ending of the French versions, wherein the unrestored swan leads the Swan-Knight to further adventures, is here omitted.

The chief motivation for the poem seems religious. The opening four lines state the possibility of God's help to the wronged, of which this narrative is to be an example. Matabryne is the direct agent of Satan (line 10). Beatrice in prison prays to the God who saved Susanna (lines 90–91). Christ sends the hind to suckle the children (line 111). The goldsmith's wife explains the growth of the half-chain as the "werke of God" (line 170). Christ sends the angel to the hermit (line 193); Enyas is Christ's representative (line 209), and the bells ring to show Christ's pleasure when Enyas is baptized (line 274). The adder and the fire come from the Cross on Enyas' shield (lines 331–32). And the poem ends "Thus the help of God restored all those wronged."

The simple religious theme and the lengthy elementary instruction given Enyas in arms permit the speculation that the poem may have been prepared as instruction for boys of about Enyas' age (line 243). Though lacking in artistic subtlety, the work is a straightforward and unified narrative with considerable simple popular appeal stemming from the marvels, the single combat, and the actions of the evil Matabryne.

HELYAS, THE KNIGHT OF THE SWAN [63]. Printed 1512 by Wynkyn de Worde. Free prose translation by Robert Copland of *La généalogie aveques les gestes . . . du . . . Godeffroy de Boulin . . .*, by Pierre d'Esrey or Desrey of Troyes, printed probably before 1500. One copy of de Worde's edition exists, as does one copy of the reprint by William Copland.

The first twenty-five chapters of this prose version cover much the same material, though in greater detail, as the *Chevalere Assigne* (summarized above). The remaining chapters (26 through 43) tell of the adventures of Helyas and his swan-brother, of Helyas' marriage and of the birth and accomplishments of his three sons: Godfrey, Baudwyn, and Eustace. The story ends with emphasis on Godfrey of Bouillon's kingship of Jerusalem.

Godefroy of Boloyne, Caxton's translation of the historical work *The Siege and Conquest of Jerusalem*, will be dealt with in the chapter devoted to Caxton (q. v.).

5. Legends of Alexander the Great

by

R. M. Lumiansky

Alexander the Great (356–23 B.C.) was the son of King Philip of Macedon. At age fourteen he was placed under the tutelage of Aristotle; at sixteen he put down a rebellion in his father's absence; at twenty he ascended the throne of his assassinated father. From 335 until his death of fever, he successfully occupied himself with stabilizing Greece and conquering a large portion of the known world.

Alexander received a great deal of attention from medieval writers. These writings fall into three groups: the legendary works derived from Pseudo-Callisthenes; the historical works derived from the tradition of Quintus Curtius, Justin, and Orosius; and the works which represent a combination of both the legendary and the historical traditions.

We are here concerned for the most part with legendary writings, almost all of which descend from a Greek prose biography, written between 200 B.C. and 200 A.D., by a native of Alexandria whom we call Pseudo-Callisthenes. Two aspects of this work are noteworthy: the claim that an Egyptian king was Alexander's father; and the detailed treatment of Alexander's travels in the East. About 300 A.D. Julius Valerius translated Pseudo-Callisthenes into Latin; an abridgement of this translation, often called the *Zacher Epitome*, was made in the ninth century. In the same century were composed a number of Latin letters between Alexander and Aristotle. About 950, Pseudo-Callisthenes was again translated into Latin, this time by Leo, Archpresbyter of Naples, whose version is called *Historia de preliis*. These accounts seem to have been extremely popular. Upon them, and upon a few other Latin works, the vernacular accounts of Western Europe are based.

There is an early twelfth-century fragment in hybrid Franco-Provençal of a poetic Alexander-book by Alberic de Pisançon. This work was partly

redone about 1165 to form the French *Decasyllabic Alexander*, and was somewhat earlier translated into German by Pfaffe Lampbrecht. The most
important French version is the lengthy twelfth-century *Roman d'Alexandre*,
written by Lambert le Tort, Alexander de Paris, and others in twelve-
syllable lines (Alexandrines). Toward the end of the twelfth century we
have two French poems about the revenge taken upon Alexander's murderers: the *Venjance Alixandre* by Jean le Nevelon, and the *Vengement Alixandre*
by Gui de Cambrai. Another important French poem, written originally
in England in the twelfth century by Thomas of Kent, is the *Roman de
toute chevalerie*, based on the *Zacher Epitome*.

Into the *Roman d'Alexandre* was incorporated from time to time imaginative
material not originally included. Two important such pieces are the *Fuerre
de Gadres* and *Voeux du paon*. The former, an expansion of an episode concerning the siege of Tyre, was written by one Eustache. The latter, sometimes called the *Roman de Cassamus*, was written about 1312 by Jacques
de Longuyon.

In Old English there are two prose pieces connected with Alexander:
Alexander's Letter to Aristotle, and the *Wonders of the East*. The various works
in Middle English are discussed below.

THE LYFE OF ALISAUNDER OR KING ALEXANDER [64]. Be-
ginning of fourteenth century. 8021 lines in four-stress couplets. Probably
London dialect. Free adaptation of the *Roman de toute chevalerie*; much
compressed; omits the episode of the *Fuerre de Gadres*. Usually considered
the best of the English Alexander-pieces.

Four Fragments of an Old Print (Wells [71]) on six leaves in the British
Museum, printed ca. 1525, including 417 lines, are fragments of this poem,
as Smithers shows in the introduction to his edition.

The poem is in two main parts. The first (lines 1–4746) tells of Alexander's
mysterious conception, his birth and youth, his coming to the throne, and
his conquest of Darius; the second (lines 4747–8021) tells of Alexander's
conquests eastward, the marvels he encountered, his seduction by Candace,
and his death by poisoning. A detailed summary of the poem will be found
on pages xv–xx of Smithers' edition (EETS, 227).

The author of this romance has presented a very skilful and attractive
poem, clearly intended for oral delivery. The couplets are noteworthy

for unusual grace and fluency, especially when read aloud; and the diction is free of the excessive repetition of tags characteristic of many metrical romances. That the author was a learned man is evident from his frequent appeals to source-authority. The tone of the poem is genial and sophisticated; even the monitory passages—such as that which claims Alexander's success to have resulted from his obeying his master's teaching (line 32), or that which treats of women's wiles (lines 7703–25)—are good-humored. The descriptions of the lands Alexander visits and of the marvels encountered therein are presented as informal geographical instruction for the audience.

Especially pleasing are the lyrical passages, not directly related to the progress of events, which serve to mark off subdivisions within the two main parts; a number of such passages serve also as indications of the time of year for the narrative, as in lines 139–46.

THE ALLITERATIVE ALEXANDER FRAGMENTS [65]. These three alliterative fragments—A (called *Alisaunder*), B (called *Alexander and Dindimus*), and C (called *Wars of Alexander*)—are regularly grouped together because they were once considered parts of a single original poem.

Fragment A. Ca. 1340–70. 1247 long lines. Region of Gloucestershire. Latin source; based in part on Orosius (lines 1–451, 901–53, 1202–47), in part on material belonging to what is called the J²-recension of the *Historia de preliis* (lines 452–900, 954–1201).

The poem tells of Philip's parentage, birth, early conquests, and marriage to Olympias (lines 1–451). Then we learn that Nectanabus, King of Egypt, is a magican who flees to Macedonia; in Philip's absence he lies with Olympias by trickery and begets Alexander; later, disguised as a dragon, he aids Philip in conquering the Lacedemonians (lines 452–900). Unable to defeat the Athenians, Philip destroys the Thebans (lines 901–53). Then he is reunited with the pregnant Olympias in Macedonia, and believes the conception to have been caused by a god; Nectanabus demonstrates to Philip the coming greatness of the child Olympias carries (lines 954–1034). The account of Alexander's birth and early years is omitted. We are told that Alexander drowns his father Nectanabus, and that he tames the ferocious horse [Bucephalus] (lines 1035–1201). Finally, the fragment breaks off at the beginning of the siege of Constantinople (lines 1202–47).

Fragment B. Ca. 1340–70. 1139 long lines. Region of Gloucestershire. Latin source: very close translation of J²-recension of the *Historia de preliis*.

The poem takes up Alexander's career at a much later date than the end of Fragment A. Alexander comes to the land of the Oxydraces or Gymnasophists, who refuse to fight against him; he, liking them, offers to grant any request they make; they ask why, if he must soon leave the earth, he wastes time fighting; he replies that by destiny he must be a conqueror (lines 1–110). Next Alexander comes to trees which disappear at sundown and which are guarded by birds spitting deadly fire (line 111–36). Then he travels to the land of the Brahmans and has to camp by the Ganges river, impassable except in July and August because of dragons and other beasts. He learns from natives on the opposite bank that Dindimus is their king, and he decides to correspond with Dindimus (lines 137–90). Now come five letters, three from Alexander and two from Dindimus (lines 191–1127). The fragment ends with the account of the pillar erected by Alexander on leaving this land (lines 1128–39).

The five letters present the chief purpose and matter of this fragment and call to mind the debate literature of the Middle Ages. In the first, (lines 191–242) Alexander asks Dindimus to instruct him in the customs of the Brahmans. The second (lines 243–811) is the most important of the five and offers the requested instruction: Dindimus describes the advantages of the simple and Godly habits of his people. In the third (lines 812–966) Alexander says the Brahmans can hardly be favored by their God, since they have no material wealth. In the fourth (lines 967–1071) Dindimus repeats his claim that Alexander's ways lead to Hell. And in the fifth (lines 1072–1127) Alexander says he sees only sin in Dindimus' customs.

Fragment C. Ca. 1450. 5677 long lines. Perhaps originally Northumbrian. Latin source: translation of a J³ᵃ-recension of the *Historia de preliis*; "the additions made by the English writer consist of an introduction, an abridged version of the *Fuerre de Gadres*, and connecting passages at the beginning or the end of the several *Passus* . . ." (Cary, p. 57).

This longest of the fragments, in twenty-seven passus, presents a full version of the romance except for the final sections concerning Alexander's poisoning and death. A summary by passus is given by Skeat (EETSES 47, p. v).

All Three Fragments. Though these alliterative fragments are often—

though not always—said to possess "literary merit," scholarly attention understandably has been directed primarily towards a number of factual questions. More specific designation of their sources would seem to depend upon further extensive cataloguing and editing of MSS of *Historia de preliis*. Dialect designation seems now as precise as we are likely to reach. Exact dating presents seemingly insurmountable difficulties because of the distance of the manuscripts from the lost originals. The characteristics of the alliterative lines are well established. Concerning authorship and the relation among the three fragments, divided opinion obtains. It was once fashionable to consider all three as descending from one lengthy Alexander-romance written by a single author, perhaps Huchown. More recently—probably most sensibly—individual authorship has been argued; however, that A and B are by a single author is still a not infrequent assertion. Further study seems unlikely to result in marked advances with this problem.

The three fragments have been called "chronicles in the epic manner" (Oakden, 2.24) because they differ so sharply from the usual romances. Instead of leisurely accounts of love and knightly endeavor, we find here rapid and energetic conquest by a superman. Fragment A is told with gusto and zest. The sections deriving from the different sources are skilfully fused. The descriptive detail throughout is memorably vivid. Its metrical technique, however, is somewhat clumsy and awkward. Fragment B has little room for narrative, since it mainly presents through the five letters moral and instructive material concerning the two ways of life. The device here seems a balancing of aspects rather than an outright debate. This writer has better control of the alliterative technique than the author of A. Fragment C, in both length and method, represents a considerable literary accomplishment and deserves more study than it has as yet received. The poem offers a vast panorama of action and an impelling dramatic conflict throughout. Events move swiftly, with Alexander always in the role of superman at the center of the action. The poet presents a memorable medieval tragedy: a fall from very high place to low.

THE CAMBRIDGE ALEXANDER-CASSAMUS FRAGMENT [66].

Fifteenth century. 566 verses; ababbcbc. Based on French *Voeux du paon*.

The fragment begins inside the besieged city with Cassamus' advice to Ydore and Betys that they make Cassyel, the captured Bawdrayn, acquainted with the lively Edee. The young people consequently hold a court of love in the Chamber of Venus, with Betys as king. The Bawdrayn and Edee make known their love for each other, as do Betys and Ydore; but Phesonas, who has rejected the besieging Clarus, says she loves no one. Then Betys as king gives answers to several questions of love: Which is more pleasant—to see the loved one, or to think of her? (he prefers the latter); What are the two most heartening aspects of love? (he says Hope and Thought); What are the most painful aspects of love? (he says Desire and Fear); What three things produce the greatest happiness for lovers? (he says Skill, Truth, and Secrecy).

At line 467 the scene shifts to the besiegers' camp. Clarus is told of Cassamus' capture of Cassyel, and Marceyn advises an immediate attack on the city to release him; but Clarus scornfully says that Cassyel is enjoying his prison and that the city will be punished in good time. Then Marceyn gives Clarus a lecture to the effect that he must be more courteous towards his followers if he expects their help against "thys kyng of Massedone" who has come to aid Cassamus. The fragment ends with the return to the camp of Clarus' four sons: Canan, Galee, Porus, and Salphadyn.

There is no way of knowing how nearly complete this translation of the *Voeux de paon* may once have been. The fragment represents no great skill in poetic creation. Greatest emphasis falls upon two admonitions: the dominant and enobling power of Love (lines 145–46, 374–75), and a king's proper behavior toward his followers (lines 515–60).

THE PROSE ALEXANDER [67]. First half of the fifteenth century. About 104 pages in the EETS edition; the manuscript has three gaps in the account (at the beginning; between leaf 18 and leaf 19; and between leaf 19 and leaf 20). Northern English. Close, slightly abridged version of J[3a]-recension of Latin *Historia de preliis*.

The text begins with Alexander's drowning of his father Anectanabus. Then follow Alexander's taming of Bucephalus, conquest of King Nicholas, reconciliation of Philip and Olympias, defiance of Darius, subjugation of Armenis, killing of Philip's slayer Pansamy, and ascension to the throne. Alexander conquers Chaledonia, Italy, other European countries, and Africa, and builds the city of Alexandria. He takes Damascus and Sidon, and besieges Tyre, which resists stoutly but finally falls. He is received as emperor by the Jews in Jerusalem, but is taunted by Darius. He then defeats several Persian groups, and, after recovering from an illness, gets the better of Darius in two battles near the river Tigris. Darius asks aid of King Porus of India: the latter cannot come. A great battle now occurs between Alexander and Darius near the river Grancus; the latter flees, and writes again to Porus for help. Two Persian traitors murder Darius; Alexander buries Darius in honorable fashion, marries his daughter Roxana, and punishes his murderers. He next defeats Porus, and the Queen of the Amazons recognizes him as Emperor. Again he marches against Porus, but his army suffers terrible hardships. In single combat he slays Porus. He visits the Gymnosophists, and sees many strange beasts and people. Then he exchanges philosophical letters with Dindimus,

King of the Brahmans. More wonders of India are met, and Alexander shrewdly outwits the Basilisk. Through the warden of the holy tree he learns of his approaching death. He spends time with Queen Candace and her sons, and later has another prophecy of his coming death. He encounters the ten tribes of Israel, ascends into the air, and descends to the sea-bottom. Bucephalus dies. Alexander visits the palace of Xerxes. He writes to Olympias and to Aristotle. In the city of Babylon Alexander is poisoned and dies at the age of 32. His body is buried in Alexandria.

This prose account has been very little studied from either the historical or the interpretative point of view. A recent critic calls it "an uninteresting prose translation . . . with little to commend it except to a student of fifteenth-century English Prose" (Cary, p. 243). Yet—for one reader at least—the piece possesses considerable appeal as a literary accomplishment. The narrative is presented by skilful intermingling of third-person exposition with frequent and effective scenes involving pointed first-person dialogue. The development of the character of Alexander, as man of destiny possessed of human frailties, lends attractive humanity to this greatest of all conquerors. And the rather simple and matter-of-fact vocabulary and tone of the North-English writer bring even the marvels of India within the realm of possibility.

THE SCOTTISH ALEXANDER BUIK [68]. 1438 (according to the epilogue). 11,138 lines in four-stress rimed couplets. Scots dialect. Translation of Old French *Fuerre de Gadres* and *Voeux du paon*. Authorship disputed.

This poem falls into two main sections, the second having two subdivisions: A. The Forray of Gadderis (lines 1–3304); B (1). The Avowis of Alexander (lines 1–8329), and B (2). The Great Battel of Effesoun (lines 8330–11138). Two episodic narratives, which grew up in connection with the Alexander legend, are here joined together to form a lengthy romance. The first part tells of the foraging expedition near Gadres during Alexander's siege of Tyre. Alexander's foragers, under Emenidus, are set upon by the army of Bevis, Duke of Gadres. Alexander comes to the rescue and finally Bevis' army is dispersed. The climax of the episode comes when Emenidus kills Gadifer, Bevis' finest knight. The second and lengthier part opens with an interview between Cassamus, the dead Gadifer's brother, and Alexander. The former wins Alexander's aid for Gadifer's two sons and one daughter against Clarus, the old and wicked King of India, who has laid siege to their city Effesoun. After considerable fighting and many amorous interludes Clarus is killed, Effesoun is delivered, and five marriages involving all the principal young people are consummated. In the course of the final battle for Effesoun various heroes attempt to carry out vows they have made over the body of a peacock shot by Porrus, Clarus' noble son. The contents of this romance are indicated in greater detail by Ritchie's summaries in his STS edition.

This poem differs greatly from such chronicle-like accounts of Alexander's life and conquests as *Kyng Alexander*, the alliterative Alexander fragments, and the *Prose Alexander*. Rather than an economical and fastmoving account of conquests centered around a superhuman hero, here we have a leisurely detailed narrative of individual performances both military and amorous. Courtly manners are described at length.

Authorship is the question which has received most scholarly attention in connection with this poem, and a controversy once raged as to whether or not John Barbour wrote it. One can safely say that Barbour is not the author, and that further attention to this question is not likely to prove fruitful.

GILBERT HAY'S BUIK OF KING ALEXANDER [69]. Fifteenth century. About 20,000 lines; four-stress rimed couplets. Scots dialect. Said to contain complete life of Alexander, including *Fuerre de Gadres* and *Voeux du paon*. French prose *Alexander* most likely source.

Only extracts of the poem have been published. The whole will be available for study when Professor A. Macdonald completes his edition for the Scottish Text Society.

THE DUBLIN ALEXANDER EPITOME [70]. Late fifteenth century. 142 lines of prose. Probably an abridged version of the Alexander material in some Caxton edition of *Dicts and Sayings of the Philosophers*.

The account opens with Alexander's address to his people just after Philip's death, to the effect that they should obey God and choose as king the man caring most for the public welfare. The people choose Alexander king. Soon Darius sends to Alexander for tribute, but the latter refuses and conquers India. Then he visits the Brahmans. Next, he encounters in one city a very righteous judge, and in another finds that no judge is needed. Finally, he writes to his mother, dies, and is buried in Alexandria.

AMORYUS AND CLEOPES [71]. According to a statement in the poem (2175-76), John Metham wrote it in 1448-49. The final hundred and six lines represent a compliment to his patrons, Miles Stapleton and his wife, and an apology for the author's poor abilities in comparison with those of Chaucer and Lydgate. Furnival called attention to the poem in 1903, but it did not become generally available until Craig's edition in 1916. Subsequently, it seems to have been seldom read.

The poem, 2211 lines long, is in seven-line stanzas generally rime royal. It is not an Alexander romance but, as Craig pointed out, it includes numerous features from the story of Alexander, who is mentioned in line 2143. A prologue of 70 lines, giving the setting, is followed by four divisions for the narrative. Though one has to agree with Metham's modest estimate of his ability as a poet, his seeming originality in shaping the materials for this poem is noteworthy. Clearly, his chief interest is religious. The high point of the poem comes in the conversion by the Christian hermit of the Persians. Thus the earlier emphasis upon Palmedon's pagan prayer, heathen worship, Venus' temple, and Christ's power is preparation for this conversion, since the Persians are convinced only after the hermit causes the image of Venus to fall and the magical sphere to vanish. For the core of his narrative, Metham used the Pyramus and Thisbe story, giving the new names Amoryus and Cleopes to the two young people. The religious intention is again evident in the original ending for this story: by a miracle of the Virgin, Amoryus and Cleopes return from death to life to be baptized and married by the hermit. In addition to the borrowings from the story of Alexander, there are echoes of the stories of Troilus and Jason. A brief summary of the poem follows:

Nero attacks Camsyre, Emperor of Persia, and kills him. Palmedon and Dydas are named kings of Persia; they settle in the chief city, Albanest, and marry; Palmedon becomes the father of Amoryus, Dydas of Cleopes. Only a stone wall divides the gardens of these two families. As the two children mature, they become outstanding in every way. A thunderbolt destroys the temple of Venus, which Dydas rebuilds at the Persians' request. Palmedon causes "Venus' secretary" to prepare a magical sphere for the new temple. The secretary dreams that the sphere will last until a "crucyffid man schal take possessyon." During the ceremony dedicating the new temple, Amoryus and Cleopes fall in love. In an eight-day tournament, Amoryus wears Cleopes' favor and overcomes all contestants. The two young people find a cranny in the wall which separates their gardens, through which they declare their love. Amoryus, aided by Cleopes' advice, slays a terrible dragon which is destroying the country.

Amoryus and Cleopes plan to meet before dawn outside the city. Cleopes, arriving first, is frightened by a lion which wipes its bloody mouth upon the handkerchief she dropped when she fled from him. Amoryus, seeing this handkerchief upon his arrival, thinks that she is dead and kills himself. Cleopes, finding him dead, then kills herself. A Christian hermit named Ore hears her final cries and comes upon the two dead lovers. He prays Christ and the Virgin to restore them to life. This miracle occurs and they immediately become Christians.

The Persians have gathered in their new temple to seek Venus' help in finding Amoryus and Cleopes. The hermit brings the two to the temple. He then destroys the image of Venus and dissolves the magical sphere. The hermit converts the people and marries Amoryus and Cleopes. Then he ordains priests and returns to the forest. Amoryus and Cleopes have a long and happy life, with many beautiful children.

6. LEGENDS OF TROY

by

R. M. Lumiansky

To medieval writers in western Europe the great war between the Greeks and the Trojans was a matter of historic truth, but to them Homer was not an honored name. They felt that his anthropomorphic treatment of the gods was sacrilegious and untrustworthy. Further, since the western countries were thought to have been founded by descendants of the Trojan heroes—Britain, for example, by Brutus, son or grandson of Aeneas—the sympathy of the inhabitants of these countries was with the Trojans rather than the Greeks. Thus the Trojans were considered speakers of Latin, and Hector—rather than Achilles, as in Homer—was taken as the central heroic figure.

Until recently scholars thought that the Homeric tradition concerning this great war was almost without influence during the Middle Ages. Atwood, however, has clearly shown that alongside the more powerful medieval tradition (discussed below) there was important and continuing classical influence—as represented by the *Excidium Troiae* and by the *Compendium Troianae-Romanae*—which can be observed in the Troy material composed in various languages during the late Middle Ages. Atwood concludes that there must have been a Latin version of the fourth to sixth centuries A.D. which was regularly used to supplement the medieval Troy tradition.

The medieval tradition begins with Dictys Cretensis' *Ephemeris belli Trojani*, a document in Latin prose. It dates from the fourth century, but is probably based on a Greek original. This account opens with the rape of Helen and continues through the return of the Greeks. Its author claims to have been present on the Greek side during the war.

Dares Phrygius' *De excidio Trojae historia* was written between 400 and 600, is in Latin prose, and is supposedly based on a Greek original. Dares is said to have been present on the Trojan side during the war. This account begins with the voyage of Jason and the Argonauts.

Benoit de Sainte-Maure, a North French poet, about 1184 finished his 30,000-line *Roman de Troie*. This version, written in Anglo-Norman, begins with the voyage of the Argonauts and concludes with the wanderings of Ulysses. Benoit bases his account mainly on Dictys and Dares, but his original treatment makes the poem one of the outstanding examples of medieval romance. Here, for the first time, appears the story of Troilus and Criseyde (called by Benoit "Briseida").

Joseph of Exeter, about 1187, wrote an excellent Latin poem in six books called *Bellum Troianum*, much influenced by Benoit.

Guido delle Colonne, a Sicilian judge, in 1287 finished his Latin prose *Historia destructionis Troiae*, one of the greatest literary hoaxes of all time. Though he claims to be presenting a hitherto undiscovered account, Guido actually prepared a close and highly abridged version of Benoit's *Roman de Troie*. Guido's *Historia* became vastly popular, a situation which can probably be attributed to its brevity, since it is both dully and crudely composed. Not until the nineteenth century was Guido's hoax discovered, and only of late years has Benoit's *Roman* begun to receive the attention it deserves.

In the various medieval languages a great many retellings of the Troy story are to be found. Consideration of all these pieces would not be appropriate here. The various Middle English versions are discussed below.

GEST HISTORIALE OF THE DESTRUCTION OF TROY [72]. Composed ca. 1350–1400. 14,044 alliterative long lines. Probably originally in Northwest Midland. Based on Guido's *Historia destructionis Troiae*.

This longest of the Middle English alliterative poems consists of a Prologue and thirty-six Books. The Prologue announces the topic and mentions authorities: Homer is not to be trusted, but Guido uses Dares and Dictys and gives a true account. The narrative proper is presented in the following stages:

```
Books 1–3   : the story of Jason and the Golden Fleece
Book 4      : the destruction of Old Troy
Book 5      : the building of New Troy
Books 6–7   : the Trojan Council and the rape of Helen
```

Books 8–13 : the Greek assembly, their journey to Troy, and their preparations
                  to besiege the city
Books 14–15: the first and second battles before Troy
Book 16   : the two months' truce and the third battle
Books 17–27: the fourth through the twenty-first battles
Books 28–29: the treachery of Aeneas and Antenor and the fall of Troy
Books 30–36: the adventures of the Greeks after the fall of Troy, ending with
                  Ulysses' death.

While following the inherited outlines for the story, the poet handles
Guido's material with great freedom and with an eye for literary effectiveness. He adds, omits, and condenses in an effort to present a balanced,
acceptable, and vigorous account. There is no effort toward a leisurely
romance; rather, the tone and manner are those of a rapidly moving
chronicle presenting historical truth. The numerous characters are clearly
conceived and vividly portrayed and the dramatic scenes are effectively
drawn. It is usual to say that the moralistic digressions—such as those
against women—impede the narrative and represent lack of artistry inherited from Guido.

Efforts to establish "Huchowne of the Awle Ryale" as the author of this
poem have not been successful.

THE SEEGE OF TROYE [73]. Composed ca. 1300–25. 2066 lines in
four-stress rimed couplets. Northwest Midlands. Based on Benoit's *Roman
de Troie*, the Latin account of Dares, and the *Excidium Troiae*.

The four manuscripts of the *Seege* vary considerably and the question of
manuscript-tradition for the poem is debated. The latest view (Hofstrand)
is that all four derive from a manuscript at least once removed from the
author's original.

The poem is independent of other Middle English Troy pieces, and
Atwood has shown that it incorporates material from the *Excidium Troiae*-
classical tradition within the general pattern of the Dictys-Dares-Benoit-
Guido-medieval tradition.

The events set forth by the poem roughly match the contents of the
Gest Historiale, with the omission of Ulysses' death, and with the addition
of Hecuba's Dream, the Youth and Judgment of Paris, and the expanded
story of Achilles—all from the classical tradition. But the whole is much
more briefly accomplished than in the *Gest*. The direct appeals to the audience and the numerous tags suggest that the original *Seege* was composed

as a minstrel romance. Descriptive passages are rare. The story is vigorously told, with a careful eye for effective dramatic appeal and unified narration. The Harley MS of the *Seege*, however, seems to have been prepared for reading rather than for recitation; the other three manuscript versions preserve the oral traits attributed to the original.

THE LAUD TROY-BOOK [74]. Composed ca. 1400. 18,664 lines in four-stress rimed couplets; alliteration frequent. Probably East Midland. Based on Guido's *Historia*, with some probable use of Benoit's *Roman*.

This poem presents generally the same material as the *Gest Historiale*, except for the account of Ulysses' death. The writer's alterations of Guido's material—for example, the de-emphasis of the Troilus and Briseida story— show clearly that he intended his poem as a Hector-romance. At every opportunity he expands the material concerning Hector and heightens that hero's role. Imagery from numerous sources is abundant and effectively used. Despite its great length, the poem is attractively presented and moves forward rapidly. One would, however, have difficulty considering it an outstanding literary accomplishment.

Lydgate's *Troy-Book* will be dealt with in the chapter devoted to that poet (see under Lydgate).

TWO SCOTTISH TROY FRAGMENTS [75]. Probably fifteenth century. In four-stress rimed couplets. Fragment A: MS Cambridge, 596 verses. Fragment B: MS Douce, lines 1–916, 1181–3118; MS Cambridge, lines 1–1562. Authorship debated; the attribution to John Barbour seems unconvincing. Used to fill gaps in Scottish manuscripts of Lydgate's *Troy-Book*. Source is Guido's *Historia*.

Fragment A. MS Cambridge (lines 1–596) begins with the inhospitable reception at Old Troy of Jason, Hercules, and the Argonauts, continues through their arrival at Colchos, and ends just before Medea's falling in love with Jason.

Fragment B. MS Douce (lines 1–916) begins with the betrayal by Aeneas and Antenor, and continues through the entry of the horse into Troy, the destruction of the city, and the death of Priam; MS Douce (lines 1181–3118) begins with the tempest which prevents the return of the

Greeks from Troy, and carries the story to its conclusion in the death of Ulysses.

Fragment B in MS Cambridge (lines 1–1562) matches MS Douce (lines 1–916), and then continues through the division of the spoils from Troy, the sacrifice of Polyxena, the argument between Ajax and Ulysses, the awarding of the Palladium to Ulysses, the departure of some of the Greeks, and the exiling of Aeneas and Antenor.

THE PROSE SIEGE OF TROY [76]. Second quarter of the fifteenth century. Brie's edition covers thirteen pages. Source is Lydgate's *Troy-Book*. Southern dialect.

This spare and straightforward prose account epitomizes the usual events of the legend from Jason's journey for the Golden Fleece through the fall of Troy. To tell of events after the fall of the city, says the writer, "wold make alonge prosses." He draws two morals from his account: "Neþer party won gretly at the ende" and "Alwey the ende of every treasoun and falsenes to sorowe and myschef at the last."

Caxton's translation, *The Recuyell of the Historyes of Troy*, will be dealt with in the chapter devoted to Caxton (q. v.).

7. LEGENDS OF THEBES

by

R. M. Lumiansky

In classic myth the city of Thebes attracted an extended and complex web of stories which trace the city's fortunes from before its foundation through its destruction. This material was generally known to the Middle Ages from Statius' *Thebaid*, the French poetic *Roman de Thèbes* (ca. 1150), and several French prose romances. Boccaccio's *Teseide* and Chaucer's *Knight's Tale* deal with parts of the legend. The story as a whole appears in Middle English in Lydgate's *Siege of Thebes* and in the briefer *Prose Siege of Thebes*.

Lydgate's *Siege of Thebes* will be dealt with in the chapter devoted to that writer (see under Lydgate).

THE PROSE SIEGE OF THEBES [77]. Composed ca. 1450. Covers about ten pages in Brie's edition. Southern dialect. Said to be retelling of Lydgate's *Siege of Thebes*.

Like the *Prose Siege of Troy*, this account is a spare and straightforward epitome. It opens with the founding of Thebes and quickly moves to the events involving Laius, Jocasta, and Oedipus. Then it recounts the fatal struggle between Eteocles and Polynices for the city, the selection of the cruel Creon as king, and Theseus' conquest and destruction of the city.

8. Eustace–Constance–Florence–Griselda Legends

by

Lillian Herlands Hornstein

The romances of this section resemble one another and several of the Miscellaneous Romances in Section 10 below in theme, story-matter, diction, style, and verse form. They embody variants of the so-called Eustace (St. Eustace, Eustache, or Placidas), Constance, Florence, and Griselda themes; all emphasize the virtue of a meek Job-like faith. The Eustace legend (see under Saints' Legends) recounts how Placidas, a worldly officer of Trajan, is converted by the appearance of Christ between the antlers of a hart. With his wife and two sons he is baptized and given the name Eustace. He accepts with patience and fortitude the misfortunes which follow: his wealth is destroyed and his homeless family dispersed, the wife being carried off by shipmen and the children borne away, one son by a lion and the other by a leopard. While employed as a journeyman, Eustace is found and recalled by Trajan to lead his armies. During the expedition, Eustace fortuitously discovers his wife and sons. Reunited, the family returns to Rome and there meets death, by burning, for refusal to sacrifice to heathen gods.

The Constance story tells of an innocent maiden who is banished by or flees from an unnatural father. She reaches a foreign land and marries its ruler. In her husband's absence she is falsely accused of giving birth to monstrous offspring and is banished with her child or children. Ultimately she is reunited to her husband and, in some versions, to her father as well. The name Constance, used to designate this type of Calumniated or Persecuted Queen, comes from the heroine of Chaucer's *Man of Law's Tale* (see under Chaucer). The Constance theme appears also in *Emare*, dealt with in the section on the Breton Lays ([87] below), and in Gower's *Confessio Amantis*, dealt with in the chapter on Gower. See also the *Earl of Toulous* [94] in the section on the Breton Lays.

The Griselda theme (so-named from the heroine of Chaucer's *Clerk's Tale*; see under Chaucer), recounts the tests of devotion to which a patient, loyal wife is subjected by her husband. Her trials reflect the combined influence of the Eustace, Constance, and Florence themes.

Many of the motifs, the veriest commonplaces of folklore, appear and reappear in romances whose essential theme is one of trial and faith. The Eustace theme of trial and separation appears in *Sir Isumbras* (see also *Apollonius of Tyre* [95]). The Constance theme occurs in *Sir Triamour*. Combinations of the themes are developed in *Octavian*, *Sir Eglamour*, and *Sir Torrent of Portyngale*. *Octavian* was possibly the conduit or bridge by which themes, wording, and expressions reached the other romances. For example, the episode of the robber beasts from the Eustace legend, adopted in *Octavian*, may have been a source for *Sir Isumbras*; robber-beasts appear also in the later *Valentine and Orson* (see [103]) and *William of Palerne* (see [11]). *Sir Eglamour* and *Sir Torrent* are much alike, whether because one imitated the other or because both derive from a common source. *Sir Triamour* is close to *Octavian*: in both the real action starts with the banishment of a Calumniated Wife; in both the real hero is the offspring, not the father. *Emare* resembles all these pieces in theme, diction, and stanza form. *Sir Launfal* (listed under Breton Lays; see [88]) is close to *Octavian*.

The self-sacrifice of a Christian maiden, her piety, pervading humility, and her monstrous offspring relate the *King of Tars* to *Le Bone Florence* and others of these pieces. Connected with the themes in this group are also those of *Lai le Freine* (see [85]), the *Nut-brown Maid*, *Chevalere Assigne* (see [62]), the *Earl of Toulous* (see [94]), and the *Knight of Curtesy and the Fair Lady of Faguell* (see [111]). *Sir Gowther* (see [93]), *Robert of Cisyle* (see [115]), *Amadace* (see [113]), *Cleges* (see [114]), and *Amis and Amiloun* (see [112]) also have elements of trial and faith which connect them with romances in this section. In these latter stories the plot includes trials of faith and piety, but the narrative also moves in the realm of love or adventure.

The additional circumstance that many of the romances of this section and of the later section of Miscellaneous Romances are found chiefly in two manuscripts (MSS Cotton Caligula A. 2, Auchinleck) and are written in similar diction and the tail-rime stanza led Trounce to argue that they constituted a "school" which had its source in the East Midlands, East Anglia; but his criteria as to dialect and provenience have not been uniformly accepted. More generally favored has been the suggestion by L. H. Loomis that scribes in a London "bookshop" produced the Auchinleck MS, from whose romances (it contains seventeen) Chaucer took hints for *Sir Thopas* (see under Chaucer). There is also the possibility that manuscripts may have been produced "through the cooperative efforts of itinerant professional scribes and educated women living in the neighborhood" (Robbins, PMLA 69.611).

The romances of these two sections may have deliberately imitated one another, but the absence of conclusive evidence for priority of composition, or popularity, or methods of dissemination makes hazardous any theory about the relationships of these romances one to the other, especially since so many details are conventional. These romances may have appropriated independently themes from the general storehouse of legends and folk-motifs; yet the patent parody of *Sir Thopas* suggests that in all likelihood by Chaucer's time a certain combination of themes, diction, and versification had reached the status of a convention.

SIR ISUMBRAS [78]. Composed in the early fourteenth century near the northern border of the East Midlands in tail-rime stanzas, aabccbddbeeb, or aabccb. Survives in nine early manuscripts: Earliest manuscript, Gray's Inn 20, fragment, 104 lines, ca. 1350; Caius Cambridge 175, 780 lines, 1425–50; Lincoln Thornton MS, 794 lines in twelve-line tail-rime, ca. 1440; Naples Royal Library 13.B.29, fragment, 122 lines in twelve-line tail-rime, ca. 1457; Cotton Caligula A.2, 798 lines in six-line tail-rime, 1450–1500; Ashmole 61, 822 lines in six-line tail-rime, 1475–1500; University College Oxford 142, fragment, one leaf (opening 15 lines), 1475–1500; Advocates 19.3.1, 837 lines in twelve-line tail-rime, 1475–1500; Douce 261 (transcript of a printing), 372 lines, 1564. Prints: Harvard University Library, John Skot, 8 leaves or fragments, imperfect, ca. 1525?; Harvard University Library, I Treveris, for John Butler or W. de Worde, one leaf and three fragments, imperfect, ca. 1530?; Westminster Abbey fragments, conjugate with Harvard Treveris fragment; British Museum W. Copland, 15 leaves, ca. 1530?; Bodleian Douce fragment f. 37, W. de Worde or Copland, one leaf (62 lines), 1530?, 1550?; Bodleian Malone 941, Copland?, one leaf (26 lines), very defective, ca. 1550. Schleich edition, 804 lines. The romance was very popular, to judge from the many allusions in medieval and renaissance texts, from the nine extant manuscripts, and from the five printings before 1550. No immediate source is known, though analogues exist in Latin, French, German, Danish. The origin stems from the legend of St. Eustace, this latter story itself having analogues in Oriental tales of Buddha.

Isumbras, happy with his wife and three sons, forgets that he owes all to God. A bird (angel) gives him a choice of suffering in youth or in old age. He chooses to suffer in youth. His horse falls dead, his hawks fly away, his property is burned. With uncomplaining patience, he accepts this just punishment for his sin. The family commences a pilgrimage. A lion bears off the eldest son, a leopard the second. A Saracen Sultan beats Isumbras and takes his wife, but leaves with him his one remaining son and a bag of gold. An eagle bears away the money, and a unicorn the child. For seven years Isumbras carries iron and stone, and learns the trade of a blower and a smithy. Then fighting in self-made armor, he defeats the Saracens during a three-day battle. For seven more years he wanders as a palmer. Near Bethlehem, an angel announces that his sins are forgiven. He is sheltered by a queen, wins a stone-heaving contest and a tournament. In a nest he finds the gold stolen by the eagle. The queen (his wife) recognizes it; a reunion follows. When Isumbras seeks to make his subjects Christian, they rebel. Isumbras and his wife are joined by three knights who, led by an angel, are respectively riding a lion, a unicorn, and a leopard. The knights help slay the pagans and reveal themselves as the sons. All live happily; after death they go to Heaven.

Characteristic incidents and well-worn phrases link the poem with a great body of folklore, romance, and saints' legends. The motif of the choice of woe was probably once a separate story absorbed into the Eustace legend (see above). The reversals of fortune, the hagiographic mood, the stress on the virtue of patience are reminiscent of *Roberd of Cisyle* (see [115]) as well as of Saints Eustace and Theophilus. Seven-year work periods recall those required as suitor-service in the *Squyr of Lowe Degre* (see [104]); robber animals appear in many romances, including *Sir Eglamour, Sir Torrent, Sir Octavian, Bevis of Hampton* (see [6]), *Valentine and Orson* (see [103]). The loss of the children is an integral part of every version. The unrecognized husband receiving the bounty of his wife is paralleled in *Bevis of Hampton* and *Guy of Warwick* (see [7]). The story of the loss and recovery of the gold, recalling the Arabian Nights, must have once been an independent Eastern tale in which lost treasure served as a recognition token. The adventures of the Job-like hero, a man tried by fate, i. e., pursued by misfortune, may seem obtrusively didactic and preposterous. But despite the insistent piety, which grows monotonous, the poem has sections which please by their vigor and blunt realism.

SIR EGLAMOUR OF ARTOIS [79]. Composed in the mid-fourteenth century in the North or on the northernmost border of the Midlands in twelve-line tail-rime stanzas (some six-line stanzas), aabccbddbeeb of four-stress iambic couplets alternating with one three-stress line. Survives in four early manuscripts: British Museum Egerton 2862, 160 lines, ca. 1400; Thornton MS, 1335 lines, ca. 1440, best text; Cotton Caligula A.2, 1311 lines, 1450–1500; Cambridge University Library Ff. 2.38, 1341 lines, 1475–1500; also a sixteenth-century fragment; and the Percy Folio MS, 1291 lines. Although the Thornton MS is in a group by itself and the others form a second, the manuscripts were probably derived from a common original no longer extant. The popularity of this romance may be inferred from the number of extant manuscripts and the printings before 1570. Dramatic versions are reported from 1444 at St. Albans to the seventeenth century in Germany.

Eglamour loves Christabelle, daughter of the Earl of Artois. To obtain her father's consent to their marriage, Eglamour must perform three feats. With the aid of a hound and a magic sword given him by his lady ("Also a swerde I give thee, / That was found in the sea"), he slays first a celebrated deer and second a huge boar, and their giant-keepers, and returns with the victims' heads on his spear. Another grateful king offers him his daughter, Organata, who is willing to wait for him for fifteen years and gives him a safety-ensuring ring. The third quest, slaying the fiery Dragon of Rome, leaves the hero victorious, but wounded. Christabelle and Degrebelle (her newborn son by Eglamour) have been set adrift by the Earl. A griffin carries off the boy. The King of Israel finds the baby and rears him as his heir. Christabelle reaches Egypt, where she is treated by her uncle-king as his daughter. When Degrebelle is fifteen, he is taken to Egypt to be married to Christabelle. Before the marriage is consummated, she recognizes him by the insignia on his shield, which shows how he had been stolen away. In a tournament against her would-be husbands, he is defeated by Eglamour, who has been seeking his wife and child, and he too is recognized by the device on his shield, depicting a woman and child in a rudderless boat. Christabelle and Eglamour are married and inherit the realm of the Earl of Artois when he dies in a fall from a tower. Degrebelle marries Organata.

The first part of the tale, concerning the love-sick knight, his confidant, weapons, and quests, deals with commonplaces of folktales and ballads (*Sir Cawline, Sir Lionel*). The second part—the adventures of the cast-out Christabelle—is a 'patchwork' of equally well-worn incidents: the calumniated wife (see Chaucer, *Man of Law's Tale*; *Emare* [87]; *William of Palerne* [*Guillaume d'Angleterre*] [11]), the loss of children (see Eustace legend, above) by robber animals (see *Isumbras, Torrent, Octavian, Valentine and Orson* [103], *Bevis* [6]), the griffin as robber beast (*Octavian, Torrent*), the recovery of treasure (*Isumbras*), the recognitions (*Torrent*). *Sir Degare* (see [92]) may have given the hint for the Oedipus-like episode; and a popular theme (Sohrab and Rustum) inspired the combat of father and son; the Eustace legend, the *King of Tars, Torrent,* and *Roberd of Cisyle* (see [115]) evoke a similar mood of piety, with prayers, masses, Holy Days, and proverbial wisdom.

The chronologico-literary relationships among these romances are difficult to reconstruct. In addition to other parallels with *Eglamour*, both *Torrent* and *Octavian* use the griffin as the robber beast and refer to their source as a "Buke of Rome" (but one need not seek such a source for poems composed of such familiar details). *Eglamour* and *Octavian* are further alike in combining the themes of the persecuted lady with the heroic exploits of her lover. *Eglamour* and *Isumbras* follow the same sequence of the stolen child and treasure. *Eglamour* and *Emare* show many verbal similarities. There is no unanimity of opinion about how or which specific influence of one romance operated upon another. Adam believed that *Eglamour* influenced *Octavian*, but Halliwell [-Phillipps], Schleich, Hibbard argue for the reverse. *Eglamour* apparently influenced *Torrent*; but some maintain that the influence worked the other way. Eglamour has also been associated with an East Anglian "school of romances" (Trounce), with *Sir Thopas* (L. H. Loomis), with Arthurian legend (R. S. Loomis, suggesting Organata to be an aphetic form of Morgana). The poem has been condemned as insipid (Schofield), fantastic (Kane), repetitive and lacking in invention (Hibbard). Despite the validity to these animadversions, *Eglamour* commands attention for its moments of grim humor and of drama.

SIR TORRENT OF PORTYNGALE [80]. Composed in the late four-teenth or early fifteenth century in the western or northwestern border of the East Midlands, in twelve-line tail-rime stanzas aabccbddbeeb. Survives in one manuscript and two early prints, MS Chetham 8009, 2668 lines, 1475–1500 (manuscript very defective, scribe probably recording from memory or from oral transmission). Prints: W. de Worde, fragment, one leaf, 43 lines, 1509?; R. Pynson, fragment, two leaves, 115 lines, 1500–15?

The cruel King of Portugal promises to permit his daughter, Desonell, to marry Torrent if he kills a giant. Task accomplished, Torrent releases the giant's captives, and their grateful fathers reward him with a sword made by Veland [Weland].

The cruel king in an anonymous letter then treacherously suggests that, before marrying, Torrent procure a special falcon for Desonell. During this search he slays a dragon and its master, a giant, and returns with both their heads. The cruel king meanwhile has promised Desonell to a Prince of Aragon, and now sends Torrent against a one-eyed giant. Torrent kills him by piercing his eye with a spear. He then defeats the Prince of Aragon in single combat and demands Desonell. The claim being made that she is already wedded to the Prince, Torrent agrees to establish his rights by a fight on an island with Aragon's champion, a giant. Torrent kills him by casting cobblestones. Desonell is divorced from the Prince and secretly grants Torrent her love, but he accedes to the King's request that the marriage be delayed for six months. Torrent gives two rings to Desonell and leaves for Norway, where he slays two dragons and a giant.

Meanwhile Desonell gives birth to twins; and her irate father, despite general pity, sets her and the babes adrift. When they land, a griffin bears off one son; a leopard, the other. One boy is rescued by St. Anthony, the other by the King of Jerusalem; Desonell is befriended by the King of Nazareth. Learning what the King of Portugal has done, Torrent orders him set adrift in a leaky boat, and himself departs for the Holy Land. After fifteen years of sieges and battles, he fights against the son reared by the King of Jerusalem, is captured, and released when the boy overhears his laments. In a joust Torrent defeats his son and from his armor is recognized by Desonell. In a tournament at Nazareth, he defeats the other son. The three are declared the best knights. The family is reunited; Desonell and Torrent are married. He is elected Emperor of Rome.

No earlier version is known. The few French words and phrases do not imply a French source. (*Eglamour* and *Octavian* similarly refer to a "Buke of Rome.")

Torrent conforms to the Eustace-Isumbras type in the separation plot, the pietistic attitude, invocations, prayers, references to saints and the rites of the Church (for this reason Adam suggests that the author was a cleric). So much like *Eglamour* in phraseology, characters, and plot (the imposition of tasks by the girl's father, the killing of far-off giants and dragons, the rescue of princesses and their offer in marriage, the birth of his child—here twins—while the hero is away, the exposure of the mother and children, the robber beasts, father-son combat, identification by the hero's coat of arms), *Torrent* is probably an amplification of *Eglamour* (Halliwell [-Phillipps]; Schleich; Hibbard; contra, Adam). The second half of *Torrent* diverges somewhat from *Eglamour*, e. g., requires a battle and two tournaments before the recognitions occur. As in *Bevis of Hampton* (see [6]), a virgin cannot be hurt by a lion; as in *Octavian* and *Valentine and Orson* (see [103]), the hero appears with this now friendly beast; as in *Guy of Warwick* (see [7]), there is an island combat; as in *Ipomadon* (see [102]), and *Valentine and Orson*, the unknown brothers joust. Trounce connects *Torrent* with an East Anglian "school of romance"; L. H. Loomis points to parallels with *Sir Thopas* and other poems of the Auchinleck MS. See the headnote to this section. The Chetham MS is so faulty that the quality of the original cannot be accurately assessed. The extant version abounds in trite phrases, repetitive incidents, trivial details, and feeble elaborations, all bespeaking the work of a crude hack-writer.

OCTAVIAN [81]. Composed in the mid-fourteenth century. Survives in three manuscripts of the mid-fifteenth century. Two manuscripts, in Northern dialect and twelve-line tail-rime aabccbddbeeb, give one version of the poem: Thornton MS, 1629 lines, one leaf wanting, ca. 1440; Cambridge University Library Ff. 2.38, 1731 lines, 1475–1500. The third manuscript is a similar but independent version in a Southeast dialect, British Museum Cotton Caligula A.2, 1962 lines, 1450–1500, in six-line stanzas riming aaabab, a lines having four, and b lines having two iambic stresses each (E. Fischer and D. Everett say the dialect is Northern Essex, MacKenzie argues for Suffolk). An imperfect W. de Worde print, 1504–06, in six-line stanzas aabaab (a in iambic tetrameter and b in iambic trimeter with some shorter b lines; there are some twelve-line stanzas) resembles Cambridge University Library Ff. 2.38.

In the Southern version, Florence, daughter of the King of France and wife of Emperor Octavian, bears twin sons. The cruel mother-in-law asserts that the children are bastards, and arranges for a pretended lover to be found in the Empress's bed. The innocent persecuted wife and her babes are driven out into a forest. One child, Florentyn, is borne off by an ape, rescued by a knight, seized by outlaws, and sold to a palmer, Clement. Clement, by occupation a butcher of Paris, pretends that Florentyn is his bastard son and rears him. The twin, young Octavian, is borne off by a tiger and both are seized by a griffin. The griffin is killed by a lioness which rears the child. Florence sails for the Holy Land. The mariners come upon the lioness; the mother rescues her child. The lioness, to the consternation of the sailors, accompanies them to Jerusalem, where Florence works embroidery and becomes chief lady to the Queen.

Meanwhile, Florentyn, adept at wrestling and casting, becomes the idol of the Parisians. His noble lineage is exhibited when he exchanges oxen for a falcon and uses gold to buy a colt. In a dream the Virgin bids him defend the Christian cause. Wearing home-made armor, he defeats the heathen Sultan's giant-champion. Paris declares noblest the butcher's craft. Florentyn by his victory wins the love of the Sultan's daughter, carries her off to Paris, and marries her. The foster-father Clement goes to the Sultan posing as the warden of King Arthur's horses, mounts the Sultan's precious unicorn, and swims it over the Seine. In a battle against the

Sultan and his Saracens, Florentyn and the Emperor Octavian and the King of Paris, with a hundred thousand nobles, are captured. The young Octavian, accompanied by the lioness, fights the Saracens and frees the prisoners. Thousands of pagans are slain by the brothers. Recognition follows. Florence and Clement tell their stories. The cruel mother-in-law is burned.

The English versions, though not dependent on one another and differing in dialect, verse, and some details, were derived from a French version (the earliest extant French manuscript is of the early fourteenth century, in octosyllabic couplets), which is the ultimate source also of versions in Danish, Dutch, German, Icelandic, Italian, and Spanish. The English versions are alike in combining the story of the calumniated wife with that of the theft of children by robber beasts, the subsequent attendance of a faithful lion upon one of them, and the shift in narrative interest from the experiences of the parents to the homely or militant activities of the sons, particularly Florentyn. As in the French, the most striking scenes are those of good-hearted, realistic comedy with the bourgeois Clement, who beats Florentyn for his lordly tastes and plays jokes on the noble guests. The Southern version, though it does in some instances follow the French word for word, tends to condense or omit, especially the love-matter, the self-analysis, and the psychological introspection. But it secures some striking scenes, especially when contrasting the innocence of the wronged queen with the dastardly behavior of her mother-in-law. This version has been praised for its homely realism and greater concentration. The author may have been a minstrel, perhaps Thomas Chestre. See *Sir Launfal* [88] and *Libeaus Desconus* [38].

In the Northern version, after seven years of childless marriage, the parents endow an abbey and thereafter the Empress bears twin sons. She is denounced by her own father. The narrative first tells continuously the story of the Empress and one son, and thereafter the story of the other son. Much is made of the love story with the Sultan's daughter, who, like heroines of sophisticated romances, has a confidante. Clement, though he attains honors, does not receive as great prominence as in the Southern version and is made the butt of burlesque incidents. The story has a hearty humor and adventurous vigor (Hibbard), but opinions vary as to the relative artistic merits of the two versions. The Northern version, closer to the French text, has been praised for its pathos and piety (and its authorship attributed to a cleric who may also have written

Isumbras) (Sarrazin); it has, on the other hand, been condemned as an unattractive, bumbling collection of marvels (Kane).

SIR TRIAMOUR [82]. Composed in the late fourteenth century in the North or Northeast Midland, in twelve-line tail-rime stanzas aabccbddb-eeb. Survives in two manuscripts and in early prints: MS Cambridge University Library Ff. 2.38, 1719 lines, 1475–1500; the Percy Folio MS, 1593 lines, ca. 1650. A Bodleian Rawlinson fragment, 75 lines (published by Halliwell [-Phillipps]), is now missing from the Bodleian. Prints: R. Pynson edition, 1503?, survives in fragments: Cambridge University Library, two leaves, 108 lines; Victoria Public Library (Australia), one leaf, 48 lines (Fenn fragment); Huntington Library, three leaves and two fragments, 140 lines (Huth fragment); Copland editions: British Museum, 1592 lines, 1561?; Bodleian, 1592 lines, 1565?.

King Ardus of Aragon, unaware that his Queen Margaret is already pregnant, prays to God to grant him an heir and goes to the Holy Land. His steward Marrok makes advances to the Queen. Repulsed, he pretends that he was merely testing her virtue. Ardus returns. The False Steward calumniates the Queen, saying that he had found her with a lover whom he killed, and was himself offered the lady's favors. The King banishes Margaret. She leaves with Roger, an old knight. Marrok, with a troop, attempts to seize the Queen; Roger and his dog fend them off while the Queen escapes. Roger is killed, and the dog keeps watch over his body. In a forest in Hungary, Margaret bears a boy, Triamour; they are rescued and become general favorites. After twelve (in one version, seven) years at Roger's grave, the dog goes to the King's palace and kills Marrok at table. He is followed back to the grave and the treason thus exposed. The King searches for Margaret. A joust is called for the hand of the daughter of the King of Hungary. In a three-day tournament, Triamour overcomes his father (neither aware of the other's identity). He also defeats Sir James, son of the Emperor of Germany. Triamour, ambushed by James, slays him. From James' troop Triamour is rescued by Ardus, and then disappears. James' father besieges Ardus, who proposes trial by combat. Triamour reappears to act as Ardus' champion, is knighted, slays the Emperor's champion, the giant Moradas, and his two giant brothers who were blocking the pass to the land of Triamour's lady. His mother reveals to Triamour that Ardus is his father. Triamour's parents are reunited at his wedding.

Triamour exhibits the familiar motifs of romances in this group: the false accuser (here a seneschal) whom the husband trusts, the calumniated and exiled wife, the faithful dog who remains at the grave of her defender, the birth of the son in a forest, the rescue of mother and child, the noble training of the son who wins a bride and defeats his father during a three-day tournament, the piled-up adventures with giants, the final reunion of the parents. The story of the faithful dog is found in the West as early as Plutarch and appears in medieval Anglo-Latin texts (Giraldus Cambrensis, *Itinerarium Cambriae*; *Gesta Romanorum*, Tale 78; Hibbard). Combined with the tale of the chaste wife and false steward, it was one of the most popular of French medieval stories, and was told of Sebilla, the persecuted wife of Charlemagne. Ballads, folktales, and dramatic versions appeared throughout Europe. *Triamour* (to line 612) preserves the only Middle English version of this combination of themes. Details like that of the pretended lover are found in the *Earl of Toulous* (see [94]); the exiling of the Queen and the combat with giants are close to *Octavian*; the birth in the woods is reminiscent of *Tristan* (see [43]) and *Bevis* (see [6]); father-son combat occurs in *Sir Degare* (see [92]) and *Sir Eglamour*. Despite the commonplaces (Bauszus) and exaggerations (Hales), the first part of the poem is neither dull nor prolix (Hibbard), and the whole exhibits masterly construction (Kane).

THE KING OF TARS [Tartary] [83]. Composed in the early fourteenth century, probably in London or its environs, in twelve-line tail-rime stanza aabaabccbddb, with considerable alliteration. Survives in three manuscripts: MS Auchinleck, 1228 lines lacking the last folio, ca. 1330; MS Vernon, 1122 lines, ca. 1390; British Museum Additional 22283, 1122 lines, ca. 1400. The manuscripts show a mixture of dialect forms: London (L. H. Loomis), East Anglia, Norfolk (Trounce), Anglia (Bliss), Midland (Dunlap), Central West Midlands for MS Vernon (Geist).

To spare her people from war, a self-sacrificing Christian princess marries a heathen sultan. When their offspring is born a formless lump of flesh, the father accuses her of having merely pretended to believe in his gods. His pleas to the heathen deities fail to restore the child; at the mother's request the infant is baptized, and immediately becomes a handsome boy. Induced by this miracle to adopt the Christian faith, the father himself changes in the baptismal water from black to white. He then joins his wife's father to convert or kill those of his vassals who do not accept Christianity.

Tales of miraculous changes from baptismal water and of the miraculous conversion of a Tartar khan are recorded in European and British chronicles of the thirteenth and fourteenth centuries (Hornstein, Spec. 16.404). By 1300, this specific story was attached to Cassanus (Ghazan), Khan of Tartary (1271-1304), who having defeated the Egyptian Sultan in 1299 was in consequence hailed by the West as an ally though he was not a Christian. These analogues (the shortest only 255 lines) may be classified by the type of monstrous birth: (A) the hairy child; (B) the half-and-half child (half-hairy, half-human and half-animal, half-black and half-white); (C) the child born a formless lump (ten versions, including the *King of Tars*). The Anglo-Latin versions belong to Group A; the *King of Tars* is fundamentally based on a version like C, but employs also the black-and-white motif of B. The poem was influenced also by the French *Florence de Rome* (Geist) and the English *Otuel and Roland* (O'Sullivan). The diction abounds with conventional pietistic expressions (Hibbard); the details from history, folklore, and romance, transformed with pious consistency, intensify the religious feeling. In analogues the disfigured child is attributed to the mother's adultery; here the defect in the offspring is thought by each parent to indicate the other's lack of faith. Despite pedestrian diction and exaggerated feelings, the earlier portions are dramatic and pathetic. The last section on the battles is anti-climactic and dull.

LE BONE FLORENCE OF ROME [84]. Composed in the late fourteenth century the North Midlands in twelve-line tail-rime stanza aabccbddbeeb. Survives in a unique version in MS Cambridge University Library Ff. 2.38, 2187 lines, 1475–1500.

Garcy, aged Emperor of Constantinople, having been refused the hand of Princess Florence, attacks her father, Otes, Emperor of Rome. Miles and Esmere, sons of the King of Hungary, defend Rome and become rival suitors for Florence. Otes is slain; Esmere, the younger brother, is captured. When released, Esmere weds Florence and becomes Emperor of Rome; but Florence will be his wife in name only, until he slays Garcy. Esmere leaves on this mission. Miles attempts to pass off a mutilated dead body as Esmere's and practises other stratagems upon Florence. He also confines her, but she is rescued by the clergy after a confession by Egravayne. Miles is imprisoned in a tower. When Esmere is victorious and about to return, Florence releases Miles, who then falsely accuses her of adultery with Egravayne. She is enticed by Miles into a forest, manages to preserve her honor, is abandoned, and rescued by Sir Tyrry. A knight whom she rejects slits the throat of Tyrry's daughter and puts the knife in the hands of the sleeping Florence. She is again sent away into a forest. There she saves a man about to be hanged, who becomes her page. He and a burgess sell her to a mariner; he pays lead instead of gold. The ship sinks. Florence is saved and reaches a nunnery. She acquires fame as a healer. To her come the ailing Esmere, Miles, the page, the burgess, the mariner. Before curing them, she makes them confess publicly. She and Esmere are reunited. "Let all who would be false bethink themselves; evil cunning is always punished."

There are nine principal incidents (Hibbard): (1) the wooing of a heroine by her brother-in-law; (2) her rejection of him and his accusation of adultery against her; (3) her condemnation; (4) flight; (5) refuge in a home where another rejected suitor murders the child of her protectors and accuses her; (6) her second flight; (7) man whom she freed from the gallows, who sells her to a ship's captain; (8) her escape when the boat is wrecked; (9) her fame as a healer which brings to her finally all her stricken persecutors. They confess their deeds. Recognition and reunion follow.

The ultimate source of these themes and their combination, whether in the Orient or the West, whether from folklore or sant's life, has not been established. Florence is one of hundreds of stories, in every language of Europe, on the same theme—an innocent persecuted wife whose sufferings are initiated by a brother-in-law when his suit is rejected; and she is finally exonerated when her fame as a healer brings together those who have wronged her (the Crescentia-Constance type). The English piece seems an abbreviated translation of a lost French version of *Florence de Rome* (Geist). Incidents are similar to those of the *King of Tars*, *Emare*, *Squyr of Lowe Degre*, with a heroine more interesting in character and behavior than the hero or villains. Despite miracles and coincidences, a sense of reality is imparted by vivid details and descriptions. The hagiographic tone, the delineation of the Seven Sins on the walls of the palace, the patient endurance of the heroine and her limitless kindliness and good nature, the pointed moralizing of the concluding lines blur the distinction between Saint's Life and Romance.

9. Breton Lays

by

Mortimer J. Donovan

The seven poems in this section exemplify the Breton lay, a type of romance perfected before 1189 by Marie de France. In her hands the Breton lay is a short narrative poem of roughly a hundred to a thousand lines, in short couplets, treating in a single adventure and without digression some aspect of love. Since it ranges from realistic story to fairy tale, it is identified most readily by its prologue and epilogue; usually a Breton source is mentioned or the setting is given as ancient Brittany or Britain. Although Marie de France claims to have heard lays rendered musically, no manuscript of a lyric Breton lay survives; whether her poems consistently relate the same story as Breton minstrels told in song is beyond proof. Certainly, however, the narrative lay is distinct from the artistic lyric lay, which developed after her time. Throughout the thirteenth century, as the characteristic prologue and epilogue were copied to advantage, the Breton lay continued to flourish. Some examples, formed as short didactic love poems, historical lays or even fabliaux, repeat conventionally Marie's claim to a Breton source and to relating the "truth." The thirteenth century vogue of the Breton lay in French is indicated by Shrewsbury School MS VII, f. 200, a title-page of a lost collection of 67 lays and other short poems from around 1270.

The English Breton lay lived equally long, and at a slightly later date, yet its history is difficult to trace. Some English examples doubtless have been lost; the few extant date mostly from the fourteenth century. There is no strong evidence that collections of lays comparable to Marie's twelve poems ever existed in English. However general, the prologue common to *Lai le Freine*, to two manuscripts of *Sir Orfeo* and to the *Franklin's Tale* provides valuable information. It not only identifies single examples of the Breton lay, but also remarks on their type. Though it states that "most" lays are about love, it allows ribaldry also as proper matter. Its familiar claim that Breton lays originate in lyric lays must be viewed as conventional assertion easily copied from any of several sources. Since, however, all the other poems in this section lack this identifying prologue, they are difficult to distinguish from other short romances. *Sir Launfal* and related poems in couplets develop from an extant lay by Marie de France; *Emare, Sir Gowther* and the *Earl of Toulous* simply mention their source in a Breton lay; *Sir Degare* is set in Brittany. That the lays in this section imitate the style of contemporary romance is evident in their verse form—short couplets or tail-rime stanzas. Chaucer's *Franklin's Tale*, which will be discussed with his other writings, is the only example in long couplets; but the complexity of its narrative structure would be the strongest reason for setting it apart.

LAI LE FREINE [85]. Beginning of the fourteenth century; 340 verses in short couplets; Southeast, or possibly Westminster-Middlesex.

In the West Country two knights live as neighbors. When one becomes the father of twins, the wife of the other remarks enviously that any mother of twins has been unfaithful. Soon, however, she herself bears twin daughters. To save herself embarrassment, she plots with the midwife to do away with one of them. The one chosen is wrapped in a rich robe and identified as well-born by means of a ring. During the night a maiden carries her as far as a distant convent and abandons her in a hollow ash tree. When the porter finds the infant, he at once informs the abbess of his discovery. The infant is christened Freine, which in French means "ash."

As Freine matures, she is accepted as the abbess' niece and at twelve years is given the few facts of her past. By now there is no fairer, more gentle, more submissive maiden in England. A young knight, Sir Guroun, wins her love and takes her away as his mistress. Later, when persuaded to marry, he happens to choose Freine's twin. The ceremony is performed, and the bride is brought to Guroun's hall.

The fragment ends here, but the story may be completed from the source.

Freine is present at the hall. Thinking the bridal bed too plainly covered, she generously places over it her own precious robe. When her mother sees the robe and learns of the ring, she confesses her guilt and identifies Freine as her own daughter. Freine's noble birth is now established. As soon as Guroun's marriage is dissolved, Freine and Guroun are happily united.

Lai le Freine, not a close rendering of one of the lays of Marie de France, departs from its source by adding, omitting and changing detail. Its long prologue (see introduction to this section) is new; it has been called a mosaic of conventional ideas found in several earlier lays. If the author of this poem composed also *Sir Orfeo*, as is possible, the close similarity of this prologue to that in the two later manuscripts of *Sir Orfeo* would be accounted for. In *Lai le Freine*, further, the setting is shifted from Brittany to the "west country" of England, which is the setting of certain French Breton lays. Many passages in the source become abbreviated and others expanded. As the infant in the story is prepared for exposure the prolonged description of night and the coming of morning makes the world of the story concrete and real. Changes from indirect to direct discourse provide a dramatic effect.

The story told belongs to the widespread medieval cycle of tales of the patient woman and in particular recalls the Griselda group (see Chaucer's *Clerk's Tale*). It builds on the motifs of the twin birth, the child separated from its parents and reunited, and the husband with two wives. The story materials are, therefore, not specifically Breton. Parallels are found in the ballad, exemplified by *Fair Annie*, in the drama and in the tale written in many European languages and extending down to recent times. Among the close parallels, Jean Renart's *Galeran de Bretagne* (ca. 1230) is the only work derived from Marie's *Lai le Fraisne*. The English *Lai le Freine* as story ranks high and has been judged with *Sir Orfeo* as the most attractive of the English Breton lays.

SIR ORFEO [86]. Beginning of the fourteenth century; 301 short couplets; Southeast or possibly Westminster-Middlesex; possibly by the author of *Lai le Freine*.

Orfeo, great harper and king of Traciens, is married to Heurodis, whose beauty is unsurpassed. One May morning, as Heurodis relaxes in her garden, she falls asleep under a grafted tree. On awakening she is distressed. She explains to Orfeo that their happy life together must end. During her sleep, she says, some knights appeared and asked her to speak with their king. Since she refused, the king himself carried her off to his kingdom; presently, he returned her to her garden and warned that she must be found under the same tree next day, her last with Orfeo. While lying under the same tree next day, she is spirited away despite her guard of a thousand knights.

Heartbroken, Orfeo appoints his steward regent and abandons himself to wandering in the forest. He lives meagerly for ten years and for solace plays his harp sweetly enough to tame wild animals. He often sees the King of Fairies and his followers hunting; where they go when they disappear, Orfeo cannot tell. One day he sees among some ladies with falcons his own Heurodis, who recognizes her lord, but does not speak. When she rides off with the others, Orfeo, with harp in hand, follows through a rocky opening until he enters a broad, sun-lit plain. Then he watches them enter a beautiful castle; posing as a minstrel, he too is admitted.

Within, he finds those taken by the fairies, including Heurodis, who is asleep under a tree. When Orfeo comes before the King and Queen of Fairies, he plays his harp so well that he is promised whatever reward he asks. He asks for Heurodis, and the King of Fairies is true to his promise. Taking Heurodis by the hand, he returns to his own kingdom.

Still unrecognized, he resolves to test his steward's good faith. Before his followers he plays his harp, which he claims belonged to a great harper long since killed in the wilderness by animals. The sorrow which the steward and others show is proof enough of their devotion to their king. Orfeo and his queen are crowned anew and live on happily.

Sir Orfeo, according to the classification of lays in its prologue, is the faery type, which contrasts with the more nearly realistic (see *Lai le Freine*). Its development has been carefully studied. Though lacking in the Auchinleck copy, its prologue appears in the two later manuscripts and must belong to the original English poem. *Sir Orfeo* probably had a French source (a lost *Lai d'Orphey* is earliest mentioned in *Floire et Blanceflor*, dating from the third quarter of the twelfth century). It developed from the myth of Orpheus and Eurydice blended with Celtic story; both chief sources tell of a mortal's loss of wife to supernatural powers and his attempt to enter their world to rescue her. The classical myth, familiar from the *Metamorphoses*, Books X and XI, and from the *Consolation of Philosophy*, Book III, Metrum 12, is still recognizable in Orfeo's harping and in the personal names, if corrupt. Though the *Wooing of Etain* has been defended as the ultimate Celtic source, it leaves unexplained such matters as the Wild Hunt, the home of the dead, and Orfeo's return in disguise and his recognition, all of which are not associated in any single analogue. Further, certain elements in the poem are peculiarly English, notably the description of Traciens as Winchester in the Auchinleck MS, and Orfeo's command that his successor be chosen by parliament.

Whatever the development of the poem, modern critics have found *Sir Orfeo* both unified and, on analysis, successful. Its beauty lies in the simple contrast of the real with the faery world. As story it is told with a deliberate simplicity and a care marred, if at all, in one way only: Orfeo's return and recognition draws attention from Heurodis' rescue and homecoming, which should be the climax of the poem.

EMARE [87]. Around 1400; 1035 verses, or 86 twelve-line stanzas riming aabccbddbeeb or aabaabccbddb; Northeast.

Emare ("the pure one"?), motherless daughter of Emperor Artyrus, is cared for by a nurse, who teaches her courtesy and embroidery. As she passes from childhood, her beauty so increases that the Emperor plans to marry her, his own daughter. He has a precious robe made for her from a richly embroidered cloth on which are represented famous lovers of romance. When Emare puts the robe on, she seems to be no earthly woman. Struck by her beauty, the Emperor now reveals to her his love. Since she stoutly rejects it, he sets her adrift in an open boat with her robe to clothe her. Only after losing her does he repent his rashness.

After several days Emare reaches a distant land called Galys, where she is rescued by the King's steward. She identifies herself as Egare ("the outcast") and, recovering her strength, joins the royal household as servant. At a feast, the King sees her in her robe and finds her beauty surpassing and unearthly. Despite the Queen Mother's protest that Emare is a devil, the King marries her. Later, while he is away fighting Saracens, a son, Segramour, is born to Emare with double king's mark. But, when the news is sent to the King, the evil Queen Mother, at whose castle the messenger stops, changes the letter to read that a devil, not a son, has been born. On hearing the news the King faints and, reviving, sends instructions that Emare should be well cared for. On the messenger's return journey, however, the Queen Mother once more intercepts the letter he is carrying, and substitutes for it another, which directs that Emare be set adrift at sea.

Emare patiently accepts this as her lord's will and, with Segramour, is placed in an open boat. After drifting many days, she is rescued by a Roman merchant, who is afraid at first when he sees her ornate robe, yet takes her into his home. Here she lives in comfort, embroiders and has the leisure to teach Segramour courtesy; yet secretly she sorrows over her misfortune. In Galys, meanwhile, the King returns from war only to discover his mother's deceit. Thinking his queen drowned for his sake, he resolves to visit Rome and seek peace of soul.

There he is lodged with the same merchant as rescued Emare. Her union with the King is effected through Segramour, who serves at table so correctly as to win admiration. He tells the King his name, identifies his mother and amid rejoicing brings the King to her chamber. About the same time, the Emperor visits Rome to do penance. When assured of his contrition, Emare asks Segramour to tell him that his daughter would see him. He comes to her, and again there is rejoicing, as her trials, patiently endured, end.

If *Emare* did not mention its source in a Breton lay, it would hardly be distinguishable from other romances associated with minstrels "who walk far and wide" and write in tail-rime stanzas. An original in French is suggested by some of its personal names, yet no immediate source is known. It is representative of the Constance story and so would be related to a large group of medieval poems of similar intention. (See the Eustace, Constance, Florence, Griselda Legends above for discussion.) Among the best known English analogues are Chaucer's *Man of Law's Tale* and Gower's tale of Constance, both derived from Trivet's *Chronique anglo-normande*. The English poems *Sir Eglamour*, *Sir Torrent*, *Octavian* and *Sir Triamour* show similarities—particularly, the first, which is related to the remote source of *Emare*.

The type of heroine represented in *Emare* is banished by an unnatural
father and exposed to a series of distresses, altogether undeserved, which
test her patience. In poems of this kind such distresses evoke pity in extreme
form and are represented artistically only with difficulty. *Emare* varies the
story pattern slightly. The heroine's distresses are rendered more severe
by an ironic misunderstanding of her beauty: when wearing her robe, she
is so beautiful as to be unearthly and so must be either *fée* or devil. Yet,
as important as her robe is in the story, it is described in 109 lines or a
tenth of the whole poem. Her courtliness takes the form of skill at embroidery, and Segramour's becomes good manners at table. Her character
at best is ill-defined and points to her chief purpose as exemplar of Christian
virtue.

SIR LAUNFAL (LAUNFALUS MILES) [88]. Later fourteenth cen-
tury; 1044 verses, or 87 twelve-line stanzas riming aabccbddbeeb; South-
east. This poem, the only known work of Thomas Chestre, is one of two
Middle English developments from *Lai de Lanval* by Marie de France.
(The second is represented by three versions in short couplets, *Sir Landeval*,
Sir Lambewell and *Sir Lamwell*, which are treated below.)

Sir Launfal, proud, generous bachelor and Arthur's steward, is renowned for
his largesse. He dislikes Guinevere because of her many lovers at court and, upon
her marriage to Arthur, is refused gifts, which she gives out to all others. Finding
a reason for leaving court, Launfal takes leave of Arthur, who offers his two
nephews as companions during the ride to Caerleon. There Launfal is met by the
Mayor, once his servant, who provides him with quarters reluctantly. The longer
generous Launfal stays, the more impoverished he becomes without Arthur's riches
to support him. His two companions presently return to court, yet agree not to
speak of his poverty, which would please Guinevere.

When the Mayor celebrates Trinity, Launfal is not invited, nor, lacking fine
clothes, does he attend church. The last three days he has not even eaten. For
solace he borrows from the Mayor's daughter saddle and bridle and, scorned by
the people, rides out unattended into the heath. His horse slips, but Launfal re-
mounts. Since the morning is warm, he rests under a tree and there laments his
misfortune. While resting, he sees two maidens coming to meet him; they summon
him to their lady, Dame Tryamour, daughter of the king of fairies. He finds her
half-clothed in an ornate pavillion and, to his surprise, is addressed as her lover;
in return for his love he is promised a magic purse, a mount, an attendant named
Gifre, and a banner insuring victory in any tournament. These Launfal accepts
and promises his love. They dine and pass the night. Before leaving next day
Launfal agrees to keep their love secret on condition that it will end if disclosed.

In his shabby clothes he returns to Caerleon. Then a troop of youths ride up
and give him the gifts which his mistress promised. The Mayor is at once more
hospitable. Launfal can practice greater largesse than ever before; he wins easily

in tournaments; at his summons his beloved visits him daily. As his good fortune increases, he is challenged to a duel by Sir Valentine, a giant knight of Lombardy, yet overcomes even him. When invited by Arthur to celebrate the feast of St. John, Launfal returns to court and finds his pride restored. During a dance Guinevere professes love for him and, in return, asks for his. Launfal is outraged by the suggestion of any disloyalty to Arthur. Then, when Guinevere claims that he has never loved a woman and no woman has ever loved him, he forgets his promise and mentions Dame Tryamour, the loveliest ever, whose maidens are lovelier than the Queen. Enraged, Guinevere tells Arthur that Launfal sought her as mistress. Launfal's woes have now doubled: Arthur is threatening to hang him; his fairy mistress and her gifts are gone. When his peers weigh the charges against him, they reduce them to one, that the accused boasted at the expense of the Queen's reputation, and they agree that he must bring forth his beloved within a year and a fortnight, or die. The stated time lapses: Dame Tryamour does not appear. As the sentence is changed, in recognition of Launfal's virtue, from death to exile, Dame Tryamour rides up and with her beauty justifies his boast. Then, blowing on Guinevere's eyes, she blinds her and, taking Launfal, rides off to the Isle of Olyroun, where the two continue to live. Once a year men can hear Launfal's horse neigh; anyone wishing to keep his arms from rusting may find an opponent in Launfal.

Thomas Chestre describes his poem simply as a "lay" and omits altogether the four-line prologue of the French *Lai de Lanval*. Scholarship has shown, in fact, that his source is based on the anonymous lay *Graelent*, which follows a simpler, less artistic form of the same story, one lacking notably an Arthurian setting. Elements in this story are accounted for in Celtic tradition: the fairy's visit to the world of mortals in search of love, her munificence, her enjoinment of her lover to secrecy, her disappearance once the love is revealed, and her fortunate return. In *Sir Launfal* two episodes unparalleled in the immediate sources, the tournament at Caerleon and the combat with Sir Valentine, reveal the freedom of the adapter, either Thomas Chestre or someone before him, to expand the story. Though *Sir Launfal* continues to hold up largesse as a knightly quality, it also allows space for the external side of chivalry as shown in these episodic passages. Certain other passages, which treat Guinevere's infidelity and the ambitious Mayor, render plausible the claim that the poem suffers a shift in purpose and, while beginning somewhat realistically, ends as the fairy type of lay.

COUPLET VERSIONS OF *LAI DE LANVAL*:

SIR LANDEVAL [89]. First half of the fourteenth century; 535 verses in short couplets; South. This version is probably derived from the same

Middle English translation, now lost, as the two versions which follow. Like these it lacks the tournament at Caerleon and the combat with Sir Valentine and, in fact, is rather close to *Lai de Lanval*. Some differences, however, are to be noted. The four-line prologue is missing, as are such touches as Launfal's meeting his beloved in the *morning* and the trembling of his horse as he approaches fairyland.

SIR LAMBEWELL [90]; SIR LAMWELL [91]: See Bibliography for description.

SIR DEGARE [92]. Before 1325; 1076 verses, in short couplets; probably Southwest Midland.

In Brittany a king unsurpassed at arms has offered his only daughter and heir to whatever suitor overcomes him in tournament; during the years no suitor succeeds. While on her way to the abbey where the deceased queen is buried, the princess becomes separated from the royal party and lost in a forest. There as her attendants rest under a chestnut tree in the heat of the morning, she moves off alone and is ravished by a knight from fairyland. On parting he leaves a pointless sword with her for the son she will bear; the point of the sword the knight himself keeps to identify his son later on. When the son is born, the mother, fearing for her reputation, secretly abandons him, but leaves in his cradle gold, silver and a pair of gloves together with a letter informing the finder that the infant is noble and should love only her whom the gloves fit. A hermit, who finds the infant and christens him Degare ("the one almost lost"), entrusts him to his sister until his tenth year and thereafter educates him himself.

Given the gold, silver and gloves and informed of the letter, Degare at twenty begins to search for his parents. With only a sapling as weapon he saves an earl from a dragon's attacks and is forthwith knighted. Since the gloves fit no one present, he continues his travels. Meeting a king offering his only daughter to any suitor who can overcome him, Degare unhorses him and so is married. Only later, when he gives her the gloves, does he discover that he has married his own mother, who at once confesses to her father her meeting with the knight from fairyland and Degare's secret birth. Armed now with the pointless sword, which his mother has kept for him, Degare sets out to find his father. He travels far in the forest where he was begotten, and reaches a castle on an island in a river. At first there is no one in the castle, but then the occupants appear, four huntresses, a dwarf and a beautiful lady with attendants. Degare conducts himself courteously, yet no one speaks to him. He is refreshed at a banquet and then reveals his love for the lady of the castle. Following her to her chamber, he lies down and is lulled to sleep by the music of a harp. Next day, after he learns that her father's death has left the castle undefended, he fights off a neighboring suitor and is promised the lady's love and land in marriage. But this he puts off until he has found his own father.

His search leads him now to a forest, where he is challenged by a knight for poaching. Though Degare protests his innocence, he accepts a fight and readies his pointless sword. But sight of the pointless sword moves his challenger to break off fighting and, by means of the missing point, which he has with him, to identify

Degare as his own son. Joyfully the two then seek out Degare's mother. As soon as his marriage to her is dissolved, the knight from fairyland, to the king's satisfaction, marries her. Accompanied by his mother, father and grandfather, Degare returns to the castle on the island and is joined to the lady to whom he earlier promised his love.

Sir Degare has been listed with the Breton lays of this section because of its setting in Brittany (in earliest readings only), its fairy elements, its length and its straightforwardness as story. It sets out to describe "wat man was" Degare, yet its interest is not his character so much as the situations involved in his search for his mother and father, from whom he is early separated. He discovers his mother in his bride and his father in his opponent in a single combat. To these familiar elements are added others which have led to the view that the poem is a composite of motives found elsewhere in medieval romance. *Sir Degare* does open by describing a possessive father somewhat like Emare's; exposes a mortal woman to a ravishing knight like Tydorel's father; causes a new-born child to be exposed, as in *Lai le Freine*; and for its climax involves its hero in a father-son combat, as in the lays *Milun* and *Doon*. Although its matter is at once traditional, the poem, especially in the Auchinleck reading, is not without power, which originates in the suspense of a search deftly handled. Later readings, admittedly, suffer from not too skilful redaction.

SIR GOWTHER [93]. Around 1400; 757 verses, or 63 twelve-line stanzas riming aabccbddbeeb; Northeast Midland.

A duke in Estryke is without heir after ten years of marriage. When his wife prays for a child by any means, she is visited in her garden by a figure who at first resembles her husband, but on parting shows himself to be a devil. Frightened, she tells her husband than an angel appeared to her and instructed her to expect a child. The child Gowther is born and, true to his father's prophecy, grows so strong as to kill his nurses and do harm to his mother. At fifteen he forges a heavy sword which only he can bear, and so terroizes everyone, including the religious, that his supposed father dies of grief and his mother is heartbroken. When an earl calls him a devil's son, Gowther forces his mother at sword's point to identify his real father.

Horrified, Gowther goes to Rome and confesses his sins to the Pope, who directs him to eat only what he can snatch from dogs and to remain silent until he receives a sign from heaven. Beginning a life of repentance, he visits the court of Almayne, where he is called "Hob the Fool." When, presently, the Saracens seek the Emperor's daughter, who has been dumb, Gowther prays for help, arms himself, and, unrecognized as Hob the Fool except by the Emperor's daughter, thrice routs the enemy before being wounded. Seeing him wounded, the maiden falls from her tower and appears to be dead. But she revives, is now able to speak and declares that Gowther is the unknown champion who saved her. The Pope, present originally for her funeral, recognizes a sign from heaven and absolves Gowther. After marriage to the Emperor's daughter Gowther rules Almayne; the earl who called him a devil's son marries Gowther's mother and rules Estryke. Despite the sin of his early life Gowther is reverenced as a saint, works miracles and intercedes for those seeking help.

Sir Gowther claims to be derived from a "lai of Breyten," but none like it survives. Gowther's "supernatural" birth, which has been related to that of Merlin, recalls also that of Tydorel in the thirteenth-century lay of the same name. But the legend of Robert the Devil, which the poem relates, is widespread and is found in forms as diverse as exemplum, ballad, drama and even opera, in Spain, Portugal, France, Germany and England: a youth begotten by the devil, on learning his paternity, is raised from extreme depravity through repentance and thereafter, disguising himself as a menial, wins a princess' hand. The late twelfth-century romance *Robert le diable*, the antecedent of *Sir Gowther* which names the legend, reaches 5078 verses and a fullness of detail impossible in a narrative lay; the related and later "Lyfe of the most Myscheuoust Robert the Deuyll," printed in 1510 by Wynkyn de Worde, and another version by Thomas Lodge, reflect the popularity of the legend in England in the sixteenth century. The legend probably has no historical basis; the Three Days' Tournament is found also in *Ipomadon*.

Not by accident one of the two manuscripts of *Sir Gowther* ends, *Explicit vita sancti*. Somewhat like a saint's life the poem records the early years and miraculous regeneration of a figure completely depraved at birth. The didactic purpose is evident. Yet, whatever the deficiencies of the poem as narrative art, paternity in the devil himself presents an extreme ill-fortune with which Gowther struggles admirably.

THE EARL OF TOULOUS [94]. Around 1400; 1224 verses, or 102 twelve-line stanzas riming aabccbddbeeb; Northeast Midland.

The Emperor of Almayne rejects the pleas of his beautiful wife that he restore to the chivalrous Sir Barnard, the Earl of Toulous, lands unjustly taken from him. In anger the Emperor raises an army against him, but is defeated and loses his trusted follower, Sir Tralabas. When Sir Barnard finds Sir Tralabas among the prisoners taken, he learns from him of the Empress' surpassing beauty and promises him freedom on condition that a meeting with her be arranged. The two set out for Almayne, Sir Barnard in the clothes of a hermit, and reach the Emperor's court. Then, when Sir Tralabas secretly informs the Empress that a mortal enemy lingers at court, he is reminded of his agreement with Sir Barnard, which she insists that he keep. When, in fact, Sir Barnard observes her beauty as she attends chapel, he wishes that she were unmarried. She responds by giving him alms and, as a love token, a ring from her finger. Next day, when Sir Barnard departs, the faithless Sir Tralabas with two followers overtakes him on the road, attempts murder, but fails so badly that all three attackers are killed and Sir Barnard escapes.

In Almayne, the Emperor, going abroad, entrusts his wife to two knights, both her undeclared lovers, who attempt to win her. One agrees to surprise the other in her chamber: if she dare refuse the wishes of either thereafter, she will be exposed as unfaithful. When she proves too strong for them, they plot a second time. They urge a youthful carver to hide naked in her chamber as if in a game for her amusement. Then, outside her chamber, their cry of infidelity leads to a discovery of the youth, who is killed before he can explain. At a special council the Empress is defended by an elderly knight, who doubts her accusers and proposes trial by champion. When Sir Barnard hears her call for a champion, he hastens to Almayne and, in an abbey one mile from court, learns from her uncle and confessor that she is innocent. Disguising himself as a monk, he too finds her innocent when he hears her confession. At once he offers himself as her champion and subdues her accusers in a combat by which she is formally cleared of guilt. The Emperor, elated, now accepts in friendship his mortal enemy, Sir Barnard. Three years later, on his death, he is succeeded by Sir Barnard, who marries the Empress and becomes father of her children.

The Earl of Toulous is, according to its own claim, a "lay of Bretayn" and may be classified as an historical lay. (See classification in Introduction to this section.) It builds on the relations of Bernard I, Count of Barcelona and Toulouse, and Empress Judith, second wife of Louis le debonnaire; in 831 the Empress was charged with adultery, but acquitted; later Bernard offered to meet in combat anyone still questioning his honor. In the present account fiction is more prominent than historic fact.

Although the poem suffers from a lack of proportion and from excessive length, it is not without virtue. It traces with delicacy the relations of a count and empress who first recognize obligations yet remain true. After a first meeting however short, they live apart by difficult choice; the ring alone reminds Sir Barnard of their love. But he quickly returns after he hears accusations against her; meets her accusers in combat after he determines for himself her innocence; and marries her after the Emperor dies. Despite the Emperor's brutality, the Empress remains loyal and indeed stands apart from other innocent, persecuted wives of medieval romance.

10. Miscellaneous Romances

by

Lillian Herlands Hornstein

The Miscellaneous Romances are much alike in their interest in love and adventure, their plots combining similar folklore materials, their localization in an exotic Orient, Persia, Egypt, or Sicily. A few seem more concerned to point a lesson than simply to entertain; a few, though grounded in chivalric ideas and attitudes, give these a new dimension by setting them in a framework of contemporary manners and morals. The combination in these romances of legendary or folktale themes, wide-ranging locales (sometimes from Spain to India), and contemporary mores results in a potpourri that, though it may disconcert the modern, fascinated the medieval audience.

For convenience, these romances are here grouped as I. Romances of Greek or Byzantine Origin; II. Composites of Courtly Romance; III. Romances on Historical Themes; IV. Romances from Family Tradition; V. Legendary Romances of Didactic Interest.

I. Romances of Greek or Byzantine Origin

Late Greek and Byzantine literature had been familiar to the Latin Middle Ages; there is still extant, for example, a portion of an Old English translation of *Apollonius of Tyre*. But with the Crusades and the ever-broadening contacts with the Near East, a new, vibrant influence came into the vernacular literature of Europe. Romances were now shaped by Eastern elements of plot and details of background, a new style, tone, and attitude. In this group notable are two Middle English romances. The fragmentary *Apollonius of Tyre* is undoubtedly a version whose ultimate source was a late Greek or Byzantine romance. *Floris and Blauncheflur*, though drawing on a vast heritage of folk-theme situations, is the most interesting of the romances for its Byzantine atmosphere and scenes.

APOLLONIUS OF TYRE [95]. Composed ca. 1376–81 at Wimborne Minster, Dorset, in a Southwest Midland dialect. The unique manuscript, Douce 216, fifteenth century, is only a fragment, about one-tenth of the original poem, comprising the final 144 lines; these long lines are divisible into quatrains abab, of irregular iambic tetrameter.

From other versions we learn of an incestuous king who will permit his daughter to marry only the man who can answer the king's riddle. Apollonius, seeking fame and fortune, arrives in the king's domain, comprehends the riddle and knows the answer, which he dare not voice since it will disclose the king's guilt. He leaves for another land where he marries a princess; he subsequently sets sail with his pregnant wife. The Douce fragment opens with Apollonius at the shrine in Ephesus when he is recalling the latter part of his story in flashback: his flight to Tarse and Cirenen (Cyrene), the birth at sea of his daughter Tharsia and the apparent death of his wife in childbirth, the subsequent false report by Strangulion and Denyse of the death of his daughter, who, however, had actually been spared by the slave Theophilus. Apollonius has now found his daughter alive. The shrine's priestess (his wife, Architrates) recognizes him, tells how she was saved from the sea. The enraged citizens stone Strangulion and Denyse. At Cirenen Apollonius rewards a fisherman who had helped him. The hero writes his adventures in two books, one for his family and the other for the shrine at Ephesus. The happy family rules over Tyre, Cirenen, Antiochia.

The story stems from pagan antiquity, but whether via Greek, Roman, or Byzantine romance is uncertain. It was affected also by folk themes of the Incestuous Father, Faithful Servitor, Evil Stepmother, Suitor Tests, Dangerous Riddle, Accidental Reunions.

The story flourished for a thousand years in hundreds of Latin narratives. The oldest vernacular version is found in two long fragments of Old English prose. But the story soon thereafter appeared in every language of Europe. Gower used the subject for the last tale in *Confessio Amantis* (see under Gower); Chaucer's Man of Law (see under Chaucer) condemned "such unnatural abominations." Translated in the fifteenth century from the *Gesta Romanorum*, in 1510 from the French (for W. de Worde), it was popular in the sixteenth century, and forms the subject of Shakespeare's *Pericles (i. e.,* Apollonius) *of Tyre* (from Gower).

FLORIS AND BLAUNCHEFLUR [96]. Composed ca. 1250 in the Southeast Midlands in lines of three or four stresses, riming in couplets. Survives in four manuscripts: Cotton Vitellius D. 3, a fragment of 451 lines, of which about half are imperfect, before 1300; MS Cambridge University Library Gg. 4.27.2, 824 lines, ca. 1300; Auchinleck MS, 861 lines, ca. 1330;

MS Egerton 2862 (Sutherland), 1083 lines, ca. 1400. The beginning of the story is lost in all the English manuscripts. Hausknecht's critical text comprises 1296 lines.

> The children, Floris, son of the King of Spain, and Blauncheflur, a captive maiden, love each other. Fearing Floris' future marriage to Blauncheflur, his parents send him away and sell the maiden to Babylonian merchants. They in turn sell her to the Emir, in whose harem she is kept as his prospective Queen. When Floris returns and sees a tomb (erected by his parents) bearing Blauncheflur's name, he attempts suicide. They reveal the truth; he goes in quest of the girl. At Babylon he learns that she is held in an inaccessible tower. He bribes the porter and is carried in a basket of flowers to the tower. The lovers are united. Found sleeping together, they are condemned to be killed. Neither is willing alone to survive the other through aid of a magic ring that can preserve one of them from death. The rivalry as to which shall die first and their pathetic story win their pardon. Floris and Blauncheflur are married and go to rule their own country. The Emir marries Clarice, friend of Blauncheflur.

The origins of the story are uncertain: parallels and resemblances have been noted in Byzantine, Greek, and Arabic romances; their exact relationship to the western versions is not clear. From twelfth-century French romances the story spread all over Europe. The oldest extant French manuscripts, of the thirteenth century, differing in style and incident, divide into two types: the "aristocratic" version and the "popular." The "aristocratic" type is an idyllic romance, sentimental and descriptive. The "popular" version is shorter (of inferior literary quality) and resembles a *chanson de geste* in its neglect of sentiment to stress physical prowess and stirring incident, e. g., Flores wins his lady by force of arms.

The English piece is one of the earliest and most charming of English romances. Close similarities with extant French texts show that the writer must have at points translated word for word some lost French original of the "aristocratic" type, antecedent to any extant text. Condensing or omitting details and descriptive matter (e. g., the accounts of the Emir's garden, the flowers), the English author secured greater unity. The simplicity of theme benefits from a simple style, weakened here, however, by excessive use of riming tags. The tale is not of combat, nor of passion, but of an idyllic love. Tender love and youthful innocence overcome all obstacles. The parents yield; the understandable rage of the Emir gives way before the devotion of the children; contrary to his previous ideas, he too makes a permanent marriage. The charm and mystery of the East complement the chivalry and sentimentality of the West. Love conquers all.

II. Composites of Courtly Romance

A few English romances, all of late origin, are in great part artificial composites of elements derived from sophisticated courtly romances. These pieces are *Sir Degrevant, Generides, Partonope of Blois, Eger and Grime, Roswall and Lillian, Ipomadon, Valentine and Orson*, the *Squyr of Lowe Degre*, and *Clariodus*.

SIR DEGREVANT [97]. Composed in the late fourteenth century in the North or Northeast Midlands (a meeting place of five dialect areas), in sixteen-line tail-rime stanzas, aaabcccbdddbeeeb, the triplets and tail-rime both in frequently two-beat lines; the lines are also highly alliterative, sometimes formulaic, occasionally linked by rime and verbal repetitions. Survives in two manuscripts, both somewhat imperfect: Thornton MS, some 1678 lines (one leaf, lines 802–1008, missing between ff. 133–34), ca. 1440 (Lincolnshire); Cambridge University Library Ff. 1.6 (Findern MS), 1904 lines, late fifteenth century (mixed Derbyshire dialect). Each manuscript is independently derived from a lost common source; Thornton version gives more evidence of original minstrel origins and oral transmission and is closer to the original dialect.

Sir Degrevant of the Table Round, famed for knightly prowess and generosity, is summoned home from a Crusade when a neighbor earl despoils the hero's hunting preserves. The earl refuses to make reparations and continues his depredations. Degrevant and his retainers hunt the trepassers as if they were deer, but the earl escapes. While Degrevant vainly challenges the earl to joust, the earl's Countess appears on the walls with her daughter Melidor. Degrevant instantly falls in love. He accosts Melidor in her garden, is threatened by her when he reveals his identity. Secretly he enters the castle, where the maid hides him overnight. He challenges a Duke of Gerle who is suing for Melidor's hand, and wins. Melidor then admits to Degrevant that she loved him at first sight, and clandestinely entertains him every night. They remain chaste. Detected by her father's steward and ambushed by her father's men, Degrevant slays his opponents. The earl then permits the marriage. After thirty years (Thornton: thirty-six years) and seven (Thornton: ten) children, Melidor dies. Degrevant goes to the Holy Land, where he is slain.

The poem—the story of a feud—is well-balanced in its action and descriptions, movement and conversation. The alliterative verse emphasizes the zestful vigor, and stanza links contribute to the variety of tone. The themes of the middle portion of the story (the secret love of an enemy's daughter, meetings in garden and bower, faithful squire and waiting-maid, wicked tale-bearer, three-day joust, courtly modesty and devotion) are

10*

commonplaces in romance. Here unusual interest derives from the realistic treatment of the feudal situation, the contrasting ideals of positions and characters, their disputes over lands and foraging (recalling the *Hunting of the Cheviot*), their large indentured retinue of archers and fighting men. Elaborated are details of social life, the glowing beauties of costume and architecture, of embroidery, jewel-work, table-fittings, wall-paintings,— picturesque items which have delighted the literary critics and inspired graphic artists like William Morris and the Pre-Raphaelites. Arthurian, Celtic, and Welsh traditions also have contributed to the poem, which shows specific similarities to the Alliterative *Morte Arthure* (see [16]), *Eger and Grime* (see [100]), and especially to the *Earl of Toulous* (see [94]).

GENERIDES [98]. Composed in the late fourteenth century in the Midlands. Survives in two independent versions: in couplets, Helmingham MS (PML M. 876), 10,086 lines, 1425–50; in seven-line stanzas (rime-royal), Trinity College Cambridge, Gale 0.5.2, 6995 lines (one leaf, 187 lines, missing after line 4619); 1475–1500. Print: Pynson fragments comprise about 450 lines in stanzas, correspond to lines 3508–87, 8371–8423, 9810–10020 of MS Helmingham; 1500?–10. The English versions possibly derive from a French original, although none has been discovered. In 1568 Thomas Purfoote was licensed to print a book *Generydes*. The two versions agree in the essential plot structure, but differ in tone and details. The couplet version (Helmingham) feeds on emotion and pathos, detailed, elaborated battle pieces and descriptions, tautological litotes formulae. The stanzaic version (Trinity College, Gale) exudes a high moral tone. It suppresses the oriental customs of the couplet version and expands the use of proverbs. Although it condenses the descriptions, it achieves a lively realism by introducing dialogue and a mildly ironic humor (Pearsall).

In the Helmingham version, King Aufreus of Ynde knows that his wife is un-faithful with his steward Amelok. On a magic stag-hunt, Aufreus meets the fairy-like Sereyne, Princess of Surre (i. e., Syria), and they have a son, Generides, who is reared by his mother. When he grows up, he goes to Aufreus' court. The Queen makes advances to him, but is unsuccessful; like Potiphar's Wife, she falsely accuses him to Amelok, who beats him. Generides departs for the court of the Sultan of Perse; he meets Princess Clarionas and they declare their love. When an envious knight reports Generides, he is imprisoned. Permitted to act as the Sultan's champion, he mortally wounds Bellyns, King of Kings. Meanwhile, Aufreus' wife has be-trayed the castle to Amelok, and Aufreus has fled to Tharse. Here he becomes

King and marries the mother of Generides. Bellyns' son, Gwynan, causes Clarionas to be abducted; Generides, disguised as a leper, rescues her. Then he departs to aid Aufreus regain Ynde. During a truce in Ynde, Generides returns to defeat Gwynan, who has invaded Perse. Aufreus' first wife sends false reports to each of the lovers, Clarionas and Generides, that the other has married, but her chicanery is revealed. When Generides defeats Amelok, the Queen dies with him. The hero weds his lady and succeeds to the thrones of Ynde and Perse.

To the two chief love stories and their involvements—the father (Aufreus-Sereyne) and the son (Generides-Clarionas)—is added a tame third one of the latter's confidant (Darrell-Lycidas). Borrowed from earlier romances and folktale, familiar patterns include the pursuit of a magic hart, a shirt washable only by the heroine, the coming of an unknown youth to court, love at first sight, exchange of rings, prophetic dreams, spying steward, false accusations, the "chaste embrace," trusted confidant, abduction, disguise as leper, father-son brother-brother combat, friendly exchange of swords while hero is sleeping. *Generides* shares these and similar themes with *Guigemar*, Chrétien's *Erec*, *Eliduc*, *Bevis of Hampton* (see [6]), *Degrevant*, *Eglamour* (see [79]), *Horn* (see [1]), *Ipomadon*, *Valentine and Orson*. The *Tristan* appears to have been the predominant influence on the love story. The incidents are well told, although there is no attempt at characterization. Of some interest is the couplet version of the begetting of the hero and the skills of his fée-like mother. The composite character of the romance and the confusion of names and places make unlikely an ultimate Eastern source.

PARTONOPE OF BLOIS [99]. Composed in the fifteenth century. Survives in six fifteenth-century manuscripts of which five are in couplets and one in stanzas. The Couplet Version was originally composed in a southerly dialect; the manuscripts are occasionally contaminated by northern scribes: the earliest manuscript is University College Oxford C. 188, 7096 lines, defective at the beginning and end, with numerous lacunae, 1425–50; the longest manuscript, despite one missing leaf after f. 19, is British Museum Additional 35288, 12,195 lines, 1475–1520; though the work of three scribes, it gives the best readings. MS Rawlinson F. 14, 6280 lines, 1475–1500, is imperfect, but supplies deficiences in the University College MS. MS Bodleian English Poetry C. 3, a fragment, 158 lines, ca. 1500 (found in the binding of a book), helps to fill the missing end of the University College MS. Clifden (Robartes) MS, is a fragment of 200 lines,

1475–1500. The Stanzaic Version is in MS Penrose [10] (Delamere), a fragment, imperfect, of 308 lines, ca. 1455, in four-stress lines in quatrains abab. The immediate French manuscript which was the source of these versions is not known; but analogues, probably close to the source texts, exist in French.

Partonope, lost while hunting a magic boar, is brought by a magic ship to a magnificent but seemingly uninhabited city; in a mysterious castle is served abundant food by invisible hands; and is guided to a splendid bed by torches. He becomes the lover of an unseen damsel, Melior, who tells him that she is empress of Byzantine, and that he must not attempt to see her for two-and-a-half years, after which they will be wed. After a year she consents to his return to his mother and uncle, the King of France, to aid his country. He performs great exploits. On this and a later visit, his mother, fearful for his soul, warns him; but he returns to Melior. Goaded by his mother, who has given him a magic lantern, he breaks the prohibition and momentarily beholds Melior's beauty; she tells him he has destroyed her power. He is cast forth in shame, goes nearly mad with despair, wishes to be devoured by wild animals or to starve to death, endures great hardships in the forest of Ardennes, and ultimately regains Melior by defeating his rivals in duels and tournaments.

The longer (couplet) English version, like the oldest western version (MS Paris Arsenal, 9744 lines), opens with Partonope; and when Melior appears, she relates the magic arts which she employed to bring the hero to her. In the other, the stanzaic version (also derived from a French source; fragmentary in English, complete in Scandinavian and Spanish texts), Melior appears first and sends messengers to seek out a worthy husband. They select Partonope, whom she then brings to her through necromancy. Structurally the poem combines two themes: that of the marriage taboo with the method of its violation (reminiscent of the late-Greek legend of Cupid and Psyche, but with sexes reversed, see Hibbard), and that of the offended fée of Celtic stories and Breton lays (Schofield). Parallels in the lays can be found for the boar hunt, magic ship, glittering palace, the fairy mistress of capricious yet generous behavior, the gift of wonderful horses, the role of minor characters, and other details. The heroine has been regarded as an avatar of and equated with Morgain la Fée (Newstead). Parallels with folktales and chivalric-courtly romances are numerous.

The English version, faithful to the order and content of the French story, is not a mere translation. It condenses descriptions, expands reflective, rhetorical elements; on occasion it openly disgrees with the original, as when it defends the purity of women. As in *Ipomadon*, the multitudinous details grow tedious; so do the innumerable episodes related by direct discourse and the continual didactic commentary upon them by the personages themselves or by the author in the first person. Commendable is the understanding of motivations, the treatment of the Saracens as human beings, and the handling of *amour courtois*. Chaucer's influence may be responsible for the poet's language, use of proverbs, and freedom in developing character.

EGER AND GRIME [100]. Composed in the mid-fifteenth century in the north, near Linlithgow on the Firth of Forth (Basilius), probably originally in stanzas (Everett, MLR 29.447). Survives in two late versions: (a) the Percy Folio MS, 1474 lines, ca. 1650; (b) prints, 2860 lines, dated 1669, 1687, 1711; all versions in four-stress couplets, occasionally irregular. Both versions derive independently from a lost original. The version in the Percy Folio MS, a "better" text (French and Hale, p. 671), may be nearer to the original than the longer version in the prints, considered corrupt and expanded; Reichel and Caldwell argue that the prints represent the original more closely.

In the version in the Percy Folio MS, Sir Eger seeks the love of Lady Winglaine; her ideal of a husband is one who has never been defeated in battle. Eger ventures into a "forbidden country" and is immediately attacked by Sir Gray-steele, a gigantic knight in gold armor and red shield. They fight on horseback and on foot with spears, swords, and knives, until Sir Eger swoons. When he recovers, he finds that his little finger has been cut off. His own horse having been killed, he takes that of another slain knight, who also has a finger missing. By nightfall Eger reaches a splendid castle, where a fair lady, Loosepaine, cares for his wounds. At his departure she gives him two shirts and two bottles of wine. Sore afflicted, he returns home to his sworn brother, Sir Grime, to whom he tells his story, overheard by an indignant Winglaine. Sir Grime arranges that Eger shall remain hidden while Grime goes to avenge him. After three days of riding, Sir Grime meets a squire who conducts him to the castle of Loosepaine. Pretending to be Sir Eger, he returns the shirts, but when she draws off his glove and sees his fingers intact, he reveals the truth and his intention to destroy Sir Gray-steele. She tells him his foe grows stronger from midnight to noon, but weaker from noon on. The next day, with the aid of the sword Erkyin (Egeking) he slays Gray-steele, cuts off his hand, and appropriates Gray-steele's golden gear and steed. Sir Grime returns to Loosepaine, who treats his wounds and tells the glad tidings to her father, Earl Gares. A marriage is arranged between Sir Grime and Loosepaine. He returns secretly to Sir Eger, who then takes over steed and armor, as if he were the victor. Eger marries Winglaine. After forty days of feasting, Grime, Eger, and Pallyas (brother of Grime) ride to Earl Gares' land, where Sir Grime marries Loosepaine. Sir Pallyas weds the daughter of Gray-steele. They live happily and have many children.

In the longer version (in the prints) (*The History of Sir Eger, Sir Gryme, and Sir Gray-Steel*), although the main plot is the same, details are changed and amplified: the name of Winglaine becomes Winliane, Loosepaine is Lillias, Grime is Grahame, and the Forbidden Land is the Land of Doubt. A new character, a burgess, aids and entertains Sir Grime. The scornful lady, Winliane, must humble herself to win back the love of Sir Eger. After Sir Grime's death, of which no details are given, Eger proclaims the truth that Grime had killed Gray-steele. Winliane angrily declares she would never have married him had she known the truth, and leaves him. Eger goes to Rome to be absolved, then to Rhodes, where he slays thousands of Saracens. After Winliane's death, he marries Lillias.

The earliest allusion to the romance comes in 1497; references thereafter are not infrequent (PFMS; Rickert). Opinion divides over which of the themes is central to the structure—the Celtic fairy mistress motif (Hibbard; R. S. Loomis), or the folktale of twin heroes—sworn brothers, represented in Grimm's *Kinder- und Hausmärchen* by *Die zwei Brüder* (Caldwell). The poem also shows reminiscences of Scandinavian influence (Hibbard; French and Hale). Related characteristics of the Otherworld—the mysterious guardian of the Forbidden Land, a Red Giant whose strength waxes and wanes with the sun, the entry into his land by a combat at the ford, the need for a magic sword to conquer him, the "love spot" between the eyebrows of the heroine, her magic powers of healing and her gorgeous fée-like abode—these and other details link the poem with Welsh-Arthurian lore. In contrast to this elusive and allusive atmosphere, the plot moves dramatically, often by direct discourse, in conversations notable for realism and humor. Pictorial and terse, gory and tender, the poem has variety and great charm.

ROSWALL AND LILLIAN [101]. Composed probably in the late fifteenth century in southern Scotland. No manuscript. Survives in two early prints: Black-letter print, 14 leaves, 846 lines (884 in Lengert's edition), in short riming couplets, Edinburgh 1663 (two copies), reprinted ca. 1679 and later; another print, Edinburgh 1775, 412 lines. The linguistic evidence as to the original dialect is inconclusive; conflicting dialect traits suggest that there was a difference between the dialect of the original composer and that of the scribe (or printers). No source is known.

Roswall, son of the King of Naples, hears three prisoners of his father bemoaning their fate; he steals the key to the prison and releases them. Spared the death penalty for this offense, Roswall is sent out of the country, accompanied by a steward. The False Steward takes advantage of the boy when he is drinking from a brook, robs him of his gold and letters of identification, and forces him to swear that he will not reveal the truth.

The False Steward presents himself at Bealm as the Prince of Naples. Roswall, calling himself Dissawar (the reason for this name is unknown), is received hospitably by a poor woman. She sends him with her son to school. The high steward of Bealm, hearing of the talents of Dissawar, takes him to the court. Princess Lillian makes him her cup-bearer and falls in love with him. To Lillian's despair, the False Steward of Naples (assumed to be the Prince of Naples) has been promised her hand; Dissawar, true to his oath, does not reveal his parentage. On the day of a tournament appointed to inaugurate the marriage festivities, the melancholy Dissawar goes to the forest to hunt. A stranger presents him with white armor and a white steed, and offers to hunt while Dissawar jousts. The White Knight upsets all his opponents, and then disappears. Dissawar returns to the palace with venison. Lillian, angry that Dissawar has spent his time hunting, expatiates on the virtues of the White Knight. The next day in the forest a knight with red armor and red horse makes the same arrangement with Dissawar. The Red Knight unseats all his rivals; again Dissawar returns loaded with venison. On the third day he is supplied in the same way with gold armor; again he wins. When he returns to the forest, his three benefactors reveal themselves as the three men whom he had released from prison. The next day despite tearful protests, Lillian is publicly married to the abhorred groom. While the wedding party is still at the dinner table, three Neapolitans enter, do obeisance to Dissawar, and reveal his identity. The False Steward confesses his deception and is hanged. Roswall and Lillian are married. Their first two sons become respectively King of Naples and King of Bealm, and the third becomes pope.

Despite the lateness of the versions, the poem is close to primitive folktales in the motifs of the male Cinderella, helpful companions, false steward, grateful friends, exchange of credentials (Lengert; Hibbard). The three-days' tournament and the hero incognito show the influence of *Ipomédon*; other incidents and phraseology are reminiscent of *Eger and Grime*. The romance influenced the ballad *The Lord of Lorn and the False Steward* (Child, 5.45). *Roswall* has the plot ingredients of popular story; and the narrative moves steadily without divagation and with much of the directness and simplicity of a ballad. A cynical reader may see no clear-cut moral conclusions in the fortuitous recognitions at the wedding feast, but the dramatic disclosure has all the elements of popular appeal—as does the theme that truth, virtue, honor will always conquer.

IPOMADON, tail-rime; THE LYFE OF IPOMYDON, couplets; IPOMEDON, prose [102]. Composed in the fourteenth and fifteenth centuries. Survives in three manuscripts: (A) MS Chetham 8009, *Ipomadon*, 8890 lines in twelve-line tail-rime stanzas aabccbddbeeb, before 1500, North Midland-Lancashire dialect (translated in the late fourteenth century from the French, Kölbing ed., p. clxxiii); (B) MS Harley 2252, *The Lyfe of Ipomydon*, 2346 four-stress lines riming in couplets, before 1500, East Midland dialect (composed before 1425, perhaps from memory, Seyferth, p. 76; Kölbing, p. lxv); (C) Longleat 257 (olim Marquis of Bath 25), *Ipomedon*, in prose, 1700 lines in the printed text, ca. 1460, of undetermined, mixed dialect (probably an independent translation). Prints: British Museum, W. de Worde, one leaf (56) lines), in couplets, 1505? ca. 1522?, corresponding roughly to Harley 2252 ff. 57^b (line 9)–58^a (lines 261–320); PML 20896, W. de Worde, another edition, 38 leaves (lacking the opening), in couplets, ca. 1530. All versions derive ultimately from *Ipomédon*, by Hue de Rotelande, ca. 1190, an Anglo-Norman poem of over 10,000 lines.

In the tail-rime *Ipomadon* (Version A), the daughter of the Duke of Calabria will wed only the most able knight in the world. Ipomadon, son of the King of Apulia, falls in love with her without having seen her; comes to her court, acts as cupbearer without revealing his identity; devotes himself to hunting and not to arms, is chided by the lady. He returns to Apulia, is knighted, then wins fame in many lands. Coming in disguise from the court of King Meleager of Sicily, he is first in a brilliant three-day tournament for which his beloved is the prize; each day he changes his horses and armor, white, red, black. The court ladies of Sicily think Ipomadon has been hunting, mock him as a fool and coward, but his inamorata does learn his identity. He departs.

On the death of his father, he becomes King of Apulia, proves himself in far lands in many adventures. Learning that his lady is besieged by a hideous suitor, the Indian Lyolyne, and again unwilling to be known, Ipomadon is dressed and shorn like a fool at Meleager's court. Assigned to the service of a scornful Maiden Messenger and her dwarf, he performs prodigies of valor. His beloved arranges to take refuge on her fleet. Ipomadon, dressed in black, Lyolyne's favorite color, defeats him, but the black armor makes it appear that the winner is Lyolyne. Meleager's heir, Capaneus, who has been active through the story, next appears against the supposed Lyolyne. In the ensuing duel, Ipomadon's head is uncovered. Capaneus declares they are brothers. The lovers too are united, various persons rewarded.

Nothing but a careful reading of the romance itself can give a proper notion of its contents or nature. The personages and incidents are numerous, the details minute and complicated. The original Anglo-French *Ipomédon*, which this English version closely follows, is an elaborate, humorous, leisurely composite of effective and striking elements. The setting—Apulia, Calabria, Sicily—is totally unrealistic (unlike that of *William of Palerne*, where the same areas are described true to their real geographic counterparts); the names are borrowed from classical sources, the *Roman de Thèbes*, or *Énéas*. The hero incognito, scorned for his unchivalric preference for hunting while in reality he is the winner of the three days' tournament, is found in folktales connected with the winning of a princess. This type appears also in Chrétien's *Cligès*, *Sir Gowther* (see [93]), Ulrich von Zatzikho-ven's *Lanzelet*, *Parténopeus de Blois*, *Richard Coer de Lyon*, *Roswall and Lillian*. The second part of the story, where the hero, playing the fool (or coward), defends a bitter-tongued maiden and her dwarf, turns on *motifs* familiar from Irish mythology and Arthurian romance, *Libeaus Desconus* (see [38]), Malory's *Tale of Sir Gareth*. Combat between relatives occurs in *Eglamour*, *Torrent of Portyngale*, *Triamour*, *Degrevant*, *Valentine and Orson* (see the section above on the Eustace, Constance, etc., Legends and elsewhere in this section). The hero's skill in skinning game and his disguise as fool resemble those of Tristan. The French versions of *Parténopeus* and *Ipomédon* show enough likeness to indicate borrowing, but which did the borrowing is not yet established. There is much direct discourse, rapid interchange of speech without narrative connection, dialogue which is sprightly and natural. The characters move with courtly breeding and gallantry; and though their conduct does not seem adequately motivated, here more than anywhere else in the romances of this section, the characters give voice to their emotional conflicts and analyze their sentiments in soliloquy and lamentation. Close to its original, a sophisticated "manufactured" romance, the poem is one of the most notable in Middle English.

The couplet *Lyfe of Ipomydon* is a greatly condensed version of the French, apparently reproduced from memory. It follows the same order of episodes as in the stanzaic *Ipomadon*, but cuts down sentiment, introspection, and conversation. Though inferior to *Ipomadon*, the couplet version is admirable for its rapidity and vigor. The same scribe who transcribed the *Lyfe* also copied the first part of the stanzaic *Morte Arthur*; but the two poems are not by the same author.

The third version, the prose *Ipomedon*, is closer to the stanzaic *Ipomadon* than to the couplet *Lyfe*. Like *Ipomadon*, the prose version was probably translated directly from a French manuscript. It occasionally condenses, as did the *Lyfe*, but is far better motivated than that version.

VALENTINE AND ORSON [103]. No manuscript extant. Translated ca. 1502, in prose, by H. Watson. Survives in printed texts: W. de Worde, Chatsworth fragment, four leaves, 1502?; another edition, W. Copland,

118 chapters, 327 pages in EETS edition, 1548–58. H. S. Bennett argues
that the Copland text is a reprint of a lost edition (1503?), not represented
by the Chatsworth fragment. Numerous printings since. The anonymous
French original used by Watson has not been found.

> King Pepin's sister Bellyssant, married to the Emperor Alexander of Constan-
> tinople, is falsely accused as an adulteress by the Archbishop whose advances she
> has repulsed. Though pregnant, she is banished, but pursued by the Archbishop.
> In the forest she bears twin sons. As she is following a bear which has carried off
> one son. King Pepin comes upon the other, left under a tree. This child, baptized
> Valentine, grows up in Pepin's court and becomes the flower of chivalry. Orson,
> reared by the bear, grows up as a savage until conquered and tamed by his brother.
> As companions, they defeat various oppressors and Saracens.
> An angelic vision instructs Valentine to go with Orson to Clerymonde, sister
> of a knight whom they had conquered; from a magic head of brass which she
> possesses they learn their own parentage and relationship. Betrayed by the giant
> Ferragus and cast into prison, they are released through the magic of Pacolet,
> are reunited with their mother, and together with Clerymonde leave Portugal.
> Other adventures follow: battles against Saracens, a family reunion with the
> Emperor of Constantinople, a charge of treason against Orson (who is falsely ac-
> cused when a knife is found in Pepin's bed), a dragon fight, the capture of Pepin
> and his twelve peers in Jerusalem, and the meeting in India with Clerymonde,
> who had been abducted. The Emperor, coming with Orson to aid Valentine, is
> unrecognized and is slain by Valentine. The penance imposed by the Pope is
> that Valentine shall live incognito and in silence for seven years under the palace
> stairs, eating only the leavings from the table. At Valentine's death the bells ring
> miraculously by themselves. Orson becomes a hermit.

Watson appears to have abbreviated the prolixities of a French version
(Dickson) into a treatment essentially designed to emphasize chivalric
character and adventure. The first half of the story relies on dialogue for
the development of the plot. The style is vigorous and idiomatic (and
less given to gallicisms than Caxton's) whether Watson is recording the
pithy interviews between honest men and false villains, the moving scenes
between lovers or between brother and brother, the magic of the Saracen
enchanter whose wooden horse conveys people to any corner of the world,
or the knowledgeable talking head of brass of the Saracen princess. The
romance has echoes in Spenser, Shakespeare, Cervantes, Bunyan. Based
on such folktale motifs as the credulous king, the accused and exiled queen,
kidnapping of children by a beast in the forest, amplified by additions from
chansons de geste, romances, saints' lives, and folk traditions, the plot forms
a compendium of the most popular elements of chivalric fiction (Dickson).
The Copland edition (1548–58) contains in addition seventy-two woodcuts, of considerable interest to bibliophiles.

THE SQUYR OF LOWE DEGRE [104]. Composed ca. 1500 in short couplets in the East Midlands. No medieval manuscripts extant. Survives in two early prints and the Percy Folio MS: W. de Worde, two fragments, 180 lines, ca. 1520; Copland print, 1132 lines, ca. 1560, a complete version (lines 1–60, 301–420 correspond to de Worde). The Percy Folio MS contains an independent and corrupt version of 170 lines, titled *The Squier*, ca. 1650. The present versions probably derive from a common source no longer extant. The story must have been familiar in the sixteenth century, for Elizabethans referred to it frequently (Mead).

A poor Squire loves the daughter of the King of Hungary. The Princess, accepting his love, imposes a seven-year trial period. An eavesdropping steward reports the conversation to the King. The latter declares his confidence in the Squire, but gives his men permission to capture him if he attempts to enter the lady's chamber; the Squire is ambushed as he comes at night to bid her farewell. He cries to her to open the door; she does not. The Squire slays the steward, whose disfigured body is then clad in the Squire's clothes. The Princess finds the body, believes it to be her lover's, embalms it, and keeps it at her bed's head for seven years. The Squire is imprisoned; but the King releases him under a pledge of secrecy to go abroad for seven years, with the promise that he will receive the lady and the realm when he returns. When the seven years have passed, the steward's body is dust; the princess is about to become an anchoress. Just then the Squire returns; the King, satisfied with her constancy, tells her the truth; the lovers are married.

The author's familiarity with other romances of exile and return is evidenced in his combining such stereotyped details as the lovers of unequal rank, the tale-bearing steward, the test of fidelity, seven-years service (see *Amis and Amiloun* [112]; *Apollonius* [95]; *Horn* [1]; *Roswall and Lillian*; *William of Palerne* [11]; and the story of Emperor Polemus in *Gesta Romanorum*). *The Squyr* probably drew to an even greater extent on *Guy of Warwick* [7]) (Mead). The most distinctive motifs—the substitution of the unrecognizable steward's body for the lover, and the preservation of that body by the heartbroken lady—have parallels in *Le Bone Florence of Rome* [84], the *Knight of Curtesy* [111], and *Eger and Grime* (Hibbard). Neither the incidents nor characters develop convincingly; nor does the poet take advantage of the emotional possibilities of his material despite the use of soliloquies of unconscionable length. But the poem has often been noted for its decorative and pictorial descriptions of food, armor, birds, plants, diversions—a glamorized view of fif-teenth-century life.

CLARIODUS [105]. Composed in the late fifteenth or early sixteenth century in Middle Scots, in five-stress couplets; based on a now-unknown English translation from the French and the French original, *Cleriadus et Meliadice*, of which only prose versions are now extant (six manuscripts and four early prints). Survives in one manuscript, MS Advocates 19.2.5, 11,801 lines, ca. 1550, imperfect at the beginning and end (commencing on folio 8, lacking two leaves at end).

> The worthy Philipon, King of England, unwilling to entrust his kingdom to the rule of a wicked younger brother, appoints as his lieutenant the good Count of Esture (Asturias), who is attended by his son Clariodus, "so fair, so young, so valiant and so wicht." The young hero (immediately smitten with love for the Philipon's daughter Meliades) defeats in single combat the king's enemy, the Duc de Jennes. When Clariodus sets out to attend the wedding of his sister, his journey is interrupted by a series of adventures which confront romance and fairy-tale heroes: he defends a lady and dwarf in distress; battles a lion who flees bleeding with Clariodus's sword in him (the lion was really a noble child transformed and unspelled only when a noble knight drew his blood); wins a third of the kingdom of Portugal; releases prisoners; persuades a felon to renounce his felonies; is accorded the highest praise in tournaments; rejects the love of the sister of the King of Spain. There is elaborate reference to the etiquette of chivalry and tournaments, of feasting and clothing. The vows here made on a peacock (cf. the *Three Kings' Sons*) are a courtly ceremonial relating to a tournament and marriage.

The familiar incidents of folklore and romance gain interest from the reversal of the usual process, for here a poet of taste and skill has transformed a prose original into verse. The couplets are smooth and easy, the diction marked by much alliteration, many doublets, and an aureate vocabulary embellished by Latin and French terms. The poetic style and the incidents sustain a courtly, society tone.

III. Romances on Historical Themes

Several English pieces are romance treatments of historical themes. These are *Richard Coer de Lyon*, *Titus and Vespasian* or the *Siege of Jerusalem*, the *Three Kings' Sons*, and Barbour's *Bruce*. Because of its effort at historical accuracy, the *Bruce* is discussed with the Chronicles (q. v.).

RICHARD COER DE LYON [106]. Composed soon after 1300, in a mixed Midland dialect of the London area (Cambridgeshire or Kent have also been suggested), in four-stress riming couplets. Survives in seven manuscripts, all imperfect; no manuscript is the source of any other. Preserved in 7262 lines. Earliest is MS Auchinleck, six fragments totalling over 1500 lines, ca. 1330 (at the beginning of the Auchinleck MS there are two twelve-line tail-rime stanzas). MS Egerton 2862 (Sutherland), 44 leaves, 7216 lines, 1375–1400; MS Arundel, 7252 lines, 1448 (Brunner's archetype for the b group); MS Douce 228, 5387 lines (lines 1269–6656), 1475–1500; MS Harley 4690, 2275 lines, 1475–1500. The preceding five manuscripts start with events leading to the Third Crusade, are relatively historical. By contrast the other two manuscripts amplify the fabulous materials: MS Caius Cambridge 175, 7212 lines, 1425–50 (Brunner's archetype for the a group); Fillingham MS, 6380 lines, ca. 1450; W. de Worde print, over 7200 lines, 1509, is the fullest version. No immediate source is known although it was once thought that the English version was compiled chiefly from the *Itinerarium peregrinorum et gesta Regis Ricardi*.

Seeking the most beautiful spouse in the world for King Henry of England, messengers meet a vessel bearing the King of Antioch and his daughter, Princess Cassadorien, on a parallel quest. Henry and the Princess are married, but she confesses that she cannot endure the presence of the Host at Mass. She bears Richard, John, and a daughter. One day, at the Elevation of the Host, she is detained in the church, and immediately flies up through the roof, bearing off her daughter, but dropping John (whose leg is injured). The third child, Richard, soon succeeds Henry. Richard, disguised successively in black, red, and white armor, tests his knights. Taking the best of them, Sir Thomas Multon and Sir Fulk Doyly, he visits the Holy Land in pilgrim's habit. He is imprisoned by the Emperor of Germany, has an affair with the Emperor's daughter, and in a match kills the Emperor's son; Richard tears out the heart of a lion sent to devour him, and finally returns to England, after being ransomed with half its wealth. Some months later he sets off with an army on a Crusade. After many losses, Richard reaches Cyprus. The Emperor of Cyprus abuses Richard's messengers, and cuts off the nose of his own steward when he protests. In anger the steward brings the treasure, the daughter, and many knights to Richard. Richard defeats and imprisons the Emperor. At Acre, he learns of terrible losses suffered by the Christians. He is ill, and longs for pork. A Saracen's head is boiled for him, a meal which he relishes. When he learns of the nature of his "pork," he laughs. Richard attempts to intimidate Saladin's messengers by serving them the heads of the pagan leaders executed for the purpose. The King dines heartily on another head set before him and remarks that the Christians need not starve so long as a Saracen is left. When the pagans deny that they have the true Cross, he slays all his prisoners except twenty, preserved to reports the news. So ends Part I.

Part II opens with a traditional lyrical May passage reminiscent of those in *Arthour and Merlin* (see [18]) and *King Alexander* (Smithers) (see [64]). The allied armies continue the war. Richard and Multon take several cities, and slay all the inhabitants. The cities assigned to be captured by the French King, Philip, are spared by the King—for a money payment. Richard berates Philip, takes the cities, and executes all their inhabitants. He gains great victories. The English and the

French besiege Babylon. Richard receives heavenly guidance for the handling of a magic steed given him by Saladin, and is thus enabled to slay hosts of pagans. After also capturing Jaffa, Richard arranges a three years' truce with Saladin, and sails for England. The author covers the next ten years of Richard's life in four lines.

The story is a combination of historical and romantic materials, the more sober versions appearing in earlier manuscripts; minute details of equipment and of siege operations are given, and there is accurate reference to geography. There is no account of the youth of Richard; the Crusade affords the chief incidents. The central interest is the superhuman, demoniac personality of Richard, a beloved and rousing leader. To account for his nature, his mother is represented as supernatural. Magic appears in the use of the Demon Horse. Twice angels come as advisers, and once St. George. The French kings are portrayed as cowards, takers of bribes, braggarts, and covetous rascals. On the basis of similarity of manner, a common author has been ascribed to this poem, *Seven Sages of Rome*, *Arthour and Merlin*, and *King Alexander*. Many scholars favor assignment of *Arthour and Merlin* and *King Alexander* to one writer; Brunner and Smithers would also ascribe Richard to him.

THE SIEGE OF JERUSALEM; TITUS AND VESPASIAN [107]. These religious romances place in an atmosphere of chivalry the life, passion, and miracles of Christ, woven into stories of the cure of Vespasian and the destruction of Jerusalem. Although it is difficult to say where legend ends and romance begins, these romances enjoyed wider popularity and diffusion than most pious tales or romances. Numerous Latin, French, and English texts draw on the same body of legend and story, but their exact dependence upon one another is not established. No text, foreign or English, is the exclusive source of these Middle English poems; and none of the Middle English manuscripts of the poem is directly descended from any other. Extant are twenty manuscripts, forming three groups: alliterative (eight manuscripts); couplet (eleven manuscripts); prose (one manuscript). The alliterative version (here called the *Siege of Jerusalem*) is shorter, perhaps slightly earlier than, and possibly influential upon, the couplet version (here called *Titus and Vespasian*).

Alliterative Version: *Siege of Jerusalem*. Composed in the last decade of the fourteenth century; original dialect Northwest Midland; original verse quatrains (EStn 16.169; Kölbing and Day). Extant in eight manuscripts, not uniform in title. Huntington HM 128, *Here begynneth þe seege of Ierusalem & how it was destroyed*, 1242 lines, East Midland, 1400–25; Laud Miscellaneous 656, no title, 1334 lines, West or Northwest Midland with Southeast Midland features, 1425–50; British Museum Additional 31042 (Thornton MS), *Hic Incepit Distruccio Jerarusalem* [sic] *Quomodo Titus et Vaspasianus obsederunt et distruxerunt Jerusalem et vi* [n] *dicarunt mortem Domini JhuXpi The Segge of Ierusalem off Tytus and Vaspasyane* (Colophon: *Explicit la sege de Jerusalem*), 1224 lines, lacks lines 289–374, Northern or Northeast, 1425–50; Lambeth 491, *Here bygynnith þe sege of Ierusalem*, 800 lines, East Midland, 1425–50; Cambridge University Library Mm. 5.14, *Incipit destruccio de Ierusalem per Titum & Vespasianum*, 1266 lines, imperfect, East Midland, 1450–75; Cotton Caligula A.2, *The Siege of Ierusalem*, 1213 lines, imperfect, East Midland, 1450–1500; Transcript of Cotton Caligula A.2 in Harvard University Library, Percy Folio MS Eng 748; Cotton Vespasian E.16, acephalous (Colophon: *Destructio Jerusalem per Vespasianum et Titum*), 362 lines, beginning at line 962 (the last 147 lines of Passus VI and all of Passus VII), East Midland, 1475–1500. Although none of these manuscripts is directly descended from any other they are related: British Museum Additional 31042 and British Museum Cotton Vespasian E. 16 form one group; British Museum Cotton Caligula A.2, Cambridge University Mm. 5.14, Lambeth 941, Huntington HM 128 form another group.

The Alliterative Version, though concentrating on the war and siege (lines 261–1334), opens with explanatory preliminaries (lines 1–260). In Gascony a vassal of Emperor Nero, one Titus, suffers from cancer of his lips; in Rome his father, Vespasian, is ill with leprosy and wasps in his nose. On his way to Rome to report to Nero that the Jews will no longer pay him tribute, the Jew Nathan is blown off course to Bordeaux. There he tells Titus that belief in the mission and miracles of Christ (including Veronica's veil) will bring healing. Titus's illness is cured as he rages and grieves over Christ's passion. Baptized, vowing revenge, he journeys to Rome. St. Peter confirms to Vespasian the story of the vernicle. Fetched to Rome by twenty knights, Veronica surrenders her veil to St. Peter, who goes with her to Vespasian. It touches him; he is healed. The "kerchief" hangs itself up in the church for all to see. The main portion of the poem now concerns the war by Titus and Vespasian to destroy Jerusalem. In a great battle outside the walls of Jerusalem, the Jews are defeated, Caiaphas and the scribes are captured and tortured to death. The Jews inside the walls still refuse to surrender. While the siege of Jerusalem continues, successive emperors in Rome die, and the crown is awarded to Vespasian, who returns to Rome. The Jews suffer terribly from famine (one Mary eats her own child); yet they reject Titus' offer of peace. Finally, they are conquered and sold thirty for a penny. Pilate commits suicide (at Viterbo or Vienne) with a knife borrowed to "paren a pear."

The Alliterative Version is artistically superior to the Couplet Version. A unified narrative concentrating on war, it yet overflows with literary reminiscences (Kölbing and Day). The principal sources are the *Vindicta salvatoris*, Higden's *Polychronicon* (see under Chronicles), *Legenda aurea* (see under Saints' Legends), with suggestions from the alliterative *Troy-Book*, the alliterative *Morte Arthure* (see [16]), *Patience* (see under the *Pearl* Poet), and the *Wars of Alexander* (see [65]). Details not found in the hitherto recognized sources do appear in Roger d'Argenteuil's *Bible en français* [*françois*], which must have been known to the poet (Moe). Fascinated with the conduct of chivalrous war, about four-fifths of the poem is concerned with the Siege of Jerusalem, the tumult of battle, and the chivalrous exercises of the attacking "knights." And when they have done their duty, they take up their tents and "trusses up their tresoure" and go singing away.

Couplet Version: *Titus and Vespasian*. Composed in the last years of the fourteenth century; original dialect London or its environs; irregular octosyllabic riming couplets; possibly later than the Alliterative Version, by which it may have been influenced (Kölbing-Day). Extant in eleven manuscripts. Herbert's edition (the "long" version) contains 5182 lines. Laud Miscellaneous 622, *The Bataile of Jerusalem*, 5166 lines, ca. 1400; Pepys 2014, 3114 lines (lacking opening 814 lines), ?1390–1420; British Museum Additional 10036, 2904 lines, imperfect at the beginning, 1400–25; British Museum Additional 36983 (MS Bedford), colophon: *þe Vengaunce of Godys deþe*, about 5154 lines, ca. 1442; Digby 230, 5166 lines, ca. 1450; British Museum Additional 36523, about 5182 lines, imperfect, 1425–50; Douce 78, 2390 lines, imperfect, 1450–75; Douce 126, 1889 lines, imperfect (begins at line 2532), first half of the fifteenth century; Harley 4733, about 5600 lines, before 1475; PML M. 898, 100 leaves, about 3851 lines, the first leaf, 40 lines, missing, mid-fifteenth century; Osborn MS (olim Derby, Knowsley Hall), fifteenth century. Additional MS 10036, Pepys MS 2014, and Morgan M. 898 form a group, the "short" Couplet Version, perhaps composed earlier than the "long" Couplet Version. The short version manuscripts are closely related, deriving from a common ancestor; but none was copied from the other (Bühler).

The Couplet Version opens with a review of the passion and resurrection, the imprisonment and miraculous release of Joseph of Arimathea (all of which is omitted from the "short" Couplet Version), prophecies of pilgrimage, servitude, and dispersion for an impenitent Israel, and the martyrdom of James. Vespasian (Waspanianus), King of Gascony and vassal of Emperor Nero, is afflicted with leprosy and wasps in his nose. Nathan the Jew, en route to Rome with tribute from Jerusalem, is blown off course to Bordeaux. There he relates to Titus, son of Vespasian, the story of Jesus, who "leched" all sickness. The steward Velosian overhears the tale; in search of a "sanatyf" (remedy) for Vespasian, Velosian travels to Jerusalem, where he finds Jacob the innkeeper and Veronica. She returns with Velosian, and together with St. Clement they visit Vespasian, who is healed by the touch of the vernicle. Vespasian and Titus sail to destroy Jerusalem, which they besiege when Pilate defies them. Vespasian returns to Rome to be crowned Emperor, but Titus continues the siege. Suffering terrible famine, the Jews eat their fellows; one of them, Mary, eats her child. Josephus secretly reports the conditions, to the joy of the emperor, who has meanwhile apparently returned to Jerusalem. Pilate surrenders; Jerusalem is destroyed. Many Jews are sold thirty for a penny; the remainder are condemned to be tortured until they die. Imprisoned at Vienne, Pilate commits suicide with a knife borrowed to "paren a pear," and is "fetched" by devils. Now follows the life of Judas. The emperor and his men are converted to Christianity by St. Clement.

The sources for this version are the Gospels, *Legenda aurea*, *Gospel of Nicodemus*, *History of Josephus* or *Hegesippus*, an unedited version of *Vindicta salvatoris*, and a lost Latin original of the French *chanson de geste La venjance Nostre Seigneur* (Kölbing and Day). Almost four times the length of the Alliterative Version, the "long" Couplet Version violates unity and coherence; at each point it intrudes and expands what should be minor incidents. So the first 800 lines are anachronistic; over-developed are the stories of Jacob the inn-keeper, of James, of Judas, of the famine, of Josephus talking over the wall, of miraculous appearances of angels, of the strange experiences of Pilate's dead body, which refuses to be buried. The "short" Couplet Version is better-planned.

Prose Version: Cleveland Public Library, MS W qO91.92–C468, the John G. White Collection (olim MS Aldenham): *Faciam[us] ho[m]i[n]em ad ymaginem n[ost]ram*, ff. 77–99, ca. 1470. This analogue opens with Adam and Eve and their expulsion from Paradise, relates the incidents of Pilate, the tormenting of Christ by the Jews, the entombment, the story of Veronica, Vespasian, the slaying of Jews and the destruction of Jerusalem. It is a translation of Roger d'Argenteuil's *Bible en français* (extant in three manuscripts) (Moe, BNYPL 70).

THE THREE KINGS' SONS [108]. A translation (ca. 1500) of a French prose tale into the Midland-London dialect survives in one magnificently illuminated manuscript. The French version, of which several

11*

manuscripts are extant, was transcribed in 1463 by a well-known callig-
rapher at the Burgundian court, one David Aubert, who may possibly
be its author. In manuscript the translation comprises 116 folios; in the
EETS edition 207 pages.

King Alfour of Sicily, sore beset by the Turks, will not permit his beautiful
daughter Iolante to marry the heathen Turkish prince, even though a truce may
thus be achieved (cf. the *King of Tars*). Instead, Alfour appeals to Christendom for
aid; and his pleas are answered independently by three princes, each of whom
adopts a *nom de guerre* to hide his identity: Philip of France (Le Despurveu, later
called Le Surnome), David of Scotland (Athys, leader of a combined army of
Scots, English, French); Humphrey of England (Ector). They join forces when
they serve incognito under the Sicilian seneschal Ferant; and each, as well as the
Turkish prince Orcays, falls violently in love with Iolante as soon as he sees her.
In pursuit of the enemy, they endure the familiar pangs and trials of outrageous
romance, crusading knights, and melodrama: their combined sufferings include
a fearsome tempest and ship-wreck, ambush, dungeons, repeated capture by princes,
hair-breadth escapes, bloody beating, strangling nigh unto death, rescue just
moments short of death on the gallows. Before the final battles, a peacock is brought
into the dining hall, and over the bird each one in the room makes a vow—the
king to defend his realm and to treat prisoners honorably, Prince Orcays to act as
peace mediator and to submit to Alfour, others to observe the same loyalty and to
fight courageously. After the Turkish Sultan is slain (his head is impaled on a
spear, cf. *Sir Eglamour*), King Alfour not only recovers his lands but is invited to
be Emperor of Germany. He then schedules "for men of royal blood" a three-day
tournament a year hence, the winner to be granted the hand of Iolante. Departing
for their own kingdoms, the three princes do not disclose their true identities.
   A year later all three return for the tournament; they are now kings (their
respective fathers having died). David and Humphrey reveal themselves at once.
But Philip comes unrecognized, in disguise as squire to his uncle, the Regent Duke
of Burgundy. The winner of the tournament is recognized to be Le Surnome when
the jousters are forced to remove their helmets as they quit the field, and only
then is made known Philip's true rank, King of France. He marries Iolante. The
others are also paired off: Humphrey with the Sultan's sister, who had followed
him and turned Christian; the Sultan with Humphrey's one sister and King David
with the other. Humphrey, David, and their wives live long and happily and have
many children. The Sultan dies childless and his widow returns to England.

Like the heroes of a crusading *chanson de geste* or a moral romance, these
princes serve not so much the earthly king of Sicily or the pagan god of
love as the true God of Heaven. When Philip resolves on his secret departure
to aid Sicily "in wars against the heathenmen" he meditates on the world's
mutability, the passion of the saints, and the means by which he, like they,
may be accepted into the eternal Kingdom of God. The chief characters
display also a kind of bourgeois good sense. The hero enjoys and excels in
such sports as running and shot-put as much as in the more noble one of
jousting. At the height of his success he asks not that he be given honors

but that the Sultan "do no more oppression nor hurt to the poor laborers and simple folk of the land." And King Alfour too says that for the good of the country he would prefer for son-in-law a poor "hardy" (i. e., competent and courageous) over a rich coward. As in a society romance (cf. *Degrevant, Clariodus*), much reference is made to minstrelsy and dancing, feasting and accoutrements, and the details of tourneying. The long-winded set speeches, the conversations, often with flashbacks and repetitions, the stylistic indulgence in doublets slow the pace of the narrative, but the high-principled protagonists keep the romance moving.

IV. Romances of Family Tradition

The titles *Melusine* and the *Romauns of Partenay (Lusignan)* are used to distinguish two late English versions of the same story of the fairy Melusine, a lamia, progenitor of the house of Lusignan.

MELUSINE [109]. Translated ca. 1500, in prose. Survives in the unique manuscript, British Museum Royal 18.B. 2, ca. 1500; occupies 371 printed pages of the EETSES edition. This is a translation corresponding closely to the French prose *Melusine* composed ca. 1387 by Jean d'Arras, and printed at Geneva 1478.

THE ROMAUNS OF PARTENAY (LUSIGNAN) [110]. Translated ca. 1500 in the Northeast Midland dialect, in 6615 lines of rime royal. Survives in the unique manuscript, Trinity College Cambridge 597 (R. 3.17), ca. 1500; ff. 1 and 88 are wanting. This is a translation of a French poetic version by La Coudrette, who composed it in octosyllabic couplets ca. 1400. La Coudrette's version is derived directly from, and is an abridgement and partial rearrangement of, the version of Jean d'Arras.

The story takes its title from the heroine, Melusine, one of the daughters of Duke Helmas and his fairy wife, Presine. He had promised never to visit her at time of childbirth; but he broke his vow. His three daughters (Melusine, Melior, and Palestine), all gifted with fairy powers, punish him by shutting him up in a mountain until he dies. The mother in turn punishes the daughters: she causes Melusine every Saturday to become a serpent from her waist downward; Melior is exiled to the Sparrow-Hawk Castle in Armenia; Palestine is compelled to guard Helmas' treasure on a mountain in Aragon. The story falls into five parts: (1) The opening section, located first in Melusine, and near the end in Partenay, deals with the incidents mentioned above. (2) In the second part Melusine marries Raymond, Count of Lusignan, and makes him vow never to visit her on a Saturday; but he breaks his vow. Melusine, now obliged to leave her home, is destined to wander as a specter. (The early passages of this section are reminiscent of the relationship between Melior and Partonope (see [99]). (3) The third part recounts the exploits of the ten sons of Raymond and Melusine, particularly those of Geoffrey of the Great Tooth. (4) The fourth part concerns Melior's adventures at Sparrow-Hawk Castle. (5) The fifth part treats of Palestine and the treasure.

The story encompasses the shopworn familar deeds of derring-do and many traditional themes: the fée-haunted fountain; marriage between a mortal and a fée; the child-birth taboo; an enchanted mountain; the sparrow-hawk castle. Included also are descriptions of architecture and feasting, and social conversation in the manner of a society novel. (*Degrevant* is the only other romance of this group which has at times a similar tone). The English versions retain the characteristics of their originals. Jean d'Arras was weak in construction, but excelled in graphic descriptions and character-drawing (notable is Geoffrey of the Great Tooth, berserker but convincing). La Coudrette reduced the text to one-third its length, eliminated most of the side episodes, and by judicious rearrangement achieved a more cohesive and dramatic development (Bourdillon). The story has continued to be popular. Tieck produced an excellent modern version for a German "Volksbuch."

THE KNIGHT OF CURTESY AND THE FAIR LADY OF FAGUELL [111].

Composed in the late fourteenth century in London or its southern environs. Survives in a unique Copland printing, in 504 four-stress lines in stanzas riming abab, 1568.

The Knight of Curtesy loves the Fair Lady of Faguell, wife of his friend and lord. She overhears him lamenting his love and joins him in the garden; in loyalty to her spouse, they vow to keep their love chaste. Another knight, envious of the riches and honors bestowed on the Knight of Curtesy, reports the secret meeting to the lord. Angry and jealous, he arranges for the Knight of Curtesy to leave—to undertake exploits.

After their first encounter, the Knight and Lady meet again only once, when she bids him farewell and gives him a tress of her yellow hair to wear on helmet or shield. One of his first adventures is the slaying of a dragon. At the siege of Rhodes (the city was in fact besieged in 1443), he is wounded by a poisoned arrow. He asks that after his death his heart be removed, wrapped in the yellow hair, and brought to his Lady. The husband intercepts the messenger, has the heart cooked and served to the wife. After the meal he tells her that she has eaten the heart of her beloved. She starves rather than again touch food. Before dying, she swears her innocence and that of the Knight of Curtesy.

An 8244-line romance (*Châtelain de Couci*) of the late thirteenth century by Jakemon Maket and the *Chronique due Chastelain de Couci et de dame de Faiel* were the ultimate sources for the abbreviated and expurgated Middle English poem. The French versions derive from two stories, one of the troubadour Guilhem de Cabestanh, and the other of the Châtelain de Couci, who loved the Dame de Faiel. (In late versions the anonymous Lady of Faiel was confused with and given the name Gabrielle de Vergi, that of the heroine of the thirteenth century *La Chastelaine de Vergi*, who died when she thought that her lover had revealed their love). That the story has any origin in fact is doubtful. The tale is a version of the Legend of the Eaten Heart known to classical and Indian literature (though the influence of these on the medieval versions is not proved), referred to in Thomas' *Tristan*, told in Boccaccio's *Decameron* (4.1, 4.9), and subsequently experiencing a long life in chronicle, drama, and balladry.

The vagueness in names and places suggests that the English author was writing from memory. The poem has been condemned for being morbid, brutal, sentimental (Rickert), and an ugly story of perverted retribution (Kane). By eliminating the pageantry, the stratagems, the elaborate love-making, the English poet avoided prolixity, but he eliminated at the same time the principal charm of the tale. Yet the pathos of the gruesome final incident is the more striking in the English version because the lovers have retained their purity and perfect loyalty.

V. Legendary Romances of Didactic Intent

It is evident from numerous exemplars that the tale or romance was regarded as an excellent vehicle for instruction, for teaching and enforcing a lesson—whether that lesson was the value of unswerving faith, the need for generosity, the evil of pride. Four romances, *Amis and Amiloun*, *Sir Amadace*, *Roberd of Cisyle*, *Sir Cleges* appear much concerned with their lesson. Occasionally, as in *Amis and Amiloun*, two versions exist—one stressing a secular theme, another what might be termed hagiographic. In these four romances, the plot and denouement depend on a supernatural intervention.

AMIS AND AMILOUN [112]. Composed toward the end of the thirteenth century in the East Midlands in twelve-line tail-rime stanzas,

aabaabccbdddb, of four-stress iambic couplets alternating with one iambic
three-stress line. Survives in four manuscripts: the earliest and best text,
MS Auchinleck, 2287 lines, ca. 1330, lacks opening and closing; MS
Egerton 2862 (Sutherland), 2186 lines, ca. 1400, supplies a trustworthy
version of the beginning and end; MS Douce 326, 2395 lines, is often faulty,
ca. 1500; MS Harley 2386 has only 894 lines, ca. 1500. No Middle English
version is the source of the other; all derive from a lost redaction of an
Anglo-Norman version.

> Amis and Amiloun, born on the same day to neighboring barons, grow up
> looking so alike and so equally notable for beauty, courtesy, and strength that they
> are undistinguishable from one another. Adopted by a Duke, they pledge absolute
> faithfulness to each other for all time. The Duke knights them and gives them high
> office. After long service Amiloun must return home to manage his estate. Each
> friend renews his troth, and each retains one of two gold cups as a token. Amiloun
> marries. The Duke's daughter, threatening Amis, forces him to become her lover.
> A jealous steward reports them to the Duke. Amis denies his guilt, and a day is
> fixed for trial by combat. Since the truth of the charge makes it impossible for Amis
> to defend himself, he appeals to Amiloun, who impersonates Amis and kills the
> steward; but Amiloun is warned by a voice from Heaven that, for taking the place
> of Amis, he will be afflicted with leprosy and poverty. Meanwhile Amis takes his
> friend's place and sleeps with his friend's wife, a sword between them. The Duke's
> daughter is then married to Amis, and bears two children. When the Duke dies,
> Amis becomes the ruler.
> Amiloun is stricken with leprosy, is cast out by his wife, and becomes a beggar.
> But he is cared for by a youth (Owaines or Amoraunt), who bears him in a cart
> to the gates of Amis. There Amis sends out wine in his token-cup. This wine Ami-
> loun pours into his own token-cup. The similarity of cups is reported to Amis,
> who assumes that his friend has been slain by the leper and beats the sick man.
> Learning his error, Amis and his wife care for Amiloun. Both friends are warned
> from Heaven that if the blood of Amis's two children is used to bathe the leper,
> he will be healed. Agonized but faithful, Amis cuts his children's throats and re-
> stores Amiloun. Amis's wife is heartbroken, but approves. When they visit the
> nursery, they find the children alive and well. The friends go to the country of
> Amiloun, who gives his lands to Amoraunt.

The Amis-Amiloun tale was one of the most popular of the Middle
Ages. Extant are versions in Latin, French, Italian, Spanish, Welsh, Dutch,
German, Norse. These are regarded as forming two groups: romantic (to
which the Middle English versions belong), and hagiographic (where the
friends suffer martyrdom fighting the heathen). The romantic version may
be closer to the primitive folktale; the intrusive feudal and hagiographic
elements may be an offshoot from a more war-like *chanson de geste*. By the
twelfth century the heroes were sometimes attached to Charlemagne, with
the spying steward a relative of Ganelon. The central theme of the poem

is the testing of ideal friendship, of the sacrifices that friends make for each other. This motif is close to a Diascuric myth, twin brothers undertaking tasks. Other themes, common in folklore and romance, include the wooing princess, jealous seneschal, judicial combat, separating sword, faithful servitor, recognition token. Some reminiscence of primitive human sacrifice may be reflected in the blood-bath, here rationalized into a miraculous restoration. The important incidents take place in spirited scenes developed by natural and affecting dialogue. The meter is facile and smooth, although the tail rime and conventional stock phrases grow monotonous, an effect not improved by the jerky full pause at the end of each stanza. The theme, which glorifies friendship at the expense of honor and family, blurs moral distinctions. The steward, defending the truth, is slain by one pretending to be the man accused. The wrongdoers, Amis and his wife, go unpunished. Poetic justice is achieved in some measure by the afflictions heaped on Amiloun and the killing of Amis's children. In the melodramatic denouement these evils are resolved happily.

SIR AMADACE [113]. Composed in the late fourteenth century in the Northwest Midlands in loose, irregular, twelve-line tail-rime stanzas, aabccbddbeeb, of four-stress iambic couplets alternating with one iambic three-stress line (MS Advocates has one six-line stanza). Survives in two manuscripts, both acephalous and both lacking verses: MS Ireland Blackburn, 852 lines, 1450-60 (South Lancashire); MS Advocates 19.3.1, 778 lines, 1475-1500. Each version was independently derived from a lost common source; the immediate source is unknown.

Both texts now open when Sir Amadace has already exhausted his estate in hospitality and largesse. Embarrassed by lack of means, he leaves home with a small retinue and a mere forty pounds. He comes upon a lady grieving beside her dead lord, who too had been overly generous, but is now denied burial because he died owing thirty pounds. Amadace, failing to soften the creditor, pays the debt and expends his last ten pounds to bury the knight. Unable further to support his retainers, he dismisses them. He is met by a knight in white, who commends him and directs him to a wrecked vessel containing equipment suitable for one courting a king's daughter. To the White Knight, Amadace pledges half his gains. The hero proves a successful jouster, shares his newly won wealth with the king, weds the princess. Ultimately the White Knight reappears and demands his share,—not only half the property, but half the wife and half the child. Grief-stricken but sustained by his wife, Amadace is about to cut her in two when the White Knight reveals himself as the grateful spirit of the buried debtor and praises the couple's sense of honor in fulfilling a pledge.

This moral romance defines the true knightly spirit as pious, courteous, generous, honoring one's word even though at great sacrifice. The two strains, folklore and romance, are skillfully synthesized. To the simple theme ultimately derived from the sacred duty of burial (cf. the Apocryphal *Book of Tobit*), have been added those of the dead held for debt, ghost thanks, spendthrift knight (see *Sir Cleges*, below), gifts shared. Romance features are highlighted in the woodland chapel and bier, the ghost as a White Knight, the shipwreck filled with gold, armor, horses, the hero's winning of lands, wealth, and a princess. *Amis and Amiloun* (see above) and *Sir Gowthar* (see [93]) may have affected the theme of child sacrifice. The charm of this composite is enchanced by realistic details: the blunt wife (though grieving, she sees the folly of her late husband's openhandedness); the humor (a canny Scot creditor); the honest self-analyses of Sir Amadace. This tale differs entirely from the French love story *Amadas et Idoine*, referred to in *Emare*, the *Confessio Amantis*, bk. 6, and *Sir Degrevant* (line 1478).

SIR CLEGES [114]. Composed in the late fourteenth century in the North Midland dialect in stanzas of twelve-line tail-rime, aabccbddbeeb, of four-stress iambic couplets alternating with one iambic three-stress line. Extant in two manuscripts: MS Advocates 19.1.11, 530 lines, 1450–1500, lacking some stanzas at end; MS Ashmole 61, 570 lines (6 lost), 1475–1500. The two manuscripts, which agree in 180 lines and in common rimes, were both written down from oral transmission and were both probably derived from a common English original. The actual source is unknown.

Sir Cleges, a knight of Uther Pendragon, distributes his largesse so liberally that he becomes poor. Consoled by his wife, he bears patiently his loneliness and meager fare. On Christmas Day as he is praying in his garden, he is amazed to see cherries growing on a tree above him. He takes the fruit to court as a present for the King. Before admitting him the porter, the usher, and the steward, each in turn demands a third of whatever recompense Cleges shall receive. The King offers him anything he wishes. Cleges asks twelve blows on anyone he names, and gives each of the three servants his share. At Uther's request, Cleges explains why. The courtiers are delighted. Uther, learning that this poor stranger is Cleges, whom he had supposed dead, makes him a steward and gives him the Castle of Cardiff and other property.

The story is a pious tale, a humorous tale, and a minstrel's tale to encourage liberality and punish greed at the Christmas season. Influenced by *Sir Amadace* (see above) and *Sir Launfal* (see [88]), the poem opens with a spendthrift knight. His first experience is a moral tale or saint's legend of a widespread Christmas-day miracle, the tree hung with fruit (unseasonable blooming). Romance then gives way to the second theme, the fabliau story of blows shared. Although many analogues have been noted for both main incidents, no other tale containing the two elements has been found. Their union in *Sir Cleges* is so well made that it is difficult to say which of the two is the principal one. The activities with the greedy servants are spirited and humorous in contrast with the earlier scenes of husband and wife grieving because they cannot celebrate the Savior's day fittingly. Cleges is unique in this period for its pleasant combination of romance, piety, and humor.

ROBERD OF CISYLE [115]. Composed in the late fourteenth century in a Southeasterly Midlands dialect, in four-stress lines riming in couplets. Survives in ten manuscripts, apparently related, but not derived from one another. The three earliest manuscripts date from the last half of the fourteenth century: Oxford Trinity College D. 57, 440 lines, ca. 1375; Bodleian Vernon, 444 lines, ca. 1390; British Museum Additional 22283, 454 lines, ca. 1400. The other manuscripts are: British Museum Additional 34801, a fragment of 46 lines, ca. 1425; Cambridge University Ff. 2.38, 516 lines, 1475–1500; Cambridge University Ii. 4.9, 374 lines, ca. 1450; Caius Cambridge 174, 470 lines, 1475–1500; British Museum Harley 525, 472 lines, ca. 1450–75; British Museum Harley 1701, 486 lines, 1425–50; Trinity College Dublin 432, 72 lines (preceded by a prologue of one stanza in seven-line rime royal), 1458–61 (begins with Robert's falling asleep, an abridgement of the story not derived from any extant manuscript). The Vernon MS shows more westerly forms than the others, perhaps influenced by the South Shropshire-Staffordshire area.

The story of King Robert of Sicily exemplifies the theme of the proud and mighty brought low, a tale of the proud king humiliated (deposed). King Robert, brother of Emperor (Valmounde) and Pope (Urban), has many virtues, but is excessively proud. He thinks more of his own high estate than of his religious duties. When at evensong he hears the Magnificat (*Deposuit potentes de sede et exaltavit humiles* [Luke 1.52]), he derides the idea that God can put down the mighty and exalt the humble. Who can bring Robert low? He falls asleep. An Angel assuming Robert's likeness and apparel leaves the church with the King's men. Robert awakens in beggar's garments to an empty church. When he protests that he is King, he is taken for a madman or a knave. Furious, he rushes to his palace; there he exchanges buffets with the incredulous porter and is thrown into a "podel." Before the Angel-King, a filthy, bedraggled Robert claims his throne. In reply he is told that he shall be the court fool, have an ape as his counselor, eat and sleep with the hounds. The Angel's reign is notable for prosperity and love. Subsequently the Angel takes the fool in his retinue on a visit to Rome to meet with the King's brothers. When even they do not recognize him, Robert recalls the fate of Nebuchadnezzar and Holofernes and confesses his own insignificance. He repents his pride and in moving prayer humbly pleads, "Lord, on thy fool thou have pity." At home again, the Angel questions Robert, "What art thou?" "Sire, a fool; and worse than a fool, if such may be." The Angel reveals himself as God's messenger sent to chasten Robert for his pride. Now that Robert is truly repentant, the Angel vanishes. In the "twynklyng of an eiȝe" Robert is again King.

This story has many analogues; in the closest, *Der nackte König* (*König im Bade*), the king is bereft of his clothing and realm while he is bathing. The origin of the legend was at one time attributed to Hindu narratives, but it now seems more likely that the core idea of the substitution, inspired by Babylonian New Year's rites, was fleshed out by Jewish-Coptic homiletics, Talmudic lore, and Western-monkish rhetoric. The immediate source of the Middle English versions is unknown; an early French romance may be predicated, though no such version is extant. Other influences on the story were legends of Nebuchadnezzar and of the French King Guisbert, and the conversion tale of Robert the Devil, which may be partly responsible for the name Robert in the English version (see *Sir Gowther* [93]). The English poem is the most dramatic and effective of the versions in its unity, piety, and lyricism. The fluid couplets shift their pauses so successfully that at times the verse achieves an almost liturgical dignity. Fully aware of the tragic ironies, reverent of the theme, the poet creates a fool-king of unusual poignancy. The story has become well-known in modern times from the rendering in Longfellow's *Tales of a Wayside Inn*.

Bibliography

TABLE OF ABBREVIATIONS

AAGRP	Ausgaben und Abhandlungen aus dem Gebiete der romanischen Philologie
AC	Archaeologica Cantiana
Acad	Academy
AEB	Kölbing E, Altenglische Bibliothek, Heilbronn 1883–
AELeg 1875	Horstmann C, Altenglische Legenden, Paderborn 1875
AELeg 1878	Horstmann C, Sammlung altenglischer Legenden, Heilbronn 1878
AELeg 1881	Horstmann C, Altenglische Legenden (Neue Folge), Heilbronn 1881
AESpr	Mätzner E, Altenglische Sprachproben, Berlin 1867–
AF	Anglistische Forschungen
AfDA	Anzeiger für deutsches Alterthum
AHR	American Historical Review
AJ	Ampleforth Journal
AJA	American Journal of Archaeology
AJP	American Journal of Philology
ALb	Allgemeines Literaturblatt
ALg	Archivum linguisticum
Allen WAR	Allen H E, Writings Ascribed to Richard Rolle Hermit of Hampole and Materials for His Biography, MLA Monograph Series 3, N Y 1927
Angl	Anglia, Zeitschrift für englische Philologie
AnglA	Anglia Anzeiger
AnglB	Beiblatt zur Anglia
AN&Q	American Notes and Queries
Antiq	Antiquity
APS	Acta philologica scandinavica
AQ	American Quarterly
AR	Antioch Review
Arch	Archiv für das Studium der neueren Sprachen und Literaturen
Archaeol	Archaeologia
Ashton	Ashton J, Romances of Chivalry, London 1890
ASp	American Speech
ASR	American Scandinavian Review
ASt	Aberystwyth Studies
Athen	Athenaeum
BA	Books Abroad
BARB	Bulletin de l'Académie royale de Belgique
Baugh LHE	Baugh A C, The Middle English Period, in A Literary History of England, N Y 1948

BB	Bulletin of Bibliography
BBA	Bonner Beiträge zur Anglistik
BBCS	Bulletin of the Board of Celtic Studies (Univ of Wales)
BBGRP	Berliner Beiträge zur germanischen und romanischen Philologie
BBSIA	Bulletin bibliographique de la Société internationale arthurienne
Bennett OHEL	Bennett H S, Chaucer and the Fifteenth Century, Oxford 1947
Best BIP	Best R I, Bibliography of Irish Philology, 2 vols, Dublin 1913
BGDSL	Beiträge zur Geschichte der deutschen Sprache und Literatur
BHR	Bibliothèque d'humanisme et renaissance
BIHR	Bulletin of the Institute of Historical Research
Billings	Billings A H, A Guide to the Middle English Metrical Romances, N Y 1901
Blackf	Blackfriars
Bloomfield SDS	Bloomfield M W, The Seven Deadly Sins, Michigan State College of Agriculture and Applied Science Studies in Language and Literature, 1952
BNYPL	Bulletin of the New York Public Library
Böddeker AED	Böddeker K, Altenglische Dichtungen des MS Harl 2253, Berlin 1878
Bossuat MBLF	Bossuat R, Manuel bibliographique de la littérature française du moyen âge, Paris 1951; supplément Paris 1955; deuxième supplément Paris 1961 [the item numbers run consecutively through the supplement]
BPLQ	Boston Public Library Quarterly
BQR	Bodleian Quarterly Record (sometimes Review)
Brandl	Brandl A, Mittelenglische Literatur, in Paul's Grundriss der germanische Philologie, 1st edn, Strassburg 1893, 2^1.609 ff, Index 2^2.345
Brown ELxiiiC	Brown C F, English Lyrics of the 13th Century, Oxford 1932
Brown Reg	Brown C, A Register of Middle English Religious and Didactic Verse, parts 1 and 2, Oxford (for the Bibliographical Society) 1916, 1920
Brown RLxivC	Brown C F, Religious Lyrics of the 14th Century, Oxford 1924
Brown RLxvC	Brown C F, Religious Lyrics of the 15th Century, Oxford 1939
Brown-Robbins	Brown C and R H Robbins, The Index of Middle English Verse, N Y 1943; see also Robbins-Cutler
Bryan-Dempster	Bryan W F and G Dempster, Sources and Analogues of Chaucer's Canterbury Tales, Chicago 1941
BrynMawrMon	Bryn Mawr College Monographs, Bryn Mawr 1905–
BSEP	Bonner Studien zur englischen Philologie
BUSE	Boston University Studies in English
CASP	Cambridge Antiquarian Society Publication
CBEL	Bateson F W, Cambridge Bibliography of English Literature, 5 vols, London and N Y 1941, 1957
CE	College English
Chambers	Chambers E K, The Mediaeval Stage, 2 vols, Oxford 1903
Chambers OHEL	Chambers E K, English Literature at the Close of the Middle Ages, Oxford 1945
CHEL	Ward A W and A R Waller, The Cambridge History of English Literature, vols 1 and 2, Cambridge 1907, 1908
CHR	Catholic Historical Review
ChS	Publications of the Chaucer Society, London 1869–1924

Ch&Sidg	Chambers E K and F Sidgwick, Early English Lyrics, London 1907; numerous reprints
CJ	Classic Journal
CL	Comparative Literature
CMLR	Canadian Modern Language Review
Comper Spir Songs	Comper F M M, Spiritual Songs from English Manuscripts of Fourteenth to Sixteenth Centuries, London and N Y 1936
Conviv	Convivium
Courthope	Courthope W J, History of English Poetry, vol 1, London 1895
CP	Classical Philology
Craig HEL	Craig H, G K Anderson, L I Bredvold, J W Beach, History of English Literature, N Y 1950
Cross Mot Ind	Cross T P, Motif Index of Early Irish Literature, Bloomington Ind 1951
Crotch PEWC	Crotch W J B, The Prologues and Epilogues of William Caxton, EETS 176, London 1928
CUS	Columbia University Studies in English and in Comparative Literature, N Y 1899–
DA	Dissertation Abstracts
DANHSJ	Derbyshire Archaeological and Natural History Society Journal
de Julleville Hist	de Julleville L Petit, Histoire de la langue et de la littérature française, vols 1 and 2, Paris 1896–99
de Ricci Census	de Ricci S and W J Wilson, Census of Medieval and Renaissance Manuscripts in the United States of America and Canada, vols 1–3, N Y 1935, 1937, 1940
Dickins and Wilson	Dickins B and R M Wilson, Early Middle English Texts, Cambridge 1950
DLz	Deutsche Literaturzeitung
DNB	Stephen L and S Lee, Dictionary of National Biography, N Y and London 1885–1900, and supplements
DomS	Dominican Studies: An Annual Review, Blackfriars Publications, London
DUJ	Durham University Journal
EA	Études anglaises
EBEP	Erlanger Beiträge zur englischen Philologie
EC	Essays in Criticism
EETS	Publications of the Early English Text Society (Original Series), 1864–
EETSES	Publications of the Early English Text Society (Extra Series), 1867–
EG	Études germaniques
EGS	English and Germanic Studies
EHR	English Historical Review
EIE, EIA	English Institute Essays (Annual), N Y 1939–
EJ	English Journal
ELH	Journal of English Literary History
Ellis EEP	Ellis G, Specimens of Early English Poetry, 3 vols, London 1811
Ellis Spec	Ellis G, Specimens of Early English Metrical Romances, 3 vols, London 1805; rvsd Halliwell, 1 vol, Bohn edn 1848 (latter edn referred to, unless otherwise indicated)
Enc Brit	Encyclopaedia Britannica, 11th edn

Engl	English: The Magazine of the English Association
E&S	Essays and Studies by Members of the English Association, Oxford 1910–
E&S Brown	Essays and Studies in Honor of Carleton Brown, N Y 1940
EStn	Englische Studien
ESts	English Studies
ETB	Hoops J, Englische Textbibliothek, 21 vols, Heidelberg 1898–1935?
Expl	Explicator
FFC	Foklore Fellows Communications
FFK	Forschungen und Fortschritte: Korrespondenzblatt der deutschen Wissenschaft und Technik
Flügel NL	Flügel E, Neuenglisches Lesebuch, Halle 1895
FQ	French Quarterly
FR	French Review
FS	French Studies
Furnival EEP	Furnivall F J, Early English Poems and Lives of Saints, Berlin 1862 (Transactions of Philological Society of London 1858)
Gautier Bibl	Gautier L, Bibliographie des chansons de geste, Paris 1897
Gayley	Gayley C M, Plays of Our Forefathers, N Y 1907
GdW	Gesamtkatalog der Wiegendrucke, Leipzig 1925–
Germ	Germania
Gerould S Leg	Gerould G H, Saints' Legends, Boston 1916
GGA	Göttingische gelehrte Anzeiger
GJ	Gutenberg Jahrbuch
GQ	German Quarterly
GR	Germanic Review
Greene E E Carols	Greene R L, The Early English Carols, Oxford 1935
GRM	Germanisch-Romanische Monatsschrift
Gröber	Gröber G, Grundriss der romanischen Philologie, Strassburg 1888–1902, new issue 1897–1906, 2nd edn 1904– (vol 2^1 1902 referred to, unless otherwise indicated)
Gröber-Hofer	Hofer S, Geschichte der mittelfranzösischen Literatur, 2 vols, 2nd edn, Berlin and Leipzig 1933–37
Hall Selections	Hall J, Selections from Early Middle English 1130–1250, 2 parts, Oxford 1920
Hammond	Hammond E P, Chaucer: A Bibliographical Manual, N Y 1908
Hartshorne AMT	Hartshorne C H, Ancient Metrical Tales, London 1829
Hazlitt Rem	Hazlitt W C, Remains of the Early Popular Poetry of England, 4 vols, London 1864–66
Herbert	Herbert J A, Catalogue of Romances in the Department of MSS of the British Museum, London 1910 (vol 3 of Ward's Catalogue)
Hermes	Hermes
Hibbard Med Rom	Hibbard L, Medieval Romance in England, N Y 1924
HINL	History of Ideas News Letter
Hisp	Hispania
HispR	Hispanic Review
HJ	Hibbert Journal
HLB	Harvard Library Bulletin
HLF	Histoire littéraire de la France, Paris 1733–; new edn 1865–
HLQ	Huntington Library Quarterly

Holmes CBFL	Cabeen D C, Critical Bibliography of French Literature, vol 1 (the Medieval Period), ed U T Holmes jr, Syracuse N Y 1949
HSCL	Harvard Studies in Comparative Literature
HSNPL	Harvard Studies and Notes in Philology and Literature, Boston 1892–
HudR	Hudson Review
IER	Irish Ecclesiastical Review
IS	Italian Studies
Isis	Isis
Ital	Italica
JAAC	Journal of Aesthetics and Art Criticism
JBL	Journal of Biblical Literature
JCS	Journal of Celtic Studies
JEGGP	Jahresbericht über die Erscheinungen auf dem Gebiete der germanischen Philologie
JEGP	Journal of English and Germanic Philology
JEH	Journal of Ecclesiastical History
JfRESL	Jahrbuch für romanische und englische Sprache und Literatur
JGP	Journal of Germanic Philology
JHI	Journal of the History of Ideas
JPhilol	Journal of Philology
JPhilos	Journal of Philosophy
JRLB	Bulletin of the John Rylands Library, Manchester
Kane	Kane G, Middle English Literature: A Critical Study of the Romances, the Religious Lyrics, Piers Plowman, London 1951
Kennedy BWEL	Kennedy A G, A Bibliography of Writings on the English Language from the Beginning of Printing to the End of 1922, Cambridge Mass and New Haven 1927
Kild Ged	Heuser W, Die Kildare-Gedichte, Bonn 1904 (BBA 14)
Körting	Körting G, Grundriss der Geschichte der englischen Literatur von ihren Anfängen bis zur Gegenwart, 5th edn, Münster 1910
KR	Kenyon Review
Krit Jahresber	Vollmüller K, Kritischer Jahresbericht über die Fortschritte der romanischen Philologie, München und Leipzig 1892–1915 (Zweiter Teil, 13 vols in 12)
KSEP	Kieler Studien zur englischen Philologie
Lang	Language
LB	Leuvensche Bijdragen, Periodical for Modern Philology
LC	Library Chronicle
Leeds SE	Leeds Studies in English and Kindred Languages, School of English Literature in the University of Leeds
Legouis	Legouis E, Chaucer, Engl trans by Lailvoix, London 1913
Legouis HEL	Legouis E and L Cazamian, trans H D Irvine and W D Mac-Innes, A History of English Literature, new edn, N Y 1929
LfGRP	Literaturblatt für germanische und romanische Philologie
Libr	The Library
Litteris	Litteris: An International Critical Review of the Humanities, New Society of Letters
LMS	London Medieval Studies
Loomis ALMA	Loomis R S, Arthurian Literature in the Middle Ages, A Collaborative History, Oxford 1959
LP	Literature and Psychology

LQ	Library Quarterly
Lund SE	Lund Studies in English
LZ	Literarisches Zentralblatt
MÆ	Medium ævum
Manly CT	Manly J M, Canterbury Tales by Geoffrey Chaucer, with an Introduction, Notes, and a Glossary, N Y 1928
Manly Spec	Manly J M, Specimens of the Pre-Shakespearean Drama, vol 1, 2nd edn, Boston 1900
Manly & Rickert	Manly J M and E Rickert, The Text of the Canterbury Tales Studied on the Basis of All Known Manuscripts, 8 vols, Chicago 1940
MBREP	Münchener Beiträge zur romanischen und englischen Philologie
MED	Kurath H and S M Kuhn, Middle English Dictionary, Ann Arbor 1952– (M S Ogden, C E Palmer, and R L McKelvey, Bibliography [of ME texts], 1954, p 15)
MH	Medievalia et humanistica
MHRA	MHRA, Bulletin of the Modern Humanities Research Association
Migne PL	Migne, Patrologiae Latinae cursus completus
Minor Poems	Skeat W W, Chaucer: The Minor Poems, 2nd edn, Oxford 1896
MKAW	Mededeelingen van de Koninklijke akademie van wetenschappen, afdeling letterkunde
ML	Music and Letters
MLF	Modern Language Forum
MLJ	Modern Language Journal
MLN	Modern Language Notes
MLQ (Lon)	Modern Language Quarterly (London)
MLQ (Wash)	Modern Language Quarterly (Seattle, Washington)
MLR	Modern Language Review
Monat	Monatshefte
Moore Meech and Whitehall	Moore S, S B Meech and H Whitehall, Middle English Dialect Characteristics and Dialect Boundaries, University of Michigan Essays and Studies in Language and Literature 13, Ann Arbor 1935
Morley	Morley H, English Writers, vols 3–6, London 1890
Morris Spec	Morris R (ed part 1), R Morris and W W Skeat (ed part 2), Specimens of Early English, part 1, 2nd edn, Oxford 1887; part 2, 4th edn, Oxford 1898
MP	Modern Philology
MS	Mediaeval Studies
MSEP	Marburger Studien zur englischen Philologie, 13 vols, Marburg 1901–11
MUPES	Manchester University Publications, English Series
NA	Neuer Anzeiger
Neophil	Neophilologus, A Modern Language Quarterly
NEQ	New England Quarterly
NLB	Newberry Library Bulletin
NM	Neuphilologische Mitteilungen: Bulletin de la Société neophilologique de Helsinki
NMQ	New Mexico Quarterly
NNAC	Norfolk and Norwich Archaeological Society
N&Q	Notes and Queries

NRFH	Nueva revista de filología hispánica
NS	Die neueren Sprachen, Zeitschrift für der neusprachlichen Unterrecht
OMETexts	Morsbach L and F Holthausen, Old and Middle English Texts, 11 vols, Heidelberg 1901–26
Oxf Ch	Skeat W W, The Works of Geoffrey Chaucer, Oxford 1894–1900 (6 vols; extra 7th vol of Chaucerian Poems)
Palaes	Palaestra, Untersuchungen und Texte
PAPS	Proceedings of the American Philosophical Society
Paris Litt franç	Paris G P B, La littérature française au moyen âge, 4th edn, Paris 1909
Patterson	Patterson F A, The Middle English Penitential Lyric, N Y 1911
Paul Grundriss	Paul H, Grundriss der germanischen Philologie, 3 vols, 1st edn, Strassburg 1891–1900; 2nd edn 1900–
PBBeitr	Paul H and W Braune, Beiträge zur Geschichte der deutschen Sprache und Literatur, Halle 1874–
PBSA	Papers of the Bibliographical Society of America
PBSUV	Papers of the Bibliographical Society, Univ of Virginia
PFMS	Furnivall F J and J W Hales, The Percy Folio MS, 4 vols, London 1867–69; re-ed I Gollancz, 4 vols, London 1905–10 (the earlier edn is referred to, unless otherwise indicated)
Philo	Philologus
PMLA	Publications of the Modern Language Association of America
PMRS	Progress of Medieval and Renaissance Studies in the United States and Canada
PP	Past and Present
PPR	Philosophy and Phenomenological Research
PPS	Publications of the Percy Society
PQ	Philological Quarterly
PR	Partisan Review
PS	Pacific Spectator
PSTS	Publications of the Scottish Text Society, Edinburgh 1884–
PULC	Princeton University Library Chronicle
QF	Quellen und Forschungen zur Sprach- und Culturgeschichte der germanischen Völker
QQ	Queen's Quarterly
RAA	Revue anglo-américaine
RadMon	Radcliffe College Monographs, Boston 1891–
RB	Revue britannique
RC	Revue celtique
RCHL	Revue critique d'histoire et de littérature
REH	The Review of Ecclesiastical History
Rel Ant	Wright T and J O Halliwell, Reliquiae antiquae, 2 vols, London 1845
Ren	Renascence
Renwick-Orton	Renwick W L and H Orton, The Beginnings of English Literature to Skelton 1509, London 1939; rvsd edn 1952
RES	Review of English Studies
RevP	Revue de philologie
RF	Romanische Forschungen
RFE	Revista de filología espanola
RFH	Revista de filología hispánica

RG	Revue germanique
RHL	Revue d'histoire littéraire de la France
Rickert RofFr, RofL	Rickert E, Early English Romances in Verse: Romances of Friendship (vol 1), Romances of Love (vol 2), London 1908
Ritson AEMR	Ritson J, Ancient English Metrical Romances, 3 vols, London 1802, rvsd E Goldsmid, Edinburgh 1884 (earlier edn referred to, unless otherwise indicated)
Ritson APP	Ritson J, Ancient Popular Poetry, 2nd edn, London 1833
Ritson AS	Ritson J, Ancient Songs from the Time of Henry III, 2 vols, London 1790, new edn 1829; rvsd W C Hazlitt, Ancient Songs and Ballads, 1 vol, London 1877 (last edn referred to, unless otherwise indicated)
RLC	Revue de littérature comparée
RLR	Revue des langues romanes
RN	Renaissance News
Robbins-Cutler	Supplement to Brown-Robbins, Lexington Ky 1965
Robbins HP	Robbins R H, Historical Poems of the 14th and 15th Centuries, Oxford 1959
Robbins SL	Robbins R H, Secular Lyrics of the 14th and 15th Centuries, 2nd edn, Oxford 1955
Robson	Robson J, Three Early English Metrical Romances, London (Camden Society) 1842
Rolls Series	Rerum Britannicarum medii aevi scriptores, Published by Authority of the Lords Commissioners of Her Majesty's Treasury, under the Direction of the Master of the Rolls, London 1857–91
Rom	Romania
RomP	Romance Philology
RomR	Romanic Review
Root	Root R K, The Poetry of Chaucer, Boston 1906
Rot	Rotulus, A Bulletin for MS Collectors
Roxb Club	Publications of the Roxburghe Club, London 1814–
RSLC	Record Society of Lancashire and Cheshire
RUL	Revue de l'Université laval
SA	The Scottish Antiquary, or Northern Notes and Queries
SAQ	South Atlantic Quarterly
SATF	Publications de la Société des anciens textes français, Paris 1875–
SB	Studies in Bibliography: Papers of the Bibliographical Society of the University of Virginia
SBB	Studies in Bibliography and Booklore
ScanSt	Scandinavian Studies
Schipper	Schipper J, Englische Metrik, 2 vols, Bonn 1881–88
Schofield	Schofield W H, English Literature from the Norman Conquest to Chaucer, N Y 1906
SciS	Science and Society
Scrut	Scrutiny
SE	Studies in English
SEER	Slavonic and East European Review
SEP	Studien zur englischen Philologie
ShJ	Jahrbuch der deutschen Shakespeare-Gesellschaft
SHR	Scottish Historical Review
Skeat Spec	Skeat W W, Specimens of English Literature 1394–1579, 6th edn, Oxford

SL	Studies in Linguistics
SN	Studia neophilologica: A Journal of Germanic and Romanic Philology
SP	Studies in Philology
Spec	Speculum: A Journal of Mediaeval Studies
SR	Sewanee Review
SRL	Saturday Review of Literature
STC	Pollard A W and G R Redgrave, A Short-Title Catalogue of Books Printed in England, Scotland, and Ireland and of English Books Printed Abroad 1475–1640, London 1926
StVL	Studien zur vergleichenden Literaturgeschichte
Summary Cat	Madan F and H H E Craster, A Summary Catalogue of Western Manuscripts Which Have Not Hitherto Been Catalogued in the Quarto Series, Oxford 1895–1953
SUVSL	Skriften utgivna av Vetenskaps-societeten i Lund
SWR	Southwest Review
Sym	Symposium
Ten Brink	Ten Brink B A K, Early English Literature, English Literature, trans Kennedy et al, vol 1, vol 2 (parts 1–2), London and N Y 1887–92 (referred to as vols 1–3)
Texas SE	Texas Studies in English
Thompson Mot Ind	Thompson S, Motif Index of Folk-Literature, 6 vols, Helsinki 1932–36
Thoms	Thoms W J, A Collection of Early Prose Romances, London 1828; part ed Morley, Carlsbrooke Library, whole rvsd edn, London (Routledge); new edn, Edinburgh 1904
TLCAS	Transactions of Lancashire and Cheshire Antiquarian Society
TLS	[London] Times Literary Supplement
TNTL	Tijdschrift voor nederlandse taal- en letterkunde
TPSL	Transactions of the Philological Society of London
Trad	Traditio, Studies in Ancient and Medieval History, Thought, and Religion
TRSL	Transactions of the Royal Society of Literature
TTL	Tijdschrift voor taal en letteren
Tucker-Benham	Tucker L L and A R Benham, A Bibliography of Fifteenth-Century Literature, Seattle 1928
UKCR	University of Kansas City Review
UQ	Ukrainian Quarterly
Utley CR	Utley F L, The Crooked Rib: An Analytical Index to the Argument about Women in English and Scots Literature to the End of the Year 1568, Columbus O 1944
UTM	University of Toronto Monthly
UTQ	University of Toronto Quarterly
VMKVA	Verslagen en mededeelingen der Koninklijke vlaamsche academie
VQR	Virginia Quarterly Review
Ward	Ward H L D, Catalogue of Romances in the Department of MSS of the British Museum, 2 vols, London 1883–93 (see Herbert for vol 3)
Ward Hist	Ward A W, A History of English Dramatic Literature to the Death of Queen Anne, 3 vols, new edn, London 1899
Wehrle	Wehrle W O, The Macaronic Hymn Tradition in Medieval English Literature, Washington 1933

WBEP	Wiener Beiträge zur englischen Philologie
Weber MR	Weber H W, Metrical Romances of the 13th, 14th, and 15th Centuries, 3 vols, Edinburgh .1810
Wessex	Wessex
WHR	Western Humanities Review
Wilson EMEL	Wilson R M, Early Middle English Literature, London 1939
WMQ	William and Mary Quarterly
WR	Western Review
Wright AnecLit	Wright T, Anecdota literaria, London 1844
Wright PPS	Wright T, Political Poems and Songs from the Accession of Edward III to That of Richard III, 2 vols, London (Rolls Series) 1859–61
Wright PS	Wright T, Political Songs of England from the Reign of John to That of Edward III, Camden Society, London 1839 (this edn referred to, unless otherwise indicated); 4 vols, rvsd, privately printed, Goldsmid, Edinburgh 1884
Wright SLP	Wright T, Spcimens of Lyric Poetry Composed in England in the Reign of Edward I, Percy Society, 2 vols, London 1896
Wülcker	Wülcker R P, Geschichte der englischen Literatur, 2 vols, Leipzig 1896
YCGL	Yearbook of Comparative and General Literature
YFS	Yale French Studies, New Haven 1948–
Yksh Wr	Horstmann C, Yorkshire Writers, Library of Early English Writers, 2 vols, London 1895–96
YR	Yale Review
YSCS	Yorkshire Society for Celtic Studies
YSE	Yale Studies in English, N Y 1898–
YWES	Year's Work in English Studies
YWMLS	Year's Work in Modern Language Studies
ZfCP	Zeitschrift für celtische Philologie (Tübingen)
ZfDA	Zeitschrift für deutsches Alterthum und deutsche Litteratur
ZfDP	Zeitschrift für deutsche Philologie
ZfFSL	Zeitschrift für französische Sprache und Literatur
ZfÖG	Zeitschrift für die österreichischen Gymnasien
ZfRP	Zeitschrift rür romanische Philologie
ZfVL	Zeitschrift für vergleichende Litteraturgeschichte, Berlin

Other Commonly Used Abbreviations

ae	altenglische	AN	Anglo-Norman	OF	Old French
af	altfranzösische	c	copyright	ON	Old Norse
engl	englische	ca	circa	pt	part
f	für	crit	criticized by	re-ed	re-edited by
me	mittelenglische	f, ff	folio, folios	rptd	reprinted
u	und	ME	Middle English	rvsd	revised
z	zu	n d	no date	unptd	unprinted

Volume-Year Correspondence Chart for Periodicals

by

Douglas A. Burger and Peter G. Beidler

Since year numbers are not given in the bibliographical entries for periodicals, this Volume-Year Correspondence Chart was compiled to provide a quick way for readers to find the year for which a given volume of a periodical was published. The periodical names (alphabetical according to abbreviation) are listed down the left-hand side of the chart, the volume numbers across the top, and the year of publication at the intersection. The full year number is given only in the first column; thereafter only the last two digits are given. For example, AJ vol 3 is for 1898; vol 12 is for 1906–07. An asterisk (*) beside the title indicates that special information is given in a footnote, which will be found arranged alphabetically by periodical abbreviation immediately following the chart. The first four double-pages cover only the first 50 volumes of the periodicals listed. For those periodicals which run to more than 50 volumes, the last double-page covers volumes 51–100. Only two periodicals (Arch and N&Q) run to more than 100 volumes, and so a second line is allowed to each of them on the chart for the second hundred volumes. The volume number in the second line of each of these is in every case 100 *plus* the volume number given on the chart (e. g., under the column headed 8, in the second line for Arch, the year for Arch vol 108 is found to be 1902). The cut-off year for the chart is 1955. In cases where that year is contained in part by two volumes (e. g., vol 31 for 1954–55 and vol 32 for 1955–56) *both* volumes are listed. If there is no volume for 1955, but one for a later year, then the next later volume is listed. If the numbering stops with a year before 1955, it may be assumed that the periodical, or at least that series of it, ends with that year (unless a footnote gives contrary information).

There are several year numbers we could have used for volume dates: (a) the year number near the volume number on the title page; (b) the year number on the cover of individual issue numbers; (c) the year number contained in the running title at the bottom of the pages of text; (d) the year number printed near other facts of publication at the bottom of the title page. Our procedure has been to use (a) whenever it exists, (b) next, then (c), and (d) only as a last resort. We have regarded année, tome, Jahrgang, Band, deel, number (when this is clearly not an individual issue number) and the like as *volume* on the chart. When two manners of numbering run concurrently we include such information in a footnote. We also include significant title changes in footnotes. We have included on the chart only "periodicals," in which volumes contain a number of articles and proceed more or less regularly. We have excluded "serial books," in which the volumes each contain only one or two articles and proceed very irregularly (e. g., vol 7 for 1917, vol 8 for 1916, vol 9 for 1920).

We would like, finally, to express our gratitude to the many librarians and journal editors who have supplied us with information for this project.

D.A.B.
P.G.B.

	Vol 1	2	3	4	5	6	7	8	9	10	11	12	13	14	15	16	17	18	19	20	21	22
AC	1858	59	60	61	63	66	68	72	74	76	77	78	80	82	83	86	87	89	92	93	95	97
Acad*	1869-0	70-1	72	73	74	74	75	75	76	76	77	77	78	78	79	79	80	80	81	81	82	82
AfDA	1876	76	77	78	79	80	81	82	83	84	85	86	87	88	89	90	91	92	93	94	95	96
AHR	1895-6	96-7	97-8	98-9	99-0	00-1	01-2	02-3	03-4	04-5	05-6	06-7	07-8	08-9	09-0	10-1	11-2	12-3	13-4	14-5	15-6	16-7
AJ	1896	97	98	99	00	01	02	03	04	05	06	06-7	07-8	09	10	11	12	13	13-4	14-5	16	16-7
AJA 1s	1885	86	87	88	89	90	91	93	94	95	96											
AJA 2s	1897	98	99	00	01	02	03	04	05	06	07	08	09	10	11	12	13	14	15	16	17	18
AJP	1880	81	82	83	84	85	86	87	88	89	90	91	92	93	94	95	96	97	98	99	00	01
ALg	1949	50	51	52	53	54	55															
Angl*	1878	79	80	81	82	83	84	85	86	88	89	90	91	92	93	95	95	96	96-7	97-8	98-9	99-0
AnglB	1890-1	91-2	92-3	93	94-5	95-6	96-7	97-8	98-9	99-0	00	01	02	03	04	05	06	07	08	09	10	11
AN&Q*	1941-2	42-3	43-4	44-5	45-6	46-7	47-8	48-0														
Antiq	1927	28	29	30	31	32	33	34	35	36	37	38	39	40	41	42	43	44	45	46	47	48
APS	1926-7	27-8	28-9	29-0	30-1	31-2	32-3	33-4	34-5	35-6	36-7	37-8	38-9	39-0	41-2	42-3	43-5	45-8	50	49	52	54
AQ	1949	50	51	52	53	54	55															
AR	1941	42	43	44	45	46	47	48	49	50	51	52	53	54	55							
Arch	1846	47	47	48	49	49	50	51	51	52	52	53	53	53	54	54	55	55	56	56	57	57
Arch 100+ ...	1898	99	99	00	00	01	01	02	02	03	03	04	04	05	05	06	06	07	07	08	08	09
Archaeol*	1770	73	75	77	79	82	85	87	89	92	94	96	00	03	06	12	14	17	21	24	27	29
ASp	1925-6	26-7	27-8	28-9	29-0	30-1	31-2	33	34	35	36	37	38	39	40	41	42	43	44	45	46	47
ASR	1913	14	15	16	17	18	19	20	21	22	23	24	25	26	27	28	29	30	31	32	33	34
ASt	1912	14	22	22	23	24	25	26	27	28	29	32	34	36								
BA	1927	28	29	30	31	32	33	34	35	36	37	38	39	40	41	42	43	44	45	46	47	48
BARB 1s	1832-4	35	36	37	38	39	40	41	42	43	44	45	46	47	48	49	50	51	52	53	54	55
BARB 2s	1857	57	58	58	58	59	59	59	60	60	61	61	62	62	63	63	64	64	65	65	66	66
BARB 3s	1881	81	82	82	83	83	84	84	85	85	86	86	87	87	88	88	89	89	90	90	91	91
BB	1897-9	99-2	02-4	04-7	07-9	09-2	12-3	14-5	16-7	18-9	20-3	23-6	26-9	30-3	33-6	36-9	40-3	43-6	46-9	50-3	53-6	
BBSIA	1949	50	51	52	53	54	55															
BGDSL*	1874	76	76	77	78	79	80	82	84	85	86	87	88	89	91	92	93	94	94	95	96	97
BHR	1941	42	43	44	44	45	45	46	47	48	49	50	51	52	53	54	55					
BIHR	1923-4	24-5	25-6	26-7	27-8	28-9	29-0	30-1	31-2	32-3	33-4	34-5	35-6	36-7	37-8	38-9	39-0	40-1	41-3	43-5	46-8	49
Blackf	1920	21	22	23	24	25	26	27	28	29	30	31	32	33	34	35	36	37	38	39	40	41
BNYPL	1897	98	99	00	01	02	03	04	05	06	07	08	09	10	11	12	13	14	15	16	17	18
BPLQ	1949	50	51	52	53	54	55															
BQR	1914-6	17-9	20-2	23-5	26-8	29-1	32-4	35-8														
BUSE........	1955-6																					
CE	1939-0	40-1	41-2	42-3	43-4	44-5	45-6	46-7	47-8	48-9	49-0	50-1	51-2	52-3	53-4	54-5	55-6					
CHR	1915-6	16-7	17-8	18-9	19-0	20-1	21-2	22-3	23-4	24-5	25-6	26-7	27-8	28-9	29-0	30-1	31-2	32-3	33-4	34-5	35-6	36
CJ*	1905-6	06-7	07-8	08-9	09-0	10-1	11-2	12-3	13-4	14-5	15-6	16-7	17-8	18-9	19-0	20-1	21-2	22-3	23-4	24-5	25-6	26
CL	1949	50	51	52	53	54	55															
CMLR	1944-5	45-6	46-7	47-8	48-9	49-0	50-1	51-2	52-3	53-4	54-5	55-6										
Conviv*	1929	30	31	32	33	34	35	36	37	38	39	40	41	42	43	47	48	49	50	51		5
CP	1906	07	08	09	10	11	12	13	14	15	16	17	18	19	20	21	22	23	24	25	26	2
DA*	1938	39-0	41	42-3	43-4	45	46-7	48	49-0	50	51	52	53	54	55							
DANHSJ.....	1879	80	81	82	83	84	85	86	87	88	89	90	91	92	93	94	95	96	97	98	99	0
DLz*	1880	81	82	83	84	85	86	87	88	89	90	91	92	93	94	95	96	97	98	99	00	0
DomS........	1948	49	50	51	52	53	54															
EA	1937	38	39	40	52	53	54	55														
EC	1951	52	53	54	55																	
EG	1946	47	48	49	50	51	52	53	54	55												
EHR	1886	87	88	89	90	91	92	93	94	95	96	97	98	99	00	01	02	03	04	05	06	•
EJ*	1912	13	14	15	16	17	18	19	20	21	22	23	24	25	26	27	28	29	30	31	32	
ELH.........	1934	35	36	37	38	39	40	41	42	43	44	45	46	47	48	49	50	51	52	53	54	

25	26	27	28	29	30	31	32	33	34	35	36	37	38	39	40	41	42	43	44	45	46	47	48	49	50
02	04	05	09	11	14	15	17	18	20	21	23	25	26	27	28	29	30	31	32	33	34	35	36	37	38
84	84	85	85	86	86	87	87	88	88	89	89	90	90	91	91	92	92	93	93	94	94	95	95	96	96
99	00	01	02	03-4	05-6	07-8	08	09	10	11	12-3	14-5	18-9	19-0	20-1	21-2	22-3	23-4	25	26	27	28	29	30	31
19-0	20-1	21-2	22-3	23-4	24-5	25-6	26-7	27-8	28-9	29-0	30-1	31-2	32-3	33-4	34-5	35-6	36-7	37-8	38-9	39-0	40-1	41-2	42-3	43-4	44-5
19-0	21	21-2	22-3	23-4	24-5	25-6	26-7	27-8	28-9	29-0	30-1	31-2	32-3	33-4	34-5	35-6	36-7	37-8	38-9	40	41	42	43	44	45
21	22	23	24	25	26	27	28	29	30	31	32	33	34	35	36	37	38	39	40	41	42	43	44	45	46
04	05	06	07	08	09	10	11	12	13	14	15	16	17	18	19	20	21	22	23	24	25	26	27	28	29
02	03	04	05	06	07	08	09	10	11	12	12	13	14	16	16	17	18	19	20	21	22	23	24	26	26
14	15	16	17	18	19	20	21	22	23	24	25	26	27	28	29	30	31	32	33	34	35	36	37	38	39
51	52	53	54	55																					
59	59	60	60	61	61	62	62	63	63	64	64	65	65	66	67	67	68	68	69	69	70	71	71	72	72
10	11	11	12	12	13	13	14	15	16	16	17	18	19	19	20	21	21	22	22	23	23	24	25	26	26
34	36	38	40	42	44	46	47	49	52	53	55	57	60	63	66	67	69	71	73	77-0	80-1	82-3	84-5	85-6	87
50	51	52	53	54	55																				
37	38	39	40	41	42	43	44	45	46	47	48	49	50	51	52	53	54	55							
51	52	53	54	55																					
68	68	69	69	70	70	71	71	72	72	73	73	74	74	75	75	76	76	77	77	78	78	79	79	80	80
93	93	94	94	95	95	96	96	97	97	98	98														
00	01	02	03	04	05	06	07	08	09	09	10	12	13	14	15	16	17	18	20	21	22	23	24	25	27
52	53	54	55																						
44	45	46	47	48	49	50	51	52	53	54	55														
21	22	23	24	25	26	27	28	29	30	31	32	33	34	35	36	37	38	39	40	41	42	43	44	45	46
-0	40-1	41-2	42-3	43-5	44-5	45-6	46-7	47-8	48-9	49-0	50-1	51-2	52-3	53-4	54-5	55-6									
-0	30-1	31-2	32-3	33-4	34-5	35-6	36-7	37-8	38-9	39-0	40-1	41-2	42-3	43-4	44-5	45-6	46-7	47-8	48-9	49-0	50-1	51-2	52-3	53-4	54-5
	31	32	33	34	35	36	37	38	39	40	41	42	43	44	45	46	47	48	49	50	51	52	53	54	55
	04	05	06	07	08	09	10	11	12	13	14	15	16	17	18	19	20	21	22	23	24	25	26	27	28
	05	06	07	08	09	10	11	12	13	14	15	16	17	18	19	20	21	22	23	24	25	26	27	28	29
	11	12	13	14	15	16	17	18	19	20	21	22	23	24	25	26	27	28	29	30	31	32	33	34	35
	37	38	39	40	41	42	43	44	45	46	47	48	49	50	51	52	53	54	55						

	Vol 1	2	3	4	5	6	7	8	9	10	11	12	13	14	15	16	17	18	19	20	21	22
Engl	1936-7	38-9	40-1	42-3	44-5	46-7	48-9	50-1	52-3	54-5												
E&S ls	1910	11	12	13	14	20	21	22	23	24	25	26	27	28	29	30	31	32	33	34	35	36
E&S ns*	1948	49	50	51	52	53	54	55														
EStn	1877	79	80	81	82	83	84	85	86	87	88	89	89	90	91	92	92	93	94	95	95	96
ESts	1919	20	21	22	23	24	25	26	27	28	29	30	31	32	33	34	35	36	37	38	39	40
Expl	1942-3	43-4	44-5	45-6	46-7	47-8	48-9	49-0	50-1	51-2	52-3	53-4	54-5	55-6								
FFK	1925	26	27	28	29	30	31	32	33	34	35	36	37	38	39	40	41	42	43	44	45	45-:
FQ	1919	20	21	22	23	24	25	26	27	28	29	30	31	32								
FR	1927-8	28-9	29-0	30-1	31-2	32-3	33-4	34-5	35-6	36-7	37-8	38-9	39-0	40-1	41-2	42-3	43-4	44-5	45-6	46-7	47-8	48-
FS	1947	48	49	50	51	52	53	54	55													
Germ*	1856	57	58	59	60	61	62	63	64	65	66	67	68	69	70	71	72	73	74	75	76	77
GQ	1928	29	30	31	32	33	34	35	36	37	38	39	40	41	42	43	44	45	46	47	48	49
GR	1926	27	28	29	30	31	32	33	34	35	36	37	38	39	40	41	42	43	44	45	46	47
GRM ls	1909	10	11	12	13	14	15-9	20	21	22	23	24	25	26	27	28	29	30	31	32	33	34
GRM ns	1950-1	51-2	53	54	55																	
Hermes*	1866	67	69	70	71	72	73	74	75	76	76	77	78	79	80	81	82	83	84	85	86	87
HINL	1954-5																					
Hisp*	1918	19	20	21	22	23	24	25	26	27	28	29	30	31	32	33	34	35	36	37	38	39
HispR	1933	34	35	36	37	38	39	40	41	42	43	44	45	46	47	48	49	50	51	52	53	54
HJ	1902-3	03-4	04-5	05-6	06-7	07-8	08-9	09-0	10-1	11-2	12-3	13-4	14-5	15-6	16-7	17-8	18-9	19-0	20-1	21-2	22-3	23-
HLB	1947	48	49	50	51	52	53	54	55													
HLQ	1937-8	38-9	39-0	40-1	41-2	42-3	43-4	44-5	45-6	46-7	47-8	48-9	49-0	50-1	51-2	52-3	53-4	54-5	55-6			
HudR	1948-9	49-0	50-1	51-2	52-3	53-4	54-5	55-6														
IS	1937-8	38-9	46-8	49	50	51	52	53	54	55												
Isis	1913	14-9	20-1	21-2	23	24	25	26	27	28	28	29	29-0	30	31	31	32	32	33	33	34	34
Ital	1924	25	26	27	28	29	30	31	32	33	34	35	36	37	38	39	40	41	42	43	44	4
JAAC	1941-2	42-3	44	45-6	46-7	47-8	48-9	49-0	50-1	51-2	52-3	53-4	54-5	55-6								
JBL	1882	83	84	85	86	87	88	89	90	91	92	93	94	95	96	97	98	99	00	01	02	C
JEGGP ls	1879	80	81	82	83	84	85	86	87	88	89	90	91	92	93	94	95	96	97	98	99	C
JEGGP ns	1921	22	23	24	25	26	27	28	29	30	31	32	33	34	35	36	37	38	39			
JEGP*	1897	98-9	00-1	02	03-5	06-7	07-8	09	10	11	12	13	14	15	16	17	18	19	20	21	22	:
JEH	1950	51	52	53	54	55																
JfRESL*	1859	60	61	62	64	65	66	67	68	69	70	71	74	75	76							
JHI	1940	41	42	43	44	45	46	47	48	49	50	51	52	53	54	55						
JPhilol	1868	69	71	72	74	76	77	79	80	82	82	83	85	85	86	88	88	90	91	92	93	
JPhilos	1904	05	06	07	08	09	10	11	12	13	14	15	16	17	18	19	20	21	22	23	24	
JRLB	1903-8	14-5	16-7	17-8	18-0	21-2	22-3	24	25	26	27	28	29	30	31	32	33	34	35	36	37	
KR	1939	40	41	42	43	44	45	46	47	48	49	50	51	52	53	54	55					
Lang	1925	26	27	28	29	30	31	32	33	34	35	36	37	38	39	40	41	42	43	44	45	
LB	1896	97-8	99	00-2	03-4	04-5	06-7	08-9	10-1	12-3	13-4	14-0	21	22	23	24	25	26	27	28	29	
LC	1944-5	46-7	47-0	50-2	54-6																	
Leeds SE	1932	33	34	35	36	37	52	52														
LfGRP	1880	81	82	83	84	85	86	87	88	89	90	91	92	93	94	95	96	97	98	99	00	
Libr ls	1889	90	91	92	93	94	95	96	97	98-9												
Libr ns	1899-0	01	02	03	04	05	06	07	08	09												
Libr 3s	1910	11	12	13	14	15	16	17	18	19												
Libr 4s	1920-1	21-2	22-3	23-4	24-5	25-6	26-7	27-8	28-9	29-0	30-1	31-2	32-3	33-4	34-5	35-6	36-7	37-8	38-9	39-0	40-1	
Libr 5s	1946-7	47-8	48-9	49-0	50-1	51	52	53	54	55												
Litteris	1924	25	26	27	28	29	30															
LMS	1937-8																					
LP	1951	52	53	54	55																	
LQ	1931	32	33	34	35	36	37	38	39	40	41	42	43	44	45	46	47	48	49	50	51	
LZ*	1850	51	52	53	54	55	56	57	58	59	60	61	62	63	64	65	66	67	68	69	70	

25	26	27	28	29	30	31	32	33	34	35	36	37	38	39	40	41	42	43	44	45	46	47	48	49	50
39	40	41	42	43	44	45	46																		
98	99	00	00	01	02	02	03	04	04	05	06	07	07	08	09	10	10	10-1	12	12	12-3	13-4	14-5	15-6	16-7
43	44-5	46	47	48	49	50	51	52	53	54	55														
49	50	53	54	55																					
51-2	52-3	53-4	54-5	55-6																					
80	81	82	83	84	85	86	87	88	89	90	91	92													
52	53	54	55																						
50	51	52	53	54	55																				
37	38	39	40	41	42	43																			
90	91	92	93	94	95	96	97	98	99	00	01	02	03	04	05	06	07	08	09	10	11	12	13	14	15
42	43	44	45	46	47	48	49	50	51	52	53	54	55												
6-7	27-8	28-9	29-0	30-1	31-2	32-3	33-4	34-5	35-6	36-7	37-8	38-9	39-0	40-1	41-2	42-3	43-4	44-5	45-6	46-7	47-8	48-9	49-0	50-1	51-2
36	36	37	38	38	39	39	40	41	42-3	44	45-6	47	47-8	48	49	50	51	52	53	54	55				
48	49	50	51	52	53	54	55																		
46	07	08	09	10	11	12	13	14	15	16	17	18	19	20	21	22	23	24	25	26	27	28	29	30	31
3	04	05	06	07	08	09	10	11	12	13	14	15	16	17	18	19	20								
6	27	28	29	30	31	32	33	34	35	36	37	38	39	40	41	42	43	44	45	46	47	48	49	50	51
7	99	01	03	04	06	10	13	14	18	20															
8	29	30	31	32	33	34	35	36	37	38	39	40	41	42	43	44	45	46	47	48	49	50	51	52	53
	41-2	42-3	44	45-6	46-7	48	49-0	50-1	51-2	52-3	53-4	54-5	55-6												
	50	51	52	53	54	55																			
	34	35	36	37	38	39	40	41	42	43	44-6	47	48	49	50	51	52	53	54	55					
	05	06	07	08	09	10	11	12	13	14	15	16	17	18	19	20	21	22	23	24	25	26	27	28	29
5	45-6																								
	75	76	77	78	79	80	81	82	83	84	85	86	87	88	89	90	91	92	93	94	95	96	97	98	99

	Vol 1	2	3	4	5	6	7	8	9	10	11	12	13	14	15	16	17	18	19	20	21	22
MÆ	1932	33	34	35	36	37	38	39	40	41	42	43	44	45	46	47	48	49	50	51	52	53
MH	1943	44	45	46	48	50	52	54	55													
MHRA	1920	21	22	23	24	25	26	27	28	29	30	31	32	33	34	35	36	37	38	39	40	41
MKAW ls* ...	1856	57	58	59	60	62	63	65	65	66	68	69	71	72	73	74	76	77	78	78	80	81
MKAW ns ...	1938	39	40	41	42	43	44	45	46	47	48	49	50	51	52	53	54	55				
ML..........	1920	21	22	23	24	25	26	27	28	29	30	31	32	33	34	35	36	37	38	39	40	41
MLF*	1915	16	17	18	20	21	22	23	24	25	26	27	28	29	30	31	32	33	34	35	36	37
MLJ	1916-7	17-8	18-9	19-0	20-1	21-2	22-3	23-4	24-5	25-6	26-7	27-8	28-9	29-0	30-1	31-2	32-3	33-4	34-5	35-6	36-7	37-8
MLN	1886	87	88	89	90	91	92	93	94	95	96	97	98	99	00	01	02	03	04	05	06	07
MLQ (Lon) ..	1897	98-9	00	01	02	03	04															
MLQ (Wash) .	1940	41	42	43	44	45	46	47	48	49	50	51	52	53	54	55						
MLR	1905-6	06-7	07-8	08-9	10	11	12	13	14	15	16	17	18	19	20	21	22	23	24	25	26	27
Monat	1899-0	00-1	01-2	02-3	03-4	05	06	07	08	09	10	11	12	13	14	15	16	17	18	28	29	30
MP	1903-4	04-5	05-6	06-7	07-8	08-9	09-0	10-1	11-2	12-3	13-4	14-5	15-6	16-7	17-8	18-9	19-0	20-1	21-2	22-3	23-4	24-
MS	1939	40	41	42	43	44	45	46	47	48	49	50	51	52	53	54	55					
Neophil	1916	17	18	19	20	20-1	21-2	22-3	23-4	24-5	25-6	26-7	27-8	28-9	29-0	30-1	31-2	32-3	33-4	34-5	35-6	36-
NEQ	1928	29	30	31	32	33	34	35	36	37	38	39	40	41	42	43	44	45	46	47	48	49
NLB.........	1944-7	48-2	52-5	55-8																		
NM	1899	00	01	02	03	04	05	06	07	08	09	10	11	12	13	14	15	17	18	19	20	21
NMQ........	1931	32	33	34	35	36	37	38	39	40	41	42	43	44	45	46	47	48	49	50	51	52
N&Q*	1849-0	50	51	51	52	52	53	53	54	54	55	55	56	56	57	57	58	58	59	59	60	60
N&Q 100+ ..	1900	00	01	01	02	02	03	03	04	04	05	05	06	06	07	07	08	08	09	09	10	1C
NRFH.......	1947	48	49	50	51	52	53	54	55													
NS*	1893-4	94-5	95-6	96-7	97-8	98-9	99-0	00-1	01-2	02-3	03-4	04-5	05-6	06-7	07-8	08-9	09-0	10-1	11-2	12-3	13-4	14-
PAPS	1838-0	41-3	43	43-7	48-3	54-8	59-0	61-2	62-4	65-8	69-0	71-2	73	74-5	76	76-7	77-8	78-0	80-1	82-3	83-4	85
PBSA	1904-5	07-8	08	09	10	11	12-3	14	15	16	17	18	19	20	21	22	23	24	25	26	27	28
Philo*	1846	47	48	49	50	51	52	53	54	55	56	57	58	59	60	60	61	62	63	63	64	6-
PMLA	1884-5	86	87	88-9	90	91	92	93	94	95	96	97	98	99	00	01	02	03	04	05	06	0:
PMRS	1923	24	25	26	27	28	29	30	31	32	33	35	37	39	40	41	42	44	47	49	51	5:
PP	1952	52	53	53	54	54	55	55														
PPR	1940-1	41-2	42-3	43-4	44-5	45-6	46-7	47-8	48-9	49-0	50-1	51-2	52-3	53-4	54-5	55-6						
PQ	1922	23	24	25	26	27	28	29	30	31	32	33	34	35	36	37	38	39	40	41	42	4-
PR	1934	35	36	37-8	38	38-9	40	41	42	43	44	45	46	47	48	49	50	51	52	53	54	5-
PS...........	1947	48	49	50	51	52	53	54	55													
PULC	1939-0	40-1	41-2	42-3	43-4	44-5	45-6	46-7	47-8	48-9	49-0	50-1	51-2	52-3	53-4	54-5	55-6					
QQ..........	1893-4	94-5	95-6	96-7	97-8	98-9	99-0	00-1	01-2	02-3	03-4	04-5	05-6	06-7	07-8	08-9	09-0	10-1	11-2	12-3	13-4	14-
RAA	1923-4	24-5	25-6	27	27-8	28-9	29-0	30-1	31-2	32-3	33-4	34-5	35-6									
RB*	1825	26	27	28	29	30	31	32	33	34	35	36	37	38	39	40	41	42	43	44	45	4
RC..........	1870-2	73-5	76-8	79-0	81-3	83-5	86	87	88	89	90	91	92	93	94	95	96	97	98	99	00	C
RCHL*	1866	67	68	69	70	72	73	74	75	76	77	78	79	80	81	82	83	84	85	86	87	8
Ren	1948-9	49-0	50-1	51-2	52-3	53-4	54-5	55-6														
RES ls	1925	26	27	28	29	30	31	32	33	34	35	36	37	38	39	40	41	42	43	44	45	
RES ns	1950	51	52	53	54	55																
RevP*	1887	88	89	90	91	92	93	94	95	96	97	98	99	00	01	02	03	04	05	06	07	▪
RF	1883	86	87	91	90	91	93	94-5	96	99	01	00	02	03	04	04	04	05	06	07	08	▪
RFH	1939	40	41	42	43	44	45	46														
RG*.........	1905	06	07	08	09	10	11	12	13	14	20	21	22	23	24	25	26	27	28	29	30	
RHL	1894	95	96	97	98	99	00	01	02	03	04	05	06	07	08	09	10	11	12	13	14	
RLC........	1921	22	23	24	25	26	27	28	29	30	31	32	33	34	35	36	37	38	39	40-6	47	
RLR*	1870	71	72	73	74	74	75	75	76	76	77	77	78	78	79	79	80	80	81	81	82	
RN..........	1948	49	50	51	52	53	54	55														
Rom.........	1872	73	74	75	76	77	78	79	80	81	82	83	84	85	86	87	88	89	90	91	92	
RomP	1947-8	48-9	49-0	50-1	51-2	52-3	53-4	54-5	55-6													

25	26	27	28	29	30	31	32	33	34	35	36	37	38	39	40	41	42	43	44	45	46	47	48	49	50
45	46	47	48	49	50-2	53-4	55-6																		
84	85	87	87	88	89	90	92	93	94	95	96	97	98	99	01	03	04	06	07	09	11	12	14	15	17
44	45	46	47	48	49	50	51	52	53	54	55														
40	41	42	43	44	45	46	47	48	49	50	51	52	53	54	55										
40-1	42	43	44	45	46	47	48	49	50	51	52	53	54	55											
10	11	12	13	14	15	16	17	18	19	20	21	22	23	24	25	26	27	28	29	30	31	32	33	34	35
30	31	32	33	34	35	36	37	38	39	40	41	42	43	44	45	46	47	48	49	50	51	52	53	54	55
32	34	35	36	37	38	39	40	41	42	43	44	45	46	47	48	49	50	51	52	53	54	55			
27-8	28-9	29-0	30-1	31-2	32-3	33-4	34-5	35-6	36-7	37-8	38-9	39-0	40-1	41-2	42-3	43-4	44-5	45-6	46-7	47-8	48-9	49-0	50-1	51-2	52-3
39-0	40-1	41-2	42-3	43-4	46	47	48	49	50	51	52	53	54	55											
52	53	54	55																						
24	25	26	27	28	29	30	31	32	33	34	35	36	37	38	39	40	41	42	43	44	45	46	47	48	49
55																									
62	62	63	63	64	64	65	65	66	66	67	67	68	68	69	69	70	70	71	71	72	72	73	73	74	74
12	12	13	13	14	14	15	15	16	16	17	18	19	20	20	21	21	22	22	23	23	24	24	25	25	26
17-8	18-9	19-0	20-1	21	22	23	24	25	26	27	28	29	30	31	32	33	34	35	36	37	38	39	40	41	42
88	89	89	90	91	92	93	93	94	95	96	97	98	99	00	01	02	03	04	05	06	07	08	09	10	11
31	32	33	34	35	36	37	38	39	40	41	42	43	44	45	46	47	48	49	50	51	52	53	54	55	
57	67	68	69	70	70	72	73	74	76	76	77	77	79	80	81	82	84	84	85	86	88	89	89	90	91
10	11	12	13	14	15	16	17	18	19	20	21	22	23	24	25	26	27	28	29	30	31	32	33	34	35
46	47	48	49	50	51	52	53	54	55																
17-8	18-9	19-0	20-1	21-2	22-3	23-4	24-5	25-6	26-7	27-8	29	30	31	32	33	34-5	35-6	36-7	37-8	38-9	39-0	40	41	42	43-4
49	50	51	52	53	54	55	56	57	58	59	60	61	62	63	64	65	66	67	68	69	70	71	72	73	74
04	05	06	07	08	09	10	11	12	13	14	15-6	17-9	20-1	22	23	24	25	26	27	28	29	30	31	32	33
91	92	93	94	95	96	97	98	99	00	01	02	03	04	05	06	07	08	09	10	11	12	13	14	15	16
49																									
11	12	13	14	15	16	17	18	19	20	21	22	23	24	25	26	27	28	29	30	31	32	33	34		
08	09	10	12	11	11	12	13	15	15	16	16	17	19	26	26-7	27-8	28	29	30	31	32	33	34	35	36
34	35	36	37	38	39																				
18	19	20	21	22	23	24	25	26	27	28	29	30	31	32	33	34	35	36	37	38	39	47	48	49	50
51	52	53	54	55																					
84	84	85	85	86	86	87	88	89	90	91	92	93-4	95	96	97	98	99	00	01	02	03	04	05	06	07
96	97	98	99	00	01	02	03	04	05	06	07	08	09	10	11	12	13	14	15-7	18-9	20	21	22	23	24

	Vol 1	2	3	4	5	6	7	8	9	10	11	12	13	14	15	16	17	18	19	20	21	22
RomR	1910	11	12	13	14	15	16	17	18	19	20	21	22	23	24	25	26	27	28	29	30	31
Rot	1931	32	33	37																		
RUL	1946-7	47-8	48-9	49-0	50-1	51-2	52-3	53-4	54-5	55-6												
SA*	1886-8	86-8	88-9	89-0	90-1	91-2	92-3	93-4	94-5	95-6	96-7	97-8	98-9	99-0	00-1	01-2	02-3					
SAQ	1902	03	04	05	06	07	08	09	10	11	12	13	14	15	16	17	18	19	20	21	22	23
SB	1948-9	49-0	50-1	51-2	52-3	54	55															
SBB	1953-4	55-6																				
ScanSt	1911-4	14-5	16	17	18-9	20	21-2	24	26-7	28-9	30-1	32-3	34-5	36-7	38-9	40-1	42-3	44-5	46-7	48	49	50
SciS	1936-7	37-8	39	40	41	42	43	44	45	46	47	48	48-9	49-0	51	51-2	53	54	55			
Scrut*	1932-3	33-4	34-5	35-6	36-7	37-8	38-9	39-0	40-1	41-2	42-3	44-5	45-6	46-7	47-8	49	50	51	52-3			
SEER	1922-3	23-4	24-5	25-6	26-7	27-8	28-9	29-0	30-1	31-2	32-3	33-4	34-5	35-6	36-7	37-8	38-9	39	39-0	41	42-3	44
ShJ*	1865	67	68	69	70	71	72	73	74	75	76	77	78	79	80	81	82	83	84	85	86	87
SHR	1903-4	04-5	05-6	06-7	07-8	08-9	09-0	10-1	11-2	12-3	13-4	14-5	15-6	16-7	17-8	18-9	19-0	20-1	21-2	22-3	23-4	24-5
SL	1942	43-4	45	46	47	48	49	50	51	52	53	54-7										
SN	1928	29	30	31-2	32-3	33-4	34-5	35-6	36-7	37-8	38-9	39-0	40-1	41-2	42-3	43-4	44-5	45-6	46-7	47-8	48-9	49-0
SP	1906	07	08	10	10	10	11	11	12	13	13	15	16	17	18	19	20	21	22	23	24	25
Spec	1926	27	28	29	30	31	32	33	34	35	36	37	38	39	40	41	42	43	44	45	46	47
SR	1892-3	93-4	94-5	95-6	97	98	99	00	01	02	03	04	05	06	07	08	09	10	11	12	13	14
SRL	1924-5	25-6	26-7	27-8	28-9	29-0	30-1	31-2	32-3	33-4	34-5	35	35-6	36	36-7	37	37-8	38	38-9	39	39-0	40
StVL	1901	02	03	04	05	06	07	08	09													
SWR*	1915-6	16-7	17-8	18-9	19-0	20-1	21-2	22-3	23-4	24-5	25-6	26-7	27-8	28-9	29-0	30-1	31-2	32-3	33-4	34-5	35-6	36-7
Sym*	1946-7	48	49	50	51	52	53	54	55													
Texas SE*	1911	14	15	24	25	26	27	28	29	30	31	32	33	34	35	36	37					
TLCAS	1883	84	85	86	87	88	89	90	91	92	93	94	95	96	97	98	99	00	01	02	03	04
TNTL	1881	82	83	84	85	86	87	88	89	90	91	92	93	94	95	96	97	98	99	00	01	02
Trad	1943	44	45	46	47	48	49-1	52	53	54	55											
TRSL 1s	1827-9	32-4	37-9																			
TRSL 2s	1843	47	50	53	56	59	63	66	70	74	78	82	83	86-9	93	94	95	97	97-8	98-9	99-0	00-
TRSL 3s	1921	22	23	24	25	26	27	28	30	31	32	33	34	35	36	37	38	40	42	43	44	45
TTL	1913	14	15	16	17	18	19	20	21	22	23	24	25	26	27	28	29	30	31	32	33	34
UKCR*	1934-5	35-6	36-7	37-8	38-9	39-0	40-1	41-2	42-3	43-4	44-5	45-6	46-7	47-8	48-9	49-0	50-1	51-2	52-3	53-4	54-5	55-
UQ	1944-5	45-6	46-7	48	49	50	51	52	53	54	55											
UTM*	1900-1	01-2	02-3	03-4	04-5	05-6	06-7	07-8	08-9	09-0	10-1	11-2	13	13-4	14-5	15-6	16-7	17-8	18-9	19-0	20-1	21-
UTQ	1931-2	32-3	33-4	34-5	35-6	36-7	37-8	38-9	39-0	40-1	41-2	42-3	43-4	44-5	45-6	46-7	47-8	48-9	49-0	50-1	51-2	52-
VQR	1925	26	27	28	29	30	31	32	33	34	35	36	37	38	39	40	41	42	43	44	45	46
WHR	1947	48	49	50	51	52	53	54	55													
WMQ 1s*	1892	93-4	94-5	95-6	96-7	97-8	98-9	99-0	00-1	01-2	02-3	03-4	04-5	05-6	06-7	07-8	08-9	09-0	10-1	11-2	12-3	13-
WMQ 2s	1921	22	23	24	25	26	27	28	29	30	31	32	33	34	35	36	37	38	39	40	41	42
WMQ 3s	1944	45	46	47	48	49	50	51	52	53	54	55										
WR*	1819-0	20	20-1	21																		
YCGL	1952	53	54	55																		
YR 1s	1892-3	93-4	94-5	95-6	96-7	97-8	98-9	99-0	00-1	01-2	02-3	03-4	04-5	05-6	06-7	07-8	08-9	09-0	10-1			
YR ns	1911-2	12-3	13-4	14-5	15-6	16-7	17-8	18-9	19-0	20-1	21-2	22-3	23-4	24-5	25-6	26-7	27-8	28-9	29-0	30-1	31-2	32-
YSCS	1937-8	38-9	40-6	47-8	49-2	53-8																
YWES	1919-0	20-1	22	23	24	25	26	27	28	29	30	31	32	33	34	35	36	37	38	39	40	4?
ZfDA*	1841	42	43	44	45	48	49	51	53	56	59	65	67	69	72	73	74	75	76	76	77	7?
ZfDP	1869	70	71	73	74	75	76	77	78	79	80	81	82	82	83	84	85	86	87	88	89	9?
ZfFSL	1879-0	80	81-2	82	83	84	85-6	86-7	87-8	88-9	89	90	91	92	93	94	95	96	97	98	99	0?
ZfÖG	1850	51	52	53	54	55	56	57	58	59	60	61	62	63	64	65	66	67	68	69	70	7?
ZfRP	1877	78	79	80	81	82	83	84	85	86	87	88	89	90	91	92	93	94	95	96	97	9?
ZfVL 1s	1886	87																				
ZfVL ns	1887-8	89	90	91	92	93	94	95	96	96	97	98	99	01	04	06	09	10				

25	26	27	28	29	30	31	32	33	34	35	36	37	38	39	40	41	42	43	44	45	46	47	48	49	50
34	35	36	37	38	39	40	41	42	43	44	45	46	47	48	49	50	51	52	53	54	55				
26	27	28	29	30	31	32	33	34	35	36	37	38	39	40	41	42	43	44	45	46	47	48	49	50	51
53	54	55																							
46-7	47-8	48-9	49-0	50-1	51-2	52-3	53-4	54-5	55-6																
90	91	92	93	94	94	95	96	97	98	99	00	01	02	03	04	05	06	07	08	09	10	11	12	13	14
27-8	47	48	49	50	51	52	53	54	55																
52-3	53-4	55																							
28	29	30	31	32	33	34	35	36	37	38	39	40	41	42	43	44	45	46	47	48	49	50	51	52	53
50	51	52	53	54	55																				
17	18	19	20	21	22	23	24	25	26	27	28	29	30	31	32	33	34	35	36	37	38	39	40	41	42
42	43	44	45	46	47	48	49	50	51	52	53	54	55												
39-0	40-1	41-2	42-3	43-4	44-5	45-6	47	48	49	50	51	52	53	54	55										
07	08	09	10	11	12	13	14	15	16	17	18	19	20	21	22-3	24	25	26	27	28	29	30-1	32	33	34-5
05	06	07	08	09	10	11	12	14	15-6	16	17	18	19	20	21	22	23	24	25	26	27	28	29	30	31
04	05-6	06-7	08-9	09-0	10-1	12	13-4	14-5	16	17	18	19													
50	53	55																							
37	38	39	40	41																					
24-5	25-6	26-7	27-8	28-9	29-0	30-1	31-2	32-3	33-4	34-5	35-6	36-7	37-8	38-9	39-0	40-1	41-2	42-3	43-4	44-5	45-6	46-7			
55-6																									
49	50	51	52	53	54	55																			
-7	17-8	18-9																							
35-6	36-7	37-8	38-9	39-0	40-1	41-2	42-3	43-4	44-5	45-6	46-7	47-8	48-9	49-0	50-1	51-2	52-3	53-4	54-5	55-6					
44	45	46	47	48	49	50	51	52	53	54	55														
	82	83	84	85	86	87	88	89	90	91	92	93	94	95	96	97	98	99	00	01	02	04	06	08	08
	94	95	96	97	98	99	00	01	02	03	04	05	06	07	08	09	10	11	12	13	15	18	20	23	26
	04	04	05	06	06	07	08	08	09	09	10	11	11	12	12-3	13	14	15	16-7	17-9	20-3	25	25-6	26-7	27
	75	76	77	78	79	80	81	82	83	84	85	86	87	88	89	90	91	92	93	94	95	96	97	98	99
	02	03	04	05	06	07	08	09	10	11	12	13	17	19	20	21	22	23	24	25	26	27	28	29	30

	Vol 51	52	53	54	55	56	57	58	59	60	61	62	63	64	65	66	67	68	69	70	71
AC	1939	40	40	41	42	43	44	45	46	47	48	49	50	51	52	53	54	54	55		
Acad*	1897	97	98	98	98	99	99	00	00	01	01	02	02	03	03	04	04	05	05	06	06
AfDA	1932	33	34	35	36	37	38	39	40	41	42	43	44	48-0	51-2	52-3	54-5	55-6			
AHR	1945-6	46-7	47-8	48-9	49-0	50-1	51-2	52-3	53-4	54-5	55-6										
AJ	1946	47	48	49	50	51	52	53	54	55											
AJA 2s	1947	48	49	50	51	52	53	54	55												
AJP	1930	31	32	33	34	35	36	37	38	39	40	41	42	43	44	45	46	47	48	49	50
Angl*	1927	28	29	30	31	32	33	34	35	36	37	38	39	40	41	42	44	44	50	51	52-3
AnglB	1940	41	42	43	44																
Arch	1873	74	74	75	76	76	77	77	78	78	79	79	80	80	81	81	82	82	83	83	84
Arch 150+	1927	27	28	28	29	29	30	30	31	31	32	32	33	33	34	35	35	35	36	36	37
Archaeol*	1888	90	92-3	94-5	96-7	98-9	00-1	02-3	04-5	06-7	08-9	10-1	12	13	14	15	16	17	20	20	21
BGDSL*	1927	28	29	30	31	32	33	34	35	36	37	38	39	40	41	42	44	45-6	47	48	49
BNYPL	1947	48	49	50	51	52	53	54	55												
DANHSJ	1929	30	31-2	33	34	35	36	37	38	39	40	41	42	43	44-5	46	47	48	49	50	51
DLz*	1930	31	32	33	34	35	36	37	38	39	40	41	42	43	44	45	46	47	48	49	50
EHR	1936	37	38	39	40	41	42	43	44	45	46	47	48	49	50	51	52	53	54	55	
EStn	1917-8	18	19-0	20	21	22	23	24	25	25-6	26-7	27-8	28-9	29	30-1	31-2	32	33-4	34-5	35-6	36-7
Hermes*	1916	17	18	19	20	21	22	23	24	25	26	27	28	29	30	31	32	33	34	35	36
HJ	1952-3	53-4	54-5	55-6																	
JBL	1932	33	34	35	36	37	38	39	40	41	42	43	44	45	46	47	48	49	50	51	52
JEGP*	1952	53	54	55																	
JPhilos	1954	55																			
LfGRP	1930	31	32	33	34	35	36	37	38	39	40	41	42	43	44	44					
LZ*	1900	01	02	03	04	05	06	07	08	09	10	11	12	13	14	15	16	17	18	19	20
MKAW 1s*	1918	19	20	22	23	23	24	24	25	25	26	26	27	27	28	28	29	29	30	30	31
MLN	1936	37	38	39	40	41	42	43	44	45	46	47	48	49	50	51	52	53	54	55	
MP	1953-4	54-5	55-6																		
NM	1950	51	52	53	54	55															
N&Q*	1875	75	76	76	77	77	78	78	79	79	80	80	81	81	82	82	83	83	84	84	85
N&Q 150+	1926	27	27	28	28	29	29	30	30	31	31	32	32	33	33	34	34	35	35	36	36
PAPS	1912	13	14	15	16	17	18	19	20	21	22	23	24	25	26	27	28	29	30	31	32
Philo*	1892	94	94	95	96	97	98	99	00	01	02	03	04	05	06	07	08	09	10	11	12
PMLA	1936	37	38	39	40	41	42	43	44	45	46	47	48	49	50	51	52	53	54	55	
QQ	1944-5	45-6	46-7	47-8	48-9	49-0	50-1	51-2	52-3	53-4	54-5	55-6									
RB*	1875	76	77	78	79	80	81	82	83	84	85	86	87	88	89	90	91	92	93	94	95
RC	1934																				
RCHL*	1917	18	19	20	21	22	23	24	25	26	27	28	29	30	31	32	33	34	35		
RF	1937	38	39	40	41	42	43	47	47	47-8	48	50	51	52	53-4	54-5	55-6				
RHL	1951	52	53	54	55																
RLR*	1908	09	10	11	12	13	14	15	16-7	18-0	21-2	23-4	25-6	26	27-8	29-2	33-6	37-9	40-7	48-0	51-4 5
Rom	1925	26	27	28	29	30	31	32	33	34	35	36	37	38	39	40-1	42-3	44-5	46-7	48-9	50
SAQ	1952	53	54	55																	
ShJ*	1915	16	17	18	19	20	21	22	24	24	25	26	27	28	29	30	31	32	33	34	35
SP	1954	55																			
SR	1943	44	45	46	47	48	49	50	51	52	53	54	55								
TLCAS	1936	37	38	39	40	41-2	43-4	45-6	47	48	49	50-1	52-3	54	55						
TNTL	1932	33	34	35	36	36-7	37-8	38-9	39-0	40-1	41-2	42-3	44	46	47-8	48-9	49-0	50-1	51-2	52-3	53
ZfDA*	1909	10	12	13	17	19	20	21	22	23	24	25	26	27	28	29	30	31	32	33	34
ZfDP	1926	27	28	29	30	31	32	33	34	35	36	37	38	39	40	41	42-3	43-4	44-5	48-9	51-2
ZfFSL	1928	29	29-0	30-1	31-2	32	33	34	35	35-7	37-8	38-9	39-0	40-2	43-4	56					
ZfÖG	1900	01	02	03	04	05	06	07	08	09	10	11	12	13	14	15	16	17-8	19-0		
ZfRP	1931	32	33	34	35	36	37	38	39	40	41	42	43	44	49	50	51	52	53	54	55

75	76	77	78	79	80	81	82	83	84	85	86	87	88	89	90	91	92	93	94	95	96	97	98	99	100
08	09	09	10	10	11	11	12	12	13	13	14	14	15	15	16										
54	55																								
86	86	87	87	87	88	88	89	89	90	90	91	91	92	92	93	93	94	94	95	95	96	96	97	97	98
39	39	40	41	41	42	42	43	43	44	48	49	50	51	53	54	55									
26	27	28	28	29	30	31	32	33	35	36	37	38	40	43	44	45	47	49	51	53	55				
53	54–5	55																							
55																									
54	55																								
2–3	44																								
40	41	42	43	44	52	53	54	55																	
24	25	26	27	28	29	30	31	32	33	34	35	36	37	38	39	40	41	42	43	44					
33	33	34	34	35	35	36	36	37	37																
87	87	88	88	89	89	90	90	91	91	92	92	93	93	94	94	95	95	96	96	97	97	98	98	99	99
38	39	39	40	40	41	41	42	42	43	43	44	44	45	45	46	46	47	48	49	50	51	52	53	54	55
35	36	37	37–8	38	39	39	40	40	41	42	43	44	44	45	46	47	48	49	50	51	52	53	54	55	
18	20	21	22–3	23–4	24–5	25–6	26–7	27–8	28–9	29–0	30–1	32	33	34	35	36–7	37–8	38–9	40–1	42–3	44	48	54	55	
99	00	01																							
54	55																								
39	40	41	43	43	46	46	48	48	50	50	50	52	52	53	54	55									
38	39	40	41	42	43	44	48–0	51–2	52–3	54–5															

13*

Notes

Acad Intermittently published as Academy and Literature.

Angl At the back of vols 4 (1881) through 8 (1885) there appears a separately paged section called Anglia Anzeiger.

AN&Q There are also two earlier journals with the same name: American Notes and Queries, Philadelphia, nos 1–4 in 1857; and American Notes and Queries: A Medium of Intercommunication for Literary Men, General Readers, etc, Philadelphia, in nine volumes beginning in 1888.

Archaeol A new series and numbering runs concurrently with the old starting with vol 51 (ns vol 1).

BGDSL The printed title page for the bound vol 67 gives the date of publication as 1945, but the covers for the individual Hefts all say 1944.

CJ This journal, published by the Classical Association of the Middle West and South Inc, with the cooperation of the Classical Associations of New England, the Pacific States, and the Atlantic States, is not to be confused with another journal of the same title (no subtitle) published in London. Vol 51 is for 1955–56 (does not appear on the chart because of space limitation).

Conviv Vols 16–21 also listed as Raccolta nuova. Vol 21 is a special edition entitled Studi in ricordo di Carlo Calcaterra and has no ordered year number. Vols 22–31 are also listed as Nuova serie.

DA Called Microfilm Abstracts for the first 11 volumes.

DLz This journal, subtitled Für Kritik der internationalen Wissenschaft, published in Berlin and Leipzig, is to be distinguished from another of the same name, without subtitle, published in Leipzig and beginning with vol 1 in 1930.

EJ At vol 17 the journal bifurcates into a college edition and a high school edition. The latter runs to the present. The college edition runs through vols 17–28 (1928–39) whereupon it is superseded by College English. Since the years for vols 17–28 are the same for both the high school and the college editions, it has not been necessary to list separately the 12 volumes of the college edition.

E&S ns Vols 1 and 2 of the new series are entitled English Studies.

Germ This journal, subtitled Vierteljahrsschrift für deutsche Alterthumskunde, is not to be confused with other journals bearing the same title. A new series and numbering runs concurrently with the old beginning with vol 13 (ns vol 1) and running to vol 37 (ns vol 25).

Hermes This journal, subtitled Zeitschrift fur klassische Philologie and published in Berlin is not to be confused with a similarly titled journal, subtitled Oder, kritisches Jahrbuch der Literatur, published in Leipzig in 35 volumes beginning in 1819.

Hisp This journal, subtitled A Journal Devoted to the Interest of the Teaching of Spanish and Portuguese, and published at Stanford, is not to be confused with other journals bearing the same title.

JEGP Vols 1–4 are called Journal of Germanic Philology.

JfRESL Vols 13–15 are also called Neue Folge 1–3.

Leeds SE There has been no official notification that this journal has ceased publication, but the combined vol 7–8 for 1952 is the last that has been sent to libraries.

LZ Listed only by year until the 1900 volume is called Jahrgang 51. Thereafter the Jahrgang is mentioned on each title page.

MKAW ls Vols 1–12 are also called 1st reek 1–12; vols 13–24, 2nd reek 1–12; vols 25–36, 3rd reek 1–12; vols 37–48, 4th reek 1–12; vols 49–52, 5th reek 1–4. Vols (or deels) 54–84 are classed into two series: the odd-numbered volumes (55, 57, 59, etc) are serie A; the even-numbered volumes (54, 56, 58, etc) are serie B. Vol 53 is classed as neither serie A nor serie B.

MLF Vols 1–10 are called Modern Language Bulletin.

N&Q Listed by year only until the 1924 volume is given as vol 146. Before that time it is divided into 12 series, each containing 12 volumes. The 13th series begins, but has only one volume.

NS Vol 51 is for 1943 (not listed on the chart because of space limitation). Subsequent volumes bear only the year, not volume numbers, and so have no place on the chart.

Philo Vols 47–96 are also called Neue Folge 1–50.

RB The numbers listed for volume numbers are année numbers. Listed concurrently with them are série listings (11 in all) which are too various to be conveniently included here.

RCHL The numbers listed for volume numbers are année numbers. Beginning with a Nouvelle série in 1876 there are also tome numbers assigned per année. Thus, année 10 (1876) contains tomes 1 and 2, année 11 (1877) contains tomes 3 and 4, etc. An exception is tome 7 for 1878 (not the expected 1879). Beginning with tome 85 (année 52, 1918) there is just one tome number per année number until the suspension of the journal in 1935.

RevP Revue de philologie française et de littérature, (Cledat) Paris. Vols 1 and 2 were called Revue des patois; vols 3–10 were called Revue de philologie française et provençale. Vols 1–19 are called tomes; from vol 20 on most are called années. There are, however, many exceptions: années 31–33 (1917–19) are comprehended in tomes 30 and 31; années 34 and 35 (1920–21) have no tome listing on the title page, but the running titles at the bottom of the pages of text give 32 and 33 respectively; années 36, 37, and 38 (1922–24) are all listed as Premier fascicule, have no année numbers on the title page, but are given tome numbers 34, 35, and 36 respectively; année 42 (1928) is also called tome 40 and Premier fascicule; année 44 (1930) is also called tome 42; année 45 (1931) is also called tome 43; année 46 (1932) has no année number on the title page, just tome 44; the next volume is called année 1933 and tome 46, with no année number given. In the chart volumes have been listed consistently by années even though several volumes do not have an année number. Another, different periodical with a similar title is Revue de philologie, de littérature, et d'histoire anciennes, Paris, which appeared in three

series, beginning in 1845 and running to the present.

RG Revue germanique; Allemagne, Angleterre, États-Unis, Pays-Bas, Scandinavie (issued under the auspices of the universities of Lille, Lyons, and Nancy). Three other periodicals have similar titles. The first is Revue moderne, Paris, beginning in 1858 and running for 55 volumes, of which vols 1–13 were called Revue germanique, vols 14–18 were called Revue germanique, française, et étrangère, and vols 19–32 were called Revue germanique et française. The second is Revue germanique, Strasbourg, in four volumes beginning in 1823 (vols 1 and 2 were called Bibliothèque allemande). The third is Revue germanique, Paris, Strasbourg, in three series, 40 volumes, beginning in 1829 (the first two series were called Nouvelle revue germanique).

RLR Vols 9–14 are also called 2s vols 1–6; vols 15–30, also 3s vols 1–16; vols 31–40, also 4s vols 1–10; vols 41–50, also 5s vols 1–10; vols 51–60, also 6s vols 1–10; vols 61–68, also 7s vols 1–8. Vol 12 is mismarked Deuxième série, tome troisième.

SA Vols 1–4 were published as Northern Notes and Queries. Properly there is no vol 2. In the preface to vol 1 the editors write, "Since they survived a second year, they think it best to make the age of the work and the number of the volumes coincide and have given a Title-page and Index for Vols. I and II (combined)." Thus, vol 1, nos 1–8, covers June 1886 to March 1888; vol 3 covers June 1888 to March 1889.

Scrut Vol 20 is a retrospect, index, and errata and has no date in the same respect as the other volumes. The publisher's date here is 1963.

ShJ Vols 1–60 were called Jahrbuch der deutschen Shakespeare-Gesellschaft. Vols 59 and 60 are also called Neue Folge 1; vols 61–83, also Neue Folge 2–24.

SWR Vols 1–9 were called Texas Review.

Sym This journal, subtitled A Journal Devoted to Modern Languages and Literatures, published by the Romance Language Dept of Syracuse University, is not to be confused with other journals bearing the same title.

Texas SE The journal stops numbering volumes after vol 17 for 1937. It uses a code applied to all Texas University bulletins, the first two digits showing the year of issue and the last two showing the position in the yearly series (thus, no 3806 is the 6th publication in 1938).

UKCR Vols 1–9 were called University Review.

UTM Entitled University Monthly from Nov 1907 to Nov 1918. Vol 13, nos 4–9, vol 14, and vol 15, no 1, are incorrectly numbered vol 14, 15, 16 respectively. Issues from Dec 1918 to Nov 1919 lack volume numbers.

WMQ ls Vols 1 and 2 were called William and Mary College Quarterly: Historical Papers.

WR The full title is Western Review and Miscellaneous Magazine. Subtitled A Monthly Publication Devoted to Literature and Science, and published in Lexington, Ky, it is to be distinguished from other Western Reviews. The best known of these is subtitled The Fraternal Magazine and is published in Chicago. Two others have no subtitle and are published in Columbus and Cincinnati.

ZfDA Vols 13–68 are also called Neue Folge 1–56. Vol 53 has no Neue Folge number, but it should be 41 since the volume before is 40 and the volume after is 42.

I. ROMANCES

GENERAL

by

Helaine Newstead

COLLECTIONS OF TEXTS, ABSTRACTS, MODERNIZATIONS.

Ritson J, Ancient English Metrical Romances, 3 vols, London 1802; rvsd E Goldsmid, Edinburgh 1884.

Ellis G, Specimens of Early English Metrical Romances, 3 vols, London 1805; rvsd J O Halliwell[-Phillips], 1 vol, Bohn edn 1848.

Weber H W, Metrical Romances of the 13th, 14th, and 15th Centuries, 3 vols, Edinburgh 1810.

Utterson E V, Select Pieces of Early English Popular Poetry, 2 vols, London 1817.

Laing D, Select Romances of the Ancient Popular Poetry of Scotland, London 1822; rvsd J Small, 1885.

Laing D, Early Metrical Tales, London 1826; rptd 1889.

Thoms W J, A Collection of Early Prose Romances, 3 vols, London 1828; rvsd H Morley et al, 1907.

Hartshorne C H, Ancient Metrical Tales, London 1829.

Madden F, Syr Gawayne, Bannatyne Club, London 1839.

Robson J, Three Early English Metrical Romances, Camden Society, London 1842.

Halliwell[-Phillipps] J O, The Thornton Romances, Camden Society, London 1844.

Hazlitt W C, Remains of the Early Popular Poetry of England, 4 vols, London 1864–66.

Furnivall F J and J W Hales, The Percy Folio MS, 4 vols, London 1867–69; re-ed I Gollancz, 4 vols, London 1905–10.

Cox (Sir) G W and E H Jones, Popular Romances of the Middle Ages, London 1871.

Ashton J, Romances of Chivalry, London 1890.

Laing D, Early Popular Poetry of Scotland and the Northern Border; rvsd W C Hazlitt, London 1895.

Weston J L, Sir Cleges, Sir Libeaus Desconus, London 1902.

Buxton E W, Stories of Early England, N Y 1907.

Darton F J H, Wonder Book of Old Romance, London 1907; 7th edn 1931.

Rickert E, Early English Romances in Verse: Romances of Friendship (vol 1), Romances of Love (vol 2), London 1908.

Ebbutt M I, Hero-Myths and Legends, N Y 1910.

Weston J L, Romance, Vision and Satire, Boston 1912.

Hibbard L, Three Middle English Romances, N Y 1911.

McKnight G H, Middle English Humorous Tales in Verse, Boston 1913.

Weston J L, Chief Middle English Poets, Boston 1914.

Krapp G P, Tales of True Knights, N Y 1921.

Barbour H B, Old English Tales Retold, N Y 1928.

French W H and C B Hale, Middle English Metrical Romances, N Y 1930 (crit F P Magoun, Spec 6.483; D Everett, YWES 11.107).

Loomis R S and R Willard, Medieval English Verse and Prose, N Y 1948 (crit B White, MLR 44.387; A C Baugh, Spec 24.128).

Williams M, Glee-Wood, N Y 1949.

Moncrieff A R H, Romance and Legend of Chivalry, London n d.

SPECIAL STUDIES.

Dunlop J, History of Prose Fiction, Edinburgh 1814; rvsd H Wilson 1888.

Wülker R, Übersicht der neuangelsächsischen Sprachdenkmäler, PBBeitr 1.57.

Kittredge G L, The Authorship of the English Romaunt of the Rose, HSNPL 1.

Gautier L, Les épopées françaises, 2nd edn, Paris 1878–97 (crit Rom 22.332; 23.485).

Ten Brink B A K, Early English Literature, English Literature, trans Kennedy et al, London and N Y 1887–92, 1.119, 164, 180, 225, 234, 253, 327, 336.

Ward H L D, Catalogue of Romances in the Department of MSS of the British Museum, 2 vols, London 1883–93.

Herbert J A, Catalogue of Romances in the Department of MSS of the British Museum, London 1910 (vol 3 of Ward's Catalogue).

Morley H, English Writers, London 1890, 3.120, 251, 264, 375.

Veitch J, The Feeling for Nature in Scottish Poetry, 2 vols, Edinburgh 1887.

de Julleville L Petit, Histoire de la langue et de la littérature française, Paris 1896–99, 1.49.

Saintsbury G, The Flourishing of Romance, Edinburgh 1897.

Ker W P, Epic and Romance, London 1897; rptd 1908, 1937.

Gautier L, Bibliographie génerale des chansons de geste, Paris 1897.

Henderson T F, Scottish Vernacular Literature, London 1898.

Billings A H, A Guide to the Middle English Metrical Romances, N Y 1901.

Gröber G, Grundriss der romanischen Philologie, Strassburg 1888–1902, 2¹ Register.

Millar J H, A Literary History of Scotland, London 1903.

Söchtig P, Zur Technik altenglischer Spielmansepen, Leipzig 1903.

Siefkin O, Das geduldige Weib in der englischen Literatur bis auf Shakspere, diss Leipzig 1903.

Nutt A, The Influence of Celtic upon Mediaeval Romance, London 1904.

Mott L F, The System of Courtly Love, London 1904.

Moorman F W, The Interpretation of Nature in English Poetry from Beowulf to Shakespeare, QF 95.58.

Schofield W H, English Literature from the Norman Conquest to Chaucer, N Y 1906, chap 5.

Deutschbein M, Studien zur Sagengeschichte Englands, Cöthen 1906.

Grossmann W, Frühmittelenglische Zeugnisse über Minstrels, Brandenburg 1906.

Kahle R, Der Klerus im mittelenglischen Versroman, Strassburg 1906.

Ward A W and A R Waller, The Cambridge History of English Literature, Cambridge 1907, 1.270.

Edwardes M, A Summary of the Literatures of Modern Europe to 1400, London 1907.

Geissler O, Religion und Aberglaube in der mittelenglischen Versromanzen, Halle 1908.

Ker W P, Romance, Oxford 1909; rptd 1913.

Hübner W, Die Frage in einigen mittelenglischen Versromanen, Kiel 1910 (crit E Borst, EStn 43.264; B Fehr, AnglB 23.308).

Körting G, Grundriss der Geschichte der englischen Literatur von ihren Anfängen bis zur Gegenwart, 5th edn, Münster 1910, p 86.

Jordan R, Die mittelenglischen Mundarten, GRM 2.124.

Lawrence W W, Medieval Story, N Y 1911; 2nd edn 1931 (crit Arch 128.449).

Creek H, Character in the Matter of England Romances, JEGP 10.429, 585.

Voltmer B, Die mittelenglische Terminologie der ritterlichen Verwandschafts- und Standesverhältnisse nach den höfischen Epen und Romanzen des 13 und 14 Jahrhunderts, Kiel 1911.

Borchers K H, Die Jagd in den mittelenglischen Romanzen, Kiel 1912.

Witter E, Das bürgerliche Leben im mittelenglischen Versroman, Kiel 1912.

Esdaile A, A List of English Tales and Prose Romances Printed before 1740, London 1912.

Dixon W M, English Epic and Heroic Poetry, London 1912.

Ker W P, Medieval English Literature, Oxford 1912.

Spence L, A Dictionary of Mediaeval Romance and Romance Writers, London 1913.

Paris G B P, La littérature française au moyen âge, 4th edn, Paris 1909, § 18.

Deters F, Die englischen Angriffswaffen zur Zeit der Einführung der Feuerwaffen (1300–1350), AF 38, 1913.

Lausterer P, Der syntaktische Gebrauch des Artikels in den älteren mittelenglischen Romanzen, Kiel 1914.

Curry W C, The Mediaeval Ideal of Personal Beauty in Metrical Romances, Legends, Chronicles, Baltimore 1916.

Willson E, Middle English Legends of Visits to the Other World and Their Relation to the Metrical Romances, Chicago 1917.

Curry W C, Middle English "brent brows," MLN 33.180.

Luick K, Über die Betonung der englischen Lehnwörter im Mittelenglischen, GRM 9.14.

Flasdieck H, Der sprachgeschichtliche Wert der mittelenglischen Überlieferung, GRM 11.361.

Crane R S, The Vogue of Medieval Chivalric Romances during the English Renaissance, Menasha Wisc 1919.

Wedel T, The Mediaeval Attitude toward Astrology, YSE 60.100.

Leach H G, Angevin Britain and Scandinavia, Cambridge Mass 1921 (crit S B Liljegren, AnglB 34.172; H Larsen, JEGP 22.147.)

Prothero R E (Baron Ernle), The Light Reading of Our Ancestors, London 1921.

Ashdown M, Single Combat in English and Scandinavian Tradition and Romance, MLR 17.113.

Funke O, Die Fügung "ginnen" mit dem Infinitiv im Mittelenglischen, EStn 56.1.

McKeehan I P, Some Relationships between the Legends of British Saints and the Medieval Romances, Univ of Chicago Abstr of Theses, Humanistic Series 2, 1923–24, p 381.

Bruce J D, The Evolution of Arthurian Romance, 2 vols, Göttingen and Baltimore 1923; 2nd edn 1928, suppl by A Hilka.

Griffin N E, A Definition of Romance, PMLA 38.50.

Bédier J and P Hazard, Histoire de la littérature française illustrée, Paris 1923, 1.15 (crit E Hoepffner, Rom 51.133).

Hibbard L, Mediaeval Romance in England, N Y 1924 (crit H R Patch, JEGP 25.108; J M Manly, MP 24.122).

Baker E A, History of the English Novel, vol 1, London 1924.

Barrow S F, The Medieval Society Romances, N Y 1924 (crit E V Gordon, YWES 5.92).

Brunner K, Romanzen und Volksballaden, Palaes 148.75.

Holthausen F, Zur Textkritik mittelenglischen Romanzen, Luick Festgabe, Marburg 1925.

Patch H R, Chaucer and Medieval Romance, Essays in Memory of Barrett Wendell, Cambridge Mass 1926, p 95.

Serjeantson M S, The Dialects of the West Midlands in Middle English, 2, Assignment of Texts, RES 3.319 (crit D Everett, YWES 8.128).

Cristensen P A, Beginnings and Endings of the Middle English Metrical Romances, Stanford Univ Abstr of Diss 2.105.

Schlauch M, Chaucer's Constance and Accused Queens, N Y 1927.

Prestage E, ed, Chivalry, A Series of Studies to Illustrate Its Historical Significance and Civilizing Influence, London 1928.

Thomas W, The Epic Cycles of Medieval England and Their Relative Importance, FQ 10.193.

Harris A E, The Heroine of the Middle English Romances, Western Reserve Univ Bull 31.4.

Walker E, Der Monolog im höfischen Epos, Stuttgart 1928.

Saintsbury G, Romance, Enc Brit, 14th edn, 19.424.

Everett D, A Characterization of the English Medieval Romances, E&S 15.98 (crit M Daunt, YWES 11.126).

Hoops R, Der Begriff "Romance" in der mittelenglischen und frühneuenglischen Literatur, AF 68 (crit K Brunner, Arch 159.107).

Weston J L, Legendary Cycles of the Middle Ages, Cambridge Medieval History, vol 6, Cambridge 1929.

Stoker R C, Geographical Lore in the Middle English Metrical Romances, Stanford Univ Abstr of Diss 4.43.

Taylor A B, An Introduction to Mediaeval Romance, London 1930 (crit D Everett, YWES 11.108).

Oakden J P, Alliterative Poetry in Middle English, 2 vols, Manchester 1930, 1935 (Part I rptd as Poetry of the Alliterative Revival, Manchester 1937).

Wilcox J, Defining Courtly Love, Papers of the Michigan Acad of Science, Arts, and Letters 12.313.

Heather P J, Precious Stones in Middle English Verse, Folklore 42.217.

Dupin H, La courtoisie au moyen âge, Paris 1931 (crit J Lods, Rom 58.156).

Baldwin C S, Three Medieval Centuries of Literature in England 1100–1400, Boston 1932 (crit D Everett, YWES 13.125).

Wilcox J, French Courtly Love in English Composite Romances, Papers of the Michigan Acad of Science, Arts, and Letters 18.575.

Eagleson H, Costume in the Middle English Metrical Romances, PMLA 47.339.

Thompson S, Motif-Index of Folk Literature, Bloomington Indiana 1932 (crit J J Parry, JEGP 34.593; A T[aylor], MP 32.439).

Koziol H, Zur Frage der Verfasserschaft einiger mittelenglischer Stabreimdichtungen, EStn 67.165.

Koziol H, Grundzüge der Syntax der mittelenglischen Stabreimdichtungen, WBEP 58 (crit A Dekker, Neophil 20.36; W Franz, DLz 54.1606).

Trounce A M, The English Tail-Rhyme Romances, MÆ 1.87, 168; 2.34, 189; 3.30 (crit D Everett, MÆ 7.29).

Taylor G, Notes on Athelston, Leeds SE 3.29; 4.47 (crit of Trounce, above).

Reinhard J R, The Survival of Geis in Mediaeval Romance, Halle 1933 (crit T M Chotzen, Museum 41.199).

Lippmann K, Das ritterliche Persönlichkeitsideal in der mittelenglischen Literatur des 13 und 14 Jahrhunders, Leipzig 1933 (crit R Hoops, AnglB 46.201).

Tuve R, Seasons and Months: Studies in a Tradition of Middle English Poetry, Paris 1933.

Whiting B J, Proverbs in Certain Middle English Romances in Relation to Their French Sources, HSNPL 15.75.

McKeehan I P, The Book of the Nativity of St Cuthbert, PMLA 48.981.

Vigneras L A and S Painter, Monday as a Day for Tournaments, MLN 48.80, 82.

Schlauch M, Romance in Iceland, N Y 1934 (crit F P Magoun, Spec 11.151; R Beck, JEGP 34.579).

Smith J M, The French Background of Middle Scots Literature, London and Edinburgh

1934 (crit R L G Ritchie, MÆ 4.44; K Brunner, AnglB 45.265).

Lewis C S, The Allegory of Love, Oxford 1936; rptd 1938.

Crosby R, Oral Delivery in the Middle Ages, Spec 11.88.

Kelly A, Eleanor of Aquitaine and Her Courts of Love, Spec 12.3.

Baker Sister I, The King's Household in the Arthurian Court from Geoffrey of Monmouth to Malory, diss Catholic Univ of America, Washington 1937.

Brie F, Die nationale Literatur Schottlands von den Anfänger bis zur Renaissance, Halle 1937.

Basilius H A, The Rhymes in Eger and Grime, MP 35.129.

Coulton G G, Mediaeval Panorama, Cambridge 1938.

Smithers G V, Notes on Middle English Texts, LMS 1.208.

West C B, Courtoisie in Anglo-Norman Literature, Oxford 1938 (crit G V Smithers, RES 15.471; H R Patch, Spec 13.479).

Van de Voort D, Love and Marriage in the English Medieval Romances, Nashville 1938.

Riedel F C, Crime and Punishment in the Old French Romances, N Y 1939 (crit E A Francis, MÆ 10.34).

Ackerman R W, Armour and Weapons in the Middle English Romances, Research Studies of the State College of Washington 7.104.

Fisher F, Narrative Art in Medieval Romances, Cleveland 1939.

Loomis R S, Chivalric and Dramatic Imitations of Arthurian Romance, Mediaeval Studies in Memory of A K Porter, Cambridge Mass 1939, 1.79.

Wilson R M, Early Middle English Literature, London 1939 (crit D Everett, MÆ 10.47; A C Baugh, MLN 56.218).

Wright C E, The Cultivation of Saga in Anglo-Saxon England, Edinburgh 1939.

Doutrepont G, Les mises en prose des épopées et des romans chevaleresques du 14e au 15e siècle, Brussels 1939.

Painter S, French Chivalry, Baltimore 1940 (crit R Kilgour, Spec 16.254).

Hatto A T, Archery and Chivalry: A Noble Prejudice, MLR 35.40.

Webster K G T, Galloway and the Romances, MLN 55.363.

Parry J J, trans, The Art of Courtly Love by Andreas Capellanus, N Y 1941 (crit M B Ogle, JEGP 41.372; T A Kirby, MLQ [Wash] 3.119).

Ackerman R W, "Dub" in the Middle English

Romances, Research Studies of the State College of Washington 9.109.

Brunner K, Der Inhalt der mittelenglischen Handschriften und die Literaturgeschichte, Angl 65.81; Die Überlieferung der mittelenglischen Versromanzen, Angl 76.66.

Dunlap A R, The Vocabulary of the Middle English Romances in Tail-Rhyme Stanza, Delaware Notes 14.1 (crit G Willcock, YWES 23.81).

Wilmotte M, Origines du roman en France, l'évolution du sentiment romanesque jusqu'en 1240, Paris 1941 (crit P de Poerck, Revue belge 33.340).

Norbert Mother M, The Reflection of Religion in English Medieval Verse Romances, Bryn Mawr 1941.

Reinhard J R, Setting Adrift in Mediaeval Law and Literature, PMLA 56.33.

Reinhard J R, Burning at the Stake in Mediaeval Law and Literature, Spec 16.186.

Olson C C, The Minstrels at the Court of Edward III, PMLA 56.601.

Loomis L H, The Auchinleck MS and a Possible London Bookshop, PMLA 57.595.

Frappier J, Les romans courtois, Paris 1943.

Hughes M J, Women Healers in Medieval Life and Literature, N Y 1943.

Cohen G, La grande clarté du moyen-âge, 4th edn, Paris [1945]; rvsd and corrected, N Y 1943 (crit B Woledge, FS 1.261).

Levy H, As myn auctor seyth, MAE 12.25.

Ackerman R W, The Knighting Ceremonies in the Middle English Romances, Spec 19.285.

Bezzola R R, Les origines et la formation de la littérature courtoise en occident, 500–1200, Paris 1944 (crit R N Walpole, RomP 1.257; E H Kantorowicz, CL 1.84; A J Denomy, Spec 23.114).

Dinkins P, Human Relationships in the Middle English Romances, Bull of Vanderbilt Univ, Abstr of Theses 45, no 11, p 13.

Cline R, The Influence of Romances upon Tournaments of the Middle Ages, Spec 20.204.

French W H, Dialects and Forms in Three Romances, JEGP 45.125.

Chambers E K, English Literature at the Close of the Middle Ages, Oxford 1945; 2nd edn 1947 (crit B White, MLR 41.426; L H Loomis, MLQ [Wash] 8.496; A C Baugh, JEGP 46.304).

Denomy A J, The Heresy of Courtly Love, N Y 1947.

Gist M A, Love and War in the Middle English Romances, Phila 1947 (crit R M Wilson, MLR 43.523; R W Ackerman, JEGP 47.295).

Sherwood M M, Magic and Mechanics in Medieval Fiction, SP 44.567.

Bezzola R R, Le sens de l'aventure et de l'amour, Paris 1947 (crit J Misrahi, RomP 4.348; W A Nitze, Spec 23.290; T Silverstein, MP 46.63).

Mathew G, Marriage and Amour Courtois in Late Fourteenth-Century England, Essays Presented to Charles Williams, Oxford 1947, p 132.

Baugh A C, A Literary History of England, N Y 1948, p 165.

Curtius E R, Europaïsche Literatur und lateinisches Mittelalter, Bern 1948 (crit E Auerback, RF 62.239, MLN 65.348; L Spitzer, AJP 70.425).

Hatzfeld H, Esthetic Criticism Applied to Medieval Romance Literature, RomP 1.305.

Castelnau J, La vie au moyen âge d'après les contemporains, Paris 1949.

Lanham M, Chastity: A Study of Sexual Morality in the English Medieval Romances, Bull of Vanderbilt Univ, Abstr of Theses 48, no 11, p 8.

Silverstein T, Andreas, Plato, and the Arabs: Remarks on Some Recent Accounts of Courtly Love, MP 47.117.

Patch H R, The Adaptation of Otherworld Motifs to Medieval Romance, Philologica, Baltimore 1949, p 115.

Cohen G, La vie littéraire en France au moyen âge, Paris 1949.

Patch H R, The Other World According to Descriptions in Medieval Literature, Cambridge Mass 1950 (crit M R Malkiel, RomP 8.52; R J Dean, RomR 42.150; C S L[ewis], MÆ 20.91).

Loomis R S, Breton Folklore and Arthurian Romance, CL 2.289.

Baugh A C, The Authorship of the Middle English Romances, MHRA 22, 1950.

Salinger G, Was the Futuwa an Oriental Form of Chivalry? PAPS 94.481.

Springer O, The "âne stegreif" Motif in Medieval Literature, GR 25.163.

Kane G, Middle English Literature: A Critical Study of the Romances, the Religious Lyrics, Piers Plowman, London 1951 (crit J R Hulbert, MP 49.205; J Lawlor, MLR 47.214).

Schoeck R J, Andreas Capellanus and St Bernard of Clairvaux: The Twelve Rules of Love and the Twelve Steps of Humility, MLN 66.295.

Bliss A J, Notes on the Auchinleck Manuscript, Spec 26.652.

Micha A, Le mari jaloux dans la littérature romanesque des 12e et 13e siècles, Studi medievali 17.303.

Bernheimer R, Wild Men in the Middle Ages, Cambridge Mass 1952.

Wilson R M, The Lost Literature of Medieval England, London 1952, p 114 (crit D Everett, MÆ 22.31).

Owings M A, The Arts in the Middle English Romances, N Y 1952 (crit C C Olson, MP 50.226).

Cohen G, La poésie en France au moyen âge, Paris 1952.

Auerback E, Mimesis, trans W Trask, Princeton 1953.

Southern R W, The Making of the Middle Ages, London 1953, p 219.

Muscatine C, The Emergence of Psychological Allegory in Old French Romance, PMLA 68.1160.

Reinhold H, Humoristische Tendenzen in der englischen Dichtung des Mittelalters, Tübingen 1953.

de Boer H, Die höfische Literatur: Vorbereitung, Blüte, Ausklang 1170–1250, Munich 1953 (crit M Wehrli, AFDA 67.93).

Baugh A C, Improvisation in the Middle English Romance, PAPS 103.418.

GENERAL AND TANGENTIAL STUDIES.

Listed below are general works and special studies which touch upon the romance as well as other Middle English writings—studies, for instance, in linguistics, versification, etc. Since it has not been possible to cite all these general and tangential works under each separate romance, the reader is advised to consult them as may seem necessary.

Bibliographical Aids. Booker J M, A Middle English Bibliography, Heidelberg 1912.

Chauvin V, Bibliographie des ouvrages arabes, 12 vols, Liège 1892–1922.

Pollard A W and G R Redgrave, A Short-Title Catalogue of Books Printed in England, Scotland, and Ireland and of English Books Printed Abroad 1475–1640, London 1926.

Edmonds C K, Huntington Library Bulletin, Supplement to the preceding item.

Kennedy A G, A Bibliography of Writings on the English Language, Cambridge Mass 1927.

Tucker L L and A R Benham, A Bibliography of Fifteenth-Century Literature, Seattle 1928.

de Ricci S and W J Wilson, Census of Medieval and Renaissance Manuscripts in the United States of America and Canada, vols 1–3, N Y 1935, 1937, 1940.

Renwick W L and H Orton, The Beginnings of

English Literature to Skelton 1509, London 1939; rvsd edn 1952.

Bateson F W, Cambridge Bibliography of English Literature, vol 1, London and N Y 1941; vol 5 (supplement), ed G Watson, 1957.

Brown C and R H Robbins, The Index of Middle English Verse, N Y 1943 (crit C F Bühler, PBSA 37.161; TLS Aug 21 1943, p 408; F L Utley, Spec 20.105).

Chambers E K, English Literature at the Close of the Middle Ages, Oxford 1945.

Farrar C P and A P Evans, Bibliography of Translations from Medieval Sources, N Y 1946 (crit E A Quain, Thought 21.698; P Boehner, Franciscan 7.99).

Bennett H S, Chaucer and the Fifteenth Century, Oxford 1947.

Cabeen D C, Critical Bibliography of French Literature, vol 1 (the Medieval Period), ed U T Holmes jr, Syracuse N Y 1949.

Bossuat R, Manuel bibliographique de la littérature française du moyen âge, Paris 1951; supplément 1955.

Williams H F, An Index of Mediaeval Studies Published in Festschriften, 1865–1946, with Special Reference to Romanic Material, Berkeley Calif 1951.

Ogden M S, C E Palmer, R L McKelvey, Middle English Dictionary: Bibliography [of ME texts], Ann Arbor Mich 1954, p 15.

Mummendey R, Language and Literature of the Anglo-Saxon Nations as Presented in German Doctoral Dissertations 1885–1950, PBSUV, Bonn 1954 (crit C D V Curtis, MLQ 16.281; M Baacke, JEGP 55.286; H M Flasieck, Angl 73.365; G Jacob, Arch 191.36).

Woledge B, Bibliographie des romans et nouvelles en prose française antérieurs à 1500, Société de publications romanes et françaises 42, Geneva 1954, MÆ 24.51.

Taylor H O, The Emergence of Christian Culture in the West (olim The Classical Heritage of the Middle Ages), Harper Torchbooks, N Y 1958.

Greenfield S B, Bibliography, in D M Zesmer, Guide to English Literature, N Y 1961.

Special Problems. Grässe J G T, Lehrbuch einer Literärgeschichte, Dresden and Leipzig 1842.

Sachs C, Beiträge zur Kunde altfranzösischer, englischer, und provenzalischer Literatur, Berlin 1857.

Child F J, The English and Scottish Popular Ballads, 5 vols, Boston Mass 1882–98.

Einenkel E, Streifzüge durch die me Syntax, Münster 1887.

Wilda O, Über die ortliche Verbreitung der zwölfzeiligen Schweifreimstrophe in Englische, Breslau 1887.

Hein J, Ueber die bildliche Verneinung in der me Poesie, Halle 1893, Angl 3 (pp 155, 220, bibl, dialect).

Willms J E, Eine Untersuchung über den Gebrauch der Farbenbezeichnungen in der Poesie Altenglands, Münster 1902.

Kaluza M, Strophische Gliederung in der me rein alliterierenden Dichtung, EStn 16.174 (crit M Day, EStn 66.245).

Potter M A, Sohrab and Rustum, London 1902.

Hoelvelmann K, Konsonantismus der altfranzösischen Lehnwörter in der me Dichtung, Kiel 1903.

Trautmann M, Zur alt- und mittelenglischen Verslehre, AnglA 5.111.

Menthel E, Zur Geschichte des Otfridischen Verses im Englischen, AnglA 8.69.

Pilch L, Umwandlung des altenglischen Alliterationsverses in den me Reimvers, Königsberg 1904.

Heuser W, Die me Entwicklung von ŭ in offener Silbe, EStn 27.391.

Ausbüttel E, Das persönliche Geschlecht unpersönlicher Substantiva, Halle 1904.

Greenlaw E A, The Vows of Baldwin: A Study in Medieval Fiction, PMLA 21.575.

Strong C, History and Relations of the Tail-Rhyme, PMLA 22.408.

Gaaf W, The Transition from the Impersonal to the Personal Construction in ME, AF 14.

Pschmadt C, Die Sage von der verfolgte Hunde, Greifswald 1911.

Leonard W E, Scansion of ME Alliterative Verse, Univ of Wisconsin Studies in Lang and Lit 11.

Jacobius H, Die Erziehung des Edelfräuleins im alten Frankreich, ZfRP Beiheft 16.

Bolte J and G Polivka, Anmerkungen zu den Kinder- und Hausmärchen der Brüder Grimm, 5 vols, Leipzig 1913–31.

Baldwin C S, Introduction to English Medieval Literature, N Y 1914; Three Medieval Centuries of Literature, Boston 1932.

Kennedy A G, Pronoun of Address in the 13th Century, Stanford Univ Publications, Univ Ser 20.

Bousset W, Die Geschichte eines Wiedererkennungemärchen, Nachrichten von der König Gesellschaft zu Göttingen, Philol hist Kl 1916, p 469; 1917, p 703.

Stidston R D, The Use of Ye in the Function of Thou in ME Literature from MS Auchinleck to MS Vernon, Stanford Univ Publications, Univ Ser 28, Stanford 1917.

Funke O, Zur Wortgeschichte der französischen Elemente im Englischen, EStn 55.7.

Holzknecht K J, Literary Patronage in the Middle Ages, Menasha Wisc 1923 (crit G G Coulton, MLR 20.478; E Fischer, AnglB 36.102).

Weaver C P, The Hermit in English Literature from the Beginnings to 1660, Nashville Tenn 1924.

Jordan R, Handbuch der me Grammatik, Heidelberg 1925.

Hecht H and L L Schücking, Englische Literatur im Mittelalter, Potsdam 1927.

Patch H S, The Goddess Fortuna in Medieval Literature, Cambridge Mass 1927.

Häusermann H W, Studien zu den Aktionsarten im Frühmittelenglischen, WBEP 54.

Swain B, Fools and Folly during the Middle Ages and the Renaissance, N Y 1932.

Döll H, Mittelenglischen Kleidernamen im Spiegel literarischen Denkmäler des 14 Jahrhunderts, Giessen 1932.

Fettig A, Die Gradadverbien im Mittelenglischen, Heidelberg 1934.

Smith M F, Wisdom and Personification of Wisdom Occurring in ME Literature before 1500, Washington D C 1935.

Ohlander W, Studies in Coordinate Expressions in ME, Lund Studies in English 5, Lund 1936.

Serjeantson M S, A History of Foreign Words in English, N Y 1936.

West V R, Der etymologische Ursprung der neuenglischen Lautgruppe /sk/, AF 83.

Kaiser R, Zur Geographie der me Wortschatze, Palaes 205, Leipzig 1937.

Wyler S, Die Adjectiv des me Schönheitsfeldes unter besonderer Berücksichtigung Chaucers, Zürich 1944.

Bennett H S, Medieval English MSS and Contemporary Taste, Edinb Bibl Soc Transactions 2.382 (on Harley 2253, BM Addit MS 31042, Camb Ff. 2.38; Lincoln 91 A.5.2); The Production and Dissemination of Vernacular MSS in the Fifteenth Century, Libr 5s 1, nos. 3, 4, p 167 (analysis of romance MS production starting with 12th century); Printers, Authors, and Readers, 1475–1557, Libr. 5s 4.157; Notes on English Retail Book Prices, 1480–1560, Libr 5s 5; English Books and Readers 1475–1557, N Y and London 1952.

Closs H M, Courtly Love in Literature and Art, Symposium 1, no 3, p 5.

Price H T, Foreign Influence on ME, Univ of Michigan Contributions in Modern Philology 10.

Purdy R R, The Friendship Motif in ME Literature, Vanderbilt Studies in the Humanities 1.

Rynell A, Rivalry of Scandinavian and Native Synonyms, Lund Studies in English 13.

Forsström G, The Verb To Be in ME, Lund Studies in English 15.

Girvan R, The Medieval Poet and His Public, English Essays Today, ed C L Wrenn and G Bullough, London 1951.

Cross T P, Motif-Index of Early Irish Literature, Bloomington Ind 1952.

Ellegård A, The Auxiliary Do, Gothenburg Studies in English 2, Stockholm 1953.

Karlberg G, The English Interrogative Pronouns, Gothenburg Studies in English 3, Stockholm 1954.

O'Dell S, A Chronological List of Prose Fiction in England 1475–1640, Cambridge Mass 1954.

Moore A K, Sir Thopas as Criticism of Fourteenth-Century Minstrelsy, JEGP 53.532 (crit J Bazire, YWES 35.62).

Everett D, Essays on ME Literature, Oxford 1955.

Enkvist N E, The Seasons of the Year: Chapters on a Motif from Beowulf to the Shepherd's Calendar, Copenhagen 1957 (Commentationes Humanarum Litterarum 22, no 4, Helsingfors 1957).

Mustanoja T F, ME Syntax, Mémoires de la Soc néophilologique de Helsinki 23.

1. ROMANCES DERIVED FROM ENGLISH LEGENDS

by

Charles W. Dunn

GENERAL.

Hardy (Sir) T D and C T Martin, Lestorie des Engles, Rolls Series no 91, 1.349; G Noack, Sagehistorische Untersuchungen zu den Gesta Herewardi, Halle 1914 (Hereward).

Wülfing J E, Laud Troy Book, EETS 121.1.

Deutschbein M, Studien zur Sagengeschichte Englands, Cöthen 1906, p 235 (crit A Stimming, DLz 27.1578; H Suchier, LZ 57.1276; J Vising, Krit Jahresber 10².113; G Binz, AnglB 18.1; W Golther, LfGRP 28.280; W P Ker, MLR 2.176; R C Boer, Museum: Maandblad voor Philologie 15.55).

Schofield, p 258.

CHEL, 1.242.

Imelmann R, J Bramis' Historia regis Waldef, BSEP 4 (crit A Brandl, Arch 128.401; reply, Imelmann, EStn 53.362).

Leach H G, Angevin Britain and Scandinavia, Cambridge Mass 1921, p 234.

Hibbard Med Rom, pp iii, 81, and passim (exhaustive).

Wilson R M, Lost Literature in Old and ME, Leeds SE 2.14; More Lost Literature, Leeds SE 5.17; Early ME Literature, London 1939, 1951, pp 21, 76, 85, 196, 199, 215, 290, 293, 294, 295; Lost Literature of Medieval England, London 1952, pp 27, 123, 132, 243.

de Lange J, Relation and Development of English and Icelandic Outlaw-Traditions, Nederlandsche Bijdragen op het Gebied van germaansche Philologie en Linguistiek 6.

Wright C E, Cultivation of Saga in Anglo-Saxon England, Edinburgh and London 1939, p 31.

Loomis L H, Sir Thopas, Bryan-Dempster, p 490.

Baugh A C, Improvisation in the ME Romance, PAPS 103.418.

Legge M D, Anglo-Norman Literature and Its Background, Oxford 1963.

[1] KING HORN.

MSS. 1, Bodl 1486 (Laud Misc 108), ff 219^b–228^a (ca 1300); 2, Camb Univ Gg. 4.27 (II), ff 6^a–13^a (ca 1260–1300); 3, Harley 2253, ff 83^a–92^b (ca 1325).

Brown-Robbins, no 166; MED, pp 12, 44.

Wright T, Specimens of Lyric Poetry, Early English Poetry 4, Percy Soc 4, London 1842, p v (Harley).

Horstmann C, Legenden des MS Laud 108, Arch 49.395; AELeg 1875, p x.

Ward, 1.447 (Harley).

Manly & Rickert, 1.178 (Camb Univ).

Brunner K, ME Metrical Romances and Their Audience, Studies in Medieval Literature in Honor of A C Baugh, Phila 1961, p 220.

Editions. Ritson AEMR, 2.91; 3.221, 439.

Michel F, Horn et Rimenhild, Bannatyne Club, Paris 1845, p 259.

Lumby J R, King Horn, EETS 14, London 1866 (crit F H Stratmann, EStn 3.270); re-ed G H McKnight, EETS 14, London 1901 (crit anon, Athen 1902².822).

AESpr, 1¹.209.

Horstmann C, King Horn nach ME Laud 108, Arch 50.39.

Wissmann T, King Horn: Untersuchungen, QF 16, Strassburg 1876 (introd) (crit A Stimming, EStn 1.351; J Zupitza, AfDA 4.149); Das Lied von King Horn, QF 45, Strassburg 1881 (edn) (crit J Koch, JEGGP 3.213; F H Stratmann, EStn 5.408; E Hausknecht, DLz 3³¹.1114; A Brandl, LfGRP 4⁴.132; B ten Brink, EStn 6.150; E Kölbing, EStn 6.153; R Wülcker, LZ 1883².61; J Zupitza, AfDA 9.181); Studien zu King Horn, Angl 4.342 (suppl) (crit J Koch, JEGGP 3.213; E Kölbing, EStn 5.287).

Hall J, King Horn, Oxford 1901 (crit anon, Athen 1902².822; O Hartenstein, EStn 31.281; W Dibelius, Arch 113.193).

French W H and C B Hale, ME Metrical Romances, N Y 1930, p 25.

French W H, Essays on King Horn, Cornell Studies in English 30, Ithaca N Y 1940, p 154 (reconstructed text) (crit anon, TLS Jan 25 1941, p 46; D Everett, RES 18.330; M Schlauch, JEGP 41.229).

Selections. Zupitza J, Alt- und mittelenglisches

Uebungsbuch, 5th edn, rvsd J Schipper, Vienna 1897, p 115.

Morris Spec, 2nd edn rvsd, 1.237, 358.

Kluge F, Mittelenglisches Lesebuch, Halle 1904; 2nd edn rvsd 1912, p 67.

Cook A S, Literary ME Reader, Boston Mass 1915, p 11.

Brandl A and O Zippel, Mittelenglische Sprach- und Literaturproben, Berlin 1917; 2nd edn, 1927, p 27.

Sampson G, Cambridge Book of Prose and Verse, Cambridge 1924, p 249.

Mossé F, Manuel de l'anglais du moyen âge 2, Moyen anglais, Paris 1949, 1.203, 2.32; trans J A Walker, Handbook of ME, Baltimore 1952, p 170.

Dickins B and R M Wilson, Early ME Texts, Cambridge 1951; rvsd 1952, p 29.

Kaiser R, Alt- und mittelenglische Anthologie, Berlin 1954 (2nd edn, 1955), p 376; Medieval English, rvsd English edn, Berlin 1958, p 397.

Modernizations and Abstracts. Lindemann H, König Horn, Festschrift zum elften deutschen Neuphilologentage, Cöln 1904, p 111.

Hibbard L A, Three ME Romances, London 1911, p 17.

Weston J L, Chief ME Poets, Cambridge Mass 1914, pp 93, 377.

Tatlock J S P, Modern Reader's King Horn, Univ of Calif Chronicle, Berkeley 1928, 30.1 (also reprint, n p 1928).

Whiting B J et al, College Survey of English Literature, N Y 1942, 1.96.

Textual Notes. Browne W H, MLN 7.267; G Tamson, Angl 19.460.

Language. Ellis A J, Early English Pronunciation, EETSES 7.480.

Thiem C, Das altenglische Gedicht King Horn, Rostock 1874.

Kölbing E, Amis and Amiloun, AEB 2, Heilbronn 1884, p xxxi (dialect).

Breier W, Zur Lokalisierung des King Horn, EStn 42.307 (phonology).

Azzalino W, Wortstellung im King Horn, Halle 1915.

Töpperwien A, Sprache und Heimat des me King Horn, Jahrbuch der philosophischen Fakultät der Georg August-Universität zu Göttingen, historisch-philologische Abteilung, 1921, 1¹.89.

Huchon R, Histoire de la langue anglaise, Paris 1930, 2.174.

Versification. Schipper J, Englische Metrik, Bonn 1881, 1.180 (crit E Einenkel, AnglA 5.47; T Wissmann, LfGRP 3⁴.133; reply, Schipper, EStn 5.488); Zur altenglischen Wortbetonung, AnglA 5.88; Paul Grundriss, 2¹.1039 (2nd edn, 2².201); Grundriss der englischen

Metrik, WBEP 2.71, 88, 112, 145, 146, 270, 271; History of English Versification, Oxford 1910, pp 79, 97, 122, 155, 156, 273.

Wissmann T, Zur me Wortbetonung, Angl 5.466.

Guest E, History of English Rhythms, ed W W Skeat, London 1882, pp 30, 171, 418, 468.

Luick K, Englische Metrik, Paul Grundriss, 2¹.994, 1004, 1007; 2nd edn, 2².154, 158, 166.

Saintsbury G A, History of English Prosody, Oxford 1906, pp 65, 70, 77; Historical Manual of English Prosody, London 1910, rptd 1926, pp 112, 149.

West H S, Versification of King Horn, Baltimore 1907.

Kaluza M, Englische Metrik, Berlin 1909, sections 105, 116, 122, 123, 126, 128, 130, 135, 167, 168; trans A C Dunstan, Short History of English Versification, London 1911, same sections.

Scripture E W, Der Versrhythmus in King Horn, Angl 52.382.

Young (Sir) G, English Prosody on Inductive Lines, Cambridge 1928, p 116.

French, Essays on King Horn (see under *Editions,* above).

Anglo-Norman Version. Michel F, Horn et Rimenhild, Bannatyne Club, Paris 1845; R Brede and E Stengel, Das anglonormannische Lied vom wackern Ritter Horn, AAGRP 8, Marburg 1883; E G W Braunholtz, Cambridge Fragments of the Roman de Horn, MLR 16.23; M K Pope, Romance of Horn by Thomas, Anglo-Norman Texts 9–10, vol 1, Oxford 1955 (crit M S La Du, RomP 10.398; M D Legge, MLR 51.258; W Stokoe, Spec 31.196; W H Trethewey, FS 10.62), Anglo-Norman Texts 12–13, vol 2, Oxford 1964. (Editions.)

Nauss M, Der Stil des anglo-normannischen Horn, Halle 1885.

Söderhjelm W, Sur l'identité du Thomas auteur de Tristan et du Thomas auteur de Horn, Rom 15.575.

Mettlich J, Bemerkungen zu dem Lied vom Ritter Horn, Beilage, Jahresbericht über das Königliche Paulinische Gymnasium zu Münster für 1889–90, Münster 1890 (rptd as diss, Münster 1895) (crit E Kölbing, Krit Jahresber 1.648; J Caro, EStn 16.306).

Freymond E, Krit Jahresber 1.395, 411.

Morsbach L, Die angebliche Originalität des King Horn, Beiträge zur romanischen und englischen Philologie, Festgabe für Wendelin Förster, Halle 1902, p 297 (crit O Hartenstein, EStn 31.281; K Luick, AnglB 13.332).

Vising J, Anglo-Norman Language and Literature, London 1923, pp 46, 61, 84, 85.

Legge M D, Anglo-Norman in the Cloisters, Edinburgh 1950, pp 35, 38, 39; Legge M D, Anglo-Norman Literature, Oxford 1963, pp 15, 49, 96, 106, 117, 145, 149, 155, 156, 367, 370.

Bossuat MBLF, nos 519–524.

Pope M K, The Romance of Horn and King Horn, MÆ 25.164.

Christmann H H, Das Verhältnis zwischen dem anglonormannischen und dem me Horn, ZfFSL 70.166.

Sources. Haigh D H, The Anglo-Saxon Sagas, London 1861, p 62.

Ward, 1.447, 468.

McKnight G H, Germanic Elements in King Horn, PMLA 15.221.

Suchier H and A Birch-Hirschfeld, Geschichte der französischen Litteratur, Leipzig 1900, p 111.

Hartenstein O, Studien zur Hornsage, 1, Heidelberg 1902; (entire) KSEP 4, Heidelberg 1902 (crit H Jantzen, Neue philologische Rundschau 1902, p 549; L Morsbach, DLz 23.2717; H Suchier, LZ 53.1534; J Vising, LfGRP 24.372; M Deutschbein, AnglB 15.333).

Schofield W H, The Story of Horn, PMLA 18.1 (offprint, Baltimore 1903) (crit C S Northup, JEGP 4.540; J Vising, Krit Jahresber 7².89; P Rajna, Rom 34.147).

Deutschbein M, Studien zur Sagengeschichte Englands, Cöthen 1906 (crit A Stimming, DLz 27.1578; H Suchier, LZ 57.1276; J Vising, Krit Jahresber 10².113; G Binz, AnglB 18.1; W Golther, LfGRP 28.280; W P Ker, MLR 2.176; R C Boer, Museum: Maandblad voor Philologie 15.55); Beiträge zur Horn- und Havelocsage, AnglB 20.16, 55.

Heuser W, Horn und Rigmel, Angl 31.105 (crit M Deutschbein, AnglB 20.16, 55; J Vising, Krit Jahresber 12².142).

Grass P, Horn und Hilde in ihrer Stellung zur germanischen Sagengeschichte, Borna-Leipzig 1911.

Peinecke A, Hornstoff und Hornballaden, Marburg 1924 (typescript).

Leidig P, Studien zu King Horn, Leipzig 1927 (crit H L Creek, JEGP 28.286).

Burgevin L G, Origin and Development of the Saga of King Horn, Harvard Univ Summaries of Theses 1931, Cambridge Mass 1932, p 212.

Oliver W, King Horn and Suddene, PMLA 46.102 (crit D Everett, YWES 12.105).

Analogues. J Grimm, Hornkind und Maid Rimenild, Museum für altdeutsche Literatur und Kunst, Berlin 1811, 2.284, 302; rptd Kleinere Schriften, Berlin 1882, 6.41.

Nyrop K, Den oldfranske Heltedigtning, Copenhagen 1883, pp 219, 298, 454; trans E Gorra, Storia dell' epopea francese, Florence 1886, Turin 1888.

Panzer F, Hilde-Gudrun, Halle 1901, pp 266, 278, 283, 302, 305, 307, 308, 320, 322, 418.

Hoyt P C, Home of the Beves Saga, PMLA 17.237.

Björkman E, Nordiska Vikingasagor i England, Nordisk Tidskrift för Vetenskap 1906.450.

Imelmann R, J Bramis' Historia regis Waldef, BSEP 4.xxxii, 1 (Aelof and Horn).

Krappe A H, The Legends of Amicus and Amelius and of King Horn, LB 16.14.

Enc Brit, 14th edn, 11.130, see under Hamlet.

Hofer S, Horn et Rimel, RF 70.278.

Later Tradition. Suchier H, Oeuvres poétiques de Philippe de Remi, SATF, Paris 1884, l.cii, cxi.

Wülfing J E, Laud Troy Book, EETS 121.1, line 21.

Luedicke V, Vorgeschichte und Nachleben des Willehalm von Orlens, Hermaea 8, Halle 1910, pp 128, 176.

Brunner K, Romanzen und Volksballaden, Palaes 148.77.

Loomis L H, Sir Thopas, Bryan-Dempster, pp 495, 501n3.

Rickard P, Britain in Medieval French Literature, Cambridge 1956, pp 125, 128.

Folkloristic and Cultural Details. Gerould G H, Forerunners of the Eustace Legend, PMLA 19.378nl (ring).

Funke O, Zum Verkleidungsmotiv im King Horn, AnglB 31.224.

Thompson Mot Ind, D 1076, D 1344.1, D 1381.7, D 1812.5.1.2, H 94.4, K 1815, K 1817.2, K 1817.3, N 836.1; G Boardman, Motif-Index of the English Metrical Romances, FFC 190.14 and passim.

McKeehan I P, Book of the Nativity of St Cuthbert, PMLA 48.993.

Patch H R, Adaptation of Otherworld Motifs, Philologica: Malone Anniversary Studies, Baltimore 1949, pp 116, 118.

Tatlock J S P, The Legendary History of Britain, Berkeley and Los Angeles 1950, pp 347, 391.

Literary Criticism. Creek H L, Character in the Matter of England Romances, JEGP 10.429, 585.

Everett D, Characterization of the Romances, E&S 15.102, 107, 110, 115, 117 (rptd Essays on ME Literature, ed P Kean, Oxford 1955, pp 5, 9, 12, 16, 19); Laȝamon and the Earliest ME Alliterative Verse, Essays on ME Literature, ed Kean, pp 38, 39.

Schaar C, The Golden Mirror, SUVSL 54.161.

Hill D M, An Interpretation of King Horn, Angl 75.157.
Baugh A C, Improvisation in the ME Romance, PAPS 103.418.

Wright T, Biographia Britannica Literaria, Anglo-Norman Period, London 1846, p 340 (Thomas); Essays on Subjects Connected with the Literature of England, London 1846, 1.101.
Paris P, Trouvères, HLF, 22.551; Körting, 1st edn, 1887, p 95; Ten Brink, 1.150, 227; Morley, 3.265; Wülcker, 1.81, 97.
Paris Litt franç, Paris 1888, pp 48, 249; Mélanges de la littérature française du moyen âge, ed M Roques, Paris 1912, pp 41, 104.
Brandl, Mittelenglische Literatur, Paul Grundriss, 1st edn, 2¹.624; Englische Literatur, Paul Grundriss, 2nd edn, 2¹.1004, 1087n.
Saintsbury G, Flourishing of Romance, Edinburgh 1897; N Y 1907, p 208; Short History of English Literature, London 1898, rptd 1907, p 87; Enc Brit, rptd 14th edn, 19.426, 427, see under Romance.
Northup C S, King Horn, Recent Texts and Studies, JEGP 4.529.
Billings, p 1; Gröber, 2¹.572; Schofield, pp 31, 260, 274; CHEL, 1.242, 319, 324, 334, 337, 344, 520; Sampson G, Concise CHEL, Cambridge 1949, pp 41, 42; Rickert RofL, pp xxvi, xxix, xxxvii.
Leach H G, Angevin Britain and Scandinavia, Cambridge Mass 1921, pp 235, 317, 328.
Hibbard Med Rom, p 83.
Enc Brit, 14th edn, 11.749, see under Horn.
Taylor A B, Introduction to Medieval Romance, London 1930, pp 96, 127, 159, 162, 187, 232, 244.
Legouis HEL, rvsd edn, London 1933, pp 89, 91.
Wilson R M, Lost Literature in Old and ME, Leeds SE 2.15n8, 17; Early ME Literature, London 1939, 1951, pp 15, 76, 198, 215, 218, 220; Lost Literature of Medieval England, London 1952, p 27.
Renwick-Orton, p 336; 2nd edn, p 351.
Wright C E, Cultivation of Saga in Anglo-Saxon England, Edinburgh and London 1939, p 31.
Baugh LHE, pp 141, 175.
Kane, pp 15, 46, 48.
Schlauch M, English Medieval Literature, Warsaw 1956, pp 144, 176, 197.
Speirs J, Medieval English Poetry, London 1957, pp 178, 193, 266n.
Gautier L, Bibliographie des chansons de geste, Paris 1897, pp 129, 258.

CBEL, 1.29, 39, 147; 5.115.
Zesmer D M and S B Greenfield, Guide to English Literature, N Y 1961, pp 110, 227, 249, 336.

[2] HORN CHILD.

MS. Advocates 19.2.1 (Auchinleck), ff 317ᵇ–323ᵇ (ca 1330).
Brown-Robbins, no 2253; MED, pp 11, 46.
Kölbing E, Vier Romanzen-handschriften, EStn 7.190.
Carr M B, Notes on a ME Scribe's Methods, Univ of Wisconsin Studies in Lang and Lit 2.153.
Loomis L H, Auchinleck MS, PMLA 57.595.
Bliss A J, Notes on the Auchinleck MS, Spec 26.653; Sir Orfeo, Oxford 1954, p ix.
Brunner K, ME Metrical Romances and Their Audience, Studies in Medieval Literature in Honor of A C Baugh, Phila 1961, p 224.
Editions. Ritson AEMR, 3.267, 282; rvsd edn, 2.216.
Michel F, Horn et Rimenhild, Bannatype Club, Paris 1845, p 341.
Caro J, Horn Childe and Maiden Rimnild, eine Untersuchung, Breslau 1886; rvsd edn, Kleine Publicationen aus der Auchinleck-HS, EStn 12.323 (crit J Vising, Krit Jahresber 1.378, E Kölbing, Krit Jahresber 1.648).
Hall J, King Horn, Oxford 1901, p 179.
Selections. Brandl A and O Zippel, Mittelenglische Sprach- und Literaturproben, Berlin 1917; 2nd edn, 1927, p 29.
Textual Notes. Holthausen F, Angl 14.309.
Language. Smith A H, Place-Names of the North Riding, English Place-Name Soc 5.129 (Cleveland).
Taylor G, Notes, Leeds SE 4.56.
Dunlap A R, Vocabulary of the ME Romances in Tail-Rhyme, Delaware Notes 14.2, 37 and passim.
Versification. Trounce A McI, English Tail-Rhyme Romances, MÆ 1.87, 168; 2.34, 189; 3.30.
Sources. Lees T, Battle of Stainmoor, Transactions of the Cumberland and Westmorland Antiquarian and Archaeological Soc 5.71; Reycross on Stainmore, Transactions of the Cumb and Westm Ant and Arch Soc 9.448.
Collingwood W G, King Eirík of York, Saga Book of the Viking Soc, London, 2.326; Battle of Stainmoor, Transactions of the Cumb and Westm Ant and Arch Soc ns 2.231.
Casson T E, Horn Childe and the Battle of Stainmoor, Transactions of the Cumb and Westm Ant and Arch Soc ns 37.30 (crit of Lees and Collingwood).

14

Schofield W H, The Story of Horn, PMLA 18.1, 66.

Brunner K, Romanzen und Volksballaden, Palaes 148.75.

See also *Sources, Analogues*, and *Later Tradition*, under KING HORN [1] above.

Relation to Chaucer. Loomis L H, Chaucer and the Auchinleck MS, E&S Brown, p 116; Chaucer and the Breton Lays, SP 38.32; Sir Thopas, Bryan-Dempster, pp 487, 489, 495, 501.

Folkloristic and Cultural Details. Wissmann T, Studien zu King Horn, Angl 4.342.

Kölbing E, Sir Tristrem, Heilbronn 1882, p xxxii.

Easter D B, Study of the Magic Elements in the Romans d'Adventure, Baltimore 1906, pp 33n150, 41n185, 45n191.

Thompson Mot Ind, D 1076, D 1317.5, D 1344.1, H 94, H 1817.1, N 836.1; G Boardman, Motif-Index of the English Metrical Romances, FFC 190.14 and passim.

Literary Criticism. Creek H L, Character in the Matter of England Romances, JEGP 10.449n28.

Everett D, Characterization of the Romances, E&S 15.115, 117 (rptd Essays on ME Literature, ed P Kean, Oxford 1955, pp 16, 19); Note on Ypotis, RES 6.446.

Kane, p 15.

Schaar C, The Golden Mirror, SUVSL 54.161.

Scott (Sir) W, Essay on Romance, Enc Brit, 1st edn, suppl; rptd Miscellaneous Prose Works, Edinburgh, 1827, 6.248, and Essays on Chivalry, Romance and the Drama, London 1887, p 5.

Warton T, History of English Poetry, ed R Price, London 1840, 1.40nu.

Ward, 1.458; Ten Brink, 1.248; Brandl, Mittelenglische Literatur, Paul Grundriss, 1st edn, 2¹.645; Englische Volkspoesie, Paul Grundriss, 2¹.853; Billings, p 12; Schofield, pp 15, 264; CHEL, 1.289, 324; Sampson G, Concise CHEL, Cambridge 1949, p 42.

Leach H G, Angevin Britain and Scandinavia, Cambridge Mass, 1921, pp 328, 331.

Hibbard Med Rom, pp 87, 97.

Wilson R M, Lost Literature in Old and ME, Leeds SE 2.15n8; Early ME Literature, London 1939, 1951, pp 76, 219; Lost Literature of Medieval England, London 1952, p 16.

Renwick-Orton, p 338; 2nd edn, p 353.

Baugh LHE, p 176n9.

Schlauch M, English Medieval Literature, Warsaw 1956, p 177.

CBEL, 1.148.

Zesmer D M and S B Greenfield, Guide to English Literature, N Y 1961, p 111.

[3] BALLAD OF HIND HORN.

Editions. Michel F, Horn et Riemenhild, Bannatyne Club, Paris 1845, pp 393, 395, 399, 407.

Child F J, English and Scottish Popular Ballads, Cambridge Mass 1882, 1.187, 502; 5.210, 287 (no 17); 4.400; 5.277 (no 252); H C Sargent and G L Kittredge, English and Scottish Ballads, Cambridge Mass 1904, p 31.

Dick J C, The Songs of R Burns, London 1903; rptd Hatboro Pa 1962, pp 335, 496 (no 348).

Bronson B H, Traditional Tunes of the Child Ballads, Princeton 1959, 1.254.

Selection. Brandl A and O Zippel, Mittelenglische Sprach- und Literaturproben, Berlin 1917, 2nd edn 1927, p 44.

Horn and Ballad Tradition. Wissmann T, King Horn, Untersuchungen, QF 16.121.

Caro J, Kleine Publicationen aus der Auchinleck-HS, Horn Childe, EStn 12.335.

Hart W M, Ballad and Epic, HSNLP 11.8, 9, 16, 19, 314.

Nelles W C, Ballad of Hind Horn, JAF 22.42.

MacSweeney J J, Hind Horn, MLR 14.210.

Brunner K, Romanzen und Volksballaden, Palaes 148.75, 76.

Gerould G H, Ballad of Tradition, Oxford 1932, pp 44, 146.

Hodgart M J C, The Ballads, London 1950, pp 76, 77.

See also KING HORN [1] above, under *Sources, Analogues*, and *Later Tradition*.

Everett D, Characterization of the Romances, E&S 15.115, 117 (rptd Essays on ME Literature, ed P Kean, Oxford 1955, pp 16, 18).

Speirs J, Medieval English Poetry, London 1957, p 184.

Warton T, History of English Poetry, ed R Price, London 1840, 1.36.

Brandl, Englische Volkspoesie, Paul Grundriss, 2¹.853.

Schofield, p 72.

CHEL, 2.410, 411, 414.

Leach H G, Angevin Britain and Scandinavia, Cambridge Mass 1921, p 329.

Hibbard Med Rom, p 85.

Baugh LHE, p 176n9; CBEL, 1.148.

[4] KING PONTHUS.

MSS. 1, Bodl 1786 (Digby 185), ff 166ᵃ–203ᵃ (ca 1450); 2, Bodl 21959 (Douce 384), ff 1ᵃ–2ᵃ (two fragments) (ca 1450–1500). PRINTS: 3, Wynkyn de Worde, London ca 1505 (fragm, 4 leaves) (STC, no 20107); 4, de Worde, London ca 1510 (fragm, 2 leaves) (STC, no 23435a, erroneously en-

titled Surdit); 5, de Worde, London 1511) (STC, no 20108).
MED, p 66.
Esdaile A, List of English Tales, Pubs of the Bibliographical Soc, London 1912, p 113.
Hodnett E, English Woodcuts, Bibliographical Soc Illustrated Monograph 22, London 1935, pp 80 (STC, no 20107), 83 (STC, no 20108), 95 (STC, no 23435a), and passim.
O'Dell S, Chronological List of Prose Fiction, Cambridge Mass, pp 26, 28, 32.
Editions. Mather F J jr, King Ponthus, PMLA 12.i (introd), 1 (edn), and offprint, Baltimore 1897 (2 MSS) (crit F Holthausen, AnglB 8.197; G Paris, Rom 26.468; P Meyer, Rom 34.142n1).
Brie F, Zwei frühneuenglische Prosaromane, Arch 118.325; Zu Surdyt, Arch 121.129 (STC, no 23435a).
Krappe E S, King Ponthus, DA 13⁵.797 (abstract) (edn of de Worde, STC, no 20108).
Excerpts. Ritson AEMR, 3.238, 277 (STC, no 20108).
Proper Names. Flutre L F, Table des noms propres dans les romans du moyen âge, Poitiers 1962, pp xv and passim.
French Source. De Montaiglon A, Le livre du chevalier de La Tour Landry, Paris 1854, p xxiii.
Thomas A, Ponthus de La Tour-Landri, Rom 34.283.
Paris G, Mélanges de la littérature française du moyen âge, ed M Roques, Paris 1912, p 336.
Dalbanne C and E Droz, Ponthus et la belle Sidoine, Livres à gravures imprimés à Lyon au quinzième siècle 3, Lyons 1926.
Bossuat MBLF, nos 4155, 7865.
Boisard P, Le roman de Ponthus et la famille de La Tour-Landry, Positions des thèses, École des chartes 1958, p 11.
Other Versions. Wüst P, Die deutschen Prosaromane von Pontus und Sidonia, Marburg 1903; Paul Grundriss, 2¹.401 (German); 2¹.451 (Dutch).
English Tradition. Watson F, Vives and the Renascence Education of Women, London 1912, p 59.
Rickard P, Britain in Medieval French Literature, Cambridge 1956, pp 122, 222, 240.
Warton T, History of English Poetry, ed R Price, London 1840, 1.41nu; 2.409nz.
Ward 1.130, 469; Ten Brink, 3.10; Billings, pp 3, 12; Gröber, 2¹.1196; Schofield, p 265; CHEL, 2.325.
Creek H L, Character in the Matter of England Romances, JEGP 10.440, 603.
Leach H G, Angevin Britain and Scandinavia, Cambridge Mass 1921, pp 166, 329, 384.

Ernle R (Lord), Light Reading of Our Ancestors, N Y ca 1927, p 106.
Hibbard Med Rom, p 87; Renwick-Orton, pp 336, 338; 2nd edn, pp 351, 353; Baugh LHE, p 176n9.
Schlauch M, English Medieval Literature, Warsaw 1956, pp 296, 309.
Hazlitt W C, Hand-Book to the Popular Literature of Britain, London 1867, p 475.
Tucker-Benham, p 137; CBEL, 1.148; Bennett OHEL, pp 310, 313.

[5] HAVELOK.

MSS. 1, Bodl 1486 (Laud Misc 108), ff 204ᵃ–219ᵇ (ca 1300); 2, Camb Univ Add 4407 (19), fragments d, e, f (1375–1400).
Brown-Robbins, no 1114; MED, pp 11, 44.
Horstmann C, Legenden des MS Laud 108, Arch 49.395; AELeg 1875, p x (Bodl).
Skeat W W, Twelve Facsmiles of OE MSS, Oxford 1892, p 26 and plate 7 (Bodl) (crit E Kölbing, EStn 17.413); A New Havelok MS, MLR 6.455 (Camb).
Hall J, King Horn, Oxford 1901, p viii (Bodl).
Brunner K, ME Metrical Romances and Their Audiences, Studies in Medieval Literature in Honor of A C Baugh, Phila 1961, p 223.
Editions. Madden F, The Ancient English Romance of Havelok the Dane, Roxb Club, London 1828.
Skeat W W, The Lay of Havelok the Dane, EETSES 4, London 1868 (corrected rpt 1889); re-ed, Oxford 1902 (crit N&Q 9s 10.400; W W Greg, MLQ (Lon) 5.154; SHR 1.446; M Förster, AnglB 14.10; F Holthausen, DLz 24.1296; H Jantzen, Neue philologische Rundschau 1903.473); A New Havelok MS, MLR 6.455 (Camb); The Lay of Havelok, 2nd end, rvsd K Sisam, Oxford 1915 (crit J W Bright, MLN 31.252; W J Sedgefield, MLR 12.125; A E H Swaen, Neophil 2.78).
Holthausen F, Havelok, OMETexts 1, London and N Y 1901 (English edn) (crit H Jantzen, Neue philologische Rundschau 1901.187; W K, LZ 52.1689; H Spies, DLz 22.346; G Binz, LfGRP 23.14; W Heuser, Arch 108.197; M Kaluza, AnglB 14.164] K D Bülbring, Museum 1905.296); 2nd corrected edn, Heidelberg 1910 (German edn); 3rd edn, Heidelberg 1928 (crit E von Erhardt-Siebold, EStn 63.417; M Day, RES 5.459; H S V Jones, JEGP 28.592; F Wild, LfGRP 52.187).
French W H and C B Hale, ME Metrical Romances, N Y 1930, p 71.
Selections. Zupitza J, Altenglisches Uebungs-

buch, Vienna 1874, p 54; Alt- und mittel-
englisches Uebungsbuch, 2nd edn rvsd,
Vienna 1882, p 82; 5th edn, rvsd J Schipper,
Vienna 1897, p 120.
Wülcker R P, Altenglisches Lesebuch, Halle
1874, 1.81, 161.
Maclean G E, Old and ME Reader, N Y 1893,
pp lvi, 85.
Morris Spec, 2nd edn rvsd 1898, 1.222, 356.
Kluge F, Mittelenglisches Lesebuch, Halle
1904; 2nd edn rvsd 1912, p 73.
Emerson O F, ME Reader, N Y 1905, rvsd
1915, pp 75, 272.
Cook A S, Literary ME Reader, Boston Mass
1915, p 17.
Brandl A and O Zippel, Mittelenglische Sprach-
und Literaturproben, Berlin 1917; 2nd edn
1927, p 47.
Sampson G, Cambridge Book of Prose and
Verse, Cambridge 1924, p 251.
Turk M H, Anglo-Saxon Reader, rvsd edn,
N Y 1927, 1930, p 222.
Mossé F, Manuel de l'anglais du moyen âge 2,
Moyen anglais, Paris 1949, 1.222, 2.39;
trans J A Walker, Handbook of ME, Balti-
more 1952, p 189.
Dickins B and R M Wilson, Early ME Texts,
Cambridge 1951; rvsd 1952, p 34.
Kaiser R, Alt- und mittelenglische Anthologie,
Berlin 1954 (and 2nd edn, 1955), p 378;
Medieval English, rvsd English edn, Berlin
1958, p 399.
Modernizations and Abstracts. Wyatt A J, The
Lay of Havelok the Dane, London 1889, 1913.
Morley, 3.267.
Hibbard L A, Three ME Romances, London
1911, p 53; R S Loomis and R Willard,
Medieval English Verse and Prose, N Y 1948,
p 76; R S and L H Loomis, Medieval Ro-
mances, N Y 1957, p 284.
Weston J L, Chief ME Poets, Cambridge Mass
1914, pp 110, 377.
Williams A T, Havelok the Dane, in Hereward
the Wake, trans D C Stedman and C J A
Oppermann, London ca 1928, p 121.
Montagu R, Havelok and Sir Orfeo, Leicester
1954, p 9, 25.
Textual Notes. Zupitza J, ZfDA 19.124; Angl
1.468; 7.145; F H Stratmann, EStn 1.423,
5.377; W H Browne, MLN 7.134, 267; 21.23;
F Holthausen, Angl 15.499; 17.441; 42.445;
AnglB 11.306; 11.359; 12.146; 49.27; 50.95;
English Miscellany Presented to Dr Furnivall,
Oxford 1901, p 176; EStn 30.343; Arch
110.100; 110.425; E Kölbing, EStn 17.297;
19.146; M Förster, Arch 107.107; L Mors-
bach, EStn 29.368; J Edwards, SHR 1.55;
H Littledale, TPSL 1903, p 161; H Bradley,

TPSL 1903, p 163; W Horn, Angl 29.132;
J H G Grattan, MLR 4.91; E Koeppel,
AnglB 23.294; K Sisam, Arch 128.194;
A S Napier, MLR 11.74; C T Onions, RES
5.328; MÆ 10.159; Philologica: Malone
Anniv Studies, Baltimore 1949, p 154;
H Matthes, AnglB 42.252; B Dickins, Leeds
SE 4.75; N R Ker, TLS Nov 14 1936, p 928;
G V Smithers, RES 13.458; English and
Germanic Stud 2.1; A MacIntosh, RES
16.189; L Whitbread, N&Q 183.366; 184.97;
186.204; 188.94; E J Dobson, English and
Germanic Stud 1.58; W J B Owen, N&Q
197.468; Anon, N&Q ns 3.236.
Language. Madden F, Glossary to the Ancient
Metrical Romance of Havelok, London 1828
(crit S W Singer, Remarks on the Glossary
to Havelok, London 1829, 1st edn and 2nd
edn rvsd; reply, F Madden, Examination of
the Remarks by Singer, London 1829).
Ellis A J, Early English Pronunciation, EETSES
7.470.
Ludorff F, Ueber die Sprache des Hauelok,
Münster 1873 (crit J Zupitza, ZfÖG 25.595).
Kölbing E, Amis and Amiloun, AEB 2, Heil-
bronn 1884, p xxxi (dialect).
Hohmann L, Ueber Sprache und Stil des
Havelok, Marburg 1886 (crit H Hupe, Angl
13.186).
Wohlfeil P, The Lay of Havelok: Ein Beitrag
zur me Sprach- und Litteraturgeschichte,
Leipzig 1890.
Schmidt F, Zur Heimatbestimmung des Have-
lok, Göttingen 1900.
Björkman E, Scandinavian Loan-Words in ME,
SEP 7.355 and passim.
Rathmann F, Die lautliche Gestaltung eng-
lischer Personennamen in Gaimars Reim-
chronik, Kiel 1906.
Wolff A, Zur Syntax des Verbums im Havelok,
Weida 1909.
Menner R J, Sir Gawain and the West Mid-
land, PMLA 37.507, 510, 513, 514, 525.
Kern J H, De Taalvormen van't middelengelse
Gedicht Havelok, MKAW 55 series A no 2
(crit F Holthausen, AnglB 35.35).
Huchon R, Histoire de la langue anglaise, Paris
1930, 2.219.
Ehrensperger E C, Dream Words in ME,
PMLA 46.82.
Ekwall E, ME o bon, Meijerbergs Arkiv för
Svensk Ordforskning, 2.23 (composed ca
1250).
Britton G C, N-Plurals in the Nouns of Have-
lok, NM 60.175 (dialect).
Flutre L F, Table des noms propres dans les
romans, Poitiers 1962, pp xii and passim.
Versification. Schipper J, Englische Metrik, Bonn

1881, 1.269; Paul Grundriss, 2^1.1044 (2nd edn, 2^2.206); Grundriss der englischen Metrik, WBEP 2.180; History of English Versification, Oxford 1910, p 187.

Wittenbrinck G, Zur Kritik und Rhythmik des Havelok, Burgsteinfurt 1891 (crit anon, AnglB 2.244; E Kölbing, EStn 16.299).

Saintsbury G A, History of English Prosody, Oxford 1906, pp 65, 69, 73, 77; Historical Manual of English Prosody, London 1926, p 149.

Guest E, History of English Rhythms, new edn, ed W W Skeat, London 1882, pp 432, 434, 468, 482.

Kaluza M, Englische Metrik in historische Entwicklung, Berlin 1909, sections 122, 125, 128, 144, 158, 167; trans A C Dunstan, Short History of English Versification, London 1911, same sections.

Young (Sir) G, English Prosody on Inductive Lines, Cambridge 1928, p 117.

Mitchell B, The Couplet System in Havelok, N&Q 10.405.

Date. Hales J W, The Lay of Havelok, Athen Feb 23 1889[1], p 244; rptd Folia Litteraria, N Y 1893, p 30 (crit F Liebermann, Deutsche Zeitschrift für Geschichtswissenschaft 4.154); W van der Gaaf, Parliaments Held at Lincoln, EStn 32.319.

Authorship. Creek H L, The Author of Havelok, EStn 48.193.

Related Versions. Kupferschmidt M, Die Haveloksage bei Gaimar, Romanische Studien 4.411 (also offprint, Bonn 1880); Ward 1.423, 940 (Gaimar); (Sir) T D Hardy and C T Martin, Lestorie des Engles, Rolls Series 91, 1.1 (Gaimar edn), 2.1 (trans), 1.290 (Lai), 2.216 (trans).

Bell A, West Saxon Genealogy in Gaimar, PQ 2.173; Glossarial and Textual Notes, MLR 43.39; Gaimar's Early Danish Kings, PMLA 65.601; L'estoire des Engleis, Anglo-Norman Texts 14–16, Oxford 1960 (edn).

Holmes CBFL, p 103 (Gaimar).

Lai d'Haveloc. Michel F, Lai d'Havelok, Paris 1833.

Kittredge G L, Sir Orfeo, AJP 7.184 and n 3.

Fahnestock E, Study of the Sources and Composition of the Lai d'Haveloc, Jamaica N Y 1915.

Vising J, Anglo-Norman Language and Literature, London 1923, pp 29, 47, 49.

Bell A, Le lai d'Havelor, Pubs of the Univ of Manchester, French Series 4, Manchester 1925 (edn of Lai and Gaimar).

Becker P A, Von den Erzählern neben und nach Chrestien, ZfRP 56.245; Der gepaarte Achtsilber in der französischen Dichtung,

Abhandlungen der philologisch-historischen Klasse der sächsischen Akademie der Wissenschaft 43^1.42.

Brereton G E, Thirteenth-Century List of French Lays, MLR 45.41.

Donovan M J, Lai du Lecheor, RR 43.85.

Legge M D, Anglo-Norman Literature, Oxford 1963, pp 32, 36, 99, 277, 282, 286, 287.

Holmes CBFL, p 97; Bossuat MBLF, nos 523, 1544, 6685 (Lai).

Putnam E K, The Lambeth Version of Havelok, PMLA 15.1 (also offprint Baltimore 1900); Skeat, Lay of Havelok, rvsd Sisam, p xvii (edn of Interpolation).

Historical Parallels. Køster K, Sagnet om Havelok Danske, Copenhagen 1868.

Storm G, Havelok the Dane and the Norse King Olaf Kuaran, Forhandlinger i Videnskabs-Selskabet i Christiania 1879 no 10; rptd, EStn 3.533 (crit G Stephens, Acad 17.343).

Heyman H E, Studies on the Havelok-Tale, Upsala 1903.

Deutschbein M, Studien zur Sagengeschichte Englands, Cöthen 1906, p 96 (crit A Stimming, DLz 27.1578; H Suchier, LZ 57.1276; J Vising, Krit Jahresber 10^2.113; G Binz, AnglB 18.1; W Golther, LfGRP 28.280; W P Ker, MLR 2.176; R C Boer, Museum: Maandblad voor Philologie 15.55); Beiträge zur Horn- und Havelocsage, AnglB 20.16, 21.

Bugge A, Havelok og Olav Trygvessøn, Aarbøger for nordisk Oldkyndighed og Historie 2s 23.233; Havelok and Olaf, trans C M E Pochin, Saga Book of the Viking Club 6^2.257.

Björkman E, Nordische Personennamen in England, SEP 37.27 (Birkabein); Zur Haveloksage, AnglB 28.333; Nordiska Vikingasagor i England, Nordisk Tidskrift för Vetenskap 1906.440.

Beaven M L R, King Edmund I and the Danes of York, EHR 33.6n22.

Liebermann F, Haveloks Prototyp, Arch 146.243.

Hill J W F, Medieval Lincoln, Cambridge 1948, p 175.

Dunn C W, Havelok and Cuaran, in Franciplegius: Medieval and Linguistic Studies in Honor of F P Magoun jr, N Y 1965, p 244.

Scandinavian Analogues. Ward H L D, EHR 10.141.

Gollancz I, Hamlet in Iceland, Northern Library 3, London 1898, p xl.

Zenker R, Boeve-Amlethus, Litterarhistorische Forschungen 32.63, 71, 73, 91, 99, 356, 377 (crit H Anders, ShJ 42.285; F Lindner, Estn 36.284; J Vising, Arch 118.226).

Olson O L, Relations of the Hrólfssaga Kraka,

Pubs of the Soc for the Advancement of Scandinavian Studies 3¹.72, 80.

Olrik A, Heroic Legends of Denmark, trans L M Hollander, N Y 1919, p 310.

Enc Brit, 14th edn, 11.130, see under Hamlet.

Welsh Analogues. Bruce J D, Vita Meriadoci, PMLA 15.332 (Havelok's influence?); Historia Meriadoci, Hesperia, Ergänzungsreihe 2.xxx.

Morriss M S, Authorship of the De ortu Waluuanii, PMLA 23.639.

Loomis R S, Latin Romances, Arthurian Literature in the Middle Ages, ed Loomis, Oxford 1959, p 475.

Havelok Tradition. Weever J, Ancient Funerall Monuments, London 1631, p 749.

Camden's Britannia, trans E Gibson, London 1695, p 471.

Brydges (Sir) S E and S Shaw, History and Ancient Description of Grimsby, The Topographer, London 1789, 1⁵.241 (quoting G Holles, Harl MS 6829).

Hearne T, Peter Langtoft's Chronicle as Improv'd by Robert of Brunne, Oxford 1725 (rptd, Work of T Hearne, 3, London 1810), 1.25.

Grime (pseud), Singular Restoration of the Ancient Seals of Grimsby, N&Q 2s 11.46; Adrian (pseud), Ancient Seals of Grimsby, N&Q 2s 11.216.

Wright T, Chronicle of Pierre de Langtoft, Rolls Series 47¹.318.

Lumby J R, Chronicon Henrici Knighton, Rolls Series 92¹.18, 27.

Peacock M, Havelok the Dane, Bygone Lincolnshire, ed W Andrews, Hull 1891, 1.33.

Wülfing J E, Laud Troy Book, EETS 121.1 (line 21).

Putnam E K, Scalacronica Version of Havelok, Trans and Proceedings of the Amer Philological Assoc 34.xci.

Brie F, Zum Fortleben der Havelok-Sage, EStn 35.359; The Brut, EETS 131 and 136, p 92.

Zettl E, Anonymous Short English Metrical Chronicle, EETS 196.18n430; 31.729.

Folkloristic and Cultural Details. Heuser W, Horn und Rigmel, Angl 31.113n.

Imelman R, J Bramis' Historia regis Waldef, BSEP 4.lii.

Ashdown M, Single Combat in English Romance, MLR 17.116; A Bell, Single Combat in the Lai d'Havelok, MLR 18.22 (crit P G Thomas, YWES 4.47).

Matter H, Englische Gründungssagen, AF 58.241.

Thompson Mot Ind, H 41.4, H 71.5, R 131.4; G Boardman, Motif-Index of the English Metrical Romances, FFC 190.14 and passim.

McKeehan I P, Book of the Nativity of St Cuthbert, PMLA 48.995.

Whiting B J, Proverbs in Certain ME Romances, HSNPL 15.111.

de Lange J, Relation and Development of English and Icelandic Outlaw-Traditions, Nederlandsche Bijdragen op het Gebied van germaansche Philologie en Linguistiek 6.42.

Stewart-Brown R, Serjeants of the Peace in Medieval England, Univ of Manchester Pubs 247, Historical ser 71, Manchester 1936, p 80.

Dickins B, The Names of Grim's Children in the Havelok Story, SN 14.114.

Heather P J, Seven Planets, Folklore 54.356.

Tatlock J S P, Legendary History of Britain, Berkeley and Los Angeles 1950, p 452.

Newstead H, The Enfances of Tristan and English Tradition, Studies in Medieval Literature in Honor of A C Baugh, Phila 1961, pp 172, 178.

d'Ardenne S R, A Neglected Manuscript, English and Medieval Studies Presented to J R R Tolkien, London 1962, p 92 (royal origin).

Literary Criticism. Creek H L, Character in the Matter of England Romances, JEGP 10.429, 585.

Everett D, Characterization of the Romances, E&S 15.101, 105, 107; rptd Essays on ME Literature, ed P Kean, Oxford 1955, pp 3, 8, 9.

Kane, pp 46, 49.

Schaar C, The Golden Mirror, SUVSL 54.161.

Spiers J, Medieval English Poetry, London 1957, pp 178, 191, 266n.

Baugh A C, Improvisation in the ME Romance, PAPS 103.418.

Wright T, Essays on Subjects Connected with the Literature of England, London 1846, 1.99.

Latham R G, On Havelok, TRSL 2s 7.71.

Körting, 1st edn, Münster 1887, pp 95, 96; Ten Brink, 1.150, 227, 232, 300; Morley, 3.265.

Ahlström A, Studier i den fornfranska Lais-Litteraturen, Upsala 1892, p 119 (crit E Freymond, Krit Jahresber 3².163).

Brandl A, Paul Grundriss, 1st edn, 2¹.644; 2nd edn, 2¹.1086.

Wülcker, 1.81, 97, 105.

Saintsbury G, Flourishing of Romance, Edinburgh 1897; N Y 1907, p 207; Short History of English Literature, London 1898, rptd 1907, pp 83, 86; Romance, Enc Brit, rptd 14th edn, 19.426.

Whistler C W, Saga of Havelok, Saga Book of the Viking Club 3.395 (crit 3.406).

Billings, p 15; Gröber, 2¹.471, 473; Schofield, pp 31, 266, 362; CHEL 1.242, 308, 319, 320, 337, 340, 343, 351, 392, 402, 447; 2.420; Rickert RofL, pp xxvi, xxix, xxxvii.

Dixon W M, English Epic and Heroic Poetry, London and N Y 1912, pp 111, 125.

Leach H G, Angevin Britain and Scandinavia, Cambridge Mass 1921, pp 200, 235, 317, 324, 330, 332, 352.

Hibbard Med Rom, p 103.

Enc Brit, 14th edn, 11.262, see under Havelok.

Taylor A B, Introduction to Medieval Romance, London 1930, pp 133, 146, 160, 163.

Legouis HEL, rvsd edn, London 1933, pp 89, 125 (crit S B Liljegren, Litteris 6.13).

Wilson R M, Lost Literature in Old and ME, Leeds SE 2.17; More Lost Literature, Leeds SE 5.19; Early ME Literature, London 1939, 1951, pp 68, 77, 84, 189, 215, 221; Lost Literature of Medieval England, London 1952, pp 27, 43n2, 50.

Renwick-Orton, pp 28, 339; 2nd edn, pp 38, 354.

Wright C E, Cultivation of Saga in Anglo-Saxon England, Edinburgh and London 1939, pp 31, 77, 115, 120, 192.

von Richthofen E, Studien zur romanischen Heldensage, Halle 1944, p 69; Estudios epicos medievales, trans J P Riesco, Madrid 1954, p 113.

Baugh LHE, p 176.

Sampson G, Concise CHEL, Cambridge 1949, pp 41, 43.

Schlauch M, English Medieval Literature, Warsaw 1956, pp 143, 144, 147, 177, 197.

CHEL, 1.520; CBEL, 1.29, 39, 42, 148; 5.115.

Zesmer D M and S B Greenfield, Guide to English Literature, N Y 1961, pp 110, 111, 119, 332, 335.

[6] BEVIS OF HAMPTON.

MSS. A Text: 1, Camb Univ Ff. 2.38 (olim no 690), ff 102ᵇ–133ᵇ (1450–1500); 2, Caius Camb 175, ff 131ᵃ–156ᵇ (1400–50); 3, Egerton 2862 (Sutherland), ff 45ᵃ–94ᵇ, 96ᵃ–96ᵇ (1375–1400); 4, Advocates 19.2.1 (Auchinleck), ff 176ᵃ–201ᵃ (ca 1330); 5, Naples, Royal Libr XIII.B.29, pp 23–79 (ca 1457). B Text: 6, Chetham 8009, ff 122ᵃ–187ᵇ (1450–1500). Fragment: 7, Trinity Camb 1117 (IV), ff 149–152 (1400–1500). PRINTS: 8, Douce fragments no 19 (Wynkyn de Worde, Westminster 1500) (STC, no 1987); 9, R Pynson (London ca 1503) (STC, no 1988); 10, W Copland (ca 1565) (STC, no 1989).

Brown-Robbins, nos 1993, *58; MED, pp 11, 27.

Schipper J, Englische Alexiuslegenden, Strassburg 1877, 1.7 (Naples MS).

Kölbing E, Vier Romanzen-handschriften, EStn 7.186, 192, 198 (Advocates, Egerton, Chetham MSS).

Duff E G, Early English Printing, London 1896, pp 7, 30, plate 12² (de Worde facs).

Duff E G, Fifteenth Century English Books, Bibliog Soc Illustrated Monog 18, Oxford 1917, p 12 (STC, no 1987).

Manly & Rickert, 1.376 (Naples MS), 1.610 (unidentified Befuitz de Hamton).

Loomis L H, The Auchinleck MS, PMLA 57.595.

Bennett H S, Chaucer and the Fifteenth Century, Oxford 1947, p 214 (Wynkyn de Worde).

Bliss A J, Notes on the Auchinleck MS, Spec 26.652; Sir Orfeo, Oxford 1954, p ix (Advocates MS).

Editions. Turnbull W B D D, Sir Beves of Hamtoun, Maitland Club Pub 44, Edinburgh 1838 (Advocates MS) (crit E Kölbing, EStn 2.317).

Kölbing E, The Romance of Sir Beues of Hamtoun, EETES 46, 48, 65 (all MSS except Trinity) (crit L Kellner, EStn 19.261] G Paris, Rom 23.486).

H W D, N&Q 10s 8.434 (note on edns).

Esdaile A, List of English Tales and Prose Romances Printed before 1740, Pubs of the Bibliographical Society, London 1912, p 163; STC, nos 1987–1996; E Hodnett, English Woodcuts, Bibliog Soc Illustrated Monog 22, London 1935, pp 90, 94, and passim; C C Mish, English Prose Fiction 1661–1700, Charlottesville Va 1952, pp 51, 56, 70; S O'Dell, Chronological List of Prose Fiction 1475–1640, Cambridge Mass 1954, pp 26, 27, 29, 36, 46, 80, 90, 96, 97, 101, 114 (later verse and prose variants).

Selections. Rel Ant, 2.59.

Sampson G, Cambridge Book of Prose and Verse, Cambridge 1924, p 275.

Modernizations and Abstracts. Hibbard L A, Three ME Romances, London 1911, p 93.

Sampson A, Sir Bevis: The Legend Retold, Southampton 1963.

Language. Schmirgel K, Stil und Sprache des me Epos Sir Beues, Breslau 1886; rptd Kölbing edn, EETES 65.xlv.

Huchon R, Histoire de la langue anglaise, Paris 1930, 2.268.

Versification. Kölbing E, Alliteration in Sir Beues, EStn 19.441.

Strong C, History and Relations of the Tail-Rhyme Strophe, PMLA 22.420.

CHEL, 1.324 and n 2.

Kaluza M, Englische Metrik, Berlin 1909,

sections 154, 177; trans A C Dunstan, Short History of English Versification, London 1911, same sections.

Source. Stimming A, Der anglonormannische Boeve de Haumtone, Bibliotheca normannica 7, Halle 1899 (edn) (crit G Paris, Rom 29.127).

Matzke J E, The Oldest Form of the Beves Legend, MP 10.19 (ME from AN).

Vising J, Anglo-Norman Language and Literature, London 1923, pp 28, 60, 61, 85.

Hibbard Med Rom, p 115.

Legge M D, Anglo-Norman Literature, Oxford 1963, pp 156, 175, 371.

Other Versions. Boje C, Die Ueberlieferung des altfranzösischen Romans von Beuve de Hamtone, Halle 1908 (offprint of pp 1–26 of following); Ueber den altfranzösischen Roman von Beuve, ZfRP, Beiheft 19 (complete bibl) (crit E Brugger, ZfFSL 35².49; L Foulet, Rom 42.314).

Vising J, Krit Jahresber 12².141; Stimming A, Der festländische Bueve de Hantone, Gesellschaft für romanische Literatur, vols 25, 30, 34, 41, 42, Dresden 1911–20 (edn of all three groups); A Wolf, Das gegenseitige Verhältnis der gereimten Fassungen des festländischen Bueve, Göttingen 1912; A Hilka, Eine neue Version des Bueve, ZfRP 44.265. (Contiental French version.)

Williams R and G H Jones, Selections from the Hengwrt MSS, London 1892, 2.119 (Welsh edn), 2.518 (trans); M Watkin, Ystorya Bown de Hamtwn, Cardiff 1958 (edn). (Welsh version.)

Robinson F N, Celtic Versions of Sir Beues, EStn 24.463; Irish Lives of Guy of Warwick and Bevis, ZCP 6.9, 273; also offprint, Halle 1907 (edn and trans). (Irish version.)

Cederschiöld G, Bevers Saga, in Fornsögur Sudrlanda, Lund 1884, pp ccxvi, ccxlvi, ccxlvii (introd); 209 (edn); 268 (combined index); also as Lunds Universitets Års-skrift, 15⁵.209, 268, 19.ccxvi, ccxlvi, ccxlvii (crit E Kölbing, PBBeitr 19.1, 24.414; replies G Cederschiöld, PBBeitr 23.257, 24.420); E Kölbing, Die Sigurðar saga þögla, ZfVL nf 10.381. (Norse version.)

Bolte J, Beiträge zur Geschichte der erzählenden Literatur des 16 Jahrhunderts, Tijdschrift voor nederlandsche taal- en letterkunde 12.311 (extracts from Dutch version).

Rajna P, I reali di Francia, Bologna 1872, 1.114 (crit G Paris, Rom 2.351); Rajna, Le origini dell' epopea francese, Florence 1884, p 382 and n 1; A da Barberino, I reali de Francia, ed G Vandelli, Bologna 1900, 2².319;

L Jordan, Ueber Boeve de Hanstone, ZfRP, Beiheft 14 (crit J Vising, Arch 122.412; E Brugger, ZfFSL 34².25; L Foulet, Rom 42.313); J Reinhold, Die franko-italienische Version des Bovo, ZfRP 35.555, 683; 36.1; H Paetz, Ueber das gegenseitige Verhältnis der Fassungen des Bueve, ZfRP, Beiheft 50; A da Barberino, I reali de Francia, ed G Vandelli and G Gambarin, Scrittori d'Italia 193, Bari 1947, bks 4, 5. (Italian versions.)

Gudzy N K, History of Early Russian Literature, N Y 1949, pp 412, 416n7 (Russian versions).

Minkoff N B, Elyeh Bohur un zayn Bove-Bukh, N Y 1950 (Yiddish version).

Gröber, 2³.386 (Rumanian version).

Folkloristic and Literary Relationships. Graf A, I complementi della Chanson d'Huon de Bordeaux, Halle 1878, p xvi.

Nyrop K, Den oldfranske Heltedigtning, Copenhagen 1883, pp 75, 157, 212, 268, 275, 282, 289, 437; trans E Gorra, Storia dell' epopea francese, Florence 1886, Turin 1888.

Panzer F, Hilde-Gudrun, Halle 1901, pp 266, 278, 320, 332, 337, 341, 418.

Hoyt P C, Home of the Beves Saga, PMLA 17.237.

Brockstedt G, Floovent-Studien, Kiel 1904 and rvsd edn 1907, pp 19, 24; Von mittelhochdeutschen Volksepen französischen Ursprungs, Kiel 1912, 2.3, 108.

Gerould G H, The Eustace Legend, PMLA 19.444.

Matzke J E, Legend of Saint George, PMLA 19.449.

Settegast F, Quellenstudien zur gallo-romanischen Epik, Leipzig 1904, p 338.

Zenker R, Boeve-Amlethus, Litterarhistorische Forschungen 32.1, 355, 380 (crit H Anders, ShJ 42.285; F Lindner, EStn 36.284; J Vising, Arch 118.226).

Deutschbein M, Studien zur Sagengeschichte Englands, Cöthen 1906, p 181 (crit A Stimming, DLz 27.1578; H Suchier, LZ 57.1276; J Vising, Krit Jahresber 10².113; G Binz, AnglB 18.1; W Golther, LfGRP 28.280; W P Ker, MLR 2.176; R C Boer, Museum: Maandblad voor Philologie 15.55).

Jordan L, Die Eustachiuslegende, Christians Wilhelmsleben, Boeve, und ihre orientalischen Verwandten, Arch 121.341.

Hibbard L A, Nibelungenlied and Beves, MLN 26.159; Jaques de Vitry and Boeve, MLN, 34.408.

Imelmann R, J Bramis' Historia regis Waldef, BSEP 4.lvi.

Enc Brit, 14th edn, 11.130, see under Hamlet.

Thompson Mot Ind, G 100; G Boardman,

Motif-Index of the English Metrical Romances, FFC 190.13 and passim.

Hofer S, Horn et Rimel, RF 70.283.

Relation to Chaucer. Loomis L H, Chaucer and the Auchinleck MS, E&S Brown, p 114; Chaucer and the Breton Lays, SP 38.32; Sir Thopas, Bryan-Dempster, pp 487, 489, 495, 511, 527, 551.

Later Bevis Tradition. Weber MR, 2.261.

Furnivall F J, Royal History of Generides, Roxb Club, Hertford 1865, p 2.

PFMS, 2.509, 517.

Murray J A H, Complaynt of Scotlande, EETSES 17.lxxx, 63.

Elyot (Sir) T, Boke Named the Gouernour, ed H H S Croft, London 1883, p 184 and n.

Ullmann J, Studien zu R Rolle, EStn 7.469 (Spec Vitae 43).

Furnivall F J, Story of England by Manning, Rolls Series 87.438 and passim.

Borrajo E M, Bevis, N&Q 8s 11.258; J B Fleming, Bevis, N&Q 8s 11.258; J B Prideaux, Bevis Marks, N&Q 8s 11.385; E Peacock, Bevis, N&Q 8s 11.396.

Greenfield B W, Heraldry of the Bargate, Papers and Proc of the Hampshire Field Club and Archaeol Soc 4².98 (Bevois and Ascupart).

Wülfing J E, Laud Troy Book, EETS 121.1 (line 15).

Curry J T, Arundel Castle, N&Q 10s 8.390; S Swithin, Arundel, N&Q 10s 8.434; W W Skeat, Arundel Castle, N&Q 10s 8.434; J E L Pickering, Arundel, N&Q 10s 8.473.

Watson F, Vives and the Renascence Education of Women, London 1912, p 59.

Zettl E, Anonymous Metrical Chronicle, EETS 196.103.

Rickard P, Britain in Medieval French Literature, Cambridge 1956, pp 136, 240, 246.

Bevis in Tapestry. Warton T, History of English Poetry, ed R Price, London 1840, 1.205; A Hussey, Bevis, N&Q 8s 11.207; J Evans, English Art 1307–1461, Oxford 1949, p 94.

Cultural Background. Easter D B, Study of the Magic Elements in the Romans d'Aventure, Baltimore 1906, pp 30, 38n176.

Hearnshaw F J C, Chivalry, ed E Prestage, N Y 1928, pp 1, 6.

Patch H R, Adaptation of Otherworld Motifs, Philologica: Malone Anniversary Studies, Baltimore 1949, pp 116, 118.

Literary Criticism. Scott (Sir) W, Essay on Romance, Enc Brit, 1st edn, suppl; rptd Miscellaneous Prose Works, Edinburgh 1827, 6.248; and Essays on Chivalry, London 1887, p 65.

Creek H L, Character in the Matter of England

Romances, JEGP 10.429, 525; Love in Mediaeval Romance, SR 24.92.

Hibbard Med Rom, p 115.

Taylor A B, Introduction to Medieval Romance, London 1930, pp 96, 126, 133, 156, 162, 225, 232.

Kane, pp 10, 46, 50.

Schaar C, The Golden Mirror, SUVSL 54.161.

Baugh A C, Improvisation in the ME Romance, PAPS 103.418.

Duval A, Beuves de Hanstone, HLF, 18.748; Trouvères, HLF, 18.701 and n 1.

Körting, 1st edn, Münster 1887, p 98; Ten Brink, 1.150, 246, 248; Brandl, pp 630, 636, 645, 653; Wülcker, 1.98.

Ker W P, Epic and Romance, London 1896, rptd N Y 1957, p 388.

Saintsbury G, Short History of English Literature, London 1898, rptd 1907, p 94; Enc Brit, rptd 14th edn, 19.427, see under Romance.

Gröber, 2¹.572, 811; Schofield, pp 15, 31, 260, 274, 477; CHEL, 1.242, 314, 320, 324, 326, 337, 339, 340, 523; 2.323; Rickert, RofL, pp xxix, xxxvii.

Leach H G, Angevin Britain and Scandinavia, Cambridge Mass 1921, pp 235, 317, 331, 382.

Ernle R (Lord), The Light Reading of Our Ancestors, N Y ca 1927, pp 12, 81, 107.

Enc Brit, 14th edn, 3.488, see under Bevis.

Crawford S J, Sir Bevis, Wessex 1³.46.

Renwick-Orton, p 342; rvsd edn, p 357.

Wright C E, Cultivation of Saga in Anglo-Saxon England, Edinburgh and London 1939, p 31.

Baugh LHE, p 179.

Sampson G, Concise CHEL, Cambridge 1949, pp 41, 42, 43.

Wilson R M, Early ME Literature, London 1939; 1951 pp 77, 215; Lost Literature of Medieval England, London 1952, p 18.

Schlauch M, English Medieval Literature, Warsaw 1956, pp 143, 144, 178, 197.

Zesmer D M and S B Greenfield, Guide to English Literature, N Y 1961, pp 112, 249.

Hazlitt W C, Hand-Book to the Popular Literature of Great Britain, London 1867, p 88.

Gautier L, Bibliographie des chansons de geste, Paris 1897, pp 69, 221.

Billings, p 36; Bossuat MBLF, nos 270–92; Supplement, no 6068; CBEL, 1.150.

[7] GUY OF WARWICK.

MSS. Tripartite version: 1, Advocates 19.2.1 (Auchinleck), ff 108ᵃ–146ᵇ, 146ᵇ–167ᵃ, 167ᵃ–175ᵇ (ca 1330). Early couplet version: 2, Caius Camb 107, pp 1–271 (ca 1475); 3,

Sloane 1044 no 625, f 345[a-b] (fragm) (ca 1375–1400). Late couplet version: 4, Camb Univ Ff. 2.38 (olim no 690), ff 161[a]–239[a] (ca 1450–1500). Fragment: 5, BM Addit 14409 (Phillipps), ff 74[a]–77[b] (ca 1325–1350). PRINTS: 6, R Pynson (London ca 1500) (STC, no 12540); 7, Douce fragments no 20 (e 14) (Wynkyn de Worde, Westminster 1500) (STC, no 12541); 8, W Copland, Book of the Most Victoryous Prince Guy, London (ca 1560) (STC, no 12542).

Brown-Robbins, nos 946, 1754, 3145, 3146, *76; MED, pp 11, 44.

Zupitza J, Zur Literaturgeschichte des Guy, Sitzungsberichte der kaiserlichen Akademie der Wissenschaften, Wien, Phil-hist Cl, 74.623.

Ward, 1.489 (Sloane), 1.490 (Addit).

Kölbing E, Vier Romanzen-handschriften, EStn 7.178, 186 (Advocates).

Duff E G, Early English Printing, London 1896, pp 19, 32, plate 25[1] (Pynson); Fifteenth Century English Books, Bibliog Soc Illustrated Monog 18, Oxford 1917, p 46 (Pynson, de Worde, Copland).

Carr M B, Notes on a ME Scribe's Methods, Univ of Wisconsin Studies in Lang and Lit, 2.153 (Advocates).

Flower R, Lost MSS, TRSL ns 18.112.

Loomis L H, Chaucer and the Breton Lays of the Auchinleck MS, SP 38.14, 32; The Auchinleck MS, PMLA 57.595.

Bennett H S, Chaucer and the Fifteenth Century, Oxford 1947, p 214 (Pynson).

Bliss A J, Notes on the Auchinleck MS, Spec 26.652, 653, 658n3; Sir Orfeo, Oxford 1954, p ix.

Editions. P(hillipps Sir) T, Romance of Guy of Warwick, Middlehill Worcestershire 1838 (BM Addit).

Turnbull W B D D, Romance of Sir Guy, Abbotsford Club 18, Edinburgh 1840, pp xxviii (Phillipps BM Addit), 1, 266, 419 (Advocates).

Zupitza J, Zur Literaturgeschichte, p 624 (Sloane) (crit E Kölbing, Germ 21.354, 365); Romance of Guy of Warwick: The Second or 15th-Century Version, EETSES 25, 26, London 1875–76 (Camb Univ) (crit E Kölbing, EStn 13.136); Romance of Guy, EETSES 42, 49, 59, London 1883, 1887, 1891 (Advocates, Caius).

Schleich G, Guy of Warwick nach Coplands Druck, Palaes 139, Leipzig 1923 (crit F Holthausen, AnglB 34.225; G H Cowling, MLR 19.222; W W Greg, MLR 19.337; U Lindelöf, NM 26.30; M Weyrauch, LZ 1924.626; M S Serjeantson, ESts 15.67).

Selections. Kaiser R, Alt- und mittelenglische Anthologie, Berlin 1954 (and 2nd edn, 1955), p 385; Medieval English, rvsd English edn, Berlin 1958, p 406.

Textual Notes. Ackerman R W, Two Scribal Errors in Guy, Research Studies of the State Coll of Washington 8[2].81; G V Smithers, Notes on ME Texts, LMS 1.214, 220.

Language. Möller W, Untersuchungen über Dialekt und Stil des Guy, Königsberg 1917 (relation to Amis and Amiloun).

Kennedy BWEL, p 169.

Strong M E, Lexical Study of Guy, Cornell Univ abstr of thesis, Ithaca 1934.

Dunlap A R, Vocabulary of the ME Romances in Tail-Rhyme, Delaware Notes 14.2, 37, and passim.

Flutre L F, Table des noms propres dans les romans, Poitiers 1962, p xvi and passim.

Versification. Schipper, 1.269.

Saintsbury G A, History of English Prosody, Oxford 1906, p 94n.

Trounce A McI, English Tail-Rhyme Romances, MÆ 1.87, 168; 2.34, 189; 3.30.

Source. Ewert A, Gui de Warewic, Paris 1932, 1933, 2 vols (edn with introd) (crit J Vising, MÆ 3.217; reply, MÆ 4.67).

Ward, 1.471, 485, 487 (AN versions); J Vising, Krit Jahresber 13[2].89; Vising, Anglo-Norman Lang and Lit, London 1923, p 60; W Schulz, Zur Handschriftenfrage der Chançun de Guillelme und des Gui, ZfFSL 46.281; M D Legge, Anglo-Norman in the Cloisters, Edinburgh 1950, pp 63, 70, 114; M D Legge, Anglo-Norman Literature, Oxford 1963, pp 162, 175, 278, 282.

Holmes CBFL, no 989; Bossuat MBLF, nos 1347–67, 4130.

Literary History. Tanner A, Die Sage von Guy, Bonn 1877 (crit E Kölbing, EStn 2.246; H Suchier, LZ 1878.1088; J Zupitza, Angl 2.191).

Weyrauch M, Die me Fassungen der Sage von Guy und ihre Vorlage, Breslau 1899; enlarged edn, Forschungen zur englischen Sprache und Litteratur 2, Breslau 1901 (crit E Björkman, Arch 110.444; F Holthausen, DLz 23.669; P Flynn, Bulletin critique de littérature 23.228; T Prosiegel, EStn 32.405).

Deutschbein M, Studien zur Sagengeschichte Englands, Cöthen 1906 (crit A Stimming, DLz 27.1578; H Suchier, LZ 57.1276; J Vising, Krit Jahresber 10[2].113; AnglB 18.1; W Golther, LfGRP 28.280; W P Ker, MLR 2.176; R C Boer, Museum: Maandblad voor Philologie 15.55).

Leach H G, Angevin Britain and Scandinavia, Cambridge Mass 1921, p 333.

London Bookshop Version. Loomis L H, The Auchinleck MS, PMLA 57.595.

Walpole R N, Source MS of Charlemagne, MLN 60.22, 25.

Smyser H M, Charlemagne and Roland, Spec 21.275.

Non-English Derivatives. Robinson F N, The Irish Lives of Guy and Bevis, ZCP 6.9 (edn and trans).

Chotzen T, Recherches sur la poésie de Dafydd ap Gwilym, Amsterdam 1927, p 140 (Welsh tradition).

Thomas H, Spanish and Portuguese Romances, Cambridge 1920, p 32 (Tirant lo Blanch).

Gesta Romanorum Tradition. Warton, History, ed Price, 1.clxxxix.

Oesterley H, Gesta Romanorum, Berlin 1872, p 563 (chap 172).

Herbert, 3.209, 219, 224, 241.

Swan C, Gesta Romanorum, pref E A Baker, London n d, pp 354, 461.

Mau P, Gydo und Thyrus, Jena 1909 (edn of German prose).

Hibbard L A, Guy of Warwick and Louvet, MP 13.181.

Girardus and Lydgate. Edwards E, Liber monasterii de Hyda, Rolls Series 45.xliii, 118 (excerpt of Girardus).

MacCracken H N, Minor Poems of John Lydgate, EETS 192.516.

Carew R, Survey of Cornwall, London 1602, p 59.

(Madden Sir F,) Clerk of Oxenforde, Gentleman's Mag Jan 1 1829, p 493.

DNB, 21.393, see under Girardus Cornubiensis.

Ward, 1.492 (Girardus), 494, 496 (Lydgate).

Schleich G, Lydgates Quelle, Arch 146.49.

Relation to Chaucer. Strong C, Sir Thopas and Sir Guy, MLN 23.73, 102.

Loomis L H, Chaucer's Jewes werk and Guy, PQ 14.371; Chaucer and the Auchinleck MS, E&S Brown, p 111; Sir Thopas, Bryan-Dempster, pp 487, 489, 490, 491, 495, 496, 500, 505, 509, 512, 516, 526, 527, 530, 534, 545, 547, 548, 551, 552; Chaucer and the Breton Lays, SP 38.14, 32.

Later English Derivatives. Ames J, Typographical Antiquities, ed W Herbert, London 1786, 2.798 (Cawood edn, 1571).

Esdaile A, List of English Tales Printed before 1740, Bibliographical Soc, London 1912, p 233.

Crane R S, The Vogue of Guy, PMLA 30.125.

Mish C C, English Prose Fiction 1661–1700, Charlottesville Va 1952, pp 2, 32, 42, 45, 62, 72.

Pleasant Song of Guy and Phyllis. Ritson J, Select Collection of English Songs, London 1783,

2.296; Ritson AS, new edn 1829, 2.193; PFMS, 2.201, 608; Ward, 1.500.

Rowlands S, Famous History of Guy (ca 1608); PFMS, 2.136 (excerpt as Guy and Amaraunt); Ward, 1.499.

Lane J, Corrected Historie of Sir Gwy, 1617, rvsd 1621, BM MS Harley 5243; Ward, 1.497.

G L, Noble and Renowned History, London 1706; H Morley, Early Prose Romances, London 1889, pp 27, 329 (edn of G L) (crit W P Reeves, The So-Called Prose Version of Guy, MLN 11.404); A C L Brown, Source of a Guy of Warwick Chap-Book, JEGP 3.22; Thoms, p 329.

Later Guy Tradition. Dugdale W, Antiquities of Warwickshire, London 1656, pp 298, 322.

Dugdale W, Baronage of England, London 1675, 1.243.

Rossus J, Historia regum Angliae, 2nd edn, ed T Hearnius, Oxford 1745, pp xxiii, 54, 97.

Nichols J, Bibliotheca topographica Britannica, London 1790, 4⁸ no 17 p 29 (Pegge's Memoir).

Weber MR, 2.261.

Hardyng J, Chronicle, ed H Ellis, London 1812, p 210.

Rows J, Roll, ed W Courthope, London 1845, passim.

Furnivall F J, Royal Historie of Generides, Roxb Club, Hertford 1865, p 2.

Wright T, Chronicle of Pierre de Langtoft, Rolls Series, 47¹.330.

Ullmann J, Richard Rolle, EStn 7.469 (Spec Vitae 45).

Kölbing E, Sir Beues, EETSES 46.123.

Kölbing E, Amis and Amiloun and Guy, EStn 9.477.

Lumby J R, Chronicon Henrici Knighton, Rolls Series 92¹.19, 24.

Zupitza J, Athelston, EStn 14.325.

Morrill G L, Speculum Gy, EETSES 75.xiii.

Liebermann F, Guy of Warwicks Einfluss, Arch 107.107.

Wülfing J E, Laud Troy Book, EETS 121.1.

Watson F, Vives, London 1912, p 59.

Zettl E, Metrical Chronicle, EETS 196.lxxviii, 22, 25, 101.

Loomis L H, Athelston Gift Story, PMLA 67.527, 529.

Folkloristic and Cultural Details. Liebrecht F, Zur Volkskunde, Heilbronn 1879, p 472.

Nyrop K, Den oldfranske Heltedigtning, Copenhagen 1883, p 245.

Adam E, Torrent, EETSES 51.107n1268 (holmgang).

Kölbing E, Zur Tristansage, Germ 34.191 (holmgang).

Weyrauch M, Umbildung des Motives vom Entzauberungskuss, StVL 2.360.

Imelman R, J Bramis' Historia regis Waldef, BSEP 4.liii.
Ashdown M, Single Combat in Romance, MLR 17.116, 123.
Beug K, Sage von König Athelston, Arch 148.189, 191, 194.
Cowardin S P jr, An Episode in Guy, Harvard Univ Summaries of Theses 1930, Cambridge 1931, p 194 (Tirri's dream).
Thompson Mot Ind, nos B 11.11, E 721.1, G 100, K 1813, N 836.1; G Boardman, Motif-Index of the English Metrical Romances, FFC 190.14 and passim.
Evans J, English Art 1307–1461, Oxford 1949, p 94n2.
Purdy R R, The Friendship Motif in ME Lit, Vanderbilt Studies in the Humanities 1.130.
Literary Criticism. Scott (Sir) W, Essay on Romance, Enc Brit, 1st edn, suppl; rptd Miscellaneous Prose Works, Edinburgh 1827, 6.187, 248.
Saintsbury G, Short History of English Literature, London 1898, rptd 1907, p 94; Enc Brit, rptd 14th edn, 19.427, see under Romance.
Creek H L, Character in the Matter of England Romances, JEGP 10.429, 585.
Everett D, Characterization of the Medieval Romances, E&S 15.100, 107, 110; rptd Essays on ME Literature, ed P Kean, Oxford 1955, pp 3, 9, 12; Note on Ypotis, RES 6.446.
Taylor A B, Introduction to Medieval Romance, London 1930, pp 96, 133, 145, 156, 162, 169, 173, 206, 208, 225, 232.
Kane, pp 7, 10, 39, 41.
Schaar C, The Golden Mirror, SUVSL 5.13n8, 161, 480.
Adams R P, Bold Bawdry, HLQ 23.44n19.
Baugh A C, Improvisation in the ME Romance, PAPS 103.418.
Blessing J H, Comparison of Some Romances with the OF, DA 20.3281.
Warton T, History of English Poetry, ed R Price, London 1840, 1.clxxxix, 80, 144, 146, 205; 3.128.
Littré E, Trouvères, HLF, 22.841.
Smith G G, Transition Period, Edinburgh 1900, pp 8, 34, 192.
PFMS, 2.509; 3.171; Körting, 1st edn, Münster 1887, p 97; Ten Brink, 1.150, 246; 2.232; S Lee, Guy of Warwick, DNB, 23.386; Morley, 3.276; Brandl, 2¹.636, 645, 670, 687; Courthope, 1.xiv, 148, 149, 323; Wülcker, 1.98, 105; Billings, p 24; Gröber, 2¹.776, 1195; Schofield, pp 15, 31, 271, 272, 477; CHEL 1.242, 314, 326, 327, 339, 340, 520; 2.199, 308, 321, 323; Rickert RofL, pp xxvi, xxix, xxxvii.

Hibbard Med Rom, pp 127, 140.
Enc Brit, 14th edn, 11.15, see under Guy of Warwick.
Wilson R M, More Lost Literature, Leeds SE 5.28, 32; Early ME Literature, London 1939, 1951, pp 77, 215; Lost Literature of Medieval England, London 1952, pp 62, 63, 129.
Renwick-Orton, p 340; rvsd edn, p 355.
Wright C E, Cultivation of Saga in Anglo-Saxon England, Edinburgh and London 1939, pp 31, 192.
Bennett OHEL, pp 214, 313.
Baugh LHE, p 178.
Sampson G, Concise CHEL, Cambridge 1949, pp 42, 43.
Schlauch M, English Medieval Literature, Warsaw 1956, pp 143, 144, 178, 179, 197.
Brydges (Sir) S E and J Haslewood, British Bibliographer, London 1814, 4.268.
Hazlitt W C, Hand-Book to the Popular Literature of Britain, London 1867, p 247.
Tucker-Benham, p 248; CBEL 1.39, 149; 5.115; Bennett OHEL, p 313.
Zesmer D M and S B Greenfield, Guide to English Literature, N Y 1961, pp 112, 249.

[8] GUY AND COLBROND.

MS. BM Addit 27879 (Percy Folio), pp 349–357 (ca 1600).
Catalogue of Additions to the MSS in the British Museum 1854–75, London 1877, 2.369; Ward 1.500.
Edition. PFMS, 2.509, 527.
Relation to Guy of Warwick. Warton T, History of English Poetry, ed R Price, London 1840, 1.93; Chambers, 1.56n6; P Christophersen, Ballad of Sir Aldingar, Oxford 1952, p 35 (canticum Colbrondi).
Gairdner J, The Paston Letters, new edn, London 1904, 1.323, 6.65 (item 5, ca 1475–83).
Wilson R M, More Lost Literature, Leeds SE 5.32; Lost Literature of Medieval England, London 1952, pp 62, 129.

For other topics, see under GUY OF WARWICK [7].

[9] GAMELYN.

MSS. 1, Bodl Barlow 20 (1450–80); 2, Bodl Hatton Donat I (1450–60); 3, Bodl Laud 600 (1430–50); 4, Bodl Laud 739 (1470–90); 5, Bodl Rawlinson Poet 149 (1450–70); 6, Christ Church Oxf 152, ff 58ᵇ–71ᵇ (1460–70); 7, Corp Christi Oxf 198, ff 61ᵃ–73ᵇ (1410–20); 8, Trinity Oxf 49 (1461–83); 9, Camb Univ Ii.3.26 (1430–50); 10, Camb Univ

Mm.2.5 (1450–60); 11, Fitzwilliam McClean 181 (1450–69); 12, Egerton 2726, ff 56–63 (18 cent transcript of Bodl Laud 600); 13, Egerton 2863 (1430–50); 14, Harley 1758, ff 46ª–55ª (1450–60); 15, Harley 7334, ff 59ª–70ᵇ (ca 1410); 16, Lansdowne 851, ff 54ᵇ–65ª (1410–20); 17, Royal 17.D.xv, ff 66ᵇ, 78ᵇ–79ª (1450–70); 18, Royal 18.C.ii, ff 56ᵇ–67ᵇ (1420–50); 19, Sloane 1685, ff 51ᵇ–62ᵇ; 20, Sloane 1686, ff 71ª–86ᵇ (1480–90); 21, Lichfield Cath 2 (1430–50); 22, Delamere (1450–60); 23, Petworth 7, ff 62ª–74ª (1420–30); 24, Glasgow Hunterian U.1.1 (1477); 25, Morgan 249 (1450–60); 26, Phillipps 8137 (1430–50).

Brown-Robbins, no 1913; MED, p 42.

Ward, 1.508, 512, 513, 514, 515 (Harl 7334, Lans, Harl 1758, Royal 18, Sloane 1685, 1686, Royal 17).

McCormick (Sir) W, MSS of Chaucer's Canterbury Tales, Oxford 1933, pp xvi, xxv, 22, 79, 86, 102, 120n, 128, 157, 180, 190, 210, 225, 259, 274, 284, 294, 302, 336, 348, 388, 406, 435, 452, 462, 485, 493, 525.

Manly & Rickert, 1.15, 55, 85, 92, 108, 130, 135, 136, 160, 183, 198, 219, 223, 225, 294, 304, 306, 309, 315, 322, 365, 372, 388, 427, 455, 476, 485, 504, 510, 535; 2.170; 2.494 charts 3, 4, 5; 2.512.

Rogers F R, Tale of Gamelyn and Editing of the Canterbury Tales, JEGP 58.49.

Editions. Urry J, Works of Geoffrey Chaucer, London 1721, p 36.

Bell J, Poetical Works of Chaucer, Poets of Great Britain, Edinburgh 1782, 6.5.

Anderson R, Works of the British Poets, Edinburgh and London 1795, 1.203.

Chalmers A, Works of the English Poets, London 1810, 1.607.

Wright T, Canterbury Tales, Percy Soc 24, London 1847, 1.176; rptd N Cooke, Universal Library, London 1853, 2²⁵.51.

Bell R, Poetical Works of Geoffrey Chaucer, Annotated Edn of the English Poets, London 1854, 1.238; rvsd W W Skeat, London 1885, 1.238.

Morris R, Poetical Works of Geffrey Chaucer, new rvsd edn, London n d, 2.138.

Furnivall F J, Ellesmere MS, ChS 1s 8, appendix (Royal 18); Hengwrt MS, ChS 1s 9, appx (Royal 17, Harl 1758); Cambridge MS, ChS 1s 10, appx (Sloane 1685, Royal 17); Corpus MS, ChS 1s 11, appx; Petworth MS, ChS 1s 12, appx; Lansdowne MS, ChS 1s 13, appx; Six-Text Print of Chaucer's Canterbury Tales, ChS 1s 14, appx (Royal 18; 17; Harl 1758; Sloane 1685; Corp; Pet; Lans); Harleian MS 7334, ChS 1s 73, appx.

Skeat W W, Tale of Gamelyn, Oxford 1884 (2nd edn, 1893; rptd Elston Press, New Rochelle N Y 1901) (crit F Lindner, EStn 9.111) (edn of Harl 7334, 1758, Corp, Lans, Pet, Royal 18, Sloane 1685).

Skeat W W, Tale of Gamelyn, Complete Works of Geoffrey Chaucer, Oxford 1894; 3.399, 403 (Canon no 143); 4.645 (normalized edn); 5.477 (notes)(6.347 (glossary).

French W H and C B Hale, ME Metrical Romances, N Y 1930, p 207 (from ChS 1s 73).

Selections. Sampson G, Cambridge Book of Prose and Verse, Cambridge 1924, p 297.

Kaiser R, Alt- und mittelenglische Anthologie, Berlin 1954 (2nd edn, 1955), p 390; Medieval English, rvsd English edn, Berlin 1958, p 413.

Modernizations. Zupitza J, Die me Vorstufe von Shakespeare's As You Like It, Jahrbuch der deutschen Shakespeare-Gesellschaft 21.69.

Rickert RofFr, pp xviii, 85, 177.

Whiting B J et al, College Survey of English Literature, N Y 1942, 1.104.

Textual Notes. Holthausen F, AnglB 40.57.

Language. Björkman E, Die Namen Ormmin, Gamelyn, Arch 119.33; Mittelenglische Personennamen auf -in, Arch 123.23, 33, 42.

Rogers, JEGP 58.49 (see under *MSS* above).

Versification. Saintsbury G A, History of English Prosody, Oxford 1906, pp 124n, 194, 241, 254, 327; Historical Manual of English Prosody, London 1910, rptd 1926, pp 165, 281, 325, 326.

Kaluza M, Englische Metrik, Berlin 1909, § 199; trans A C Dunstan, Short History of English Versification, London 1911, same section.

Outlaw Tradition. Lindner F, Tale of Gamelyn, EStn 2.94, 321.

Prideaux W F, Who Was Robin Hood, N&Q 7s 2.424.

Child F J, English and Scottish Popular Ballads, Cambridge Mass 1888, 3.12 (no 115); 3.144 (no 128).

de Lange J, Relation and Development of English and Icelandic Outlaw-Traditions, Nederlandsche Bijdragen op het Gebied van germaansche Philologie en Linguistiek 6.32, 42.

Steel A, Richard II, Cambridge 1941, p 68.

Keen M, The Outlaws of Medieval Legend, London and Toronto 1961, pp 78, 224.

Relation to Chaucer. Tyrwhitt T, Introductory Discourse to the Canterbury Tales, Poetical Works of Geoffrey Chaucer, London 1843, p lvii (§ xiii).

Brusendorff A, Chaucer Tradition, London and Copenhagen 1925, pp 72, 126.

Tatlock J S P, Canterbury Tales in 1400, PMLA 50.112.
Loomis L H, Sir Thopas, Bryan-Dempster, pp 488, 495, 500, 505, 515.
Relation to Shakespeare. Furness H H, As You Like It, New Variorum Edition of Shakespeare, Phila 1890, 8.310.
Courthope, 4.123.
Bullough G, Narrative and Dramatic Sources of Shakespeare, London 1958, 2.143.
Other Problems. Mahew A L, The Name of Ote, N&Q 6s 11.145.
Shannon E F jr, Medieval Law in Gamelyn, Spec 26.458.
Thompson Mot Ind, L 101 (unpromising hero); G Boardman, Motif-Index of the English Metrical Romances, FFC 190.13 and passim.
Saintsbury G, Short History of English Literature, London 1898, rptd 1907, p 325.
Snell F J, Age of Chaucer, London 1901, p 1.
Leach H G, Angevin Britain, Cambridge Mass 1921, p 351.
Ward, 1.508, 516; Ten Brink, 2.183, 188; 3.271; Morley, 5.320; Brandl, 2¹.658; Schofield, p 279; CHEL, 1.321, 410, 521; 2.162, 164, 178, 194, 211, 215, 216, 467; 3.279, 358; G Sampson, Concise CHEL, Cambridge 1949, pp 41, 42, 263; Rickert RofL, pp xxix, xxxvii, xxxviii; Hibbard Med Rom, p 156; Renwick-Orton, p 343; 2nd edn, p 359; Chambers OHEL, p 132; Baugh LHE, p 194; Kane, pp 46, 48.
Schlauch M, English Medieval Literature, Warsaw 1956, pp 180, 197.
Hammond, pp 175, 229, 425; CBEL, 1.151; 5.116; Bennett OHEL, p 310.
Griffith D D, Bibliography of Chaucer, Seattle 1955, p 265.
Zesmer D M and S B Greenfield, Guide to English Literature, N Y 1961, p 112.

[10] ATHELSTON.

MS. Caius Camb 175, ff 120ª–131ª (ca 1420).
Brown-Robbins, no 1973; MED, pp 11, 26.
Editions. Hartshorne AMT, pp ix, 1.
Rel Ant, 2.85.
Zupitza J, Die Romanze von Athelston, EStn 13.331; 14.321.
Hervey (Lord) F, Corolla Sancti Eadmundi, London 1907, pp 525, 669.
French W H and C B Hale, ME Metrical Romances, N Y 1930, p 177.
Trounce A McI, Athelston, Publications of the Philological Soc 11, London 1933 (crit N&Q 165.413; TLS Oct 5 1933, p 674; A Brandl, Arch 164.295; G H Gerould, MÆ 3.57; J R Hulbert, MP 32.107; H C Matthes,

GRM 22.408; D Everett, RES 11.112 and YWES 14.120; M S Serjeantson, ESts 17.100; E Fischer, AnglB 47.259; W H French, MLN 51.340; H S V Jones, JEGP 35.418; F Wild, LfGRP 57.386); rvsd reissue, EETS 224, London 1951 (identical pagination) (crit N&Q 197.22).
Modernization. Rickert RofFr, pp xvi, 67, 175.
Textual Notes. Zupitza, edn, p 343.
Taylor G, Leeds SE 4.47.
Onions C T, End of One's Kin, MÆ 7.118.
Language. Trounce A McI, ME Tail-Rhyme Romances, MÆ 1.87, 1.168, 2.34, 2.189, 3.30 (crit D Everett, YWES 13.94, 14.118).
Taylor G, Leeds SE 4.47.
Dunlap A R, Vocabulary of the ME Romances in Tail-Rhyme, Delaware Notes 14.2, 37, and passim.
Versification. Trounce, MAE, 1.168; edn, p 52.
Sources and Analogues. Stubbs W, Willelmi Malmesbiriensis De gestis regum, Rolls Series 90, London 1889, 2.lxxx (Emma's ordeal).
Gerould G H, Social and Historical Reminiscences in Athelston, EStn 36.193 (sworn brotherhood; Alryk and Becket).
Brandl, 2nd edn, 2¹.1087 (King Athelstan ballads).
Liebermann F, Gesetze der Angelsachsen, Halle 1903–16, 2.386 no 13c (cf no 13b Emma).
Hibbard L A, Athelston a Westminster Legend, PMLA 36.223 (Emma); Med Rom, p 143.
Beug K, Die Sage von König Athelston, Arch 148.181, 191.
McKeehan I P, St Edmund of East Anglia: The Development of a Legend, Univ of Colorado Studies 15.67.
Baugh A C, A Source for Athelston, PMLA 44.377 (Walter Map).
Wilson R M, More Lost Literature, Leeds SE 5.29; Lost Literature of Medieval England, London 1952, p 63.
Boardman G, Motif-Index of the English Metrical Romances, FFC 190.13 and passim.
Bryan-Dempster, pp 494, 505, 542 (Sir Thopas parallels).
Everett D, Characterization of the English Medieval Romances, E&S 15.107; rptd Essays on ME Literature, ed P Kean, Oxford 1955, p 9.
Baugh A C, Improvisation in the ME Romance, PAPS 103.418.
Wilson R M, Early ME Literature, London 1939, 1951, p 215.
Schlauch M, English Medieval Literature and Its Social Foundations, Warsaw 1956, pp 179, 190, 197.

Brandl, p 670; Billings, p 32; Schofield, pp 275, 477; CHEL, 1.319, 519; Rickert RofFr, p xvi; RofL, p xxxvii; Hibbard Med Rom, p 143; Renwick-Orton, p 342; rvsd edn, p 358; Baugh LHE, p 180; Kane, p 54; CBEL, 1.150; 5.115.

[11] WILLIAM OF PALERNE.

MS. King's Camb 13, ff 4ᵃ–9ᵇ, 11ᵃ–86ᵃ (ca 1360–75).
Brown-Robbins, no *54; MED, pp 11, 83.
Hartshorne AMT, p xxiv.
Editions. Madden F, The Ancient English Romance of William and the Werwolf, Roxb Club, London 1832.
Skeat W W, Romance of William of Palerne, EETSES 1, London 1867 (rptd 1890).
Selections. Hartshorne AMT, pp xxiv, 256.
Wülcker R P, Altenglisches Lesebuch, Halle 1879, 2.76, 261.
Morris Spec, 2.138, 318.
Sampson G, Cambridge Book of Prose and Verse, Cambridge 1924, p 310.
Textual Notes. Stratmann F H, EStn 4.99; W H Browne, MLN 7.268; E A Kock, Angl 26.367.
Language. Bryant J, Observations upon the Poems of Rowley, London 1781, p 14.
Madden F, Glossary to the Ancient English Romance of William and the Werwolf, London 1832.
Hardwick C and H R Luard, Catalogue of the MSS Preserved in the Library of the Univ of Cambridge, Cambridge 1867, 5.189 (MS glossary).
Asklöf I, Essay on the Romance of William, Stockholm 1872.
Schüddekopf A, Sprache und Dialekt des me Gedichtes William of Palerne, Erlangen 1886 (crit E Hausknecht, DLz 7.1755; M Kaluza, EStn 10.291).
Pitschel E, Zur Syntax des William of Palerne, Marburg 1890.
Hulbert J R, The West Midland of the Romances, MP 19.1.
Menner R J, Sir Gawain and the West Midland, PMLA 37.512, 515, 517.
Serjeantson M S, Dialects of the West Midlands, RES 3.56, 59, 60, 329.
Huchon R, Histoire de la langue anglaise, Paris 1930, 2.245.
Oakden J P, Alliterative Poetry in ME, Dialectal and Metrical Survey, Manchester 1930 (rptd as Poetry of the Alliterative Revival, Manchester 1937), pp 55, 153, 248 (crit W van der Gaaf, ESts 13.142); Alliterative Poetry in ME, Survey of the Traditions,

Manchester 1935, pp 24, 38, 176, 181, 312.
Whiting B J, Proverbs in Certain ME Romances, HSNPL 15.107.
Versification. Rosenthal F, Die alliterierende englische Langzeile, Angl 1.414, 415, and passim.
Schipper, Englische Metrik, 1.196; Grundriss der englischen Metrik, WBEP 2.76, 83; History of English Versification, Oxford 1910, pp 86, 93.
Guest E, History of English Rhythms, ed W W Skeat, London 1882, pp 240, 242, 447, 482, 692.
Luick K, Die englische Stabreimzeile, Angl 11.566; Englische Metrik, Paul Grundriss, 2¹.1013 (2nd edn, 2².164).
Saintsbury G A, History of English Prosody, Oxford 1906, pp 102, 181n; Historical Manual of English Prosody, London 1910, rptd 1926, pp 48, 221.
Oakden, Alliterative Poetry (see *Language,* above).
Relation to Alliterative Alexander. Trautmann M, Ueber Verfasser und Entstehungszeit einiger alliterirender Gedichte, Leipzig 1876 (another edn, Halle 1876); H Koziol, Zur Frage der Verfasserschaft einiger Stabreimdichtungen, EStn 67.167.
Source. Michelant H, Guillaume de Palerne, SATF, Paris 1876.
Delp W S, Étude sur la langue de Guillaume de Palerne, Paris 1907 (glossary, index of names).
Flutre L F, Table des noms propres dans les romans, Poitiers 1962, pp xii and passim.
Kaluza M, William of Palerne und seine französische Quelle, EStn 4.197, 274 (notes on Michelant edn), 280 (notes on Skeat edn).
McKeehan I P, Guillaume de Palerne a Medieval Best Seller, PMLA 41.785.
Dunn C W, The Foundling and the Werwolf, A Literary-Historical Study of Guillaume de Palerne, Univ of Toronto Dept of English Studies and Texts 8, Toronto 1960 (crit F J Byrne, SN 32.358; M D Legge, EHR 76.699; H Newstead, RomP 15.188; W Rothwell, FS 15.253; N B Spector, MP 58.208; H F Williams, Spec 36.123; M Williams, Folklore 71.273).
French Prose Version. Williams H F, Les versions de Guillaume de Palerne, Rom 73.64.
English Prose Version. Brie F, Zwei frühneuenglische Prosaromane, Arch 118.318 (edn); A Esdaile, List of English Tales, Publications of the Bibliographical Soc, London 1912, p 137.

Irish Prose Version. O'Rahilly C, Eachtra Uilliam, Dublin 1949 (edn and trans) (crit H F Williams, RomP 3.306; C W Dunn, Spec 32.849).

Cultural and Folkloristic Topics. Hertz W, Der Werwolf, Stuttgart 1862, p 65.

Smith K F, Historical Study of the Werwolf, PMLA 9.41n1.

Heyman H E, Studies on the Havelok-Tale, Upsala 1903, p 107 (dream).

Kittredge G L, Arthur and Gorlagon, HSNPL 8.150 (werwolf).

Tibbals K W, Elements of Magic in William of Palerne, MP 1.355.

Easter D B, Study of the Magic Elements in the Romans d'Adventure, Baltimore 1906, pp 5n24, 8, 27, 39n180.

Watson F, Vives and the Renascence Education of Women, London 1912, p 59.

Barrow S F, Medieval Society Romances, Columbia Univ Studies in English and Comp Lit, N Y 1924, pp 14, 16, 32, 115, 133.

Hulbert J R, Hypothesis Concerning the Alliterative Revival, MP 28.413, 415 (patronage).

Thompson Mot Ind, B 442, B 575, D 113.1.1, K 521.1, N 836.1, R 131.3.3, R 169.3; 5.451 (D 0), 452 (D 800), 455 (D 1700); G Boardman, Motif-Index of the English Metrical Romances, FFC 190.15 and passim.

Literary Criticism. Creek H L, Character in the Matter of England Romances, JEGP 10.444n24, 45n29, 596n46, 598.

Kane, pp 8, 9, 46, 51.

Everett D, The Alliterative Revival, Essays on ME Literature, ed P Kean, Oxford 1955, pp 48, 53.

Schaar C, The Golden Mirror, SUVSL 54.161, 480.

Waldron R A, Oral-Formulaic Technique and ME Alliterative Poetry, Spec 32.792.

Blessing J H, Comparison of Some ME Romances with the OF, DA 20.3281.

Saintsbury G, Short History of English Literature, London 1898, rptd 1907, p 105.

Körting, 1st edn, Münster 1887, p 99; Ten Brink, 1.334; Morley, 3.284; Brandl, 2¹.660; Wülcker, 1.113; Billings, p 41; Schofield, p 312; CHEL, 1.312, 318, 325, 352, 399, 422, 524; G Sampson, Concise CHEL, Cambridge 1949, p 46; Hibbard Med Rom, p 214.

Paris G, Mélanges de la littérature française du moyen âge, ed M Roques, Paris 1912, pp 45, 111.

Lot-Borodine M, Le roman idyllique, Paris 1913, p 248 (crit F L Critchlow, MLN 29.188).

Ker W P, English Literature, Medieval, London n d, pp 73, 142.

Thomas P G, English Literature before Chaucer, London 1924, p 129.

Enc Brit, 14th edn, 10.969, see under Guillaume de Palerne.

Taylor A B, Introduction to Medieval Romance, London 1930, pp 137, 152, 158, 164.

Legouis HEL, rvsd edn, London 1933, pp 107, 109.

Renwick-Orton, p 341; 2nd rvsd edn, p 356.

Chaytor H J, From Script to Print, An Introd to Medieval Literature, Cambridge 1945, p 105.

Baugh LHE, pp 194, 232.

Schlauch M, English Medieval Literature, Warsaw 1956, pp 189, 199.

CBEL, 1.29, 40, 156; Holmes CBFL, pp 82, 139; Bossuat MBLF, nos 1368–1373, 6250.

Zesmer D M and S B Greenfield, Guide to English Literature, N Y 1961, p 112.

2. ARTHURIAN LEGENDS

by

Helaine Newstead

BIBLIOGRAPHIES.

Weston J L, King Arthur and His Knights, a Survey, London 1905.

Brown A C L, The Round Table before Wace, Boston 1900 (notes to later pieces).

Magoun F P, An Index of Abbreviations in Miss Alma Blount's Unpublished Onomasticon Arthurianum, Spec 1.90.

Chambers E K, Arthur of Britain, London 1927, p 283.

Bruce J D, The Evolution of Arthurian Romance, 2nd edn, Baltimore 1928, 2.380.

Gray H J B, Bibliography of Recent Arthurian Literature, Arthuriana 1.67; F M Williams, Arthurian Bibliography, Arthuriana 2.83.

Parry J J, A Bibliography of Critical Arthurian

Brayer E, Manuscrits de romans bretons photographiés à L'Institut de recherche et d'histoire des textes, BBSIA 6.79.

National Library of Wales, Bibliotheca Celtica: A Register of Publications Relating to Wales and the Celtic Peoples and Languages, 3 ser 1, 1953.35 (Arthurian literature).

Woledge B, Bibliographie de romans et nouvelles en prose française antérieurs à 1500, Geneva 1954 (crit A Ewert, FS 9.88).

Gröber, p 1254 and under individual names; Paris Litt franç, § 53; de Julleville Hist, 1.340; Krit Jahresber; Enc Brit, see under Arthur, Lancelot, Tristram, Merlin, Perceval, Holy Grail, Gawain; Körting, § 101 anm; CHEL, 1.513; Billings, p 85.

Wells J E, CBEL 1.130 (bibl to 1933).

GENERAL TREATMENTS.

Ritson J, Life of King Arthur, London 1825; A B Hopkins, Ritson's Life of King Arthur, PMLA 43.251.

Rhŷs J, Studies in the Arthurian Legend, Oxford 1891.

Zimmer H, Beiträge zur Namenforschung in den altfranzösischen Arthurepen, ZfFSL 13¹.1.

Hoeppner A B, Arthurs Gestalt in der Literatur Englands, diss Leipzig 1892.

Pütz F, Zur Geschichte der Entwicklung der Artursage, ZfFSL 14¹.161.

MacCallum M W, Tennyson's Idylls of the King and Arthurian Story, Glasgow 1894.

Wülcker R P, Die Arthursage in der englischen Literatur, Leipzig 1895.

Saintsbury G, Flourishing of Romance, Edinburgh 1897.

Ker W P, Epic and Romance, London 1897, 1908, chap 5.

Newell W W, King Arthur and the Table Round, Boston 1897.

Nutt A, Les derniers travaux allemands, RC 12.181.

Brown A C L, The Round Table before Wace, Boston 1900 (crit G P[aris], Rom 29.634).

Lot F, Études sur la provenance du cycle arthurien, Rom 25.1; Rom 28.1, 321; Rom 30.1.

Nutt A, Celtic and Mediaeval Romance, London 1899.

Dickinson W H, King Arthur in Cornwall, N Y 1900 (crit W A Nitze, MLN 17.429).

Paton L A, Studies in the Fairy Mythology of Arthurian Romance, Boston 1903 (crit J Koch, EStn 34.377; W A Nitze, MLN 19.80).

Briggs W D, King Arthur in Cornwall, JEGP 3.342.

Kittredge G L, Arthur and Gorlagon, HSNPL 8.149.

Weston J L, King Arthur and His Knights, a Survey, London 1905.

Moorman F W, The Interpretation of Nature in English Poetry from Beowulf to Shakespeare, Strassburg 1905, p 61.

Fletcher R H, The Arthurian Material in the Chronicles, Boston 1906 (crit P M[eyer], Rom 36.335).

Mott L F, The Round Table, PMLA 20.231.

Maynadier G H, The Arthur of the English Poets, Boston 1907.

Sommer H O, ed, Vulgate Version of the Arthurian Romances, 7 vols and Index, Washington 1908–16.

Blount A, An Arthurian Onomasticon, RadMon 15, Boston 1910, p 25.

Jones W L, King Arthur in History and Legend, Cambridge 1911 (crit T Mühe, AnglB 24.298).

Lawrence W W, Medieval Story, N Y 1911.

Loth J, Contributions à l'étude des romans de la Table Ronde, Paris 1912 (crit E Brugger, ZfFSL 47.218).

Sommer H O, The Structure of the Livre d'Artus and Its Function in the Evolution of the Arthurian Prose Romances, Paris and London 1914 (crit W Golther, LfGRP 36.154).

Leach H G, Angevin Britain and Scandinavia, Cambridge Mass 1921.

Liebermann F, Die Eigenname Arthur vor Galfrids Einfluss, Arch 141.235; Die angebliche Entdeckung einer brythonischen Geschichte aus Römerzeit: Galfrid von Monmouth und Tysilio, Arch 144.31.

Parry J J, Modern Welsh Versions of the Arthurian Stories, JEGP 21.572.

Bruce J D, Desiderata in the Investigation of the Old French Prose Romances, MP 20.339.

Schoepperle G, Arthur in Avalon and the Banshee, Vassar Medieval Studies, New Haven 1923, p 9.

Cross T P, The Passing of Arthur, Manly Anniversary Studies, Chicago 1923, p 284.

Mead W E, ed, Middleton's Chinon of England, EETS 165, introd.

Gordon G, The Trojans in Britain, E&S 9.1.

Malone K, Artorius, MP 22.367; The Historicity of Arthur, JEGP 23.463 (crit E V Gordon, YWES 5.96; J Loth, RC 42.307).

Baker E A, The History of the English Novel, London 1924, pp 63, 82, 108, 148.

Johnson W B, The Arthurian Legend in Brittany, The Nineteenth Century and After 98.756.

Loomis R S, Medieval Iconography and the Question of Arthurian Origins, MLN 40.65.

Plesner K F, Engelsk Arthur-Digtning, Köbenhavn 1925.

Ten Bensel E v d V, The Character of King Arthur in English Literature, Amsterdam 1925 (crit J J Parry, MLN 42.417; M Gaster, Folklore 37.404).

Entwistle W J, The Arthurian Legend in the Literature of the Spanish Peninsula, London 1925 (crit C S Northup, MP 24.481; E G Gardner, MLR 21.333).

Snell F J, King Arthur's Country, London 1926.

Spence L, Arthurian Tradition in Scotland, Scots Magazine Apr 1926, p 17.

Singer S, Die Artussage, Bern 1926 (crit E Brugger, ZfFSL 50.161; F Piquet, RG 18.38).

Robinson J A, Two Glastonbury Legends, King Arthur and St Joseph of Arimathea, Cambridge 1926 (crit M Foerster, DLz 48.1061; F Klaeber, AnglB 38.133; D Everett, YWES 7.89).

Gerould G H, King Arthur and Politics, Spec 1.33; 2.448; A C L Brown, A Note on the Nugae of G H Gerould's King Arthur and Politics, Spec 2.449.

Loomis L H, Arthur's Round Table, PMLA 41.771 (crit A C L Brown, MP 25.242).

Van Hamel A G, Koning Arthurs Vader, Neophil 12.34.

Jones T G, Some Arthurian Material in Keltic, ASt 8.37.

Slover C H, Early Literary Channels between Britain and Ireland, Texas SE 6.5; 7.5 (crit J J Parry, JEGP 29.136; A C L Brown, MLN 44.407).

Crawford O G S, Lyonesse, Antiq 1.5.

Bruce J D, Mordred's Incestuous Birth, Medieval Studies in Memory of G S Loomis, Paris and N Y 1927, p 197.

Chambers E K, Arthur of Britain, London 1927 (crit G H Gerould, Spec 3.259; K Malone, MLN 43.481; A H Krappe, RomR 19.121).

Loomis R S, Celtic Myth and Arthurian Romance, N Y 1927 (crit J A Robinson, Dublin Review 94[374].33; E Brugger, ZfFSL 54.81; W J Gruffydd, Y Llenor 6.187; A C L Brown, T P Cross, ZfCP 18.114; J J Parry, JEGP 27.246; H R Patch, Spec 4.117).

Bruce J D, The Evolution of Arthurian Romance, Göttingen and Baltimore 1923, 2nd edn 1928 (with bibliographical supplement by A Hilka; crit 1st edn, R S Loomis, JEGP 23.582; W A Nitze, MP 22.99; 2nd edn,

L S[uttina], Studi medievali 3.160; J A Robinson, Dublin Review 94[374].33).

Jaffray R, King Arthur and the Holy Grail, N Y 1928.

Faral E, La légende arthurienne, 3 vols, Paris 1929 (crit A C L Brown, Spec 6.305; R S Loomis, MLN 46.176; J Loth, Moyen âge 41.289; A C Baugh, MP 29.357).

Loomis L H, The Round Table Again, MLN 44.511.

Weston J L, Legendary Cycles of the Middle Ages, Cambridge Mediaeval History, vol 6, N Y and Cambridge 1929.

Weston J L, Enc Brit, 14th edn 1929 (articles on Arthurian legend and Holy Grail rewritten; others abridged with some titles added to bibliographies; those on Arthur and the Round Table replaced by anonymous compilations).

Northup C S, King Arthur, the Christ, and Some Others, Miscellany in Honor of F Klaeber, Minneapolis 1929, p 309.

Parsons A E, The Matter of Britain, TLS 1929, p 1002.

Robinson J A, Recent Studies of the Arthurian Legend, Dublin Review 94(374).33 (Bruce, Chambers, Griscom, Faral etc).

MacCulloch J A, The Arthurian Legend, Folklore Society, Papers and Transactions, London 1930, p 198.

Loomis R S, Some Names in Arthurian Romance, PMLA 45.416.

Loomis R S, The Scientific Method in Arthurian Studies, Studi medievali 3.288.

Taylor A B, An Introduction to Mediaeval Romance, London 1930.

Gardner E G, The Arthurian Legend in Italian Literature, London 1930 (crit J Loth, Moyen âge 43.98; J A Noonan, MÆ 2.82).

Brugger E, The Hebrides in Arthurian Literature, Arthuriana 2.7.

Loomis L H, Arthurian Tombs and Megalithic Monuments, MLR 26.408.

Cons L, Avallo, MP 28.385.

Slover C H, Avalon, MP 28.395.

Lewis C B, Classical Mythology and Arthurian Romance, London 1932 (crit J J Parry, Spec 9.336; E V[inaver], MÆ 3.204; H R Patch, MLN 49.415).

Baldwin C S, Three Medieval Centuries of Literature in England 1100–1400, Boston 1932 (chaps 3–6).

Morgan Sister M L, Galahad in English Literature, diss Catholic Univ, Washington 1932.

Millican C B, Spenser and the Table Round, Cambridge Mass 1932, p 1.

MacCulloch J A, Medieval Faith and Fable, London 1932.

Tristram, Lancelot, and Courtly Love, TLS 1932, p 597.

Knowles J, The Legends of King Arthur and His Knights, London 1932.

Byrne Sister M of the Incarnation, The Tradition of the Nun in Medieval England, diss Catholic University, Washington 1933 (crit H R Patch, MLN 49.274).

Loomis R S, The Visit to the Perilous Castle: A Study of the Arthurian Modifications of an Irish Theme, PMLA 48.1000.

Raglan Lord, The Hero of Tradition, Folklore 45.212.

Nitze W A, The Exhumation of King Arthur at Glastonbury, Spec 9.355.

Schlauch M, Romance in Iceland, N Y 1934.

Smith J M, The French Background of Middle Scots Literature, London and Edinburgh 1934.

Loomis C G, King Arthur and the Saints, Spec 8.878.

Loomis R S, By What Route Did the Romantic Tradition of Arthur Reach the French? MP 33.225 (crit J Vendryes, Études celtiques 2.367).

Loomis R S, The Modena Sculpture and Arthurian Romance, Studi medievali 9.1.

Thompson J W, Ancient Celtic Symptoms in Arthurian Romance, Transactions Hon Soc of the Cymmrodorion for 1936, p 137.

Crawford O G S, Arthur and His Battles, Antiq 9.277.

Oakeshott W F, Arthuriana at Winchester, Wessex 3.74.

Baker Sister I, The King's Household in the Arthurian Court, Washington 1937 (crit K Brunner, LfGRP 61.26).

Reid M C J, The Arthurian Legend; Comparison of Treatment in Modern and Mediaeval Literature; a Study in the Literary Value of Myth and Legend, Edinburgh 1938 (crit E V[inaver], RES 16.331).

Loomis R S and L H, Arthurian Legends in Medieval Art, N Y 1938 (crit H R Patch, RomR 30.192; F Ranke, GR 14.219).

Wilson R M, Early Middle English Literature, London 1939, p 201.

Tatlock J S P, The Date of the Arthurian Saints' Legends, Spec 14.345.

Nitze W A and A Taylor, Some Recent Arthurian Studies, MP 36.307.

Brodeur A G, Arthur dux bellorum, Univ of Calif Publ in English 3, no 7, 1939, p 237 (crit W A Nitze, MLN 57.64).

Newstead H, Bran the Blessed in Arthurian Romance, N Y 1939 (crit T Jones, MLR 35.402; A H Krappe, Spec 15.117; G Frank, RomR 31.293).

Nitze W A, Arthurian Romance and Modern Poetry and Music, Chicago 1940 (crit A F J Remy, RomR 32.300).

Reinhard J R, Burning at the Stake in Mediaeval Law and Literature, Spec 16.186.

Loomis R S, The Spoils of Annwn, PMLA 56.887.

Loomis R S, The Arthurian Legend before 1139, RomR 32.3.

Loomis R S, King Arthur and the Antipodes, MP 38.289.

Giffin M E, Cadwalader, Arthur, and Brutus in the Wigmore Manuscript, Spec 16.109.

Sneyers G, Les romans de la Table Ronde, Brussels 1941.

Savage J H J, Insula Avallonis, Transactions of the American Philological Assoc 73.405.

Sparnaay H, De Weg van Koning Arthur, Groningen 1942.

Frappier J, Les romans courtois, Paris 1943 (selections and commentary).

Foulon C, Les voyages merveilleux dans les romans bretons, Paris 1943.

Krappe A H, Avallon, Spec 18.303.

Cross T P, Early Irish Literature in Its Relation to Arthurian Romance, PMLA 59.1335.

Sandoz E, Tourneys in the Arthurian Tradition, Spec 19.389.

Wieruszowski H, King Arthur's Round Table: An Academic Club in Fourteenth Century Tuscany, Trad 2.502.

McHugh S J, The Lay of the Big Fool: Its Irish and Arthurian Sources, MP 42.197.

Loomis R S, Morgain la Fée and the Celtic Goddesses, Spec 20.183.

Krappe A H, Arturus Cosmocrator, Spec 20.405.

Scherer M, About the Round Table, N Y 1945 (crit L H Loomis, Spec 21.359; T A Kirby, MLN 62.216).

Bar F, Les routes de l'autre monde, Paris 1946.

Newstead H, The Traditional Background of Partonopeus de Blois, PMLA 61.916.

Bowditch H, Another Printed Version of the Arms of the Knights of the Round Table, Spec 21.490.

Loomis R S, From Segontium to Sinadon— the Legends of a Cité Gaste, Spec 22.520.

Gruffydd W J, The Arthurian Legend and the Mabinogion, Welsh Review 6.244 (notes by T J Morgan, 262).

Spence L, Scotland in Mediaeval Romance, Scots Magazine Apr 1947, p 37.

Housman J E, Higden, Trevisa, Caxton and the Beginnings of Arthurian Romance, RES 23.209.

Vinaver E, ed, The Works of Sir Thomas Malory, 3 vols, Oxford 1947.

Newstead H, The Besieged Ladies in Arthurian Romance, PMLA 63.803.

Hole C, British Folk-Heroes, London 1948.

Loomis R S, Arthurian Tradition and Chrétien de Troyes, N Y 1949 (crit J Frappier, Rom 72.118; H Newstead, Spec 24.591; J Marx, Études celtiques 5.456; J J Parry, MLQ [Wash] 13.99; H R Patch, RomP 3.310).

Loomis R S, Le folklore breton et les romans arthuriens, Annales de Bretagne 56.203 (English version, CL 2.289).

Nitze W A, Arthurian Names: Arthur, PMLA 64.585 (correction, 1235).

Pauphilet A, Le legs du moyen âge, Melun 1950.

Patch H R, The Other World, Cambridge Mass 1950 (crit R J Dean, RomR 42.148).

Tatlock J S P, The Legendary History of Britain, Berkeley Calif 1950 (crit T Jones, Llên Cymrū 1.189; H Newstead, Latomus 10.53; T P Cross, MP 48.211; K Malone, MLN 66.332; R S Loomis, RomR 42.150).

Frappier J, Le roman breton, Introduction: des origines à Chrétien de Troyes, Paris 1950.

Foulon C, Enchanted Forests in Arthurian Romance, YSCS 1949–52.1 (trans C H Gillies).

Dickins B and R M Wilson, Early Middle English Texts, Cambridge 1951; 2nd rvsd impression 1952 (selections; crit S Einarsson, MLN 68.575).

Swansea and Brecon, the Lord Bishop of, Vespasian A XIV, Archaeologia Cambrensis 101.91 (unptd MS of Welsh saints' lives containing Arthurian material).

Kane G, Middle English Literature, London 1951 (crit J R Hulbert, MP 49.205).

Ackerman R W, An Index of the Arthurian Names in Middle English, Stanford 1952 (crit J A W Bennett, MLR 49.221; J Frappier, RomP 7.372; R S Loomis, Spec 29.244).

Denomy A J, The Round Table and the Council of Rheims 1049, MS 14.143.

Bivar A D H, Lyonnesse: The Evolution of a Fable, MP 50.162.

Loomis R S, Edward I, Arthurian Enthusiast, Spec 28.114.

Reinhold H, Humoristische Tendenzen in der englischen Dichtung des Mittelalters, Tübingen 1953.

Starr N C, King Arthur Today, Gainesville Florida 1954.

Zumthor P, Histoire littéraire de la France médiévale (6e–14e siècles) Paris 1954, p 193 (crit M R[oques], Rom 75.256).

Loomis R S, Wales and the Arthurian Legend, Cardiff 1956 (crit H Newstead, Spec 33.105).

Köhler E, Ideal und Wirklichkeit in der höfischen Epik: Studien zur Form und frühen Artus- und Graldichtung, ZfRP 97, Tübingen 1956 (crit H Newstead RomP 12.326).

Loomis R S, Arthurian Tradition and Folklore, Folklore 69.1.

Loomis R S, Objections to the Celtic Origin of the Matière de Bretagne, Rom 79.47.

Loomis R S, Scotland and the Arthurian Legend, Proc of the Soc of Antiquaries of Scotland, 89.1.

Harward V J jr, The Dwarfs of Arthurian Romance and Celtic Tradition, Leiden 1958 (crit H Newstead, MLN 76.51).

Schirmer W F, Die frühen Darstellungen des Arthurstoffes, Köln u Opladen 1958.

Newstead H, King Mark of Cornwall, RomP 11.240.

Loomis R S, ed, Arthurian Literature in the Middle Ages, Oxford 1959. (An international collaboration, with chapters by the foremost Arthurians.)

Loomis R S, Morgain la Fee in Oral Tradition, Rom 80.337.

Parry J J, The Historical Arthur, JEGP 58.365.

Loomis R S, The Development of Arthurian Romance, London 1963.

Paris Litt franç, § 53; HLF, 30.1; Gröber, 2¹.288, 363, 469, 495, 551, 585, 996; de Julleville Hist, 1.255; ten Brink, 1.134, 140, 164, 171, 187.

Sommer H O, ed, Malory's Morte Darthur, London 1889–91, vol 3.

Billings, p 85; Schofield, pp 159, 475; CHEL, 1.270; Körting, § 101; Renwick-Orton; Baugh LHE, pp 165, 173, 185.

Leach M and J Fried, edd, Funk and Wagnalls Standard Dictionary of Folklore, Mythology, and Legend, 2 vols, N Y 1949–50, articles either by R S Loomis or MacE Leach on Arthur, Celtic Folklore, Fisher King, Galahad, Gawain, Grail, Guinevere, Isolt, Joseph of Arimathea, Kay, Lancelot, Loathly Lady, Mabinogion, Merlin, Mordred, Morgain le Fay, Pellinor, Percival, Round Table, Tristan, Vivien.

Anderson G K et al, A History of English Literature, N Y 1950.

Willcock G D, Middle English II: Before and After Chaucer, YWES 33.67.

I. The Whole Life of Arthur

[12] EARLY TRADITIONS.

Gildas. Chambers E K, Arthur of Britain, pp 2, 234 (text).

Faral E, ed, La légende arthurienne, Paris 1929, 1.1.

Lot F, De la valeur historique du De excidio, Medieval Studies in Memory of G S Loomis, N Y 1927, p 229.

Anderson A O, The Dating Passage in Gildas' De excidio, ZfCP 17.403; Gildas and Arthur, 17.404.

Anscombe A, King Arthur in Gildas, N&Q, 155.115, 324.

Nennius. Mommsen T, ed, Historia Brittonum, Mon Germ Hist, Berlin 1898, 13.111.

Faral E, La légende arthurienne, 1.56; 3.1.

Lot F, Nennius et l'Historia Brittonum: Étude critique, suivie d'une édition des diverses versions de ce texte, Paris 1934.

Giles J A, Six Old English Chronicles, London 1848, 1901 (trans).

Zimmer H, Nennius vindicatus, Berlin 1893 (crit R Thurneysen, ZfDP 28.80).

O'Rahilly C, Ireland and Wales: Their Historical and Literary Relations, London 1924 (crit E K, Studies [Dublin] 13.321; E Ekwall, History 12.250).

Chambers E K, Arthur of Britain, pp 1, 238.

Crawford O G S, King Arthur's Last Battle, Antiq 5.236; Arthur and His Battles, Antiq 9.277.

Anderson A O, Nennius's Chronological Chapter, Antiq 6.82.

Johnston P K, The Victories of Arthur, N&Q, 166.381; 167.65.

White G H, The Victories of Arthur, N&Q 166.466.

Williams I, Notes on Nennius, BBCS 7.380 (crit T J Morgan, YWMLS 6.192; J Vendryes, Études celtiques 2.386).

Thurneysen R, Zu Nemnius (Nennius), ZfCP 20.97 and 185 (Nochmals Nemnius).

Jackson K, Nennius and the Twenty-Eight Cities of Britain, Antiq 12.44.

Wade-Evans A W, Nennius's History of the Britons, London 1938.

Nitze W A, Bédier's Epic Theory and the Arthuriana of Nennius, MP 39.1.

Jackson K, Arthur's Battle of Breguion, Antiq 23.48.

Jackson K, Once Again Arthur's Battles, MP 43.44.

Jackson K, Language and History in Early Britain, Edinburgh 1953, pp 47, 119, 121.

Jackson K, The Britons in Southern Scotland, Antiq 29.77.

Welsh Arthurian Traditions. Loth J, Les Mabinogion, 2nd edn, Paris 1913.

O'Rahilly C, Ireland and Wales, London 1924.

Jones T G, Some Arthurian Material in Keltic, ASt 8.37.

Gruffydd W J, Math Vab Mathonwy, Cardiff 1928 (crit I Williams, Archaeologia Cambrensis 83.353; R S Loomis, Spec 4.134).

Ellis T P and J Lloyd, The Mabinogion, a New Translation, Oxford 1929 (crit W J Gruffydd, RES 6.205; J J Parry, Spec 6.139).

Jones G and T, The Mabinogion, a New Translation, London 1948, 1949 (crit W J Gruffydd, MÆ 21.91; H I Bell, Welsh Review 7.298).

Gruffydd W J, Mabon Vab Modron, Y Cymmrodor 42.129 (in Arthurian literature, especially in Kulhwch and Olwen).

Van Hamel A G, The Game of the Gods, Arkiv för Nordisk Filologi 6.218 (Welsh Arthurian material).

Jackson K, Studies in Early Celtic Nature Poetry, Cambridge 1935 (Myrddin).

Williams I, The Gododdin Poems, Transactions of the Anglesey Antiquarian Society, 1935, p 25.

Williams I, Canu Aneirin, Cardiff 1938.

Jackson K, The Gododdin of Aneirin, Antiq 13.25 (detailed commentary on Williams, Canu Aneirin).

Gresham C A, The Book of Aneirin, Antiq 16.237 (précis, checked by Williams, of his Welsh introd to Canu Aneirin).

C[rawford] O G S, A Note on Catterick (supplement to Jackson, Antiq 13.25).

Loomis R S, The Spoils of Annwn, PMLA 56.887.

Gruffydd W J, Rhiannon: An Inquiry into the Origins of the First and Third Branches of the Mabinogi, Cardiff 1953 (crit J Marx, Études celtiques 6.404; A O H Jarman, Llên Cymru 3.123).

Bromwich R, The Character of the Early Welsh Tradition, Studies in Early British History, ed N K Chadwick, Cambridge 1954, p 83.

The Modena Sculpture and Other Early Traditions. Loomis R S, The Story of the Modena Archivolt and Its Mythological Roots, RomR 15.266; The Date, Source, and Subject of the Arthurian Sculpture at Modena, Medieval Studies in Memory of G S Loomis, N Y 1927, p 209.

Gerould G H, Arthurian Romance and the Date of the Relief at Modena, Spec 10.355.

Loomis R S, The Modena Sculpture and Arthurian Romance, Studi medievali 9.1.

Loomis R S, Geoffrey of Monmouth and the Modena Archivolt: a Question of Precedence, Spec 13.221 (reply to Gerould).

Loomis R S and L H, Arthurian Legends in Medieval Art, N Y 1938, p 31.

Bruce J D, Evolution of Arthurian Romance, 1.3.

Tatlock J S P, The English Journey of the Laon Canons, Spec 8.454.

Loomis R S, By What Route Did the Romantic Tradition of Arthur Reach the French? MP 33.225.

Loomis R S, The Arthurian Legend before 1139, RomR 32.3.

Loomis R S, Arthurian Tradition and Chrétien de Troyes, N Y 1949, p 3.

Chadwick N K, The Lost Literature of Celtic Scotland: Caw of Pritden and Arthur of Britain, Scottish Gaelic Studies 7.115.

[13] GEOFFREY OF MONMOUTH.

Editions. Schulz A (San Marte), Historia regum Britanniae, Halle 1854.

Griscom A, The Historia regum Britanniae of Geoffrey of Monmouth, N Y 1929 (crit E Faral, Rom 55.482; E Brugger, ZfFSL 57.257; E K Chambers, RES 6.199).

Faral E, La légende arthurienne, vol 2, Paris 1929 (Vita Merlini, Historia).

Parry J J, A Variant Version of Geoffrey of Monmouth's Historia, Kastner Miscellany, Cambridge 1932, p 364.

Hammer J, Geoffrey of Monmouth, Historia regum Britanniae, a Variant Version, Cambridge Mass 1951 (crit T Jones, Llên Cymru 2.261; J J Parry, JEGP 51.237).

Parry J J, The Vita Merlini, Urbana 1925 (crit E Brugger, ZfFSL 49.368; R S Loomis, JEGP 26.423).

Giles J A, Six Old English Chronicles, London 1848, 1901 (trans).

Evans S, The Histories of the Kings of Britain by Geoffrey of Monmouth, London 1903 (trans, Everyman's Library); rvsd CW Dunn, N Y 1958).

Date. Faral E, Geoffrey de Monmouth: les faits et les dates de sa biographie, Rom 53.1.

Lloyd J E, Geoffrey of Monmouth, EHR, 57.460.

Tatlock J S P, The Date of Henry I's Charter to London, Spec 11.461.

Chambers E K, The Date of Geoffrey of Monmouth's History, RES 1.431; 3.332.

Griscom A, The Date of Composition of Geoffrey of Monmouth's Historia, Spec 1.129.

Parry J J, The Date of the Vita Merlini, MP 22.413.

Tatlock J S P, Geoffrey of Monmouth's Vita Merlini, Spec 18.265.

Tatlock J S P, Certain Contemporaneous Matters in Geoffrey of Monmouth, Spec 6.206.

Tatlock J S P, Geoffrey of Monmouth's Motives for Writing His Historia, PAPS 79, 4.695.

Sources and Literary Relationships. Fletcher R H, Two Notes on the Historia regum Britanniae, PMLA 16.461.

Windisch E, Das keltische Britannien bis zu Kaiser Arthur, Leipzig 1912, p 123.

Matter H, Englische Grundungssagen von Geoffrey of Monmouth bis zur Renaissance, Heidelberg 1922.

Cross T P, The Passing of Arthur, Manly Anniversary Studies, Chicago 1923, p 284.

Parry J J, Celtic Tradition and the Vita Merlini, PQ 4.193.

Van Hamel A J, Koning Arthurs Vader, Neophil 12.34.

Nitze W A, Geoffrey of Monmouth's King Arthur, Spec 2.317.

Loomis R S, Geoffrey of Monmouth and Arthurian Origins, Spec 3.16.

Gollancz I, Chivalry in Medieval English Poetry, in Chivalry, ed E Prestage, London 1928, chap 7 (Geoffrey).

Parry J J, The Triple Death in the Vita Merlini, Spec 5.216.

Loomis L H, Geoffrey of Monmouth and Stonehenge, PMLA 45.400.

Tatlock J S P, Geoffrey and King Arthur in Normannicus Draco, MP 31.1, 113.

Loomis C G, King Arthur and the Saints, Spec 8.478.

Tatlock J S P, Geoffrey of Monmouth's Estrildis, Spec 11.121.

Hutson A E, Geoffrey of Monmouth, Transactions of the Hon Soc of the Cymmrodorion for 1937, p 361.

Baker Sister I, The King's Household in the Arthurian Court from Geoffrey of Monmouth to Malory, Washington 1937, p 24.

Parry J J, Geoffrey of Monmouth and the Paternity of Arthur, Spec 13.271.

Hutson A E, British Personal Names in the Historia regum Britanniae, Berkeley 1940 (crit G Jones, MLR 36.121).

Jackson K, The Motive of the Three-Fold Death, Feil-Sgribhinn Eoin MhicNeill, Dublin 1941, p 535.

Loomis R S, The Arthurian Legend before 1139, RomR 32.3.

Loomis R S, The Spoils of Annwn, PMLA 56.907.

Piggott S, The Sources of Geoffrey of Monmouth, Antiq 15.269, 305.

Jones E v B, Geoffrey of Monmouth's Account of the Establishment of Episcopacy in Britain, JEGP 40.360.

Hammer J, Geoffrey of Monmouth's Use of the Bible, JRLB 30.293.

Hammer J, Remarks on the Sources and Textual History of Geoffrey of Monmouth's Historia regum Britanniae, Quarterly Bulletin of the Polish Institute of Arts and Sciences of America 2.501.

Caldwell R A, Wace's Brut and the Variant Version of Geoffrey of Monmouth's Historia regum Britanniae, Abstr, BBSIA 6.109.

Caldwell R A, Geoffrey of Monmouth, Wace, and the Stour, MLN 69.237.

Caldwell R A, The History of the Kings of Britain in College of Arms MS Arundel XXII, PMLA 69.643.

Tatlock J S P, Legendary History of Britain, Berkeley 1950.

Newstead H, About Geoffrey of Monmouth, Latomus 10.52.

Williams S, Geoffrey of Monmouth and the Canon Law, Spec 27.184.

Influence. Perrett W, The Story of King Lear from Geoffrey of Monmouth to Shakespeare, Berlin 1904.

Fletcher R H, Arthurian Material in the Chronicles, Boston 1906.

Taylor R, The Political Prophecy in England, N Y 1911.

Brandenburg H, Galfrid von Monmouth und die frühmittelenglischen Chronisten, Berlin 1918.

Leach H G, Angevin Britain and Scandinavia, Cambridge Mass 1921, p 130.

Entwistle W J, Geoffrey of Monmouth and Spanish Literature, MLR 17.381.

Gordon G, The Trojans in Britain, E&S 9.9.

Parsons A E, The Trojan Legend in England, MLR 24.253, 394.

Parry J J, The Welsh Texts of Geoffrey of Monmouth's Historia, Spec 5.424.

Millican C B, The First English Translation of the Prophecies of Merlin, SP 28.720.

Hammer J, Some Leonine Summaries of Geoffrey of Monmouth's Historia regum Britanniae and Other Poems, Spec 6.114.

Tatlock J S P, The Dragons of Wessex and Wales, Spec 8.223.

Allen H E, The Ancren Riwle and Geoffrey of Monmouth, MLR 29.172.

Tatlock J S P, Geoffrey of Monmouth and the Date of the Regnum Scotorum, Spec 9.135.

Hammer J, A Commentary on the Prophetia Merlini, Spec 10.3; 15.409.

Van Hamel A G, The Old Norse Version of the Historia regum Britanniae and the Text of Geoffrey of Monmouth, Études celtiques 1.197.

Parry J J, ed, Brut Y Brenhinedd: Cotton Cleopatra Version, Cambridge Mass 1937 (crit W J Gruffydd, MÆ 19.44; H I Bell, History 23.65).

Hammer J, Une version métrique de l'Historia regum Britanniae de Geoffrey de Monmouth, Latomus 2.131.

Jones E v B, The Reputation of Geoffrey of Monmouth 1640–1800, Berkeley 1944.

Keeler L, Geoffrey of Monmouth and the Late Latin Chroniclers 1300–1500, Berkeley 1946.

Keeler L, The Historia regum Britanniae and Four Mediaeval Chroniclers, Spec 21.24.

Dickins B, A Yorkshire Chronicler (William of Newburgh), Transactions of the Yorkshire Dialect Soc 5, pt 35, p 17.

Kendrick T D, British Antiquity, London 1950.

Pähler H, Strukturuntersuchungen zur Historia regum Britanniae des Geoffrey of Monmouth, Bonn 1958.

Chambers E K, Arthur of Britain, pp 20, 58.

Bruce J D, Evolution of Arthurian Romance, 1.18.

Ward, 1.203; CHEL, 1.284; DNB, Geoffrey of Monmouth (bibl).

[14] WACE.

Le Roux de Lincy A J V, ed, Le roman de Brut par Wace, 2 vols, Rouen 1936–38.

Faral E, La légende arthurienne, Paris 1929.

Arnold I, ed, Wace, Le roman de Brut, 2 vols, Paris 1938, 1940 (crit C Fahlin, SN 11.85).

Mason E, trans, Arthurian Chronicles Represented by Wace and Layamon, London 1912, rptd 1921, 1928 (trans of Arthurian parts).

Fletcher R H, Arthurian Material in the Chronicles, Boston 1906.

Ulbrich A, Über das Verhältniss von Wace's Roman de Brut zu seiner Quelle, der Historia regum Britanniae des Gottfried von Monmouth, RF 26.181.

Hopkins A B, The Influence of Wace on the Arthurian Romances of Crestien de Troiies, Menasha Wis 1913 (bibl).

Waldner L, Wace's Brut und seine Quellen, Karlsruhe 1914.

Arnold I, Wace et l'Historia regum Britanniae de Geoffroi de Monmouth, Rom 57.1.

Hoepffner E, L'Eneas et Wace, Archivum Romanicum 15.248; 16.162.

Arnold I, The Brut Tradition in the English

Manuscripts, Kastner Miscellany, Cambridge 1932, p 1.

Keins J P, Zur sozialen und literarischen Stellung des Dichters Wace, Archivum Romanicum 16.515.

Pelan M, L'influence du Brut de Wace sur les romanciers français de l'époque, Paris 1931 (crit E Hoepffner, Rom 58.292; M Wilmotte, Moyen âge 44.222).

Houck M, Sources of the Roman de Brut of Wace, Berkeley 1941.

Delbouille M, Le témoignage de Wace sur la légende arthurienne, Rom 74.172.

Caldwell R A (see above, under GEOFFREY OF MONMOUTH [13]).

Tatlock J S P, Legendary History of Britain, Berkeley 1950, p 463.

CHEL, 1.293; Gröber, 2¹.635.

LAYAMON: See under Chronicles.

[15] ARTHUR.

MS. Longleat, Liber rubeus Bathoniae 1428 (Marquis of Bath's MS), ff 42^b–46^b (ca 1425).

Editions. Furnivall F J, Arthur: A Short Sketch of His Life in English Verse, EETS 2, 1864; re-ed 1869; rptd 1889, 1895.

Language. Bülbring K D, Geschichte der Ablaute der starken Zeitwörter innerhalb des Südenglischen, QF 63.49.

Moore S, S Meech, H Whitehall, ME Dialect Characteristics and Dialect Boundaries, Essays and Studies in Engl and Comp Lit, Univ of Michigan, 13.51.

Brandl, § 70; Körting, § 101; Schofield, p 255; Wülcker, 1.110; Billings, p 190.

[16] MORTE ARTHURE.

MS. Lincoln Cath 91 (Thornton), ff 53^a–98^b (ca 1440).

Madden F, Syr Gawayne, London 1839, p 1 (description of MS).

Editions. Halliwell[-Phillips] J O, The Alliterative Romance of the Death of King Arthur, London 1847 (edition limited to 75 copies).

Brock E, EETS 8, 1871, rptd 1898, 1904, re-ed of G G Perry, EETS 8, 1865.

Banks M M, Morte Arthure, London 1900 (crit F Holthausen, AnglB 12.235; H Spies EStn 35.101).

Björkman E, Morte Arthure, Heidelberg 1915 (crit J Koch, EStn 51.115; W Viëtor, AnglB 29.129).

Selections. Wülcker R P, Altenglisches Lesebuch, Halle 1879, 2.109.

Brandl A and O Zippel, Mittelenglisches Sprach- und Literaturproben, Berlin 1917, p 75.

Sampson G, Cambridge Book of Prose and Verse, Cambridge 1924, p 313.

Modernizations. Boyle A, Morte Arthure, ed L A Paton, London 1912, rptd 1936 (Everyman's Library).

Weston J L, Romance, Vision and Satire, Boston 1912, p 139 (modernized selections in verse).

Loomis R S and R Willard, Medieval English Verse and Prose, N Y 1948, p 128 (modernized selections in verse).

Textual Notes. Banks M M, Notes on the Morte Arthure Glossary, MLQ (Lon) 6.64.

Edwards J, Old Oaths and Interjections, SHR 1.56 (notes on lines 1166–69, 3776–79).

Björkman E, Notes on the Morte Arthure and Its Vocabulary, Minneskr t Prof Axel Erdmann, Uppsala 1913, p 34.

Holthausen F, Zur alliterierenden Morte Arthure, AnglB 24.240; 34.91; 36.188.

Language. Andrew S P, The Dialect of Morte Arthure, RES 4.418.

Oakden J P, Alliterative Poetry in ME, Manchester 1930, 1.63, 153, 255.

Koziol H, Grundzüge der Syntaxe der me Stabreimdichtungen, WBEP 58 (crit M Calloway, Lang 10.212; D Everett, YWES 13.110).

Versification. Luick K, Die englische Stabreimzeile im 14, 15, und 16 Jahrhundert, Angl 11.392, 563.

Mennicken F, Versbau und Sprache in Huchown Morte Arthure, BBA 5 (crit K Luick, AnglB 12.33; F Holthausen, EStn 30.269).

Reicke C, Untersuchungen über den Stil der me Gedichte Morte Arthure, etc, Königsberg 1906.

Björkman E, Zum alliterierenden Morte Arthure, Angl 39.253.

Greg W W, J P Oakden, The Continuity of the Alliterative Tradition, MLR 27.453; 28.233.

Hulbert J R, Quatrains in the Middle English Alliterative Poems, MP 48.73.

Date. Brown C, Somer Soneday, Studies in English Philology: A Miscellany in Honor of F Klaeber, Minneapolis 1929, p 362.

Eagleson H, Costume in the Middle English Metrical Romances, PMLA 47.339.

Schröder E, Zur Datierung des Morte Arthure, Angl 60.396.

Authorship. Lübke H, Awntyrs of Arthure, diss Berlin 1883, p 30.

Brown J T T, Poems of D Rate, SA 12.5; Huchown of the Awle Ryale, Glasgow 1902.

Millar G H, Literary History of Scotland, London 1903, p 5.

Henderson T F, Scottish Vernacular Literature, 3rd edn, Edinburgh 1910, p 31.

Neilson G, Huchown's Morte Arthure and the Annals of 1327–64, SA 16.229; Antiquary 38.73, 229.

Neilson G, Three Dates in Morte Arthure, Athen 1902².758; The Viscount of Rome in Morte Arthure, Athen 1902².602.

Neilson G, Morte Arthure and the War of Brittany, N&Q 9s 10.161; The Baulked Coronation of Arthur, 381, 403.

Björkman E, Zur Huchown-Frage, EStn 48.171.

Koziol H, Zur Frage der Verfasserschaft einiger me Stabreimdichtungen, EStn 67.171.

Andrew S O, Huchown's Works, RES 5.12 (crit D Everett, YWES 10.132).

Sources and Literary Relationships. Branscheid P, Über die Quellen des stabreimenden Morte Arthure, AnglA 8.179.

Neilson G, Three Footnotes, Furnivall Miscellany, Oxford 1901, p 383.

Griffith R H, Malory, Morte Arthure, and Fierabras, Angl 32.389.

Bruce J D, The Development of the Mort Arthur Theme in Mediaeval Romance, RomR 4.403 (crit E Brugger, ZfFSL 47.98).

Bruce J D, Mordred's Incestuous Birth, Medieval Studies in Memory of G S Loomis, N Y 1927, p 197.

Vinaver E, The Legend of Wade in the Morte Arthur, MÆ 2.135.

O'Loughlin J L N, The Middle English Alliterative Morte Arthure, MÆ 4.153.

Gordon E V and E Vinaver, New Light on the Text of the Alliterative Morte Arthure, MÆ 6.81.

Vorontzoff T, Malory's Story of Arthur's Roman Campaign, MÆ 6.99.

Arnold I, Malory's Story of Arthur's Roman

Campaign, MÆ 7.74 (comment on preceding item).

Baker Sister I, The King's Household, Washington 1937, p 127.

Parks G B, King Arthur and the Roads to Rome, JEGP 45.164.

Hammerle K, Das Fortunamotiv von Chaucer bis Bacon, Angl 65.90.

Loomis L H, The Athelstan Gift Story: Its Influence on English Chronicles and Carolingian Romances, PMLA 67.521.

Oakden J P, Alliterative Poetry in Middle English, Manchester 1935, 2.35.

Everett D, Essays on Middle English Literature, ed P Kean, Oxford 1955, p 46 (the Alliterative Revival).

Matthews W, The Tragedy of Arthur: A Critical Study of the ME Alliterative Poem Morte Arthure, Berkeley and Los Angeles 1960 (crit H Newstead, RomP 16.118).

Wülcker R P, Die Arthursage in der englischen Literatur, Leipzig 1895, p 12.

Brandl, § 75; Körting, § 103; Ten Brink, 3.49; Sommer ed of Malory, 3.148; Schofield, p 253; Billings, p 181; Chambers OHEL, p 190; Baugh LHE, p 191; Kane, p 69.

[17] THE LEGEND OF KING ARTHUR.

MS. BM Addit 27879 (Percy Folio), pp 179–80 (ca 1650).

Editions. PFMS, 1.497; re-ed I Gollancz, London 1905–10.

Percy Reliques, bk 7, no 5.

Child F J, Ballds, Boston 1857, 1.106 (not in later edns).

Millican C B, The Original of the Ballad Kinge: Arthur's Death in the Percy Folio MS, PMLA 46.1020.

Friedman A, The First Draft of Percy's Reliques, PMLA 69.1233.

Wells J E, CBEL, 1.132, 136 (bibl to 1933).

II. Merlin and the Youth of Arthur

THE MERLIN LEGEND.

Schulz A (San Marte), Die Sagen von Merlin, 1853.

Paris G and R Ulrich, edd, Huth-Merlin, Paris 1886 (introd).

Sommer H O, ed, Vulgate Version of the Arthurian Romances, vol 2, Washington 1908–16.

Rhŷs J, Studies in the Arthurian Legend, Oxford 1891.

Mead W E, Outlines of the History of the Legend of Merlin, EETS 112 (introd).

Ward H L D, Lailoken or Merlin Silvester, Rom 22.504.

Gaster M, The Legend of Merlin, Folklore 16.407.

Weston J L, The Legend of Merlin, Folklore 17.230.

Lot F, Études sur Merlin, Annales de Bretagne 15.324, 505.

Brugger E, L'enserrement Merlin: Studien zur

Merlinsage, ZfFSL 29^1.56; 30^1.169; 31^1.239; 33^1.145; 34^1.99; 35^1.1.

Maynadier G H, The Arthur of the English Poets, Boston 1907, chaps 3, 6.

Taylor R, Political Prophecy in England, N Y 1911, chaps 1–3 (crit R W Bond, MLR 11.347).

Paton L A, Les prophécies de Merlin, 2 vols, N Y 1926–27 (crit E G Gardner, MLR 23.85; J S P Tatlock, Spec 3.416).

Cranmer-Byng L, Who Was Merlin? Quarterly Review 252.293.

Millican C B, The First English Translation of the Prophecies of Merlin, SP 28.720.

Chadwick H M and N K, The Growth of Literature, Cambridge 1932, 1.105, 123 (crit A H Krappe, Spec 8.270).

Krappe A H, La naissance de Merlin, Rom 59.12.

Owenby E S, Merlin and Arthur, Bull of Vanderbilt Univ, Abstr of Theses 33, no 9, p 11.

Schiprowski P E A, Merlin in der deutschen Dichtung, Breslau 1933.

Weiss A M, Merlin in German Literature, Catholic Univ Studies in German 3, Washington 1933.

Krappe A H, L'enserrement de Merlin, Rom 60.79.

Jackson K, The Motif of the Three-Fold Death, Feil-Sgribhinn Eoin MhicNeill, Dublin 1940, p 535.

Zumthor P, La délivrance de Merlin, Contribution à l'étude des romans de la Table Ronde, ZfRP 62.370.

Paton L A, Notes on Merlin in the Historia regum Britanniae of Geoffrey of Monmouth, MP 41.88.

Zumthor P, Merlin le prophète, Lausanne 1943 (crit A O H Jarman, Llên Cymru 1.198).

Smith R M, King Lear and the Merlin Tradition, MLQ (Wash) 7.153.

Tatlock J S P, Legendary History of Britain, Berkeley 1950, p 171.

Bernheimer R, Wild Men in the Middle Ages, Cambridge Mass 1952.

Daube D, The Date of the Birth of Merlin, Aberdeen Univ Review 35.49, 147.

Jackson K, A Further Note on Suibhne Geilt and Merlin, Eigse 7.112.

Ackerman R W, Arthur's Wild Man Knight, RomP 9.115.

Chambers E K, Arthur of Britain, London 1927, chap 2 and bibl.

Billings p 114; Bruce, Evolution of Arthurian Romance, 1.129, 395; 2.312, 393; Ward, 1.278, 371, 384; Gröber, 2.193, 371, 406, 489, 725, 909, 997, 1006; Schofield, p 248;

Wells, CBEL, 1.131(a), 133(a), 138(n,p). See also above under GEOFFREY OF MONMOUTH [13].

[18] ARTHOUR AND MERLIN.

MSS. 1, Bodl 21880 (Douce 236), ff 1^b–36^b (late 15 cent); 2, Harley 6223, f 123^a (late 15 cent); 3, BM Addit 27879 (Percy Folio), pp 145–178 (ca 1650); 4, Lincoln's Inn 150, ff 13^a–27^b (before 1425); 5, Advocates 19.2.1 (Auchinleck MS), ff 201^a–256^a (ca 1330); 6, Bodl 21698, ff 1^a–141^b (transcript about 1800 of Auchinleck version).

Kölbing E, Fier Romanzen-Handschriften, EStn 7.178 (Auchinleck and Lincoln's Inn 150).

Carr M B, Notes on an English Scribe's Methods, Univ of Wisconsin Studies in Language and Literature, Madison 1918, 2.158.

Loomis L H, The Auchinleck MS and a Possible London Bookshop of 1330–1340, PMLA 57.595.

Editions. Turnbull W D, Arthour and Merlin, a Metrical Romance, Abbotsford Club, Edinburgh 1838 (Auchinleck MS; Harley 6223 fragment, p x).

Kölbing E, Arthour and Merlin, Leipzig 1890 (Auchinleck text, pp 1–262; Lincoln's Inn and Douce in parallel columns, pp 275–370; crit K D Bülbring, EStn 16.251; E Koeppel, AnglB 2.105).

PFMS, 1.417, 420, 279 (re-ed I Gollancz, London 1905–10).

Selections. Zupitza J, Alt- und mittelenglisches Übungsbuch, 11th edn, Vienna 1915, 1922, p 144.

Modernizations. Weston J L, Chief Middle English Poets, Boston 1910, p 119.

Textual Notes. Holthausen F, AnglB 31.198.

Smithers G V, Notes on Middle English Texts, LMS 1.208.

Language. Mackenzie B A, A Special Dialectal Development of OE ea in Middle English, EStn 61.386.

Moore S, S Meech, H Whitehall, ME Dialect Characteristics and Dialect Boundaries, Essays and Studies in Engl and Comp Lit, Univ of Michigan, 13.54, 55 (dialect of MSS Douce 236 and Lincoln's Inn 150).

Liedholm A, A Phonological Study of the ME Romance Arthour and Merlin (MS Auchinleck), Uppsala 1941 (crit S B Liljegren, AnglB 53.13).

French W H, Dialects and Forms in Three Romances, JEGP 45.125.

Trounce A McI, The English Tail-Rhyme Romances, MÆ 1.87, 168; 2.34, 189; 3.30.

Sources and Literary Relations. Gaster M, Jewish Sources of and Parallels to the Early English Romance of King Arthur and Merlin, London 1887 (crit Rom 18.204).

Wheatley H, Prose Merlin, EETS 10.xvi; 112.lv.

Wedel T O, Medieval Attitude Toward Astrology, YSE 60.107.

Ackerman R W, Arthur's Wild Man Knight, RomP 9.115.

Loomis R S, Vandeberes, Wandlebury, and de l'Espine, RomP 9.162.

Brandl, § 36; Körting, § 109; Ten Brink, 1.244; 3.10; Schofield, p 251; CHEL, 1.298, 353, 446; Billings, p 111; Dunlop, History of Prose Fiction, 1.146 (rvsd H Wilson, 1888).

[19] PROSE MERLIN.

MSS. 1, Camb Univ Ff.3.11 (late 15 cent); 2, MS Rawlinson Misc olim 1262 later 1370 (fragm extending from p 317, line 15 [my lyf tyme] to p 317, line 34 [thei ben] of Wheatley's edn) (late 15 cent, noted by E Kölbing, Arthour and Merlin, Leipzig 1890, p xxi).

Editions. Wheatley H B, Merlin, a Prose Romance, EETS 10, 21, 36, 112.

Selections. Cranner-Byng L, Selections from the Prose Merlin, London 1930 (crit H L Savage, MLN 46.482).

Textual Notes. Richter G and G Stecher, Beiträge zur Erklärung und Textkritik, EStn 20.397; 28.1.

Sources and Literary Relations. Workman S B, Fifteenth Century Translation as an Influence on English Prose, Princeton Univ

Studies in Engl 18, Princeton 1940 (planograph reprod).

Fox M, Merlin in the Arthurian Prose Cycle, Arthuriana 2.20.

Baker Sister I, The King's Household, Washington 1937, p 124.

Ackerman R W, Arthur's Wild Man Knight, RomP 9.115.

Körting, § 109anm; EETS 112.lxiii.

[20] LOVELICH'S MERLIN.

MS. Corpus Christi Coll Camb 80, ff 88[b]–200d (before 1450).

Editions. Kock E A, EETSES 93,112, 185 (crit D Everett, RES 9.94).

Selections. Furnivall F J, Seynt Graal or the Sank Ryal, Roxburghe Club, London 1861, 1863, 2.393 (146 lines from f 135[a]).

Furnivall F J, Henry Lovelich's History of the Holy Grail, EETSES 20, 28.

Kölbing E, Arthour and Merlin, Leipzig 1890, p 373 (lines 1–1638).

Authorship. Bradley H, Henry Lonelich the Skinner, in Collected Papers, Oxford 1928, p 233.

Skeat W W, The Translator of the Graal, Athen 1902[2].684; The Author of the Holy Grail, Athen 1902[2].758.

Ackerman R W, Henry Lovelich's Name, MLN 67.531.

Literary Relations. Ackerman R W, Herry Lovelich's Merlin, PMLA 67.473.

Ackerman R W, Arthur's Wild Man Knight, RomP 9.115.

Schofield, p 250; Billings, p 123; Kölbing, Arthour and Merlin, pp xviii, clxxx; see below under History of the Holy Grail.

III. Lancelot and the Last Years of Arthur

THE LANCELOT LEGEND.

Bruce J D, ed, Mort Artu, an Old French Prose Romance of the 13th Century, Being the Last Division of Lancelot du Lac, Halle 1910.

Sommer H O, ed, Vulgate Version of the Arthurian Romances, vols 3–5, Washington 1908–16.

Frapper J, ed, La mort le roi Artu, Paris 1936; 2nd edn Geneva 1954.

Paton L A, Sir Lancelot of the Lake, N Y 1929 (translation and commentary; crit E G Gardner, MLR 25.356; R S Loomis, MLN 45.274).

Paris G, Études sur les romans de la Table Ronde: Lancelot du Lac, Rom 12.459.

Rhŷs J, Studies in the Arthurian Legend, Oxford 1891, pp 127, 145.

Sommer H O, Malory, Le Morte Darthur, London 1891, 3.176.

Weston J L, The Legend of Sir Lancelot du Lac, London 1901 (crit J Koch, EStn 32.113; S Singer, AnglB 14.168; W W Greg, Folklore 12.486; Rom 31.174).

Weston J L, The Three Days' Tournament, London 1902.

Paton L A, Studies in the Fairy Mythology of Arthurian Romance, Boston 1903.

Maynadier G H, The Arthur of the English Poets, Boston 1907, p 84.

Lot F, Étude sur le Lancelot en prose, Paris

1918; re-impression Paris 1954 (including also M Lot-Borodine, Le double esprit et l'unité du Lancelot en prose, 1925, and Lot's rev, Rom 64.111 of J Frappier, Étude sur la Mort le roi Artu; crit G Schoepperle, JEGP 20.262; J D Bruce, RomR 10.377).

Bruce J D, The Composition of the Old French Prose Lancelot, RomR 9.241, 353; 10.48, 97.

Lot F, L'origine du nom de Lancelot, Rom 51.423.

App A, Lancelot in English Literature, Washington 1929 (crit R S Loomis, Spec 5.104; J J Parry, JEGP 29.448).

Cross T P and W A Nitze, Lancelot and Guenevere: A Study in the Origins of Courtly Love, Chicago 1930 (crit K G T Webster, MLN 46.53; J Vendryes, RC 48.399).

Lot F, Sur la date du Lancelot en prose, Rom 57.137.

Krappe A H, Arthur and Charlemagne, EStn 68.351.

Frappier J, Étude sur la Mort le roi Artu, Paris 1936 (crit F Lot, Rom 64.111).

Lewis C S, The Allegory of Love, Oxford 1936 (rptd 1938), p 23.

Walsche M O'C, The Fabulous Geography of Lanzelet, LMS 1.93.

Strassberg S, Die Entführung und Befreiung der Königin Ginevra, Berlin 1937.

Krappe A H, Avallon, Spec 18.303.

Lloyd J E, The Death of Arthur, BBCS 11.158.

Loomis R S, Arthurian Tradition and Chrétien de Troyes, N Y 1949, p 187.

Loomis R S, The Descent of Lancelot from Lug, BBSIA 3.69.

Loomis R S, Bruce's Conception of the History of Lancelot, BBSIA 6.101 (abstr).

Webster K G T and R S Loomis, Ulrich von Zatzikhoven's Lanzelet, N Y 1951 (translation and commentary; crit J Marx, Études celtiques 6.373; G F Jones, MLN 69.537).

Webster K G T, Guinevere, a Study of Her Abductions, Milton Mass 1951 (crit H Newstead, JEGP 52.250; J Frappier, RLC 27.101).

Billings, p 195; P Paris, Romans de la Table Ronde, p 3; HLF, 30; Ward, 1.345; Bruce, Evolution of Arthurian Romance, 1.192.

Wells, CBEL, 1.131(b), 138(l), 139(v), 140(w), bibl to 1933; Bruce, Evolution of Arthurian Romance, 2.397; M Reid, The Arthurian Legend, Edinburgh 1938, p 87.

[21] LANCELOT OF THE LAIK.

MS. Camb Univ Kk.1.5.vii, ff 1ª–42ᵇ (late 15 cent).

Editions. Stevenson J, Maitland Club, London 1839.

Skeat W W, Lancelot of the Laik, EETS 6 (2nd edn rvsd 1870).

Gray M M, Lancelot of the Laik, PSTS 2 (1912).

Selections. Wülcker R P, Lesebuch 2.115.

Language. Skeat, edn, p xv.

Date. Vogel B, Secular Politics and the Date of Lancelot of the Laik, SP 40.1.

Literary Relations. Veitch J, Feeling for Nature in Scottish Poetry, Edinburgh 1887, 1.146.

Hubert H, The Kingis Quhair, The Quare of Jelusy, and Lancelot of the Laik, Jahrbuch der philosophischen Facultät der deutschen Universität in Prag, 1926–27.

Weston J L, The Three Days' Tournament, London 1902.

Brandl, § 138; Körting, § 108; Billings, p 192; Schofield, p 239.

[22] SIR LANCELOT DU LAKE.

MS. BM Addit 27879 (Percy Folio), pp 36–37 (ca 1650).

Editions. Percy, Reliques, vol 1, bk 2, no 9.

PFMS, 1.84 (re-ed I Gollancz, London 1905–10).

Billings, p 200n.

[23] LE MORTE ARTHUR.

MS. Harley 2252, ff 88ª–133ᵇ (late 15 cent).

Editions. Panton G A, Le Morte Arthur, Roxburghe Club, London 1819.

Furnivall F J, Le Morte Arthur, London 1864.

Bruce J D, Le Morte Arthur, EETSES 88, 1903.

Hemingway S B, Le Morte Arthur, N Y 1912 (crit C S Northup, JEGP 12.486).

Paton L A, Morte Arthur: Two Early English Romances, London 1912 (rptd 1936, Everyman's Library), p 95.

Selections. Brandl A and O Zippel, Mittelenglische Sprach- und Literaturproben, Berlin 1917, p 80.

Sampson G, Cambridge Book of Prose and Verse, Cambridge 1924, p 291.

Modernizations. Newell W W, King Arthur and the Table Round, Boston 1897, 2.199 (abridged, in prose).

Weston J L, Chief Middle English Poets, Cambridge Mass 1914, p 262 (selection in verse).

Textual Notes. Weymouth R F, Transactions of the London Philological Soc 1860–61, p 279.

Sommer H O, Acad 38.450, 479.

Language. Seyferth P, Sprache und Metrik des me strophischen Gedichtes Le Morte Arthur und sein Verhältniss zu The Lyfe of Ipomedon, BBGRP 8.

Sources and Literary Relations. Branscheid P, Über die Quellen des Stabreimenden Morte Arthure, AnglA 8.179.

Mead W E, Selections from Malory's Morte Darthur, Boston 1897, pp 293, 305.

Bruce J D, The Middle English Metrical Romance Le Morte Arthur: Its Sources and Its Relation to Sir Thomas Malory's Morte Darthur, Angl 23.67; H O Sommer, On Dr Douglas Bruce's Article The Middle English Romance Le Morte Darthur, Angl 29.429; J D Bruce, A Reply to Dr Sommer, Angl 30.209.

Bruce J D, The Development of the Mort Arthur Theme in Mediaeval Romance, RomR 4.403.

Wilson R H, Malory, the Stanzaic Morte Arthur, and the Mort Artu, MP 37.125.

Donaldson E T, Malory and the Stanzaic Le Morte Arthur, SP 47.460.

Byrne Sister M of the Incarnation, The Tradition of the Nun in Medieval England, Washington 1932, p 154.

Baker Sister I, The King's Household, Washington 1937, p 130.

Brandl, § 125; Körting, § 103 anm; Billings, p 200; Schofield, pp 238, 255; Ward, 1.405; Baugh LHE, pp 191, 306; Kane, p 66.

[24] KING ARTHUR'S DEATH.

MS. BM Addit 27879 (Percy Folio), pp 180–182 (ca 1650).

Editions. Percy, Reliques, bk 7, no 4.

PFMS, 1.501 (re-ed I Gollancz, London 1905–10).

Child F J, Ballads (1857), 1.40 (not in later edn).

Sommer H O, ed, Le Morte Darthur, London 1889–91, 3.269.

Sources. Millican C B, The Original of the Ballad King Arthur's Death in the Percy Folio MS, PMLA 46.1020.

Friedman A B, Percy's Folio Manuscript Revalued, JEGP 73.524.

Friedman A B, The First Draft of Percy's Reliques, PMLA 69.1233.

Billings, p 208n.

IV. Gawain

THE GAWAIN LEGEND.

Weston J L, The Legend of Sir Gawain, London 1897 (rptd 1900; crit Rom 26.630).

Weston J L, The Legend of Perceval, London 1906, 1.282.

Weston J L, Sir Gawain at the Grail Castle, London 1903 (trans from the First Continuation of Le conte del Graal, Diu Crône, and the Prose Lancelot).

Maynadier G H, The Wife of Bath's Tale, London 1901 (crit J L Weston, Folklore 12.373; P Rajna, Rom 32.233; J Koch, EStn 30.460).

Bruce J D, Historia Meriadoci and De ortu Waluuanii, Baltimore 1913 (introd to De ortu).

Heller E K, Studies on the Story of Gawain in Chrestien and Wolfram, JEGP 24.463.

Ray B K, The Character of Gawain, Dacca Univ Bull, 11.8.

Whiting B J, Proverbs in Certain Middle English Romances in Relation to Their French Sources, HSNPL 15.75.

Webster K G T, Galloway and the Romances, MLN 55.363.

Whiting B J, The Wife of Bath's Tale, Bryan-Dempster, p 223.

Whiting B J, Gawain: His Reputation, His Courtesy, and His Appearance in Chaucer's Squire's Tale, MS 9.189.

Loomis R S, Arthurian Tradition and Chrétien de Troyes, N Y 1949, p 146.

Nitze W A, The Character of Gauvain in the Romances of Chrétien de Troyes, MP 50.219.

Markman A M, Sir Gawain of Britain: A Study of the Romance Elements in the British Gawain Literature, DA 15.1613 (Michigan).

Rhŷs J, Arthurian Legend; HLF, 30.23,29; Enc Brit, see under Gawain.

Wells, CBEL, 1.131(c), 134(c,d), 135(f), 136(g), 138(k,m), 139(q,r,s,t,u) (bibl to 1933); Reid, Arthurian Legend, p 59.

[25] SIR GAWAIN AND THE GREEN KNIGHT.

MS. BM Cotton Nero A.x, ff 91^a–124^b (ca 1400).

Gollancz I, Pearl, Cleanness, Patience, and Sir Gawain, reproduced in Facsmile from the Unique MS, EETS 162, 1923 (rptd 1931; crit W W Greg, MLR 19.223).

Greg W W, A Bibliographical Paradox Cotton Nero A.x, Libr 13.188.

Oakden J P, The Scribal Errors of the MS Cotton Nero A.x, Libr 14.353 (reply to Greg).

Loomis R S and L H, Arthurian Legends in Medieval Art, N Y 1938, p 138 (discussion of MS illustrations).

Hill L L, Madden's Divisions of Sir Gawain and the Large Initial Capitals of Cotton Nero A.x, Spec 21.67.

Editions. Madden F, Syr Gawayne, Bannatyne Club, London 1839.

Morris R, EETS 4, 1864; rvsd 1869; rvsd I Gollancz 1897.

Tolkien J R R and E V Gordon, Sir Gawain and the Green Knight, Oxford 1925, corr impression 1930 (crit J H G Grattan, RES 1.484; J R Hulbert MP 23.246; O F Emerson, JEGP 26.248; R J Menner, MLN 41.397).

Gollancz I, M Day, M S Serjeantson, Sir Gawain and the Green Knight, EETS 210, 1938 (crit H L Savage, MLN 39.342; TLS Jan 25 1941, p 46; E G Bowen, G Jones, MÆ 13.58; A MacDonald, MLR 36.527).

Ford B, Sir Gawayne and the Grene Knight, The Age of Chaucer, London 1956, p 351 (normalized text based on Tolkien and Gordon).

Selections. AESpr 1.311.

Kluge F, Mittelenglisches Lesebuch, Halle 1912, p 104.

Cook A S, A Literary Middle English Reader, Boston 1915, p 53.

Brandl A and O Zippel, Mittelenglische Sprach- und Literaturproben, Berlin 1917, p 58.

Sisam K, Fourteenth Century Verse and Prose, Oxford 1921, p 44.

Sampson G, Cambridge Book of Prose and Verse, Cambridge 1924, p 334.

Brunner K and R Willmair, Mittelenglisches Lesebuch für Anfänger, Heidelberg 1929, p 30.

Mossé F, Manuel de l'anglais du moyen-âge, Paris 1949, Engl trans J A Walker, Baltimore 1952.

Modernizations. Weston J L, Sir Gawain and the Green Knight, London 1898 (prose, condensed; crit E Kölbing, EStn 26.399; Rom 28.164).

Stucken E, Gawân, ein Mysterium, Berlin 1901 (dramatization).

Cox J H, Knighthood in Germ and Flower, Boston 1910, p 93.

Weston J L, Romance, Vision and Satire, Boston 1912 (verse).

Kirtlan E J B, Gawain and the Green Knight, London 1912, new edn, 1913 (crit P G Thomas, EStn 47.250).

Neilson W A and K G T Webster, Chief British Poets of the Thirteenth and Fourteenth Centuries, Boston 1916, p 19; also printed with mod of Piers Plowman, Boston 1917.

Watt H A and J B Munn, Ideas and Forms in English and American Literature, Chicago 1925, p 115 (J L Weston, prose).

Andrew S L, Sir Gawain and the Green Knight, N Y 1929 (in the original meter; crit D Everett, YWES 10.126; F E Farley, Spec 5.222).

Banks T H jr, Sir Gawain and the Green Knight, N Y 1929 (crit D Everett, YWES 10.126; F E Farley, Spec 6.222).

Gerould G H, Old English and Medieval Literature, N Y 1929, p 85; rvsd edn 1933 (prose).

Gerould G H, Beowulf to Shakespeare, pt 1, N Y 1938, p 132.

Ridley M R, The Story of Sir Gawain and the Green Knight in Modern English, Leicester 1944 (some omissions; crit G Willcock, YWES 25.62).

Pons E, Sir Gauvain et le Chevalier Vert, Paris 1946 (crit B White, MLR 43.253; H L Savage, JEGP 47.44).

Hare K, Sir Gawayne and the Green Knight, London 1918; 2nd edn, Stratford 1948 (introd, notes by R M Wilson; crit H L Savage, MLN 66.489).

Loomis R S and R Willard, Medieval English Verse and Prose, N Y 1948, p 156 (Banks version).

Williams M, Glee-Wood, N Y 1949, p 362 (modernized selections).

Jones G, Sir Gawain and the Green Knight, London 1953.

Textual Notes. Skeat W W, Rare Words in Middle English, TPSL 1891–94, p 359.

Skeat W W, English Etymologies, TPSL 1903–06, pp 247, 359.

Napier A S, Notes on Gawain and the Green Knight, MLN 17.85 (lines 143–44, 228–29, 680–81, 777, 893, 1008–09, 1283–84, 1331, 1443–44, 1998–99).

Kullnick M, Studien über den Wortschatz in Sir Gawain, Berlin 1902.

Wright E M, Notes on GGK, EStn 36.209.

Chambers R W, Sir Gawain and the Green Knight lines 697–702, MLR 2.167.

Thomas P G, The Middle English Alliterative Poem Gawain and the Green Knight, EStn 47.311.

Brett C, Notes on GGK (lines 681, 966–67, 1439–40, 1729–32), MLR 8.160.

Brett C, Notes on Cleanness and GGK, MLR 10.188 (lines 151–61, 210–14, 1235–40, 1489–97).

Knott T A, The Text of Gawain and the Green Knight, MLN 30.102.

Ekwall E, A Few Notes on English Etymology and Word History, AnglB 29.195 (line 1710).

Brett C, Notes on Passages of Old and Middle English, MLR 14.1.

Sundén K F, Några Förbisedda Skandinaviska Lånord i Gawain and the Green Knight, Göteborgs Högskolas Årsskrift 26.140.

Emerson O F, Two Notes on Gawain and the Green Knight, MLN 36.212 (lines 160, 864–70).

Emerson O F, Notes on Sir Gawain and the Green Knight, JEGP 21.363.

Jackson I, Sir Gawain's Coat of Arms, MLR 15.77; 17.289 (lines 619–20).

Hare K, TLS Sept 6 1923; C T Onions, Aug 16, Sept 20 1923 (lines 530–31, crit Hare); Feb 11 1926, Feb 5 1931.

Hulbert J R, The Name of the Green Knight, Manly Anniversay Studies, Chicago 1923, p 12.

Wright E M, The Word Abloy in GGK line 1174, MLR 18.86; M Day, The Word Abloy in GGK, MLR 18.337.

Förster M, Der Name des Green Knight, Arch 147.194.

Holthausen F, Zu Sir Gawain and the Green Knight, AnglB 35.32.

Menner R J, Notes on GGK, MLR 19.204 (lines 171, 864–70, 1264–67).

Onions C T, Notes on Sir Gawain and the Green Knight, N&Q 146.203, 244, 285 (lines 28, 69, 110, 155, 573, 1931, 155–57, 185, 194, 261–62, 290, 440, 670, 773–74, 822, 890, 958, 1015, 1174, 1533, 1695–96, 1710, 2018, 2101–02).

Emerson O F, Shakespearean and Other Feasts, SP 22.161.

Self-Weeks W, GGK: Harled, N&Q 148.122.

Snell B S, Four Notes on GGK, N&Q 148.75, 122.

Onions C T, Fade in Sir Gawain, TLS Jan 20 1927, Feb 3 1927; K Sisam, TLS Jan 27, March 17 1927.

Sisam K, Sir Gawain lines 147–50, N&Q 195.239 (fade).

Magoun F P, Anmerkungen zum Glossar des Tolkien-Gordonschen Sir Gawain and the Green Knight, Angl 52.79.

King R W, Notes on GGK, RES 5.449.

Sundén K F, Etymology of ME Trayþ(e)ly and Runisch, Renusch, SN 2.41.

Savage H L, GGK line 1704, MLN 44.249.

Savage H L, Fnasted in Sir Gawain line 1702, PQ 9.209.

Sundén K F, Etymology of the ME Verbs Roþe, Roþele, and Ruþe, Grammatical Miscellany Offered to O Jespersen, London 1930, p 109.

Savage H L, Notes on Gawain and the Green Knight, PMLA 46.169 (lines 296, 310, 493, 722, 1006, 1028, 1147, 1154, 1161, 1324, 1380, 1423, 1467, 1563, 1595, 1602, 1603, 1604, 1690–96, 1701, 1714, 1726, 1913, 2251).

Savage H L, A Note on Gawain and the Green Knight lines 700–02, MLN 46.455.

Andrew S O, The Text of Gawain and the Green Knight, RES 6.175.

Mathews J C, Sir Gawain line 133: An Emendation, PQ 9.215.

Menner R J, Middle English Lagmon (GGK line 1729) and Modern English lag, PQ 10.162.

Whiting E K, ed, The Poems of John Audelay, EETS 184.xxiv.

King R W, A Note on GGK 2414 ff, MLR 29.435.

Savage H L, A Note on GGK line 2035, MLN 49.232.

Smith J H, Gawain's Leap: GGK line 2316, MLN 49.462.

MacDonald A, GGK lines 14 ff, MLR 30.343.

Savage H L, A Note on GGK line 1700, MÆ 4.199.

Savage H L, Scrape in GGK, TLS Sept 26 1936; correction, Oct 31 1936.

Wright E M, Sir Gawain and the Green Knight, JEGP 34.157, 339; 35.313; 38.1.

Magoun F P, Sir Gawain and Mediaval Football, ESts 19.208.

Magoun F P, Kleine Beiträge zur Sir Gawain, Angl 61.129.

Perry L M, GGK line 2511, MLR 32.80.

Savage H, Brow or Brawn?, MLN 52.36 (lines 1454–61).

Savage H L, A Note on Sir Gawain line 1795, MLN 55.604.

Richardson M E, A Note on GGK line 877, N&Q 180.96.

Kökeritz H, GGK line 1954, MLN 58.373.

Kökeritz H, Two Interpretations, SN 14.277 (line 1954).

Savage H L, Methles in GGK, MLN 58.46.

White B, Chevisaunce as a Flower Name, RES 21.317 (Shepherds Calendar and GGK).

Whitbread L, A Reading in Sir Gawayne, N&Q 189.189.

Savage H L, Lote Loteȝ in GGK, MLN 60.492.

Savage H L, GGK lines 875–77, Expl 3, item 58.

Savage H L, GGK lines 206–07, Expl 4, item 41.

Chapman C O, Ticius to Tuskan, GGK line 11, MLN 63.59.

Dowden P J, GGK lines 620, 625, MLR 44.229.

Pons E, Note sur GGK (line 790) Embaned, Mélanges Hoepffner, Paris 1949, p 71.

Savage H L, The Green Knight's Molaynes, Philologica: Malone Anniversary Studies, Baltimore 1949, p 167.

Jackson I, GGK, a Note on Fade, line 149, N&Q 195.24.

Clark J W, Paraphrases for God in the Poems Attributed to the Gawain Poet, MLN 65.232.

Smithers G V, A Crux in GGK, N&Q 195.134.

Chapman C O, An Index of Names in Pearl, Purity, Patience, and Sir Gawain, Cornell Studies in Engl 38, Ithaca 1951 (crit R W Ackerman, JEGP 50.538; H L Savage, Spec 27.364).

Clark J W, On Certain Alliterative and Poetic Words in the Poems Attributed to the Gawain Poet, MLQ (Wash) 12.389.

Bonjour A, Werre and Wrake and Wonder (GGK line 16), ESts 32.70.

Onions C T, Middle English gawne, a Correction of Some Notes, MÆ 22.110.

White B, Two Notes on Middle English, Neophil 37.114 (GGK line 295).

MacDonald A, A Note on GGK, ESts 35.15 (line 385).

Clark C, The Green Knight Shoeless: A Reconsideration, RES 6.174.

Luttrell C A, The Gawain Group: Cruxes, Etymologies, Interpretations, Neophil 39.207.

Pearsall D A, A Rhetorical Descriptio in GGK, MLR 50.129.

Language. Schwahn F, Die Conjugation in Sir Gawain und den sogenannten Early English Alliterative Poems, Strassburg 1884.

Fick W, Zum me Gedicht von der Perle: eine Lautuntersuchung, Kiel 1885.

Knigge F, Die Sprache des Dichters von Sir Gawain, der sogenannten Early English Alliterative Poems, and De Erkenwalde, Marburg 1886.

Heuser W, Offenes und geschlossenes ee im W M Dialekt, Angl 19.451.

Schmittbetz K R, Das Adjektiv im Verse von Syr Gawain, Angl 32.1, 163, 359.

Day M K, The Weak Verb in the Work of the Gawain Poet, MLR 14.413.

Hulbert J R, The West Midland of the Romances, MP 19.1.

Menner R J, Sir Gawain and the Green Knight and the West Midland, PMLA 37.503.

Flasdieck H, Studien zur me Grammatik, AnglB 36.240.

Menner R J, Four Notes on the West Midland Dialect, MLN 41.454.

Serjeantson M S, The Dialects of the West Midlands in Middle English, II, Assignment of Texts, RES 3.327.

Andrew S O, The Preterite in North-Western Dialects, RES 5.431.

Whitehall H, A Note on North-West Midland Spelling, PQ 9.1.

Gordon E V and C T Onions, Notes on the Text and Interpretation of Pearl, MÆ 1.126 (line 1710).

Oakden J P, Alliterative Poetry in Middle English, A Survey of the Traditions, 2 vols, Manchester 1930, 1935 (crit D Everett, YWES 11.92; C T Onions, RES 9.89; W W Greg, The Continuity of the Alliterative Tradition, MLR 27.453; J R Hulbert, MP 28.483).

Oakden J P, The Continuity of the Alliterative Tradition, MLR 28.233 (reply to Greg).

Koziol H, Grundzüge der Syntax der me Stabreimdichtungen, WBEP 58.

Clark J W, The Gawain Poet and the Substantival Adjective, JEGP 49.60.

Akkatral T, A Point of Syntax in Sir Gawain and the Green Knight, N&Q 198.322.

Bazire J, ME ē and ę in the Rhymes of GGK, JEGP 51.234.

Versification. Rosenthal F, Die alliterierende englische Langzeile im 14 Jahrhundert, Angl 1.414.

Fuhrmann J, Die alliterierenden Sprachformeln in Morris' Early English Alliterative Poems und in GGK, diss Kiel, Hamburg 1886.

Luick K, Die englische Stabreimzeile im 14, 15, und 16 Jahrhundert, Angl 11.572.

Trautmann M, Zur Kenntniss und Geschichte der me Stabzeile, Angl 18.83.

Kaluza M, Studien zum germanischen Alliterationsvers, Berlin 1900 (crit K Luick, AnglB 12.33).

Kuhnke B, Die alliterierende Langzeile in der me Romanze GGK, Berlin 1900 (crit K Luick, AnglB 12.33).

Fischer J, Die Stabende Langzeile in der Werken des Gawain-Dichters, BBA 11.1 (crit K Luick, AnglB 12.46).

Fischer J and F Mennicken, Zur me Stabzeile, BBA 11.139.

Thomas J, Die alliterierende Langzeile des Gawayn-Dichters, diss Jena 1908.

Schumacher K, Studien über den Stabreim in der me Alliterationsdichtung, BSEP 11, 1914.

Day M, Strophic Division in Middle English Alliterative Verse, EStn 66.245.

Borroff M, Sir Gawain and the Green Knight: A Stylistic and Metrical Study, YSE 152, New Haven 1962.

Renoir A, An Echo to the Sense: The Patterns of Sound in Sir Gawain and the Green Knight, English Miscellany 13.9.

Date and Authorship. Trautmann M, Der Dichter Huchown und seine Werke, Angl 1.109, 188.

Trautmann M, Über die Verfasser und Entstehungszeit einiger alliterierenden Gedichte, Halle 1878.

Gollancz I, Ralph Strode, DNB.

Bradley H, A New Theory as to Huchown, Athen Dec 22 1900, p 826.

Neilson G, Sir Hew of Eglintoun and Huchown of the Awle Ryale, Proc Phil Soc, Glasgow 32.111.

Neilson G, Huchown of the Awle Ryale, Transactions of the Glasgow Arch Soc, 1900.

Brown J T T, Huchown of the Awle Ryale, Glasgow 1902.

Brown C F, Note on the Question of Strode's Authorship of the Pearl, PMLA 19.146.

Reicke C, Untersuchungen über den Stil der me Gedichte Morte Arthur, the Destruction of Troy, the Wars of Alexander, the Siege of Jerusalem, Sir Gawain and the Green Knight, Königsberg 1906.

Hamilton G L, Capados and the Date of GGK, MP 5.365.

Gollancz I, Pearl, London 1921, p xlvi (the Medieval Library edn).

Cargill O and M Schlauch, The Pearl and Its Jeweller, PMLA 43.118.

Hulbert J R, A Hypothesis Concerning the Alliterative Revival, MP 28.405.

Rickert E, New Life Records of Chaucer, TLS Oct 4 1928; H W Garrod, TLS Oct 11 1928; I Gollancz, TLS Oct 25 1928.

Chapman C O, The Authorship of the Pearl, PMLA 47.346.

Koziol H, Zur Frage der Verfasserschaft einiges me Stabreimdichtungen, EStn 67.165.

A L E, Sir Gawain and the Green Knight and Pearl, N&Q 170.27.

Savage H L, Enguerrand de Coucy VII and the Campaign of Nicopolis, Spec 14.423.

Robbins R H, A Gawain Epigone, MLN 58.361.

Clark J W, Observations on Certain Differences in Vocabulary between Cleanness and GGK, PQ 28.261.

Robbins R H, The Poems of Humfrey Newton, Esquire, 1466–1536, PMLA 65.249 (the Gawain Epigone of MLN 58.361).

Braddy H, Sir Gawain and Ralph Holmes the Green Knight, MLN 67.240.

Highfield J R L, The Green Squire, MÆ 22.18 (Simon Newton, fl 1363–80, in the West Midlands).

Sources and Literary Relations. Thomas M C, Sir Gawayn and the Green Knight, a Comparison with the French Perceval, diss Zürich 1883 (crit G P[aris], Rom 12.376).

Steinbach P, Über den Einfluss des Crestien de Troies auf die altenglische Litteratur, diss

Leipzig 1885, p 48 (crit A Brandl, LfGRP 9.211; M Kaluza, EStn 12.89).

Weston J L, The Legend of Sir Gawain, London 1897.

Hulbert J R, Syr Gawain and the Grene Knight, MP 13.433, 689.

Kittredge G L, A Study of Sir Gawain and the Green Knight, Cambridge Mass 1916.

Schaubert E von, Der englische Ursprung von Syr Gawayn and the Greene Knyght, EStn 57.331 (crit P G Thomas, YWES 4.52).

McKeehan I P, St Edmund of East Anglia: The Development of a Romantic Legend, Univ of Colorado Studies 15.18 (parallel to GGK).

Garrett R M, The Lay of Sir Gawayne and the Green Knight, JEGP 24.125.

Loomis R S, Celtic Myth and Arthurian Romance, N Y 1927, p 59, 69–84, 114.

Loomis R S, Gawain, Gwri, and Cuchulainn, PMLA 43.384.

Gollancz I, Chivalry, ed E Prestage, London 1928, p 175.

Becker P A, Der grüne Ritter, Arch 159.275.

Loomis R S, The Visit to the Perilous Castle, a Study in the Arthurian Modifications of an Irish Theme, PMLA 48.1000.

Buchanan A, The Irish Framework of Gawain and the Green Knight, PMLA 47.315.

Nitze W A, Is the Green Knight Story a Vegetation Myth? MP 33.351.

Gerould G H, The Gawain Poet and Dante, PMLA 51.31.

L O E, The Inner Side of the Shield, N&Q 170.8.

Bayley A R, The Five Wounds, N&Q 171.266; J R F, The Five Wounds N&Q 171.335; E J G Forse, The Five Wounds, N&Q 171.300.

Dickins B, A Yorkshire Chronicler (William of Newburgh), Transactions of the Yorkshire Dialect Soc 5, pt 35, p 19.

Löhmann O, Die Sage von Gawain und dem grünen Ritter, Königsberg 1938 (crit J R Hulbert, MLN 55.159; K Brunner, AnglB 49.336; H L Savage, JEGP 38.445).

Krappe A H, Who Was the Green Knight? Spec 13.206.

Vogel H, Étude du personnage de Gauvain dans Sir Gawain and the Green Knight, Bull de la Faculté des lettres de Strasbourg 19.77 (abstr).

Loomis R S, More Celtic Elements in GGK, JEGP 42.149.

Coomaraswamy A K, Sir Gawain and the Green Knight: Indra and Namuci, Spec 19.104.

Chapman C O, Virgil and the Gawain Poet, PMLA 60.16.

Smith R M, Guingambresil and the Green Knight, JEGP 45.1.

Watson M R, The Chronology of Sir Gawain and the Green Knight, MLN 64.85.

Loomis R S, Arthurian Tradition and Chrétien de Troyes, N Y 1949, p 278.

Eagan J T, The Import of Color Symbolism in Sir Gawain and the Green Knight, St Louis Univ Studies 1.11.

Baughan D E, The Role of Morgan le Fay in Sir Gawain and the Green Knight, ELH 17.241.

Pons E, Y a-t-il une psychologie proprement anglaise du caractère de Gauvain?, BBSIA 3.103 (abstr).

Chapman C O, Chaucer and the Gawain-Poet, a Conjecture, MLN 68.521.

Zimmer H, Gawan beim grünen Ritter, Deutsche Beiträge zur geistiges Überlieferung, Chicago 1953.

Engelhardt G J, The Predicament of Gawain, MLQ (Wash) 16.218.

Bricriu's Feast, ed G Henderson, Irish Texts Society 2, 1899.

Veitch J, Feeling for Nature in Scottish Poetry, Edinburgh 1887, 1.13.

Bruce J D, The Breaking of the Deer in GGK, EStn 32.23.

Gollancz I, Gringolet, Gawain's Horse, Saga Book of the Viking Club, 5.104.

Jackson I, Sir Gawain and the Green Knight Considered as a Garter Poem, Angl 37.393.

Jahrmann J, Syr Gawain and the Green Knight and Stucken's Gawân, NS 26.405.

Ray B K, The Character of Gawain, Dacca Univ Bull 11.8.

Savage H L, The Significance of the Hunting Scenes in Sir Gawain and the Green Knight, JEGP 28.1.

Plessow G, Gotische Tektonik in Wortkunstwerk, Munich 1931.

Chapman C O, The Musical Training of the Pearl Poet, PMLA 46.177.

Savage H L, Hunting in the Middle Ages, Spec 8.30.

Baker Sister I, The King's Household, Washington 1937, p 116.

Savage H L, Sir Gawain and the Order of the Garter, ELH 5.146.

Obrecht D, Le thème et la langue de la chasse dans Sir Gawain and the Green Knight, Bulletin de la Faculté des Lettres de Strasbourg 17.22 (abstr).

Colgrave B, Sir Gawayne's Green Chapel, Antiq 12.351 (addit note by O G S C[raw-ford]; The Bridestones East of Congleton, Cheshire).

Savage H L, Historical Background of Sir Gawain and the Green Knight, Year Book of the Amer Philosoph Soc 1939, p 231.

Brewer D S, Gawain and the Green Chapel, N&Q 193.13.

Davies R J, Gawayn and the Green Chapel, N&Q 193.194 (reply to Brewer).

Ong W J, The Green Knight's Harts and Bucks, MLN 65.536.

Savage H L, Hunting Terms in Middle English, MLN 66.216 (comment on Ong, MLN 65.536).

Savage H L, The Feast of Fools in Sir Gawain and the Green Knight, JEGP 51.537.

Speirs J, Sir Gawain and the Green Knight, Scrut 16.274; J Bayley, 17.128; Speirs, 17.130; Q D Leavis, 17.253.

Reinhold H, Humoristische Tendenzen in der englischen Dichtung des Mittelalters, Tübingen 1953, p 118.

Chambers OHEL, p 75.

Everett D, Essays on ME Literature, ed P Kean, Oxford 1955, p 68.

Savage H L, The Gawain-Poet: Studies in His Personality and Background, Chapel Hill 1956.

Markman A M, The Meaning of Sir Gawain and the Green Knight, PMLA 72.574.

Ackerman R W, Gawain's Shield: Penitential Doctrine in Gawain and the Green Knight, Angl 76.254.

Friedman A B, Morgan le Fay in Sir Gawain and the Green Knight, Spec 35.260.

Bloomfield M W, Sir Gawain and the Green Knight: An Appraisal, PMLA 76.7.

Schnyder H, Sir Gawain and the Green Knight: An Essay in Interpretation, Cooper Monographs 6, Bern 1962.

Berry F, The Age of Chaucer, ed B Ford, London 1954, p 148.

Brandl, § 74; Körting, § 105; Ten Brink, 1.337; CHEL, 1.363, 525; Ward, 1.337; HLF, 30.71; Billings, p 100; Chambers, 1.117, 185; Baugh LHE, p 236; Kane, p 73.

See also under Pearl, Patience, Purity.

[26] THE GRENE KNIGHT.

MS. BM Addit 27879 (Percy Folio), pp 203–210 (ca 1650).

Editions. Madden F, Syr Gawayne, London 1839, pp 224, 352.

PFMS, 2.56.

Child F J, English and Scottish Popular Ballads, Boston 1857, 1.35 (not in later edns).

Sources and Literary Relations. Hulbert J R, Syr Gawayn and the Grene Knyʒt, MP 13.460, 695, 701, 714.

Kittredge G L, A Study of Gawain and the

Green Knight, Cambridge Mass 1916, pp 122, 282, 296.

Day M, Sir Gawain and the Green Knight, EETS 210.xxxviii (parallels and differences).

Brandl, § 113; Schofield, p 217; Billings, p 209; Kane, p 15.

[27] THE TURKE AND GOWIN.

MS. BM Addit 27879 (Percy Folio), pp 38–46 (ca 1650).

Editions. Madden F, Syr Gawayne, London 1839, pp 243, 355.

PFMS, 1.88.

Sources and Literary Relations. Maynadier G H, The Wife of Bath's Tale, London 1901, p 148.

Hulbert J R, Syr Gawayn and the Grene Knyʒt, MP 13.697, 703.

Kittredge G L, A Study of Gawain and the Green Knight, Cambridge Mass 1916, pp 118, 200, 274, 296.

Loomis R S, Celtic Myth and Arthurian Romance, N Y 1927, pp 100, 300.

Kurvinen A, Sir Gawain and the Carl of Carlisle, Helsinki 1951, p 103.

Walpole R N, The Pèlerinage de Charlemagne, Poem, Legend, and Problem, RomP 8.173 (ME parallels including The Turke and Gowin).

Brandl, § 105; HLF, 30.68; Schofield, p 218; Billings, p 211.

[28] SYRE GAWENE AND THE CARLE OF CARELYLE.

MS. National Library of Wales, Aberystwyth, Porkington MS 10, ff 12ª–26ᵇ (before 1475).

Kurvinen A, MS Porkington 10, Description with Abstracts, NM 54.33 (also described in her edn of Sir Gawain and the Carl of Carlisle, Helsinki 1951, p 27).

Editions. Madden F, Syr Gawayne, London 1839, pp 187, 344.

Ackerman R W, Syre Gawene and the Carle of Carelyle, Univ of Michigan Contributions in Modern Philology 8, Ann Arbor 1947 (crit J R Hulbert, MP 46.203).

Kurvinen A, Sir Gawain and the Carl of Carlisle, Helsinki 1951, pp 114–58 (even-numbered pages; crit R W Ackerman, JEGP 51.244; C O Chapman, Spec 27.226).

Textual Notes. Holthausen F, Zum Sir Gawain and the Carl of Carlisle, Arch 190.315.

Language. Ackerman, edn, p 4; Kurvinen, edn, p 29.

Date. Ackerman, edn, p 8; Kurvinen, edn, p 28.

Versification. Kurvinen, edn, p 33.

Relation to Percy Folio Carle of Carlile. Kurvinen, edn, p 64.

Sources and Literary Relations. Hulbert J R, Syr Gawayne and the Grene Knyʒt, MP 13.696.

Kittredge G L, A Study of Gawain and the Green Knight, Cambridge Mass 1916, pp 41, 87, 226, 256.

Loomis R S, Celtic Myth and Arthurian Romance, N Y 1927, p 98.

Buchanan A, The Irish Framework of Gawain and the Green Knight, PMLA 47.331.

Loomis R S, The Visit to the Perilous Castle, PMLA 48.1007.

Kurvinen, edn, p 80.

Bernheimer R, Wild Men of the Middle Ages, Cambridge Mass 1952, p 29.

Baker Sister I, The King's Household, Washington 1937, p 118.

Brandl, § 125; HLF, 30.68; Schofield, p 218; Billings, p 215.

[29] THE CARLE OFF CARLILE.

MS. BM Addit 27879 (Percy Folio), pp 448–455 (ca 1650).

Kurvinen, edn, p 54. (See below under *Editions.*)

Editions. Madden F, Syr Gawayne, London 1839, pp 256, 365.

Child F J, English and Scottish Popular Ballads, Boston 1857, 1.58.

PFMS, 3.275.

Kurvinen A, Sir Gawain and the Carl of Carlisle, Helsinki 1951, pp 115–59 (odd-numbered pages).

Language, Versification, Date. Kurvinen, edn, pp 55, 63; p 56; p 63.

Sources and Literary Relations. See above under Syre Gawene and the Carle of Carelyle [28].

Loomis R S, Arthurian Tradition and Chrétien de Troyes, N Y 1949, p 286.

Schofield, p 218; Billings, p 217.

[30] THE AWNTYRS OFF ARTHURE AT THE TERNE WATHELYNE.

MSS. 1, Bodl 21898 (Douce 324), ff 1ª–11ᵇ (late 15 cent); 1a, Bodl 21883 (19 cent transcript by Douce), f 1ª; 2, Lambeth 491.B, ff 275ª–286ᵇ (before 1450); 3, Lincoln Cath 91 (Thornton), ff 154ª–161ᵇ (ca 1440); 4, Ireland Blackburn, ff 5ª–15ᵇ (ca 1450).

Bülbring K D, Über die Handschrift Nr 491 der Lambeth-Bibliothek, Arch 86.385.

Dickins B, The Date of the Ireland Manuscript, Leeds SE 2.62; A E Schmidt, B Dickins, The Ireland MS, TLS 1933, pp 896, 909.

Hooper A G, The Lambeth Palace MS of the Awntyrs off Arthure, Leeds SE 3.67.

YWES 26.236 (Ireland MS, from Harmsworth Library, notice of sale).

Editions. Pinkerton J, Scotish Poems, London 1792, 3.197 (edn of Douce MS).

Laing D, Ancient Popular Poetry of Scotland, Edinburgh 1822; new edn, J Small 1885; rvsd W C Hazlitt 1895, 1.4 (edn of Thornton MS).

Madden F, Syr Gawayne, London 1839, pp 95, 326 (Thornton and Douce).

Robson, p 1 (Ireland MS).

Amours F J, Scottish Alliterative Poems, PSTS 27, 1897 (Douce MS, even-numbered pp 116–70; Thornton MS, odd-numbered pp 117–71; all MSS).

Modernizations. Weston J L, Romance, Vision, and Satire, Cambridge MSS 1912, p 109.

Textual Notes. Holthausen F, Zur Textkritik me Gedichte, AnglB 36.187.

Language. Hulbert J R, The West Midland of the Romances, MP 19.1.

Menner R J, Sir Gawain and the Green Knight and the West Midland, PMLA 37.503.

Serjeantson M S, The Dialects of the West Midlands in ME, II, Assignment of Texts, RES 3.328.

Moore S, S Meech, H Whitehall, ME Dialect Characteristics and Dialect Boundaries, Essays and Studies in Engl and Comp Lit, Univ of Michigan, 13.53.

Hooper A G, The Awntyrs off Arthure: Dialect and Authorship, Leeds SE 4.62.

Oakden J P, Alliterative Poetry in ME, Manchester 1930, 1.113, 217; 2.47 (1935).

Versification. Lübke H, The Aunters of Arthur, diss Berlin 1883.

Luick K, Zur Metrik der me Reimend-alliterierenden Dichtung, Angl 12.452.

Medary M P, Stanza-Linking in ME Verse, RomR 7.243.

Brown L, On the Origin of Stanza-Linking in English Alliterative Verse, RomR 7.271.

Tatlock J S P, Dante's Terza Rima, PMLA 51.90.

Authorship. Trautmann M, Der Dichter Huchown und seine Werke, Angl 1.129.

Lübke H, The Aunters of Arthur, diss Berlin 1883.

Bradley H and G Neilson, Athen 1903[1].498, 626, 657, 689, 754, 816; 1903[2].221.

Andrew S O, Huchown's Works, RES 5.14.

Webster K G T, Galloway and the Romances, MLN 55.363.

Veitch J, Feeling for Nature in Scottish Poetry, Edinburgh 1887, 1.139.

Neilson G, Crosslinks between the Pearl and the Awntyrs, SA 16.67.

Baker Sister I, The King's Household, Washington 1937, p 120.

Billings, p 173; Brandl, § 75; Ten Brink, 1.336; HLF, 30.96; Gröber, 2[1].519; Schofield, p 218; CHEL, 1.325, 347; Körting, § 102; Kane, p 52.

[31] GOLAGRUS AND GAWAIN.

MSS. No MS extant. PRINT: Chepman W and A Myllar, The Knightly Tale of Golagros and Gawane, Edinburgh 1508, Advocates Libr H.30.a.

Editions. Pinkerton J, Scotish Poems, London 1792, 3.65.

Facsimile edn of Chepman and Myllar 1508, rptd D Laing, Edinburgh 1827 (76 copies).

Madden F, Syre Gawayne, London 1839, pp 131, 336.

Trautmann M, Golagrus und Gawan, Angl 2.395.

Amours F J, Scottish Alliterative Poems, PSTS 27, 1897.

Stevenson G, Pieces from the Macculloch and the Gray MSS together with the Chepman and Myllar Prints, PSTS 65, 1918, p 67.

Textual Notes. Edwards J, Old Oaths and Interjections, SHR 1.57 (lines 809–10, 265).

Skeat W W, SHR 1.296.

Holthausen F, Zur Textkritik me Gedichte, AnglB 36.185.

Language. Noltemeyer O, Über die Sprache . . . diss Marburg 1889.

Hahn O, Zur Verbal und Nominal-Flexion bei den schottischen Dichtern, Berlin 1889.

Bearder J W, Über den Gebrauch der Praepositionen, Halle 1894.

Luick K, Zur Metrik des me Reimend-alliterierenden Dichtung, Angl 12.438.

Oakden J P, Alliterative Poetry in ME, Manchester 1930, 1.113, 217.

Authorship. Trautmann M, Der Dichter Huchown und seine Werke, Angl 1.109.

Sources and Literary Relations. Trautmann M, Golagrus and Gawan, Angl 2.402.

Neilson G, History in the Romance of Golagros and Gawayne, Proc Royal Phil Soc of Glasgow, 1902.

Thomas M C, Syr Gawayne and the Grene Knight, Zurich 1883, p 87.

Brown C, Somer Soneday, Klaeber Miscellany, Minneapolis 1929, p 362.

Ketrick P J, The Relation of Golagros and Gawane to the Old French Perceval, diss Catholic Univ, Washington 1931 (crit D Everett, YWES 12.101; J J Parry, JEGP 31.426; J Vendryes, RC 50.87).

Oakden J P, Alliterative Poetry in ME, Manchester 1935, 2.48.

Lascelles M M, Alexander and the Earthly Paradise in Mediaeval English Writings, MÆ 5.79 (pt 2 includes Golagros and Perceval).

Webster K G T, Galloway and the Romances, MLN 55.363.

Craigie W, The Scottish Alliterative Poems, Proc British Academy 1942, p 217.

Baker Sister I, The King's Household, Washington 1937, p 122.

Brandl, § 133; Körting, § 106; HLF, 30.41; Schofield, p 320; Billings, p 168; CBEL, 1.139; Renwick and Orton, pp 366, 411; Bennett OHEL, p 312.

[32] THE AVOWYNGE OF KING ARTHUR, SIR GAWAN, SIR KAYE, AND SIR BAWDEWYN OF BRETAN.

MS. Ireland Blackburn, ff 35ᵃ–59ᵃ (ca 1450).

Dickins B, The Date of the Ireland MS, Leeds SE 2.62.

Editions. Robson J, Three Early English Metrical Romances, London 1842.

French W H and C B Hale, ME Metrical Romances, N Y 1930, p 607.

Ireland MS, ed J Smith, Pubs and Abstrs of Theses by Members of Leeds Univ 1937–38, p 19 (abstr).

Language. Serjeantson M S, The Dialects of the West Midlands in ME, II, Assignment of Texts, RES 3.328.

Moore S, S Meech, H Whitehall, ME Dialect Characteristics and Dialect Boundaries, Essays and Studies in Engl and Comp Lit, Univ of Michigan, 13.53.

Tihany L, The Avowynge of King Arthur: A Morphological and Phonological Study of Words in Rhyme and of Certain Non-Rhyming Words, Summaries of Doctoral Dissertations, Northwestern Univ, 1936, 4.5 (abstr).

Versification. Bülbring K D, Untersuchungen zur me Metrik, SEP 50.511.

Luick K, Zur me Verslehre, Angl 38.268; 39.274.

Medary M P, Stanza-Linking in ME Verse, RomR 7.243.

Brown L, On the Origin of Stanza-Linking in English Alliterative Verse, RomR 7.271.

Sources and Literary Relations. Thomas M C, Sir Gawayne and Green Knight, diss Zürich 1883.

Greenlaw E, The Vows of Baldwin in the Avowynge of Arthur, PMLA 21.575.

Reinhard J R, Some Illustrations of the Mediaeval Gab, Essays and Studies in Engl and Comp Lit, Univ of Michigan, 8.37.

Brandl, § 75; HLF, 30.111; Schofield, p 222; Billings, p 178.

[33] YWAIN AND GAWAIN.

MS. Cotton Galba E.ix, ff 4ᵃ–25ᵃ (before 1425).

Editions. Ritson AEMR 1.1; 3.219, 437 (rptd E Goldsmid, Edinburgh 1891).

Schleich G, Ywain and Gawain, Oppeln, Leipzig 1887 (crit M Kaluza, EStn 12.83; F Holthausen, Angl 14.319).

Selections. French W H and C B Hale, ME Metrical Romances, N Y 1930, 1485.

Modernizations. Weston J L, Chief Middle English Poets, Cambridge Mass 1914, p 228.

Textual Notes. Schleich G, Collationen zu me Dichtungen, EStn 12.139.

Kölbing E, Zu Ywain and Gawain, EStn 24.146.

Lister W, Notes on the Text of the ME Romance Ywaine and Gawin, MLR 35.56.

Language. Lindheim B von, Studien zur Sprache des MS Cotton Galba E.ix, enth eine Darstellung d Sprache des 1 u 5 Schreibers des gen MS bzw der Texte Ywain u Gawain, The Seven Sages of Rome, The Pricke of Conscience, WPEB 59, 1937 (crit K Wittig, AnglB 49.306; K Brunner, EStn 73.253; F Holthausen, LfGRP 60.178).

Lindheim B von, Sprachliche Studien zu Texten des MS Galba E.ix, Angl 61.65.

Date. Eagleson H, Costume in the Middle English Metrical Romances, PMLA 47.339.

Sources and Literary Relations. Steinbach P, Über den Einfluss des Crestien de Troies auf die altenglische Litteratur, diss Leipzig 1885 (crit M Kaluza, EStn 12.89).

Schleich G, Über das Verhältniss des me Romance Ywain and Gawain zu ihrer altfranzösischen Quelle, Berlin 1889 (crit M Kaluza, EStn 15.429).

Weston J L, Ywain and Gawain and Le Chevalier au Lion, MLQ (Lon) 2.98; 31.94.

Foerster W, Kristian von Troyes Ywain, 2nd edn, A Hilka, Halle 1926.

Reid T B W, Chrétien de Troyes Yvain, Manchester 1942, rptd 1948 (photographic reprod of Foerster's text with new introd, notes, glossary).

Brown A C L, Iwain: A Study on the Origins of Arthurian Romance, Boston 1903.

Zenker R, Forschungen zur Artusepik: Ivainstudien, Beihefte zur ZfRP 70, Halle 1921 (crit W A Nitze, MP 20.101).

Brodeur A G, The Grateful Lion, PMLA 39.485.

Bruce J D, Evolution of Arthurian Romance, Baltimore 1928, 1.67.

Chotzen T M, Le lion de Owein (Yvain) et ses prototypes celtiques, Neophil 18.51, 131.

Whiting B J, Proverbs in Certain Middle English Romances in Relation to Their French Sources, HSNPL 15.75.

Brugger E, Yvain and His Lion, MP 38.267.

Loomis R S, Arthurian Tradition and Chrétien de Troyes, N Y 1949, p 269.

Harris J, The Role of the Lion in Chrétien de Troyes' Yvain, PMLA 64.1143.

Ackerman R W, Arthur's Wild Man Knight, RomP 9.115.

Gröber, 2¹.501; Paris Litt franç, § 57; Brandl, § 64; Körting, § 104; Dunlop, Hist of Fiction, 1.266; Schofield, p 230; Ward, 1.392; Billings, p 153; CBEL, 1.134 (bibl to 1933).

[34] THE WEDDYNGE OF SIR GAWEN AND DAME RAGNELL.

MS. Bodl 11951 (Rawlinson C 86), ff 129ᵃ–140ᵃ (ca 1500).

Editions. Madden F, Syr Gawayne, London 1839, p 297.

Sumner L, The Weddynge of Sir Gawen and Dame Ragnell, Smith College Studies in Modern Languages 5, no 4, 1924 (crit C B, MLR 21.345).

Whiting B J, Bryan-Dempster, p 242 (reprint of Sumner text).

Modernizations. Saul G B, The Wedding of Sir Gawain and Dame Ragnell, N Y 1934 (crit H L Savage, MLN 51.136).

Reinhard J R, Mediaeval Pageant, N Y 1939, p 75.

Sources and Literary Relations. Webster K G T, Galloway and the Romances, MLN 55.363.

Stokes W, The Marriage of Sir Gawain, Acad 41.399 (Irish analogues).

Nutt A, The Marriage of Sir Gawain and the Loathly Damsel, Acad 41.425 (Irish analogues).

Weston J L, The Legend of Sir Gawain, London 1897, p 49.

Maynadier G H, The Wife of Bath's Tale, London 1901.

Kittredge G L, A Study of Gawain and the Green Knight, Cambridge Mass 1916, p 269.

Loomis R S, Celtic Myth and Arthurian Romance, N Y 1927, p 298.

Loomis R S, Arthurian Tradition and Chrétien de Troyes, N Y 1949, p 377.

[35] THE MARRIAGE OF SIR GAWAINE.

MS. BM Addit 27879 (Percy Folio), pp 46–52 (ca 1650).

Editions. Percy, Reliques, 1794, 3.350.

Ritson AEMR, l.cx.

Madden F, Syr Gawayne, London 1839, p 288.

PFMS, 1.105.

Child F J, The English and Scottish Popular Ballads, Boston 1857, 1.288; 1882, 1.288.

Clouston W A, Chaucer Soc Originals and Analogues, 2nd ser, 22.483.

Whiting B J, Bryan-Dempster, p 235 (reprint of PFMS, 1.105).

Sources and Literary Relations. Görbing F, The Ballad The Marriage of Sir Gawain, Angl 23.405.

Weston J L, Legend of Sir Gawain, London 1897, p 48.

Maynadier G H, The Wife of Bath's Tale, London 1901.

Skeat W W, Oxf Ch 3.447.

Coomaraswamy A K, On the Loathly Bride, Spec 20.391.

See under THE WEDDYNGE OF SIR GAWEN AND DAME RAGNELL [34] and also Chaucer's WIFE OF BATH'S TALE.

[36] THE JEASTE OF SYR GAWAYNE.

MSS. 1, Bodl 21835 (Douce 261), ff 15ᵃ–25ᵇ, transcript ca 1564 of an early print by E B; PRINT: 2, Harley 5927 Arts 32 (single leaf from early print).

Brown-Robbins, no *13.

Editions. Madden F, Syr Gawayne, London 1839, pp 207, 348.

Sources and Literary Relations. Bennett R E, The Sources of the Jeaste of Syr Gawayne, JEGP 33.57.

Roach W, The Continuations of the Old French Perceval of Chrétien de Troyes: The First Continuation, Phila 1949, 1.69 (French text).

Brandl, § 113; Schofield, p 228; Billings, p 213.

[37] KING ARTHUR AND KING CORNWALL.

MS. BM Addit 27879 (Percy Folio), pp 24–31 (ca 1650).

Editions. Madden F, Syr Gawayne, London 1839, p 275.

Child F J, The English and Scottish Popular Ballads, Boston 1882, 1.274.

Sources and Literary Relations. Briggs W D, King Arthur and King Cornwall, JEGP 3.342.

Webster K G T, Arthur and Charlemagne, EStn 36.337.

Reinhard J R, Some Illustrations of the Mediaeval Gab, Essays and Studies in Engl and Comp Lit, Univ of Michigan, 8.27.

Krappe A H, Mediaeval Literature and the Comparative Method, Spec 10.270 (includes King Arthur and King Cornwall).

Loomis R S, Arthurian Tradition and Chrétien de Troyes, N Y 1949, p 134.

Walpole R N, The Pèlerinage de Charlemagne, Poem, Legend, and Problem, RomP 8.173 (ME parallels including King Arthur and King Cornwall).

[38] LIBEAUS DESCONUS.

MSS. 1, Bodl 6922* (Ashmole 61), ff 38ᵇ–59ᵇ late 15 cent); 2, Cotton Calif A.II, ff 42ᵇ–57ᵃ (late 15 cent); 3, BM Addit 27879 (Percy Folio), pp 317–346 (ca 1650; transcript of an early print); 4, Lambeth 306, ff 73ᵃ–107ᵇ (late 15 cent); 5, Lincoln's Inn 150, ff 1ᵃ, 4–12ᵇ (before 1425); 6, Naples, Royal Library XIII.B 29, ff 87–113 (1457).

Brown-Robbins, no 1690.

Kölbing E, Vier Romanzen-Handschriften, EStn 7.194 (Lincoln's Inn).

Kaluza M, Libeaus Desconus, Leipzig 1890, p xvii (relations of MSS).

Manly & Rickert, 1.376 (description of Naples MS).

Editions. Ritson AEMR, 2.1 (rptd E Goldsmid, Edinburgh 1891; Cotton Calig MS).

Hippeau C, Le bel inconnu, Paris 1860, p 241 (Cotton Calig MS).

PFMS, 2.415.

Kaluza M, Libeaus Desconus, Leipzig 1890 (critical text; crit K D Bülbring, EStn 17.118; G Paris, Rom 20.297).

Selections. Rel Ant, 2.68, 65 (Naples MS).

Sampson G, Cambridge Book of Prose and Verse, Cambridge 1924, p 281.

Modernizations. Weston J L, Sir Cleges; Sir Libeaus Desconus, London 1902 (crit G Binz, AnglB 15.332).

Language. Wilda O, Über die örtliche Verbreitung der zwölfzeiligen Schweifreimstrophe in England, Breslau 1887, p 8.

Bülbring K D, Geschichte der Ablaute der starken Zeitwörter innerhalbs des Südenglischen, QF 63.30, 49.

Kaluza, edn, p lxxiv.

Fischer E, Der Lautbestand des südmittelenglischen Octovian, verglichen mit seiner Entsprechungen im Lybeaus Desconus und im Launfal, Heidelberg 1927 (crit E von Erhardt-Siebold, JEGP 28.547; L von Hibler, EStn 64.71).

Trounce A McI, The English Tail-Rhyme Romances, MÆ 1.87, 168; 2.34, 189; 3.30.

Dunlap A R, The Vocabulary of the ME Romances in Tail-Rhyme Stanzas, Delaware Notes 14.1.

Authorship. Sarrazin G, ed, Octavian, Heilbronn 1865, p xxv.

Kaluza M, Thomas Chestre, Verfasser des Launfal, Libeaus Desconus, und Octavian, EStn 18.165 (crit A McI Trounce, MÆ 2.196).

Sarrazin G, Noch Einmal Thomas Chestre, EStn 22.331.

Sources and Literary Relations. Kölbing E, Zur Überlieferung und Quelle des me Gedichtes Lybeaus Desconus, EStn 1.121, 362.

Paris G, Guinglain ou Le bel inconnu, Rom 15.1.

Mennung A, Der Bel Inconnu des Renaut de Beaujeu in seinem Verhältniss zum Lybeaus Desconus, Carduino und Wigalois, Halle 1890 (crit G Paris, Rom 20.297; M Kaluza, LfGRP 3.84).

Schofield W H, Studies on the Libeaus Desconus, Boston 1895 (crit E Philipot, Rom 26.290; Rom 25.638).

Saran F, Über Wirnt von Grafenberg und den Wigalois, PBBeitr 21.253; 22.151.

Broadus E K, The Red-Cross Knight and Libeaus Desconus, MLN 18.202.

Taylor A, The Motif of the Vacant Stake in Folklore and Romance, RomR 9.21.

Magoun F P, The Source of Chaucer's Rime of Sir Thopas, PMLA 42.833.

Dickson A, The Earl of Westmoreland and Boeve de Hantone, PMLA 43.570.

Williams G P, ed, Renaud de Beaujeu, Le bel inconnu, Paris 1929.

Dennis L, Blandamour in the Percy-Ritson Controversy, MP 29.232.

Everett D, The Relationship of Chestre's Launfal and Lybeaus Desconus, MÆ 7.29.

Loomis L H, Sir Thopas, Bryan-Dempster, p 486.

Wilson R H, The Fair Unknown in Malory, PMLA 58.1.

McHugh S J, The Lay of the Big Fool: Its Irish and Arthurian Sources, MP 42.197.

Loomis R S, From Segontium to Sinadon—the Legends of a Cité Gaste, Spec 22.520.

Loomis R S, Arthurian Tradition and Chrétien de Troyes, N Y 1949, p 79.

Newstead H, Kaherdin and the Enchanted Pillow: An Episode in the Tristan Legend, PMLA 65.302.

Whiting B J, Proverbs in Certain Middle English Romances in Relation to Their French Sources, HSNPL 15.75.

Wedel T O, Medieval Attitude Toward Astrology, YSE 60.105 (crit J Caro, AnglB 34.310).

Patch H R, The Other World, Cambridge Mass 1950, p 289.

Brandl, § 70; Körting, § 107; HLF, 30.171; Ward, 1.400; Schofield, p 226; CHEL, 1.329; Billings, p 134; Gröber, 2¹.513.

V. Perceval

THE PERCEVAL LEGEND.

Heinrich G A, Le Parcival de Wolfram d'Eschenbach et la légende du Saint-Graal, Paris 1855.

Birch-Hirschfeld A, Die Sage vom Gral, Leipzig 1877.

Martin E, Zur Gralsage, Strassburg 1880.

Hertz W, Die Sage von Parzival und dem Graal, Breslau 1882.

Nutt A, Studies on the Legend of the Holy Grail, London 1888, p 37 (crit G Paris, Rom 18.588; H Zimmer, Göttingische gelehrte Anzeiger June 10 1890).

Heinzel R, Über die französischen Gralromane, Denkschr der Kaiserl Akad der Wiss, philhist Klasse 40 Abh 3, Vienna 1891.

Harper G M, Legend of the Holy Grail, PMLA 8.77; MLN 8.316.

Wechssler E, Untersuchungen zu den Gralromanen, ZfRP 23.135.

Martin E, ed, Wolframs von Eschenbach Parzival und Titurel, Halle 1900, 1903.

Newell W W, The Legend of the Holy Grail and the Perceval of Crestien of Troyes, Cambridge Mass 1902.

Hoffmann W, Die Quellen des Didot Perceval, Halle 1905 (crit E Brugger, ZfFSL 30².7).

Weston J L, The Legend of Sir Perceval, 2 vols, London 1906, 1909 (crit E Brugger, ZfFSL 31².122; 36².31; M J Minckwitz, Rom 36.311; G Huet, Rom 39.99; F Lot, Biblio de l'École de chartes 70.564; J F D Blöte, ZfDA Anzeiger, 22.24; 34.242).

Williams M R, Essai sur la composition du roman gallois de Peredur, Paris 1909 (crit R Thurneysen, ZfCP 8.185).

Windisch E, Das keltische Britannien bis zu Kaiser Arthur, Leipzig 1912.

Woods G B, Reclassification of the Perceval Romances, PMLA 27.524.

Zenker R, Zur Mabinogion-Frage, Halle 1912.

Pace R B, The Death of the Red Knight in the Story of Perceval, MLN 31.53.

Loomis R S, The Tristan and Perceval Caskets, RomR 8.196.

Weston J L, From Ritual to Romance, Cambridge 1920.

Golther W, Parzival und der Gral in der Dichtungen des Mittelalters und der Neuzeit, Stuttgart 1925 (crit A Hilka, ZfRP 46.497; F Piquet, RG 17.213; E Brugger, ZfFSL 52.315).

Weston J L, The Relative Position of the Perceval and Galahad Romances, MLR 21.385.

Brown A C L, The Irish Element in King Arthur and the Grail, Medieval Studies in Memory of G S Loomis, N Y 1927, p 95.

Brugger E, Bliocadran, the Father of Perceval, Medieval Studies in Memory of G S Loomis, N Y 1927, p 147.

Bruce J D, Evolution of Arthurian Romance, Baltimore 1928, 1.219; 2.8, 145.

Thompson A W, The Elucidation, a Prologue to the Conte del Graal, N Y 1931.

Hilka A, Der Percevalroman (Li Contes del Graal), Halle 1932 (crit A W Thompson, MP 30.434; W Golther, LfGRP 54.24; M Wilmotte, Rom 59.453).

Nitze W A and T A Jenkins, Le haut livre du Graal, Perlesvaus, 2 vols, Chicago 1932, 1937 (crit M Wilmotte, Moyen âge 43.33; E Brugger, ZfRP 59.554; J J Parry, Spec 7.570; reply by Nitze, 8.116; R S Loomis, RomR 23.265).

Roach W, Eucharistic Tradition in the Perlesvaus, ZfRP 59.10.

Newstead H, Bran the Blessed in Arthurian Romance, N Y 1939.

Roach W, The Didot Perceval, Phila 1941 (crit J Marx, Études celtiques 5.426; R S Loomis, RomR 33.168; A W Thompson, MLN 58.628; J J Parry, MP 40.213).

Loomis R S, The Spoils of Annwn, PMLA 56.887.

Brown A C L, The Origin of the Grail Legend, Cambridge Mass 1943 (crit W J Gruffydd, MLR 39.202; M Schlauch, Spec 19.502; R S Loomis, RomR 25.82, and Rev of Religion, March 1944, p 295; W A Nitze, MP 41.200).

Brugger E, Der schöne Feigling in der arthurischen Literatur, ZfRP 61.1; 63.123, 275; 65.121, 289; 67.289.

Loomis R S, The Combat at the Ford in the Didot Perceval, MP 43.63.

Newstead H, Perceval's Father and Welsh Tradition, RomR 36.3.

Newstead H, The Grail Legend and Celtic Tradition, Franco-American Pamphlets 3 ser no 5, N Y 1945.

Loomis R S, Arthurian Tradition and Chrétien de Troyes, N Y 1949.

Nitze W A, Perceval and the Holy Grail, Univ of Calif Pubs in Modern Philology 28, no 5, Berkeley 1949, p 281 (crit E Brugger, ZfRP 68.123; W Roach, Spec 25.290).

Roach W, The Continuations of the Old French Perceval of Chrétien de Troyes, Phila, vol 1, 1949; vol 2, 1951; vol 3, 1952, 1955 (glossary by L Foulet).

Marx J, La légende arthurienne et le Graal, Paris 1952.

Bruce, Evolution of Arthurian Romance, 2.398; W Roach, Holmes CBFL, p 130.

See under SIR PERCEVAL OF GALLES [39], The Grail Legend.

[39] SIR PERCEVAL OF GALLES.

MS. Lincoln Cath 91 (Thornton), ff 161ª–176ª (ca 1440).

Editions. Halliwell[-Phillips] J O, The Thornton Romances, London 1844, p 1.

Schleich G, Collationen zu me Dichtungen, EStn 12.139 (collation of first 1060 lines of Halliwell's edn with the MS).

Ellis F S, Syr Percyvelle of Galles, Kelmscott Press, London 1895 (William Morris; rpt of Halliwell).

Campion J and F Holthausen, Sir Perceval of Gales, Heidelberg 1913 (crit W Golther, LfGRP 35.154; M Förster, ZfRP 38.116).

French W H and C B Hale, ME Metrical Romances, N Y 1930, p 531.

Modernizations. Weston J L, The Chief ME Poets, Cambridge Mass 1914, p 236.

Textual Notes. Holthausen F, lines 687, 1876, 2279, Angl 44.78.

Language. Ellinger J, Über die sprachlichen und metrischen Eigentümlichkeiten in The Romance of Sir Perceval of Galles, Troppau 1889.

Ellinger J, Syntaktische Untersuchungen zu der Sprache der me Romanze von Sir Perceval of Galles, Troppau 1893.

Versification. Luick K, Die englische Stabreim-zeile im 14, 15, und 16 Jahrhundert, Angl 12.437.

Luick K, Paul Grundriss, 2².168.

Bülbring K D, Untersuchungen zur me Metrik, SEP 50.510.

Medary M P, Stanza-Linking in ME Verse, RomR 7.243.

Brown L, On the Origins of Stanza-Linking in English Alliterative Verse, RomR 7.271.

Finsterbusch F, Der Versbau der me Dichtungen Sir Perceval of Galles und Sir Degrevant, WBEP 49.1.

Sources and Literary Relations. Steinbach P, Über den Einfluss des Crestien de Troies auf die altenglische Literatur, Leipzig 1885.

Strucks C, Der junge Parzival in Wolframs von Eschenbach Parzival, Crestien's Conte del Gral, Sir Perceval, und Carduino, diss Münster, Leipzig 1910.

Griffith R H, Sir Perceval of Galles, Chicago 1911 (crit J L Weston, Rom 40.625; J D Bruce, RomR 4.125; E Brugger, ZfFSL 44.137).

Pace R B, Sir Perceval and the Boyish Exploits of Finn, PMLA 32.598.

Brown A C L, The Grail and the English Sir Perceval, MP 16.553; 17.361; 18.201, 661; 22.79, 113 (crit A Bell, MLR 21.78; J Vendryes, RC 43.193; J J Parry, JEGP 25.433).

Sparnaay H, Verschmelzung legendarischer und weltlicher Motive in der Poesie des Mittelalters, Groningen 1922.

Bruce J D, The Evolution of Arthurian Romance, Baltimore 1928, 1.309.

Webster K G T, Galloway and the Romances, MLN 55.363.

Loomis L H, Sir Thopas, Bryan-Dempster, p 486.

Brown A C L, The Origin of the Grail Legend, Cambridge Mass 1943, p 202.

McHugh S J, Sir Percyvelle: Its Irish Connections, Ann Arbor 1946 (crit G Murphy, Studies, Educ Co of Ireland, 37.368).

Newstead H, The Besieged Ladies in Arthurian Romance, PMLA 63.803.

Loomis R S, Arthurian Tradition and Chrétien de Troyes, N Y 1949, pp 364, 398, 405.

Paris Litt franç, §§ 59, 60; Brandl, § 79; Körting, § 108n; Dunlop, Hist of Fiction, 1.172; CHEL, 1.327; Gröber, 2¹.504; Schofield, p 229; Billings, p 125; Baugh LHE, p 192; Kane, p 76.

CBEL, 1.131(d), 137(j) (bibl to 1933).

VI. The Holy Grail

THE GRAIL LEGEND.

Heinrich G A, Le Parcival de Wolfram d'Eschenbach et la légende du Saint Graal, Paris 1855.

Birch-Hirschfeld A, Die Sage vom Gral, Leipzig 1877.

Martin E, Zur Gralsage, Strassburg 1880.

Nutt A, Studies on the Legend of the Holy Grail, London 1888.

Heinzel R, Über die französischen Gralromane, Vienna 1891.

Harper G M, The Legend of the Holy Grail, PMLA 8.77; MLN 8.316.

Wechssler E, Über die verschiedenen Redaktionen des Robert von Boron zugeschriebenen Graal-Lancelot-cyclus, Halle 1895 (crit G Paris, Rom 24.472).

Wechssler E, Die Sage vom heiligen Graal, Halle 1898.

Nutt A, Legends of the Holy Grail, London 1902.

Newell W W, The Legend of the Holy Grail, Cambridge Mass 1902.

Maynadier G H, The Arthur of the English Poets, Boston 1907, p 106.

Peebles R J, The Legend of Longinus, Baltimore 1911 (crit A C L Brown, MLN 28.21; G Schoepperle, JEGP 13.350).

Weston J L, The Quest of the Holy Grail, London 1913.

Nitze W A, Concerning the Word Graal, Greal, MP 13.481.

Fisher L A, The Mystic Vision in the Grail Legend and in the Divine Comedy, N Y 1917 (crit W A Nitze, E H Wilkins, MP 16.433; J L Gerig, RomR 11.87).

Rosenberg A, Longinus in England, Berlin 1917.

Brown A C L, From Cauldron of Plenty to Grail, MP 14.385.

Brown A C L, The Grail and the English Sir Perceval, MP 16.553; 17.361; 18.201, 661; 22.79, 113.

Nitze W A, On the Chronology of the Grail Romances, MP 17.151, 605.

Bruce J D, Galahad, Nascien, and Some Other Names in the Grail Romances, MLN 33.129.

Weston J L, From Ritual to Romance, Cambridge 1924 (crit W A Nitze, MLN 35.352; T P Cross, MP 18.679).

Sparnaay H, Verschmelzung legendarischen und weltlicher Motive in der Poesie des Mittelalters, Groningen 1922 (crit G Ehris-

mann, Anz deut Altertum und deut Lit 43.63; A H Krappe, JEGP 23.591).

Nitze W A, On the Chronology of the Grail Romances 2. The Date of Robert de Boron's Metrical Joseph, Manly Anniversary Studies, Chicago 1923, p 300.

Pauphilet A, La Queste del Saint Graal, roman du 13e siècle, Paris 1923 (photog reprod, Paris 1949).

Gardner E G, The Holy Grail in Italian Literature, MLR 20.443.

Golther W, Parzival und der Gral in der Dichtung des Mittelalters und der Neuzeit, Stuttgart 1925.

Brown A C L, Did Chrétien Identify the Grail with the Mass? MLN 4.226.

Robinson J A, Two Glastonbury Legends, N Y 1926 (King Arthur and Joseph of Arimathea).

Comfort W W, The Quest of the Holy Grail, London 1926 (trans of Vulgate romance).

Nitze W A, ed, Robert de Boron, Le roman de l'Estoire dou Graal, Paris 1927.

Brown A C L, The Irish Element in King Arthur and the Grail, Medieval Studies in Memory of G S Loomis, N Y 1927, p 95.

Nitze W A, The Identity of Brons in Robert de Boron's Metrical Joseph, Medieval Studies in Memory of G S Loomis, N Y 1927, p 138.

Bruce J D, Evolution of Arthurian Romance, Baltimore 1928, 1.219; 2.114.

Jaffray R, King Arthur and the Holy Grail, N Y 1928.

Pennington W, An Irish Parallel to the Broken Sword of the Grail Castle, MLN 43.534.

Loomis R S, Bron and Other Figures in the Estoire del Saint Graal, MLR 24.416.

Brugger E, Der Gralpassus bei Helinandus, ZfFSL 53.147.

Weston J L, article on Grail rvsd for 14th edn Enc Brit.

Lot-Borodine M, Autour du Saint Graal, à propos de travaux récents, Rom 56.526; 57.147.

Loomis R S, The Head in the Grail, RC 47.39.

Loomis R S and J S Lindsay, The Magic Horn and Cup in Celtic and Grail Tradition, RF 45.71.

Lot F, Les Auteurs du Conte de Graal, Rom 57.117.

Morgan Sister M L, Galahad in English Literature, diss Catholic Univ, Washington 1932.

Brown A C L, Another Analogue of the Grail Story, Kastner Miscellany, Cambridge 1932, p 85.

Gazay J, Études sur les légendes de sainte Marie-Madeleine et de Joseph d'Arimathie, Annales du midi 51.5, 113, 225 (crit A J, Rom 66.409).

Burdach K, Der Graal: Forschungen über seinen Ursprung und seinen Zusammenhang mit den Longinuslegende, Stuttgart 1938 (crit W A Nitze, MP 37.315; R S Loomis, GR 14.221; F Ranke, AfDA 64.20; S Hofer, ZfRP 61.538).

Newstead H, Bran the Blessed in Arthurian Romance, N Y 1939.

Nitze W A, What Did Robert de Boron Write? MP 41.1.

Viscardi A, Il Gral, Giuseppe d'Arimatea, l'abbazia di Glastonbury e le origini cristiane della Britania, Cultura neolatina 2, no 1, 1941.

Brown A C L, The Origin of the Grail Legend, Cambridge Mass 1943.

Loomis R S, The Irish Origin of the Grail Legend, Spec 8.415.

Newstead H, The Grail Legend and Celtic Tradition, N Y 1945.

Nitze W A, The Waste Land: A Celtic Arthurian Theme, MP 43.58.

Finlay Sister M G, Joseph of Arimathea and the Grail, diss Columbia, Microfilm Abstracts 11.110.

Vendryes J, Les éléments celtiques de la légende du Graal, Études celtiques 5.1.

Lot-Borodine M, Le symbolisme du Graal dans l'Estoire del Saint-Graal, Neophil 34.65.

Loomis L H, The Holy Relics of Charlemagne and King Athelstan: The Lances of Longinus and St Mauricius, Spec 25.437.

Loomis L H, The Passion Lance Relic and the War Cry Monjoie in the Chanson de Roland and Related Texts, RomR 41.241.

Nelli R, ed, La lumière du Graal, Paris 1951 (crit R S Loomis, RomP 5.322).

Marx J, Le héros du Graal, Lumière du Graal, Paris 1951, p 90.

Viscardi A, La quête du Graal dans les romans du moyen âge italien, Lumière du Graal, Paris 1951, p 263.

Lot-Borodine M, Les apparitions du Christ aux messes de l'estoire et de la queste del Saint Graal, Rom 72.202.

Marx J, La légende arthurienne et le Graal, Paris 1952 (crit R Lejeune, Moyen âge 60.181; R S Loomis, Spec 27.407; J Frappier, Rom 73.248; W A Nitze, RomP 7.86; G Murphy, Eigse 7.134; A Micha, ZfRP 70.428).

Nitze W A, The Fisher King and the Grail in Retrospect, RomP 6.14.

Nitze W A, Messire Robert de Boron: Enquiry and Summary, Spec 28.279.

Loomis R S, Grail Problems, RomR 45.12 (reply to Nitze RomP 6.14).

Marx J, Le Graal chez Robert de Boron et l'Abbaye de Glastonbury, BBSIA 3.96; Robert de Boron et Glastonbury, Moyen âge 59.69.

Frappier J, Le Graal et la Chevalerie, Rom 75.165.

Adolf H, Visio Pacis: Holy City and Grail, Univ Park Pa 1960 (crit H Newstead, GR 37.218).

Bruce, Evolution of Arthurian Romance, 2.398; Roach W, Holmes CBFL, p 130; Billings, p 99; Körting, § 101 anm, § 110; Ten Brink, 1.171; Schofield, p 240; Ward, 1.340; Enc Brit, see under Grail.

See under The Perceval Legend, Sir Perceval of Galles [39], Arthurian Legends, General.

[40] JOSEPH OF ARIMATHIE.

MS. Bodl Poet A.1 (Vernon MS), ff 403[a]–404[b] (ca 1390).

Editions. Skeat W W, Joseph of Arimathie: Otherwise Called The Romance of the Seint Graal or Holy Graal, EETS 44, 1871 (rptd 1924) p 1.

Language. Hulbert J R, The West Midland of the Romances, MP 19.1.

Menner R J, Sir Gawain and the Green Knight and the West Midland, PMLA 37.503.

Oakden J P, Alliterative Poetry in ME, Manchester 1930, 1.58, 153.

Koziol H, Grundzüge der Syntax der me Stabreimdichtungen, WBEP 58.

Greg W W, The Continuity of the Alliterative Tradition, MLR 27.453.

Oakden J P, The Continuity of the Alliterative Tradition, MLR 28.233.

Versification. Luick K, Die englische Stabreimzeile im 14, 15, und 16 Jahrhundert, Angl 11.569.

Hulbert J R, Quatrains in the ME Alliterative Poems, MP 48.73.

Oakden J P, Alliterative Poetry in ME, Manchester 1935, 2.41.

Brandl, § 73; Körting, § 110; Ten Brink, 1.332; Dunlop, Hist of Fiction, 1.159; Schofield, p 247; Billings, p 96; Kane, p 27. See under The Grail Legend.

[41] THE HISTORY OF THE HOLY GRAIL.

MS. Corp Christi Camb 80, ff 197[a]–198[b], 1[a]–88[b] (leaves misplaced; date, before 1450).

Editions. Furnivall F J, Henry Lovelich, History of the Holy Grail, EETSES 20, 24, 28, 30, 95 (ed D Kempe).

Authorship. Bradley H, Henry Lonelich the Skinner, Athen 1902². 587 (also in Collected Papers of Henry Bradley, Oxford 1928, p 233).

Skeat W W, The Translator of the Graal, Athen 1902². 654, 758.

Ackerman R W, Henry Lovelich's Name, MLN 67.531.

Sources and Literary Relations. Gazay J, Études sur la légende de Sainte Marie-Madeleine et de Joseph d'Arimathie, Annales du midi 51.5, 113, 225, 337.

Finlay Sister M G, Joseph of Arimathea and the Grail, diss Columbia, Microfilm Abstracts 11.110.

Ackerman R W, Herry Lovelich's Merlin, PMLA 67.473.

Brandl, § 113; Schofield, p 246; Billings, p 109; Kane, p 16. See under Lovelich's Merlin [20], The Grail Legend.

[42] THE PROSE LYFE OF JOSEPH,
DE SANCTO JOSEPH,
HERE BEGYNNETH, A PRAYSING.

MSS. No MS extant. PRINT: A Treatyse taken out of a boke which somtyme Theodosius the Emperour founde in Iherusalem in the pretorye of Pylate of Ioseph of Ar-

mathy, printed by Wynkyn de Worde, 1511(?), ff 1–6.

Edition. Skeat W W, Joseph of Arimathie, EETS 44.27.

MSS. No MS extant. PRINT: De Sancto Joseph Ab Arimathia, The Kalendre of the New Legende of Englande, printed by Richard Pynson, 1516, f lviii.

Edition. Skeat W W, Joseph of Arimathie, EETS 44.33.

MSS. No MS extant. PRINT: Here begynneth the Lyfe of Joseph of Arimathia, printed by Richard Pynson, 1520, ff 1^b–8^b.

Edition. Skeat W W, Joseph of Arimathie, EETS 44.37.

MSS. No MS extant. PRINT: A Praysing to Joseph, printed by Richard Pynson 1520, ff 8^b–10.

Edition. Skeat W W, Joseph of Arimathie, EETS 44.50.

Hucher E, ed, Le Saint-Graal ou le Joseph d'Arimathie, Le Mans 1875–78.

Weidner G, ed, Der Prosaroman von Joseph von Arimathea, Oppeln 1881.

Körting, § 110 anm; Billings, p 109; HLF, p 30; de Julleville Hist, 1.341; Gröber, 2¹.502, 724, 996, 1195; Paris Litt franç §§ 57, 59, 60; J D Bruce, Evolution of Arthurian Romance, 2.398; W Roach, Holmes CBFL, p 130; CBEL, 1.132(e), 134(c), 138(o), 140(x) (bibl to 1933); M Reid, The Arthurian Legend, p 128.

VII. Tristram

THE TRISTRAM LEGEND.

Editions and Translations of Texts. Michel F, Tristan, Recueil de ce qui reste des poèmes relatifs à ses aventures, 3 vols, London 1835–39.

Lichtenstein F, Eilhart von Oberge [Tristrant], Strassburg 1877.

Kölbing E, Die nordische und die englische Version der Tristansage, 2 vols, Heilbronn 1878–82.

Bechstein R, Gottfried von Strassburg, Tristan, 3rd edn, Leipzig 1890.

Löseth E, Le roman en prose de Tristan, Paris 1891 (detailed analysis based upon the Paris MSS).

Bédier J, Le roman de Tristan par Thomas, 2 vols, SATF, Paris 1902, 1905.

Muret E, Le roman de Tristan par Béroul, SATF, Paris 1903; 3rd edn rvsd, Paris 1928; 4th edn rvsd L M Defourques, Paris 1947.

Cross T P, A Welsh Tristan Episode, SP 17.93 (text and trans).

Ranke F, Gottfried von Strassburg, Tristan und Isold, Munich 1925.

Williams I, Trystan ac Esyllt, BBCS 5.115.

Ewert A, The Romance of Tristran by Béroul, Oxford 1939.

Johnson F C, La grant ystoire de Monsignor Tristan li Bret, Edinburgh 1942 (first part of Prose Tristan from Edinburgh MS).

Hoepffner E, La folie Tristan d'Oxford, 2nd edn, Paris 1943.

Zeydel E H, The Tristan and Isolde of Gottfried von Strassburg, Princeton 1948 (trans of about half the text).

Hoepffner E, La folie Tristan de Berne, 2nd edn, Paris 1949.

Closs A, Tristan und Isolt, a Poem by Gottfried von Strassburg, 2nd edn, Oxford 1947 (selections).

Wind B, Les fragments du Tristan de Thomas, London 1950.

Loomis R S, The Romance of Tristram and Ysolt by Thomas of Britain, N Y 1923, 1931; new rvsd edn 1951 (trans of Thomas's version).

Studies. Sudre L, Les allusions à la légende de Tristan dans la littérature du moyen âge, Rom 15.534.

Zimmer H, Beiträge zur Namenforschung in den altfranzösischen Arthurepen, ZfFSL 13.1.

Röttiger W, Der heutige Stand der Tristanforschung, Hamburg 1897.

Paris G, Poèmes et légendes du moyen âge, Paris 1900, p 113.

Bossert A, La légende chevaleresque de Tristan et Iseult, essai de littérature comparée, Paris 1902.

Deutschbein M, Eine irische Variante der Tristan-Sage, AnglB 15.16.

Golther W, Tristan und Isolde in den Dichtungen des Mittelalters und der neuen Zeit, Leipzig 1907.

Maynadier G H, The Arthur of the English Poets, Boston 1907, p 153.

Loth J, Contributions à l'étude des romans de la Table Ronde, Paris 1912 (crit G Schoepperle, RomR 3.431; A Smirnov, Rom 43.119).

Schoepperle G, Tristan and Isolt, a Study of the Sources of the Romance, Frankfurt, London 1913 (crit J D Bruce, MLN 29.213; W A Nitze, JEGP 13.444; F Lot, Rom 43.126).

Loomis R S, A Sidelight on the Tristan of Thomas, MLR 10.304.

Loomis R S, Illustrations of Medieval Romance on Tiles from Chertsey Abbey, Univ of Illinois Studies in Lang and Lit, Urbana 1916.

Levi E, I lais brettoni e la leggenda di Tristano, Studj romanzi 14.1.

Loomis R S, The Tristan and Perceval Caskets, RomR 8.196.

Singer S, Arabische und europäische Poesie im Mittelalter, Abhand der Preussischen Akad der Wissenschaften, phil-hist Klasse, Berlin 1918.

Loomis R S, Notes on the Tristram of Thomas, MLR 14.38.

Hamilton G L, Tristan's Coat of Arms, MLR 15.425.

Leach H G, Angevin Britain and Scandinavia, Cambridge Mass 1921, pp 169, 331.

Deister J L, Bernart de Ventadorn's Reference to the Tristan Story, MP 19.287.

Loomis R S, Tristram and the House of Anjou, MLR 17.24.

Kelemina J, Geschichte der Tristansage nach den Dichtungen des Mittelalters, Vienna 1923 (crit F Piquet, RG 15.453; W Golther, LfGRP 46.149).

Thurneysen R, Eine irische Parallele zur Tristan-Sage, ZfRP 43.385.

Brugger E, Loenois as Tristan's Home, MP 22.159.

Loomis R S, Bleheris and the Tristram Story, MLN 39.319.

Van Hamel A G, Tristan's Combat with the Dragon, RC 41.331.

Tregenza W A, The Relation of the Oldest Branch of the Roman de Renart and the Tristan Poems, MLR 19.301.

Loomis R S, Problems of the Tristan Legend: Bleheris, the Diarmaid Parallel, Thomas's Date, Rom 53.82.

Vinaver E, Études sur le Tristan en prose, Paris 1925 (crit E Brugger, ZfFSL 51.131).

Murrell E S, Girart de Roussillon and the Tristan Poems, Chesterfield 1926.

Krappe A H, Balor with the Evil Eye, N Y 1927, p 154.

Vinaver E, The Love Potion in the Primitive Tristan Romance, Medieval Studies in Memory of G S Loomis, N Y 1927, p 75.

Lot-Borodine M, Tristan et Lancelot, Medieval Studies in Memory of G S Loomis, N Y 1927, p 21.

Ranke F, Isoldes Gottesurteil, Medieval Studies in Memory of G S Loomis, N Y 1927, p 84.

Brugger E, Almain and Ermonie as Tristan's Home, MP 25.269; 26.1.

Bruce J D, Evolution of Arthurian Romance, Baltimore 1928, 1.152.

Krappe A H, Petitcrû, RC 45.318.

Scheludko D, Orientalisches in der altfranzösischen erzählenden Dichtung, ZfFSL 51.255.

Aitken D F, The voyage à l'aventure in the Tristan of Thomas, MLR 23.468.

Van Dam J, Tristanprobleme, Neophil 15.18, 88, 183.

Krappe A H, Der Zwerg im Tristan, RF 45.95.

Remigereau F, Tristan maître de vénerie dans la tradition anglaise et dans le roman de Tristan, Rom 58.218.

Witte A, Der Aufbau der ältesten Tristandichtungen, ZfDA 70.161.

Anderson M D, The Mediaeval Carver, Cambridge 1935.

Loomis R S and L H, Arthurian Legends in Medieval Art, N Y 1938, pp 42, 57.

Delpino M, Elementi celtici ed elementi classichi nel Tristan di Thomas, Archivum Romanicum 23.312.

Newstead H, Kaherdin and the Enchanted Pillow: An Episode in the Tristan Legend, PMLA 65.290.

Pauphilet A, Le legs du moyen âge, Melun 1950, p 107.

Panvini B, La leggenda di Tristano e Isotta; studio critico, Firenze 1951.

Bivar A D H, Lyonnesse: The Evolution of a Fable, MP 50.162.

Bailey H W and A S C Ross, Idrisi or Lyonesse, JCS 2.32.

Bromwich R, Some Remarks on the Celtic Sources of Tristan, Transactions of the Honourable Society of the Cymmrodorion for 1953, p 32.

Marx J, Quelques remarques sur un passage du Roman de Tristan en prose et sur ses analogies avec des récits celtiques, Annuaire 1954–55 de l'École pratique des hautes études, sect des sciences réligieuses, Paris 1954, p 3.

Lejeune R, Mentions de Tristan chez les Troubadours, BBSIA 6.96 (abstr).

Marx J, Observations sur un épisode de la légende de Tristan, Recueil de Travaux offert à C Brunel, Paris 1955, p 265.

Lejeune R, Rôle littéraire d'Aliénor d'Aquitaine et de sa famille, Cultura neolatina 14.1.

Roques M, Sur l'équitation féminine au moyen âge, à propos d'un épisode du Tristan de Thomas, Mélanges . . . offerts à C Bruneau, Geneva 1954, p 219.

Paris G, Rom 15.481; Brandl, § 51; Körting, § 118; Ten Brink, 1.237; HLF, 19.687; Billings, p 85; de Julleville Hist, 1.259, 340; Schofield, p 201; Enc Brit, see under Tristram.

Bruce J D, Evolution of Arthurian Romance, 2.384 (bibl).

Küpper H, Les études françaises sur la légende de Tristan et Iseult, RG 26.322; 27.23.

Küpper H, Bibliographie zur Tristansage, Deutsche Arbeiten der Universität Köln, Heft 17, Jena 1941 (crit J Horrent, Revue Belge 23.357, additional items).

Adams R D A, A Tristan Bibliography, Univ of Southern Calif Lang and Lit Series 4, Los Angeles 1943.

Newstead H, Holmes CBFL, pp 123, 258.

Newstead H, The Enfances of Tristan and English Tradition, in Studies in Medieval Literature in Honor of A C Baugh, ed M Leach, Phila 1961, p 169.

Newstead H, The Tryst beneath the Tree: An Episode in the Tristan Legend, RomP 9.269.

[43] SIR TRISTREM.

MS. Advocates 19.2.1 (Auchinleck MS), ff 281^a–299^b (ca 1330).

Kölbing E, Vier Romanzen-Handschriften, EStn 7.189.

Carr M B, Notes on an English Scribe's Methods, Univ of Wisconsin Studies in Language and Literature, Madison 1918, 2.153.

Editions. Scott W, Sir Tristrem, Edinburgh 1804.

Kölbing E, Die nordische und die englische Version der Tristansage, Heilbronn 1882, 2.1.

McNeill G P, Sir Tristrem, PSTS 8, 1886 (crit E Kölbing, EStn 10.287).

Selections. Mätzner H, AESpr, Berlin 1867, 1.231.

Eyre-Todd G, Early Scottish Poetry, Glasgow 1891, p 21.

Kluge F, Mittelenglisches Lesebuch, Halle 1912, p 89.

Brandl A and O Zippel, Mittelenglische Sprach- und Literaturproben, Berlin 1917, p 53.

Modernizations. Weston J L, Chief ME Poets, Cambridge Mass 1914, p 141.

Textual Notes. K[ölbing] E, Nachträgliches zum Tristan, EStn 2.533.

Powell Y, A Few Notes on Sir Tristrem, EStn 6.463.

Kölbing E, Vier Romanzen Handschriften, EStn 7.189.

Kölbing E, Kleine Beiträge zur Erklärung, Textkritik, und Phräseologie me Dichter, EStn 13.133.

Edwards J, Old Oaths and Interjections, SHR 1.56 (lines 1875–76).

Holthausen F, Zur Erklärung und Textkritik der me Romanze Sir Tristrem, Angl 39.373.

Swaen A E H, Sir Tristrem 297, Angl 41.182.

Holthausen F, Zur Textkritik des Sir Tristrem, AnglB 39.183.

Holthausen F, Zur Erklärung und Textkritik des Sir Tristrem, Angl 58.374.

Language. Raiter G W, Phonology and Morphology of the Auchinleck Sir Tristrem, Summaries of Doctoral Dissertations . . . Northwestern Univ, 1935, 3.5 (abstr).

Vogel B D, The Dialect of Sir Tristrem, JEGP 40.538.

Vogel B D, Wortgeographische Belege and Sir Tristrem, JEGP 41.478.

Versification. Medary M P, Stanza-Linking in ME Verse, RomR 7.243.

Brown L, On the Origin of Stanza-Linking in English Alliterative Verse, RomR 7.271.

Sources and Literary Relations. Deutschbein M, Studien zur Sagengeschichte Englands, Cöthen 1906, p 169.

Skeat W W, The Romance of Sir Tristrem, SHR 6.58.

Henderson T F, Scottish Vernacular Literature, Edinburgh 1910, p 25.

Dempster G and J S P Tatlock, Bryan-Dempster, p 393 (the trouthe motif in the Franklin's Tale).

Smith R M, Gernemuþe and the Benighted Geography of the Minstrels, MLN 64.70.

Ten Brink, 1.238; Schofield, p 208; Billings, p 85; HLF, 19.687; Körting, § 118; Brandl, § 51; Baugh LHE, p 192; Kane, p 23.

CBEL, 1.132(f), 133(b) (bibl to 1933); see under The Tristram Legend.

VIII. Arthur of Little Britain

[44] ARTHUR OF LITTLE BRITAIN.

MSS. No MS extant.

Editions. Lord Berners, Sir John Bourchier, The Hystorie of Arthur of Lytell Brytayne, London 1555(?).

Bourchier John, Lord Berners, The History of the Valiant Knight Arthur of Little Britain, a Romance of Chivalry, ed E V Utterson, London 1814 (rptd from edn by R Copland for R Redborne, 1550(?) 1555(?); another edn, T East, London, 1581).

French Source. Le livre du vaillant et preux cheualier Artus, fils du duc de Bretagne [Jean de la Fontaine], Lyon 1453; 1496; Michel le Noir, Paris 1514 (most widely circulated version).

Woledge B, Les manuscrits du Petit Artus de Bretagne, Rom 63.393.

Lozinski G, Encore un manuscrit du Petit Artus de Bretagne, Rom 64.104.

Lecoy F, Encore un manuscrit du Petit Artus de Bretagne, Rom 73.241.

Sources and Analogues. Loomis R S, Celtic Myth and Arthurian Romance, N Y 1927, pp 172, 302.

Schlauch M, The Reimundar Saga Keisarasonar as an Analogue, ScanSt 10.189.

Schlauch M, Romance in Iceland, N Y 1934, pp 65, 161, 162.

Loomis R S, Arthurian Tradition and Chrétien de Troyes, N Y 1949, p 206.

Lewis C S, English Literature in the Sixteenth Century, Oxford 1954, p 151.

3. Charlemagne Legends

by

H. M. Smyser

CONTINENTAL VERNACULAR BACKGROUNDS.

Unger C R, ed, Karlamagnus Saga ok Kappa hans, Christiania 1860 (a compendium containing the Olive and Landres, as a survival, an Otuel, a Roland, and other significant matters).

Paris G, Histoire poétique de Charlemagne, 2nd edn, Paris 1865.

Ludlow J M, Popular Epics of the Middle Ages of the Norse-German and Carolingian Cycles, London 1865.

Rajna P, Contributi alla storia dell' epopea e del romanzo medievale, Rom 14.398; 17.161, 355; 18.1; 23.36; 26.34.

Gautier L, Les épopées françaises du moyen âge, Paris 1878–97, esp vol 3; Bibl des chansons de geste, Paris 1897.

de Julleville Hist, vol 1, chap 2 (bibl, p 168).

Church A J, Stories of Charlemagne, N Y 1902.

Gröber, 2¹.447, 461, 535, 792 (see also Register).

Weston J L, The Romance Cycle of Charlemagne, 2nd edn, London 1905 (a brief work, chiefly valuable for its bibl).

Paris Litt franç, §§ 18–42 (p 35), esp §§ 24, 25 (p 44).

Bédier J, Les légendes épiques, 4 vols, Paris 1908–13.

Bullfinch T, Legends of Charlemagne, Everyman Library, N Y 1911.

Leach H G, Angevin Britain and Scandinavia, Cambridge Mass 1921, p 253.

Koschwitz E, Karls des Grossen Reise nach Jerusalem und Constantinopel, 5th edn, Leipzig 1923 (the Pèlerinage de Charlemagne).

Ker W P, Epic and Romance, 2nd edn, London 1926, chaps 1, 4.

Weston J L, Legendary Cycles of the Middle Ages, in the Cambridge Medieval History, 6.815, esp 816–24.

Holmes U T, A History of Old French Literature, N Y 1937, esp chaps 7–9.

Mortier R, ed, Les textes de la Chanson de Roland, Paris 1940–44 (many pages of facsimile are included and besides the French texts of the Roland are printed Pfaffen Konrad, the Grandes chroniques, the Turpin, Carmen de Prodicione, and Ronsasvals).

Bossuat MBLF, p 11 and suppl, p 21.

Crosland J, The OF Epic, Oxford 1951 (crit G Frank, MLN 67.135).

Queirazza G G, ed, La Chanson de Roland nel testo assonanzato franco-italiano, Turin 1954.

Aebischer P, Rolandiana borealia, la Saga af Runzivals Bardaga et ses dérivés scandinaves comparés à la Chanson de Roland, Publications de la Faculté des Lettres de l'Université de Lausanne, Lausanne 1954 (crit A Burger, SN 27.126; F Lecoy, Rom 76.383).

Rychner J, Les chansons de geste; essai sur l'art épique des jongleurs, Geneva 1955.

Menéndez Pidal R, La Chanson de Roland et la tradition épique des Francs, 2nd edn, rvsd by R Louis in coöperation with the author and trans from the Spanish by I-M Cluzel, Paris 1960 (crit W M Hackett, MLR 58.153).

de Mandach A, Naissance et développement de la chanson de geste en Europe, I: la geste de Charlemagne et de Roland, Publications romanes et françaises, 69, Geneva 1961 (extensive bibl; crit C Meredith Jones, Spec 37.634).

See also under ORIGINS OF THE CHANSON DE GESTE.

LATIN BACKGROUNDS.

Castets F, ed, The Pseudo-Turpin, Montpellier 1880.

Grant A J, trans and ed, Early Lives of Charlemagne, London 1905 (Eginhard; Monk of St Gall).

Rauschen G, ed, Die Legende Karls des Grossen im 11 und 12 Jahrhundert, Leipzig 1890 (contains the Descriptio qualiter Karolus Magnus clavum et coronam Domini a Constantinopoli Aquis Grani detulerit).

Thoron W, ed, Chronicle of the Pseudo-Turpin (Vat MS Codex C 128, coll with BM Addit 12213), Boston 1934 (crit F M Powicke, MÆ 4.122).

Meredith Jones C, ed, Historia Karoli Magni et Rotholandi, ou Chronique du Pseudo-

Turpin, Paris 1936 (critical edn; crit H M Smyser, JEGP 36.433; A. Hämel, Spec 13.248; F M Powicke, Spec 13.364).

Walpole R N, Note to the Meredith Jones edn of the Pseudo-Turpin, Spec 22.260 (on the particular version of the Turpin which proliferated in Britain, and on its provenience).

Smyser H M, ed, The Pseudo-Turpin, ed from Bib Nat, Fonds Lat 17656 with an Annotated Synopsis, The Mediaeval Acad of America, Cambridge Mass 1937 (crit F M Powicke, Spec 13.364; C Meredith Jones, AHR 39.954).

Walpole R N, Philip Mouskés and the Pseudo-Turpin Chronicle, Univ of Calif Press 1947 (crit J M Wallace-Hadrill, MÆ 17.37).

Lambert E, L'historia Rotholandi du Pseudo-Turpin et le Pèlerinage de Compostelle, Rom 69.362 (on the origin of the Turpin).

Burger A, Sur les relations de la Chanson de Roland avec le récit du faux Turpin et celui du Guide du Pèlerin, Rom 73.242 (argues for a lost poem in Latin hexameters as a common source).

Walpole R N, The Pèlerinage de Charlemagne: Poem, Legend, and Problem, RomP 8.173.

ORIGINS OF THE CHANSON DE GESTE.

Paris G, Histoire poétique, pp 37–52 (theory of lost cantilenae).

Rajna P, Origini dell'epopea francese, Florence 1884 (Germanic origins; crit G Paris, Rom 13.598).

Bédier J, Les légendes épiques, esp 3.200–477 (the genre arose in and was exploited by monasteries and shrines of the pilgrimage routes; crit F Lot, Rom 42.593).

Lot F, Études sur les légendes épiques françaises, with an introduction by R Bossuat, Paris 1958 (contains the review of Bédier above and articles from Romania as follows: 27.1; 52.75, 257; 53.325, 449; 54.357; 66.238; 70.192, 355; traditionalist, finding historical echoes in the chansons, while granting great role to pilgrimage routes in the development of the genre).

Healey E, The Views of Ferdinand Lot on the Origins of the Old French Epic, SP 36.433.

Fawtier R, La Chanson de Roland, Étude historique, Paris 1933 (traditionalist).

Frank G, Historical Elements in the Chansons de Geste, Spec 14.209 (eclectic theory basically in accord with Lot).

Mortier R, La Chanson de Roland: Essai d'interprétation du problème des origines, Paris 1939 (crit H Gavel, as below).

Gavel H, Les problèmes de la Chanson de Roland; nouvelles hypothèses, Annales du midi 61.106 (an excellent summary).

Irving T B, Roncesvalles: A Basque and Arab Epic, Eusko-Jakintsa 2.457 (deals with Arab and Spanish traditions; poorly documented).

Pei M A, French Precursors of the Chanson de Roland, N Y 1948 (crit A G Hatcher, MLN 64.354).

Siciliano I, Les origines des chansons de geste, Paris 1951 (a Bédierist).

Alonso D, La primitiva epica francesa a la luz de una nota emilianse, Madrid 1954 (crit B Woledge, YWMLS 16.43; R N Walpole, RomP 9.370).

Bossuat MBLF, p 12 and suppl, Paris 1955, p 21.

de Riquer M, Los cantares de gesta franceses, Madrid 1952; Les chansons de geste françaises, 2nd edn, Paris 1957 (full account of the eclectic position).

Knudson C A, Bibl of theories of the origin of the chanson de geste, in the Cabeen Critical Bibl of Fr Lit, 1, rvsd edn, Syracuse Univ Press 1952, pp 50, 243.

Holmes U T, The Post-Bédier Theories on the Origins of the Chanson de Geste, Spec 30.72.

Walpole R N, The Nota Emilianse: New Light (but how much?) on the Origins of the Old French Epic, RomP 10.1.

Horrent J, Ferdinand Lot et les origines des légendes épiques françaises, Moyen âge 65.321.

Aebischer P, Études sur Otinel; de la chanson de geste à la saga norroise et aux origines de la legende, Berne 1960 (crit P le Gentil, RomP 16.105).

Dougherty D M, The Present Status of Bédier's Theories, Sym 14.289.

See also above, under CONTINENTAL VERNACULAR BACKGROUNDS: P Aebischer, J Rychner, R Menéndez Pidal, A de Mandach.

ENGLISH CHARLEMAGNE ROMANCES: GENERAL.

Paris G, Histoire poétique, p 154.

Lee S, The Charlemagne Romances in France and England in edn of Huon of Bordeaux, EETSES, London 1882, 40.vii-xxiii.

Paris G, Review of edns by Herrtage and Hausknecht, Rom 11.149.

Ward, 1.546; Brandl, § 125: 2¹.609, see also Index, 2².345; Billings, esp pp 47–84; Gröber, 2¹.447, 791.

Griffith R H, Malory's Morte Darthur and Fierabras, Angl 32.389 (sees the combat of Oliver and Fierabras retold of Gawain and Priamus).

Kirchhoff J, Zur Geschichte der Karlssage in der engl Lit des Mittelalters, diss Marburg 1913 (on the introduction, dissemination, and influence of the Charlemagne romances in England; a somewhat sketchy account in 87 pages).

Baker E A, History of the English Novel, London 1924, 1.217.

Thomas W, The Epic Cycles of Medieval England and Their Relative Importance, FQ 10.193 ("the cycle of Charlemagne and his peers must have struck the hearers as alien to Great Britain and thus failed to secure any permanent standing in English literature").

Taylor A B, Introduction to Medieval Romance, London 1930, p 16.

Smyser H M, Studies in the Engl Charlemagne Romances, Harvard Summaries of Theses, Harvard Univ Press 1932, p 286.

Wells J E, Bibliography of Charlemagne Romances to 1933, CBEL, 1.140 B.

Herrtage, Hausknecht, O'Sullivan, and others, Introductions to EETSES 34, 35, 36–41, 43–45, 50, and EETS 198, London 1879–1935.

Wilson R M, Early ME Literature, London 1939, chap 9, esp pp 199–201.

Baugh LHE, p 185, esp p 188 (religious aspects).

Kane, pp 15, 27, 39.

Crosland J, The OF Epic, Oxford 1951, esp pp 230–41.

Renwick-Orton, 2nd edn, London 1952, pp 42, 371 (the former portion, by Renwick, offers critical judgments based chiefly on the Fillingham Firumbras).

Everett D, A Characterization of the English Medieval Romances, in Essays on ME Literature, Oxford 1955, p 19 (articulates what is practically a consensus of critics: that the audience was popular, not fashionable, and that only insatiable demand for romances drove writers to "uncongenial" Charlemagne material).

SPECIAL TOPICS.

John Barbour, The Bruce, ed W W Skeat, EETSES 55, London 1870, bk 3, lines 435–66 (Robert the Bruce reads the romance of Ferumbras to his men; cf Loomis, Athelstan Gift Story, as below, p 534).

Baugh A C, The Authorship of the Middle English Romances, MHRA 22.13, esp 23–27 (finds strong evidence of clerical authorship in the Charlemagne romances).

Loomis L H, The Saint Mercurius Legend in Medieval England and in Norse Saga, Philologica: Malone Anniversary Studies, Baltimore 1949, p 132; The Holy Relics of Charlemagne and King Athelstan: the Lances of Longinus and St Mauricius, Spec 25.437; The Passion Lance Relic and the War Cry Monjoie in the Chanson de Roland and Related Texts, RR 41.241; The Athelstan Gift Story: Its Influence on English Chronicles and Carolingian Romances, PMLA 67.521, esp 530–37 (of Mrs Loomis' four kindred "relic" studies, this last alone comes explicitly into English Charlemagne romances).

Tonguc S, The Saracens in the ME Charlemagne Romances, Litera 5.17 (cf C Meredith Jones, The Conventional Saracen, in [53] below).

[45] *OLIVE AND LANDRES.

(A lost romance surviving only in an Old Norwegian translation.)

Unger C R, ed, Karlamagnus Saga ok Kappa hans, Christiania 1860, p xv and pt 2: Af Fru Olif ok Landres Syni hennar, p 50.

Meyer P and G Huet, edd, Doon de la Roche, SATF, Paris 1921 (an analogue of *Olive and Landres).

Leach H G, Angevin Britain and Scandinavia, Cambridge Mass 1921, p 241.

Schlauch M, Chaucer's Constance and Accused Queens, N Y 1927, p 95; Romance in Iceland, Princeton N J 1934, p 182.

Smyser H M, The ME and ON Story of Olive, PMLA 56.69.

Ward, 1.671 (on Doon de la Roche).

Smyser H M, trans, The Story of Landres, in H M Smyser and F P Magoun Jr, Survivals in Old Norwegian of Medieval English, French, and German Literature, Conn Coll Monograph 1, New London Conn 1941.

Larsen H, Olive and Landres, JEGP 40.526.

Smyser H M, Olive Again, MLN 61.535.

Wilson R M, The Lost Literature of Medieval England, London 1952, p 121 (crit D Everett, MÆ 22.31).

I. The Firumbras Group

SOURCES.

MSS of the Destruction-Fierabras Tradition. Gröber G, Die handschriftlichen Gestaltungen der Ch de g Fierabras u ihre Vorstufen, Leipzig 1869 (crit K Bartsch, JfRESL 11.219).

Ward, 1, 615 (on Fierabras).

Smyser H M, A New MS of the Destruction de Rome and Fierabras [Egerton 3028]—see below under LITERARY RELATIONS IN THE DESTRUCTION-FIERABRAS TRADITION.

British Museum, Catalogue of Additions to the MSS, 1916–20, London 1933, p 338 (description of Egerton 3028).

Wirtz I, Studien zur Handschrift IV,578 der Provinzialbibl zu Hannover, der Ch de g Fierabras, diss Göttingen 1935 (discusses the MS published in part by Gröber and its relations; finds that the Fierabras portion does not differ radically from the version published by Kroeber and Servois: a contribution toward a critical edn then planned by A Hilka; crit J Storost, ZfRP 60.404).

Christ K, Der provenzalische Fierabras, ZfRP 56.192 ("zur Geschichte einer Hs u einer Ausgabe").

Flower R, Lost MSS, Essays by Divers Hands, TRSL ns 18.116 (describes Egerton 3028; some of its relationships; its acquisition).

Brandin L, La Destruction, Rom 64.18—see below under Editions (description of Egerton 3028).

Jodogne O, Fragments, Lettres Romanes 6.240 —see below under Editions (lists all Fierabras MSS).

Editions. de Reiffenberg F, Chronique rimée of Philippe Mouskés, vol 1, Brussels 1836, lines 4664–4717 (summary of the Balan; reprinted in the beginning of Jarník, as below).

Kroeber A and G Servois, Fierabras, Anciens poètes de la France 4, Paris 1860 (the basic MS is BN 12603; readings have been supplied from BN 1499, BM Royal 15 E vi, and Vatican Queen of Sweden 1616).

Gröber G, La Destruction de Rome (Hanover MS), Rom 2.1 (crit, with corrections, L Brandin, Rom 28.489); answer to Brandin, ZfRP 24.447.

Stokes W, ed and trans, Irish Prose Fierabras, RC 19.14, 118, 252, 364.

Brandin L, La Destruction de Rome et Fierabras, MS Egerton 3028, Rom 64.18 (edits and describes the unique MS of this version).

Jodogne O, Fragments de Mons: II: Fierabras, Lettres romanes 6.240 (edits two fragments, of 120 lines, and lists all now-known Fierabras MSS; avers the need of a new edition).

LITERARY RELATIONS IN THE DESTRUCTION-FIERABRAS TRADITION.

Bédier J, La composition de Fierabras, Rom 17.22 (relationship of Fierabras to Balan).

Reichel C, Die me Sir Fyrumbras und ihr Verhältnis zum af und prov Fierebras, diss Breslau 1892 (see below under ASHMOLE SIR FIRUMBRAS [47]: *Sources and Literary Relations*).

Friedel V, Deux fragments du Fierabras: Étude critique sur la tradition de ce roman, Rom 24.1.

Lauer P, Le poème de la Destruction de Rome et ses origines de la cité léonine, Mélanges d'archéologie et d'histoire de l'École française de Rome, Rome 1899, 19.307.

Roques M, L'élément historique dans Fierabras, Rom 30.161.

Jarník H, Studie über die Komposition der Fierabrasdichtungen, Halle 1903 (a thorough analysis, with review of earlier contributions; crit M Roques, Rom 33.430; R Mehnert, ZfRP 60.49).

Ettmayer K, Zur Destruction de Rome, ZfRP 38.663 (on origins; crit, with further considerations, A Stimming, Die Entwickelungsgeschichte der Destruction de Rome, ZfRP 40.550).

Bédier J, Légendes épiques, 2.256; 4.156.

Griffith R H, Malory's Morte Darthur and Fierabras, Angl 32.389 (sees the combat of Oliver and Fierabras retold of Gawain and Priamus).

O'Sullivan M I, A Study of the Fillingham Text of Firumbras and Otuel and Roland, London 1927 (reprinted as Introduction of the O'Sullivan edn as cited below).

Smyser H M, The Sowdon of Babylon and Its Author, HSNPL 13.185 (crit R Mehnert, ZfRP 60.49); A New MS of the Destruction de Rome and Fierabras [Egerton 3028], HSNPL 14.339 (summary and analysis of this version, in a MS acquired by the BM in 1920).

O'Sullivan M I, Firumbras and Otuel and Roland, EETS 198, London 1935 (see below; discussion of relationships, pp xv-xlii).

Mehnert R, Neue Beiträge zum Handschriftenverhältnis der Ch de g Fierabras, diss Göttingen 1938 (crit J Storost, ZfRP 60.404); Alte und Neue Fierabras-Fragen, ZfRP 60.49 (objects to the authority which Smyser claims for the Egerton DFi and Sowdon and Provençal Fi in the reconstruction of the original DFi).

Irving T B, Roncesvalles: A Basque and Arab Epic, Ensko-Jakintza 2.457 (undocumented account of Spanish allusions to Fierabras and Floripas).

Baugh L H E, p 186 (the Firumbras Group in general).

Loomis L H, The Athelstan Gift Story: Its Influence on English Chronicles and Carolingian Romances, PMLA 67.521, see esp 533–37.

Konick M, The Authorship of Sir Ferumbras: Ashmole MS 33, DA 13.233 (in microfilm; Publication no 4940; charts the relationships of all known versions of Fierabras).

Schutz A H, Vernacular Books in Parisian Private Libraries of the Sixteenth Century, Univ of N Carolina Studies in the Romance Languages and Literatures 25.48 (gives important bibl).

[46] SOWDON OF BABYLON.

(A version of the Destruction de Rome and Fierabras.)

MS. Garrett no 140 (Garrett Bldg, Baltimore); formerly Phillips 8357, ff 1^a–41^a (ca 1450). de Ricci Census, p 893.

Regarding transcriptions of this MS by George Steevens or by Steevens and George Ellis, Bodl Douce 175 and Phillipps 8332, see R N Walpole, Charlemagne and Roland, Univ of California Publications in Modern Philology 21, no 6, p 440n13.

Editions. The Romaunce of the Sowdone of Babylone Who Conquered Rome, Roxburghe Club 71, London 1854.

Hausknecht E, The Sowdone of Babylone, EETSES 38, London 1881 (crit G Paris, Rom 11.149; textual emendations, F Holthausen, Angl 15.200).

Selections and Abstract. Ellis Spec, 379 (here called Sir Ferumbras).

French W H and C B Hale, ME Metrical Romances, N Y 1930, p 239 (lines 1491–3226, from Hausknecht's text).

Language and Sources. Hausknecht E, Über Spr und Quelle des me Heldengedichts vom Sowdan of Babylon, diss Berlin 1879 (crit T Wissmann, LfGRP 1.99; G Gröber, ZfRP 4.163).

Kirchhoff J, Zur Geschichte der Karlssage, Marburg 1913, p 46.

Ackerman R, Arthur's Wild Man Knight, RomP 9.117 (on the giant Agolafre).

Authorship. Smyser H M, The Sowdon of Babylon and Its Author—see above under SOURCES and under LITERARY RELATIONS IN THE DESTRUCTION-FIERABRAS TRADITION.

Paris G, Histoire poétique, p 251; Gautier, Les épopées françaises, 3.366; Billings, p 47; Körting, § 95; Schofield, p 154; J Crosland, OF Epic, Oxford 1951, p 238; Kane, p 27.

[47] THE ASHMOLE SIR FIRUMBRAS.

MS. Bodl 25166–67 (Ashmole 33), ff 1^a–77^b (ca 1380).

Black W H, A Descriptive, Analytical and Critical Catalogue of Ashmolean MSS, Oxford 1845, p 14.

Fischer W, Zur . . . Sir Ferumbras, as below under *Textual Matters.*

Konick M, The Authorship of Sir Ferumbras (see below under *Authorship*), esp p 3.

Edition. Herrtage S J, Sir Ferumbras, EETSES 34, London 1879 (crit F H Stratmann, LfGRP 1.374; C Reichel, EStn 18.270; E Hausknecht, Angl 7.160; G Paris, Rom 11.149).

Selections. Zupitza J and J Schipper, Alt- und mittelenglisches Übungsbuch, 12th edn, rvsd by A Eichler, Vienna 1922, p 173 (lines 1104–59 from Herrtage's edition).

MacLean G E, Old and ME Reader, London 1898, p 111 (lines 1104–59 from Zupitza).

Sampson G, Cambridge Book of Prose and Verse, Cambridge 1924, p 289 (lines 602–55).

Textual Matters. Browne W H, MLN 12.223 (on line 3555: For vilentyne he fond ynow & play).

Fischer W, Zur . . . Sir F: Das Verhältnis des ersten Entwurfs [lines 331–759] zur Reinschrift, Arch 142.25.

For textual emendations, see Stratmann, Reichel, and Hausknecht under Herrtage S J, edn, above.

Language. Herrtage, edn, p xviii.

Carstens B H, Zur Dialektbestimmung des me Sir F, diss Kiel 1884 (Southwestern; crit G Sarrazin, LfGRP 5.388).

Bülbring K, Gesch des Ablauts der starken Zeitwörter innerhalb des Südenglischen, QF 63.35 (two pages on strong verbs of Ashmole Firumbras).

Morsbach L, Mittelenglische Grammatik, Halle 1896, pp 6, 10 (finds Ashmole Firumbras Southwestern).

Heuser W, Festländische Einflüsse in Mittelenglischen, BBA 12.178.

Moore S, S B Meech, H Whitehall, ME Dialect Characteristics and Dialect Boundaries, Essays and Studies in Engl and Comp Lit, Univ of Michigan, 13.52 (locates the text at Exeter).

MED, p 12.

See also Konick below, under *Authorship,* p 207 (in the thesis).

Versification. Baugh L H E, p 186; see also Konick below, under *Authorship,* p 223 (in the thesis).

Date. Herrtage, edn, p xvi; MED, p 12.

Authorship. Konick M, The Authorship of Sir Ferumbras: Ashmole MS 33 of the Bodl Libr, diss Univ of Pennsylvania, DA 13.233 (in microfilm; no 4940; page numbers elsewhere in the present bibl refer to the thesis itself).

Sources and Literary Relations. Reichel C, Die me Sir Fyrumbras und ihr Verhältnis zum af und prov Fierebras, diss Breslau 1892 (derives, via one or more intermediaries, from the original independently of Provençal and of the French texts known to Gröber).

Kirchhoff J, Zur Geschichte der Karlssage, Marburg 1913, p 45.

Jodogne O, Fragments de Mons, II: Fierabras, Lettres romanes 6.240.

See also Konick above under *Authorship,* passim, esp p 11.

Literary Criticism. Billings, p 52; Schofield, p 154; Baugh L H E, p 186; J Crosland, OF Epic, p 235; Kane, p 15.

Brandl, § 70; Körting, § 94. For background material, see especially Jarník, Kroeber and Servois, G Paris, L Gautier, Bédier, and Gröber under the headings preceding this.

[48] THE FILLINGHAM FIRUMBRAS.

MS. The so-called Fillingham MS, now BM Addit 37492, ff 1^a–30^a (1475–1500).

Rotographs of Fillingham MS, BM Addit 37492; Modern Language Deposit no 1 in Library of Congress and New York Public Library Reading Room.

Ellis Spec, pp 357–79.

British Museum, Catalogue of Additions to the MSS, 1906–10, London 1912, p 53.

Edition. O'Sullivan M I, Firumbras and Otuel and Roland, ed from MS BM Addit 37492, EETS 198, London 1935 (crit H R Patch, MLN 51.490; H Marcus, AnglB 47.235; G L Brook, MÆ 8.67; G V Smithers, RES 14.461).

O'Sullivan M I, A Study of the Fillingham Text of Firumbras and Otuel and Roland, diss Bryn Mawr 1925, London 1927 (this study of relationships, style, language, etc, was reprinted as the introd to the edn cited above).

Renwick-Orton, p 42.

Jodogne O, Fragments de Mons, II: Fierabras, Lettres romanes 6.240 (background material only).

Loomis L H, The Athelstan Gift Story: Its

Influence on English Chronicles and Carolingian Romances, PMLA 67.535.
Konick M, The Authorship of Sir Firumbras, p 32.

[49] CAXTON'S CHARLES THE GRETE.

Editions. [Caxton W,] Thystory and lyf of the noble and crysten prynce Charles the grete, Westminster, W. Caxton, 1485 (Harvard has a facsimile of the unique copy, BM C.10.b.9).
Herrtage S J, The Lyf of the Noble and Chrysten Prynce, Charles the Grete, translated from the French by William Caxton and printed by him 1485, EETSES 36, 37, London 1880, 1881 (Introduction in 2.v-xii; crit G Paris, Rom 11.149).
Sources and Background. [Bagnyon] Fierabras, Geneva, Adam Steinchaber, 1478; Geneva, Symon du Jardin, 1480 (Harvard has a facsimile of BM copy, G10531, of this edn).
Herrtage S J, ed, Sir Ferumbras, EETSES, London 1879, 34.v; also edn as above, 2.v.
Vincent of Beauvais, Speculum historiale, Erlangen 1893.
Paris G, Histoire poétique de Charlemagne,

p 157 (on the relationship of Caxton to Bagnyon); Rom 10.634 (brief notice concerning Bagnyon).
Rauschen G, Die Legende Karls des Grossen im 11 und 12 Jahrhundert, Leipzig 1890 (contains the Descriptio).
Schofield, p 155.
Kirchhoff J, Zur Geschichte der Karlssage, Marburg 1913, p 47.
Besch E, Les adaptations en prose des Ch de geste au 15e et 16e siècle, Revue du seizième siècle 3.155, esp 167 (discussion of the prose French Fierabras).
Byles A T, in Chivalry, ed E Prestage, London 1928, p 183.
Meredith Jones C, ed, Historia Karoli Magni (Pseudo-Turpin), Paris 1936.
Doutrepont G, Les mises en prose des épopées et des romans chevaleresques du 14e au 16e siècles, Brussels 1939, p 94 (on Bagnyon).
Crosland J, The Old French Epic, Oxford 1951, p 241.
Jodogne O, Fragments de Mons, II: Fierabras, Lettres romanes 6.240.
Konick M, The Authorship of Sir Ferumbras, p 15.

II. The Otinel (Otuel) Group

[50] OTINEL AND BACKGROUND OF OTUEL LEGENDS.

Edition. Guessard G and H Michelant, Otinel, Anciens poètes de la France, Paris 1859 (based on MS Vatican Queen of Sweden 1616, with supplementary use of Phillips MS 8345).
Treutler H, Die Otinelsage im Mittelalter, EStn 5.97.
Langlois E, Deux fragments épiques: Otinel . . ., Rom 12.433 (293 lines).
Rajna P, Contributi alla storia dell' epopea, Rom 18.1 (esp p 35, on the origin of the names Otinel and Garsie).
Bédier J, Légendes épiques 2.269.
Leach H G, Angevin Britain and Scandinavia, Cambridge Mass 1921, pp 237, 249.
Bianchi D, La leggenda di Otinel, Nuovi studi medievali [orig ser] 2 (pt 2) 264.
Aebischer P, Études sur Otinel, Berne 1960 (crit P le Gentil, RomP 16.105).
HLF, 26.269; Gröber, 2¹.545; Gautier Bibl, 155.

[51] *CHARLEMAGNE AND ROLAND.

(A lost romance represented by the Roland and Vernagu of the Auchinleck MS and the Otuel and Roland of the Fillingham MS, qv.)

Paris G, Histoire poétique, Paris 1865, p 156.
Walpole R N, Charlemagne and Roland: A Study of the Source of Two ME Metrical Romances, Roland and Vernagu and Otuel and Roland, Univ of California Publications in Modern Philology 26, no 6, 1944, p 385 (crit U T Holmes, Spec 19.511; J Monfrin, Rom 69.548); The Source Manuscript of Charlemagne and Roland and the Auchinleck Bookshop, MLN 60.22 (the MS is BM Addit 40142; crit L H Loomis, MLQ [Wash] 6.349).
Smyser H M, Charlemagne and Roland and the Auchinleck MS, Spec 21.275.
Schofield, p 154; Baugh L H E, p 187.
Descriptio—see Rauschen, ed, under LATIN BACKGROUNDS, above; cf. Bédier, Légendes épiques, 4.122.
Pseudo-Turpin—see LATIN BACKGROUNDS, above, for edns.

[52] THE AUCHINLECK MS AND THE LOOMIS BOOKSHOP THEORY.

National Libr of Scotland, Advocates 19.2.1 (the Auchinleck MS); 334 folios (1330–40).
Scott Sir W, ed, Sir Tristrem, Edinburgh 1811,

pp cvii-cxxvi (description of the MS and contents).

Kölbing E, Vier Romanz Handschriften, EStn 7.178 (description of the MS and contents).

Booker J M, A ME Bibliography, Heidelberg 1912, p 54 (date).

Carr M B, Notes on an English Scribe's Methods [in the Auchinleck MS], Univ of Wisconsin Studies in Lang and Lit, Madison 1918, 2.153 (on the RV scribe's treatment of OE ā).

O'Sullivan M I, ed, Firumbras and Otuel and Roland, EETS, London 1935, 198.lv (parallels between OR and RV and Otuel a Knight).

Zettl E, ed, Short Metrical Chronicle, EETS, London 1935, 196.xvi (date).

Loomis L H, Chaucer and the Auchinleck MS: Thopas and Guy of Warwick, Essays and Studies in Honor of Carleton Brown, NYU Press 1940, p 111; Chaucer and the Breton Lays of the Auchinleck MS, SP 38.14; The Auchinleck MS and a Possible London Bookshop of 1330–40, PMLA 57.595 (the basic article of the Bookshop Theory).

Walpole R N, Charlemagne and Roland, as above under *CHARLEMAGNE AND ROLAND [51], esp pp 420–33; The Source MS of CR and the Auchinleck Bookshop, MLN 60.22.

Loomis L H, The Auchinleck Roland and Vernagu and the Short Chronicle, MLN 60.94.

Smyser H M, Charlemagne and Roland and the Auchinleck MS, Spec 31.275; The List of Norman Names in the Auchinleck MS, Mediaeval Studies in Honor of J D M Ford, Cambridge Mass 1948, p 283n4 (date).

Smithers G V, Two Newly-Discovered Fragments from the Auchinleck MS, MÆ 18.1 (of King Alisaunder and Richard Coeur de Lion).

Bliss A J, Notes on the Auchinleck MS, Spec 26.652 (detects 6 scribes vs Kölbing's 5 and reassigns various works; notes scribal collaboration, p 656).

Loomis L H, The Athelstan Gift Story: Its Influence on English Chronicles and Carolingian Romances, PMLA 67.530.

[53] ROLAND AND VERNAGU.

(See also *CHARLEMAGNE AND ROLAND [51], above.)

MS. See under AUCHINLECK MS [52], above. Ff 263[a]–267[b].

Editions. Nicholson A, The Romances of Roland and Vernagu and Otuel from the

Auchinleck Manuscript, Abbotsford Club, Edinburgh 1836.

Herrtage S J, The Taill of Rauf Coilyear, Roland and Vernagu, and Otuel, EETSES 39, London 1882, p 37.

Abstract. Ellis Spec, p 346.

Textual Matters. (See also under *Sources and Literary Relations*, below.) Wächter W, Untersuchungen über die beiden me Gedichte Roland and Vernagu and Otuel, Berlin 1885.

Holthausen F, Textual Notes to Herrtage's edn, Angl 21.366.

Language. Herrtage, edn, p xiv (East Midland with Southwestern influence).

Wächter W, Untersuchungen, p 33 (Northeast Midland).

Carr M B, Notes on an English Scribe's Methods (as above under AUCHINLECK MS [52]).

Trounce A McI, English Tail-Rhyme Romances, MÆ 3.46 (Suffolk or North Essex).

Jordan R, ed H C Matthes, Handbuch der me Grammatik, Heidelberg 1934, p 6 (loosely Southwestern with Northern rhymes).

MED, p 11.

Versification. Wilda O, Über die örtliche Verbreitung der zwölfzeiligen Schweifreimstrophe in England, diss Breslau 1887.

Kaluza M, ed, Libeaus Desconus, Leipzig 1890, p lvii.

Sources and Literary Relations. Paris G, Histoire poétique, pp 53, 337.

Gautier L, Les épopées françaises, 3.397.

Wächter W, Untersuchungen, p 7.

Wilda O, Über die örtliche Verbreitung (as above, under Versification).

Kirchhoff J, Zur Geschichte der Karlssage, Marburg 1913, p 43.

Trounce A McI, The English Tail-Rhyme Romances, MÆ 1.87, 168; 2.34, 189; 3.30 (crit D Everett, YWES 13.94, 14.118).

Smyser H M, The Engulfed Lucerna of the Pseudo-Turpin, HSNPL 15.61 (relationships of lines 278–304).

Walpole R N, Charlemagne and Roland: A Study (as above, under *CHARLEMAGNE AND ROLAND [51]), esp chaps 3–5.

Loomis L H, The Auchinleck Roland and Vernagu and the Short Chronicle, MLN 60.94 (lines 109–23 as a borrowing from the chronicle; The Saint Mercurius Legend, Philologica: Malone Anniversary Studies, Baltimore 1949, pp 132–43, esp p 141n).

Walpole R N, Stanzas 26 and 27 of the ME Romance Roland and Vernagu, MÆ 20.40 (a popular etymology probably introduced by the translator).

Loomis L H, The Athelstan Gift Story: Its Influence on English Chronicles and Carolingian Romances, PMLA 67.521, esp 531.

Meredith Jones C, The Conventional Saracen of the Songs of Geste, Spec 17.201.

Ten Brink, 1.245; Gautier Bibl, 155; Brandl, § 3, p 645; Billings, p 58; Schofield, p 154; Körting, § 100.

[54] OTUEL AND ROLAND.

(See also *CHARLEMAGNE AND RO-LAND [51], above.)

MS. The so-called Fillingham MS, now BM Addit 37492, ff 30^b–76^a (1475–1500). See under FILLINGHAM FIRUMBRAS [48], above.

Edition. O'Sullivan M I, Firumbras and Otuel and Roland, edited from BM Addit 37492, EETS 198, London 1935 (for crit of this edn, see under FILLINGHAM FIRUMBRAS [48], above).

O'Sullivan M I, A Study of the Fillingham Text of Firumbras and Otuel and Roland, diss Bryn Mawr, London 1927 (this study of relationships, style, language, etc, was later used as the introd to the edn cited above).

Walpole R N, Syr Bertram the Baner in the ME Romance Otuel and Roland, MLN 62.179 (on the meaning of Baner).

Paris, Histoire poétique, p 154; Billings, p 60.

[55] OTUEL A KNIGHT.

MS. See under AUCHINLECK MS [52], above. Ff 268^a–277^b.

Editions. Nicholson A, Otuel a Knight, Abbotsford Club, Edinburgh 1836.

Herrtage S J, The Taill of Rauf Coilyear, Roland and Vernagu, and Otuel, EETSES 39, London 1882, pp 65–116.

Abstract. Ellis Spec, p 357.

Textual Matters. Holthausen F, Angl 21.369 (note to line 154: & be þe hod Otuwel nam).

Koeppel E, Eine historische Anspielung in the Romance of Otuel, Arch 107.392 (on the Douglas larder of the year 1307 and line 1128).

Language. Herrtage, edn, p xiv.

Sources and Literary Relations. Paris G, Histoire poétique, p 155.

Gautier L, Les épopées françaises, 3.397.

Treutler H, Die Otinelsage im Mittelalter, EStn 5.126.

Wächter W, Untersuchungen über die beiden me Gedichte Roland and Vernagu and Otuel, Berlin 1885.

Ten Brink, 1.245 (a rather confused account of Charlemagne and Roland, with what is evidently meant to be a reference to Otuel a Knight).

Gragger J, Zur me Dichtung Sir Otuel, Graz 1896.

Kirchhoff J, Zur Geschichte der Karlssage, Marburg 1913, p 44.

O'Sullivan M I, Introduction to edn of Firumbras and Otuel and Roland, p xlii (relations of Otuel a Knight to Fillingham Otuel and Roland and to other versions of Otuel [Otinel]).

Brandl, § 37; Billings, p 67; Schofield, p 153; Körting, § 96.

[56] THE SEGE OF MELAYNE.

MS. A Thornton MS, BM Addit 31042, ff 66^b–79^b (ca 1450).

Edition. Herrtage S J, The Sege off Melayne, etc, EETSES 35, London 1880 (crit G Paris, Rom 11.151; see also below).

Textual Matters, Versification, Language. Herrtage, edn, p xii.

Kölbing E, EStn 5.467 (emendations of Herrtage's text).

Bülbring K D, EStn 13.156 (emendations of Herrtage's text).

Wilda O, Über die örtliche Verbreitung der Schweifreimstrophe, diss Breslau 1887, p 65.

Holthausen F, Angl 40.402 (textual notes).

Dannenberg B, Metrik and Sprache der me Romanze The Sege off Melayne, diss Göttingen 1890 (holds that both author and scribe were northern).

Date. Herrtage, edn, p xiii; MED, p 72.

Sources and Literary Relations. Gautier L, Les épopées françaises, 2.304 (suggests that Sege was perhaps a preface to Otinel as the Destruction de Rome was to Fierabras; the same suggestion was made by Gaston Paris to Herrtage at about the same time; see Herrtage's edn, as above, p ix).

Kirchhoff J, Zur Geschichte der Karlssage, Marburg 1913, p 45.

Trounce A McI, English Tail-Rhyme Romances, MÆ 1.87, 168; 2.34, 189; 3.30.

Brandl, § 79 (here classified with other tail-rhyme romances); Billings, p 63; Schofield, p 154; Gautier Bibl, 201; Kane, p 15.

[57] DUKE ROLAND AND SIR OTUEL OF SPAIN.

MS. A Thornton MS, BM Addit 31042, ff 82^a–94^a (ca 1450).

Ward, 1.953; British Museum, Catalogue of Additions to the MSS, 1876–81, London 1882, p 148.

Edition. Herrtage S J, The Sege off Melayne, The Romance of Duke Rowlande and Sir Ottuel of Spayne, etc, EETSES 35, London 1880 (crit G Paris, Rom 11.151).

Textual Matters. Holthausen F, Textual Notes on Roland and Otuel, Angl 40.397.

Date. Herrtage, edn, p xiii; MED, p 69.

Sources and Literary Relations. Wilda O, Über die örtliche Verbreitung der Schweifreimstrophe, diss Breslau 1887, p 17.

Engler H, Quelle und Metrik der me Romanze Duke Rowlande and Sir Otuell of Spayne, diss Königsberg 1901.

Kirchhoff J, Zur Geschichte der Karlssage, Marburg 1913, p 46.

Trounce A McI, The English Tail-Rhyme Romances, MÆ 1.87, 168; 2.34, 189; 3.30.

Brandl, § 79; Billings, p 71; Schofield, p 153; Körting, § 97; Kane, p 15.

III. Detached Romances

[58] THE SONG OF ROLAND.

MS. BM Lansdowne 388, ff 381ᵃ–395ᵇ (1475–1500).

Ward, 1.631.

Edition. Herrtage S J, The Sege off Melayne, The Romance of Duke Rowland and Sir Otuell of Spayne, together with a Fragment of the Song of Roland, from the unique MS Lansdowne 388, EETSES 35, London 1880 (crit G Paris, Rom 11.151).

Summary. Michel F, ed, La Chanson de Roland, Paris 1837, Appendix no 8, p 279 (the English poem analyzed with over 100 lines quoted).

Textual Matters. Holthausen F, textual notes, EStn 51.16.

Language. Schleich, as below, pp 6 and 307 respectively; Herrtage, edn, p xxv; MED, p 11.

Date. Schleich, as below, pp 3 and 313 respectively; Herrtage, edn, p xxx; MED, p 75.

Sources and Literary Relations. Schleich G, Prolegomena ad Carmen de Rolando Anglicanum, Burg 1879 (crit R P Wuelcker, Angl 3.401; T Wissmann, LfGRP 1.334).

Schleich G, Beiträge zum me Roland, Angl 4.307.

Wichmann C, Das Abhängigkeitsverhältnis des ae Rolandsliedes zur af Dichtung, diss Münster 1889.

Stengel E, Das af Rolandslied, Leipzig 1900, vol 1 (critical edn).

Kirchhoff J, Zur Geschichte der Karlssage, Marburg 1913, p 46.

Mortier R, ed, Les textes de la Chanson de Roland, Paris 1940–44, vol 1, introd, esp pp viii-ix and xv.

Literary Criticism. Crosland J, The Old French Epic, Oxford 1951, p 231.

Paris, Histoire poétique, p 155; Gautier, Les épopées françaises, 3.493; Ten Brink, 1.244; Brandl, § 113; Gröber, 2¹.463; Billings, p 73; Schofield, p 151; Körting, § 93; Baugh LHE, p 186; Gautier Bibl, 192.

[59] THE TAILL OF RAUF COILYEAR.

Editions. The Taill of Rauf Coilyear, St Andrews: Robert Lekpreuik 1572 (the only known copy of this edition was discovered in the Advocates' Library in 1821; it is the basis of all later editions, no MS of the poem being known; cf W A Craigie, ed, The Asloan MS, Edinburgh and London 1923–24, p xv).

Laing D, Select Remains of the Ancient Popular Poetry of Scotland; re-ed by John Small, 1885; rvsd by W C Hazlitt, Early Popular Poetry of Scotland, London 1995, 1.212.

Herrtage S J, The Taill of Rauf Coilyear, EETSES 39, London 1882 (crit G Paris, Rom 11.150).

Tonndorf M, The Tail of Rauf Coilyear, Berlin 1894.

Amours F J, Rauf Coilyear, Scottish Alliterative Poems, PSTS 27, 38, Edinburgh 1892, 1897.

Browne W H, The Taill of Rauf Coilyear, Baltimore 1903 (crit F Melbus, EStn 36.256; O Ritter, AnglB 17.67).

Selections. Browne W H, Selections from the Early Scottish Poets, Baltimore 1896, p 94 (lines 1–323, 363–453, 480–570).

Analysis with Quotation. Henderson T F, Scottish Vernacular Literature, 3rd rvsd edn, Edinburgh 1910, p 77.

Modernization. Whiting B J, Ralph the Collier, College Survey of English, N Y 1942, 1.138.

Language. Tonndorf, edn, p 10; Browne, edn, p 35.

Versification. Oakden J P, Alliterative Poetry in ME, Manchester 1930, pp 117, 217.

Oakden J P and E R Innes, Alliterative Poetry in ME, Manchester 1935, p 50.
Date. Herrtage, edn, p vi; Tonndorf, edn, p 13; Browne, edn, p 30; Smyser, as below, p 135.
Sources and Literary Relations. John the Reeve, PFMS, 2.550; J Wenzig, Westslawischer Märchenschatz, Leipzig 1857, p 179; Maria von Ploennies, Die Sagen Belgiens, Köln 1846, p 249.
Tonndorf M, Rauf Coilyear, Halle diss 1893 (reprinted as an introd to Tonndorf's edn, above).
Kirchhoff J, Zur Geschichte der Karssage, Marburg 1913, p 47.
Kittredge G L, A Study of Gawain and the Green Knight, Cambridge Mass 1916, pp 101, 305 (on the "courtesy lesson" in Rauf).
Smyser H M, The Taill of Rauf Coilyear and Its Sources, HSNPL 14.135 (contains bibl of analogues and echoes, including Otinel and Fierabras, qv, above).
Brandl, § 135; Billings, p 79; Schofield, p 153; Körting, § 99; Baugh LHE, p 186.

[60] THE FOURE SONNES OF AYMON.

Editions. Caxton W, The Right Pleasaunt and Goodly Historie of the Foure Sonnes of Aymon, London, 1489–91.
Richardson O, The Foure Sonnes of Aymon, EETSES 44, 45, London 1884, 1885.
Modernization and Abstract. Steele R, Renaud of Montauban: First Done into English by William Caxton and now Abridged and Retranslated, London 1897.
Guerber H, Legends of the Middle Ages, N Y 1924, p 152.
Source and Background Materials. Les quatre filz Aymon, [Lyons 1480?] (BM C.22.c).
Castets F, Les quatre fils Aymon, ed with an introd, RLR 49.97, 368; 50.97, 216, 344; 51.67, 143, 289, 407; 52.16, 130, 193 (see esp 50.170 and 49.424; this edn appeared in book form, Montpellier 1909; crit P Meyer, Rom 33.296).
Ward, 1.619.
Bédier J, Légendes épiques, 4.189 (under the title Renaud de Montauban).
Besch E, Les adaptations en prose des chansons de geste au 15e et au 16e siècle, Revue du seizième siècle 3.155.
Byles A T, Chivalry, ed E Prestage, London 1928, p 183 (background material for the genre).
Doutrepont G, Les mises en prose des épopées, Brussels 1939, p 184 and passim.
Gröber, 2¹.547 (on the origin of Renaud de Montauban); Schofield, p 156; Baugh LHE, p 301; Gautier Bibl, 158.

[61] THE BOKE OF DUKE HUON OF OF BURDEUX.

Editions. Bourchier, Sir John (Lord Berners), The Boke of Duke Huon of Burdeux, [London, Wynkyn de Worde?, ca 1534].
Lee S, The Boke of Duke Huon of Burdeux, EETSES 40, 41, 43, 50, London 1882–87.
Modernization and Abstract. Steele R, Huon of Bordeaux: Done into English by Sir John Bourchier, Lord Berners; and now Retold, London 1895.
Guerber H, Legends of the Middle Ages, N Y 1924, p 163.
Authorship. Greenwood A D, CHEL 2.383 (on Berners' career and his style).
Lee S, DNB 2.920 (see under Bourchier; article on John Bourchier, Lord Berners).
Source and Background Materials. Huon de Bordeaux, Paris, Michael Lenoir, 1513 (BM 12431.i.12).
Guessard F and C Grandmaison, Huon de Bordeaux, Paris 1860 (edn of the French version; see under Ruelle, below).
Longnon A, L'élément historique de Huon de Bordeaux, Rom 8.1.
Paris G, Poèmes et légendes du moyen âge, Paris 1900, p 24; Sur Huon de Bordeaux, Rom 29.209.
Besch E, Les adaptations en prose des chansons de geste, Revue du seizième siècle 3.155.
Ebert W, Vergleich der beiden Versionen von Lord Berners Huon of Bordeaux, diss Halle 1917 (the 1st and 3rd edns [1534 and 1601] are meant; the 2nd edn [probably of 1570] is lost).
Byles A T, Chivalry, ed E Prestage, London 1928, p 183 (background material for the genre).
Krappe A H, Über die Quellen des Huon de Bordeaux, ZfRP 54.68 (on the sources, especially of Auberon, in folklore and literature).
Doutrepont G, Les mises en prose des épopées, Brussels 1939, p 139 and passim.
Ruelle P, Rom 72.424 (projected new edn of the French version); Huon de Bordeaux, Paris, Presses universitaires de France 1961.
Owen D D R, The Principal Source of Huon de Bordeaux, FS 7.129 (thinks a chief source of the French epic to be a version of Huon d'Auvergne).
Gröber, 2¹.549; Schofield, p 157 (influence on Spenser, Shakespeare, and Keats); Paris Litt franç, § 25; Gautier Bibl, 132.

4. LEGENDS OF GODFREY OF BOUILLON

by

R. M. Lumiansky

GENERAL.

Pigeonneau H, Le cycle de la Croisade et de la famille de Bouillon, St Cloud 1877.

Gröber, 2¹.471, 575.

Paris Litt franç, § 29.

Jaffray R, The Two Knights of the Swan, N Y 1910.

Hibbard L A, Mediaeval Romance in England, N Y 1924, p 239.

Frey A L, The Swan-Knight Legend, Nashville 1931.

Renwick W L and H Orton, The Beginnings of English Literature, N Y 1940, p 357 (includes bibl).

Andressohn J C, The Ancestry and Life of Godfrey of Bouillon, Bloomington 1947 (Indiana Univ Publications, Social Science Series, no 5).

Origins. Lot F, Le mythe des Enfants-Cygnes, Rom 21.62.

Blöte J F D, der historische Schwanritter, ZfRP 21.176, 251 (crit G Paris, Rom 26.581).

Blöte J F D, Das Aufkommen des Clevischen Schwanritters, ZfDA 42.1 (crit G Paris, Rom 27.334).

Blöte J F D, Die Sage vom Schwanritter in der Brogner Chronik von c 1211, ZfDA 44.407.

Blöte J F D, Der Ursprung der Schwanritter-tradition in Englischen Adelsfamilien, EStn 29.337.

Paris G, Mayence et Nimègue dans le Chevalier au Cygne, Rom 30.404.

Blöte J F D, Mainz in der Sage vam Schwan-ritter, ZfRP 27.1.

Huet G, Sur quelques formes de la légende du Chevalier au Cygne, Rom 34.206.

Sparnaay H, Verschmelzung legendarischer und weltlicher Motive in der Poesie des Mittelalters, Groningen 1922, p 135 (crit A H Krappe, JEGP 23.591; W Fischer, AnglB 35.171).

Krüger A G, Die Quellen der Schwanritter-dichtungen, Gifhorn (Hannover) 1936 (crit A Taylor, MP 35.100; H Rosenfeld, Arch 171.72).

Krogmann W, Die Schwanrittersage, Arch 171.1.

Hibbard Med Rom, p 251.

Boekenoogen G J, ed, Historie van den Ridder Metter Swane, Nederlandsche Volksboeken 3, Leiden 1931 (bibl by Blöte).

CBEL, 1.146.

[62] CHEVALERE ASSIGNE.

MS. BM Cotton Calig A.2, ff 125ᵇ–129ᵇ (ca 1460).

Editions. Utterson B, Roxb Club 1820.

Gibbs H H, EETSES 6, London 1868.

French W H and C B Hale, ME Metrical Romances, N Y 1930, p 859.

Textual. Holthausen F, Zur Alt- und Mittel-englischen Dichtungen, Angl 21.441.

Language. Krüger A G, Zur me Romanze Chevalere Assigne, Arch 77.167.

Oakden J P, Alliterative Poetry in ME, Manchester 1930, 1.61, 153.

Versification. Kaluza M, Strophliche Gliederung in der me rein alliterierenden Dichtung, EStn 16.174.

Hulbert J R, Quatrains in ME Alliterative Poems, MP 48.73 (quatrain-division exists in Chevalere Assigne).

Literary Criticism. Oakden J P, Alliterative Poetry in ME, Manchester 1935, 2.40.

Kane, pp 9, 20 (artistically poor).

Other Versions. Todd H A, La naissance du Chevalier au Cygne, PMLA 4.i (French; crit G Paris, Rom 19.314).

Boekenoogen (as above under General; Dutch).

Liebermann F, Chevalier au Cygne in England, Arch 107.106.

Loomis C G, Two Miracles in the Chevalere Assigne, EStn 73.331 (self-ringing bells and magically increasing metal).

Ward, 1.708; Brandl, § 73; Billings, p 228; Schofield, p 315; Hibbard Med Rom, p 239; Baugh LHE, p 194.

[63] HELYAS, THE KNIGHT OF THE SWAN.

MSS. No MS extant. PRINT: Copland R, The History of Helyas, Knight of the Swan, translated from the French, Paris 1504; rptd by W Copland, London 1550?; rptd by Wynkyn de Worde, London 1512; de Worde's text published by Grolier Club, N Y 1901. Thoms, London (Routledge), p 691 (reprints R Copland's text).

Ashton J, Romances of Chivalry, N Y 1887, p 207 (rpt of R Copland's text). Hibbard Med Rom, p 244.

GODEFROY OF BOLOYNE: See under Caxton.

Edition. Colvin M N, EETSES 64, London 1893.

5. LEGENDS OF ALEXANDER THE GREAT

by

R. M. Lumiansky

GENERAL.

Biography. Robson E I, Alexander the Great: A Biographical Study, London 1929.
Wilcken U, Alexander der Grosse, Leipzig 1931.
Weigall A E P B, Alexander the Great, N Y and London 1933.
Wright F A, Alexander the Great, London 1934.
Robinson C A, Alexander the Great, N Y 1947.
Robinson C A, The History of Alexander the Great, Brown Univ Studies 16, Providence 1953 (index to and translations of the pertinent historical documents).
Savill A F, Alexander the Great and His Time, London 1955 (bibl included).
Early Development of the Legend. Müller C, ed, Pseudo-Callisthenes, Arriani Anabasis et Indicie, Paris 1846 (based on beta-type MS).
Meusel H, ed, Psuedo-Callisthenes, Jahrbücher für Classische Philologie, neue Folge, Supplementband 5.700 (uses Leiden MS).
Kroll W, ed, Historia Alexandri Magni (Pseudo-Callisthenes), vol 1 (Recensio Vetusta), Berlin 1926 (no further vols have appeared).
Ausfeld A, Die Orosius-Recension der Historia de preliis und Babiloths Alexanderchronik, Festschrift der Badischen Gymnasien 1886, p 99.
Budge E A W, History of Alexander the Great, Cambridge 1889.
Hertz W, Aristoteles in den Alexanderdichtungen des Mittelalters, Munich 1890.
Héron P, La légende d'Alexandre et d'Aristote, Rouen 1892.
Carraroli D, La leggenda di Alessandre Magno, Turin 1892 (summarizes research to date on formation and development of the legend).
Budge E A W, Life and Exploits of Alexander the Great, 2 vols, London 1896 (edn and trans of Ethiopic text).

Hamilton G L, A New Redaction of the Historia de preliis and the Date of Redaction J[3], Spec 2.113.
Magoun F P, Gests of King Alexander of Macedon, Cambridge Mass 1929 (introd has sect on early history of the legend; crit C Brett, MLR 24.466; D Everett, RES 6.329; L von Hibler, AnglB 41.242; H R Patch, Spec 5.117).
Magoun F P, The Harvard Epitome of the Historia de preliis (Recension I[2]), HSNPL 14.115.
Magoun F P, A Prague Epitome of the Historia de preliis Alexandri Magni (Recension I[2]), HSNPL 16.119 (introductory comment on the state of Alexander-studies and on the transmission of the legend).
Hilka A and F P Magoun, A List of Manuscripts Containing Texts of the Historia de preliis Alexandri Magni, Recensions I[1], I[2], I[3], Spec 9.84.
Thomson S H, An Unnoticed Abridgment of the Historia de preliis (Redaction I[2]–I[3]), Univ of Colorado Studies in the Humanities, series B, 1.3.241 (found in Chetham Library, Manchester, MS Mum. A.4.102: A.5.18).
Baugh LHE, p 181.
Merkelbach R, Die Quellen des griechischen Alexander-Romans, Munich 1954 (bibl included).
Haight E H, The Life of Alexander of Macedon, N Y 1955 (trans of Kroll, see above).
Cary G, The Medieval Alexander (ed D J A Ross), Cambridge 1956 (very important treatment of the development of and the medieval attitude towards the legend; crit C F Bühler, PBSA 50.7).
The Old English Pieces. Rypins S, ed, Three Old English Prose Texts in MS Cotton Vitellius A XV, EETS 161, London 1924.

Anderson G K, The Literature of the Anglo-Saxons, Princeton 1949, p 377 (bibl, p 382).

Förster M, Zur altenglischen Mirabilien-Version, Arch 117.367.

Pfister F, Auf den Spuren Alexanders des Grossen in der alteren englischen Litteratur, GRM 16.81.

The French Versions. Michelant H, ed, Li romans d'Alixandre par Lambert le Tors et Alexandre de Bernay, Stuttgart 1846.

Meyer P, Les premiers compilations françaises d'histoire ancienne, Rom 4.7.

Meyer P, Alexandre le Grand dans la littérature française du moyen âge, 2 vols, Paris 1886.

Magoun F P, The Compilation of St Albans and the Old French Prose Alexander Romance, Spec 1.225 (source of OF Prologue is a work like Latin compilation of St Albans).

Aebischer P, Fragments d'un manuscrit du Roman d'Alexandre de Lambert le Tort et Alexandre de Bernay, Archivum Romanicum, 9⁴.366.

Armstrong E C, The Authorship of the Vengement Alixandre and of the Venjance Alixandre, Princeton 1926.

Edition of the Medieval French Roman d'Alexandre. Elliott Monographs Series, nos 36–41, Princeton: vol 1 (EM 36), M S La Du, Text of Arsenal and Venice Versions, 1937; vol 2 (EM 37), E C Armstrong, D L Buffum, B Edwards, L F H Lowe, Version of Alexandre de Paris, text, 1937; vol 3 (EM 38), A Foulet, Version of Alexandre de Paris, variants and notes to Branch 1, 1949; vol 4 (EM 39), E C Armstrong and A Foulet, Le roman du Fuerre de Gadres d'Eustache, 1942; vol 5 (EM 40), F B Agard, Version of Alexandre de Paris, variants and notes to Branch 2, 1942; vol 7 (EM 41) B Edwards and A Foulet, Version of Alexandre de Paris, variants and notes to Branch 4, 1955. Additional vols will be forthcoming.

Edwards B, ed, Le vengement Alixandre, Princeton 1928.

Ham E B, ed, Five Versions of the Venjance Alixandre, Princeton 1935.

Ham E B, Branch 2 of the French Alexander, MP 42.123 (critique of vols 4 and 5 of the Princeton edition cited above).

German Version. Knizel K, ed, Lamprechts Alexander nach den drei Texten, mit den Fragmenten des Alberic von Besançon, Germanische Handbibliothek 6, Halle 1884.

Müller H E, ed, Die Werke des Pfaffen Lamprecht, vol 12, Munich 1923 (Vorau Alexander text).

Maurer F, ed, Das Alexanderlied des Pfaffen Lamprecht, Leipzig 1940.

Italian Versions. Storost J, Studien zur Alexandersage in der alteren italienischen Literatur: Untersuchungen und Texte, Halle 1935.

Hebrew Version. Wallach L, Yosippon and the Alexander Romance, Jewish Quarterly Review 37.407 (Hebrew version belongs to the 12th cent recension J²).

Miscellaneous General Items. Becker H, Die Brahmanen in der Alexandersaga, ZfDP 23.424.

Ogle M B, The Perilous Bridge and Human Automata, MLN 35.132 (story of perilous bridge occurs in various versions of the Alexander legend).

Duncan T S, The Alexander Theme in Rhetoric, Washington Univ Studies, Humanistic Series, 9.315 (theme very popular among Greek rhetoricians).

Manly J M, The Romance of Alexander, TLS, Sept 22 1927, p 647 (cites mention in an English legal document of 1381–82 of "a book of Romance of King Alexander in verse").

Lascelles M, Alexander and the Earthly Paradise in Mediaeval English Writings, MAE 5.31.

Matthews W, The Tragedy of Arthur, Univ of Calif Press 1960 (includes discussion of medieval treatments of Alexander and their influence upon the alliterative Morte Arthure).

Saintsbury G, The Flourishing of Romance, N Y 1897, p 148.

Taylor A B, An Introduction to Medieval Romance, London 1930, p 118.

Hamilton G L, Quelques notes sur l'histoire de la Légende d'Alexandre le Grand en Angleterre au moyen âge, Mélanges de philologie et d'histoire offerts à M Antoine Thomas, Paris 1927, p 195.

de Julleville Hist, 1.229; Morley, 3.286; Ward, 1.94; Gröber, 2¹.579, 817; Paris Litt franç, § 44; Körting, § 111; Renwick-Orton, N Y 1940, pp 357, 390 (includes bibl).

CBEL, 1.142.

Magoun F P, Gests of Alexander, Cambridge Mass 1929 (footnotes carry many references; no bibl as such).

Berzuna J, A Tentative Classification of Books, Pamphlets and Pictures Concerning Alexander the Great and the Alexander Romances, privately printed 1939 (sect on romances begins p 75; many items not included).

Cary G, The Medieval Alexander, Cambridge 1956, p 378 (very full listing; footnotes give items not always included in bibl).

[64] THE LYFE OF ALISAUNDER OR KING ALEXANDER.

MSS. 1, Bodl 1414 (Laud Misc 622; formerly Laud I.74), ff 27^b–64^a (ca 1400); 2, Lincoln's Inn (London) 150, ff 28^a–90^a (end of 15 cent); 3, Advocates 19.2.1 (Auchinleck), ff 278^a–279^a (1330–40; a fragment); 4, Univ of St Andrews, two fragments totaling 150 lines, probably originally contained in Auchinleck MS; 5, British Museum, six printed leaves (see Bagford Ballads, under *Editions* below).

Smithers G V, Two Newly-Discovered Fragments from the Auchinleck MS, MÆ 18.1 (on the fragments found by N R Ker in the Libr of Univ of St Andrews).

Smithers G V (see below, under Editions), EETS 237.1 (description, history, and affiliation of MSS).

Editions. Weber MR, 1.3.

Smithers G V, Kyng Alisaunder, vol 1, EETS 227, London 1952 (texts, summary); vol 2, EETS 237, London 1957 (introd, commentary, glossary).

Bagford Ballads, vol 1, no 27, London 1878, ed J W Ebsworth (the six leaves in the British Museum).

Bülbring K D, Vier neue Alexanderbruchstücke, EStn 13.145 (includes descriptive comment upon the six leaves in the British Museum).

Selections. AESpr, 1.242 (taken from Weber, lines 2049–2546).

Warton T, The History of English Poetry, London 1871, 2.205, 4.102.

Sampson G, Cambridge Book of Prose and Verse, Cambridge 1924, p 263 (lines 6658–6727).

French W H and C B Hale, ME Metrical Romances, N Y 1930, p 789 (lines 3857–4281, 6684–6743).

Brandl A and O Zippel, ME Literature (Mittelenglische Sprach- und Literaturproben), 2nd edn, N Y 1949, p 66 (lines 7826–8030, with some French parallels).

Kaiser R, Alt- und Mittelenglische Anthologie, 2nd edn, Berlin 1955 (lines 139–215, 1439–1551).

Textual Notes. Kölbing E, Kleine Beiträge zur Erklärung, Textkritik, und Phraseologie me Dichter, EStn 13.138 (comments on lines 3584–4059).

Kölbing E, Kleine Beiträge zur Erklärung und Textkritik me Dichtungen, EStn 17.298 (comments on lines 3605–07, 3614, 3619, 3739, 3913, 4027, 4042, 4045).

Language. Mackenzie B A, A Special Development of OE ēa in ME, EStn 61.386.

Moore S, S B Meech, and H Whitehall, ME Dialect Characteristics and Dialect Boundaries, Essays and Studies in Engl and Comp Lit, Univ of Michigan, 13.54.

French W H, Dialects and Forms in Three Romances, JEGP 45.125 (this poem, Arthour and Merlin, and Richard Coeur de Lion are in same Midland dialect).

Smithers G V, EETS 237.40 (language, provenance, vocabulary).

Authorship. Kölbing E, ed, Arthour and Merlin, Leipzig 1890, p lx.

Neilson G, Huchown of the Awle Ryale, Glasgow 1902, p 59.

Hamilton G L, Quelques notes sur l'histoire de la légende d'Alexandre le Grand en Angleterre au moyen âge, Mélanges de philologie et d'histoire offerts à M Antoine Thomas, Paris 1927, p 196 and n 5.

French W H, Dialects and Forms in Three Romances, JEGP 45.125 (rejects Kölbing's view that this poem is by same author as Arthour and Merlin and Richard Coeur de Lion).

Baugh A C, The Authorship of the ME Romances, MHRA 22.17 (clerical authorship).

Smithers G V, EETS 237.58 (author may have been in orders).

Source. Meyer P, Alexandre le Grande in littérature française du moyen âge, Paris 1886, 2.294 (comparison with French version).

Hildenbrand T, Die altfranzösische Alexanderdichtung Roman de toute chevalerie des Thomas von Kent und die me Kyng Alisaunder, Bonn 1911.

Lascelles M, Alexander and the Earthly Paradise in Medieval English Writings, MÆ 5.85.

Smithers G V, EETS 237.15.

Miscellaneous Topics. Bülbring K D, Vier neue Alexanderbruchstücke, EStn 13.145 (relationship of fragments to poem).

Kittredge G L, Zwei Berichtigungen, EStn 14.392 (six printed leaves had been reported earlier than Bülbring's article).

Searles C, Some Notes on Boiardo's Version of the Alexander-Sagas, MLN 15.90 (comparison of Italian with Kyng Alisaunder).

Eagleson H, Costume in the ME Metrical Romances, PMLA 47.344 (costume is realistic).

Tuve R, Seasons and Months, Paris 1933, p 179 (seasonal introductions used to indicate chronology).

Heather P J, The Seven Planets, Folklore 54.338, 344, 351, 352 (medieval attitudes towards planets).

Ten Brink, 1.241; Brandl, § 36; Schofield, p 300; HLF 24.501; Körting, § 111; Kane, pp 42, 44 (imaginative, literarily outstanding).

Magoun F P, Gests of King Alexander of Macedon, Cambridge Mass 1929, p 34.

Baugh LHE, p 182.

Cary G, The Medieval Alexander, Cambridge 1956, p 37, 241.

Smithers G V, EETS 237.

[65] THE ALLITERATIVE ALEXANDER FRAGMENTS.

MSS. For Fragment A (Alisaunder): Bodl 3832 (Greaves 60), ff 1^b–20^a (ca 1600).

For Fragment B (Alexander and Dindimus): Bodl 2464 (Bodley 264), ff 209^a–217^b (15 cent).

For Fragment C (Wars of Alexander): 1, Bodl 6925 (Ashmole 44), ff 1^a–97^b (15 cent); 2, Trinity Dublin D.4.12, ff 1^a–41^b (15 cent; f 40 is lost).

Hessels J H, The Dublin MS of the Alliterative Romance of Alexander, EStn 3.531 (this MS supplies lines missing in MS Ashmole 44 for Fragment C).

Skeat W W, Twelve Facsimiles of Old English Manuscripts, Oxford 1892, p 34 (facsimile of f 51 of MS Ashmole 44).

Editions. For Fragment A: Skeat W W, The Gestes of the Worthie King and Emperour, Alisaunder of Macedonie, EETSES 1, London 1867, p 177; F P Magoun, Gests of King Alexander of Macedon, Cambridge Mass 1929, p 121.

For Fragment B: Stevenson J, The Alliterative Romance of Alexander, Roxb Club 1849, p 197; W W Skeat, Alexander and Dindimus, EETSES 31, London 1878; F P Magoun, Gests of King Alexander of Macedon, Cambridge Mass 1929, p 171.

For Fragment C: Stevenson J, The Alliterative Romance of Alexander, Roxb Club 1849, p 1, W W Skeat, The Wars of Alexander, EETSES 47, London 1886.

Textual Notes. Smithers G V, Notes on ME Texts, London Medieval Studies, 1.208 (on lines 321f of Fragment B).

Language. Henneman J B, Untersuchungen über das me Gedicht Wars of Alexander, Berlin 1889 (Fragment C).

Henneman J B, The Interpretation of Certain Words and Phrases in the Wars of Alexander, MLN 5.242 (lines 1066, 1945, 2420, 2447, 5349, 800, 1000, 4919, 1040, 1782, 4747 of Fragment C).

Hulbert J R, The West Midland of the Romances, MP 19.1 (should be called North Midland; concerns all three fragments).

Menner R J, Sir Gawain and the Green Knight and the West Midland, PMLA 37.503 (vs Hulbert, MP 19.1; language is West Midland; concerns all three fragments).

Oakden J P, Alliterative Poetry in ME, Manchester 1930, 1.47 (Fragment A), 1.50 (Fragment B), 1.97 (Fragment C).

Versification. Rosenthal F, Die alliterierende englische Langzeile im 14 Jahrhundert, Angl 1.145 (Fragments A and B).

Luick K, Die englische Stabreimzeile im 14, 15, und 16 Jahrhundert, Angl 11.553 (all three fragments).

Kaluza M, Strophische Gliederung in der me rein alliterierenden Dichtung, EStn 16.169 (Fragment C; uses 8-line strophe).

Steffens H, Versbau und Sprache des me stabreimenden Gedichtes The Wars of Alexander, BBA 9 (Fragment C).

Deutschbein M, Zur Entwicklung des englischen Alliterationsverses, Halle 1902 (Fragments A and B).

Oakden J P, Alliterative Poetry in ME, Manchester 1930, 1.247 (Fragments A and B), 1.255 (Fragment C).

Day M, Strophic Division in ME Alliterative Verse, EStn 66.245 (all three fragments; use quatrains).

Hulbert J R, Quatrains in ME Alliterative Poems, MP 48.73 (all three fragments; use quatrains).

Dates. Oakden J P, Alliterative Poetry in ME, Manchester 1930, 1.153 (all three fragments).

Authorship. Trautmann M, Über Verfasser und Entstehungszeit einiger alliterierenden Gedichte des Altenglischen, Halle 1876 (A and B are fragments of same poem).

Bradley H, The English Gawain-poet and the Wars of Alexander, Acad Jan 14 1888, p 27 (Fragment C; similarities of vocabulary).

Henneman J B, Untersuchungen über das me Gedicht Wars of Alexander, Berlin 1889 (Fragment C).

Neilson G, Wars of Alexander, Athen, 1900^1.591; 1902^1.784 (Fragment C derived from Hunterian MS T.4.1 of De preliis Alexandri).

MacCracken H N, Concerning Huchown, PMLA 25.529 (not author of Fragment C).

Andrew S O, Wars of Alexander and Destruction of Troy, RES 5.267 (Fragment C not by same author as Destruction of Troy; crit unfavorably, D Everett, YWES 10.131).

Oakden J P, Alliterative Poetry in ME, Manchester 1930, 1.247 (Fragments A and B), 1.255 (Fragment C).

Koziol H, Zur Frage der Verfasserschaft einiger me Stabreimdichtungen, EStn 67.166 (Fragments A and B), 67.171 (Fragment C).

Day M, ed, Sir Gawain and the Green Knight,

EETS 210, London 1940, p xiii (Fragment C not conclusively connected with Pearl Poet).

Baugh A C, The Authorship of the Middle English Romances, MHRA 22.17 (Fragment A; clerical authorship).

Sources. Henneman J B, Untersuchungen über das me Gedicht Wars of Alexander, Berlin 1889 (Fragment C).

Hamilton G L, A New Redaction (J³ᵃ) of the Historia de preliis and the Date of Redaction J³, Spec 2.113 (source of Fragment C).

Lascelles M, Alexander and the Earthly Paradise in Mediaeval English Writings, MÆ 5.93 (all three fragments).

Literary Evaluation. Oakden J P, Alliterative Poetry in ME, Manchester 1935, 2.24 (Fragment A), 2.27 (Fragment B), 2.28 (Fragment C).

Kane, pp 9, 57, 59 (Fragments A and B; plain style, literarily successful).

Ten Brink, 1.293 (Fragment A), 1.333 (Fragment B); Brandl, §§ 73, 125 (all three fragments); Schofield, p 301 (Fragment C): Körting, § 111A, B (all three fragments).

Wedel T O, Mediaeval Attitude Toward Astrology, YSE 60.104 (Fragment C).

Baugh LHE, p 182 (Fragments A and B), p 183 (Fragment C).

Cary G, The Medieval Alexander, Cambridge 1956, p 48 (Fragments A and B), p 57 (Fragment C).

[66] THE CAMBRIDGE ALEXANDER-CASSAMUS FRAGMENT.

MS. Camb Univ Ff. 1.6, ff 142ᵃ–153ᵇ (15 cent).

Edition. Rosskopf K, Editio Princeps des me Cassamus (Alexanders-Fragmentes), Munich 1911, p 51.

Holthausen F, Zum me Cassamus-bruchstück, EStn 51.23 (suggests several emendations to Rosskopf's text).

Magoun F P, Gests of King Alexander of Macedon, Cambridge Mass 1929, p 30.

Cary G, The Medieval Alexander, Cambridge 1956, p 32.

[67] THE PROSE ALEXANDER.

MS. Lincoln Cath 91 (olim A.i.17) (Thornton), ff 1ᵃ–49ᵃ (1430–1440).

Halliwell[-Phillipps] J O, ed, The Thornton Romances, Camden Soc 1844, p xxvi (description of the MS).

Wooley R M, Catalogue of the MSS of the Lincoln Cathedral Chapter Library, Oxford 1927, p 51 (description of the MS).

Editions. Westlake J S, The Prose Life of Alexander, EETS 143, London 1913 (for 1911; text only; no apparatus).

Hamilton G L, A New Redaction of the Historia de preliis (J³ᵃ) and the Date of Redaction J³, Spec 2.113 (source, date).

Magoun F P, Gests of King Alexander of Macedon, Cambridge Mass 1929, p 56.

Cary G, The Medieval Alexander, Cambridge 1956, p 56.

[68] THE SCOTTISH ALEXANDER BUIK.

MSS. No MS extant (date of composition, 1438, given in text).

Editions. History of Alexander the Great, printed by Alexander Arbuthnet ca 1580 (only copy belongs to Earl of Dalhousie).

Weber M R, l.xxxi (comment on Arbuthnet's print), l.xxiii (summary of Arbuthnet's print).

Laing D, The Buik of the Most Noble and Vailyeand Conqueror Alexander the Great, Bannatyne Club 1831 (rpt of Arbuthnet's text).

Ritchie R L G, The Buik of Alexander, PSTS ns no 17 (vol 1), 1925, no 12 (vol 2), 1921, no 21 (vol 3), 1927, no 25 (vol 4), 1929 (French text parallel; introduction mainly devoted to argument for John Barbour's authorship).

Neilson G, John Barbour, Poet and Translator, TPSL 1899–1902, p 320 (includes Alexander Buik among Barbour's works).

Smith J M, French Backgrounds of Middle Scots Literature, Edinburgh and London 1934, p 7 (cites theories of Ritchie and Nielson for Barbour's authorship).

Ham E B, Three Neglected Manuscripts of Voeux du Paon, MLN 46.78 (three important MSS of French source overlooked by Ritchie, Thomas, and P Meyer).

Rheinhard J R, Some Illustrations of the Medieval Gab, Essays and Studies in Engl and Comp Lit, Univ of Michigan, 8.47 (makes use of Voeux de Paon).

Whiting B J, Proverbs in Certain ME Romances in Relation to Their French Sources, HSNPL 15.85 (proverbs translated literally; doubts Barbour's authorship).

Laing D, Adversaria, Edinburgh 1867, p 1 (the hitherto unpublished preface for the 1831 Bannatyne reprint).

Hermann A, Untersuchungen über das Schottische Alexanderbuch, Halle 1893 (author a disciple of Barbour; treats sources, language, metre, text).

Gröber, 2¹.818, 891; Schofield, p 303 (accepts Barbour's authorship).

Magoun F P, Gests of King Alexander of Macedon, Cambridge Mass 1929, p 28.

Baugh LHE, p 300 (Barbour's authorship doubtful).

Cary G, The Medieval Alexander, Cambridge 1956, p 35.

Geddie W, A Bibliography of Middle Scots Poets, PSTS 61, Edinburgh 1912, p 66 ("Barbour's Alexander").

[69] GILBERT HAY'S BUIK OF KING ALEXANDER.

MSS. The MS situation for this piece is not fully clear. Apparently two MSS exist, although most scholars concerned (e g Wells, p 106) have considered only one. The edition in preparation for the STS by Professor A Macdonald will presumably clarify this state of affairs. I have not had opportunity to examine the MSS.

1, BM Addit 40732; 2, Taymouth Castle, ff 1ᵃ–129ᵇ (middle 16 cent).

Hermann A, The Taymouth Castle MS of Sir Gilbert Hay's Buik of Alexander, Berlin 1898 (description; crit O Glöde, EStn 27.140).

Hermann A, The Forraye of Gadderis; The Vows; Extracts from Sir Gilbert Hay's Buik of King Alexander the Conqueror, Ostern 1900 (excerpts from MS; crit O Glöde, EStn 33.259).

Ritchie R L G, ed, The Buik of Alexander, vol 1, PSTS 1925, p lxiii (on Taymouth MS).

Ritchie R L G, ed, The Buik of Alexander, vol 4, PSTS 1929, p 443 ("One of the *two* MSS at Taymouth Castle—the discovery of the second is signalized by Laing in his edition of Dunbar (1834, vol I, p 317)—was acquired in 1923 by the British Museum: Add MS 40732. It is that used by Laing for his privately printed, and very rare *Extracts from the Buike of King Alexander the Conqueroure* (? 1834). Both MSS were seen at Taymouth by Cosmo Innes (see his *Black Book of Taymouth*, 1855) but the second had disappeared before 1896 when Hermann began his work on the other MS, which presumably is still at Taymouth. For this information we are indebted to Mr Herbert J M Milne of the British Museum, who has made a full description of the MS.")

Brown-Robbins, no *55 (the prose version by Hay indicated here does not exist).

Edition. None has been prepared.

Author. Stevenson J H, ed, Gilbert of the Haye's Prose Manuscript, vol 44, PSTS 1901, p xxiii (detailed biographical sketch).

Source. Smith J M, French Backgrounds of Middle Scots Literature, Edinburgh and London 1934, p 139.

Lascelles M, Alexander and the Earthly Paradise in Mediaeval English Writings, MÆ 5.81.

Magoun F P, Gests of King Alexander of Macedon, Cambridge Mass 1929, p 29.

Cary G, The Medieval Alexander, Cambridge 1956, p 35.

[70] THE DUBLIN ALEXANDER EPITOME.

MS. Trinity Dublin, D.4.12, ff 45ᵇ–47ᵃ (after 1477).

Bühler C F, ed, The Dicts and Sayings of the Philosophers, EETS 211, London 1941 (for 1939), p 358 ("a copy made from some Caxton edition").

Edition. Skeat W W, The Wars of Alexander, EETSES 47, London 1886, p 279 (description of MS, p xviii; dialect, p xix).

Pfister F, Eine orientalischer Alexandergeschichte in me Prosabearbeitung, EStn 74.19 (source relationship).

Magoun F P, Gest of King Alexander of Macedon, Cambridge Mass 1929, p 62.

Cary G, The Medieval Alexander, Cambridge 1956, p 60.

[71] AMORYUS AND CLEOPES.

MS. Princeton Univ Libr, Garrett Collection, The Works of John Metham, ff 17ᵃ–56ᵇ (1448–49), Norfolk.

Edition. Craig H, The Works of John Metham, EETS 132, London 1916 (for 1906; description of MS p vii; concerning Metham p x).

Furnivall F J, Athenaeum 1903¹.598 (notice of MS; brief summary of poem).

Furnivall F J, Political, Religious, and Love Songs, EETS 15, London 1903, p 301 (summary of poem; edition of Prologue and Epilogue).

Moore S, Patrons of Letters in Norfolk and Suffolk, PMLA 27.196 (extracts from Furnivall's summary; treatment of Metham's life).

6. LEGENDS OF TROY

by

R. M. Lumiansky

GENERAL.

Development of the Legend. Dunger H, Die Sage vom trojanischen Kriege in den Bearbeitungen des Mittelalters und ihre antiken Quellen, Leipzig 1869.

Piper P H E, Höfische Epik, Stuttgart 1892, 1.282.

Sommer H O, ed, The Recuyell of the Historyes of Troye, 2 vols, London 1894, 1.xvii (crit G Paris, Rom 24.295).

Wager C H A, ed, The Seege of Troy, N Y and London 1899, p xi.

Griffin N E, Un-Homeric Elements in the Medieval Story of Troy, JEGP 7.32 (shows spirit of antagonism towards Homer).

Taylor H O, The Classical Heritage of the Middle Ages, N Y 1901, p 39.

Taylor H O, The Mediaeval Mind, N Y and London 1911, chap 32, § 4.

Root R K, ed, The Book of Troilus and Criseyde, Princeton 1926, p xxi.

Barnicle M E, ed, The Seege or Battayle of Troy, EETS 172, London 1927, p 216.

Hofstrand G, The Seege of Troy: A Study in the Intertextual Relations, Lund 1936, p 196.

Atwood E B, The Excidium Troie and Medieval Troy Literature, MP 35.115 (this classical version of the legend was current and influential in the middle ages).

Young A M, Troy and Her Legend, Pittsburgh 1948, p 48.

Early Latin Versions. Körting G, Dares and Dictys, Halle 1874.

Simonsfield H, ed, Compendium historiae Trojanae-Romanae, Neues Archiv der Gesellschaft für ältere Deutsche Geschichtskunde 11.241 (story similar to that found in Excidium Troiae).

Greif W D, Die mittelalterlichen Bearbeitungen der Trojanersage: Ein neuer Beitrag sur Dares- und Dictysfrage, Marburg 1886.

Griffin N E, Dares and Dictys: Introduction to the Study of the Medieval Versions, Baltimore 1907.

Atwood E B, The Rawlinson Excidium Troie: A Study of Source Problems in Mediaeval Troy Literature, Spec 9.379 (this classical version was known to medieval writers).

Oldfather W A, Notes on the Excidium Troie, Spec 11.272 (additional notes for Atwood's edition, Spec 9.379).

Atwood E B and V K Whitaker, edd, Excidium Troiae, Cambridge Mass 1944 (valuable introd and bibl of analogous texts).

Benoit, Joseph of Exeter, and Guido. Joly A, ed, Benoit de Seinte-More et le Roman de Troie, Paris 1870–71.

Constans L, ed, Le Roman de Troie par Benoit de Sainte-Maure, SATF, 6 vols, Paris 1904–12.

Sedgwick W B, The Bellum Troianum of Joseph of Exeter, Spec 5.49 (examination of metre, grammar, style, text, vocabulary).

Riddehough G B, A Forgotten Poet: Joseph of Exeter, JEGP 46.254 (Bellum Troianum merits careful attention).

Riddehough G B, Joseph of Exeter: The Cambridge Manuscript, Spec 24.389 (this previously neglected MS throws light on many difficult passages in Bellum Troianum).

Griffin N E, ed, Guido de Columnis, Historia destructionis Troiae, Cambridge Mass 1936 (crit R K Root, Spec 12.523).

Italian and Slavic Versions. Gorra E, Testi inediti di storia Trojana, Torino 1887.

Bationskof T, Rom 18.303 (crit of a book in Russian which discusses Slavic Troy versions).

Miscellaneous General Items. Tatlock J S P, The Siege of Troy in Elizabethan Literature, Especially in Shakespeare and Heywood, PMLA 30.673.

Curry W C, The Judgment of Paris, MLN 31.114 ("The wisdom-offer of Pallas . . . is not of classical growth").

Atwood E B, Robert Mannyng's Version of the Troy Story, Texas SE 18.5 (the 300-line digression on Troy derives from a classical not a medieval account).

Loomis R S, Morgain la Fee and the Celtic Goddess, Spec 20.183 (points to a traditional feud between Morgain and Hector).

Kane, pp 20, 44 (story very attractive for medieval audiences).

Presson R K, Shakespeare's Troilus and Cressida and the Legends of Troy, Madison 1953.

See also the section on Chaucer's TROILUS AND CRISEYDE.

General Comment on ME Versions. Heeger G, Die Trojanersage der Britten, Munich 1886 (crit G P[aris], Rom 15.449).

Baker E A, The History of the English Novel, London 1924, 1.229.

Gordon G, The Trojans in Britain, E&S 9.9 (traces through medieval English writings the idea of descent from Trojans).

Parsons A E, The Trojan Legend in England, MLR 24.253, 394 ("some instances of its application to the politics of the times").

Taylor A B, An Introduction to Medieval Romance, London 1930, p 120.

Atwood E B, English Versions of the Historia Trojana, Abstracts of Dissertations of the Univ of Virginia, 1931–32, p 3.

Renwick-Orton, N Y 1940, pp 359, 390 (includes bibl).

Baugh LHE, p 255.

Hinton N D, A Study of the ME Poems Relating to the Destruction of Troy, DA 17.2010.

Wager C H A, ed, The Seege of Troy, N Y and London 1899, p 117 ("selected bibliography relating to medieval Troy Cycle").

CBEL, 1.144.

Rey A and A G Solalinde, Essayo de una bibliographia de las leyendas Troyanas en la literatura Española, Indiana Univ Publications, Humanities Series, no 6, Bloomington 1942.

[72] GEST HISTORIALE OF THE DESTRUCTION OF TROY.

MS. Univ of Glasgow, Hunterian 388, ff 2^a–214^b (ca 1450). The folios are somewhat out of order; see EETS 56, p liii.

Fiston W, The Ancient Historie of the Destruction of Troy, London 1596.

Wood G R, A Note on the Manuscript Source of the Alliterative Destruction of Troy, MLN 67.145 (curious spellings copied from certain MSS of Guido's Historia).

Edition. Panton G A and D Donaldson, The Gest Historiale of the Destruction of Troy, EETS 39, 56, London 1866, 1874.

Selections. MacLean G E, An Old and Middle English Reader, N Y and London 1893, p 104 (lines 1–97).

Wülfing J E, Das Laud Troy-Book, EStn 29.384 (prints lines 316–413, 4471–4511 from Panton-Donaldson edn).

Zupitza J, Alt- und Mittelenglisches Übungsbuch, Vienna 1902, p 162 (lines 1–98).

Sisam K, Fourteenth Century Verse and Prose, Oxford 1921, p 68 (lines 1–98, 12463–12547).

French W H and C B Hale, ME Metrical Romances, N Y 1930, p 809 (lines 1–98, 4699–4782, 8592–8673).

Kaiser R, Alt- und Mittelenglische Anthologie, 2nd edn, Berlin 1955 (lines 1–80, 10252–11254).

Language, Versification, and Author. Trautmann M,

Der Dichter Huchown und seine Werke, Angl 1.123.

Bock W, Zur Destruction of Troy: Eine Sprach- und Quellenuntersuchung, Halle 1883.

Luick K, Die englische Stabreimzeile im 14, 15, und 16 Jahrhundert, Angl 11.393.

Morley, 6.241 (Huchown the author).

Hulbert J R, The West Midland of the Romances, MP 19.1 (not *West* Midland).

Menner R J, Sir Gawain and the Green Knight and the West Midland (vs Hulbert, MP 19.1; is West Midland).

Andrew S O, Wars of Alexander and Destruction of Troy, RES 5.267 (language, Northwest Midland; author, not same for both).

Oakden J P, Alliterative Poetry in ME, Manchester 1930, 1.67 (dialect), 1.155 (versification), 1.255 (author).

Koziol H, Zur Frage der Verfasserschaft einiger mittelenglischer Stabreimdichtungen, EStn 67.171, 172 (Gest Historiale and Wars of Alexander not by same author; Gest Historiale and Morte Arthure not by same author).

Hulbert J R, Quatrains in ME Alliterative Poems, MP 48.73 (Gest Historiale does not make use of quatrains).

See also the items concerning Huchown under MORTE ARTHURE [16].

Source. Bock W, Zur Destruction of Troy: Eine Sprach- und Quellenuntersuchung, Halle 1883.

Brandes H, Die me Destruction of Troy und ihre Quelle, EStn 8.398.

Neilson G, Huchown's (?) Codex, Athen 1900¹.751 (argues that Hunterian MS T.4.1 is source of Huchown's Gest Historiale).

Style. Reicke K, Untersuchungen über den Stil der me Morte Arthure, Königsberg 1906.

Influence. Kölbing E and M Day, edd, The Siege of Jerusalem, EETS 188, London 1932, p xxvi (Siege borrows several passages from Gest Historiale).

Literary Criticism. Oakden J P, Alliterative Poetry in ME, Manchester 1935, 2.32.

Kane, pp 10, 11, 27, 45, 56, 58 (original, learned, emotional, rhetorical, unduly elaborated).

Brandl, § 125; Körting, § 112 (E Kölbing, crit of Körting—1887 edn—, EStn 11.285); Baugh LHE, p 184; Baugh A C, The Authorship of the ME Romances, MHRA 22.22 (clerical authorship).

[73] THE SEEGE OF TROYE.

MSS. 1, BM Egerton 2862, ff 111^b–134^a (ca 1400); 2, BM Harley 525, ff 1^a–34^b (early

15 cent); 3, Coll of Arms Arundel XXII, ff 1^a–8^b (14 cent); 4, Lincoln's Inn 150, ff 90^b–108^b (end of 14 or beginning of 15 cent).
The editions listed below include comment on the MSS.
Ward, 1.84; Baugh LHE, p 183.
Kölbing E, Vier Romanzen-Handschriften, EStn 7.191, 194 (description of MS Egerton 2862—formerly Duke of Sutherland's—and of MS Lincoln's Inn 150).
Caldwell R A, Joseph Holland: Collector and Antiquary, MP 40.295 (early history of MS Arundel XXII).
Editions. Zeitsch A, Zwei me Bearbeitungen der Historia de Excidio Trojae des Phrygiers Dares, Arch 72.11 (edn of MSS 2 and 4).
Wager C H A, The Seege of Troye, N Y and London 1899 (edn of MS 2; crit G L Hamilton, MLN 15.188).
Barnicle M E, The Seege or Batayle of Troye, EETS 172, London 1927 (edn of MSS 1, 2, 3, and 4; crit E Ekwall, AnglB 41.233; L von Hibler, EStn 65.98).
Hibler-Lebmannsport L, Das me Versgedicht The Seege of Troye: vol 1, Ein philologische Untersuchung nebst einem Abdruck der drei Handschriften; vol 2, Text; Graz 1928 (uses MSS 1, 2, and 4; crit W van der Gaff, ESts 11.146; E Ekwall, AnglB 41.233; C S Northup, JEGP 30.90).
Text. Fick W, Zur me Romanz Seege of Troye, Breslau 1894 (relationship of texts).
Hibler L von, Methodisches zur Ermittlung der Schreiberindividualität im me Handschriften, dargestellt an der Seege of Troye, Angl 51.354.
Hibler L von, Die Individualität des A-Schreibers (MS Arundel XXII) der Seege of Troye, Angl 60.39.
Hofstrand G, The Seege of Troye: A Study in the Intertextual Relations of the ME Romance The Seege or Batayle of Troye, Lund 1936 (includes precise survey of earlier views; crit L von Hibler, AnglB 48.194; A Kihlbom, ESts 19.27).
Language. Zeitsch A, Uber Quelle und Sprache des me Gedichtes Seege oder Batayle of Troy, Kassel 1883.
Bülbring K, Geschichte der Ablaute der Starken Zeitworten, Strassburg 1889, p 34.
Moore S, S B Meech, and H Whitehall, ME Dialect Boundaries and Characteristics, Essays and Studies in Engl and Comp Lit, Univ of Michigan, 13.54 (on dialect of MS 4).
Sources. Zeitsch A, as under *Language.*
Granz E T, Uber die Quellengemeinschaft des

me Gedichtes Seege oder Batayle of Troye und des mittelhochdeutschen Gedichtes vom trojanischen Kriege des Konrad von Wurzburg, Leipzig 1888 (argues for an expanded Roman de Troie).
Schofield, p 289 (assumes an expanded Roman de Troie).
Atwood E B, The Youth of Paris in the Seege of Troye, Texas SE 21.7; The Story of Achilles in the Seege of Troye, SP 39.489; The Judgment of Paris in the Seege of Troye, PMLA 57.343 (each article presents careful evidence to show role of Excidium Troiae as source).
Kane, pp 20, 27 (poem crudely sensational).
Baugh A C, The Authorship of the ME Romances, MHRA 22.15 (clerical authorship).

[74] THE LAUD TROY-BOOK.

MS. Bodl 1502 (Laud 595), ff 1^a–275^a (beginning 15 cent).
Edition. Wülfing J E, The Laud Troy Book, EETS 121, 122, London 1902–04 (no introd, very little apparatus; vol 121: crit R K R[oot], JEGP 5.367).
Comment. Kempe D, A ME Tale of Troy, EStn 29.1 (treats MS, date, relation to Guido and Benoit, portrayal of contemporary life, and style of poem).
Wülfing J E, Das Laud-Troybook, EStn 29.374 (comments in detail on Kempe's article, EStn 29.1).
Wülfing J E, Das Bild und die bildliche Verneinung im Laud-Troy-Book, Angl 27.555, 28.29 (gives detailed catalogue, with index, of images).
Hofstrand G, The Seege of Troy, Lund 1936, p 193 (dialect East Midland).
Baugh LHE, p 184.
Kane, pp 8, 10, 26 (tedious, of intermediate quality).
Baugh A C, The Authorship of the ME Romances, MHRA 22.22, 27 (clerical authorship).

LYDGATE'S TROY-BOOK: See under Lydgate.

[75] TWO SCOTTISH TROY FRAGMENTS.

MSS. Inserted in two MSS of Lydgate's Troy-Book (both 15 cent). Fragment A: Camb Univ Kk.5.30, ff 1^a–9^a (596 lines; beginning corresponds to Troy-Book, 1.876). Fragment

B: 1, Bodl 21722 (Douce 148), ff 290ᵃ–
300ᵃ (lines 1–916), ff 307ᵃ–335ᵇ (lines 1181–
1562 and continuing to line 3118); 2,
Camb Univ Kk.5.30, ff 304ᵇ–323ᵇ (lines
1–1562).

Edition. Horstmann C, Barbour's, des schottischen Nationaldichters, Legendensamm-
lung nebst den Fragmenten seines Trojaner-
krieges, 2 vols, Heilbronn 1881, 2.215 (includes notes on the MSS, 2.217, 228).

Author. Bradshaw H, On Two Hitherto Unknown Poems by John Barbour, Cambridge
Antiquary Soc, 3.111 (identification and
attribution of the fragments).

Paton G A and D Donaldson, The Gest Historiale of the Destruction of Troy, EETS 56,
London 1874, p x (by Barbour).

Ten Brink, Berlin 1877, 2.405 (by Barbour).

Buss P, Sind die von Horstmann herausgegeben
schottischen Legenden ein Werk Barbere's?
Angl 9.495 (fragments not by Barbour).

Koeppel E, Die Fragmente von Barbour's
Trojanerkrieg, EStn 10.373 (not by Barbour).

Prothero G W, A Memoir of Henry Bradshaw,
London 1888, p 133 (on Bradshaw's discovery and attribution of the fragments).

Bradshaw H, Collected Papers, Cambridge
1889, p 58 (rpt of the article from Cambridge
Antiquary Soc, 3.111).

Brandl, § 76 (by Barbour).

Neilson G, John Barbour, Poet and Translator,
TPSL 1899–1902, p 316 (by Barbour).

Wülfing J E, Das Laud-Troybook, EStn 29.383
(by Barbour).

Schofield, p 290 (authorship disputed).

Körting, § 112C (by Barbour).

Ritchie R L G, ed, The Buik of Alexander,
PSTS, Edinburgh and London 1925, 1.ccxxii
(by Barbour).

Language. Farish J, Some Spellings and Rhymes
in the Scots Sege of Troy, ESts 38.200 (*o* for *a*
results from influence of dialects of the Midlands).

[76] THE PROSE SIEGE OF TROY.

MS. Bodl 12908 (Rawlinson Misc D.82), ff
11ᵃ–24ᵇ (middle of 15 cent; see below, under
THE PROSE SIEGE OF THEBES [77].)

Editions. Griffin N E, The Sege of Troy, PMLA
22.157 (introd treats MS and sources).

Brie F, Zwei me Prosaromane: The Sege of
Thebes und die Sege of Troy, Arch 130.40,
269 (introd treats MS and sources; Brie
seems unaware of Griffin's edn).

Combellack C R B, The Composite Catalogue
of the Seege of Troye, Spec 26.624 (the
catalogue of ships in the Prose Siege of Troy
is a conflation of four lists of names; Lydgate
main source for piece).

THE RECUYELL OF THE HISTORYES
OF TROY: See under Caxton.

7. LEGENDS OF THEBES

by

R. M. Lumiansky

GENERAL.

French Versions. Constans L, ed, La légende
d'Oedipe, Paris 1881.

Constans L, ed, Roman de Thèbes, Paris 1890
(crit P Meyer, Rom 21.107; reply by
Constans, RLR 35.612).

Fisher F, Narrative Art in Medieval Romances,
Cleveland 1939, p 1 (analyzes technique in
Roman de Thèbes).

de Julleville Hist, 1.173, 252; Gröber, 2¹.528;
Paris Litt franç, § 47; CBEL, 1.146.

LYDGATE'S SIEGE OF THEBES: See
under Lydgate.

[77] THE PROSE SIEGE OF THEBES.

MS. Bodl 12908 (Rawlinson Misc D.82), ff
1ᵃ–10ᵇ (middle of 15 cent; see above, under
THE PROSE SIEGE OF TROY [76]).

Edition. Brie F, Zwei mittelenglische Prosaromane: The Sege of Thebes und The Sege
of Troy, Arch 130.40, 269 (comments on
date and source).

8. Eustace–Constance–Florence–Griselda Legends

by

Lillian Herlands Hornstein

GENERAL.

Marbach G O, Geschichte von Griseldis und dem Markgrafen Walter, Volksbücher no 1, Leipzig 1838.

Rel Ant, Griselda 2.68.

Unger C R, Karlamagnussaga ok Kappa Hans, Christiana 1860, p 50.

PFMS, 3.421 (Patient Grisell).

Ker W P, Epic and Romance, N Y 1897.

Köhler R, Griselda, in Ersch & Gruber, Allgemeine Encyklopädie 1. § 91, p 413, rptd Kleinere Schriften, Berlin 1900, 2.501; Die Griseldis-Novelle als Volksmärchen, Archiv für Literaturgeschichte, 1.409; ZfRP 3.272 (crit of H Kunst, Das Obras didacticas y dos legendes sacados de manuscritos de la Biblioteca del Escorial, Madrid 1878).

Steinbach P, Über den Einfluss des Crestien de Troies auf die altenglische Literatur, Leipzig 1885, p 41.

Wheatley H B, ed, The History of Patient Grisel, 1619, Chap Books Folklore Tracts ls no 4, London 1885.

Adam E, Sir Torrent of Portyngale, EETSES 51.xxii.

Wilda O, Über die örtliche Verbreitung der zwölfzeiligen Schweifreimstrophe in Englische, Breslau 1887.

Westenholz F, Die Griseldis-Sage in der Literaturgeschichte, Heidelberg 1888 (crit W F Biedermann, ZfVL 2.111).

Wannenmacher F X, Die Griseldissage auf der Iberischen Halbinsel, Strassburg 1894 (crit A L Stiefel, LfGRP 16.415).

Ogden P, A Comparative Study of the Poem Guillaume d'Angleterre, Baltimore 1900.

Gough A B, The Constance-Saga, Palaes 23 (crit E Eckhardt, EStn 32.110; L Pineau, RCHL 54.212; M W, LZ 53.1433).

Kittredge G L, Arthur and Gorlagon, HSNPL 8.241.

Siefken O, Der Konstanze-Griseldistypus in der englischen Literatur bis auf Shakspere (part printed as Das geduldige Weib in der englischen Literatur, Rathenow 1903), Leipzig 1904.

Gerould G H, Forerunners, Congeners, and Derivatives of the Eustace Legend, PMLA 19.335.

Jordan L, Die Eustachiuslegende, Chr Wil-

helmsleben, Boeve de Hanstone und ihre orientalischen Verwandten, Arch 121.341.

Lawrence W W, The Banished Wife's Lament, MP 5.400.

Rickert E, ed, Romance of Emare, EETSES 99.xxxii, xcix.

Monteverdi A, La leggenda di S Eustachio, Studi medievali 3.169, 392 (I testi della legenda).

Pschmadt C, Die Sage von der verfolgten Hunde, Greifswald 1911, pp 32, 45.

Däumling H, Studie über den Typus des Mädchens ohne Hände innerhalb des Konstanzezyklus, München 1912.

Rockwood R E, A Spanish Patient Persecuted Wife Tale of 1329, RR 7.235.

Leach H G, Angevin Britain and Scandinavia, Cambridge Mass 1921, p 241.

Hibbard Med Rom, pp 1–48, 267–89.

Petersen H, Les origines de la légende de Saint Eustache, NM 26.65.

Wesselski A, Märchen des Mittelalters, Berlin 1925, pp 29, 200.

Holmes U T, La leggenda di St Eustachio, Nuovi studi medievali, 3.223.

Murray J, The Eustace Legend in Medieval England, MHRA, 1.35.

Schlauch M, Chaucer's Constance and Accused Queens, N Y 1927, chaps 3–5 (crit N&Q 153.161; H Lange, AnglB 39.334; C H Herford, MLR 23.65; G H Gerould, JEGP 28.285; H R Patch, EStn 67.112); Man of Law's Tale, Bryan-Dempster, p 155; Historical Precursors of Chaucer's Constance, PQ 29.402 (crit G D Willcock, YWES 30.77).

Laserstein K, Der Griseldis-stoff in der Weltliteratur, Weimar 1926; reissued in Forschungen zur neueren Literaturgeschichte 58, Duncker 1928 (crit E Sauer, Euphorion 29.322; W Wurzbach, LfGRP 50.241).

Malone K, Patient Griseldus, RR 20.340 (analogue).

Schick J, Die Urquelle der Offa-Konstanze-Saga, Britannica, M Förster zum 60 Geburstag, Förster Festschrift, Leipzig 1929, p 31.

Griffith D D, Origin of the Griselda Story, Univ of Washington Studies, Publications in Lang and Lit 8, no 1, Seattle 1931; rptd Univ of Chicago Libraries 1932 (crit D Everett, YWES 12.90; H J Rose, Folklore, 43.111; P Meissner, AnglB 44.78; A M[onteverdi], Studi medievali 6.141; J W Ashton, PQ 13.88).

Cate W A, The Problem of the Origin of the Griselda Story, SP 29.389 (crit D Everett, YWES 13.88).

Golenistcheff-Koutouzoff É, L'histoire de Griseldis en France au 14e et au 15e siècle, Paris 1933 (crit J Raith, AnglB 45.235).

Krappe A H, The Offa-Constance Legend, Angl 61.361.

Robinson F N, ed, The Complete Works of Geoffrey Chaucer, Boston 1933, Notes, p 794 (Man of Law's Tale), p 813 (Clerk's Tale), p 842 (Sir Thopas); 2nd edn 1957, pp 692, 710, 736.

Hornstein L H, Trivet's Constance and the King of Tars, MLN 55.354.

Loomis L H, Chaucer and the Auchinleck MS: Thopas and Guy of Warwick, E&S Brown, p 111; The Tale of Sir Thopas, Bryan-Dempster, p 486; The Auchinleck MS and a Possible London Bookshop of 1330–1340, PMLA 57.595.

Severs J B, The Clerk's Tale, Bryan-Dempster, p 288; The Literary Relationships of Chaucer's Clerkes Tale, YSE 96, New Haven and London 1942 (crit D Everett, YWES 32.57, and MÆ 13.47; B R, TLS 1942, p 444; R Pratt, Spec 17.577; G Dempster, MP 40.285, and 41.6; W F Bryan, JEGP 43.250).

Jones G and T Jones, Mabinogian, London 1948, pp xv, xvi (Eustace, calumniated wife).

Patch H R, The Other World According to Descriptions in Medieval Literature, Cambridge Mass 1950, p 258.

Wickert M, Chaucer's Konstanze und die Legende der guten Frauen, Angl 69.1, 89 (crit G D Willcock, YWES 30.62).

Craig B M, L'estoire de Griseldis (MS Bibliothèque National fr 2203), University of Kansas Publications, Humanistic Studies no 31, Lawrence Kansas 1954 (first serious French play with non-religious theme).

Isaacs N D, Constance in Fourteenth Century England, NM 59.260.

Dunn C W, The Foundling and the Werwolf, A Literary-Historical Study of Guillaume de Palerne, Univ of Toronto Dept of English Studies and Texts no 8, Toronto Canada 1960.

See also under EUSTACE; EMARE [87]; Chaucer's MAN OF LAW'S TALE, CLERK'S TALE, TALE OF SIR THOPAS.

[78] SIR ISUMBRAS.

MSS. 1, Bodl 6922* (Ashmole 61), ff 9ᵃ–16 (1475–1500); 2, Bodl 21835 (Douce 261),

ff 1ᵃ–7ᵇ, imp transcript of printing (1564, after Copland); 3, Univ Coll Oxf 142, p 237, fol 128 (1475–1500); 4, Caius Camb 175 (A.9), ff 98ᵇ–107ᵇ (1425–50); 5, BM Cotton Calig A.2 (olim Cotton Vesp D.8), ff 130ᵃ–134ᵃ (1450–1500); 6, Advocates 19.3.1 (olim Jac V.7.27), art 7, ff 48ᵃ–56ᵇ (1475–1500); 7, Gray's Inn 20 (ca 1350); 8, Lincoln Cath 91 (olim A.5.2, olim A.1.17) (Thornton), ff 109ᵃ–114ᵃ (ca 1440); 9, Naples Royal Libr 13.B.29, p 114 (1457); 10, Harvard Univ, Percy Folio MS Eng 748, vol 3, ff 51–81 (transcript) (ca 1767). PRINTS: 11, Bodl Douce fragm f 37, W de Worde ? or W Copland ?, one leaf, 62 lines (ca 1530? 1550?) (STC, no 14281); 12, Bodl 1119 (Malone 941), Copland ?, ff 9ᵃ–9ᵇ, one leaf, 26 lines, very defective (ca 1550?); 13, BM C 21c61, Garrick Collection, W Copland, 15 leaves (ca 1530?) (STC, no 14282); 14, Harvard Univ, John Skot, 8 leaves or fragm, imp (ca 1525?) (STC, no 14280.1); 15, Harvard Univ, I Treveris, for John Butler or W de Worde, 1 leaf and 3 fragm, imp (ca 1530?) (STC, no 14280.2); 16, Westminster Abbey fragm, conjugate with item 15.

Brown-Robbins, no 1184; MED, p 50.

Halliwell [-Phillipps], see under *Editions* below, pp xviii, xxvii (Thornton MS).

Ward, 1.180, 760.

Zupitza J, Die Romanze von Athelston, EStn 14.321 (MS Caius Camb 175); Zum Sir Isumbras, Arch 88.72 (Malone 941); 90.148 (PFMS text).

Everett D, A Note on Ypotis, RES 6.446 (MS Ashmole 61, Cotton Calig A.2).

Manly & Rickert, 1.376, 377 (MS Naples Royal Libr 13.B.29).

Bliss A J, Sir Orfeo, London 1954, p xi (MS Ashmole 61).

Editions. Utterson E V, Select Pieces of Early Popular Poetry, London 1817, 1.77 (BM C 21c61, Copland print).

Halliwell [-Phillipps] J O, Thornton Romances, Camden Soc 30, London 1844, p 88 (Thornton MS), and selections from some of the other MSS, pp 267–69; rptd F S Ellis, Sir Isumbras, 1897.

Rel Ant, 2.67 (MS 13.B.29, Naples Royal Libr).

Kölbing E, Das Neapler Fragment von Sir Isumbras, EStn 3.200 (MS 13.B.29, Naples Royal Libr).

PFMS, 1.532, n 2 (fragm MS Malone 941), lines completed by J Zupitza, Zum Sir Isumbras, Arch 88.72, and corrected Arch 90.148; see T Percy, Reliques of Ancient English Poetry, ed H B Wheatley, London 1886, 3.369.

Ellis F S, Sir Isumbras, Kelmscott Press 1897 (text from Halliwell [-Phillipps], Thornton Romances).

Schleich G, Sir Ysumbras: Eine englische Romanze des 14 Jahrhunderts, im Aschluss an die vorarbeiten J Zupitza, Palaes 15.65 (Caius Camb 175, and readings of all MSS) (crit M Kaluza, Krit Jahresber, 6².362; L Duvau, Moyen âge 2s 5.418; W Heuser, AnglB 12.333; F Holthausen, LfGRP 23.16; M W in LZ 53.1433).

Brown C, A Passage from Sir Isumbras, EStn 48.329 (Univ Coll Oxf MS 142).

D'Evelyn C, The Gray's Inn Fragment of Sir Ysumbras, EStn 52.73 (Gray's Inn MS 20).

Selections. Sampson G, Cambridge Book of Prose and Verse, Cambridge 1924, p 284 (after Halliwell [-Phillipps], Thornton Romances).

Abstract. Ellis Spec, p 479 (Caius Camb 175).

Language. Zupitza J, The Romance of Guy of Warwick, EETSES 25–26, notes, p 413 and passim.

Adam E, Torrent of Portyngale, EETSES 51.xxi.

Ogden P, Comparative Study of Guillaume of Angleterre, Baltimore 1900, p 3.

Lindberg H, Satire on Blacksmiths, Arch 101.395; see contra, Trounce, MÆ 3.36.

Trounce A McI, The English Tail-Rhyme Romances, MÆ 1.87, 168, 2.34, 189, 3.30; Athelston, EETS 224.1 (the South of the East Midlands).

Manly & Rickert, 1.377 (MS Naples is East Midland with some Northern features).

Dunlap A R, The Vocabulary of ME Romances in Tail-Rhyme Stanza, Delaware Notes ns 36, no 3, p 31 (disagrees with Trounce; argues that vocabulary is not a good guide for localization of dialect).

Versification. Curtius F J, An Investigation of the Rimes and Phonology of the Middle-Scotch Romance Clariodus, Angl 16.449.

CHEL, 1.322.

Luick K, Zur me Verslehr, Angl 38.290; Nachtrag, Angl 39.274.

Trounce, MÆ 1.87, 168; 2.34, 189; 3.36, 40, and passim.

Date. Sarrazin G, Octavian, AEB 3.xviii, xliv.

Ostermann L, Entstehungszeit des Isumbras, BBA 12.97.

Everett D, A Note on Ypotis, RES 6.446; A Characterization of the English Medieval Romances, E&S 15; rptd Essays on ME Lit, ed P Kean, Oxford 1955, p 16.

Manly & Rickert, 1.377 (MS Naples contains date 1457).

Author. Sarrazin, Octavian, AEB 3.xlv, xviii.

Relations with Folktales. Thompson Mot Ind, B 141, B 141.1 (prophetic bird; bird gives warning); B 557 (unusual animal as riding-horse); H 91.1 (recognition through gold found in eagle's nest, cf H 151.8 (husband attracted by wife's power of healing, recognition follows); H 1562.2 (test of strength: lifting stone); J 214 (choice: suffering in youth or old age); L 412 (rich man made poor to punish pride); N 251 (man pursued by misfortune); N 527 (treasure carried by bird to nest); N 730, N 731, N 741 (accidental reunion of families); R 13.0.1 (children carried off by animals); R 154.1, R 154.2 (sons rescue parents); T 292 (wife sold unwillingly by husband).

Cross Mot Ind, B 141; J 214; N 251; N 730; R 13.0.1; T 292.

Chauvin V, Bibliographie des ouvrages arabes, Leipzig and Liège 1900, 4.204.

Weston J L, The Three Days' Tournament, London 1902, pp 1, 34.

Gerould G H, The Grateful Dead, Folklore Soc 60, London 1908, pp 2, 35, 92.

Bousset W, Die Geschichte eines Wiedererkennungsmärchen und Placidaslegende, Nachrichten von der K Gesellschaft zu Göttingen, Philol hist Kl (1916), p 469; (1917) p 703 (parallels in Turkish, Jewish, Oriental folktales).

Dickson A, Valentine and Orson, N Y 1929, pp 100, 103n11, 104.

Relations with the Ballad. Furnivall F J, ed, Captain Cox, His Ballads and Books, Ballad Soc 7, London 1871, pp xiii, xxxiii.

Child F J, English and Scottish Popular Ballads, 5 vols, Boston 1882–98, 2.513a (cf Old Robin of Portingale, no 80).

Relations with Eustace Legend. Gerould G H, Forerunners, Congeners, and Derivatives of the Eustace Legend, PMLA 19.365; The Hermit and the Saint, PMLA 20.529, 543.

Jordan L, Die Eustachiuslegende, Chr Wilhelmsleben, Boeve de Hanstone und ihre orientalischen Verwandten, Arch 121.364.

Garbe R, Contributions of Buddhism to Christianity, The Monist 21.538 (trans from Deutsche Rundschau, 1910–11).

Günter H, Buddha in der abendländischen Legende, Leipzig 1922, pp 8–19, 126 (Eustachius).

Krappe A H, La leggenda di S Eustachi, Nuovi studi medievali, 3.233, 238, 254; An Oriental Theme in Sir Ysumbras, EStn 67.175 (Armenian parallel) (crit D Everett, YWES 13.96); Florent et Octavien, Rom 65.364,

367 (Isumbras only version with three children).

Murray J, The Eustace Legend in Medieval England, MHRA 1.35.

Schlauch M, Historical Precursors of Chaucer's Constance, PQ 29.405.

Relations with Chaucer. Loomis L H, Sir Thopas, in Bryan-Dempster, pp 488, 502, 513.

Atkins J W H, English Literary Criticism: The Medieval Phase, Cambridge 1943, p 153.

Relations with Other Romances, Typical Phrases. Halliwell [-Phillipps], Thornton Romances, p xviii (Robert of Sicily, Arabian Nights).

Sarrazin, Octavian, AEB 3.xliv (Octavian influenced Isumbras).

Ward, 1.759 (Guillaume d'Angleterre).

Adam E, Sir Torrent of Portyngale, EETSES 51.xxiv (parallels).

Ogden P, A Comparative Study of Guillaume d'Angleterre, Baltimore 1900, pp 8, 9, 14.

Trounce, MÆ 3.36; Athelston, EETS 224, passim (parallels to Athelston, Beves).

Schlauch M, Romance in Iceland, N Y and London 1934, p 63.

Steinbach P, Über den Einfluss des Crestien de Troies auf die ae Literatur, Leipzig 1885, p 41.

Owst G R, Literature and Pulpit in Medieval England, Cambridge 1933, pp 13, 15.

Thomas P G, English Literature before Chaucer, London 1924, p 113.

Atkins J W H, English Literary Criticism: The Medieval Phase, Cambridge 1943, p 153.

Schlauch M, English Medieval Literature and Its Social Foundations, Warsaw 1956, p 190.

Ward, 1.180, 760; Brandl, § 79; Schofield, p 313; CHEL, 1.351 (by J W H Atkins); Körting, § 95anm; Baugh LHE, p 193; Kane, pp 13, 15.

Hibbard Med Rom, pp 3, 10, new edn, 1960, p 349; CBEL, 1.156; Renwick-Orton, p 379.

[79] SIR EGLAMOUR OF ARTOIS.

MSS. 1, Bodl 21835 (Douce 261), f 26ª, fragm, transcript of printing (1564); 2, Camb Univ Ff. 2.38 (More 690), ff 71ª–79ª (1475–1500); 3, BM Cotton Calig A.2 (olim Cotton Vesp D.8), ff 5ᵇ–13ª (1450–1500); 4, BM Egerton 2862 (olim Trentham-Sutherland MS), f 148ª–148ᵇ, single leaf (ca 1400); 5, BM Addit 27879 (Percy Folio), pp 296–313 (ca 1650); 6, Lincoln Cath 91 (olim A.5.2, olim A.1.17) (Thornton), ff 138ᵇ–146ᵇ (ca 1440); 7, Harvard Univ, Percy Folio MS Eng 748, vol 4, ff 47ª–63ᵇ, transcript (ca 1767) of no 3 above. PRINTS: 8, Camb Univ one leaf, 59 lines, [W de Worde] (ca 1500) (STC,

no 7541); 9, Nat Libr Scotland, W Chepman and A Myllar, Edinb 1508 (?), pp 53–88, imp (STC, no 7542); 10, Camb Univ, three fragments, R Bankes [or J Rastell (?)], London 1523–28; 11, Bodl, S Selden 45(5), imp, fragm, Wm Copland, n d [1548–69 (?)] (STC, no 7543); 12, BM, Garrick Collection, 20 leaves, J Walley, London [1570 (?)] (STC, no 7544); 13, Huntington Libr, Sir Eglamour, HN Libr Bull Suppl to STC, Cambridge Mass 1933, p 44, no 7544.

Brown-Robbins, no 1725; MED, p 39.

Halliwell [-Phillips], Thornton Romances, Camden Soc 30, London 1844, pp xxii, xxxvi (MS Camb Univ Ff. 2.38).

Ward, 1.766, 820 (MS Cotton Calig A.2).

Madan F, ed, The Day-Book of John Dorne, Oxford Hist Soc, Collectanea 1s, 1885, no 152.

Kölbing E, Vier Romanzen-Handschriften, EStn 7.191.

Schleich, see under *Editions*, pp 91, 101, 105, 115.

Aldis H G, Note on a Pseudo Chepman and Myllar Fragment, Publns Edinb Bibl Soc 9.86.

Duff E G, Fifteenth Century English Books, London 1917, p 37, no 135.

Barnicle M E, The Seege or Batayle of Troye, EETS 172, p xv (MS Egerton 2862).

Loomis L H, Sir Thopas, Bryan-Dempster, p 488n3.

Ringler W, A Bibliography and First-line Index of English Verse Printed through 1500; A Supplement to Brown-Robbins Index, [PBSA 49.166.

Editions. Laing D, The Knightly Tale of Gologros and Gawane, Edinb 1827, no 9 (Chepman and Myllar print, with missing leaves supplied from Walley print).

Halliwell [-Phillipps] J O, Thornton Romances, Camden Soc 30, London 1844, p 121 (MS Camb Univ Ff. 2.38), p 273 (extracts from Copland printing, collation with MS Thornton, Lincoln Cath; MS Douce 261, MS Cotton Calig A.2, BM).

PFMS, 2.338.

Kölbing E, Vier Romanzen-Handschriften, EStn 7.193 (MS Egerton 2862).

Hall J, Bruchstücke eines alten Druckes des Eglamour of Artois, Arch 95.308 (Bankes fragments).

Schleich G, Sir Eglamour: Eine englische romanze des 14 Jahrhunderts auf Grund der gesamten Überlieferung, Palaes 53 (critical text, MS Thornton, with variants from other texts) (crit F Holthausen, AnglB 17.291;

P Doin, RCHL 62.153; MW in LZ 58.737; M Konrath, Arch 118.441; E Björkman, EStn 39.433; R Dyboski, ALb 17.399; rptd A S Cook, Sir Eglamour, see below).

Cook A S, Sir Eglamour, N Y 1911 (with modernized punctuation).

Stevenson G S, Pieces from the Makulloch and the Gray MSS, together with the Chepman and Myllar Prints, STS 65.117.

Beattie W, The Chepman and Myllar prints; Nine Tracts from the First Scottish Press, Edinb 1508, Followed by Two Other Tracts in the Same Volume in the Nat Libr of Scotland, Edinb 1950 [Hartwith facsimile], pp xi, 53, no 3 (crit TLS May 26, 1950, p 332; A F Johnson, Libr 5s, 5.153; S Reid, Spec 26.448; A Macdonald, RES 2.161; A Brown, MLR 46.80).

Whitrow M, Index to Theses Accepted for Higher Degrees in the Universities of Great Britain and Ireland 1957–58, vol 8, London 1960, p 8, no 141 (E F Richardson, Oxford St Hugh's, an edition of Sir Eglamour of Artois).

Abstract. Ellis Spec, p 527 (after Walley printing).

Language, Dialect. Zupitza J, The Romance of Guy of Warwick, the Second or 15th-Century Version, EETSES 25, 26, p 406 and passim.

Adam E, Torrent of Portyngale, EETSES 51.xxvii (Guillame d'Angleterre), xxxi.

Zielke A, Untersuchungen zu Sir Eglamour of Artois, Kiel 1889, pp 6, 48.

McKnight G H, King Horn, EETS 14.140 and passim.

Rickert E, Emare, EETSES 99.xlvii.

Barnicle, Seege or Batayle of Troye, EETS 172.xxiv.

Trounce A McI, The English Tail-Rhyme Romances, MÆ 1.87, 168; 2.34, 189; 3.30, and passim; Chaucer's Imperative with as, MÆ 2.68.

Dunlap A R, Vocabulary of ME Romances in Tail-Rime, Delaware Notes 14s, passim.

Date. Zielke, Untersuchungen zu Sir Eglamour, pp 48, 60.

Versification. Curtius F J, An Investigation of the Rimes and Phonology of the Middle-Scotch Romance Clariodus, Angl 16.413, 449.

Luick K, Zur me Verslehr, Angl 38.290.

Trounce, see above under *Language.*

Sources. Zielke, Untersuchungen zu Sir Eglamour, p 60 (urges French source; contra, Hibbard Med Rom, p 277).

Schleich G, Ueber die Beziehungen von Eglamour und Torrent, Arch 92.343 (crit E Kölbing, Krit Jahresber 4.2.430).

Siefken O, Das geduldige Weib in der engl

Literatur bis auf Shakspeare, Rathenow 1903, p 52.

Relations with Folktales. Thompson Mot Ind, D 1081 (magic sword); D 1344.1 (magic ring renders invulnerable); H 91.1 (recognition through gold found in eagle's nest); H 111 (identification by garment); H 335, H 335.0.1 (bride helps suitor); H 335.3 (task to kill ferocious animal; H 335.3.5, H 336 (suitors assigned quests); H 1154.2 (task: capturing deer); H 1161 (task: killing beast); N 730 (accidental reunion of families); N 731.1 (shield with emblem of rescuer); N 731.2 (father-son combat); N 836.1 (king adopts hero); R 13.0.1 (faithful servant); R 13.0.1 (children carried off by animal); S 141, S 431.1 (exposure in boat); T 412 (mother-son incest).

Cross Mot Ind, D 1344; H 336; N 731.2; R 13.0.1; S 141; T 412.

Potter M A, Sohrab and Rustum, London 1902, p 52.

Siefken O, Das geduldige Weib, Rathenau 1904, pp 44, 52.

Pschmadt C, Die Sage von der verfolgten Hinde, Greifswald 1911, p 68.

Rank O, Das Inzest-Motiv in Dichtung und Sage, Leipzig und Wien, 2nd edn, 1926, pp 171, 315.

Schlauch M, Chaucer's Constance and Accused Queens, N Y 1927, p 117.

Luthi M, Das europäische Volksmärchen Form und Wesen, Bern 1947, p 84 (wish for child is central motif in folktales).

Dunn C W, The Foundling and the Werwolf, A Literary-Historical Study of Guillaume de Palerne, Univ of Toronto Dept of Engl Studies and Texts 8, Toronto Canada 1960, p 88.

Relations with Eustace Legend. Gerould G H, Forerunners, Congeners, and Derivatives of the Eustace Legend, PMLA 19.439.

Murray J, Eustace Legend in Medieval England, MHRA 1.35.

Relations with the Ballad. Courage Crowned with Conquest, Sir Eglamore Fought with a Dragon, London 1672.

PFMS, p 74.

Furnivall F J, ed, Captain Cox, His Ballads and Books, Ballad Soc 7, London 1871, pp xii, xxviii.

Roxb Ballads, 9 vols, Hertford 1874–99, vol 2, ed W Chappell, London 1874, p 55.

Ebsworth J W, The Bagford Ballads, Ballad Soc, Hertford 1878, in list p lxx, no 191.

Child F J, English and Scottish Popular Ballads, 5 vols, Boston 1882–1898, 1.208, 2.500 (Ballad of Sir Lionel, no 18); 2.511 (Ballad of Sir Cawline, no 61); 2.451; 4.196 (Ballad of Sir Eglamore).

Brunner K, Romanzen und Volksballaden, Palaes 148.78 Anglica 2 (Sir Lionel, Torrent, Degrevant, Eger and Grime).

Caldwell J R, Eger and Grime, HSCL, Cambridge Mass 1933, 9.60.

Chambers OHEL, 2.166 (modern version of Sir Lionel).

Leach M E, The Ballad Book, N Y 1955, pp 100 (Sir Lionel, no 18), 185 (Sir Aldingar, no 59) (compares Eger and Grime).

Relations with Chaucer. Kölbing E, Zu Chaucer's Sir Thopas, EStn 11.495.

Hammond, p 288.

Young K, Origin and Development of Troilus, Chaucer Soc 2s, 1908, p 46.

Loomis L H, Sir Thopas, Bryan-Dempster, pp 488, 497, 499, 533, 543, 545, 547, 548.

Relations with Other Romances. Halliwell [-Phillipps], Thornton Romances, p xxii (Eglamour influenced Torrent).

Zielke O, Sir Orfeo: Stil und Überlieferung des Gedichtes, Breslau 1879 (rptd with text 1880), pp 5 and passim (similar phrasing); Untersuchungen zu Sir Eglamour of Artois, Kiel 1889, p 60.

A am E, Torrent of Portyngale, EETSES 51.xxiv, xxx (incest motif from the legend of Pope Gregory or Sir Degaré).

Schleich G, Ueber die Beziehungen von Eglamour und Torrent, Arch 92.343.

Brandl, 2.708 (urges common source with Torrent; contra Schleich, Arch 92.343).

Ogden P, A Comparative Study of Guillaume d'Angleterre, Baltimore 1900, pp 10, 14, 16.

McKnight, King Horn, EETS 14.140, notes to lines 315, 319, 320, and passim.

Rickert E, Emare, EETSES 99.xlvii.

Caldwell, HSCL 9.60.

McKeehan I P, The Book of the Nativity of St Cuthbert, PMLA 48.989 (casting adrift).

Meyerstein E H W, TLS 1933, p 248 (Coleridge's possible source for the name Christabel).

Trounce, MÆ 3.32 (Octavian influenced Eglamour).

Chambers OHEL, 2.65.

Casson L F, The Romance of Sir Degrevant, EETS 221.lxiv.

Loomis R S, Arthurian Tradition and Chrétien de Troyes, N Y 1949, p 124 and n 23.

Kane, p 22 (parallels to Emare).

Smithers G V, Kyng Alisaunder, EETS 237.87.

Isaacs N D, Constance in Fourteenth-Century England, NM 59.260.

Baskerville C R, Some Evidence for Early

Romantic Plays in England, MP 14.37, 229; An Elizabethan Eglamour Play, MP 14.759.

Thomas P G, English Literature before Chaucer, London 1924, p 113.

Atkins J W H, English Literary Criticism: The Medieval Phase, Cambridge 1943, p 153.

Everett D, Characterization in the English Medieval Romances, E&S 15.98, rptd Essays on ME Literature, ed P Kean, Oxford 1955, p 21.

Schlauch M, English Medieval Literature and Its Social Foundations, Warsaw 1956, p 190.

Ward, 1.766, 820; Brandl, § 79; Schofield, p 313; CHEL, 1.352; Körting, § 113; Bennett OHEL, 2.214; Baugh LHE, pp 193, 195; Kane, pp 14, 22.

Hibbard Med Rom, pp 274, 278, new edn, 1960, p 348; Renwick-Orton, p 379; CBEL, 1.157(k).

[80] SIR TORRENT OF PORTYNGALE.

MSS. 1, Chetham 8009 (Chetham Libr, Manchester), ff 76^a–119^b (late 15 cent). PRINTS: 2, Bodl [Douce fragm e.20(1)] [W de Worde], one leaf, imp (1509?) (STC, no 13075 note); 3, Bodl [Douce fragm e.20(2)] [R Pynson], 2 leaves, imp (1500–15?) (STC, no 24133).

Brown-Robbins, no 983; MED, p 79.

Halliwell [-Phillipps] J O, Account of the European MSS in the Chetham Library at Manchester, Manchester 1842, pp 16, 113.

Kölbing E, Vier Romanzen-Handschriften, EStn 7.195, 344.

Bennett H S, English Books and Readers, N Y and London 1952, p 268 (Douce fragm: W de Worde; STC, no 13075 note).

Editions. Halliwell [-Phillipps] J O, Torrent of Portugal, London 1842 (MS Chetham 8009), Appendix p 113 (Douce fragm; STC, no 24133) (crit E Kölbing, Collationen V, EStn 7.344 (MS Chetham 8009), 347 (Douce fragm; STC, no 24133).

Adam E, Sir Torrent of Portyngale, EETSES 51 (MS Chetham 8009); p 93 (Douce fragm; STC, no 24133); (introd identical with Breslau diss 1887) (crit R [P] W[ülker], Angl 11.542; M Kaluza, EStn 12.432; E Koeppel, LfGRP 11.17; F Zupitza, EStn 15.1; E Kölbing, Krit Jahresber 4.2.430).

Textual Matters. Kölbing E, Kleine Beiträge zur Erklärung me Dichter, EStn 13.136; cf F Zupitza, EStn 13.379, 382.

Holthausen F, Zu alt- und me Dichtungen, Angl 17.401; Zu me Romanzen, Torrent of Portyngale, Angl 42.429.

Language, Dialect. Adam, edn, pp vi, x (western borders of East Midland).

Trounce A McI, The English Tail-Rhyme Romances, MÆ 1.87, 168; 2.34, 189; 3.30 and passim (Norfolk).

Renwick-Orton, p 379 (East Midlands).

Dunlap A R, The Vocabulary of the ME Romances in Tail-Rhyme Stanza, Delaware Notes 14s, pp 33, 34n90, 36 (West Midland).

Versification. Curtius F J, An Investigation of the Rimes and Phonology of the Middle-Scotch Romance Clariodus, Angl 16.450.

Sources and Analogues. Halliwell [-Phillipps], Thornton Romances, Camden Soc 30, London 1844, p xxii.

Steinbach P, Über den Einfluss des Chrestiens de Troies auf die altenglische Literatur, Leipzig 1885, p 41.

Brandl, 2.708.

Schleich G, Über die Beziehungen von Eglamour und Torrent, Arch 92.343, 364.

Hibbard Med Rom, pp 280, 132n11.

Trounce, MÆ 3.34 (relation to Eglamour, Horn Child).

Relations with Folktales. Thompson Mot Ind, A 515; A 531; B 11.11; cf B 575, B 847; F 531.1.1.1 (one-eyed giant); G 511.1; H 94; H 126 (identification by coat of arms); H 310, H 335, H 335.0.1 (bride helps suitor); H 335.3.1 (killing dragon); H 336, H 1211 (suitor assigned severe tests); cf H 1236.2 (quest over path guarded by dangerous animal); H 1238 (quest accomplished with aid of wife); H 1561.2.1; N 731.2 (father-son combat); N 733; N 312, R 13.0.1 (children carried off by animals); N 836.1 (king adopts hero); R 111.1.4 (rescue of princess from giant); S 141, S 322.1, S 431.1, S 451 (cast-off wife and children exposed in boat, at last reunited with husband); T 31.1 (hero in service of lady's father); T 481.1 (birth of child).

Cross Mot Ind, A 515; A 531; B 11.11; H 310, H 336, H 1211; N 731.2; R 13.0.1; R 111.1.4; S 322.1; S 350; S 141; T 581.1.

Siefken O, Das geduldige Weib, Rathenow 1903, p 56.

Schlauch M, Chaucer's Constance and Accused Queens, N Y 1927, p 117; English Medieval Literature and Its Social Foundations, Warsaw 1956, p 190.

Isaacs N D, Constance in Fourteenth-Century England, NM 59.260.

Weland the Smith. Halliwell [-Phillipps], edn, p vii.

Depping G B and F Michel, Wayland Smith, A Dissertation on a Tradition of the Middle Ages, London 1847.

Zupitza F, Ein Zeugnis für die Wieland-sage, ZfDA 19.129.

Schofield W H, The Lays of Graelent and Lanval, PMLA 15.172 (on Wayland).

Maurus P, Die Wielandsage in der Literatur, Munchener Beiträge z rom u engl Philologie, 25.1; Die Wielandsage, Weitere neuzeitliche Bearbeitungen, Munich 1910.

Wilson R M, Early Middle English Literature, London 1939, p 198; 2nd edn 1951.

Relations with Eustace Legend. Gerould G H, Forerunners, Congeners, and Derivatives of the Eustace Legend, PMLA 19.439, 441.

Krappe A H, La leggenda di S Eustachio, Nuovi studi medievali, 3.236, 245.

Murray J, Eustace Legend in Medieval England, MHRA 1.35.

Relations with the Ballad. Child F J, The English and Scottish Popular Ballads, 5 vols, Boston 1882–1898, 2.510, 5.297 (parallels to King Estmere, no 60); 3.510n (parallels to Ipomydon).

Smith W, Elements of Comedy in English and Scottish Ballads, Vassar Medieval Studies, New Haven 1923, p 85n5 (flytings of warriors before battle).

Brunner K, Romanzen und Volksballaden, Palaes 148.78 (Anglica 2) (relation to Sir Lionel, Eglamour, Eger and Grime).

Christophersen P, The Ballad of Sir Aldingar, Oxford 1952, p 51n3.

Relations with Chaucer. Kölbing E, Zu Chaucer's Sir Thopas, EStn 11.495.

Hammond, p 288.

Loomis L H, Sir Thopas, in Bryan-Dempster, pp 503, 513, 514, 540, 547.

Atkins J W H, English Literary Criticism: The Medieval Phase, Cambridge and N Y 1943, p 153.

Other Relations, Similar Phrases. Halliwell [-Phillipps], Thornton Romances, p xxii (Torrent an amplification of Eglamour).

Adam, edn, p xxiv (Isumbras), p xxv (Octavian), pp xxvi, xxx (Eglamour).

Mead W E, The Squyr of Lowe Degre, Boston etc 1904, pp xxvii, xxix.

Schleich, see above under *Sources and Analogues.*

Rickert E, Emare, EETSES 99.xlvii.

Reinhard J R, The OF Romance of Amadas et Ydoine, An Historical Study, Durham N C 1927, p 42.

Dickson A, Valentine and Orson, N Y 1929, pp 107, 132n106, 143.

Trounce, MÆ 3.34 (Eglamour, Horn Childe).

McKeehan I P, The Book of the Nativity of St Cuthbert, PMLA 48.989 (casting adrift).

Casson L F, Degrevant, EETS 221.lxiii.

Trounce, MÆ 1.102 (Relation to Germanic heroic style).

Thomas P G, English Literature before Chaucer, London 1924, p 113.

Everett D, A Characterization of English Medieval Romances, E&S 15.98; rptd Essays on ME Literature, ed P Kean, Oxford 1955, p 21.

Atkins J W H, English Literary Criticism: The Medieval Phase, Cambridge 1943, p 153.

Schlauch M, English Medieval Literature and Its Social Foundations, Warsaw 1956, p 190.

Ten Brink, 1.317; Brandl, § 125; Schofield, p 313; CHEL, 1.352; Körting, § 113; Hibbard Med Rom, p 279; Bennett OHEL, 2.164, 316; Baugh LHE, p 193; Kane, pp 14, 54.

Tucker-Benham, p 258; Hibbard Med Rom, p 281, new edn, 1960, p 350; CBEL, 1.159; Bennett OHEL, 2.316; Renwick-Orton, p 379.

[81] OCTAVIAN.

MSS. Northern Versions: 1, Camb Univ Ff. 2.38 (More 690), ff 90^a–101^b (1475–1500); 2, Lincoln Cath 91 (olim A.5.2, olim A.1.17) (Thornton), ff 98^b–117, leaf wanting between ff 102, 103 (ca 1440). Southern Versions: 3, BM Cotton Calig A.2 (olim Cotton Vesp D.8) ff 22^b–33 (1450–1500); 4, Harvard Univ, Percy Folio MS Eng 748, vol 5, ff 1–34, transcript of Cotton Calig A.2 (ca 1767). PRINT: 5, Huntington Libr 14615, W de Worde, 12 leaves (1504–06) (STC, no 18779).

Brown-Robbins, no 1774 (Southern), no 1918 (Northern); MED, p 63.

Halliwell [-Phillipps] J O, Thornton Romances, Camden Soc 30, London 1844, p xxv (Thornton MS), xlii (Camb Univ Ff. 2.38).

Hazlitt W C, Hand-book of the Popular, Poetical, and Dramatic Literature of Great Britain, London 1867, p 427.

Hodnett E, English Woodcuts 1480–1535, Illustrated Monographs, no 22, Bibliographical Soc, London, Oxford 1935, no 1121.

Mead H R, A New Title from De Worde's Press, Libr 5s 9.45.

Editions. Weber MR, 3.157 (MS Cotton Calig A.2).

Halliwell [-Phillipps] J O, The Romance of the Emperor Octavian, London 1848, Percy Soc 14 (Camb Univ Ff. 2.38, with variants from MS Thornton).

Sarrazin G, Octavian: Zwei me Bearbeitungen der Sage, AEB 3 (ME Manuscripts and Bodl Hatton 100) (crit E Hausknecht, LfGRP 7.137; K Breul, EStn 9.456).

Reiss E A, The Northern ME Octavian, An Edition and Commentary [Harvard], An

Index to American Doctoral Dissertations, 1959–1960, University Microfilms, Ann Arbor Mich 1960, p 115.

Selections. Kaluza M, Libeaus Desconus, Die me Romanze vom schönem Unbekannten nach sechs Hss critisch heraug, AEB 5, Leipzig 1890, p clxiii (crit E Freymond, Krit Jahresber 1.422; E Kölbing, ibid, 1.648).

Mead, Libr 5s 9.46, 47 (facsimiles, title page, first page, HN Lib [STC, no 1877]).

Language, Dialect, Verse. Weber MR, 1.lviii.

Kölbing E, Amis and Amiloun, AEB 2.xxviii.

Kaluza, AEB 5.lxxxii; Englische Metrik, Berlin 1909, trans A C Dunstan, London 1911, §§ 150, 180.

Curtius F J, An Investigation of the Rimes and Phonology of the Middle-Scotch Romance Clariodus, Angl 16.450.

Skeat W W, The Use of d for th in ME, N&Q 9s 10.321.

Mackenzie B A, A Special Dialectal Development of OE $\bar{e}a$ in ME, EStn 61.386 (OE $\bar{e}a$ rhymes as a tense vowel); The Early London Dialect, Oxford 1928, § 344 (crit H M Flasdieck, AnglB, 42.46; cf G V Smithers, Kyng Alisaunder, EETS 237.41).

Fischer E, Der Lautbestand des südme Octavian vergl mit seinen Entsprechungen im Lybeaus Desconus und im Launfal, AF 63.184, 195 (crit Arch 154.145; R Willard, MLN 43.567; D Everett, YWES 8.127; E von Erhardt-Siebold, JEGP 28.547; F Wild, LfGRP 50.183; L von Hibler, EStn 64.71; M S Serjeantson, RES 5.455; W van der Gaff, ESts 11.27; E Ekwall, AnglB 41.14); Ea in Südmostme und die Heimat des Südl 'O', EStn 64.1 (places Octavian in north Essex) (crit D Everett, YWES, 10.151).

Everett D, A Note on Ypotis, RES 6.446.

Trounce A McI, The English Tail-Rhyme Romances, MÆ 1.104, 108; 2.53, 68; 3.36, 40; Chaucers Imperative with as, MÆ 2.68; Athelston, A ME Romance, EETS 224.52, 57 (places Octavian in East Anglia).

Serjeantson M S, A History of Foreign Words in English, N Y 1936, p 64 (Scandinavian fleyne, a little ship).

Dunlap A R, The Vocabulary of the ME Romances in Tail-Rhyme Stanza, Delaware Notes 14s, p 1 and passim.

Gordon E V, ed, Pearl, Oxford 1953, p 89n3.

Smithers, EETS 237, 54n1, 65.

Date. Kaluza, Libeaus Desconus, pp ix, clxiii.

Fischer, AF 63.4, 6.

Trounce, Athelston, EETS 224.55 (Octavian composed ca 1340).

Scribe. Skeat W W, The Use of d for th in ME, N&Q 9s 10.321.

Author. Sarrazin, AEB 3.xxv, xxix (S version, Thomas Chestre), xliv (N version, cf Isumbras, Lybeaus Desconus).

Kaluza M, Thomas Chestre, Verfasser des Launfal, Libeaus Desconus und Octovian, EStn 18.165, 185.

DNB, see under Chestre, Thomas.

Billings, p 142.

Bennett H S, The Author and His Public, E&S 23.8.

Sources and Analogues. Conybeare J J, The Romance of Octavian, Emperor of Rome, Abridged from a MS in the Bodleian Libr, Oxford 1809 (OF, Eng transl, notes); rptd with additional notes by E M Goldsmid, Edinb 1882, Aungervyle Soc Reprints, 1s nos 8, 9.

Simrock K, Geschichte von Kaiser Octavianus, Leipzig 1836 (Die deutschen Volksbücher 2.251) (German version).

Rajna P, Storie di Fioravante, Bologna 1872, p 444 (bibl) (Italian version).

Vollmöller K, Octavian, Altfrz Roman nach der Oxforder Hs Bodl Hatton 100 zum ersten Mal herausgegeben, AEB 3 (crit A Mussafia, ZfRP 6.628; G P, Rom 11.609, 34.167; E Stengel, LfGRP 4.268); cf HLF, 26.303.

Streve P, Die Octaviansage, Halle 1884, p 50 (relation to Eustace legend and French version).

Eule R, Untersuchungen über die nordengl Version des Octavian, Halle 1889 (crit of Vollmöller).

Brockstedt G, Floovent-Studien, Kiel 1904.

Settegast F, Floovent und Julian nebst einem Anhang über die Oktaviansage, Halle 1906, Beihefte z ZfRP 9.52; cf Hibbard Med Rom, p 271.

Schofield, p 313.

Kittredge G L, A Study of Gawain and the Green Knight, Cambridge Mass 1916, p 128.

Franken G, Wunder und Taten der Heiligen, Bucher des Mittelalters, ed F Vonderlayen, Munchen 1925, pp 168, 182.

Krzyżanowski J, ed, Historja o cesarzu Otonie, 1569, Kraków 1928 (Slavic version).

Kessler L, Der Prosaroman vom Kaiser Oktavian, Limburg a d L 1930; rptd Frankfurt 1932, p 1490 (German version).

Whiting B J, Proverbs in Certain ME Romances in Relation to their French Sources, HSNPL 15.103 (crit D Everett, YWES 15.106).

Bateson F H, Le Chanson de Floovant, Paris 1938 (crit F Lecoy, Rom 65.245).

Krappe A H, Florent et Octavien, Rom 65.359, 364, 371.

Andolf S, Floovant, Chanson de geste du 12e siècle, Uppsala 1941 (crit E Gamillscheg, ZfFSL 65.249).

Baird H L Jr, [Octavien] Un análisis lingüístico y filológico del Emperedor Otas de Roma [text del MS del Escorial], Chicago 1955 (Spanish version).

Relations with Folktales. Thompson Mot Ind, B 443 (helpful lion); B 520; B 575 (animal as constant attendant of man); H 335; K 2101.1 (cruel mother-in-law); K 2110.1 (calumniated wife); K 2112, K 2215 (woman slandered as adulteress); N 215 (robbing animal); N 251 (man pursued by misfortune); R 13.0.1 (children carried off by animals); cf R 131.13 (palmer rescues abandoned child); S 51 (cruel mother-in-law); S 143 (abandonment in forest); S 410 (persecuted wife); S 451 (outcast wife at last united with husband and children); T 587.1 (birth of twins an indication of unfaithfulness). V 331.1 (conversion to Christianity through miracle).

Cross Mot Ind, B 575, B 576.1; K 2110.1; K 2112; K 2218.1; R 13.0.1; S 51; V 331.1.

Potter M A, Sohrab and Rustum, London 1902, p 87.

Brown A C L, Iwain, a Study in the Origins of Arthurian Romance, HSNPL 8.132, Cambridge Mass 1903, (faithful lion borrowed from saint's legend) (crit W Nitze, MLN 19.82); The Knight of the Lion, PMLA 20.673.

Siefken O, Das geduldige Weib, Rathenow 1903, p 48.

Greenlaw E A, The Vows of Baldwin: A Study in Medieval Fiction, PMLA 21.602, 607, 616.

Hibbard Med Rom, pp 29, 35, 271n3.

Schlauch M, Chaucer's Constance and Accused Queens, pp 86, 93, 99n11, 107.

Dickson A, Valentine and Orson, N Y 1929, p 107.

Krappe A H, Florent et Octavian, Rom 65.359, 360n1.

Relations with Eustace Legend. Gerould G H, Forerunners, Congeners, and Derivatives of the Eustace Legend, PMLA 19.436.

Jordan L, Die Eustachiuslegende, Chr Wilhelmsleben, Boeve de Hanstone und ihre orientalischen Verwandten, Arch 121.345.

Relations with the Ballad. Child F C, English and Scottish Popular Ballads, 5 vols, Boston 1882–1898, 2.33n; 2.41, 510; 3.508 (cf Ballad of Sir Aldingar, no 59).

Christophersen P, Ballad of Sir Aldingar, Oxford 1952, pp 39, 114, 147 (parallels to Eustace legend).

Relations with Chaucer. Hammond, p 288.

Loomis L H, Sir Thopas, in Bryan-Dempster, pp 502, 515, 547, 553.

Loomis L H, Chaucer and the Breton Lays of the Auchinleck MS, SP 38.14.

See under LIBEAUS DESCONUS [38], SIR LAUNFAL [88].

Other Relations, Similar Phrases. Ward, 1.759 (Guillaume d'Angleterre).

Kölbing E, Amis and Amiloun, AEB 2.xxviii.

Sarrazin, edn, pp xxiii, xxviii (S) (Launfal, Lybeaus Desconus); p xl (N) (Amis and Amiloun).

Adam E, Torrent of Portyngale, EETSES 51.xxi, xxiv, xxv (Torrent, Isumbras).

Kaluza, Libeaus Desconus, AEB 5.clviii, clix, clxiii (Octavian).

Rickert E, The Romance of Emare, EETSES 99.xlvii (Octavian influenced Emare).

Schofield, p 313.

Hibbard Med Rom, p 269 (Emare, Earl of Toulous, Chevalier Assigne), p 295 (Lay le Freine), p 39n8.

Fischer E, Der Lautbestand des Südme Octavian vergl mit sein Entsprechungen im Lybeaus Desconus und im Launfal, AF 63.184, and passim.

Dickson A, Valentine and Orson, N Y 1929, p 48n58.

Trounce, MÆ 1.96 (relation to Isumbras, Eglamour, Torrent, Amis and Amiloun, Amadace, Cleges); Athelston, EETS 224.45.

Schlauch M, Romance in Iceland, N Y 1934, p 154.

Krappe A H, Florent et Octavian, Rom 65.364 (relation to Isumbras), 367 (Beves), 371 (La Reine Sibille and the Eustache Legend).

Casson L F, The Romance of Sir Degrevant, EETS 221.lxiii.

Bossuat R, Florent et Octavian, Chanson de geste du 14e siècle, Rom 73.289.

Baskerville C R, Some Evidence for Early Romantic Plays in England, MP 14.230 (an old play ca 1443).

Whiting, HSNPL 15.103 (crit D Everett, YWES 15.106).

Magoun F P, The History of Football from the Beginnings to 1871, Kölner Anglistische Arbeiten 31.8.

Thomas P G, English Literature before Chaucer, London 1924, p 113.

Voretzsch K, Introduction to the Study of OF Literature, trans F M Du Mont, N Y 1931, p 394.

Schlauch M, English Medieval Literature and Its Social Foundations, Warsaw 1956, p 190.

Ward, 1.762; HLF, 26.303; Gröber, 2¹.798; Brandl, §§ 70, 79; Schofield, pp 184, 313;

Körting, § 113; Bennett OHEL, 2.106; Baugh LHE, p 193; Kane, p 29.

Gautier L, Bibliographie des chansons de geste, 2nd edn 1897, p 103; Hibbard Med Rom, pp 267, 272, new edn 1960, p 349; Tucker-Benham, p 253; Renwick-Orton, p 379; CBEL, 1.156(g); Holmes CBFL, nos 594, 594.1, 687.1, 716, 717; Bossuat MBLF, nos 368–70.

[82] SIR TRIAMOUR.

MSS. 1, Bodl (Rawlinson MS), fragm, 75 lines (MS now missing); 2, Camb Univ Ff.2.38 (More 690), ff 79ᵇ–90 (1475–1500); 3, BM Addit 27879 (Percy Folio), pp 210–232 (ca 1650); 4, Harvard Univ, Percy Folio MS Eng 748, vol 4, ff 65ᵃ–84ᵇ (transcript) (ca 1767). PRINTS: 5, Camb Univ [R Pynson], 2 leaves (ca 1503?) (STC, no 24301.5) (olim STC, no 24302); 6, Victoria Public Libr (Australia), [R Pynson], 1 leaf, Fenn fragm no 16 (1503?) (STC, no 24301.5); 7, Huntington Libr, [R Pynson], 3 leaves and 2 fragm, Huth fragm no 6 (1503?) (STC, no 24301.5) (olim STC, no 24303); 8, BM C21060, Garrick Collection, w (sic) Copland, (1561?) (STC, no 24303); 9, Bodl, S Selden d.45 (4), W (cap) Copland, A-F4 (1565?) (STC, no 24303.5).

Brown-Robbins, no 1177; MED, p 79.

Halliwell [-Phillipps] J O, Thornton Romances, Camden Soc 30, London 1844, pp xxxvi, xlii (Camb Univ Ff.2.38).

Kaluza M, Libeaus Desconus, AEB 5, Leipzig 1890, p x (Percy Folio).

Erdman-Schmidt, see below, under *Editions*, p l.

J O Halliwell and the Bodleian, Bodleian Libr Record 2.237.

Editions. Utterson E V, Select Pieces of Early English Popular Poetry, London 1816, 1.1; Select Pieces of Early Popular Poetry, London 1817, 1.1 (BM Copland).

Halliwell [-Phillipps] J O, Sir Tryamoure, Percy Soc 16, London 1846 (Camb Univ Ff.2.38), p 61 (Rawlinson MS), p 59 (variants from BM Copland, leaf 7ᵇ, somewhat normalized spellings).

PFMS, 2.78 (MS BM Addit 27879).

Bauszus H, Die me Romanze Sir Triamour, Königsberg 1902 (critical text, lines 1–144 from Camb Univ Ff.2.38, PFMS) (crit M Kaluza, Krit Jahresber 8.2.172).

Erdman-Schmidt A J, Syr Tryamowre, Utrecht 1937 (Camb Univ Ff.2.38) (crit S T R O d'Ardenne, ESts 20.217; G L Brook MÆ 8.70).

Record P D, An Index to Theses Accepted for

Higher Degrees in the Universities of Great Britain and Ireland (1950–51), vol 1, London 1953, p 17, no 370 (Allum J, Syr Tryamoure; A Literary and Linguistic Study and an Investigation of Textual Relations [together with parallel texts] [London, University College]).

Abstract. Ellis Spec, p 491 (BM Copland).

Language, Dialect. Zupitza J, The Romance of Guy of Warwick, the Second or 15th-Century Version, EETSES 25, 26, pp 345, 352, 382, 413, 423, and passim.

Kaluza M, Englische Metrik, Berlin 1909, trans A C Dunston, London 1911, § 178.

Trounce A McI, English Tail-Rhyme Romances, MÆ 2.190; Athelston, EETS 224.43, 58.

West V R, Der etymologische Ursprung neuenglischen Lautgruppe /sk/, AF 83.70.

Erdman-Schmidt, edn, pp 5, 23 (Scandinavian element), 25 (French element).

Dunlap A R, The Vocabulary of the ME Romance in Tail-Rhyme Stanza, Delaware Notes 14s, p 1 and passim.

Sources and Analogues. Paris G, Histoire poétique de Charlemagne, Paris 1865, rptd 1905, p 389 (Franco-Italian versions).

Hazlitt W C, Handbook to the Popular, Poetical, and Dramatic Literature of Great Britain, London 1867, p 616 (Summary of French and Italian versions).

Köhler R, Zu der altspan Erzählung von Karl und Sibille, JfRESL 12.286; rptd Kleinere Schriften, Berlin 1900, 2.273.

Gautier L, Les épopées françaises, Paris 1880, 3.684.

Bonilla y san Martin A, Libros de Caballerias, Madrid 1907, 1.503.

Baker A T, Fragments de la Chanson de la Reine Sibile, Rom 44.1.

Relations with Folktales. Thompson Mot Ind, B 301.2, B 575, D 699.2 (faithful animal at master's grave, avenges his murder); G 511.1 (battle with giants); H 331.2 (suitor contest: tournament); K 2112.2 (woman slandered as adulteress); K 2242 (treacherous steward); cf K 2277 (treacherous dwarf); L 224 (hero refuses reward); N 731.2 (father-son combat); S 143; S 162.1 (fighting on stumps of legs); S 451 (outcast wife united with husband).

Potter M A, Sohrab and Rustum, London 1902, p 90.

Siefken O, Das geduldige Weib, Rathenow 1903, p 62.

Greenlaw E A, The Vows of Baldwin: A Study in Medieval Fiction, PMLA 21.615, 620.

Schlauch M, Chaucer's Constance and Accused Queens, N Y 1927, pp 104n25, 105.

The Faithful Dog. Guessard F and L Larchey, Parise la Duchesse, Paris 1860; Guessard, Macaire, Paris 1866 (French and Italian versions of Queen Sebilla and the faithful dog).

Baugart F, Die Tiere in altfranzösische Epos, Marburg 1885, p 177.

Kreitz E, Die Tiere in den Hauptwerken der älteren schottischen Literatur, Bad Lauchstädt 1932, p 8 (Barbour's Bruce).

Viscardi J, Le chien de Montargis, étude de folklore juridique, Paris 1932.

Malone K, Rose and Cypress, PMLA 43.407, 437 (faithful dog, faithless steward).

Relations with the Ballad. Furnivall F J, ed, Captain Cox, His Ballads and Books, London 1871, Ballad Soc 7, pp xii, xxix.

Child F J, The English and Scottish Popular Ballads, 5 vols, Boston 1882–1898, 2.40, 59 (Sir Aldingar no 59), (source; giant fighting on his stumps); 5.176.

Nessler K, Geschichte der Ballade Chevy Chase, Berlin 1911, pp 88, 90, 93.

Brunner K, Romanzen und Volksballaden, Palaes 148.80 (Anglica 2) (cf Sir Aldingar).

Christophersen P, Ballad of Sir Aldingar, Oxford 1952, pp 39, 121.

Other Relations, Similar Phrases. Kittredge G L, Arthur and Gorlagon, HSNPL 8.254n1.

Bauszus, edn, p 42 (parallels to Beves of Hamtoun, Launfal, Libeaus Desconus, Octavian, Squyr of Lowe Degre, Ywain and Gawain).

Greenlaw E A, The Vows of Baldwin: A Study in Medieval Fiction, PMLA 21.615, 620.

Hibbard Med Rom, pp 12, 25n5, 29, 35, 285, 286n6 (parallels to Earl of Toulous, Emare, Florence of Rome, Octavian).

Dickson A, Valentine and Orson, N Y 1929, pp 72, 166.

Christophersen P, Ballad of Sir Aldingar, pp 39, 121 (parallels to Crescentia, Sibille, Florence).

Smithers G V, Kyng Alisaunder, EETS 237.69, 125, 152.

Loomis L H, Sir Thopas, Bryan-Dempster, p 544.

Brooks C, ed, The Correspondence of Thomas Percy and Richard Farmer, in The Percy Letters, ed D N Smith and C Brooks, Louisiana State Univ Press 1946, 2.xi, 7 (influence on Spenser).

Thomas P G, English Literature before Chaucer, London 1924, p 113.

Schlauch M, English Medieval Literature and Its Social Foundations, Warsaw 1956, p 190.

Gröber, 2¹.643, 811; Brandl, § 113; Schofield, p 313; Bennett OHEL, 2.164, 316; Baugh LHE, p 194; Craig HEL, p 82; Kane, p 31.

Gautier L, Bibliographie des chansons de geste, Paris 1897, p 143; Hibbard Med Rom, pp 283, 288, new edn, 1960, p 350; Tucker-Benham, p 256; CBEL, 1.159(q), 5.116(q); Renwick-Orton, p 380.

[83] THE KING OF TARS.

MSS. 1, Bodl 3938 (Vernon, Bodl Poet A.1), ff 304^b (col 2)–307^a (col 1) (ca 1390); 2, BM Addit 22283 (Simeon), ff 126^a (col 3)–128^b (col 1) (ca 1400); 3, Advocates 19.2.1 (Auchinleck), ff 7^a–13, imp (ca 1330).
Brown-Robbins, no 1108; MED, p 50.
Ritson AEMR, 3.222, 321.
Ward, 1.767 (Simeon MS close to Vernon MS).
Kölbing E, Vier Romanzen-Handschriften, EStn 7.177.
Bliss A J, Notes on the Auchinleck Manuscript, Spec 26.652 (crit G D Willcock, YWES 32.89); The Auchinleck Life of Adam and Eve, RES ns 7.406n1.
Loomis L H, The Auchinleck Manuscript and a Possible London Bookshop of 1330–1340, PMLA 57.595 (crit G D Willcock, YWES 23.85); Sir Thopas, in Bryan-Dempster, p 489n2.
Editions. Ritson AEMR, 2.156 (Vernon MS), 3.320n.
Krause F, Kleine Publicationen aus der Auchin-leck-Hs IX The King of Tars, EStn 11.1, 33 (Vernon and Auchinleck MSS with variants from Simeon) (crit F Holthausen, Angl 15.195; R J Geist, Notes on The King of Tars, JEGP 47.178).
Abstract, Selection. Warton T, The History of English Poetry, London 1840, 1.188 (MS Vernon).
Textual Matters. Holthausen F, The King of Tars, Angl 15.195.
Roberts W F J, Ellipsis of the Subject Pronoun in ME, LMS 1.107 (on Krause's insertion of the subject in line 679).
Geist R J, On the Genesis of the King of Tars, JEGP 42.266 (emends line 1217 Auchinleck MS); Notes on the King of Tars, JEGP 47.173.
Bliss A J, Notes on The King of Tars, N&Q ns 2 (1955) no 11, p 461 (emends lines 550–55, 1117–22 of Auchinleck MS) (crit B J Timmer, YWES 36.71, R G Thomas, YWES 36.97).
Language, Dialect. AEB, 2.xiv; Krause, edn, p 14.
Carr M B, Notes on an English Scribe's Methods, Univ of Wisconsin Studies in Language and Literature, Madison 1918, 2.153 (OE ā in Auchinleck MS).

Trounce A McI, The English Tail-Rhyme Romances, MÆ 1.94, 2.50 (places King of Tars in East Anglia, probably Norfolk); Athelston, EETS 224.50 (dialect of the Auchinleck manuscript is East Anglian).
Brunner K, The Seven Sages of Rome, EETS 191.xxv (Scribe A from London).
Zettl E, Anonymous Short Metrical Chronicle, EETS 196.xvi (Scribe Y from London).
Taylor G, Notes on Athelston, Leeds SE 4.47 (opposes Trounce's criteria for Norfolk dialect).
Dunlap A R, The Vocabulary of the ME Tail-Rhyme Romances, Delaware Notes 14s, p 33 and n 87 (dialect is East Midland).
Loomis L H, Chaucer and the Breton Lais of the Auchinleck MS, SP 38.15 (London origin).
Geist, JEGP 47.175 (London origin for the Auchinleck version of the King of Tars).
Bliss A J, Sir Orfeo, London 1954, p xvii (dialect of Auchinleck MS is Anglian).
Verse. Krause, edn, p 8; Trounce, MÆ 1.94, 2.50, and passim.
Date, Provenance. Loomis L H, PMLA 57.595; Sir Thopas, in Bryan-Dempster, p 489n2.
Bennett H S, Medieval English Manuscripts and Contemporary Taste, Edinb Bibl Soc Transactions, Edinb 1946, 2.382 (supports Loomis's theory of the provenance of the Auchinleck manuscript).
Leach M E, Amis and Amiloun, EETS 203, p xc n 1 (supports Loomis's date).
Sources and Analogues. Krause, edn, pp 24, 28 (German, Anglo-Latin chronicle); AEB, 4.xl; Geist, JEGP 42.260.
Holthausen F, The King of Tars, Angl 15.195.
Hibbard Med Rom, p 45 (additional Chronicle versions).
O'Sullivan M I, Firumbras and Otuel and Roland, EETS 198.lxvii (Otuel and Roland influenced King of Tars).
Hornstein L H, New Historical Sources for the King of Tars, PMLA 53.1360; Trivet's Constance and the King of Tars, MLN 55.354 (crit G D Willcock, YWES 21.73); New Analogues to the King of Tars, MLR 36.433 (crit G D Willcock, YWES 22.73); The Historical Background of the King of Tars, Spec 16.404.
Relations with Folktales. Thompson Mot Ind, D 57 (change in person's color); D 741.2 (disenchantment of monster child when baptized); D 1812.5.1.2 (bad dream an evil omen); T 11.1; T 104; T 550 (monstrous birth); T 551.1.1 (child born as formless lump of flesh); T 551.4.1 (child born beautiful on one side, hairy on other); V 81; V 123;

V 331.1; V 331.3; V 332; V 381 (image blamed for misfortune).
Cross Mot Ind, D 57; D 1812.5.1.2; T 550; T 551.1.1; T 551.4.1; V 331.1.
Hibbard Med Rom, p 48n6 (misbegotten child in Theseus of Cologne).
Hornstein L H, A Folklore Theme in the King of Tars, PQ 20.82 (crit G D Willcock, YWES 22.72).
Relations with the Ballad. Child F J, The English and Scottish Popular Ballads, 5 vols, Boston 1882-1898, 2.511b (cf Child Wyet, no 66).
Relations with Chaucer. Robinson F N, ed, The Complete Works of Chaucer, Cambridge, Mass 1933, p 846, 2nd edn, 1957, p 750, n to line 905, Sir Thopas (parallels to The King of Tars, Libeaus Desconus, Isumbras).
Schlauch M, The Man of Law's Tale, Bryan-Dempster, p 158.
Relations with Other Romances. Zielke O, Sir Orfeo, Breslau 1879, passim (similar phrases).
Lüdtke G, The Erl of Tolous and the Emperes of Almayn, Berlin 1881, p 290 (similar endings).
Krause, edn, p 12.
Kölbing E, Sir Beues de Hamtoun, EETSES 46.xlv; AEB 4.lx.
Holthausen, Angl 15.195.
Hibbard Med Rom, p 15 (parallels to Florence of Rome).
O'Sullivan M I, A Study of the Fillingham Text of Firumbras and Otuel and Roland, London 1927, p 67; EETS 198.lxvii.
Geist, JEGP 42.265, and notes 28, 29 (parallels to Otuel and Roland, Le Bone Florence); JEGP 47.175 (parallels to Roland and Vernagu).
Walpole R N, Charlemagne and Roland, A Study, Cambridge 1944, p 391.
Smyser, H M, Charlemagne and Roland and the Auchinleck MS, Spec 21.287 (Firumbras and Otuel and Roland influenced the King of Tars).
Loomis R S, Arthurian Tradition and Chrétien de Troyes, N Y 1949, pp 93, 199.
Bliss A J, Notes on the King of Tars, N&Q ns 2, no 11, 462 (parallels to Richard Coeur de Lyon and Kyng Alisaunder).
Everett D, A Characterization of the English Medieval Romances, E&S 15.98; rptd Essays on ME Literature, ed P Kean, Oxford 1955, p 11.
Schlauch M, English Medieval Literature and Its Social Foundations, Warsaw 1956, p 189.
Brunner K, ME Metrical Romances and Their Audience, Studies in Medieval Literature in Honor of A C Baugh, ed M Leach, Phila 1961, p 225.

Ward, 1.767; Ten Brink, 1.252; Brandl, § 38; Schofield, p 312; Körting, § 114anm; Baugh LHE, p 195; Kane, p 19.
Hibbard Med Rom, p 45, new edn, 1960, p 349; CBEL, 1.154(c), 5.116(c); Renwick-Orton, p 380.

[84] LE BONE FLORENCE OF ROME.

MS. Camb Univ Ff.2.38 (More 690), ff 239^b–254^a (1475-1500).
Brown-Robbins, no 334; MED, p 41.
Halliwell [-Phillipps] J O, Thornton Romances, Camden Soc 30, London 1844, pp xxxvi, xlv.
Editions. Ritson AEMR, 3.1.
Viëtor W, Le Bone Florence, Marburg 1893 (Text), W A Knobbe, Über die me Dichtung Le Bone Florence, Marburg 1899 (Introd) (crit F Holthausen, AnglB 10.129; A Wallensköld, DLz 1900.422; E Stengel, Krit Jahresber 6.2.72; W Heuser, EStn 29.123; M Weyrauch, Arch 110.446).
Summary. Edwardes M, A Summary of the Literatures of Modern Europe to 1400, London 1907, p 252 (French version).
Christophersen P, The Ballad of Sir Aldingar, Oxford 1952, p 39.
Textual. Kölbing E, Kleine Beiträge zur Erklärung und Textkritik englischer Dichter, EStn 3.103.
Holthausen F, Zu me Romanzen, 7: Le bone Florence of Rome, Angl 41.497.
Language, Dialect. Lüdtke G, The Erl of Tolous and the Emperes of Almayn, Berlin 1881, p 54.
Zupitza J, The Romance of Guy of Warwick, the Second or 15th-century Version, EETSES 25, 26, p 353.
Curtius F J, An Investigation of the Rimes and Phonology of the Middle-Scotch Romance Clariodus, Angl 16.449.
Trounce A McI, The English Tail-Rhyme Romances, MÆ 1.87, 168, 2.34, 189, 3.40, 43, and passim; Athelston, EETS 224.55.
Dunlap A R, The Vocabulary of the ME Romances in Tail-Rhyme Stanza, Delaware Notes 14s, p 1 and passim.
Bennett OHEL, 2.311 (N Midland).
Sources and Analogues. Mussafia Ad, Über eine italienesche metrische Darstellung der Crescentia Saga, Sitzungsberichte der phil-hist Classe der Kais Akad der Wissenschaften, Vienna 1865, 51.589, or 2.589.
Ward, 1.711 (MS Landsdowne 362, BM).
Suchier H, ed, Oeuvres poétiques de Philippe de Remi Sire de Beaumanoir, SATF 1884, 1885, 17, part 1, pp xxv, xxxvii, liv.

Wenzel R, Die Fassungen der Sage von Florence de Rome und ihr gegenseitiges Verhältnis, Marburg 1890 (French text, other versions) (crit E Freymond, LfGRP 13.266).

Furnivall F J, ed, Hoccleve, Minor Poems, EETSES 61.140 (Latin Gesta Romanorum).

Rickert E, The Romance of Emare, EETSES 99.xlvi.

Teubert S, Crescentia-Studien, Halle 1906, p 6.

Wallensköld A, Le conte de la Femme Chaste convoitée par son beau-frère, Étude de littérature comparée, Acta societatis scientiarum Fennicae, Helsingfors 1907, 34.81; Florence de Rome, Chanson d'Aventure du premier quart du 13ᵉ siècle, SATF 1907, 1909, 58, 64 (French and other texts, introd) (crit H Suchier, ZfRP 35.752); L'origine et l'évolution du conte de la Femme Chaste (Légende de Crescentia), NM, Helsingfors 1912, p 67 (story in part of Oriental origin).

Karl L, Florence de Rome et la Vie de deux saints de Hongrie, RLR 52.163.

Stefanović S, Die Crescentia-Florence Sage, eine kritische Studie ueber ihren Ursprung und ihre Entwicklung, RF 29.461.

Hilka A, Zum Crescentiastoff, Arch 133.135 (Latin parallels, from Breslau, Munich MSS).

Chaytor H J, A Fragment of the Chanson D'Aventure, Florence de Rome, MHRA 1.48 (leaf of French version).

Schlauch M, Chaucer's Constance and Accused Queens, N Y 1927, pp 108, 128 (summary Middle Dutch Seghelijn van Jerusalem).

Whiting B J, Proverbs in Certain ME Romances in Relation to Their French Sources, HSNPL 15.118 (crit D Everett, YWES 15.106).

Geist R J, On the Genesis of the King of Tars, JEGP 42.260, 265n29.

Aebischer P, Fragments de la Chanson de la Reine Sebile et du roman de Florence de Rome, conservés aux archives cantonale de Sion, Studi medievali, ns 16.135 (Florence p 153).

Relation with Folktales. Thompson Mot Ind, D 1213 (magic bell); D 1601.18.1 (self-ringing bell); H 151.8 (husband attracted by wife's power of healing); K 2110.1 (calumniated wife); K 2112 (woman slandered as adulteress); K 2116 (innocent woman accused of murder); K 2155.1.1 (bloody knife left in innocent person's bed brings accusation of murder); K 2211.1 (treacherous brother-in-law); cf N 251; N 730, N 741 (accidental reunion); S 451 (outcast wife at last reunited with husband); T 321 (saved by miracle); T 425 (brother-in-law seduces, seeks to seduce sister-in-law).

Grundtvig S, A Olrik, H G Nielsen, Danmarks Gamle Folkeviser, 11 vols (1853–1948), Copenhagen 1853, 1.193; 3.782; 4.730.

Child F J, The English and Scottish Popular Ballads, 5 vols, Boston 1882–1898, 2.34, 3.235.

Siefken O, Das gedüldige Weib, Rathenow 1903, pp 35, 39, 42.

Stefanović S, Ein Beitrag zur angelsächsischen Offsage, Angl 35.483; cf Angl 32.398.

Tatlock J S P, Notes on Chaucer, MLN 29.98.

Barry P, Bells Rung Without Hands, MLN 30.28.

Hibbard Med Rom, p 16 (miraculous ringing of bells).

Schlauch, Chaucer's Constance and Accused Queens, p 109 (importance of fairy tale analogues).

Dickson A, Valentine and Orson, A Study in Late Medieval Romance, N Y 1929, p 72.

Fahlin C, La femme innocente exilée dans une forêt, Motif folklorique de la littérature médiévale, Mélanges de philologie offerts at K Michaëlsson, Göteborg 1952, p 147 (crit B Woledge, YWMLS 14.35).

Relations with the Ballad. Child, English and Scottish Popular Ballads, 2.41, 510.

Christophersen P, The Ballad of Sir Aldingar, Oxford 1952, pp 112, 118, 121.

Other Relations and Similar Phrases. Kölbing, see above under *Textual*, pp 103, 105.

Rickert E, Emare, EETSES 99.xlvii.

Hibbard Med Rom, pp 12, 15, 16 (Bénoit's Roman de Troie, King of Tars).

Chambers OHEL, 2.65 (15th cent play).

Smithers G V, Kyng Alisaunder, EETS 237.87.

Schlauch M, English Medieval Literature and Its Social Foundations, Warsaw 1956, p 190.

HLF, 26.335; Ward, 1.711; Gröber, 2¹.798, lines 910, 919; Brandl, § 79; Schofield, p 313; Paris Litt franç, § 27; Körting, § 86 vorbem; Bennett OHEL, 2.164; Baugh LHE, p 194; Kane, pp 31, 35.

Gautier L, Les épopées françaises, 5.103; Hibbard Med Rom, p 21, new edn 1960, p 348; Renwick-Orton, p 380; CBEL, 1.158(o); Bennett OHEL, 2.311; Holmes CBFL, nos 697, 711, 712; Bossuat, nos 249–53, 1339–42, 6058.

9. BRETON LAYS

by

Mortimer J. Donovan

GENERAL.

Marie de France. Warnke K, Die Lais der Marie de France, Bibliotheca Normannica 3, 3rd edn, Halle 1925 (crit E Hoepffner, Neophil 11.141; O Schultz-Gora, ZfRP 46.314). Ewert A, Marie de France, Lais, Oxford 1944 (crit E J Arnould, MÆ 14.69; U T Holmes Jr, Spec 20.114). Lods J, Les lais de Marie de France, Paris 1959. Fox J C, Marie de France, EHR 25.303, 26.317; U T Holmes Jr, New Thoughts on Marie de France, SP 29.1; Further on Marie de France, Sym 3.335; F Nagel, Marie de France als dichterische Persönlichkeit, RF 44, Erlangen 1930; E A Francis, Marie de France et son temps, Rom 72.78; W S Woods, Femininity in the Lais of Marie de France, SP 47.1; R Lejeune, Rôle littéraire d'Aliénor d'Aquitaine et de sa famille, Cultura neolatina 14.38. (On the identity and times of Marie de France.) Foulet L, Thomas and Marie in Their Relation to the Conteurs, MLN 23.205; A Ahlström, Marie de France et les lais narratifs, Kungl Vetenskaps- och Vitterhets-Samhälles, Handlingar 3rd ser 29 no 3, Göteborg 1925, p 1; E Hoepffner, Les lais de Marie de France, Paris 1935; R S Loomis, Le folklore breton et les romans arthuriens, Annales de Bretagne 56.203 (English translation CL 2.289); C Foulon, Marie de France et la Bretagne, Annales de Bretagne 60.243 (abstr BBSIA 6.37); M Donovan, Priscian and the Obscurity of the Ancients, Spec 36.75. (Sources and literary relations.) Foulet L, Marie de France et les lais bretons, ZfRP 29.19, 293 (crit J Bédier, Rom 34.479, 35.137); Warnke, Die Lais der Marie de France, p xx; E Hoepffner, Les deux Lais du Chèvrefueille, Mélanges Paul Laumonier, Paris 1935, p 41; M de Riquer, La aventure, el lai y el conte en Maria de Francia, Filologia romanza 1955, fasc 1.1; J Frappier, Remarques sur la structure du lai; essai de définition et de classement (Extr de la littérature, Colloques de Strasbourg, avril 1959, p 23); E Hoepffner, The Breton Lais, in Loomis ALMA, p 112; Smithers G V, Story Patterns in Some Breton Lays, MÆ 22.61 (crit B J Timmer, YWES 34.18). (The narrative lay as a form.)

Schiött E, L'amour et les amoureux dans les lais de Marie de France, Lund 1889; C Conigliani, L'amore e l'avventura nei Lais di Maria di Francia, Archivum Romanum 2.201; S F Damon, Marie de France: Psychologist of Courtly Love, PMLA 44.968; L Spitzer, Marie de France—Dichterin von Problemmärchen, ZfRP 50.29; The Prologue to the Lais of Marie de France, MP 41.96 (crit H A Hatzfeld, RomP 1.319); F Schürr, Komposition und Symbolik in den Lais der Marie de France, ZfRP 50.556; E Eberwein, Zur Deutung mittelalterlicher Existenz, Kölner Romanistische Arbeiten 7, Bonn and Cologne 1933, p 27; E Hoepffner, Aux origines de la nouvelle française, Oxford 1939; D W Robertson, Marie de France, Lais, Prologue 13–15, MLN 64.336; M Allen, The Literary Craftsmanship of Marie de France, diss Univ of Virginia, DA 14.1714. (Themes and problems of composition.)

Other Breton Lays. For editions of French lays see Holmes CBFL and Bossuat MBFL below. Meissner R, Die Strengleikar: Ein Beitrag zur Geschichte der altnordischen Prosaliteratur, Halle 1902 (ON versions). Brereton G, A Thirteenth Century List of French Lays and Other Narrative Poems, MLR 45.40 (evidence of vogue in 13 cent). Donovan M J, Lai du Lecheor: A Reinterpretation, RomR 43.81 (Lecheor as a parody of a changing form). Hofer S, Bemerkungen zur Beurteilung des Horn- und Mantellai, RF 65.38.

Relations with Other Forms. Everett D, A Characterization of the English Medieval Romances, E&S 15.121 (rptd in Essays on Middle English Literature, ed P Kean, London 1955). Hodgart M, The Ballads, London 1950, p 75. Hertz W, Spielmannsbuch, Stuttgart and Berlin 1886; 3rd edn 1905, introd. Leach H G, Angevin Britain and Scandinavia, Cambridge Mass 1921, pp 199, 399. Bruce J D, The Evolution of Arthurian Romance, Göttingen and Baltimore 1923, 1.52, 2.175. Voretzsch C, Einführung in das Studium der altfranzösischen Literatur, 3rd edn, Halle 1925, p 269 (trans F du Mont, N Y 1931). Harris J, Marie de France: The Lays Gugemar,

Lanval and a Fragment of Yonec, N Y 1930, introd.

French W H, Essays on King Horn, Cornell Univ Studies in Engl 30, Ithaca 1940, p 1.

Wilson R M, The Lost Literature of Medieval England, London 1952, p 136.

de Julleville Hist, 1.285, 340; Gröber, 2¹.496, 590; Schofield, p 179; Paris Litt franç, § 55; Holmes CBFL, Syracuse N Y 1947, 1.94; Bossuat MBLF, p 140, Supplement, p 42.

[85] LAI LE FREINE.

MS. Advocates 19.2.1 (Auchinleck), ff 261ª–262ᵇ (1330–40); 340 lines; lacks ending.

Kölbing E, Vier Romanzen-Handschriften, EStn 7.177; A J Bliss, Notes on the Auchinleck Manuscript, Spec 26.652. (Description and contents of the Auchinleck MS.)

Carr M B, Notes on an English Scribe's Methods, Univ of Wisconsin Studies in Lang and Lit, Madison 1918, 2.153 (on the scribe's treatment of O E ā in Auchinleck MS).

Bliss A J, Sir Orfeo Lines 1–46, English and Germanic Studies, Univ of Birmingham, 5.7 (f 261ª supplies lines missing from Sir Orfeo in Auchinleck MS).

Editions. Weber MR, 1.357.

Varnhagen H, Lai le Freine, Angl 3.415 (crit J M Garnett, AJP 1.495).

Wattie M, The ME Lai le Freine, Smith Coll Studies in Mod Lang 10, no 3, Northampton 1929 (crit F P Magoun Jr, Spec 5.239).

Modernizations and Abstracts. Ellis Spec, p 538.

Luquiens F B, Four Lays of Marie de France, N Y 1903, p 25.

Rickert RofL, p 47.

Mason E, French Mediaeval Romances from the Lays of Marie de France and Other French Legends, London 1911, p 61.

Textual Matters. Holthausen F, Lay le Freine, v 91, Angl 13.360.

Brugger E, Eigennamen in den Lais der Marie de France, ZfFSL 49.201, 381.

Language. Laurin A, An Essay on the Language of Lai le Freine, diss Upsala 1869.

Sources. Warnke, Die Lais der Marie de France, pp 54, cvi, 262; Ewert, Marie de France, Lais, pp 35, 169. (Text of OF Lai le Fraisne and notes.)

Matzke J E, The Lay of Eliduc and the Legend of the Husband with Two Wives, MP 5.211.

Hoepffner, Les lais de Marie de France, p 109.

Adler A, Höfische Dialektik im Lai du Fresne, GRM 42.55.

Stemmler T, Die me Bearbeitungen zweier Lais der Marie de France, Angl 80.243.

See studies under EUSTACE-CONSTANCE-FLORENCE-GRISELDA LEGENDS; Chaucer's CLERK'S TALE, MAN OF LAW'S TALE.

Prologue. Zupitza J, Zum Lay le Freine, EStn 10.41.

Foulet L, The Prologue of Sir Orfeo, MLN 21.46.

Guillaume G, The Prologues of the Lai le Freine and Sir Orfeo, MLN 36.458.

Relations with Chaucer. Foulet L, Le prologue du Franklin's Tale et les lais bretons, ZfRP 30.698.

Loomis L H, Chaucer and the Breton Lays of the Auchinleck MS, SP 38.14.

Relations with the Ballad. Child F J, English and Scottish Ballads, Boston 1857, 3.191 (edn of ballad Fair Annie).

Küchler W, Schön Annie, Fraisne und Griselda, NS 35.492.

Other Versions. Foulet L, Galeran de Bretagne, Classiques français du moyen âge, Paris 1925.

Ten Brink, 1.259; Brandl, § 29; Schofield, p 192; Körting, § 133; Kane, p 46; Hibbard Med Rom, p 294; CBEL, 1.151.

[86] SIR ORFEO.

MSS. 1, Bodl 6922* (Ashmole 61), ff 151ª–156ª (late 15 cent); 2, Harley 3810, ff 1ª–10ª (early 15 cent); 3, Advocates 19.2.1 (Auchinleck), ff 300ª–303ª (1330–40).

EStn 7.178; Spec 26.652; Carr, Univ of Wisconsin Studies in Lang and Lit 2.153; English and Germanic Studies, Univ of Birmingham, 5.7.

Editions. Ritson AEMR, 2.248 (MS Harley 3810).

Laing D, Selected Remains of Ancient Popular Poetry of Scotland, London 1822; rvsd W C Hazlitt, Early Popular Poetry of Scotland, London 1895, 1.64 (Auchinleck MS).

Halliwell [-Phillips] J O, Illustrations of the Fairy Mythology of A Midsummer Night's Dream, London 1845, p 36; rptd W C Hazlitt, Fairy Tales, Legends and Romances, London 1875, p 83, and SA 16.30 (MS Ashmole 61).

Zielke O, Sir Orfeo, Breslau 1880 (critical edn, all MSS; crit E Einenkel, AnglA 5.13; F Lindner, EStn 5.166; T Wissmann, LfGRP 2.135).

Shackford M, Legends and Satires, Boston 1913, p 141 (Auchinleck MS, after Laing).

Cook A S, A Literary Middle English Reader, Boston 1915, p 88 (Auchinleck MS completed from Harley, after Zielke).

Sisam K, Fourteenth Century Verse and Prose,

Oxford 1921, p 13 (Auchinleck MS with Harley 1–24, 33–46).

French W H and C B Hale, ME Metrical Romances, N Y 1930, p 321 (Auchinleck MS completed from Harley, with Sisam's variants from all MSS).

Ford B, The Age of Chaucer, London 1954, p 271 ("normalized" text, based on Sisam; lines 1–24 omitted).

Bliss A J, Sir Orfeo, London 1954 (full texts of all three MSS; crit K Brunner, Angl 73.216; S R T O d'Ardennes, RES ns 8.57; P Hodgson, MLR 50.325; L H Loomis, JEGP 55.290; M L Samuels, MÆ 24.56; H M Smyser, Spec 31.134).

Selections. Sampson G, Cambridge Book of Prose and Verse, London 1924, p 265 (Auchinleck MS).

Kaiser R, Alt- und mittelenglische Anthologie, Berlin 1955, p 386 (lines 281–595 from Auchinleck MS).

Modernizations. Rickert RofL, p 32.

Hunt E E, Sir Orfeo, Adapted from the Middle English, Cambridge Mass 1909; rptd R S Loomis and R Willard, Medieval English Verse and Prose, N Y 1948, p 95.

Weston J L, Chief Middle English Poets, Boston 1914, p 133.

Williams M, Glee-Wood, N Y 1949, p 112 (modernized selections).

Montagu R, Havelok and Sir Orfeo, London 1954, pp 16, 97.

Loomis R S and L H Loomis, Medieval Romances, N Y 1957, p 311.

Textual Matters. Holthausen F, Zu me Romanzen: Sir Orfeo, Angl 42.425.

Tucker S, A Note on the Lai of Sir Orfeo, v 514, English and Germanic Studies 2.39.

Donovan M, Herodis in the Auchinleck Sir Orfeo, MÆ 27.162.

Gray D, Sir Orfeo, Line 565, Arch 198.167.

Bullock-Davies C, Ympe Tre and Nemeton, N&Q ns 9.6.

Language. Serjeantson M S, The Dialects of the West Midlands in ME, RES 3.330.

Sources. Kittredge G L, Sir Orfeo, AJP 7.176.

Davies C, Marie de France, TLS 29 Nov 1934, p 856; Sir Orfeo and De Nugis, MLN 51.492; Notes on the Sources of Sir Orfeo, MLR 31.354.

Loomis R S, Sir Orfeo and Walter Map's De Nugis, MLN 51.28; Arthurian Tradition and Chrétien de Troyes, N Y 1949, p 162.

Smithers G V, Story-Patterns in Some Breton Lays, MÆ 22.85.

Severs J B, The Antecedents of Sir Orfeo, in Studies in Medieval Literature in Honor of A C Baugh, ed M Leach, Phila 1961, p 187.

Bullock-Davies C, Classical Threads in Orfeo, MLR 56.161.

Rota F, Echi di miti e legende in un poemetto medievale inglese, Letteratura moderne 8.439.

Allen D, Orpheus and Orfeo: The Dead and the Taken, MÆ 33.102.

Virgil, Georgics, bk 4; Ovid, Metamorphoses, bks 10–11; Boethius, De consolatione philosophiae, bk 3, met 12. (Versions of the classical story.)

O'Curry E, On the Manners and Customs of the Ancient Irish, Dublin 1873, 2.192; H d'Arbois Jubainville, Cours de littérature celtique, Paris 1884, 2.311; A H Leahy, Heroic Romances of Ireland Translated into English Prose and Verse, London 1905, 1.23; T P Cross and C H Slover, Ancient Irish Tales, N Y 1936, p 82. (Versions of the Wooing of Etain.)

Gaelic Journal 2.307; Cross and Slover, Anc Irish Tales, p 488. (Versions of the Adventures of Connla the Fair.)

Patch H R, The Other World According to Descriptions in Medieval Literature, Smith Coll Studies in Mod Lang ns 1, Cambridge Mass 1950, p 243.

Prologue. Brugger E, Ueber die Bedeutung von Bretagne, Breton, ZfFSL 20.154.

EStn 10.42; MLN 21.46; 36.458.

Relations with Chaucer. ZfRP 30.698; SP 38.14.

Relations with the Ballad. Child, English and Scottish Ballads, 1.215 (edn of ballad King Orfeo).

Gummere F B, The Popular Ballad, Boston 1907, p 224.

Brunner K, Romanzen und Volksballaden, Palaes 148.79.

Wimberly L C, Folklore in the English and Scottish Ballads, Chicago 1928, p 332.

Other Versions. Marshall L E, Greek Myths in Modern English Poetry, Studi di filologia moderna 5.203.

Wirl J, Orpheus in der englischen Literatur, WBEP 40, Vienna 1913.

See under Henryson, ORPHEUS AND EURYDICE.

Hertz, Spielmannsbuch, introd.

Ker W P, English Literature: Mediaeval, N Y and London 1912, p 121.

Hill D, The Structure of Sir Orfeo, MS 23.136.

Carpinelli F, Sir Orfeo, Expl 19, item 13 (on lines 103–12).

HLF, 29.499; Ward, 1.171; Ten Brink, 1.260; Brandl, § 29; Gröber, 2¹.593; Schofield, p 184; Körting, § 133; Kane, p 80; Hibbard Med Rom, p 195, CBEL, 1.151.

[87] EMARE.

MS. Cotton Calig A.ii, ff 71ᵃ–76ᵃ (15 cent).
Glauning O, Lydgate's Minor Poems, EETSES 80, London 1900, p xxxvii.
Editions. Ritson AEMR, 2.204; E Kölbing, EStn 15.248 (collation of R with MS).
Gough A B, Emaré, Old and Middle English Texts 2, London N Y and Heidelberg 1901 (crit W Dibelius, Arch 110.196; F Holthausen, AnglB 13.46).
Rickert E, The Romance of Emaré, EETSES 99, London 1906 (diss Univ of Chicago 1907).
French and Hale, Metrical Romances, p 423 (edn from MS, with some of Rickert's emendations).
Textual Matters. Gough A B, On the ME Metrical Romance Emaré, diss Kiel 1900.
Sources. Lücke E, Das Leben der Constance bei Trivet, Gower and Chaucer, Angl 14.77.
Gough A B, On the Constance Saga, Palaes 23, Berlin 1902.
Siefken O, Der Konstanze-Griseldistypus, Rathenow 1904; Das geduldige Weib, diss Leipzig 1904.
Däumling H, Studien uber den Typus des Mädchens ohne Hände, Munich 1912; J Knedler, The Girl without Hands, Harv Univ Abstracts of Diss 1937, p 274.
Schlauch M, Chaucer's Constance and Accused Queens, N Y 1929.
Wickert M, Chaucer's Konstanze und die Legende der guten Frauen, Angl 69.101.
Wilda O, Ueber die örtliche Verbreitung der zwölfzeiligen Schweifreimstrophe in England, diss Breslau 1887.
Trounce A McI, The English Tail-Rhyme Romances, MÆ 1.81, 168; 2.34, 189; 3.30 (crit D Everett, YWES 13.94; 14.118).
See under EUSTACE-CONSTANCE-FLORENCE-GRISELDA LEGENDS; Chaucer's CLERK'S TALE, MAN OF LAW'S TALE.
Ward, 1.418; Schofield, p 189; Brandl, § 80; Kane, p 22; Hibbard Med Rom, p 23; CBEL, 1.152.

[88] SIR LAUNFAL (LAUNFALUS MILES).

MS. Cotton Calig A.ii, ff 33ᵇ–40ᵃ (15 cent).
Glauning, Minor Poems, EETSES 80, p xxxvii; Rickert, Emaré, EETSES 99, p ix.
Editions. Ritson AEMR, 2.1.
Halliwell [-Phillips], Illustrations of the Fairy Mythology of A Midsummer Night's Dream, p 2; rptd Hazlitt, Fairy Tales, p 48.
Erling L, Li lais de Lanval, Kempten 1883.
Kaluza M, Thomas Chestre, Verfasser des Launfal, Libeaus Desconus und Octovian, EStn 18.168.
French and Hale, Metrical Romances, p 343.
Bliss A, ed Thomas Chestre: Sir Launfal, London 1960.
Selection. Sampson, Cambridge Book of Prose and Verse, p 238.
Modernizations. Weston J L, Four Lais Rendered into English Prose from the French of Marie de France, London 1900, p 31; Chief Middle English Poets, p 204; rptd W Blair and W K Chandler, Approaches to Poetry, N Y and London 1935, p 90; 2nd edn 1953.
Rickert RofL, p 57.
Textual Matters. ZfFSL 49.201, 381; A Bliss, The Spelling of Sir Launfal, Angl 85.275; A Bliss, The Hero's Name in the Middle English Version of Lanval, MÆ 27.80.
Language. Fischer E, Die Lautbestand des südmittelenglischen Octovian verglichen mit seinen Entsprechungen im Lybeaus Desconus und im Launfal, AF 63, Heidelberg 1927.
Mills M, The Composition and Style of the Southern Octovian, Sir Launfal, and Libeaus Desconus, MÆ 31.88.
Bülbring K, QF 63.30.
Authorship. Sarrazin G, Octovian, AEB 3, Heilbronn 1885, introd; EStn 18.168; M Kaluza, Libeaus Desconus, Leipzig 1890, introd; DNB, Thomas Chestre; J Harris, A Note on Thomas Chestre, MLN 46.24; D Everett, The Relation of Chestre's Launfal and Lybeaus Desconus, MÆ 7.29 (crit G Willcock, YWES 19.88).
Sources. Warnke, Die Lais der Marie de France, pp 86, cxxx and 263; Ewert, Marie de France, Lais, pp 58 and 172. (Text of OF Lanval and notes.)
Grimes E M, The Lays of Desiré, Graelent and Melion, N Y 1928 (edn of Graelent).
Rychner J, ed, Marie de France, Le lai de Lanval, Paris 1958.
Schofield W H, The Lays of Graelent and Launfal, PMLA 15.121; The Lay of Guingamor, HSNPL 5.221 (crit G P, Rom 27.323); W C Stokoe Jr, The Work of the Redactors of Sir Launfal, Richard Coeur de Lion and Sir Degaré, diss Cornell Univ, Abstracts 1946 (1947), p 26; The Sources of Sir Launfal: Lanval and Graelent, PMLA 63.392; E Hoepffner, Graëlent ou Lanval? Recueil de travaux offerts à M Clovis Brunel, Paris 1955, 2.1; T Stemmler, Die me Bearbeitungen zweier Lais der Marie de France, Angl 80.243. (Relationship of Lanval and Graelent and sources of Sir Launfal.)
Cross T P, The Celtic Fée in Launfal, Kittredge Anniversary Papers, Boston 1913, p 377;

The Celtic Elements in the Lais of Lanval and Graelent, MP 12.585; H Newstead, The Traditional Background of Partonopeus de Blois, PMLA 61.925; R S Loomis, Wales and the Arthurian Legend, Cardiff 1956, p 112; R Ackerman, English Rimed and Prose Romances, in Loomis ALMA, p 516.

MÆ 22.62; Hoepffner, Les lais de Marie de France, p 56; S Hofer, Zur Beurteilung der Lais der Marie de France, ZfRP 66.414; Die Komposition des Lai Desiré, ZfRP 71.69.

Francis E A, The Trial Scene in Lanval, Mélanges M K Pope, Manchester 1939, p 115.

Münster K, Untersuchungen zu Thomas Chestre's Launfal, diss Kiel 1886.

Kolls A, Zur Lanvalsage, Berlin 1886.

Wilda O, Ueber die örtliche Verbreitung der Schweifreimstrophe, diss Breslau 1887; MÆ 1.81, 168; 2.34, 189; 3.30.

Relations with the Ballad. Child, English and Scottish Ballads, 1.258 (edn of Tam Lin) and 1.109 (edn of Thomas Rymer).

Wimberly L C, Folklore in the English and Scottish Ballads, Chicago 1928, p 167.

Corso T, I Temi folklorici nei lais di Maria di Francia, Folklore—Revista di tradizioni populari 6.33.

Brandl, §§ 70, 113; Billings, p 144; Gröber, 2¹.595; Schofield, p 181; Körting, § 125; Kane, p 34; Hibbard Med Rom, p 97; CBEL, 1.152.

[89] SIR LANDEVAL.

MS. Bodl 11951 (Rawlinson C 86), ff 119^b– 128^a (1480–1508).

Editions. Kittredge G L, Sir Launfal, AJP 10.1 (crit J Zupitza, Arch 88.68).

Zimmermann R, Sir Landeval, diss Königsberg 1900.

CBEL, 1.152.

See *Sources* and *Relations with the Ballad,* under SIR LAUNFAL [88].

[90] SIR LAMBEWELL.

MS. Additional 27879 (Percy Folio), ff 29^b– 33^b (ca 1650).

Editions. PFMS, 1.144. Kolls A, Zur Lanvalsage, Berlin 1886.

CBEL, 1.153.

See *Sources* and *Relations with the Ballad,* under SIR LAUNFAL [88].

[91] SIR LAMWELL.

MS. 1, Camb Univ Kk.V.30, f 11 (ca 1612), first 90 lines. PRINTS: 2, Malone 941 (prob

16 cent), eight printed leaves; 3, Douce Fragments e.40, one leaf of 61 lines.

Editions. PFMS, 1.522, 533; Kolls, Zur Lanvalsage (Malone 941 and Douce Fragments e.40).

Libr 35 6.233 (an early edn, probably by John Rastell, active 1516–33).

Furnivall F J, Captain Cox, His Ballads and Books, Ballad Society, London 1871, p xxxi; rptd Robert Laneham's Letter, New Shakspere Society, London 1890 (Camb Univ Kk.V.30).

CBEL, 1.153.

See *Sources* and *Relations with the Ballad,* under SIR LAUNFAL [88].

[92] SIR DEGARE.

MSS. 1, Bodl 14528 (Rawlinson F. 34), ff 10^b– 17^b (15 cent); 2, Bodl 21835 (Douce 261), ff 8^a–14^a (1564), four fragments, 350 lines; 3, Camb Univ Ff.II.38, ff 257^b–261^b (c 1450), 602 lines; 4, Egerton 2862, ff 95, 97 (end 14 cent), two fragments of 161 lines; 5, Additional 27879 (Percy Folio), ff 183^b– 189^a (c 1650); 6, Advocates 19.2.1 (Auchinleck), ff 78^b–84^b (1330–40). PRINTS: 7, de Worde, ca 1502–34 (Pierpont Morgan Library); 8, Copland, ca 1548–68 (BM C.21.c.66); 9, John King, 1560 (Selden D 45 [3]).

EStn 7.178; Spec 26.652; Carr, Univ of Wisconsin Studies in Lang and Lit, 2.153. (Description of the Auchinleck MS.)

Faust G P, Sir Degare, A Study of the Text and Narrative Structure, Princeton Studies in English 11, Princeton 1935 (crit M B Carr, MLN 53.153; G L, Arch 170.140; J R H, MP 34.97; H Marcus, AnglB 48.37; F Mossé, RAA 13.334; J P Oakden, MLR 34.256; G V Smithers, RES 13.470).

Editions. Utterson E V, Select Pieces of Early Popular Poetry, London 1817, 1.113 (Copland's print).

Laing D, Sire Degarre, Abbotsford Club Publications 28, Edinburgh 1849; French and Hale, Metrical Romances, p 287 (Auchinleck MS completed from MS Camb Univ Ff.ii.38).

PFMS, 3.16 (Percy Folio MS).

Carr M B, Sire Degarre, diss Univ of Chicago, Abstracts of Theses, Humanities Ser, 1923– 24, 2.369 (all MSS and prints except Rawlinson).

Schleich G, Sire Degarre, ETB 19, Heidelberg 1929 (edn all MSS; crit C Brett, RES 7.92; K Brunner, Arch 157.276; D Everett, YWES 9.117; J Koch EStn 65.271; M Serjeantson, ESts 15.67; C Slover, MP 28.377).

Abstracts. Ellis Spec, p 574; Ashton J, Romances of Chivalry, London 1890, p 103 (abstracts of Copland).
Sources. MÆ 22.79; Faust, Sir Degare, p 41 (narrative structure).
Potter M A, Sohrab and Rustum, London 1902; T P Cross, A Note on Sohrab and Rustum in Ireland, JCS 1.176.
Donovan M J, Sir Degare: Lines 992–97, MS 15.206 (historical parallel).
SP 38.14 (relations with Chaucer).
Evaluation. Slover C, Sire Degarre: A Study in a Mediaeval Hack Writer's Methods, Texas SE, 11.6 (crit D Everett, YWES 12.105); Faust, Sir Degare, p 41.
Stokoe W C, The Double Problem of Sir Degaré, PMLA 70.518.
HLF, 24.505; Kaluza, Libeaus Desconus, p cliv; Ten Brink, 1.252; Brandl, § 50; Schofield, p 187; Hibbard Med Rom, p 301; CBEL, 1.153.

[93] SIR GOWTHER.

MSS. 1, Royal 17.B.xliii, ff 116ª–131ᵇ (second half 15 cent); 2, Advocates 19.3.1, ff 11ª–28ª (second half 15 cent).
Editions. Utterson E V, Select Pieces of Early Popular Poetry, London 1817, 1.157 (Royal 17.B.xliii).
Breul K, Sir Gowther, Oppeln 1886 (both MSS; crit A Brandl, AfDA 14.205; E Einenkel, AnglA 7.6; G Sarrazin, LfGRP 5.16; Rom 15.160).
Sources. Ravenel F, Tydorel and Sir Gowther, PMLA 20.152; M Ogle, The Orchard Scene in Tydorel and Sir Gowther, Rom R 13.37; MÆ 22.77.
Weston J L, The Three Days' Tournament, London 1902.
Wilda O, Ueber die örtliche Verbreitung der Schweifreimstrophe, diss Breslau 1887; MÆ 1.81, 168; 2.34, 189; 3.30.
Other Versions. Löseth E, Robert le Diable, Roman d'aventure, SATF, Paris 1902.
Meyer P, L'enfant voué au diable, Rom 33.162 (edn of La vie saint Sauveur l'ermite).
Crane R S, An Irish Analogue of the Legend of Robert the Devil, RomR 5.55.
Herbert I, Roberte the Deuyll, London 1798 (from de Worde or Pynson's text); W J Thoms, A Collection of Early Prose Romances, Lon-

don 1828, p 167 (de Worde's text); rptd 1858 and 1906; rptd Robert the Deuyl, Edingburgh 1904; Hazlitt Rem, 1.217 (de Worde's text); C M Lancaster, Saints and Sinners in Old Romance: Poems of Feudal France and England, Nashville 1942 (modernization).
Ward, 1.416, 728; Brandl, § 80; Billings, p 227; Schofield, p 187; Kane, p 32; Hibbard Med Rom, p 49; CBEL, 1.153.

[94] THE EARL OF TOULOUS.

MSS. 1, Bodl 6922* (Ashmole 61), ff 27ᵇ–38ª (late 15 cent); 2, Bodl 6926 (Ashmole 45), ff 3ª–31ᵇ (15 cent); 3, Camb Univ Ff.II.38, ff 63ª–70ᵇ (15 cent); 4, Lincoln Cath 91, ff 114ᵇ–122ª (1430–40).
Editions. Ritson AEMR, 3.105; French and Hale, Metrical Romances, p 381 (Camb Univ Ff. II.38).
Lüdtke G, The Erl of Tolous and the Emperes of Almayn, Sammlung englischer Denkmäler 3, Berlin 1881 (critical edn, all MSS; crit F Doenne, AnglA 5.4; G Sarrazin, EStn 7.136; T Wissmann, LfGRP 3.179).
Selection. Emerson O F, Middle English Reader, N Y 1908, 1915, p 105 (Camb Univ Ff.II.38, lines 895 to end).
Modernization. Rickert RofL, p 80.
Textual Matters. Holthausen F, Zum Erl of Tolous, AnglB 27.171.
Sources. Paris S, Le Roman du Comte de Toulouse, Annales du Midi 12.1; J Bolte, Graf von Toulouse, Bibliographie des litterarischen Vereins in Stuttgart 222, Tübingen 1901.
Thomas A, Le Roman de Goufier de Lastours, Rom 34.55.
Casson L F, The Romance of Sir Degrevant, EETS 221, London 1949, pp lxvi, lxxi.
Siefken O, Das geduldige Weib, diss Leipzig 1904, p 66.
Wilda O, Ueber die örtliche Verbreitung der Schweifreimstrophe, diss Breslau 1887; MÆ 1.81, 168; 2.34, 189; 3.30.
Relations with the Ballad. Child, English and Scottish Ballads, 3.234 (edn of ballad Sir Aldingar).
Christophersen P, The Ballad of Sir Aldingar, Oxford 1952, pp 38, 127.
Brandl, § 80; Schofield, p 196; Kane, p 35; Hibbard Med Rom, p 35; CBEL, 1.153.

10. MISCELLANEOUS ROMANCES

by

Lillian Herlands Hornstein

I. Romances of Greek or Byzantine Origin

[95] APOLLONIUS OF TYRE.

MS. Bodl 21790* (MS Douce 216), 2 leaves, ff 17, 18 (15 cent).

Brown-Robbins, no *51.

Malone E, The Plays and Poems of William Shakespeare, London 1821, 21.3.

Editions. Halliwell [-Phillips] J O, A New Boke about Shakespeare and Stratford-on-Avon, London 1850, p 1 (MS Douce 216).

Smyth A H, Shakespeare's Pericles and Apollonius of Tyre: A Study in Comparative Literature, PAPS 37.206; rptd Phila 1898, p 49 (after Halliwell [-Phillipps]), partly normalized spellings.

Raith J, Die alt- und me Apollonius-Bruchstücke, Studien und Texte zur englischen Philologie 3, Munich 1956, p 1 (facsimile), p 78 (transcript) (crit R M Wilson, YWES 37.74).

Selections. Malone E, The Plays and Poems of William Shakespeare, London 1821, 21.221 (6 lines).

Warton T, History of English Poetry from the Twelfth to the Close of the Sixteenth Century, ed W C Hazlitt, London 1871, 2.303.

Language, Dialect. Smyth, edn, p 49.

Helming E M, The Absolute Participle in the Apollonius of Tyre, MLN 45.175 (OE version).

Sources and Analogues. Thorpe B, The Anglo-Saxon Version of Apollonius of Tyre, London 1834 (with trans) (crit J Zupitza, Angl 1.463).

Madden F, Gesta Romanorum [no 153], Roxb Club 1838 (Harl MS 7333).

Herrtage S J H, Gesta Romanorum, EETSES 33.525, no 153.

Hagen H, Der Roman von König Apollonius von T in seinen verschiedenen Bearbeitungen, Berlin 1878.

Riese A, ed, Historia Apollonii regis Tyri, Leipzig 1893 (Latin).

Singer S, Apollonius von Tyrus: Untersuchungen über das Fortleben des antiken Romans in spätern Zeiten, Halle 1895 (crit W v Wurzbach, Krit Jahresber 4².9; AnglB 10.98).

Zupitza J, Die ae Bearbeitung der Apollonius von Tyrus, Archiv 97.17.

Märkisch R, Die ae Bearbeitung der Erzählung von Apollonius von Tyrus, Berlin 1899, Palaes 6 (crit M Förster, EStn 28.111).

Klebs E, Die Erzählung von Apollonius aus Tyrus: Eine geschichtliche Untersuchung über ihre lateinische Urform und ihre spätern Bearbeitungen, Berlin 1899, pp 114, 460, 472 (crit C Weyman, DLz 21.675; S Singer, AnglB 10.233).

Smyth, edn, pp 10, 25 (German versions), 31 (Scandinavian), 34 (Dutch), 37 (Hungarian), 38 (Italian), 39 (Spanish), 41 (French), 43 (Greek), 47 (English).

Gower, Confessio Amantis, bk 8, line 271, ed G C Macaulay, Oxford 1901, 2.393.

Lewis C B, Die altfranz Prosaversionen des Apollonius-Romans nach allen bekannten Handschriften, Breslau 1912 and RF 34.1 (crit E Faral, Rom 43.443; M Delbouille, Rev belge de phil et hist, 7.1194).

Rohde E, Der griechische Roman u seine Vorläufer, 3rd edn, Leipzig 1914, pp 408, 495, 600.

Marden C C, Libro de Apolonio, An Old Spanish Poem, Baltimore and Paris 1917–22, Elliott Monographs in Romance Lang and Lit 5 (crit Holmes CBFL, 1.881).

Delbouille M, La version de l'historia Apollonii Regis Tyri conservé dans le Liber Floridus du Chanoine Lambert, Rev belge de phil et hist, 7.1194, 8.1195.

Grismer R L and E Atkins, The Book of Apollonius, Minneapolis 1936 (trans of Old Spanish Libro de Apolino) (crit W J Entwistle, MÆ 6.242).

Haight E H, More Essays on Greek Romances, N Y 1945, pp 142, 168, 178.

Janssen A A P, Narratio neo-graeca, Nijmegen 1954 (Modern Greek, Latin, French).

Goolden P, The Old English Apollonius of Tyre, Oxford Eng Monographs 6, Oxford 1958, Introduction (crit R M Wilson, YWES 39.75; H D Meritt, Spec 35.603; O K Schram, RES 11.194; E G Stanley, MLR 55.428).

Relations with Folktales. Thompson Mot Ind, C 822 (dangerous riddle); H 310 (suitor tests); H 541.1 (riddle propounded); L 161 (poor squire); N 251 (man pursued by misfortune); N 730 (accidental reunion); S 322.4

(evil stepmother); T 411, T 411.1 (incest motif).

Kemble J M, The Dialogue of Salomon and Saturnus, London 1848, p 114.

Rank O, Das Inzest-Motif in Dichtung und Sage, Leipzig 1912; 2nd edn, Leipzig u Wien 1926, p 346.

Goepp P H, The Narrative Material in Apollonius of Tyre, ELH 5.154, 164.

Relations with the Ballad. Child F J, English and Scottish Popular Ballads, 5 vols, Boston 1882–1898, 1.416, 485, 5.245 (cf Sir Andrew Barton, no 167).

Other Relations. Halliwel [-Phillipps] J O, The Remarks of Mr. Karl Simrock on the Plots of Shakespeare's Plays, London 1850, Shakespeare Soc 43.116.

Vesselovsky A, Iz istorii literaturnavo obstehenia vostoka i Zapada, Slavianskaia Skazania, Solomonge i Kitovrase i Zapadnya legendy o Marolfe i Merline, St Petersburg 1872 (Merlin).

Smyth, edn, pp 48, 206 (versions through Lillo), 83 (Amis).

Mead W E, The Squyr of Lowe Degre, Boston 1904, p xxvii.

Bédier J, Le roman de Tristan par Thomás, SATF 1.94 note one (Tristan).

Faral E, Rom 43.443 (Tristan).

Deutschbein M, Studien zur Sagengeschichte Englands, Clöthen 1906, p 35 note one.

Teubert S, Crescentia-Studien, Halle a S 1916, p 6 (Florence of Rome).

Marden, Libro de Apolonio, p xxii (Guillaume d'Angleterre).

Schlauch M, Chaucer's Constance and Accused Queens, N Y 1927, pp 75n23, 132 (Chaucer, Gower, Trivet); Romance in Iceland, N Y 1934, p 63.

Chapman C O, Beowulf and the Latin Apollonius of Tyre, MLN 46.439.

Goepp, ELH 5.154 (Constance group), 157 (Tristan).

Hornstein L H, Trivet's Constance and the King of Tars, MLN 55.354.

Wickert M, Chaucers Konstanze und die Legende der guten Frauen, Angl 69.100.

Delbouille M, A propos de la patrie et de la date de Floire et Blanchefleur (version aristocratique), Mélange Mario Roques, Paris 1952, 4.64.

Arthos J, Pericles, Prince of Tyre: A Study in Dramatic Use of Romantic Narrative, Shakespeare Quarterly 4.257; N&Q 171.450.

Bibliography Early Printings. Esdaile A J K, List of English Tales and Prose Romances Printed before 1740, London 1912, p 11.

Bennett OHEL, 2.305 (Gesta Romanorum).

O'Dell S, A Chronological List of Prose Fiction in English Printed in England and Other Countries 1475–1640, Cambridge, Mass 1954, p 119.

OE Versions. Körting, § 68a; Wülcker, § 622; Paul Grundriss, 2nd edn, 2¹.1132; Baugh LHE, p 104; Renwick-Orton, p 244; CBEL, 1.93.

Heusinkveld A H and E J Bashe, A Bibliographical Guide to OE, Iowa City 1931, p 108.

Gudzy N K, The History of Early Russian Literature, trans S W Jones, N Y 1949, p 405.

Schlauch M, English Medieval Literature and Its Social Foundations, Warsaw 1956, p 190.

Ten Brink, 1.114, 169; Ward 1.161; Gröber 2¹.1197; Schofield, p 306; Herbert 3.182 (W de Worde).

Farrar C P and A P Evans, Bibliography of English Translations from Medieval Sources, Columbia Records of Civilization Sources and Studies 39, N Y 1946, nos 323–25.

Hibbard Med Rom, pp 171–72, new edn 1960, p 347; Renwick-Orton, p 383; CBEL, 1.94; Holmes CBFL, no 881; Bossuat MBLF, nos 1241–50, 4095 (versions in other languages).

[96] FLORIS AND BLAUNCHEFLUR.

MSS. 1, Camb Univ Gg.4.27.2, ff 1ᵃ–5ᵇ (ca 1300); 2, BM Cotton Vitell D.3, ff 6–8, fragm (before 1300); 3, BM Egerton 2862 (olim Trentham-Sutherland), ff 98ᵃ–111ᵃ (ca 1400); 4, Advocates 19.2.1 (Auchinleck), ff 100ᵃ–104ᵇ (ca 1330).

Brown-Robbins, no *45; MED, p 41.

Kölbing E, Vier Romanzen-Handschriften, EStn 7.178, 186 (Auchinleck MS), 193 (MS Egerton 2862).

Meyer P, Fragments d'une ancienne histoire de Marie et de Jésus, Rom 16.248, 253, 254 (Cotton Vitellius D.3).

Ward, 1.716.

Barnicle M E, The Seege or Batayle of Troye, EETS 172.ix n 3 (MS Egerton 2862).

Bliss A J, Notes on the Auchinleck MS, Spec 26.652.

Editions. Hartshorne C H, Ancient Metrical Tales, London 1829, p 81 (Auchinleck MS) (crit Laing, see next item, p ix).

Laing D, A Penni Worth of Witte: Florice and Blauncheflour, Abbotsford Club 29, Edinb 1857, pp v, 15 (Auchinleck MS).

Lumby J R, King Horn, Floriz and Blauncheflur, The Assumption of Our Lady, EETS 14 (MSS Camb Univ Gg.4.27.2, Cotton Vitellius D.3).

Hausknecht E, Floris and Blauncheflur, Sammlung engl Denkmäler 5, Berlin 1885 (composite text, all MSS) (crit G Lüdtke, AnglA 8.150; E Kölbing, EStn 9.92; C Stoffel EStn 9.389).

McKnight G H, re-ed of Lumby, EETS 14 (MSS Camb Univ Gg.4.27.2, Cotton Vitellius D.3, Egerton 2862) (crit Athen 2.822).

Taylor A B, Floris and Blancheflour, Oxford 1927 (MSS Egerton 2862 and Auchinleck, with missing lines supplied from other MSS) (crit D Everett, RES 4.220; L von Hibler, AnglB 39.329; C B, MLR 23.387; F Karpf, NS 37.421).

French W H and C B Hale, ME Metrical Romances, N Y 1930, p 823 (MS Egerton 2862).

Selections. Emerson O F, A ME Reader, N Y 1905, rev edn 1915, pp 35, 263 (MS Camb Univ Gg.4.27.2).

Dickins B and R M Wilson, Early ME Texts, N Y 1951, 3rd rvsd edn 1956, p 43 (MS Camb Univ Gg.4.27.2).

Abstract. Ellis Spec, p 453 (Auchinleck MS).

Modernizations. Leighton Mrs, Medieval Legends, London 1895; The Sweet and Touching Tale of Fleur & Blanchefleur, London 1922 (from the French).

Darton F J H, A Wonder Book of Old Romance, N Y 1907, p 355.

Rickert RofL, p 1.

Textual Matters. Zupitza J, Verbesserungen und Erklaerungen, Floriz, Angl 1.473 (Lumby, edn, p 58, lines 257, 261, 318, 465, 549, 555, 701).

Kölbing E, Kleine Beiträge zur Erklärung und Textkritik englischer Dichter, Floriz und Blauncheflur, EStn 3.99 (crit of Lumby and Zupitza, Angl 1.473).

Emerson O F, A ME Reader, N Y 1915, p 263.

Holthausen F, Zu me Romanzen, Floris and Blauncheflur, Angl 40.408.

Carr M B, Notes on an English Scribe's Methods, Univ of Wisconsin Studies in Lang and Lit, Madison, Wisc 1918, 2.153 (OE ā in Auchinleck MS).

Prins A A, Two Notes on the Prologue of Chaucer's Canterbury Tales, ESts 30.42 (meaning of Chyvachie, line 67).

Dickins and Wilson, Early ME Texts, p 181.

Language, Dialect. Mackenzie B A, A Special Dialectical Development of OE ēa in ME, EStn 61.386 (Suffolk: OE ēa rhymes as a tense vowel); The Early London Dialect, Oxford 1928, §§ 328, 344 (Middlesex: OE a > o before a nasal) (crit H M Flasdieck, AnglB 42.46; G V Smithers, Kyng Alisaunder, EETS 237.41).

Dickins and Wilson, Early ME Texts, p 179 (Southeast Midland).

Sources and Analogues. Paris P, Les romanciers françois, Paris 1833.

Du Méril M E, Floire et Blanceflor, Paris 1856 (Byzantine source).

Schwalbach F C, Die Verbreitung der Sage von Flore und Blanceflor in der europaeischen Literatur, Koenigl Wilhelms-Gymn zu Krotischin zu Ostern 1869, p 14.

Sundmacher H, Die altfr und mhd Bearbeitungen der Sage von Flore und Blanscheflur, Göttingen 1872.

Scheler A, ed, Li roumans de Berte aus grans piés, Bruxelles 1874.

Herzog H, Die beiden Sagenkreise von Flore und Blanscheflur, Germ 29.137.

Kölbing E, Krit Jahresber 4².435 (relations of Norse Saga—Flóres saga ok Blankiflur, Altnordissche saga-bibliothek 5, Halle 1896).

Huet G, Sur l'origine de Floire et Blanchefleur, Rom 28.348; 35.95 (crit J H Reinhold, Rom 35.335); Quelques remarques sur les sources de Floire et Blanceflor, Rev de philol franç et de littérature 19.163, 165.

Paris G, Rom 28.439 (review of V Crescini, Il cantari di Fiorio e Biancifiore, Bologna 1899).

Trénet J, L'Ancien Testament et la langue française du moyen âge, Paris 1904, p 590 (infl of Book of Esther).

Reinhold J, Quelques remarques sur les sources de Floire et Blanceflor, Rev de philol français et de littérature, 19.163; Floire et Blanche-flor, Étude de littérature comparée, Paris 1906, p 32 (crit W Golther, ZfFSL 31.163; P A Becker, LfGRP 29.156; G G[röber], ZfRP 30.753; L Lécureux, Rom 37.310).

Basset R, Les sources arabes de Floire et Blancheflor, Revue des traditions populaires, 22.24 (parallels to Arabian Nights).

Johnstone O M, The Origin of the Legend of Floire and Blanchefleur, Matzke Memorial Vol, Stanford Calif 1911, p 125; see also ZfRP 32.705; Flügel Memorial Vol, Stanford Calif 1916, p 193; ZfRP 55.197 (crit E A Francis, YWMLS 6.43) (use of Ovid).

Ernst L, Flore und Blantscheflur: Studie zur Vergleichenden Literaturwissenschaft, QF 118.62.

Leendertz P jr, ed, Floris ende Blancefloer van Diederic van Assenede, Leiden 1912 (crit J W Muller, Museum 20.131; J Reinhold, LfGRP 37.107).

Decker O, Flos unde Blankeflos, Rostock 1913 (crit J Reinhold, LfGRP 38.362).

Faral E, Recherches sur les sources latines des contes et romans courtois du moyen âge, Paris 1913, p 32n2.

Leach H G, Angevin Britain and Scandinavia, Cambridge, Mass 1921, p 158.

Singer S, Arabische und europäische Poesie im Mittelalter, ZfDA 52.77 (parallels to Arabian Nights).

Reinhold J, Nowoodkryty rękopis palatyńsky poematu: Floire et Blancheflor, Rozprawy Wydziaku Filologicznego PAU 62, no 4.

Schlauch M, Romance in Iceland, N Y and London 1934, p 181.

Pelan M, Floire et Blancheflor, publication de la Faculté des Lettres de l'Université de Strassbourg, Textes d'études 7, Paris 1937, nouvelle edn 1956 (crit I D O A[rnold], MÆ 8.225; R Levy, MLN 72.463).

Wirtz W, Flore et Blancheflor, Frankfurter Quellen und Forschungen 15, Frankfort 1937 (crit A Jeanroy, Rom 63.534; I D O A[rnold], MÆ 8.225).

Krüger F, Li romanz de Floire et Blancheflor, Romanische Studien 45, Berlin 1938 (crit (crit I D O A[rnold], MÆ 8.225; E Gamillscheg, ZfSL 62.452).

Keyser P de, Floris ende Blancefoer, eine middeleeuwsche idylle door Diederik van Assende, Klassike Galerie n 25, Antwerpen 1945.

Delbouille M, A propos de la patrie et de la date de Floire et Blanchefleur (version aristocratique), Mélange Mario Roques, Paris 1952, 4.53, 64.

Relations with Folktales. Thompson Mot Ind, D 1076, D 1380.11, D 1381.7 (magic ring protects); D 1388.0.1; H 411.11 (magic spring as chastity test); K 1340 (entrance into girl's room by trick) cf K 2357.10; L 162 (lowly heroine marries prince-king).

Relations with the Ballad. Child F J, The English and Scottish Popular Ballads, Boston 1882–1898, 5 vols, 1.269; 2.500a, 502a, 510b; 5.175 (cf no 60, King Estmere).

Relations with Romances. Mead W E, Squyr of Lowe Degre, Boston 1904, p xxxiii.

Hibbard Med Rom, pp 187, 191 (Emare, Partonopeus of Blois, Aucassin and Nicolette, Amis and Amiloun, Apollonius, Pyramus and Thisbe).

Taylor, edn, pp 11, 16, 23 (Amis and Amiloun, Huon of Bordeaux, Squyr of Lowe Degre).

Uri S P, Some Remarks on Partonopeus de Blois, Neophil 37.89.

Bliss A J, Sir Orfeo, London 1954, p xxxi.

Smithers G V, Kyng Alisaunder, EETS 237.73, 84, 119.

Special Problems. Johnstone O M, The Descrip-tion of the Emir's Orchard in Floire et Blancheflor, ZfRP 32.705.

Lot-Borodine M, Le roman idyllique au moyen-âge, Floire, Paris 1913, p 9 (crit F L Critchlow, MLN 29.188).

Spargo J W, The Basket Incident in Floire and Blancheflor, NM 28.69.

Blanck A, Floires et Blancheflor et l'épisode de Haidée dans le Don Juan de Byron, Mélanges offerts à F Baldensperger, Paris 1930, 1.54.

Wilson R M, More Lost Literature, II, Leeds SE 6.43 (correcting J C Russell on a Lost Work of Banastre in Dict of Writers of 13 Cent England, BIHR, p 183); Early ME Literature, London 1939, 2nd edn 1951, pp 169, 227.

Heather P J, The Seven Planets, Folklore 54.357 (lines 249–54).

Other Problems. McKeehan I P, The Book of the Nativity of St Cuthbert, PMLA 48.992.

Smith M F, Wisdom and the Personification of Wisdom Occurring in ME Literature before 1500, Washington 1935, pp 50, 168.

Sherwood M, Magic and Mechanics in Medieval Fiction, SP 44.567.

Brunner K, ME Metrical Romances and Their Audience, Studies in Medieval Literature in Honor of A C Baugh, ed M Leach, Phila 1961, p 230.

Snell F J, The Fourteenth Century, Edinburgh and London 1913, p 47.

Ker W P, English Literature, Medieval, N Y and London [Home Univ Lib] [1912], p 120.

Thomas P G, English Literature before Chaucer, London 1924, p 113.

Everett D, A Characterization of the English Medieval Romances, E&S 15.98, rptd in Essays on ME Literature, ed P Kean, Oxford 1955, p 3.

Voretzsch K, Introduction to the Study of OF Literature, trans F M Du Mont, N Y 1931, p 349.

Wilson, Early ME Literature, p 226.

Schlauch M, English Medieval Literature and Its Social Foundations, Warsaw 1956, p 188.

Ward, 1.714; Gröber, 2¹.490, 527, 859; Ten Brink, 1.236; Brandl, § 38; Schofield, p 306; CHEL, 1.343; Paris Litt franç, § 51; Körting, § 114; Baugh LHE, p 193; Kane, p 47.

Körting G, Encykl der rom Phil, 2.497, 3.320; Hibbard Med Rom, pp 184, 187, new edn, 1960, p 348; Renwick-Orton, p 384; CBEL, 1.153(a); Bossuat MBLF, nos 1319–38, Suppl 6245–47; Holmes CBFL, nos 901–07.

II. Composites of Courtly Romance

[97] SIR DEGREVANT.

MSS. 1, Camb Univ Ff.1.6 (Findern), ff 96ᵃ–
109ᵇ, imp (late 15 cent); 2, Lincoln Cath 91
(olim A.5.2, olim A.1.17) (Thornton), ff
130ᵃ–138ᵇ, imp (ca 1440).
Brown-Robbins, no 1953; MED, p 36.
Ogden M S, The Liber de Diversis Medicinis,
EETS 207.x.
Robbins R H, The Findern Anthology, PMLA
69.610n3, 611, 619, 626, no 27.
Editions. Halliwell [-Phillipps] J O, Thornton
Romances, Camden Soc 30, London 1844,
p 177 (Camb Univ Ff.1.6, with variant
readings from Thornton MS) (crit E Kölbing,
Kleine Beiträge zur Erklärung und Text-
kritik englischer Dichter, EStn 3.100;
Schleich, edn).
Schleich G, Collationen zu me Dichtungen:
Sir Degrevant, EStn 12.140 (collation first
96 lines of both MSS).
Ellis F S, The Romance of Sir Degrevant,
Kelmscott Press, Hammersmith 1896 (Halli-
well [-Phillipps] text).
Luick K, Sir Degrevant, Vienna and Leipzig
1917, WBEP 47 (both MSS).
Casson F, The Romance of Sir Degrevant,
A Parallel Text Edition, EETS 221 (crit
G D Willcock, YWES 30.77; TLS, Sept 2
1949, p 566; G L Brook, MÆ 19.77; A
McIntosh, RES ns 2.68; H Marcus, Angl
70.322; B White MLR 47.384).
Modernization. Rickert RofL, p 106.
Summary. Wilcox J, French Courtly Love in
English Composite Romances, Papers of
Michigan Acad of Science, Arts and Letters,
18.580.
Textual Matters. Schleich G, Collationen zu me
Dichtungen, EStn 12.140.
Holthausen F, Zu me Dichtungen, Angl 44.78.
Language, Dialect. Tolkien J R R, The Devil's
Coach-Horses, RES 1.333.
Dunlap A R, The Vocabulary of the ME Ro-
mances in Tail-Rhyme Stanza, Delaware
Notes 14s, p 30 (Degrevant influenced by
vocabulary of the alliterative poems).
Robbins, PMLA 69.630 (Findern MS mixed
dialect, southern Derbyshire).
Versification. Luick K, Die englische Stabreim-
zelle im 14, 15, und 16 Jahrhundert, Angl
11.392; Zur Metrik der me reimendallite-
rierenden Dichtung, Angl 12.440, 442; see
also AnglB 12.33; Zu me Verslehre, Angl
38.269, 307.
Kaluza M, A Short History of English Versi-

fication, trans A C Dunstan, London 1911,
pp 200, 231.
Bülbring K D, Untersuchungen zu me Metrik,
SEP 50.511 (Festschrift für L Morsbach).
Medary M P, Stanza-Linking in English Alliterative Verse, RomR 7.244, 255.
Brown A C L, On the Origin of Stanza-Linking
in English Alliterative Verse, RomR 7.281
(inventiveness of author, influence of Welsh
poetry, no evidence of a French original).
Finsterbusch F, Der Versbau der me Dich-
tungen Sir Perceval of Gales und Sir Degre-
vant, WBEP 49, pp 64, 74, 75, 80, 99, 106,
131, 161 (crit Casson, edn, p xxxvi).
Willcock, crit of Casson edn, YWES 30.77.
Date, Scribe. Hibbard Med Rom, p 306 (minstrel
authorship).
Ogden, EETS 207.xi (MS Lincoln Cath 91).
Robbins, PMLA 69.611, 623, 626, 630 (Findern
MS) (later 15 cent).
Sources and Analogues. Rickert RofL, xlvii.
Hibbard Med Rom, pp 307 (Celtic), 309 (Eger
and Grime), 310 (Erle of Toulous).
Casson, edn, pp lxii, lxiii n (opposes Rickert's
historical identification), lxv (discounts Hib-
bard's evidence of Celtic influence), lxvi
(Lay of Guigemar), lxviii (Welsh, Celtic
parallels), lxix (Alliterative Morte Arthure),
lxxi (Earl of Toulous).
Relations with Folktales. Thompson Mot Ind,
E 501 (lover as hunter; H 1227 (quest-
pilgrimage); K 1641 (trickster killed by
intended victim); P 361 (faithful servant);
P 365 (treacherous steward); T 11.1 (love
from mere mention or description); T 24
(symptoms of love).
Relations with the Ballad. Rickert RofL, xlvii.
Nessler K, Geschichte der Ballade Chevy Chase,
Berlin 1911, pp 88, 90.
Relations with Chaucer. Loomis L H, Sir Thopas,
in Bryan-Dempster, pp 498, 509, 547.
Relations with Arthurian Romance. Loomis R S,
The Combat at the Ford in the Didot Per-
ceval, MP 43.69; Arthurian Tradition and
Chrétien de Troyes, N Y 1949, pp 93n45,
415.
Tolkien J R R and E V Gordon, Sir Gawain
and the Green Knight, Oxford 1925, p 84,
note to line 110.
Other Problems, Similar Phrases. Lüdtke G, The
Erl of Tolous and the Emperes of Almayn,
Berlin 1881.
Mead W E, Squyr of Lowe Degre, Boston 1904,
p xxvii.
Brunner K, Romanzen und Volksballaden,

Palaes 148.78 (Eglamour, Kilwch and Olwen, Eger and Grime).

Wilcox J, French Courtly Love in English Composite Romances, Papers of Michigan Acad of Science, Arts, and Letters 18.581.

Casson, edn, pp lxii, lxiii (Amis and Amiloun, Octavian, Cleges, Torrent of Portyngale, Squyr of Low Degre, Generydes, Roswall and Lillian); lxiv (Partenopeus of Blois, Ipomedon, Eglamour); lxvi (Erle of Tolous); 116 (notes), 117 note to line 21 (Triamour, Beves, Alexander), lxxiv (influence on Wm Morris and the Pre-Raphaelites), lxxvi (Erle of Tolous, Squyr of Lowe Degre).

Brandl, § 79; Schofield, p 311; W P Ker, CHEL, 1,322; Körting, § 86 vorbem; P G Thomas, English Literature before Chaucer, London 1924, p 115; Baugh LHE, pp 194, 197; TLS, Sept 2 1949, p 566 (review of Casson edn); Kane, pp 10, 51, 66, 90.

Schlauch M, English Medieval Literature and Its Social Foundations, Warsaw 1956, p 191.

Hibbard Med Rom, pp 307 note 2, 311; new edn, 1960, p 348; Tucker-Benham, p 256; Renwick-Orton, p 384; CBEL, 1.158(n), 5.116(n); Casson, edn p lxxvi.

[98] GENERIDES.

MSS. Version B: 1, Trinity Camb 1283 (Gale 0.5.2), ff 1^a–37^b, imp, (1475–1500). Version A: 2, PML M876 (Helmingham) (olim Tollemache), ff 103^b–152^b (1425–50). PRINTS: 3, Trinity Camb [Pynson, 1500–05?], The History of the excellent knyght Generides, 3 leaves, fragms (STC, no 11721); 4, State Libr of Victoria, Melbourne, Australia, Pynson, 1 leaf (Huth fragm) (1510); 5, Huntington Libr, Pynson, 4 leaves (Huth fragm) (1510) (STC, no 11721.5).

Brown-Robbins, no 70 (Version A), no 1515 (Version B); MED, p 42.

Pearsall D A, Notes on the Manuscript [Trinity Camb 1283] of Generydes, Libr 5s 16.205, 208.

Editions. Furnivall F J, A Royal Historie of the Excellent Knight Generides, ed from the unique MS of John Tollemache, MP, Roxb Club 85 (Helmingham MS, and early printed fragments, pp xxv, xxxiii, and postscript).

Wright W A, Generydes, A Romance in Sevenline Stanzas, EETS 55, 70 (MS Trinity Camb 1283) (crit F Holthausen, Angl 23.125, 249; Arch 106.351).

Summary. Faverty F E, The Story of Joseph and Potiphar's Wife in Med Literature, HSNPL 13.92.

Wilcox J, French Courtly Love in English Composite Romances, Papers of the Michigan Acad of Science, Arts, and Letters 18.582.

Textual Matters. Zupitza J, Verbesserungen und Erklaerungen, Generides, Angl 1.481.

Zirwer O, Zur Textkritik der me Generides-Romanzen, EStn 17.23; Untersuchungen zu den beiden me Generides-Romanzen, Breslau 1889.

Kölbing E, Zur Textkritik der strophischen dichtung Generydes, EStn 17.49.

Holthausen F, Beiträge zur Textkritik der me Generydes-romanze (ed Wright, EETS 55, 70), Festskrift tillägnad Oscar Ekman, Göteborg 1898 (crit M Kaluza, DLz 21.1443); Angl 23.125, 249; Arch 106.351.

Language, Dialect, Verse. Furnivall, edn, pp xxi, xxii (Midland with Northern mixture).

Zupitza J, The Romance of Guy of Warwick, the Second or 15th-century Version, EETSES 25, 26, pp 345, 358, 359, 383, 409.

Wilcox, Papers of the Michigan Acad of Science, Arts, and Letters 18.581 (Midland).

Pearsall D A, The Assembly of Ladies and Generydes, RES ns 12.229, 233.

Sources and Analogues. Zirwer, Untersuchungen zu den beiden me Generides-Romanzen, p 32.

Howe W D, A Dissertation Entitled Sir Generides; Its Origin, History, and Literary Relations, Unpublished MS, 1899, Harvard Univ Libr, chap 3, p 46.

Settegast F, Quellenstudien zur galloromanischen Epik, Leipzig 1904, p 232.

Schofield, p 310 (French source).

Hibbard Med Rom, pp 231 (French influence), 233 (Indian, Persian, Byzantine parallels).

Pearsall, RES ns 12.229, 234.

Relations with Folktales. Thompson Mot Ind, B 183, F 898.15 (magic boar); D 1812.5.1.2 (dream an evil omen); F 302.3.1; H 94 (recognition by ring); H 151.6, K 1816 (heroine in menial disguise); H 331.2 (suitor contest: tournament); K 1818.1 (disguise as leper); K 2111 (Potiphar's wife); K 2112 (woman slandered as adulteress); K 2213, T 230 (treacherous, faithless wife); K 2242, P 365 (treacherous steward); N 251 (man pursued by misfortune); N 730, N 741 (reunion of families); N 774 (adventure pursuing enchanted animal); P 314 (combat of disguised friends); P 361 (faithful servant); R 111.1.4 (rescue of princess); S 322.4 (evil stepmother); T 24 (symptoms of love).

Potter M A, Sohrab and Rustum, London 1902, pp 56, 207 (Appendix A).

Hibbard L A, Chaucer's Shapen was my Sherte, PQ 1.222; Med Rom, pp 234n4, 235.

Malone K, Rose and Cypress, PMLA 43.437.

Faverty, HSNPL 13.92, 101.
Schlauch M, Chaucer's Constance and Accused Queens, N Y 1927, p 117.
Relations with the Ballad. Child F J, The English and Scottish Popular Ballads, Boston 1882–1898, 5 vols, 2.12^b, 2.511, 5.292^b (cf no 66, Lord Ingram and Chiel Wyet, Sword of Chastity).
Christophersen P, The Ballad of Sir Aldingar, Oxford 1952, pp 114, 115n1, 116n (crit G D Willcock, YWES 33.81; F Mossé, EA 6.146; S Thompson, MLN 69.369).
Relations with Chaucer. Young K, The Origin and Development of the Story of Troilus and Criseyde, Chaucer Soc 2s 40, 1908, p 46 (faithful friend).
Loomis L H, Sir Thopas, Bryan-Dempster, p 548.
Pearsall, RES ns 12.229.
Other Problems and Literary Relations. Nuck R, King Roberd of Cisyle, Berlin 1887, p 53.
Zirwer, Untersuchungen zu den beiden me Generides-Romanzen, pp 22, 32.
Jentsch F, Die me Romanze Richard Coeur de Lion und ihre Quellen, EStn 15.232.
Watson F, ed of J L Vives, Institutione Faemenae Christianae (1529), London 1912, pp 58, 59.
Hibbard Med Rom, pp 153 (Richard), 207 (Partonopéus), 234 (Guigemar, Erec), 236 (Tristan), 237 (Horn).
Dickson A, Valentine and Orson, N Y 1929, pp 110, 143, 173.
Wilcox, Papers of Michigan Acad of Science, Arts, and Letters 18.582 (Eric and Enide, Eastern legends).
McKeehan I P, The Book of the Nativity of St Cuthbert, PMLA 48.981, 988 (supernatural origin).
Whiting B J, Proverbs in Certain ME Romances, HSNPL 15.109 (crit D Everett, YWES 15.106).
Casson L F, Sir Degrevant, EETS 221.lxiii, 145.
Pearsall, RES ns 12.229, 236.
Brandl, § 108; Schofield, p 310; CHEL, 1.324; Körting, § 116; Bennett OHEL, 2.164; Baugh LHE, p 194; Kane, pp 33, 46, 48; Lewis OHEL, 3.123.
Schlauch M, English Medieval Literature and Its Social Foundations, Warsaw 1956, p 189.
Hibbard Med Rom, pp 231, 238, new edn 1960, p 348; Tucker-Benham, p 248; Renwick-Orton, p 384; CBEL, 1.159; Bennett OHEL, 2.225, 312.

[99] PARTONOPE OF BLOIS.

MSS. Version A: 1, Bodl 14507 (Rawl Eng Poetry F. 14), ff 8–92, imp 1475–1500);

2, Bodl 30516 (Rawl Eng Poetry C. 3) (formerly New College), ff 6, 7 (1475–1500); 3, Univ Coll Oxf C. 188, ff 1–91^b, begins and ends imp (1425–50); 4, BM Addit 35288, ff 2^a–154 (1475–1500); 5, Clifden (Robartes), 2 fragm (1475–1500). Version B: 6, Penrose (olim Delamere, Vale Royal), ff 164^a–166^a (ca 1455).
Brown-Robbins, no 4132 (Version A, couplets), no 4081 (Version B, stanzas); MED, p 64.
Furnivall F J, N&Q 4s 9 (1892), p 353 (MS Penrose, olim Delamere, Vale Royal).
Robbins R H, The Speculum Misericordie, PMLA 54.935, 937 (MS Penrose).
Manly & Rickert, 1.108 (MS Penrose).
Editions. Buckley W E, The OE Version of Partonope of Blois, Roxb Club 82, London 1862 [MS Univ Coll Oxf 188, MS Bodl 30516 (Rawl Eng Poetry C. 3), selections from MS Bodl 14507 (Rawl Eng Poetry F. 14)] (crit E Kölbing, Beiträge zur vergleichenden Geschichte der romantischen Poesie und Prosa des Mittelalters, Breslau 1876, p 80).
N[ichols] R C, A Fragment of Partonope of Blois, from a Manuscript at Vale Royal, in Possession of Lord Delamere, Roxb Club 98, London 1873 (now MS Penrose); rptd Bödtker EETSES 109.481, see Bödtker below).
Wülcker R, Zu Partonope of Blois, Angl 12.607 (MS Clifden [Robartes] with corresponding portions from MS 188 Univ Coll Oxf, and a preceding portion from MS Rawl Eng Poetry F 14) (crit E Kölbing, Fragmente von Partonope, EStn 14.435).
Bödtker A T, The ME Versions of Partonope of Blois, EETSES 109 (all MSS; MS BM Addit 35288 is basic text), pp viii, 481, reprints MS Penrose, after R C N[ichols].
Summary. Ward, 1.699 (French version).
Wilcox J, French Courtly Love in the English Composite Romances, Papers of the Michigan Acad of Science, Arts, Letters 18.576.
Newstead H, The Traditional Background of Partonopéus de Blois, PMLA 61.916 (crit G D Willcock, YWES 27.88).
Language, Dialect. Scott E J L, Catalogue of Additions to the MSS in the British Museum 1894–1899, London 1901, p 1282.
Robbins, PMLA 54.937 (Penrose, Midland with Northern features).
Manly & Rickert, 1.408.
Date. Holmes U T, History of Old French Literature, N Y 1937, p 152.
Robbins, PMLA 54.935.
Manly & Rickert, 1.109.
Authorship. Kölbing E, Ueber die verschiedenen Gestaltungen der Partonopeus-Sage, Germa-

nistische Studien, Suppl to Germania, ed
K Bartsch, Vienna 1875, 2.77 (author of
French text).
Ward, 1.701.
Martin H, L'Explicit de Partonopeus de Blois
dans le MS BN Acq franç 7516, Rom 65.226
(Walter Map either author or inspirer).
Sources and Analogues. See below, under *Other
Versions, Relations with Folktales, Other Rela-
tions.*
Kölbing E, Beiträge zur vergleichenden Ge-
schichte der romantischen Poesie und Prosa
des Mittelalters, Breslau 1876, Über die
englischen Versionen der Partonopeussage,
pp 80, 90.
Weingartner F, Die me Fassungen der Partonopeus-Sage, und ihr Verhältniss zum altfranzösischen Originale, Breslau 1888, pp 13,
45 (crit E Freymond, Krit Jahresber 1.387).
Uri S P, Some Remarks on Partonopéus de
Blois, Neophil 37.83.
Other Versions: French. Robert A C M, ed, and
G A Crapelet, pub, Partonopeus de Blois,
publié pour la première fois d'après le manuscrit de la Bibliothèque de l'Arsenal, collection des anciens monuments de l'histoire et
de la langue françoise no 12, Paris 1834,
2 vols; A Fourrier, Le courant réaliste dans
le roman courtois en France au moyen-âge,
Paris 1960, pp 316–17, 385 and notes.
Other Versions: German. Massman H F, Partonopéus und Melior, Berlin 1847 (OF, MHG,
Middle Dutch).
Moret A, L'originalité de Conrad de Wurzbourg
dans son poème Partonopier und Meliur;
étude comparative du poème moyen-haut-
allemand et des manuscrits français, avec
rapprochement des versions anglaises, espa-
gnoles, néerlandaises, italienne, bas-alle-
mande, islandaise et danoise, Société d'édi-
tion du Nord, Lille 1933 (crit M Roques,
Rom 62.143).
Warren F M, Notes on the romans d'aventure,
MLN 13.343, 345, 347.
Other Versions: Scandinavian. Kölbing E, Über
die nordischen Gestaltungen der Partonopeus
Sage, Breslau 1873.
Bödtker A T, Parténopeus de Blois, étude com-
parative des versions islandaise et danoise,
Videnskabs-Selskabets Skrifter 2, Hist-Filos
Kl no 3, Christiana 1904, pp 26, 45 (crit
E Stengel, DLz [1905], 26.34).
Leach H G, Is Gibbonssaga a Reflection of
Partonopeus? Medieval Studies in Memory
of G S Loomis, N Y and Paris 1927, p 113.
Other Versions: Spanish. Bödtker A T, Par-
ténopeus in Catalonia and Spain, MLN
21.234.

Buchanan M A, Partinuplés de Bles, MLN 21.3
(bibl of Spanish chapbook).
Relations with Folktales. Thompson Mot Ind,
B 183, B 291.3, E 501.4.3 (magic boar);
B 301 (faithful animal); B 312.1 (helpful
animal as gift); B 401 (helpful horse);
C 31.1.1 (tabu: looking at supernatural wife
too soon); D 1123, D 1425, D 1427, D 1523.2
(magic object [ship] draws lover to woman);
D 2004.3.1, D 2006.1 (forgetfulness of fiancée
by drinking); E 501.4.3 (wild hunt); F 111
(journey to earthly paradise); F 242.2 (magic
boat); F 302, F 302.3.1 (fairy mistress entices
man into fairyland); F 302.3.3.1 (fairy
avenges self on inconstant husband); F 302.6
(fairy mistress leaves man when he breaks
tabu); H 217 (decision by single combat);
H 218 (judicial combat); H 331.2 (suitor
contest: tournament); K 1816 (disguise as
menial); K 2242 (treacherous steward);
L 431.1 (haughty mistress); P 361 (faithful
squire); Q 113 (knighthood as reward);
Q 471.1 (persecuted queen); R 222 (three
days' tournament); S 51 (cruel mother-in-
law); T 11, T 11.1 (falling in love with
person not yet seen); T 93.1 (disappointed
lover becomes wild man); T 111 (marriage
of mortal and supernatural being).
Cross Mot Ind, E 501.4.3; F 111; F 242.2;
F 302.3.1; K 1816; R 222; T 93.1.
Relations with Story of Cupid and Psyche. Ward,
1.700.
Lang A, Introd to William Aldington's trans
of Cupid and Psyche, London 1887.
Kawczyński M, Parténopeus de Blois, poemat
francuski z wieku xii, Sonderabzug aus dem
Bulletin de l'Académie des Sciences de
Cracovie, July 1901, p 123 (crit W Foerster,
LfGRP 23.28); Ist Apuleius im Mittelalter
bekannt gewesen (Mit einem anhang zu
Parténopeus?), Bausteine zur romanische
Philologie, Festgabe für A Mussafia, Halle
1905, p 193.
Reinhold J H, Quelques remarques sur les
sources de Floire et Blanceflor, Rev de philol
français et de litérature 19.163.
Stumfall B, Das Märchen von Amor und
Psyche in seinem Fortleben, MBREP 39.8.
Huet G, Le roman d'Apulée: était-il connu au
moyen âge, Moyen âge 22.22, 29.44.
Gough A, Notes to L Friedländer, Roman Life
and Manners, London 1913, 4.99.
Tegethoff E, Studien zum Märchentypus von
Amor und Psyche, Bonn, Leipzig 1922, p 124.
de Meyer M, Amor et Psyche, Folkliv 2 (1938),
p 197.
Newstead H, The Traditional Background of
Partonopeus de Blois, PMLA 61.919n7 (fairy

tales), 944 (Psyche); 919 (Breton lais), 923 Morgain la Fée) (crit G D Willcock, YWES 27.88).

Thompson S, The Folktale, N Y 1946, pp 97, 100.

Lüthi M, Das europäische Volksmärchen, Form und Wesen, Bern 1947, pp 85, 112.

Spence L, The Fairy Tradition in Britain, London 1948, p 200.

Swahn J O, The Tale of Cupid and Psyche (Aarne-Thompson 425, 428), Lund 1955, p 382.

Relations with Chaucer. Smith R M, Three Notes on the Knight's Tale, MLN 51.320 (crit D Everett, YWES 17.77).

Parr J, Chaucer and Partonope of Blois, MLN 60.486 (crit D Everett, YWES 26.49).

Whiting B J, A Fifteenth Century English Chaucerian: The Translator of Partonope de Blois, MS 7.40.

Everett D, Chaucer's Good Ear, RES 23.201, rptd Essays on ME Literature, ed P Kean, Oxford 1955, p 141.

Other Relations. Rose W S, Partenopex de Blois; A Romance in Four Cantos, Freely Translated from the French of M le Grand, London 1807, notes pp 103, 105 (Melusine).

Kölbing E, Partonopeus-Sage, Germanistische Studien, Suppl to Germania, 2.55, 77.

Foerster W, LfGRP 23.28 (crit of Kawczyński, relation to Chrétien de Troyes).

Carter C H, Ipomedon, an Illustration of Romance Origins, Haverford Essays, Studies in Modern Literature [for] Francis B Gummere, Haverford Pa 1909, p 253.

Otto S, Das Einfluss des Roman de Thebes auf altfranzösischen Literatur, Göttingen 1909, p 59.

Cross T P, The Celtic Origin of the Lay of Yonec, RC 31.414; The Celtic Fée in Launfal, Kittredge Anniversary Papers, Boston and London 1913, p 377 (magic hunt; fairy mistress); Celtic Elements in Lanval and Graelent, MP 12.592n2.

Pschmadt C, Die Sage von der verfolgten Hinde, Griefswald 1911, pp 66, 88, 95, 122.

Leendertz P, Floris ende Blancefloer, Leiden 1912, p 40 (Eastern origins).

Watson F, ed of J L Vives, Institutione faeminae Christianae (1529), London 1912, pp 58, 59 (reputation of Partonope in 16 cent).

Brown A C L, From Cauldron of Plenty to Grail, MP 392n4 (magic boat).

Ogle M B, The Stag-Messenger Episode, Am Journal of Philology 37.390, 393, 411 (classical, oriental parallels).

Puckett H W, The Fay, Particularly the Fairy Mistress in Middle High German, MP 16.297.

Ashdown M, Single Combat in Certain Cycles of English and Scandinavian Tradition and Romance, MLR 17.126, 130.

Hibbard Med Rom, pp 6 n one, 211n25 (Ipomedon influenced Partonope), 205n9, 212 (Celtic elements).

Voretzsch K, Introduction to the Study of OF Literature, trans F M Du Mont, N Y 1931, p 352 (Ywain, Lancelot, Guingamor).

Moret, see above, *Other Versions* (Bibl MHG, Low German, Dutch, Old Norse, Danish, ME, Spanish).

Reinhard J R, The Survival of Geis in Mediaeval Romance, Halle 1933, p 267 (the taboo, Celtic parallels).

Whiting B J, Proverbs in Certain ME Romances, HSNPL 15.94 (crit D Everett, YWES 15.106).

Martin H, L'explicit de Partonopeus de Blois, Rom 65.226.

Wright H G, An Allusion to the Romance of Partonope of Blois in the Fifteenth Century Tale of Guiscardo and Ghismonda, MLR 38.340 (crit G D Willcock, YWES 24.66).

Loomis R S, Morgain La Fée and the Celtic Goddesses, Spec 20.189; Arthurian Tradition and Chrétien de Troyes, N Y 1949, pp 90, 93 (French versions, Celtic-Arthurian parallels).

Newstead H, The Traditional Background of Partonopéus de Blois, PMLA 61.916, 919 (Breton lais), 934, 938, 946 (French versions, Celtic-Arthurian parallels, Morgain la Fée).

Williams H F, Floriant and Florete, Univ of Michigan Publications in Language and Literature 23, Ann Arbor 1947, p 26 (crit H D Learned, Symposium 2.136) (magic boat).

Casson L F, Sir Degrevant, EETS 221.lxiv.

Kane, pp 36, 40 (Degrevant, Firumbras, William of Palerne, Chevalier Assigne).

Wilson R M, The Lost Literature of Medieval England, London 1952 (crit D Everett, MÆ 22.33).

Smithers G V, Story Patterns in Some Breton Lays, MÆ 22.61 (crit B J Timmer, YWES 34.78); Kyng Alisaunder, EETS 257.150 note to line 7250 (judicial combat).

Uri S P, Some Remarks on Partonopéus de Blois, Neophil 37.83, 97.

Albrecht W P, The Loathly Lady in Thomas of Erceldoune, Univ of New Mexico Publications in Lang and Lit 11, Albuquerque 1954, pp 30, 61.

Eisner S, A Tale of Wonder: A Source Study of the Wife of Bath's Tale, Wexford, Ireland 1957, chap 6 (crit K Malone, SN 30.261).

Dunn C W, The Foundling and the Werwolf,

A Literary-Historical Study of Guillaume de Palerne, Univ of Toronto Dept of English Studies and Texts 8, Toronto 1960, pp 68, 72.

Rickard R, Britain in Medieval French Literature, Cambridge 1956, p 167n8.

Other Problems. Webster K G, The Twelfth Century Tourney, Kittredge Anniversary Papers, Boston and London 1913, pp 227, 229, 233.

Ashdown M, Single Combat in Certain Cycles of English and Scandinavian Tradition and Romance, MLR 17.126, 130.

Barrow S F, The Medieval Society Romances, N Y 1924, p 139.

Reinhard, Survival of Geis in Medieval Romance, p 267.

Wilcox J, French Courtly Love in the English Composite Romances, Papers of the Michigan Acad of Science, Arts and Letters 18.583, 586.

Fisher F, Narrative Art in Medieval Romance, Cleveland O, 1938, pp 23, 58 (French version).

Everett D, Chaucer's Good Ear, RES 23.201, rptd in Essays on ME Literature, Oxford 1955, p 141 and nn 4, 5.

Ward, 1.690, 698; Gröber, 2¹.586; Brandl, § 113; Paris Litt franç, § 51, p 84, and bibl; Schofield, p 307; Körting, § 103anm2; Bennett OHEL, 2.106, 164; Baugh LHE, p 194; Kane, pp 8, 36, 51, 80, and passim.

Thomas P G, English Literature before Chaucer, London 1924, p 116.

Wilson R M, The Lost Literature of Medieval England, London 1952 (crit D Everett, MÆ 22.33).

Schlauch M, English Medieval Literature and Its Social Foundations, Warsaw 1956, p 189.

Hibbard Med Rom, p 212, new edn, 1960, p 349; Tucker-Benham, p 253; Voretzsch, Introduction to OF Literature, p 354; Renwick-Orton, p 385; CBEL, 1.159, 5.116 (t); Newstead, PMLA 61.916; Bennett OHEL, 2.314; Bossuat MBLF, nos 1381–87, 6252; Holmes CBFL, nos 892–93.

Uri, Neophil 37.97 (editions in foreign languages).

Swahn, The Tale of Cupid and Psyche (Aarne-Thompson 425, 428), p 382.

Schmitt F A, Stoff- und Motivgeschichte der deutschen Literatur: eine Bibliographie, begründet von K Bauerhorst, Berlin 1959, p 6, Amor nos 91, 92.

[100] EGER AND GRIME.

MSS. 1, BM Addit 27879 (Percy Folio), pp 124–145 (ca 1650). PRINTS: 2, BM, The History of Sir Eger, Glasgow, Robert Sanders, 1669, 4° (Wing, STC, no 2139); 3, HN, [anr edn] [Glasgow, Robert Sanders?], 1687, 24° (Wing, STC, no 2140); 4 [anr edn] Aberdeen (Laing text), 1711, (almost identical with no 3 above).

Brown-Robbins, no 1624; no early MSS extant.

Laing D, Early Popular Poetry of Scotland, Edinb 1822, Advertisement describing Sir Egeir, Sir Gryme, and Sir Gray Steill.

Furnivall F J, ed, Captain Cox, His Ballads and Books, Ballad Soc 7, London 1871; rptd J H H Murray, The Complaynt of Scotland, EETSES 17, 18, p lxxix, p 63.

Rickert Rof Fr, p 182.

Editions. See above under *MSS*, nos 2, 3, 4.

Laing D, Early Metrical Tales including the History of Sir Egeir, Sir Gryme and Sir Gray-Steill, Edinb 1826, p 1 (Aberdeen print 1711); rptd in Early Scottish Metrical Tales, Glasgow and London 1889, p 53; rvsd W C Hazlitt, Early Popular Poetry of Scotland and the Northern Border, Rearranged and Revised, London 1895, 2.119, 131.

PFMS, 1.341 (Introd), 342n2, 354 (Percy Folio, BM Addit 27879); rptd J W Hales, Folio Literaria, Essays and Notes on English Literature, N Y 1893, p 40.

French W H and C B Hale, ME Metrical Romances, N Y 1930, p 671 (Percy Folio).

Caldwell J R, Eger and Grime; a parallel text edition of the Percy and the Huntington-Laing versions of the romance, HSCL 9, Cambridge Mass 1933 (crit A C Baugh, Bibl PMLA 48.1311; TLS, Apr 5 1934, p 246; D Everett, YWES 14.121; D Everett, MLR 29.446; A T[aylor], MP 31.323; A Taylor, JAF 47.265; A B[randl], Arch 165.138; H Marcus, AnglB 45.233; H Koziol, EStn 70.270; K[emp] M[alone], MLN 51.415).

Abstract. Ellis Spec, p 546 (1711 edn).

Warton T, History of English Poetry, ed W C Hazlitt, London 1871, 2.33.

Hazlitt W C, Early Popular Poetry of Scotland, 2.119.

Caldwell J R, Eger and Grime, Harvard Univ Summary of Theses, Cambridge Mass 1930, p 192; edn, p 51.

Retelling. Rickert Rof Fr, p 137 (The Story of Gray-Steel).

Moncrieff A R H, Romances and Legends of Chivalry, N Y 1934, p 335 (The Forbidden Island).

Textual Matters. PFMS, 1.363 (lines 305, 974).

Kölbing E, Kleine Beiträge zur Erklärung und Textkritik englischer Dichter, EStn 3.101, 3.105.

Reichel G, Studien zu der schottischen Romanze: The History of Sir Eger, Sir Grime and Sir Gray-Steel, Breslau 1893, rptd in EStn 19.15 (crit E Kölbing, Krit Jahresber, 4².435).

Language, Dialect, Versification. Rickert RofFr, p xx.

Basilius H A, The Rhymes in Eger and Grime, MP 35.129 (northern, but not characteristically Scottish) (crit Bibl PMLA 52.1237; M S Serjeantson, YWES 18.98).

Sources and Analogues. Reichel, EStn 19.8, 15. Rickert RofFr, pp xx, xxiii, 183 (Teutonic elements).

Van Duzee M, A Medieval Romance of Friendship: Eger and Grime, N Y 1963.

Relations with the Folktale. Thompson Mot Ind, H 57.2 (recognition by missing finger); H 335, H 933 (princess sets hero tasks); K 3 (substitute in contest); Q 598 (fighting all who pass); S 161.1 (mutilation: cutting off fingers).

Gerould G H, The Grateful Dead, Folklore Soc 60, 1907, chap 2: The Lady and the Monster.

Peebles R J, Blood Brotherhood in the ME Romances, PMLA 29, Appendix, p xxvii, no 53.

Dickson A, Valentine and Orson, A Study in Late Medieval Romance, N Y 1929, p 42 n42.

Cross Mot Ind, H 335, K 3, S 161.

Loomis R S, Arthurian Tradition and Chrétien de Troyes, N Y 1949, p 165n12; Wales and the Arthurian Legend, Cardiff 1956, p 85.

Relations with Ballad. PFMS, 1.74, 75n (Sir Lionel, Sir Aldingar).

Child F J, The English and Scottish Popular Ballads, Boston 1882–98, 1.208 (Sir Lionel, no 18), 2.56 (Sir Cawline, no 61), 3.306 (Sir Eglamour, Sir Triamour, Hunting of Cheviot).

Nessler K, Geschichte der Ballade Chevy Chase, Berlin 1911, p 93.

Taylor D, The Lineage and Birth of Sir Aldingar, JAF 65.139.

Christophersen P, The Ballad of Sir Aldingar, London, N Y 1952.

Leach M, The Ballad Book, N Y 1955, pp 100, 185.

Brunner K, Romanzen und Volksballaden, Palaes 148.78 (relation to Sir Lionel).

The Combat at the Ford. Thurneysen R, Keltoromanisches, Halle 1884, p 20.

Zenker R, Lai de l'Épine, ZfRP 17.246.

Weston J L, Legend of Sir Gawain, London 1897, p 12; Legend of Sir Perceval, London 1906, 2.207.

Cross T P, Celtic Elements in the Lays of Lanval and Graelent, MP 12.604n1.

Dickson A, Valentine and Orson, A Study in Late Medieval Romance, p 69n16.

Loomis R S, The Combat at the Ford in the Didot Perceval, MP 43.65 and note 10; rptd in Wales and the Arthurian Legend, p 94; Arthurian Tradition and Chrétien de Troyes, p 276.

Literary Relations including Arthurian. Reichel, EStn 19.8, 15.

Jefferson B L, A Note on the Squyr of Lowe Degre, MLN 28.109 (Knight of Curtesy).

Brown A C L, Iwain, A Study in Romance Origins, HSNPL 8, Boston 1903, p 34 (Chrétien de Troyes' Iwain).

Rickert RofFr, Introduction, pp xx, 158, 183, 184.

Cross, MP 12.718.

Kittredge G L, A Study of Gawain and the Green Knight, Cambridge Mass 1916, p 104.

Hibbard Med Rom, pp 276n2, 314, 318 (Ywain and Gawain), pp 316 (Irish hero Diarmaid), 309 (Degrevant), 318 (Nibelungen).

Loomis R S, Celtic Mythology and Arthurian Romance, N Y 1927, pp 84, 86; Arthurian Tradition and Chrétien de Troyes, pp 93n45, 276, 277, 415 (Lai de l'Espine, Ywaine, Pwyll); Vandeberes, Wandlebury and the Lai de l'Espine, RomP 9.166 (William A Nitze Testimonial Volume, 4, part 1); Wales and the Arthurian Legend, p 85.

Caldwell, edn, pp 62, 98 (fairy mistress), 103, 110 (otherworld champion), 186 (Melusine) (and notes).

Brunner K, Romanzen und Volksballaden, Palaes 148.78 [Anglica 2] (Sir Torrent, Sir Eglamour, Sir Lionel).

Other Problems. Rickert RofFr, p 158 (women doctors in the Middle Ages).

Wilson R M, The Lost Literature of Medieval England, London 1952, p 132.

Enkvist N E, The Seasons of the Year: Chapters on a Motif from Beowulf to the Shepherds Calendar, Copenhagen 1957, Commentationes humanarum litterarum 22, no 4, Helsingfors Finland 1957, p 128.

Lowell J R, Essay on Chaucer, in Literary Essays, Collected Works, Boston 1890, 3.327.

Ker W P, Epic and Romance, London and N Y 1899, p 442.

Henderson T F, Scottish Vernacular Literature, London 1898, 2nd edn rvsd 1900, p 39.

Leach H G, Angevin Britain and Scandinavia, Cambridge Mass 1921, p 334.

Hammond E P, English Verse between Chaucer and Surrey, Durham N C 1927, p 32.

Schlauch M, English Medieval Literature and Its Social Foundations, Warsaw 1956, p 296.

Speirs J, Medieval English Poetry, London 1957, pp 119n1, 201.

Schofield, p 232; Rickert RofFr, introd p xxiv; Renwick-Orton, p 117; Baugh LHE, p 193; Kane, p 31.

Hibbard Med Rom, pp 309, 312, 313; new edn, 1960, p 348; CBEL, 1.160(y), 5.117(y); Bennett OHEL, 2.311; Lewis OHEL, 3.68, 597.

[101] ROSWALL AND LILLIAN.

MSS. No MS extant. PRINTS: 1, Bodl Douce PP 157, The pleasant history of Roswal and Lillian, 14 leaves, [1663?], 8°; 2, Bodl Douce PP 173, The pleasant history of Roswal and Lillian, Newcastle, [n d], 12°; 3, BM, The Pleasant History of Roswal and Lillian, 12 pages, [1700?], 12°; 4, Natl Libr Scotland (Advocates), The Pleasant history of Roswall and Lillian, Edinburgh, by I H, 1663, 4° (Wing, STC, no P 2550).

Editions. Laing D, A Pleasant History of Roswall and Lillian, Edinb 1882 (reproduction of 1663 text), printed for D Laing's Select Remains of the Ancient Popular Poetry of Scotland, Edinb 1822, but issued separately.

Laing D, Early Metrical Tales, Edinb 1826, p 263 [Roswall and Lillian based on Edinb 1663 text and other prints], rptd in Early Scottish Metrical Tales, London and Glasgow 1889 [Roswall and Lillian, pref p 43 and text p 283].

Hazlitt W C, Early Popular Poetry of Scotland, London 1895, 2.239 (revising Laing's Select Remains, 1822, and Early Popular Poetry, 1826).

Lengert O, Die schottische Romanze Roswall and Lillian, EStn 16.321 (parallel text edition of Edinb 1663, Natl Libr Scotland, Newcastle prints compared with prints of 1679 and Edinb 1775, Douce, Bodl; EStn 17.341 (commentary and notes).

Abstract, Summary. Ellis Spec, p 578.

Child F J, English and Scottish Popular Ballads, London 1882–98, 5 vols, 5.43.

Hazlitt W C, Tales and Legends of National Origin or Widely Current in England from Early Times, London 1892, p 385.

Modernization. Rickert RofFr, p 117, introd p xx, p 179 (notes).

Sources and Analogues, Relations with Folktales. Thompson Mot Ind, E 501 (lover as hunter); F 601.2, G 671, N 801 (grateful helpers in suitor tests); H 331.2, R 222 (three days'

tournament); K 1816, K 1816.0.3 (disguise as menial); L 101 (male Cinderella).

Arfert P, Das Motiv von der untergeschobenen Braut, Rostock 1878, p 50.

Köhler R, Albanische Märchen übersetzt von G Meyer mit Anmerkungen von R Köhler, Archiv für Litteraturgeschichte, Leipzig 1884, pp 137, 142.

Weston J L, The Three Days' Tournament, London 1902, pp 34, 37n1.

Maynadier H, The Arthur of the English Poets, Boston 1907, p 223.

Carter C H, Ipomedon, Haverford Essays, Haverford 1909, p 245.

Schoepperle G, Tristan and Isolt, Frankfurt a Main, London 1913, 1.206 (substitute bride).

Bolte J and G Polivka, Anmerkungen zu den kinder- u Hausmärchen der Brüder Grimm, Leipzig 1918, 2.273 [Grimm no 89], 3.94 [Grimm no 136] (helpful companions).

Loomis L H, Sir Thopas, Bryan-Dempster, p 550 (catalogue lists).

Relations with the Ballad. PFMS, 1.180 (The Lord of Learne).

Child, English and Scottish Popular Ballads, 5.43, 47 (The Lord of Lorn and the False Steward, no 271).

Roxb Ballads, ed C Hindley, London 1874, 2.348.

Hazlitt, Early Popular Poetry of Scotland, 2.239 and note.

Brunner K, Romanzen und Volksballaden, Palaes 148.75, 81 [Anglica 2].

Falconer A F, ed, The Correspondence of Thomas Percy and David Dalrymple, Lord Hales: The Percy Letters, ed D N Smith and C Brooks, Barton Rouge La 1954, 4.15.

Other Relations. Jentsch F, Die me Romanze Richard Coeur de Lion u ihre Quellen, EStn 15.233.

Panzer F, Hilde-Gudrun, Halle 1901, p 266 (Apollonius of Tyre).

Mead W E, Squyr of Lowe Degre, Boston etc 1904, pp xx, xxvii, xxx, and passim.

Casson L F, Sir Degrevant, EETS 221.lxiii, lxiv, 145.

Cline R H, The Influence of Romances on Tournaments of the Middle Ages, Spec 20.210 (on three-day tournaments).

Henderson T F, Scottish Vernacular Literature, 2nd edn, London 1900, p 39.

Ward, 1.734; Schofield, pp 118, 188; Körting, § 92; Hibbard Med Rom, pp 290, 293, new edn 1960, p 350; CBEL, 1.160(z).

[102] IPOMADON.

MSS. 1, BM Harley 2252, ff 54a–84a (ca 1500) (Version B); 2, BM Longleat 257 (Marquis of Bath 25), ff 90^a–106^b (ca 1460) (Version C, prose); 3, Chetham's Libr, Manchester, Chetham 8009, ff 188^a–332^a (ca 1500) (Version A). PRINTS: 4, BM (The Metrical Romance of Ipomydon), Bagford Ballads, 1 leaf, W de Worde (ca 1522) (STC, no 5732.5; olim STC, no 14128); 5, PML 20896 (The Life of Ipomydon), 38 leaves, imp, W de Worde (ca 1530) (STC, no 5733).

Brown-Robbins, no 2142 (Version B, couplets), no 2635 (Version A, stanzas); MED, p 50.

Ward, 1.755 (Harley 2252).

Kölbing E, Vier Romanzen-Handschriften, EStn 7.195 (Chetham); MS 25 der Bibliothek des Marquis of Bath, EStn 10.204 (Longleat 257).

Manly & Rickert, 1.339, 341 (MS Longleat 257, f 98b contains autograph of Richard III).

Flower R, Lost Manuscripts, Essays by Divers Hands, TRSL ns 18.112 (name of a 14 cent owner).

Editions. W de Worde, see above under *MSS.* Weber MR, Lyfe of Ipomydon, 2.279; see introd 1.1; notes, 2.478, 3.361 (Harley 2252, BM).

Kirschten W, Ueberlieferung und Sprache der me Romanze The Lyfe of Ipomydon, Marburg 1885, p 2 (BM W de Worde, Bagford Ballads, 54 lines).

Bülbring K D, Vier Neue Alexanderbruchstücke, EStn 13.153, Anhang 1.

Kölbing E, Hue de Rotelande's Ipomedon in drei englischen Bearbeitungen, Breslau 1889, p 3 (stanzaic), p 257 (couplet), p 323 (prose) (crit Athen 1889, no 3220; A Brandl, DLz 10.1681; J M Garnett, AJP 10.348; M Kaluza, EStn 13.482; R W, LZ, 1889, p 1779; R W[ülcker], Angl 12.476; J Zupitza, LfGRP 11.142; G L Kittredge, Anmerkungen zum me Ipomadon A, EStn 14.386; E Freymond, Krit Jahresber 1.388).

Selections. Warton T, History of English Poetry from the Twelfth to the Close of the Sixteenth Century, London 1840, vol 1, § 5, p 194; ed W C Hazlitt 1871, 2.184.

Bennett H S, England from Chaucer to Caxton, London 1928, p 118 (Harley 2252 [Version B], after Kölbing), 22 lines to show a young page's training.

French W H and C B Hale, ME Metrical Romances, N Y 1930, p 649 (Chetham 8009 [Version A]).

Abstract, Summary. Ellis Spec, p 505.

Wilcox J, French Courtly Love in the English Composite Romances, Papers of the Michigan Acad of Science, Arts, and Letters 18.576.

Textual Matters. Kirschten W, Ueberlieferung

und Sprache der me Romanze the Lyfe of Ipomydon, Marburg 1885 (crit Weber's text).

Köppel E, Zur Textkritik des Ipomadon, EStn 14.371.

Kittredge G L, Ammerkungen zum me Ipomadon A, EStn 14.386.

Kellner L, Syntaktische Bemerkungen zu Ipomadon, EStn 18.282.

Willert H, Ipomadon, Strophe 37, EStn 38.131.

Holthausen F, Zu me Romanzen: Lyfe of Ipomydon, Angl 40.412; Ipomadon, Angl 41.463.

Language, Dialect, Versification. Kirschten, Ueberlieferung und Sprache der Lyfe of Ipomydon (crit Weber's text).

Kölbing, edn, p clxiii (Northwest Midland, Lancashire), p lxv (method of translator).

Kellner, EStn 18.282.

Curtius F J, An Investigation of the Rimes and Phonology of the Middle Scotch Romance Clariodus, Angl 16.450.

Jong R R de, On ME Rhymes in end(e) and ent(e), EStn 21.325.

Seyferth P, Sprache und Metrik des me strophischen Gedichtes Le Morte Arthur und sein Verhältnis zu The Lyfe of Ipomydon, Berlin 1895, BBGRP 8.75, 76 (§§ 41, 42).

Reicke C, Untersuchungen über den Stil der me alliterierenden Gedichte Morte Arthur, The Destruction of Troy, The Wars of Alexander, The Siege of Jerusalem, Sir Gawayn and the Green Knight, ein Beitrag zur Lösung der Huchown-frage, Königsberg 1906, pp 12, 28, 44, 56, 61, 70, 80, and passim (verse). CHEL, 1.324.

Trounce A McI, The English Tail-Rhyme Romances, MÆ 1.87, 168, and passim; 2.34, 189, and passim; 3.36, 40, 41 (opposes Kölbing's criteria for the dialect), 42 (date 1350), 43, 47; Athelston, London 1933, rvsd, EETS 224.50 (Northeast Midland dialect), 55 (run-on lines), 57 (verse accent).

Craigie W, rev of J A Falconer's The Northern Element in English Literature, ESts 17.106.

Serjeantson M S, A History of Foreign Words in English, N Y 1936, p 145 (French words—technical character, lists of passions, stones).

Manly & Rickert, 1.339.

Dunlap A R, The Vocabulary of the ME Tail-Rhyme Stanza, Delaware Notes, 14s, passim.

Author. Seyferth, BBGRP 8.75.

Billings A H, A Guide to the ME Metrical Romances Dealing with the Cycles of Charlemagne and Arthur, N Y 1901, YSE 9.208.

Sources and Analogues. French Version. Ward, 1.728.

Kölbing E and E Koschwitz, Hue de Rote-

lande's Ipomedon: ein französischen Aben-
teuerroman des 12 Jahrhundert, Breslau
1889, p xv (fragment printed by E Stengel,
ZfRP 6.394).

Mussafia A, Sulla critica del testo del romanzo
in francese antico Ipomedon, Wien 1890,
Sitzungsber der Wiener Akad 121, item 13
(crit E Freymond, Krit Jahresber 1.388).

Livingston C H, Manuscript Fragments of a
Continental French Version of the Roman
d'Ipomedon, MP 40.117.

Warren F M, Notes on the romans d'aventure,
MLN 13.343, 345.

Carter C H, Ipomedon, an Illustration of Ro-
mance Origins, Haverford Essays, Studies in
Modern Literature [for F B Gummere],
Haverford Pa 1909, p 239 (crit M Kaluza,
Krit Jahresber 13².584).

Otto S, Der Einfluss des Roman de Thèbes
auf die altfranz Literatur, Göttingen 1909,
p 62.

Hahn W, Der Wortschatz des Dichters Hue de
Rotelande, Berlin 1910.

Gay L M, Hue de Rotelande's Ipomedon and
Chrétien de Troyes, PMLA 32.468.

Voretzsch K, Introduction to the Study of OF
Literature, trans F M Du Mont, N Y 1931,
p 346 (Chrétien de Troyes, lais, romances of
antiquity).

Wilson R M, Early ME Literature, London
1939, 2nd edn 1951, p 78.

Relations with the Folktale. Thompson Mot Ind,
H 151.10, N 731.2, N 733 (combat of unknown brothers); H 331.2 (suitor contest:
tournament); K 1816, 1816.0.3 (disguise as
menial); K 1818.3 (disguise as fool); L 113.2
(menial heroine); L 431.1 (haughty mistress);
M 181 (magic horse); R 169.1, R 222 (disguised knight—3 days' tournament); T 11.1
(love from mere mention); T 24 (symptoms
of love); T 31, T 31.1 (lovers' meeting: hero
in service of heroine, her uncle).

Cosquin E, Contes populaires Lorraine, Rom
8.545.

Ward, 1.734.

Potter M A, Sohrab and Rustum, London
1902, p 207.

Carter, Ipomedon, Haverford Essays, pp 239,
256, 263.

Bruce J D, Evolution of Arthurian Romance,
Hesperia 8, Göttingen 1925, 1.212, 371n8.

Cross T P, Celtic Elements in Lanval and
Graelent, MP 12.612n3.

Moore O H, Jaufre Rudel and the Lady of
Dreams, PMLA 29.527.

Malone K, Rose and Cypress, PMLA 43.399.

Dickson A, Valentine and Orson, N Y 1929,
pp 107, 143, 188n63.

Schlauch M, Romance in Iceland, N Y and
London 1934, p 64.

Loomis R S, Arthurian Tradition and Chrétien
de Troyes, N Y 1949, p 445.

Relations with the Ballad. Furnivall F J, ed,
Captain Cox, His Ballads and Books, Ballad
Soc 7, London 1871, p cxlii.

Child F J, The English and Scottish Popular
Ballads, Boston 1882–98, 2.510b (King
Estmere, no 60), 5.47.

Proverbs. Kittredge, EStn 14.386.

Whiting B J, Proverbs in Certain ME Romances, HSNPL 15.76 (crit D Everett, YWES
15.105).

Relations with Chaucer. Kittredge, EStn 14.391.

Young K, The Origin and Development of the
Story of Troilus and Criseyde, Chaucer Soc
1908, 2s, 40, p 46 (faithful squire).

Trounce A McI, The English Tail-Rhyme
Romances, MÆ 1.87, 168.

Smith R M, Three Notes on the Knight's Tale,
MLN 51.320 (alliterative description of
tournament) (crit D Everett, YWES 17.77).

Loomis L H, Sir Thopas, in Bryan-Dempster,
pp 486, 495; Ipomadon A (stanzaic, MS
Chetham), pp 505, 514, 520, 546, 548;
Ipomydon B (couplet, MS Harley 2252),
pp 502, 510, 513, 514, 520.

Dunlap A R, The Vocabulary of the ME
Romances in Tail-Rhyme Stanza, Delaware
Notes 14s, p 29 (compared with Sir Tho-
pas).

Parr J, Chaucer and Partonope of Blois, MLN
60.486.

Everett D, Chaucer's Good Ear, RES 23.201
(crit D Everett, YWES 28.71); rptd Essays
on ME Literature, ed P Kean, Oxford 1955,
p 141.

Relations to Arthurian Romances. Potvin C, ed,
Perceval le Gallois ou le Conte du Graal,
Société des bibliophiles belges 21, Mons 1866,
lines 43719–44056.

Ward, 1.734 (Sir Gowther), 1.735 (Launcelot).

Seyferth P, Sprache und Metrik des me strophischen Gedichtes Le Morte Arthur und sein
Verhältnis zu The Lyfe of Ipomydon,
BBGRP 8.75, 76 (crit F Holthausen, LZ,
1895, p 1562).

Weston J L, The Three Days' Tournament,
London 1902, p 34.

Maynadier G H, The Arthur of the English
Poets, Boston 1907, p 223 (three days'
tournament, other parallels).

Carter, Ipomedon, Haverford Essays, p 248
(Lancelot), p 255 (Le Bel Inconnu), p 261
(Tristan), p 270.

Gay L M, Hue de Roteland's Ipomedon and
Chrétien de Troyes, PMLA 32.469.

Bruce J D, The Evolution of Arthurian Romance, Göttingen 1923, pp 217, 247n8.

Muchnic H, The Coward Knight and the Damsel of the Cart, PMLA 43.327 (three days' tournament, handsome coward).

Loomis R S, Celtic Myth and Arthurian Romance, N Y 1927, pp 27, 215; Malory's Beaumains, PMLA 54.656; Arthurian Tradition and Chrétien de Troyes, N Y 1949, pp 225, 338, 351, and passim.

Other Relations, Typical Phrases. Jentsch F, Die me Romanze Richard Coeur de Lion, EStn 15.233 (Richard).

Kittredge G L, A Study of Gawain and the Green Knight, Cambridge Mass 1916, pp 100, 128, 135.

McKnight G H, King Horn, EETS 14.139, 140, 141, notes to lines 239, 250, 387, 595, and passim.

Carter, Ipomedon, Haverford Essays, p 250 (Chrétien's Cligès); p 254 (Roswall and Lillian); p 255 (Richard Coeur de Lion).

Schlauch M, Chaucer's Constance and Accused Queens, N Y 1927, p 119 (Sicily as scene of action).

Trounce, The English Tail-Rhyme Romances, MÆ 3.36, 40, 43, 47 (Le Bone Florence); Athelston, EETS 224.43, 45, Introduction, and passim (Amis and Amiloun, Octavian, Cleges).

Casson L F, The Romance of Sir Degrevant, EETS 221.liv.

Smithers G V, Kyng Alisaunder, EETS 237.154.

Legge D, rev of Gaimar's L'estoire des Engles, MLR 56.265.

Watson F, edn R Hyrde's trans of Vives' Institutione faeminae Christianae, London 1912, pp 58, 59.

Webster K G T, The Twelfth-Century Tourney, Kittredge Anniversary Papers, Boston and London 1913, pp 229, 231, 233.

Barrow S F, The Medieval Soc Romances, N Y 1924.

Malone K, Rose and Cypress, PMLA 43.399.

Wilcox, French Courtly Love in the Engl Composite Romances, Papers of Mich Acad of Science, Arts, and Letters 18.576.

Fisher F, Narrative Art in Medieval Romance, Cleveland O 1938, p 58 (French version).

Cline R H, The Influence of Romances on Tournaments, Spec 20.210 (different colored armor).

Baugh A C, Improvisation in the ME Romances, PAPS 103.420.

Warton T, History of English Poetry, London 1840, 1.35; 140; ed W C Hazlitt 1871, 1.194.

Ker W P, Epic and Romance, London and N Y 1899, p 441; English Literature, Medieval, N Y and London, 1912, pp 103, 106.

Thomas P G, English Literature before Chaucer, London 1924, p 116.

Wilson R M, Early ME Literature, London 1939, 2nd edn 1951, p 78.

Schlauch M, English Medieval Literature and Its Social Foundations, Warsaw 1956, p 189.

Dunn C W, The Foundling and the Werwolf, A Literary-Historical Study of Guillaume de Palerne, Univ of Toronto Department of English Studies and Texts 8, Toronto 1960, p 84, notes 114, 115.

Ward, 1.728, 738, 755; Gröber, 2¹.585; Brandl, §§ 80, 125; HLF, 24.504; Schofield, p 310; CHEL, 1.285, 291, 349, 313; Körting, § 103anm2; Bennett OHEL, 2.164, 314; Baugh LHE, pp 141, 193; PAPS 103.420; Kane, p 28.

Hibbard Med Rom, pp 224, 229; new edn 1960, p 349; Renwick-Orton, p 385; CBEL, 1.155(f); Bossuat MBLF, nos 1150, 1153, 1154, 1157, 1160 (Protheselaus); Holmes CBFL, nos 910–12 (Protheselaus).

[103] VALENTINE AND ORSON.

MSS. No MS extant. PRINTS: 1, Duke of Devonshire, Chatsworth, W de Worde, 4 leaves, fragm (1502?) (or 1503–05) (corresponding to ff C³–D² of print no 2, HN, listed next), trans H Watson; 2, Huntington Libr (olim Britwell), W Copland for John Walley, 239 leaves (photostat in Columbia Univ Libr), London 1548–58, imp (possibly a reprint of a lost edition) (STC, no 24572ª); 3, BM (c.34.1.17) and Yale Univ Libr (olim Britwell), W Copland, 246 leaves, London 1562–67, probably set from print no 2, HN (STC, no 24572); 4, BM Harl 5919 (Bagford Collection C.72; no 43), one leaf, f Hh 3, same as print no 3, above; 5, An abridgment, Bodl and BM, London 1637 (STC, no 24573).

Dickson, see below, under *Editions*, pp xi, xiv, xvii, xliv (woodcuts); see below, *Study*, p 285.

Esdaile A, A List of English Tales and Prose Romances Printed before 1740, London 1912, p 133.

Editions. Dickson A, Valentine and Orson, trans from the French by Henry Watson, EETS 204 (based upon print no 2, above) (pp 18–32 give parallel text from print no 1, above) (pp 307–315 from print no 3, above, BM copy) (crit TLS, Aug 28 1937, p 620; A Brandl, Arch 173.82; F Delotte, Rev de l'université de Bruxelles, Oct-Nov 1938, 1.89; H Marcus, AnglB 49.10; E E Wardale, MLR

33.60; N&Q March 26 1938, 174.234; G D Bone, MÆ 8.231; K M[alone], MLN 55.242).

Selection. Dickson, Study 1929, p 281. Nugent E M, The Thought and Culture of the English Renaissance, Cambridge 1956, p 597 (Copland print 1548).

Retelling, Summary. Ashton J, Chapbooks of the Eighteenth Century, London 1882, p 109; Romances of Chivalry Told and Illustrated in Facsimile, London 1887, p 235.

Littlewood S R, Valentine and Orson, The Twin Knights of France, London 1919.

Harris J R, Valentine and Orson: A Study in Twin-Cult, Contemporary Review, 126.324.

Dickson A, Valentine and Orson; A Study in Late Medieval Romance, N Y 1929, pp 4, 297, nos 67, 69; p 298, no 74 (crit R Bossuat, RCHL 96.549; A Taylor, MLN 44.412; D Everett, YWES 10.130, 13.96; D Everett, RES 6.331; TLS May 1 1930, p 373; F Neri, Giornale storico della lett ital, 98.348; A H Krappe, MLN 47.493, 48.485; H Marcus, AnglB 44.77; M Delbouille, Moyen âge 44.42; A Hilka, ZfRP 53.620; S Hofer, ZfFSL 58.355; MLN 48.207; Correspondence, MLN 49.68 [replies to Krappe]; R O Frick, Schweizer Volksbunde 21.114; Z f österreich Volksbunde 38.44).

Language. Brie F W D, Skelton-Studien, EStn 37.18.

Pompen F A, The English Versions of the Ship of Fools, London 1925, pp 282, 287.

Date. Gröber, 2¹.792 (hypothetical French verse original; Valentin and Namelos).

Dickson, Study 1929, pp 5n8, 265 (French Valentine and Orson); edn, p ix (French Valentine and Orson).

Sources and Analogues, Other Versions. Klemming G E, Namnlös och Valentin, Stockholm 1846, p vii.

Seelmann W, Valentin und Namelos, Leipzig 1884, pp ix, xxv, xxx, xxxiii, liii, lvii.

Frölicher H, Thüring von Ringoltingen's Melusin, Wilhelm Ziely's Oliver und Artus und Valentin und Orsus, und das Berner Cleomades-Fragment mit französischen Quellen verglichen, Zurich 1889.

Dickson, Study 1929, pp 3 (and n 5), 8, 10, 155, 156; edn, pp ix, xvii, xix (French text).

Dieperink G J, Studien zum Valentin und Namelos, Haarlem 1933, p 157.

Relations with the Folktale. Thompson Mot Ind, A 515.1.1, A 515.1.2, T 685.1 (twins as culture heroes, as adventurers); B 443; B 535, B 563; B 631, B 635.1 (animal nurse); F 601.5, F 610.1, G 671, H 94 (identification by ring); H 151.10, Z 210.1 (extraordinary

companion, brothers, wild man); K 2110.1, K 2112, K 2116 (calumniated wife); K 2231 (treacherous mistress); L 111.1, L 111.2 (foundling hero); N 312, N 738, N 765, Q 523.3 (penance-eating food offered to dogs); Q 598 (fighting all who pass through forest); R 13.0.1 (separation; carried off by beasts); T 685; and passim, numerous references.

Jahrbücher der Literatur, Wien 1825, 31.138 (Charlemagne Romances; review of G Dunlop, The History of Fiction, 2nd edn, Edinburgh 1816).

Potter M A, Sohrab and Rustum, London 1902, p 208 (cf Dickson, Study 1929, p 98 and notes).

Gerould G H, Forerunners, Congeners, and Derivatives of the Eustace Legend, PMLA 19.334, 439.

Rank O, Das Inzest-Motiv in Dichtung und Sage, Leipzig und Wien 1912, 2nd edn 1926, p 421.

Harris, Contemporary Review 126.323.

Krappe A H, La leggenda di S Eustachio, Nuovi studi medievali, 3.223.

Schlauch M, Chaucer's Constance and Accused Queens, N Y 1927, pp 86, 93, 98, and passim; Romance in Iceland, London 1934, pp 155, 166.

Rajna P, Per le origini e la storia primitiva del Ciclo brettone, Studi medievali ns 3.225 (puer sine nomine).

Spargo J W, Virgil the Necromancer, Cambridge Mass 1934, pp 132, 364, 367, 368, 411.

Bernheimer R, Wild Men in the Middle Ages, Cambridge Mass 1952, pp 17, 71, and p 201 note 55.

Relations with the Ballad. PFMS, 2.390 (The Emperor and the Childe); Reliques of Ancient English Poetry, ed H B Wheatley, London 1876–77, 3.291 (reference in St George for England), 3.265 (Valentine and Ursine, hero found on St Valentine's Day).

Child F J, The English and Scottish Popular Ballads, 5 vols, Boston 1882–98, 3.330 (Valentine and Ursine), 3.234 (Sir Aldingar), 3.173 (Sir Cauline).

Ebsworth J W, The Bagford Ballads, Hertford 1878, p lvi.

Christophersen P, Ballad of Sir Aldingar, Oxford 1952, pp 41, 149.

Robinson M G and L Dennis, edd, The Correspondence of Thomas Percy and Thomas Warton, The Percy Letters, ed D N Smith and C Brooks, Baton Rouge La 1951, 3.65.

Falconer A F, ed, The Correspondence of Thomas Percy and David Dalrymple, Lord Hales: The Percy Letters, ed D N Smith and C Brooks, Baton Rouge La 1954, 4.24 and n34.

Other Literary Relations and Allusions. Hole R, Arthur, or The Northern Enchantment, 1789, Preface p vii, quoted by R P Bond, SP 28.505.

Seelmann, p xxviii (Cervantes; flying horse, talking head).

Kittredge G L, A Study of Gawain and the Green Knight, Cambridge Mass 1916, p 185.

Harris, Contemporary Review 126.331 (Shakespeare).

Dickson, Study 1929, Index and pp 34, 48n59 (Apollonius), 100, 168 (Eustace), 106, 198n (Octavian, Torrent), 107 (Parzival), 110 (Generides); 189, 209 (Floris and Blaunchefleur, Seven Sages, Tristan), 72, 199 (Contance story), 215 (Don Quixote); Le roman de la Violette, Rev belge de philologie et d'histoire 12.1480 (Violette, Perceval); edn, pp li (Spenser), lix, lxi (Cervantes), lxii (Bunyan).

Golder H, Bunyan and Spenser, PMLA 45.216; Bunyan's Giant Despair, JEGP 30.361.

Caldwell J R, Eger and Grime, Cambridge Mass 1933, HSCL 9.110.

Warton T, History of English Poetry, ed C W Hazlitt, London 1871, 2.339, 3.195.

Gautier L, Les épopées françaises, 2nd edn, Paris 1878–97, 2.604.

Gudzy N K, The History of Early Russian Literature, trans S W Jones, N Y 1949, p 419.

Ward, 1.850; Schofield, p 318; CHEL, 2.369; Baugh LHE, p 301.

Hibbard Med Rom, p 10 (St Eustace); CBEL, 1.735; Bossuat MBLF, nos 4083–84.

[104] THE SQUYR OF LOWE DEGRE.

MSS. 1, BM Addit 27879 (Percy Folio), pp 444–446 (ca 1650). PRINTS: 2, BM [Garrick Collection], Here begynneth Undo Youre Dore, W Copland, 21 leaves (ca 1560), 4° (STC, no 23112); 3, Huntington Libr 62181, ff A ii, A vii, A viii, [Here Begynneth unto Youre Dore], W de Worde, 3 fragm (ca 1520), 4° (STC, no 23111.1).

Brown-Robbins, no 1644; MED, p 75.

Dibdin T F, The Library Companion or the Young Man's Guide, and the Old Man's Comfort, in the Choice of a Library, London 1825, 2nd edn, pp 657n, 666n.

Hazlitt W C, Bibliographical Collections and Notes on Early English Literature, 4s, London 1903, see under Squire.

Editions. Ritson AEMR, 3.145 (BM Copland) (crit E Kölbing, Kleine Beiträge zur Er-

klärung und Textkritik englischer Dichter, EStn 3.103).

Dibdin T F, Reminiscences of a Literary Life, London 1836, 2 vols, 2.912 (HN de Worde).

Hazlitt Rem, 2.21 (BM Copland) (crit J R Lowell, Literary Essays, in Collected Works, Boston 1890, 1.331).

PFMS, 3.263.

Mead W E, The Squyr of Lowe Degre, A ME Metrical Romance, Boston 1904 (all texts) (crit G Binz, AnglB 17.7; Archiv 117.465; M Weyrauch, EStn 37.408).

McCallum J D, English Literature, The Beginnings to 1500, N Y 1929, p 372; rptd 1932, p 402 (BM Copland, about 100 lines omitted).

French W H and C B Hale, ME Metrical Romances, N Y 1930, p 721 (BM Copland).

Selections. Warton T, History of English Poetry, London 1840, 1.175 (lines 91–104, 739–852 BM Copland from Ritson AEMR, 3.145); ed W C Hazlitt 1871, 2.167 § 5.

Sampson G, Cambridge Book of Prose and Verse, Cambridge 1924, p 301 (BM Copland).

Retelling. Hazlitt W C, Tales and Legends of National Origin or Widely Current in England from Early Times, London 1892, p 367.

Modernization. Rickert RofL, p 153.

Sources and Analogues. Tunk P, Studien zur me Romance The Squyr of Lowe Degre, Breslau 1900 (argues against a direct French source) (crit M Kaluza, Krit Jahresber 6².362, 8².173, Polemus in English Gesta Romanorum as source).

Weyrauch M, Zur Komposition, Enstehungszeit und Beurteilung der me Romanze Squyr of Lowe Degre, EStn 31.177.

Mead, edn, pp xxv, xxxvii (Squyr modelled on Guy of Warwick).

Jefferson B L, A Note on the Squyr of Lowe Degre, MLN 28.102 (originality of the theme).

Relations with Folktales. Thompson Mot Ind, H 317.1 (seven year service imposed on suitor); H 387.1 (bride's constancy tested by seven years mourning); K 1644; L 161 (lowly hero marries princess); T 85.4 (lover's body kept for years by grieving mistress).

Luthi M, Das europäische Volkmärchen Form und Wesen, Bern 1947, p 96 (poor man wins princess and throne).

Relations with the Ballad. Furnivall F J, Captain Cox, His Ballads and Books, Ballad Soc 7, London 1871, pp xii, xxiii.

Ebsworth J W, The Bagford Ballads, Ballad Soc, Hertford 1878, p lxxvi.

Child F J, The English and Scottish Popular Ballads, 5 vols, Boston 1882–98, 1.255 (no 27), 2.512 (no 73).

Relations with Sir Thopas. Loomis L H, ⁺Sir Thopas, in Bryan-Dempster, pp 550, 551, 555, 558 (catalogue lists).

Falconer A F, ed, The Correspondence of Thomas Percy and Thomas Warton: The Percy Letters, ed by D N Smith and C Brooks, Baton Rouge La 1951, 3.19, 21.

Other Relations. Zielke O, Sir Orfeo, Stil und Überlieferung des Gedichtes, Breslau 1879, rptd with text, 1880, pp 12, 15, 20, and passim.

Hall J, King Horn, Oxford 1901, p vii.

Mead, edn, p xxvii (Apollonius, Amadas de Gaul, William of Palerne, Amis and Amiloun, King Horn, Roswall and Lillian, Guy of Warwick, Torrent of Portyngale).

Jefferson, MLN 28.102 (Knight of Curtesy and the Fair Lady of Faguell, Eger and Grime).

McCausland E, The Knight of Curtesy and the Fair Lady of Faguell, Smith Coll Studies in Modern Lang 4, Northampton Mass 1922, pp xii, xvi.

Hibbard Med Rom, pp 265 (Florence of Rome; substitution of mutilated body), 266n7 (Knight of Courtesy).

Reinhard J R, The Old French Romance of Amadas et Ydoine, an Historical Study, Durham N C 1927, pp 41, 42, 62, 185.

Wilcox J, French Courtly Love in English Composite Romances, Papers of Michigan Acad of Science, Arts, and Letters 18.575, 587.

Luthi M, Das europäische Volksmärchen Form und Wesen, Bern 1947, pp 84, 96.

Casson L F, The Romance of Sir Degrevant, EETS 221.lxiii, lxv, 144n to line 1593, and passim.

Thomas P G, English Literature before Chaucer, London 1924, p 116.

Everett D, A Characterization of the English Medieval Romances, E&S 15.98, rptd in Essays on ME Literature, ed P Kean, Oxford 1955, p 6.

Schlauch M, English Medieval Literature and Its Social Foundations, Warsaw 1956, p 191.

Brandl, § 113; Schofield, p 310; CHEL, 1.321, 351; Körting, § 86 vorbem; Bennett OHEL, 2.164, 316; Baugh LHE, p 193; Kane, pp 66, 89, 96.

Hibbard Med Rom, pp 263, 266, new edn 1960, p 350; Tucker-Benham, p 257; Renwick-Orton, p 385; CBEL, 1.159(u).

[105] CLARIODUS.

MS. Advocates 19.2.5, ff 8–162, imp (ca 1570).

Editions. Irving D, ed, Clariodus: A Metrical Romance, Printed from a MS of the Sixteenth Century, Maitland Club 9, Edinburgh 1830.

Chapman R L, An Edition of the Middle Scots Romance Clariodus, DA 13.382.

Summary. Spence L, A Dictionary of Medieval Romance and Romance Writers, London 1913, p 64.

Language. Curtis F J, An Investigation of the Rimes and Phonology of the Middle-Scotch Romance Clariodus, Angl 16.387, 17.1.

Lenz K, Zur Lautlehre der französischen Elemente in den schottischen Dichtungen von 1500–1550 (G Douglas, W Dunbar, D Lyndesay, Clariodus), mit Bemerkungen zur Wortbildung und Wortbedeutung, Marburg 1913, pp 6, 7, 13 and passim.

Source. Smith J M, The French Background of Middle Scots Literature, Edinburgh and London 1934, p 24.

Millar J H, A Literary History of Scotland, London 1903, p 221.

Gröber, 2¹.158; W P Ker, CHEL, 1.291; Schofield, p 318.

Ward 1.383; Holmes CBFL, nos 1295–96. (French version: Cleriadus et Meliadice).

III. Romances on Historical Themes

[106] RICHARD COER DE LYON.

MSS. 1, Bodl 21802 (Douce 228), ff 1ᵃ–40ᵇ, imp (late 15 cent); 2, Caius Camb 175, ff 1–98, imp (1425–50); 3, BM Egerton 2862 (olim Trentham-Sutherland), ff 1ᵃ–44ᵇ, imp (ca 1400); 4, BM Harley 4690, ff 106ᵃ–115, imp (1450–1500); 5, BM Addit 31042 (Fillingham), ff 125ᵃ–163, imp (1425–50); 6, Coll of Arms, HDN 58 (olim Arundel),

ff 250ᵃ–275, imp (ca 1448); 7, Advocates 19.2.1 (Auchinleck), ff 326 and 327, imp (ca 1330); 8, Univ of Edinb 218, Div 56, ff 3, 4, two fragm, originally between ff 326 and 327 of Auchinleck MS; 9, Univ of St Andrew's Fragment 2, one bifolium originally between ff 326 and 327 of Auchinleck MS. PRINTS: 10, Bodl (Coynes 734), John Rylands Libr, Manchester, W de Worde, Rycharde cuer de Lyon (1509) (STC, no

21007); 11, Bodl, BM, PML 20931 (Landsdowne), W de Worde, Kynge Rycharde Cuer du Iyon (1528) (STC, no 21008).

Brown-Robbins, no 1979; MED, p 69.

Laing D, A Penni Worth of Witte, Abbotsford Club 29, Edinb 1857, pp ii, v (Auchinleck MS).

Arber Stationers' Registers, London 1875, 1.179 (Thomas Purfoote, 1568–69).

Ward, 1.949 (MS Harley 4690), 1.944 (Fillingham MS).

Kölbing E, Vier Romanzen-Handschriften, EStn 7.190 (Auchinleck MS), 191 (MS Egerton 2862).

Herrtage S J H, Sege of Melayne, EETSES 35.viii (Harley 4690; Fillingham MS).

McKerrow R B, Printers' & Publishers' Devices in England & Scotland 1485–1640, Bibl Soc Illustrated Monographs 16, London 1913, no 21.

Brunner K, Hs Brit Mus Additional 31042, Arch 132.327.

Carr M B, Notes on an English Scribe's Methods, Univ of Wisconsin Studies in Language and Literature, Madison Wisc 1918, 2.153 (OE ā in Auchinleck MS).

The [London] Times, Feb 10 1949, p 6 g.

Smithers G V, Two Newly-Discovered Fragments from the Auchinleck MS, MÆ 18.1; Kyng Alisaunder, EETS 237.4 (crit K Brunner, Angl 76.549, 550).

Trounce A McI, Athelston, EETS 224.1 (Caius Camb 175).

Bliss A J, Notes on the Auchinleck Manuscript, Spec 26.653, 656, no 48 (description and contents of Auchinleck MS) (crit G D Willcock, YWES 32.89).

Editions. W de Worde, see above, under *MSS*, 10, 11.

Weber MR, 2.1, 248 (MSS Caius Camb 175, Douce 228, and W de Worde 1528 edn), see 1.xlv (cf Ellis Spec, p 282).

Laing D and W B Turnbull, Owen Miles and Other Inedited Fragments of Ancient English Poetry, Edinb 1837, p 59, no 2 (Auchinleck MS), lines 674–1774, 2763–2936.

Kölbing E, Kleine Publicationen aus der Auchinleck-hs, Zwei Fragmente von King Richard, EStn 8.115 (prints 352 lines); Kleine Beiträge zur Erklärung me Dichter, EStn 13.138.

Paris G, Le roman de Richard Coeur de Lion, Rom 26.355 (Auchinleck text parallels to Weber's print).

Brunner K, Der me Versroman über Richard Löwenherz; kritische Ausgabe nach alten Handschriften mit Einleitung, Anmerkungen und deutscher Übersetzung, WBEP 42, Wien

und Leipzig 1913 (MS Caius Camb 175 with variants from all MSS and W de Worde) (crit Academy 1914, 1.202; M Förster, LZ 65.480; R Immelman, DLz 35.2375; N Y Nation, 99.2561, July 30 1914, p 138; J Koch, EStn 49.126; F Holthausen, AnglB 27.131; R S Loomis, JEGP 15.455).

Selections. Wülcker R P, Altenglisches Lesebuch, Halle 1874, 1.95 (lines 6657 to end) (crit E Kölbing, EStn 17.299).

Weston J L, Chief ME Poets, Boston, N Y etc 1914; new edn, London 1922, pp 123, 126 (modernized from Weber MR).

Bennett H S, England from Chaucer to Caxton, N Y 1928, p 240 (from Weber MR, 2.171, lines 4295–4415).

Funke O, A ME Reader: Texts from the 12th to the 14th cent, Bibliotheca Anglicana, Texts and Studies, 7, 7a, Bern 1944, p 41 (from Brunner, p 424 f).

Kaiser R, Medieval English, Berlin 1958; 3rd edn, rptd 1959, p 410, lines 1–234 (MS Caius Camb 175).

Baugh A C, Improvisation in the ME Romance, PAPS 103.438 (Fillingham MS, lines 241–264), 439 (MSS Auchinleck and Douce 228, lines 19–36), and passim.

Abstract. Ellis Spec, p 282 (after MS Caius Camb 175).

Percy T, Reliques of Ancient English Poetry, ed H B Wheatley, London 1886, 3.355, 372 (after W de Worde, 1528 edn).

Brunner, WBEP 42.12.

Summary. Ward, 1.944.

Textual Matters. Zupitza J, Richard Coeur de Lion, EStn 7.179; Die Romanze von Athelston, EStn 14.321 (on MS Caius Camb 175).

Kölbing E, EStn 7.178, 190; EStn 8.115; EStn 11.497n1; EStn 13.138 (on Auchinleck MS); Kleine Beiträge zu Erklärung und Textkritik me Dichtungen, EStn 17.299.

N Y Nation 99, no 2561, July 30 1914, p 138 (line 3151).

Baugh, PAPS 103.434, 438.

Language, Dialect, Verse. Schipper J, Englische Metrik, Bonn 1882, 1.258.

Kölbing E, Arthour and Merlin, AEB 4, pp CII, LX (Southeast Midland near Kent).

Kaluza M, A Short History of English Versification from the Earliest Times to the Present Day, trans A C Dunstan, London 1911, p 228.

Brunner WBEP 42, pp 24, 48; Arch 132.316, 327; Die Reimsprache der sogenannten kentischen Fassung der Sieben weisen Meister, Arch 140.199, 205 (Southeast Midland, The London Area, Kent); Die englische

Sprache, ihre geschichtliche Entwicklung, Halle 1951, 1.148.

Loomis R S, JEGP 15.456, 463 (Kent).

Mackenzie B A, A Special Dialectal Development of OE ēa in ME, EStn 61.386; Early London Dialect, Oxford 1928, pp 12, 121 OE ēa rhymes as tense vowel; dialect is Essex) (crit H M Flasdieck, AnglB 42.33, 46; G V Smithers, Kyng Alisaunder, EETS 237.41).

Smith R N, Two Chaucer Notes, MLN 51.314 (the name Topyas).

French W H, Dialects and Forms in Three Romances, JEGP 45.130 (mixed Midland dialect).

Smithers, Kyng Alisaunder, EETS 237.31, 42 (London) (crit K Brunner, Angl 76.549).

Penttilä E, Sense-Development of Verbs Denoting Emission of Light, NM 59.169 (ME glent).

Baugh, PAPS 103.421, 428, and passim (epic formulas, predictable complements).

Date. Ward, 1.946 (on real people mentioned in poem).

Kölbing E, Arthour and Merlin, AEB 4, CII, LX.

Paris G, Le roman de Richard Coeur de Lion, Rom 26.361 (about 1230).

Bülbring K, Sidrac in England, Festgabe für Wendelin Foerster, Halle 1902, Beiträge zur romanischen und englischen Philologie, p 447.

Loomis R S, JEGP 15.456 (about 1250).

French W H, Dialects and Forms in Three Romances, JEGP 45.125 (1275–1300).

Authorship. Kölbing E, Arthour and Merlin, AEB 4, pp LX, LXXIII, CII (same author for Richard and Arthour and Merlin) (crit E Freymond, Krit Jahresber 1.425; Kölbing, ibid, 1.648).

Brunner, edn, p 58; Arch 140.199.

Loomis R S, JEGP 15.456.

Smithers G V, Notes on ME Texts, LMS 1.208; Kyng Alisaunder, EETS 237.9, 41.

Stokoe W C jr, The Work of the Redactors of Sir Launfal, Richard Coeur de Lion, and Sir Degaré, Cornell Univ Abstr of Theses, 1946–47, p 26.

Sources, Literary-Historical Relations. Needler G H, Richard Coeur de Lion in Literature, Leipzig 1890 (crit LZ Feb 21 1891, p 272; H Varnhagen, DLz 12.418; F Jentsch, R Coeur de Lion, EStn 16.142; G Paris, Le roman de Richard Coeur de Lion, Rom 26.353).

Jentsch F, Die me Romanze Richard Coeur de Lion und ihre Quellen, EStn 15.161 (source in the Itinerarium peregrinorum et gesta regis Ricardi and other chronicles (crit

G Paris Rom 26.369; F Liebermann, Deutsche Zeitschrift für Geschichtswissenschaft 7.E61; E Freymond, Krit Jahresber 8².295).

Paris G, La légende de Saladin, Journal des savants, mai-août 1893, p 284; Le roman de Richard Coeur de Lion, Rom 26.361 (original AN poem composed from historical, pseudo-historical, and oral traditions); Paris Litt franç §§ 69, 88.

Lodeman F E, Le pas Saladin, MLN 12.21.

Thomas A, La légende de Saladin en Poitou, Journal des savants 1908, p 467.

Brunner K, Richard Coeur de Lion, WBEP 42.49, 51, 61, 73 (supplements Paris, particularly on oral, fabulous traditions); Angl 76.449, 450.

Immelman R, Englische und romanische Philologie und Literaturgeschichte, DLz 35.2375.

Loomis R S, Richard Coeur de Lion and the Pas Saladin in Medieval Art, PMLA 30.509; JEGP 15.464 (author a minstrel).

Norgate K, Richard the Lion Heart, London 1924, p 34.

Cartellieri A, Richard Löwenherz, Probleme der englischen Sprache und Kultur, Festschrift für Johannes Hoops, Germanische Bibliothek 2.20, Heidelberg 1925, p 131.

Wilkinson C, Richard Coeur de Lion, London 1933 (crit H A Cronne, History 19.150).

Paris G, ed, Ambroise, L'estoire de la guerre sainte (1190–1192), Collection des documents inédits sur l'histoire de France, 1897, trans M J Hubert, with notes by J T La Monte, The Crusade of Richard the Lion Hearted, Records of Civilization 34, N Y 1951.

Wilson R M, Early ME Literature, London 1939, 2nd edn 1951, p 218 (history a subject for romance).

Kelly A, Eleanor of Aquitaine and the Four Kings, Cambridge Mass 1950.

Baugh, PAPS 103.434.

Labande E-R, Pour une image véridique d'Aliénor d'Aquitaine, Bull de la Société des antiquaires de l'ouest 4s 2.180.

Benton J F, The Court of Champagne as a Literary Center, Spec 36.551.

Legends about Eleanor. Berger E, Les aventures de la reine Aliénor, Histoire et légende, comptes rendus de l'Académie des inscriptions et belles lettres, Paris 1906, p 702.

Chambers F M, Some Legends concerning Eleanor of Aquitaine, Spec 16.459.

Chapman R L, A Note on the Demon Queen Eleanor, MLN 70.393 (crit B J Timmer, YWES 36.66).

Lejeune R, Le rôle littéraire de la famille d'Aliénor d'Aquitaine, Cahiers de civilisation

médiévale, 10ᵉ–12ᵉ siècles, 1ʳᵉ annee, no 3, juillet-septembre 1958, p 322.
Relations with Folktales. Thompson Mot Ind, B 184.1 (magic horse); D 1076, D 1358.1 (eating courageous animal's heart); D 1380.11, D 1388.0.1 (magic ring protects); D 1425, D 1427 (magic object draws lover, compels one to follow), D 1812.3.3, D 1812.5.1.2 (future revealed in dream); D 1846.3 (magic horse renders rider invulnerable); E 714.4.1 (eaten heart gives one the owner's qualities; cf K 952.3); G 60 (human flesh eaten unwittingly); H 1301.1 (quest for most beautiful bride); H 1561.1, R 222 (test of valor; three days' tournament); K 521.4.3 (escape in humble disguise), cf K 1816.0.3 (menial disguise of princess's lover); K 1817.2, K 2357.2 (disguise as pilgrim); M 181 (magic horse); V 39.2 (wicked woman unable to endure presence of host at mass).
Paris G, La légende de Saladin, Journal des savants, mai 1893, p 489 (traces theme of gift of demon horse).
Weston J L, The Three Days' Tournament, London 1902, p 34.
Kittredge G L, Arthur and Gorlagon, HSNPL 8, Cambridge Mass 1903, p 194n2.
Jackson K H, A Celtic Miscellany, Cambridge Mass 1951, p 56 § 9 (analogue: how Celchar killed the brown mouse).
Chapman R L, MLN 70.393.
Bordman G M, The Folklore Motifs in the Matter of England Romances, DA 19.764.
Relations with the Ballad. Child F J, English and Scottish Ballads, Boston 1882–98, 5 vols, 2.511b, 2.513a, 3.55 (cf with no 80, Old Robin of Portingale); 3.508 (cf with no 61, Sir Cawline), 3.220.
Relations with Chaucer. Loomis L H, The Auchinleck MS and a Possible London Bookshop of 1330–40, PMLA 57.595 (short metrical chronicle borrows from Richard); Sir Thopas, Bryan-Dempster, pp 486, 495, 549, 553, 557.
Other Relations, Typical Phrases. Paris G, Sur un épisode d'Aimeri de Narbonne, Rom 9.542.
Kölbing E, Arthour and Merlin, AEB 4, Leipzig 1890, pp lxxiii, clii (Ipomadon).
Needler G H, Richard Coer de Lion in Literature, Leipzig 1890.
Jentsch F, EStn 15.232 (similar phrases in Generides, Arthour and Merlin, Ipomadon, Sir Gowther, Roswall and Lillian, Sir Beves of Hamtoun).
Kittredge, A Study of Gawain and the Green Knight, Cambridge Mass 1916, p 221 (the game of exchanging buffets).
Loomis R S, PMLA 30.509, 513 (Richard's

career in art); Arthurian Tradition and Chrétien de Troyes, N Y 1949, p 93.
Magoun F P jr, The Gests of King Alexander of Macedon, Two ME Alliterative Fragments: Alexander A and Alexander B, Cambridge Mass 1929, p 29 (cf E C Armstrong, A Foulet, and F B Agard, edd, Fuerre de Gadres, Princeton 1942, p 109, The Medieval French Roman d'Alexandre, vols 4, 5 being Elliot Monographs nos 39, 40).
Panzer F W, Gahmuret: Quellenstudien zu Wolframs Parzival, Heidelberg 1940, pp 39, 59–70 (argues that Richard was the historical prototype for Gahmuret the Angevin) (crit M F Richey, YWMLS 11.296).
Stokoe W C jr, The Double Problem of Sir Degaré, PMLA 70.518.
Mossé F, Points de vue nouveaux sur la poésie anglaise au moyen âge, EA 5.41.
Smithers, Kyng Alisaunder, EETS 237.31 (stylistic formulae found in OF epic).
Baugh, PAPS 103.422.
Reinhard J R, The Survival of Geis in Medieval Romance, Halle 1933, p 293.
Tuve R, Seasons and Months, Studies in a Tradition of ME Poetry, Paris 1933, pp 23, 180.
Culbert T, The Single Combat in Medieval Heroic Narrative, DA 18.1416.
Enkvist N E, The Seasons of the Year: Chapters on a Motif from Beowulf to the Shepherd's Calendar, Copenhagen Denmark 1947, Commutationes humanarum litterarum 22, no 4, Helsingfors Finland 1957, p 79.
Ward, 1.944; Gröber, 2¹.661, 665, 675, 765; Ten Brink, 1.242; Brandl, § 36; Schofield, p 314; J W H Atkins, CHEL, 1.317; H Bradley, CHEL, 1.399; Paris Litt franç, §§ 69, 88, and bibl; Körting, § 122; Baugh LHE, pp 142, 179; Kane, p 43.
Ker W P, English Literature, Medieval, N Y and London 1912, p 121.
Thomas P G, English Literature before Chaucer, London 1924, p 112.
Brie F, Die nationale Literatur Schottlands von den Anfängen bis zur Renaissance, Halle/Saale 1937, p 91.
Levy H L, As Myn Auctor Seyth, MÆ 12.29n1.
Schlauch M, English Medieval Literature and Its Social Foundations, Warsaw 1956, p 180.
Ford B, The Age of Chaucer, London 1954, p 38.
Hibbard Med Rom, pp 147, 155, new edn 1960, p 350; Tucker-Benham, p 254; Renwick-Orton, p 386; CBEL, 1.150(h), 157, 5.115; Bossuat MBLF, no 2384; Holmes CBFL, no 2340.

[107] THE SIEGE OF JERUSALEM; TITUS AND VESPASIAN.

Alliterative Version:

MSS. 1, Bodl 1059 (Laud Misc 656), ff 1^b–19^a (1425–50); 2, Camb Univ Mm. 5.14, ff 186^a–205^b, imp (1450–75); 3, Cotton Calig A.2, ff 111^a–125, imp (1475–1500); 4, Cotton Vesp E.16, ff 70^a–75^b, lines 1–957 lacking (1475–1500); 5, BM Addit 31042 (Thornton), ff 50^a–66, imp (1425–50); 6, Lambeth 491, ff 206^a–227^b (1425–50); 7, Huntington HM 128 (olim Ashburnham 130), ff 205^a–216^a, imp (1400–25); 8, Harvard Univ, Percy Folio MS Eng 748, vol 4, ff 9–29^b (transcript of no 3, above [ca 1767]).

Brown-Robbins, no 1583; MED, p 72.

Herrtage S J, The English Charlemagne Romances, Part 2, The Sege of Melayne, EETSES 35.viii and facsimile, leaf 66, BM Addit 31042 (Thornton signature and last lines of the Siege).

Skeat W W, Piers Plowman, EETS 54.xxiv (Laud Misc 656).

Furnival F J, Adam Davy's 5 Dreams about Edward II, EETS 69.7.

Ward, 1.180 (Cotton Calig A.2), 185 (Cotton Vespasian E.16), 929 (BM Addit 31042).

Bülbring K D, Über die Handschrift Nr 491 der Lambeth Bibliothek, Arch 86.384.

Rickert E, Emare, EETSES 99.ix (Cotton Calig A.2).

Brunner K, Hs British Museum Additional 31042, Arch 132.316.

Hulbert J R, The Text of the Siege of Jerusalem, SP 28.602, rptd in J J Royster Memorial Studies, Chapel Hill N Car 1931, p 70 (crit D Everett, YWES 12.108).

Hooper A G, The Lambeth Palace MS of the Awntyrs off Arthure, Leeds SE 3.37.

Editions. Steffler G, Sege of Jerusalem, Emden 1891 (Laud Misc 656) (crit E Kölbing, Krit Jahresber 4².429; AnglB 2.244).

Kölbing E and M Day, The Siege of Jerusalem, ed from MS Laud 656 with variants from all other extant MSS, EETS 188 (crit TLS, Nov 2 1933, p 754; D Everett, YWES 13.100; N&Q 164.180; K Brunner, AnglB 45.72; C Brett, MLR 29.83; E Ekwall, ESts 19.214).

Selection. Warton T, History of English Poetry, London 1840, 2.105 (Cotton Calig A.2 and Laud Misc 622).

Summary. Ward, 1.181, 928.

Gryting L A T, The Oldest Version of the Twelfth-Century Poem La Venjance Nostre Seigneur, Univ of Michigan Contributions in Modern Philology, Ann Arbor Mich 1952, 19.6 (summary of French texts).

Textual Matters. Hulbert, SP 28.602.

Language, Dialect. Pipeclay P, N&Q 2s 4.114, Aug 8 1857.

Kopka F M, The Destruction of Jerusalem; ein me alliterierendes Gedicht, Breslau 1887, p 5 (crit J Z[upitza], Arch 86.384 n 1; E Kölbing, Krit Jahresber 4².429).

Björkman E, Scandinavian Loan Words in ME, SEP 7, 11, Halle 1900, 1902, pp 11 n 2, 295.

Reicke C, Untersuchungen über den Stil der me alliterierenden Gedichte Morte Arthur, The Destruction of Troy, The Wars of Alexander, The Siege of Jerusalem, Sir Gawayn and the Green Knight, ein Beitrag zur Lösung der Huchown-Frage, Königsberg 1906, pp 26, 44, 52, 65, 70, 80, and passim.

Schumacher K, Studien über den Stabreim in der me Alliterationsdichtung, BSEP 11, Bonn 1914, pp 2, 33, 42, and passim.

Kölbing and Day, edn, pp xi, xv (North Midland of a Westerly character).

Oakden J P, Alliterative Poetry in ME: A Survey of the Tradition, English Series Univ of Manchester 19, 22, Manchester 1930, 1935, 1.70, 154.

Kellogg A B, The Language of the Alliterative Siege of Jerusalem especially MS Laud Misc 656, Chicago 1943, pp 49, 61, and passim.

Everett D, The Alliterative Revival, Essays on ME Literature, ed P Kean, Oxford 1955, p 58.

Waldron R A, Oral-Formulaic Technique and Alliterative Poetry, Spec 32.795.

Benson L D, The Rede Wynde in the Siege of Jerusalem, N&Q 7s 205.363.

Versification. PFMS, 3.xxx.

Ward, 1.180.

Reicke, Stil der me alliterierenden Gedichte, pp 34, 40 (examines especially the second half-lines).

Oakden, Alliterative Poetry in ME, 1.70, 153.

Day M, Strophic Division in ME Alliterative Verse, EStn 66.245 (crit D Everett, YWES 12.99) (Cotton Calig A.2, Camb Univ Libr Mm. 5.14); Kölbing and Day, edn, p ix.

Casson L S, Sir Degrevant, EETS 221.xxxix, xl.

Hulbert J R, Quatrains in ME Alliterative Poems, MP 48.73, 75, 81.

Waldron, Spec 32.795.

Date. Skeat, Piers Plowman, EETS 54, Preface 3.xxiv (MS Laud Misc 656, early 15 cent).

Authorship. Neilson G, Huchown of the Awle Ryale (Sir Hew of Eglintown), the Alliterative Poet, Glasgow 1902, p 30 (from Transactions, Glasgow Archeological Soc 1900).

McCracken H N, Concerning Huchown, PMLA 25.207 (disagreeing with Neilson).

Couplet Version:

MSS. 1, Bodl 1414 (Laud Misc 622), ff 71^b–72^b, 1–21^b (ca 1400); 2, Bodl 1831 (Digby 230), ff 195^a–223^b (ca 1450); 3, Bodl 21652 (Douce 78), ff 19^a–75^b, imp (1450–75); 4, Bodl 21700 (Douce 126), ff 69^a–83, imp (first half 15 cent); 5, Magdalen Camb Pepys 2014 (olim Pepys 37), ff 23^a–35^b, imp (?1390–1420); 6, BM Harley 4733, ff 40^b–127^a (before 1475); 7, BM Addit 10036, ff 2^a–61^b, imp at beginning (1400–25); 8, BM Addit 36523, ff 1^a–71^a (1425–50); 9, BM Addit 36983 (Bedford), ff 216^a–255 (ca 1442); 10, Pierpont Morgan Libr Morgan M 898, 100 leaves, imp at beginning (first half 15 cent); 11, Osborn MS, New Haven Conn (olim Derby, Knowsley Hall), ff 1^a–38^b, imp at end (15 cent).

Prose Version:

MS. Cleveland Public Libr W q091.92–C468, John G White Collection (olim Aldenham), ff 77–99 (ca 1470).

Brown-Robbins, no 1881; MED, p 79.

Ward, 1.187 (BM Addit 10036).

Hulme W H, The ME Harrowing of Hell and the Gospel of Nicodemus, EETSES 100.xxii and note 4 (lines 395–666 on Nicodemus lacking in MS Pepys 2014).

Kölbing E and M Day, The Siege of Jerusalem, ed from MS Laud Misc 656 with variants from all other extant MSS, EETS 188.3 (Appendix 2) (Harley 4733).

Smithers G V, Kyng Alisaunder, EETS 237.1, 2, 3 (Laud Misc 622).

Bühler C F, The New Morgan Manuscript of Titus and Vespasian, PMLA 76.20.

Editions. Fischer R, Vindicta Salvatoris—me Vengeaunce of Goddes deth or Bataile of Jerusalem, Arch 111.285; 112.25 (MS Pepys 2014, Magdalen Camb) (crit W Suchier, Arch 122.159).

Herbert J A, Titus and Vespasian or the Destruction of Jerusalem in rhymed couplets, Roxb Club 146 (BM Addit 36523, with collation of 4 other MSS) (crit W Suchier, Arch 122.159).

Selections. Warton T, History of English Poetry, London 1840, vol 2, § 6, pp 4, 105 (Cotton Calig A.2, Laud Misc 622).

Language. Arvidson J M, The Language of Titus and Vespasian or the Destruction of Jerusalem, MS Pepys 37, Lund 1916.

Hulbert J R, Quatrains in ME Alliterative Poems, MP 48.74 (Laud Misc 622).

Author. Furnivall F J, Adam Davy's 5 Dreams about Edward II, EETS 69.7 (author not Davy).

Ward, 1.187.

Bergau F, Untersuchungen über Quelle und Verfasser des me Reimgedichts: The Vengeaunce of Goddes Deth (The Bataile of Jerusalem), Königsberg 1901 (crit W Suchier, Arch 108.199; M Kaluza, Krit Jahresber 6^2.363; Kölbing and Day, EETS 188.xxv).

All Versions:

Sources and Analogues. Goodwin C W, The Anglo-Saxon Version of the Legend of St Veronica, Cambridge Antiquarian Soc, Cambridge 1851, p vi.

HLF, 22.412.

Meyer P, Du manuscrit de la BN fr 25415, La prise de Jerusalem ou La vengeaunce de Jésus-Christ, Bulletin SATF, 1.32, 53; Notice du MS de l'Arsenal 5201, La prise de Jerusalem ou La vengeance de Jésus-Christ, Rom 16.56; Notice sur deux anciens manuscrits français, Notices et extraits des MSS de la Bibliothèque Nationale, Paris 1890, 33^1.71.

Graf A, Roma nella memoria e nelle immaginazioni del medio evo, 2 vols, Turin 1882–83, edn 1923, p 285.

Ward, 1.178 (Latin versions), 928 (Rabbinic legend); 189.

Kopka, The Destruction of Jerusalem, p 31.

Langlois E, Notices des manuscrits français et provençaux de Rome anterieurs au 16e siècle, Notices et extraits des MSS de la Bibliothèque Nationale, Paris 1890, 33^2.233.

Dobschütz E von, Christusbilder: Untersuchungen zur christliche Legende, Leipzig 1899, in Texte und Untersuchungen zur Geschichte der altchristlichen Literatur, NF 3.157, 197, 335, and passim.

Suchier W, Über das altfranzösische Gedicht La venjance Nostre Seigneur (Sauveur), Halle 1899 (MSS, sources), rptd ZfRP 24.161, 25.94, 256.

Bergau F, Untersuchungen über Quelle und Verfasser des me Reimgedichts: The Vengeaunce of Goddes Deth (The Bataile of Jerusalem), Königsberg 1901 (crit W Suchier, Arch 108.199; Kölbing and Day, edn, p xxv).

Herbert J A, Titus and Vespasian, Roxb Club 146.vi.

Duparc-Quioc S, La conquête de Jerusalem, Positions de thèses de l'École des chartes, 1937, p 140; Les manuscrits de La conquête de Jerusalem, Rom 65.183.

Gryting L A T, La venjance Nostre Seigneur, Univ of Michigan Contributions in Modern Philology 19, Ann Arbor Mich 1952, (crit B Woledge, YWMLS 14.34; F A G Cowper, Spec 28.884; G R de Lage, Moyen âge

60.190; F W A George, MÆ 23.104; H H Lucas, MLR 49.78; A Långfors, NM 54.284; R C D Perman, French Sts 8.61).

Relations with the Folktale. Thompson Mot Ind, C 53 (refusing credit to God); D 1381.4.1 (Christ's coat of mercy protects Pilate from punishment); D 1502.4, D 2161.1, D 2161.4.9 (magic object, baptism, cures leprosy); F 950.1 (sickness cured by Veronica's napkin); F 955 (miraculous cure for leprosy; rage at hearing for first time of Christ's passion causes cure); N 365, Q 242 (incest punished); Q 221.2 (punishment for opposition to Christ at Crucifixion); Q 556.1 (curse for participation in Crucifixion); V 34.1, V 121, V 211, V 221.0.1 (sacrament, relics of saint cure disease).

Relations with Shakespeare. TLS 1924 for all the following: R C Rhodes, Apr 17, p 240; May 22, p 322; W W Gregg, May 1, p 268; May 15, p 304; J S Smart, May 8, p 268; June 5, p 356; J M Robertson, May 29, p 340.

Other Relations. Neilson, Huchown of the Awle Ryale, pp 33, 89 (Troy and Alexander legends, and Morte Arthur).

McKeehan I P, Some Relationships between the Legends of British Saints and Medieval Romance, Univ of Chicago Abstracts of Theses, Humanistic Series 2.383.

Oakden, Alliterative Poetry in ME, 2.95, 100 (parallels with other alliterative pieces).

Warton T, History of English Poetry, London 1840, 2.105 (Cotton Calig A.2); ed Hazlitt, London 1871, 2.201 (Laud 622).

Ward, 1.161, 176 (French versions), 180, 187, 929; 2.641 (Vernicle miracles).

Everett D, Essays on Middle English Literature, ed P Kean, Oxford 1955, p 58.

Gröber, 2¹.658; Brandl, §§ 70, 73; Schofield, p 378; Paris Litt franç, § 140; Körting, § 110 end; Oakden, Alliterative Poetry in ME, 2.44; Baugh LHE, p 195; Kane, pp 9, 19, 45, 50, and passim.

Gautier L, Les épopées françaises, 2nd edn, Paris 1878–97, 5.137.

Esdaile A, A List of English Tales and Prose Romances Printed before 1740, London 1912, p 81 (W de Worde edns).

STC, no 14517–19 (Pynson, de Worde).

Renwick-Orton, p 386; CBEL, 1.157. 5.116(1) (couplet version), 1.158(m) (alliterative version); Manly & Rickert, 1.610, 618 (references to Sege of Jerusalem in 15 cent book lists); Bossuat MBLF, nos 6189, 6597.

Kellogg, The Language of the Alliterative Siege of Jerusalem, p 63.

O'Dell S, A Chronological List of Prose Fiction in English Printed in England and Other Countries 1475–1640, Cambridge Mass 1954, p 27 (16 cent translations and printings).

[108] THE THREE KINGS' SONS.

MS. Harley 326, ff 18ᵃ–123ᵇ (ca 1500).

Editions. Furnivall F J, The Three Kings' Sons (Englisht from the French), edited from the unique MS Harleian 326, about 1500 AD, EETSES 67, pt 1 (the text).

Summary. Spence L, A Dictionary of Medieval Romance and Romance Writers, London 1913, p 354.

Baker E A and J Packman, A Guide to the Best Fiction, new and enlarged 3rd edn, N Y 1932, p 465.

Author-Scribe (D Aubert). Paris G, Histoire poétique de Charlemagne, 1865, p 96.

Ward 1.783,377; Bossuat MBLF, nos 430,442 (Aubert as author of other works).

Fisher J H, ed, The Tretyse of Love, EETS 225.xiv n 4, xv.

Bédier J et P Hazard, Littérature française, Paris 1948, 1.160 (French backgrounds).

Schlauch M, Antecedents of the English Novel 1400–1600 (from Chaucer to Deloney), Warsaw and London 1963, p 54 notes 15 and 16.

Farrar C P and A P Evans, Bibl of English Translations from Medieval Sources, N Y 1946, no 412.

Ward 1.377, 782; Schofield, p 318; Bennett OHEL, 2.317; Gröber 2¹.1144.

IV. Romances of Family Tradition

[109] MELUSINE.

See also ROMAUNS of PARTENAY [110].

MSS. 1, BM Royal 18.B.2, ff 1–219ᵇ (ca 1500), in prose. PRINT: 2, Bodl, John of Arras [Melusine, or a tale of the serpent fairy], fragm, W de Worde? (1510?) (STC, no 14648).

MED, p 59.

Bourdillon F W, Some Notes on Two Early Romances: Huon de Bordeaux and Melusine, Libr 4s 1.33 (illustrations in the texts).

Editions. Donald A K, Melusine Compiled (1382–94 AD) by Jean D'Arras, Englisht about 1500; ed from a unique MS in the BM, EETSES 68 (Royal 18.B.2).

Modernization, Abstract. Wigand O, Geschichte von der edlen und schönen Melusina, Volksbücher 3, ed G O Marbach, Leipzig 1838.

Leighton Mrs, trans, The Mysterious History of Melusina, or the Legend of Lusignan, Medieval Legends, London 1895.

Sources and Analogues: French Version. Jean d'Arras, L'histoire de la Belle Melusine, Geneva 1478; facsimile, ed W J Meyer, Soc suisse des bibliophiles, Neuchâtel 1924.

Nodot F, Histoire de Melusine, tirée des chroniques de Poitou et qui sert d'origine à l'ancienne maison de Lusignan, Paris 1698–1700.

Brunet C, Mélusine, Bibliothèque elzévirenne, Paris 1854.

De Saivre L, Le mythe de la Mère Lusine, Extraits des mémoires de la Société de statistique, sciences, lettres et arts de Deux Sèvres 20, Saint-Maixent 1883, Niort 1885 (crit H Gaidoz, RC 6.122).

Schorbach K, Die Historie von der schönen Melusine, Zeitschrift für Bücherfreunde, 1.132, 134.

Bourdillon, Libr 4s 1.31 (relationship to Partenay).

Marchand J, La légende de Mélusine selon le roman commencé le mercredi devant la Saint-Clement d'Hiver, l'an 1387, achevé sept ans après par Jean d'Arras, Paris 1927.

Hoffrichter L, Die ältesten französischen Bearbeitungen der Melusinensage, Romanistische Arbeiten 12, Halle 1928 (relationship of French versions) (crit W Suchier, DLz 49 part 2, nf 5, 1928, p 2203; RomR 20.369).

Stouff L, Melusine, ou, la Fée de Lusignan, Publ de l'université de Dijon 5, Paris 1932 (trans Jean d'Arras into modern French).

Workman S K, Fifteenth Century Translations as an Influence on English Prose, Princeton 1940, p 183 (French version, fragm, de Worde).

Boussuat MBLF, no 4142 (English and Geneva texts contain a passage lacking in the French MSS).

Schultz A H, Lusignan in Provençal Biographies, SP 43.1 (parallels to the Swan Knight).

Loomis R S, Arthurian Tradition and Chrétien de Troyes, N Y 1949, pp 93n45 (date), 415.

Painter S, The Houses of Lusignan and Chalellérault, Spec 30.314 (genealogical accounts).

Sources and Analogues: German Version. See PARTENAY [110] below.

Biltz K, Zur deutschen Bearbeitung der Melusinasage, Zeitschrift für Deutschkunde, Ergänzungsheft 3, Festschrift R Hildebrands, Leipzig 1894, p 1.

Bourdillon, Libr 4s 1.31, 32.

Thüring von Ringoltingen, Melusine, ed K Schneider, Texte des spätern Mittelalters, 9 (from La Coudrette), Berlin 1958, p 30.

Relations with Folktale. See above under *Sources and Analogues.* Thompson Mot Ind, B 652.2 (marriage to serpent-maiden); C 31.1.2, C 31.1.4, C 151 (tabu: looking at supernatural wife on certain occasion: in childbirth); E 501, E 501.11.1.2 (lover as hunter); F 302, F 302.2, F 302.6, T 111 (fairy mistress leaves man when he breaks tabu); Q 431, Q 433 (punishment for broken tabu: banishment, imprisonment); The Folktale, N Y 1946, p 247 (fairy lover, tabus).

Wigand O, Geschichte von der edlen und schönen Melusina, Volksbücher 3, ed G O Marbach, Leipzig 1838.

Keightley T, Fairy Mythology, London 1847, p 480.

Baring-Gould S, Curious Myths of the Middle Ages, 2 vols, London 1868, 1.471.

Nowack M, Die Melusinasage, ihr mythische Hintergrund, ihre Verwandtschaft mit anderen Sagenkreisen und ihre Stellung in der deutschen Literatur, Freiburg 1886 (nature myth, connection with Indian tales) (crit E Mogk, LfGRP 8.345).

Kohler J, Der Ursprung der Melusinensage: Eine ethnologische Untersuchung, Zeitschrift für Bücherfreunde, Leipzig 1895 (crit L F, LZ, 1895, p 1598; M Hippe, ZfVL 10.257; A H[auser], Euphorion 3.245).

Köhler R, Kleinere Schriften zur neueren Literaturgeschichte Volkskunde und Wortforschung, ed J Bolte, 3 vols, Weimar 1900, 3.265 nn 1, 2.

Baudot J, Les Princesses Yolande et les Ducs de Bar de la famille de Valois, 1, Melusine, Paris 1900.

MacCulloch J A, The Childhood of Fiction, London 1905, p 325; Medieval Faith and Fable, London 1932, p 50.

Rickert E, Emare, EETSES 99.xlv (motif of jealous mother-in-law).

Bolte J and G Polívka, Anmerkungen zu den Kinder- u Hausmärchen der Brüder Grimm, Leipzig 1913–32, 2.269.

Gough A B, Notes to L Friedlander, Roman Life and Manners, London and N Y 1913, 4.99.

Hartland E S, The Romance of Melusine, Folklore 24.187 (primitive customs related to tabus in the romance).

Hastings J, ed, Encyclopaedia of Religion and Ethics, N Y 1921, 11.410b.

Beckwith M W, Polynesian Analogues to the Celtic Otherworld and Fairy Mistress Themes, New Haven 1923, Vassar Medieval Studies, ed C F Fiske, pp 29, 48.

Wesselski A, Märchen des Mittelalters, Berlin 1925, p 156, no 57 (Kaiser und Bärin), p 247 (notes).

Schlauch M, Chaucer's Constance and Accused Queens, N Y 1927, p 54 (relation to Cupid and Psyche, breaking of tabu); Romance in Iceland, N Y 1934, pp 167, 185 (mortal man, fairy mistress).

Dickson A, Valentine and Orson, N Y and London 1929, p 117 (human parent at times assumes beast-form).

Griffith D D, The Origin of the Griselda Story, Univ of Washington Publications in Lang and Lit, Seattle Wash 1931, 8.23.

Kohl R, Das Melusinenmotiv, Niederdeutsche Zeitschrift für Volkskunde, 11.183.

Reinhard J R, Survival of Geis in Medieval Romance, Halle 1933, pp 260, 266, 273.

Caldwell J R, Eger and Grime, HSCL, Cambridge Mass 1934, 9.103, 186.

Loomis R S, see below under *Other Relations.*

Patch H S, The Other World According to Descriptions in Medieval Literature, Cambridge Mass 1950, p 269 (discovery of fairy mistress).

Van Gennep A, Manuel de folklore française contemporaine, Paris 1938, 4.L51 (bibl).

Albrecht W P, The Loathly Lady in Thomas of Erceldoune with a Text of the Poem Printed in 1652, Univ of New Mexico Publications in Lang and Lit, Albuquerque 1954, 11.33, 60, 67 (crit W Schmidt-Hidding, Angl 73.524; J Kinsley, MAE 25.55).

Relations with the Ballad. Child F J, The English and Scottish Popular Ballads, 5 vols, Boston 1882–98, 1.179, 5.226a, 236 (childbirth tabu; cf no 15, Lusome Brand, no 90, Jellon Grame).

Other Relations including Arthurian. Frölicher H, Thüring von Ringoltingen's Melusine und Valentine und Orsus mit französischen Quellen vergleichen, Zurich 1889.

Paton L A, Studies in the Fairy Mythology of Arthurian Romance, Boston and Cambridge 1903, 2nd edn (with preface and bibl R S Loomis), N Y 1960, pp 100n1, 111, 222.

Caldwell, HSCL 9.103, 187.

Mulertt W, Rabelais und die Melusinen-Geschichte, ZfFSL 62.325 (Melusine a sister of Morgan le Fée).

Cross T P, The Celtic Elements in the Lays of Lanval and Graelent, MP 12.718.

Loomis R S, The Combat at the Ford in the Didot Perceval, MP 43.66, 69; Arthurian Tradition and Chrétien de Troyes, N Y 1949, pp 93n45, 415.

Uri S P, Some Remarks on Partonopéus de Blois, Neophil 37.83 (parallel between Melior and Melusine).

Albrecht, The Loathly Lady in Thomas of Erceldoune, pp 37, 38, 41.

Chapman R L, A Note on the Demon Queen Eleanor, MLN 70.393, 395 (crit B J Timmer, YWES 36.66).

Ackerman R W, English Rimed and Prose Romance, Arthurian Literature in the Middle Ages, ed R S Loomis, Oxford 1959, p 483n4 (dedication trans from French text).

Bowers R H, Chaucer's Troilus as an Elizabethan Wanton Book, N&Q 7s 205.371.

Eisner S, A Tale of Wonder, Wexford 1957, chap 6 (crit K Malone, SN 30.261).

Dunn C W, The Foundling and the Werwolf, A Literary-Historical Study of Guillaume de Palerne, Univ of Toronto Department of English Studies and Texts, Toronto Canada 1960, 8.68, 72.

Weaver C P, The Hermit in English Literature from the Beginnings to 1660, Nashville Tenn, pp 99–100.

Warton T, The History of English Poetry, London 1840, preface by R Price, 1.35.

Lowell J R, Literary Essays, Collected Works, Boston 1890, 3.361.

Voretzsch K, Introduction to the Study of Old French Literature, trans F M Du Mont, 3rd edn, N Y 1925, p 482 (bibl).

Gudzy N K, History of Early Russian Literature, trans S W Jones, N Y 1949, p 420.

Schlauch M, English Medieval Literature and Its Social Foundations, Warsaw 1956, p 296.

Ward, 1.687; Gröber, 2¹.1082; Schofield, p 316; Körting, p 133n; Hibbard Med Rom, p 207; Baugh LHE, p 194; Kane, p 17.

Renwick-Orton, p 386; CBEL, 1.160(w), 5.117(w); Bennett OHEL, 2.314. French versions: de Julleville Hist, 1.344; H Gausseron, N&Q 5s 6.324; Bossuat MBLF, nos 4139–51, 6792.

[110] ROMAUNS OF PARTENAY (LUSIGNAN).

See also MELUSINE [109].

MS. MS Trinity Camb 597 (R.3.17), ff 1ᵃ–124ᵇ, 2 folios wanting, (ca 1500).

Brown-Robbins, no *27; MED, p 64.

Ward, 1.692.

Editions. Skeat W W, The Romauns of Parthenay, or of Lusignan: Otherwise Known as

the Tale of Melusine, Translated from the French of La Coudrette (about 1500–1520), ed from a unique manuscript in the library of Trinity College, Cambridge, with an introd, notes, and glossarial index, EETS 22, rvsd edn 1899.
Language. Skeat W W, William of Palerne, EETSES 1.228; edn, p xiv (edn 1899, pp xvii, xx) (Midland, East Anglian).
Hattendorf G A, Sprache und Dialekt der altenglischen Romans of Partenay, Göttingen 1887.
Versification. Skeat, edn, EETS 22.i, iv (edn 1899, p vii).
Patch H S, The Other World, Cambridge Mass 1950, pp 269n122, 270n128 (verse of La Coudrette).
Date. James M R, Western MSS in the Library of Trinity College, Cambridge 1901, 2.66 (English version ca 1486).
Farrar C P and A P Evans, Bibl of English Translations from Medieval Sources, N Y 1946, no 1036 (Coudrette's version finished ca 1401).
Albrecht W P, The Loathly Lady in Thomas of Erceldoune with a Text of the Poem Printed in 1652, Univ of New Mexico Publications in Lang and Lit, Albuquerque N Mex 1954, 11.8.
Sources and Analogues, Relations to Folktale, Other Relations. See also MELUSINE [109].
Michel F, Mellusine par Couldrette, Niort 1854.
Skeat, edn, EETS 22.iii, xiii (immediate source is French MS Ll. 2.5, Camb Univ).
Ward, 1.692 (cf BM Addit 6796, other versions).
Hattendorf, Sprache und Dialekt der ae Partenay, p 6.
Bourdillon F W, Some Notes on Two Early Romances: Huon de Bordeaux and Melusine, Libr 4s 1.32, 33.
Hoffrichter L, Die ältesten französischen Bearbeitungen der Melusinensage, Romanistische Arbeiten 12, Halle 1928.
Albrecht W P, A Seventeenth-Century Text of Thomas of Erceldoune, MÆ 23.88; The Loathly Lady, Univ of N Mex Publ in Lang and Lit 11.37, 39.
Thüring von Ringoltingen, Melusine, ed K Schneider, Texte des spätern Mittelalters 9, Berlin 1958, p 31.
Ward, 1.692; Brandl, § 108; Schofield, p 316; Körting, § 133n; Baugh LHE, p 194; Kane, p 17 (crit J Lawlor, MLR 47.214).
Renwick-Orton, p 387; CBEL, 1.160(x). For bibl see also final items under MELUSINE [109].

[111] THE KNIGHT OF CURTESY AND THE FAIR LADY OF FAGUELL.

MSS. No MS extant. PRINT: Bodl, W Copland, 10 leaves (1568).
Brown-Robbins, no 1486; MED, p 50.
Editions. Ritson AEMR, 3.193.
Hazlitt Rem, 2.65, 4.363.
McCausland E, The Knight of Curtesy and the Fair Lady of Faguell, A Study of the Date and Dialect of the Poem and Its Folklore Origins, Smith College Studies in Modern Languages, Northampton Mass 1922, 4.1 (crit H M Flasdieck, AnglB 34.265; Arch 146.286; Zeitschrift für französischen und englischen Unterricht 24.5).
Modernization. Kemp-Welch A, The Chatelaine of Vergi; A 13th Century French Romance, Done into English, London 1903, rptd 1907, 1909 (from Raynaud's French edn) (crit E B Schlatter, La Chastelaine de Vergi, Univ of Wisconsin Studies in Lang and Lit, 20.44).
Rickert RofL, p 141.
Barrow S F, The Medieval Soc Romances, N Y 1924 (from the French Châtelain de Coucy), p 122.
Dialect. Brandl, § 113 (South Midland).
Arch 146.286 (Northern rhymes).
McCausland, edn, p vii (London dialect).
Verse. CHEL, 1.300 (ballad measure).
Sources and Analogues: Chatelain de Coucy. Crapelet G A, ed, L'histoire du Châtelain de Coucy et de la Dame de Fayel, Paris 1829.
Michel F, ed, Chansons du Châtelain de Coucy, Paris 1830 (includes the Chronique).
Paris G, Le roman du Châtelain de Couci, Rom 8.343, 361; HLF, 28.352 (imitations, parallels, authorship); La légende du Châtelain de Couci dans l'Inde, Rom 12.359 (Indian parallels).
Ahlström A, Studier i den Fornfranska Lais—Literaturen, Upsala 1892, p 130 (Germanic parallels).
Matzke J E, The Legend of the Eaten Heart, MLN 26.1; The Roman du Châtelain de Couci and Fauchet's Chronique, Studies in Honor of A Marshall Elliott, Baltimore 1913, 1.1 (French versions not from one another but from a common source).
Matzke J E and M Delbouille, edd, Le roman du Castelain de Couci et de la Dame de Fauel, SATF 90, Paris 1936 (crit A Långfors, Rom 63.535).
Sources and Analogues: Châtelain de Vergi. Raynaud G, La Chastelaine de Vergi, Rom 21.145, 165 (text), Paris 1910 (crit E S Sheldon, RR 2.214); 2nd edn 1912 (crit R

W[eeks], RR 6.112); 3rd edn (with L Foulet) 1921, pp vi, vii (bibl of reviews).

Lorenz E, Die Kastellanin von Vergi in der Literatur Frankreichs, Italiens, der Niederlande, Englands und Deutschlandes, mit einer deutscher Übersetzung der altfranzösischen Versnovelle und einem Anhänge: Die Kastellan von Couci sage als Gabrielle de Vergi, Halle 1909 (crit E Stengel, DLz 30.2728; A L Stiefel, Krit Jahresber 12².45; Archiv 124.180).

Whitehead F, La Chastelaine de Vergi, Manchester 1944, p vii n 1.

Frappier J, La Chastelaine de Vergi, Publication Faculté lettres de Strasbourg, fasc 105, Mélanges, 1945; Études littéraires, Paris 1946, p 89 (bibl of all later versions).

Sources and Analogues: Boccaccio Version. Zupitza J, Die me Bearbeitung von Ghismonda und Guiscardo, Vierteljahrsschrift für Kultur und Literatur der Renaissance, Berlin 1886, 1.63 (the story in the 16th cent).

Lee A C, ed, The Decameron, Its Sources and Analogues, London 1909, pp 116, 143.

Hauvette H, Le 39e nouvelle du Décamérone et la Légende du coeur mangé, Rom 41.184, 193 (opposes theory of Oriental origins).

Jones E N, Boccaccio and His Imitators, Chicago 1910, p 23.

Smythe B, Trobador Poets, N Y and London 1911, p 169 (Guilhem de Cabestanh).

Långfors A, Le Troubadour Gilhem de Cabestanh, Extrait des annales du midi, 26.199.

Relations with Folktale. See above, *Sources and Analogues.*

Thompson Mot Ind, B 11.11 (fight with dragon); Q 478.1 (adulteress caused to eat lover's heart); Q 491.5.

Cross Mot Ind, G 91.1; Q 478.1.

Herbert, pp 134, 472, 574.

Swynnerton C, Four Legends of King Rasálu of Sialkot, Folklore Journal 1.129, 143; The Adventures of the Panjáb Hero Rájá Rasálu and Other Folk Tales of the Panjáb,

Calcutta 1884, p 103; Romantic Tales from the Panjáb, Westminster 1903, p 109.

Clouston W, Popular Tales and Fiction, Edinb 1887, 2.191.

Patzig H, Zur Geschichte der Herzmäre, Berlin 1891.

Siefken O, Das geduldige Weib, Rathenow 1903, p 69.

Matzke J E, The Legend of the Eaten Heart, MLN 26.1.

Malone K, Rose and Cypress, PMLA 43.413, 430 (embalmed head of lover).

Lecoy F, Un épisode du Protheselaus et le conte du mari trompé, Rom 76.477 (crit B Woledge and H P Clive, YWMLS 17.55).

Relations with the Ballad. Furnivall F J, Captain Cox, His Ballads and Books, Ballad Soc 7, London 1871, pp xii, xxiv.

Child F J, The English and Scottish Popular Ballads, [5 vols, Boston 1892–98, 5.33 (no 269, Lady Diamond 5.29).

Other Literary Relations. Schofield W H, The Lays of Graelent and Lanval, PMLA 15.123.

Matzke, Studies in Honor of A Marshall Elliott, 1.15 (relation to Tristan).

Mead W, Squyr of Lowe Degre, Boston 1904, p xxxiv.

Schelling F, Elizabethan Drama 1558–1642, 2 vols, Boston and N Y 1908, 1.197.

Jefferson B L, A Note on the Squyr of Lowe Degre, MLN 28.109 (Knight of Curtesy, Eger and Grime).

Everett D, A Characterization of the English Medieval Romances, E&S 15.98, rptd in Essays on ME Literature, ed P Kean, Oxford 1955, p 9.

Brandl, § 113; Schofield, p 200; Kane, pp 20, 22.

de Julleville Hist, 1.343 (Le Chatelaine de Couci); Paris Litt franç, § 66; Hibbard Med Rom, pp 253, 261, new edn, 1960, p 349; Renwick-Orton, p 387; CBEL, 1.160(v); Bossuat MBLF, nos 1161–76; Holmes CBFL, nos 976, 983.1, 2251–54 (Chatelain de Coucy).

V. Legendary Romances of Didactic Intent

[112] AMIS AND AMILOUN.

MSS. 1, Bodl 21900 (Douce 326), ff 1ª–13 (ca 1500); 2, BM Egerton 2862 (olim Trentham-Sutherland), ff 135ª–147ᵇ, imp (ca 1400); 3, BM Harley 2386, ff 131ª–137ᵇ, 138, imp (ca 1500); 4, Advocates 19.2.1 (Auchinleck), ff 48ᵇ–61, imp (ca 1330).

Brown-Robbins, no 821; MED, p 25.

Kölbing E, Vier-Romanzen Handschriften, EStn 7.178 (Auchinleck MS), 7.191 (Egerton 2862).

Barnicle M, Seege or Batayle of Troye, EETS 172.xv (Egerton 2862).

Bliss A J, Notes on the Auchinleck Manuscript, Spec 26.652, 654.

Editions. Weber MR, 2.367, 478, 1.lii (Auchinleck MS).

Kölbing E, Amis and Amiloun zugleich mit der altfranzösischen Quelle, nebst einer Beilage Amícus ok Amilíus Rímur, AEB 2 (all MSS with French, Latin, and Norse texts) (crit E Einenkel, Angl 8 Anz 27; C Stoffel, EStn 9.175; K Breul, EStn 9.456; A Brandl, AfDA 13.92).

Leach M, Amis and Amiloun, EETS 203 (Auchinleck MS, with first 97 lines and last 112 lines supplied from BM Egerton 2862, and with variants from other MSS, pp 10, 107 (MS Harley 2386), p 108 (MS Egerton 2862), p 109 (MS Douce 326) (crit M S Serjeantson, YWES 18.94; K Brunner, AnglB 49.259; W Héraucourt, MLR 33.575, EStn 73.260; G V Smithers, MÆ 8.159; A McIntosh, RES 16.76).

Selections. Cook A S, A Literary ME Reader, Boston etc 1915, p 81 (from Kölbing edn).

Sampson G, Cambridge Book of Prose and Verse, Cambridge 1924, p 258 (from Kölbing edn).

Abstract. Ellis Spec. p 584.

Modernizations, Translations. Morris W, On the Friendship of Amis and Amile, Hammersmith 1894; rptd in Old French Romances, London 1896, p 29; 2nd edn 1914; rptd Portland Me 1896; 5th edn 1899 (trans from the French).

Rickert RofFr, p 1 (from the French).

Darton F J H, A Wonder Book of Old Romance, N Y 1907; 7th edn, 1931, p 379.

Weston J L, Chief ME Poets, Boston etc 1914, p 174.

Michaut G, Amis et Amiles in Floire et Jeanne; contes des 13ᵉ siècle, Paris 1923, p 121 (modern French).

Summary. Saintsbury G, A Short History of French Literature, Oxford 1901, 6th edn, p 14.

Textual Matters. Kölbing E, Zur Ueberlieferung der Sage von Amis und Amiles, PBBeitr 4.271, 282; Zu Amis and Amiloun, EStn 2.295, 5.465, 9.477; Kleine Beiträge zur Erklärung me Dichter, EStn 13.134.

Holthausen F, Zu me Romanzen, 5, Amis and Amiloun, Angl 41.456.

Carr B M, Notes on an English Scribe's Methods, Univ of Wisconsin Studies in Lang and Lit, Madison 1918, 2.153 (OE ā in Auchinleck MS).

Smithers G V, Notes on ME Texts, LMS 1.214 (line 2135, bod- "to experience").

Bliss, Spec 26.652, 654.

Language, Dialect, Versification. Lüdtke G, The

Erl of Tolous and the Emperes of Almayn, Berlin 1881, p 54.

Kölbing, edn, pp xiv (verse), xxiv (dialect, xxviii (inflections), xxxvii; xlii (formulas), lxvi (alliteration); EStn 13.134.

Modersohn H, Die Realien in den altfranzösischen Chansons de Geste Amis et Amiles und Jourdains de Blaivies, Lingen 1886, passim.

Curtius F J, An Investigation of the Rimes and Phonology of the Middle Scotch Romance Clariodus, Angl 16.1450.

Gough A B, Emare, London 1901, pp ix, 36.

Gerould G H, Social and Historical Reminiscences in the ME Athelston, EStn 36.196 (northern East Midlands).

Reicke C, Untersuchungen über den Stil der me alliterierenden Gedichte Morte Arthur, The Destruction of Troy, The Wars of Alexander, The Seige of Jerusalem, Sir Gawayn and the Green Knight, ein Beitrag zur Lösung der Huchown-Frage, Königsberg 1906, pp 18 (verse), 28, 54, 60, and passim.

Kaluza M, Englische Metrik, Berlin 1909, § 178; trans A C Dunstan, A Short History of English Versification from the Earliest Times to the Present Day, London 1911, p 229.

Möller W, Untersuchungen über Dialekt und Stil des me Guy of Warwick und des strophischen Teiles des Guy zu Amis und Amiloun, Königsberg 1917, pp 47, 49, 84 (northern quality).

Trounce A McI, The English Tail-Rhyme Romances, MÆ 1.94, 2.42, 44 (places Amis in Norfolk); Athelston, EETS 224.57, 59 (verse accent) (crit G Taylor, Notes on Athelston, Leeds SE 4.56: argues for a non-East Anglian origin).

Dunlap A R, The Vocabulary of the ME Romances in Tail-Rhyme Stanza, Delaware Notes 14s, passim.

Sources and Analogues. Hofmann K, Amis et Amiles und Jourdains de Blaivies, Erlangen 1852; 2nd edn 1882 (French, Latin, other versions from 1100–1600); Erster Nachtrag zur Einleitungen in Amis et Amiles, RF 1.

Warton T, History of English Poetry, ed W Hazlitt 1871, 1.275, 2.192 (Gesta Romanorum).

Gaidoz H, L'amitié d'Amis et Amiles, RC 4.201, 204 (Welsh text and transl into French).

Kölbing E, Zu Amis and Amiloun, EStn 2.295, 5.465; edn, p cxxi; PBBeitr 4.271 (no extant poem is the immediate source of the English version).

Schweiger P, Die Sage von Amis und Amiles, Berlin 1885, published also ZfRP 9.419

(argues for Germanic origins, stresses parallels with Nibelungenlied) (crit E Kölbing, EStn 9.149; [G Paris], Rom 14.318).

Köhler R, Aufsätze über Märchen und Volkslieder, Berlin 1894, p 31; Die Legende von dem beiden treuen Jacobsbrüdern, Kleinere Schriften, Berlin 1900 (Italian versions).

Panzer F, Hilde-Gudrun, Halle 1901, p 274 (Turkish parallels).

Gerould, EStn 36.196 (folk custom of sworn brotherhood).

Bédier J, Les légendes épiques, Paris 1908, 2.170, 189; 2nd edn 1917, p 184 (hagiographical tradition).

Körner K, Über die Ortsangaben in Amis et Amiles, ZfFSL 33.195 (geographical relations to epic traditions).

Potter M A, Ami et Amile, PMLA 23.471.

Evans J G, Kymdeithas Amlyn ac Amic, Llanbedrog 1909 (Welsh version a direct transl from Latin).

Konrad von Würzburg, Englehart und Engletrue, ed P Gereke, Altdeut Text Bibl 17, Halle 1912.

Huet G, Ami et Amile, Les origines de la légende, Moyen âge, 30.162.

Frenken G, Wunder und Taten der Heiligen, München 1925, p 139 (legend originated ca AD 773).

Krappe A H, The Science of Folklore, London 1930, p 124 (origin from a pair of Celtic Dioskouroi).

Ogle M B and D M Schullian, edd, Rudolphi Tortarii carmina, Papers and Monographs of the American Acad in Rome, Rome 1933, 8.260, Epistula 3, line 123 (crit E Faral, Revue critique d'histoire et de litérature ns 100.450 [source is a lost chanson de geste]).

Schlauch M, Romance in Iceland, N Y and London 1933, p 179 (bibl).

Ruggieri R M, Il processo di Gano nella Chansòn di Roland, Firenza 1936.

Bar F, Les épitres latines de Raoul le Tourtier (1065?–1114?) : études des sources: la légende d'Ami et d'Amile, Paris 1937, pp 58, 99; le Mabinogi de Pwyll, prince de Dyvet et la légende d'Ami et Amile, Rom 68.168.

Wilson R M, Early ME Literature, London 1939; 2nd edn 1951, p 74 (story attached to Charlemagne).

Woledge B, Ami et Amile: les versions en prose française, Rom 65.433.

Remy P, La lèpre thème littéraire au moyen-âge, Moyen âge 52.195, 214, 227 (sources oriental and Biblical).

Asher J A, Amis et Amilies, An Exploratory Survey, Auckland Univ College Modern Language 1s, Auckland 1952 (crit F White-head, MÆ 24.120 (gives author as Ashton, sic).

Pasquali C, Origini italiane della legenda di A e A, Cultura neolatina, 13.218 (crit B Woledge, YWMLS 17.50).

Relations with Folktale. Thompson Mot Ind, F 577.1, (friends identical in appearance); H 121 (identification by cup); H 217 (decision by single combat); H 218 (judicial combat); K 3 (substitute in contest); M 253 (friends in life and death); P 314 (combat of disguised friends); S 268 (child sacrificed to provide blood for friend); T 351 (sword of chastity).

Kölbing, edn, p cvi; PBBeitr 4.306.

Flach J, Le compannage dans les chansons de geste, Études romanes dédiées à Gaston Paris, Paris 1891, p 141, rptd in Origines de l'ancienne France, Paris 1893, 2.427.

Jacobs J, Introduction to OF Romances, p xv, ed Morris, 1896, see Morris above under *Modernizations, Translations*.

Panzer F, Hilde-Gudrun, Halle 1901, p 274 (Turkish parallel).

Harris J R, The Dioscuri in the Christian Legends, London 1903, p 21; Cult of the Heavenly Twins, Cambridge 1906, p 58 (use of similar names).

Gerould G H, The Grateful Dead, Folklore Soc 60, London 1908, pp 39, 136 (relation to Isumbras, Amadas); Social and Historical Reminiscences in the ME Athelston, EStn 36.194, 196.

Heller B, L'épée, symbole et gardienne de chasteté, Rom 36.36; 37.162.

Potter M A, Ami et Amilie, PMLA 23.471 (argues that legend was a märchen, not basically feudal or Christian).

Bolte J and G Polívka, Anmerkungen zu der Kinder- und Hausmärchen der Brüder Grimm, Leipzig and Berlin 1913, 1.56, 528 (nos 60, 85).

Barry P, Bells Ringing Without Hands, MLN 30.29.

Krappe A H, The Legend of Amicus and Amelius, MLR 18.152, 154, 163 (crit P G Thomas, YWES 4.48); The Legends of Amicus and Amelius and of King Horn, Leuvensche Bijdragen 16.14; The Science of Folklore, pp 101, 217 (cure of leprosy in human blood bath).

Aarne-Thompson, Type 516.

Leach, edn, pp xxxiv, xliii, xlv n 8 (bibl on motif of the separating sword), lxxxviii.

Caldwell J R, Eger and Grime, Cambridge, Mass 1933, HSCL 9.70 (theme of sworn brotherhood), 9.85.

Bauerfeld W, Die Sage von Amis and Amiles,

ein Beitrag zur me Freundschaftssage, Haale/Saale 1941, pp 55, 106.

Cross F577.1; H218; K3; T351.

Relations with the Ballad. Child F J, The English and Scottish Popular Ballads, Boston 1882–98, 2.127, 511a; 5.292b (Lord Ingram and Chiel Wyat; no 66, sword of chastity).

Relations with Chaucer. Loomis L H, Sir Thopas, Bryan-Dempster, pp 486, 494; no 3 (minstrel comments), p 497; no 29 (hero's pastimes—riding), p 511; no 38 (hero's pastimes—sleeping in forest), p 514; no 69 (hero's praise), p 545; The Auchinleck MS and a London Bookshop, PMLA 57.595 (Amis and Amiloun borrows from Guy of Warwick).

Other Literary Relations. Koch J, Über Jourdains de Blaivies, Königsberg 1875 (attempt to identify Amis and Amiloun with Duke William IV of Aquitaine and Count William of Angoulême).

Kaluza M, Libeaus Desconus, AEB 5.lxxxxviii (Octavian, Ipomadon).

McKnight G H, King Horn, EETS 14.140, notes to lines 315, 319, 420, and passim.

Panzer, Hilde-Gudrun, p 266 (Apollonius).

Mead W E, Squyr of Lowe Degre, Boston and N Y etc 1904, pp xxvii, xxix (Apollonius, Guy of Warwick, King Horn, Squyr of Lowe Degre, Torrent of Portyngale, William of Palerne).

Deutschbein M, Studien zur Sagengeschichte Englands, 1 Teil, Du Wikingersage, Göthen 1906, p 31 (Apollonius).

Ayres H M, The Faerie Queene and Amis and Amiloun, MLN 23.177.

Schoepperle G, Tristan and Isolt, London and Frankfurt a Main 1913, Index (separating sword).

Trounce, MÆ 1.94 (Amis and Amiloun and King of Tars); Athelston, A ME Romance, TPSL, London 1933, 11.6 (crit G H Gerould, MÆ 3.59), rvsd, reissued; Athelston, EETS 224.4, 11, 42 (parallels in plot and theme), 51 (Amis and Amiloun and Guy of Warwick).

Caldwell, Eger and Grime, HSCL 9.71.

Dickins B, The Owl and the Nightingale and the Saint William Window in York Minster, Leeds SE 5.68 (judicial combat).

Smithers, Notes on ME Texts, LMS 1.208; Kyng Alisaunder, EETS 237.84, 150, 154.

Casson L F, Sir Degrevant, EETS 221.lxiii (secret love), lxiv (steward).

Mills L J, One Soul in Bodies Twain, Bloomington Ind 1937, p 39.

Remy, La lèpre, Moyen âge 52.195, 214, 227.

Baugh A C, Improvisation in the ME Romances, PAPS 103.420.

Thomas P G, English Literature before Chaucer, London 1924, p 117.

Everett D, A Characterization of the English Medieval Romances, E&S 15.98, rptd in Essays on ME Literature, ed P Kean, Oxford 1955, p 9.

Wilson R M, Early ME Literature, London 1939; 2nd edn 1951, pp 73, 74.

Schlauch M, English Medieval Literature and Its Social Foundations, Warsaw 1956, p 190.

Ward, 1.202, 674, 677; Gröber, 2^1.458, 549, 570, 993, 1088; Ten Brink, 1.250; Brandl, § 52; HLF, 22.288; Schofield, p 309; CHEL, 1.350; Paris Litt franç, § 27; Körting, § 115; Baugh LHE, pp 141, 193; Kane, pp 15, 28, 30.

Gautier L, Les épopées françaises, 2nd edn, Paris 1878–97, 2.308; 5.52, 212.

Chauvin V, Bibliographie des ouvrages arabes, Liège 1892–1922, 8.194.

Frenken G, Wunder und Taten der Heiligen, ed F Vonderleyen, München 1925, p 226.

Hibbard Med Rom, pp 65, 71, new edn 1960, p 347; Renwick-Orton, p 387; CBEL, 1.154(b), 5.116(b); Bossuat MBLF, nos 179–93, 4015, 6051–52; Holmes CBFL, nos 801–19, cf nos 820–23.

[113] SIR AMADACE.

MSS. 1, Advocates 19.3.1 (olim Jac V.7.27), ff 68^a–84^a (1475–1500); 2, Ireland Blackburn, Hale Hall, Liverpool, ff 16^a–34^b (1450–60) (photograph in Univ of Leeds Libr).

Brown-Robbins, no *62; MED, p 25.

Dickins B, The Date of the Ireland Manuscript, Leeds SE 2.62.

Editions. Weber MR, 3.243 (MS Advocates 19.3.1); see 1.x.

Robson J, Three Early English Metrical Romances, Camden Soc 18, London 1842, p 27 (Ireland Blackburn MS).

Stephens G, Ghost Thanks, or the Grateful Unburied, A Mythic Tale in Its Oldest European Form, Sir Amadace, Cheapinghaven [Copenhagen] 1860 (Both text: from Weber, from Robson).

Smith M N, An Edition of the Ireland and Edinburgh Texts of Sir Amadace, Leeds Univ Libr, unpubld, Leeds SE 3.64.

Modernization. Rickert RofFr, p 49.

Weston J L, Chief ME Poets, Boston and N Y etc 1914; new edn, London 1922, p 216.

Textual Matters. Kölbing E, Kleine Beiträge zur Erklärung u Textkritik englischer Dichter, EStn 3.101 (lines 614, 428, Weber edn).

Trounce A McI, Chaucer's Imperative with as, MÆ 2.68 ("os lette," line 386, Chaucer and author of Amadace got the construction from the same source).

Language, Dialect. Hulbert J R, The West Midland of the Romances, MP 19.3.

Serjeantson M S, The Dialects of the West Midlands in ME, RES 3.328 (Ireland Blackburn MS from South Lancashire); A History of Foreign Words in English, New York 1936, p 97 (Northwest Midlands).

Oakden J P, Alliterative Poetry in ME; The Dialect and Metrical Survey, Manchester 1930, p 114 (Carlisle).

Trounce A McI, The English Tail-Rhyme Romances, MÆ 2.190; see also MÆ 2.68.

Dickins B, The Date of the Ireland MS, Leeds SE 2.62 (crit D Everett, YWES 14.124).

Moore S, S B Meech, H Whitehall, ME Dialect Characteristics and Dialect Boundaries, in Essays and Studies in Engl and Comp Lit, Univ of Michigan, 13.53.

Dunlap A R, The Vocabulary of the ME Romances in Tail-Rhyme Stanza, Delaware Notes 14s, passim.

Versification. Luick K, Zur me Verslehre, Angl 38.286, 290, 299, 337.

Date. Wyld H C, Short History of English, 3rd edn rvsd, N Y 1927, p 101 (Ireland Blackburn MS, ca 1400–13).

Serjeantson, RES 3.328 (accepts Wyld's date).

Hibbard Med Rom, pp 73, 77 (Ireland Blackburn MS, 15 cent; but combination of themes dates from 13 and 14 cent).

Dickins, Leeds SE 2.64 (Ireland Blackburn MS cannot be dated before 1450).

Bennett OHEL, 2.165 (scribe of Advocates 19.3.1).

Sources and Analogues. Hippeau C, Amadas et Idoine, Paris 1863, introd p xv (possible source for opening lines of Sir Amadace).

Hippe M, Untersuchungen zur me Romanze von Sir Amadas, Arch 81.141 (crit G P[aris], Rom 18.197).

Hibbard Med Rom, pp 75, 73 (no French source has been found; story of Amadas et Ydoine is not the source of Sir Amadace, nor the same).

Relations with Folktale. Thompson Mot Ind, E 341, H 972 (grateful dead); L 114.2, Q 42.1, Q 42.1.3 (spendthrift knight-hero); M 241.1 (dividing the winnings: half of the bride demanded).

Cross Mot Ind, E 341.

Stephens G, Notes, Corpse Arrest, Folklore Record 3, Publications of the Folklore Soc, London 1879, p 199 (crit F Liebrecht, EStn 4.134).

Köhler R, Die dankbaren Toten und der gute Gerhard, Kleinere Schriften zur Märchenforschung, ed J Bolte, Weimar 1898, 1.5, 21 (zu dem Märchen von dem dankbaren Toten).

Gerould G H, The Grateful Dead, the History of a Folk Story, Folklore Soc 60, London 1907, pp 33, 37, 153, 162, and passim; Social and Historical Reminiscences in the ME Athelston, EStn 36.200.

Kittredge G L, A Study of Gawain and the Green Knight, Cambridge Mass 1916, p 210 (thankful dead man).

Bolte J and G Polívka, Anmerkungen zu den Kinder- und Hausmärchen der Brüder Grimm, Leipzig 1913–31, 3.509, no 217 (der dankbare Tote).

Benary W, Hervis von Metz u die Sage von dankbaren Toten, ZfRP 37.60.

McKnight G H, ME Humorous Tales in Verse, Boston and London 1913, p xiii (spendthrift knight).

Hibbard Med Rom, p 76 (origins in the sacred duty of burial).

Tatlock J S P, Levenoth and the Grateful Dead, MP 22.211.

Wesselski A, Märchen des Mittelalters, Berlin 1925, p 36, no 12, Der Lohn für das Begrabnis, p 200 (notes).

Relations with the Ballad. Child F J, The English and Scottish Popular Ballads, Boston 1882–98, 3.508 (Sir Cawline, no 61; A True Tale of Robin Hood, no 154).

Other Relations, Typical Phrases. Dutz H, Der Dank des Todten in der engl Literatur, Jahresber Staats-Oberrealschule, Troppau 1894, pp 10, 12 (Peele's Old Wives' Tale).

Gerould, Folklore Soc 60.2, 35, 92 (Amis and Amiloun, and Isumbras).

Holthausen F, Sir Amadas und Peele's Old Wives' Tale, Arch 117.177.

Hibbard Med Rom, pp 76 (Amis and Amiloun), 77 notes 6, 7 (Cleges, Sir Gowther).

Weston, Chief ME Poets, p 378.

Fisher F, Narrative Art in Medieval Romance, Cleveland 1938, p 78 (Amadas et Ydoine).

Ker W P, CHEL 1, chap 13, Metrical Romances, p 237; Medieval English Literature, Home Univ Libr, London n d, pp 102, 113, 176.

Thomas P G, English Literature before Chaucer, London 1924, p 117.

Schlauch M, English Medieval Literature and Its Social Foundations, Warsaw 1956, p 190.

Gröber, 2¹.531; Brandl, § 75; HLF, 24.505; Schofield, p 322; Paris Litt franç, § 66; Körting, § 86anm; Baugh LHE, p 194; Kane, p 19.

Hibbard Med Rom, pp 73, 78, new edn 1960, p 347; Renwick-Orton, p 387; CBEL, 1.154(d), 5.116(d).

[114] SIR CLEGES.

See also under Tales.

MSS. 1, Bodl 6922* (Ashmole 61), ff 67^b–73^a (1475–1500); 2, Advocates 19.1.11 (olim Jac V.6.21), ff 71^a–79^b, imp (1450–1500).

Brown-Robbins, no 1890; MED, p 33.

Bliss A J, Sir Orfeo, Oxford 1954, pp xi, xii.

Editions. Weber MR, 1.331 (MS Advocates 19.1.11).

Morley H, Shorter English Poems, London and N Y etc 1876, p 24 (rpts Weber with modernized spellings).

Treichel A, Sir Cleges, Ein me Romanze, EStn 22.374 (both texts) (crit L Frankel, Krit Jahresber, 4².485).

McKnight J H, ME Humorous Tales in Verse, Boston and London 1913, p 38 (MS Bodl 6922* with MS Advocates 19.1.11 used to supply lacunae) (crit K Brunner, EStn 49.286).

French W H and C B Hale, ME Metrical Romances, N Y 1930, p 877 (MS Advocates 19.1.11).

Modernizations. Weston J L, Sir Cleges, Sir Libeaus Desconus (prose), Arthurian Romances Unrepresented in Malory 5, London 1902 (also with imprint N Y 1902), p 3 (crit G Binz, AnglB 15.332).

Thomson C L, Tales of the Middle Ages, London 1905, p 120.

Hadow G E and W H, The Oxford Treasury of English Literature, Oxford 1906, 1.37 (condensed from Weber MR).

Darton F J H, A Wonder Book of Old Romance, N Y 1907; 7th edn 1931, p 67, Sir Cleges and the Cherries.

Krapp G P, Tales of True Knights, N Y 1921, p 3 (retelling abridged).

Language, Dialect. Trounce A McI, The English Tail-Rhyme Romances, MÆ 1.94.

Dunlap A R, The Vocabulary of the ME Tail-Rhyme Stanza, Delaware Notes 14s, passim.

Sources and Analogues. Weston, Sir Cleges, p 71n.

McKnight, edn, p lxxiv (oral dissemination; a minstrel story; the two texts come from a common source).

Relations with Folktales. Thompson Mot Ind, D 2145.2.2, F 971.5 (fruit magically grows in winter); H 1023.3 (task: bringing berries in winter); K 187 (strokes shared); L 114.2, Q 42.1, Q 42.1.3 (spendthrift knight); cf

E 341.1, H 972 (tasks accomplished with help of grateful dead).

Cross Mot Ind, Q 42.1.3 (excessive hospitality causes chieftain to become poor; cf E 341).

Clouston W, Popular Tales and Fiction, N Y 1887, p 467.

Bédier J, Les fabliaux, Paris 1895, p 220 (strokes shared).

Weston, Sir Cleges, p 72n.

McKnight, edn, pp lxiii (spendthrift knight), lxv (miracle of ripe fruit), lxix (strokes shared).

Hibbard Med Rom, p 79n2 (impossible tasks), p 80 n 1 (strokes shared).

Frenken G, Wunder und Taten der Heiligen, München 1925, pp 119, 219n.

Reinhard J R, Strokes Shared, JAF 36.380.

MacCulloch J A, Medieval Faith and Fable, London 1932, pp 47, 310n8 (blossoming branches, relation to Tannhauser myth).

Other Relations, Typical Phrases. Robson J, Sir Amadace, Camden Soc 18, London 1842, p xxvi.

Leach H G, Angevin Britain and Scandinavia, Cambridge Mass 1921, p 228.

Casson L F, Sir Degrevant, EETS 221.145 (note to line 1593).

Loomis C G, Sir Cleges and Unseasonable Growth, MLN 53.591 (parallels to miracles of Irish saints).

Speirs J, Medieval English Poetry, London 1957, p 331n (First Towneley Shepherds' Play).

Brandl, § 114; Schofield, p 322 (summary); J W H Atkins, CHEL, 1.350; Körting, § 157n2; Bennett OHEL, 2.164; Baugh LHE, p 194; Kane, p 19.

Schlauch M, English Medieval Literature and Its Social Foundations, Warsaw 1956, p 190.

Hibbard Med Rom, pp 79, 80, new edn 1960, p 347; Tucker-Benham, p 256; Renwick-Orton p 388; CBEL, 1.158(p), 5.116(p); Bennett OHEL, 2.315.

[115] ROBERD OF CISYLE.

MSS. 1, Bodl 3938, English Poetry A.1 (Vernon), ff 300^a (col 3)–301^a (col 3) (ca 1390); 2, Trinity Oxf D. 57, ff 165^a–167^a (ca 1375); 3, Camb Univ Ff.2.38 (olim More 690), ff 254^a–257^b (1475–1500); 4, Camb Univ Ii.4.9, ff 87^b–93^b (ca 1450); 5, Caius Camb 174, pp 456–468 (1475–1500); 6, BM Harley 525, ff 35^a–43^b (1450–75); 7, BM Harley 1701 (olim Harley Plutarch 1701), ff 92–95 (1425–50); 8, BM Addit 22283 (Simeon), ff 90^b (col 3)–91^b (col 2) (ca 1400); 9, BM Addit 34801, f 2, one leaf, early 15 cent;

10, Trinity Dublin 432 B, ff 60^a–61^b (1458–61).

Brown-Robbins, no 2780; MED, p 71.

Halliwell [-Phillipps] J O, Thornton Romances, Camden Soc 30, London 1844, p xlv (Camb Ff.2.38); Some Account of the Vernon Manuscript, London 1848.

Ward, 1.763, 765.

Hornstein L H, King Robert of Sicily: A New Manuscript, PMLA 78.453.

Editions. Utterson E V, Kyng Roberd of Cysylle, London 1839, privately printed; anr edn, London, Beldornie Press 1839.

Halliwell [-Phillipps] J O, Nugae poeticae, London 1844, pp 49, 71 (Camb Univ Ff. 2.38).

Hazlitt Rem, 1.264 (Camb Univ Ff.2.38, Utterson, Halliwell [-Phillipps]).

Horstmann C, Sammlung ae Legenden, Heilbronn 1878, p 209 (Vernon MS and variants in footnotes); Nachträge zu den Legenden, Archiv 62.416, 417 (Camb Univ Ii.4.9), p 421 (Caius Camb 174), p 426 (Camb Univ Ff.2.38).

Nuck R, Roberd of Cisyle, Berlin 1887, p 38 (critical edn).

French W H and C B Hale, ME Metrical Romances, N Y 1930, p 933 (Vernon MS).

Brotanek R, Mittelenglische Dichtungen aus der Handschrift 432 des Trinity College in Dublin, Halle 1940, p 36 (crit F Holthausen, AnglB 51.97; W Horn, Archiv 177.120; H Marcus, DLz 61.668; F Schubel, EStn 75.88; A A Prins, ESts 25.81).

Ford B, The Age of Chaucer, London 1954, p 289, ("normalized" text, lines 318, 361–64 omitted, opening stanza modernized).

Hornstein L H, King Robert of Sicily: A New Manuscript, PMLA 78.453.

Selections. Warton T, History of Poetry, London 1840, 1.183 (MS Harley 525); rvsd W C Hazlitt, London 1871, 2.174 (MS Vernon).

Cook A S, Literary ME Reader, Boston and N Y etc 1915, p 167 (from Horstmann, Sammlung ae Legenden).

Abstract. Ellis, p 474 (MS Harley 1701); rptd C Swan, Gesta Romanorum, rvsd by W Hooper, London 1912, p 374; rptd N Y 1959.

Modernization. Hunt L, A Jar of Honey from Mount Hybla, London 1848, p 68.

Longfellow H W, King Robert of Sicily (The Sicilian's Tale) in Tales of a Wayside Inn, Boston 1863, p 55.

McCarthy J, The Proud Prince, N Y 1903, p 99 (adaptation, novelized).

Darton F J H, A Wonder Book of Old Romance, London 1907; 7th edn 1931, p 56.

Textual Matters. Kölbing E, Kleine Beiträge zur Erklärung me Dichter, EStn 13.136.

Horstmann C, Roberd of Cisyle, Archiv 62.430 (on lines 341–42).

Date. Horstmann C, Canticum de creatione, Angl 1.287 (dates MS Trinity Oxf D. 57, at 1375).

Hibbard Med Rom, pp 60, 61 (legends assimilated by middle 13 C and written down 14 C).

Hornstein L H, King Robert of Sicily: Analogues and Origins, PMLA 79.13.

Language, Dialect. Nuck, edn, p 30 (southern part of East Midland).

Allen H E, Manuscripts of the Ancren Riwle, TLS Feb 8 1936, p 116.

Serjeantson M, The Index of the Vernon MS, MLR 32.246, no 342 (South Shropshire, South Staffordshire area).

Holthausen, AnglB 51.97.

Authorship. Westra C M, A Talkyng of the Loue of God, 'S-Gravenhage 1950, p xv (MS Vernon not written by same scribe as BM 22283 [MS Simeon]).

Sources and Analogues. Relations with the Folktale. Thompson Mot Ind, B 29.9 (man-ape); H 797.1 (What does God do? He brings low the proud and exalts the lowly); L 400 (pride brought low); L 411 (proud king displaced by angel); P 672.2 (cutting off hair as insult); Q 330, Q 331 (pride punished); Q 523.3 (penance: eating food offered to dogs).

Hazlitt Rem, 1.265 (Robert the Devil).

Jean de Condé, Li dis dou Magnificat, Dits et contes de Baudouin de Condé et son fils, ed A Scheler, Bruxelles 1866, 2.355, 455n.

Varnhagen H, Ein indisches Märchen auf seiner Wanderung durch die asiatischen und europäischen Litteraturen, Berlin 1882, pp 16, 52, 65 (crit F Liebrecht, EStn 6.259; K Nyrop, Zur Volkskunde, LfGRP 4.146); Longfellow's Tales of a Wayside Inn und ihre Quellen nebst Nachweisen und Untersuchungen über die vom Dichter bearbeiten Stoffe, Berlin 1884, p 16 (crit F Liebrecht, EStn 8.328; J Koch, Angl 7, Anz p 143).

Child F J, The English and Scottish Popular Ballads, Boston and New York 1882–98, 1.405, 2.506, no 45.

Breul K, Sir Gowther, Oppeln 1886, pp x, 132.

Lévi J, L'orgueil et présomption de Salomon, Revue des études juives, 1888, 17.58 (Jerusalem Talmud story of Solomon points to Jewish origin, not Indian).

Chauvin V C, Bibliographie des ouvrages arabes ou relatifs aux Arabes, Liège 1892–1922, pt 2, p 161, no 51.

Köhler R, Der nackte König, Kleinere Schriften 2, Berlin 1900, p 208 (story of Solomon from the Babylonian Talmud).

Kittredge G R, Arthur and Gorlagon, HSNPL, Cambridge Mass 1903, 8.251n2, at p 252.

Jacob G, Xoros Kardash, Berlin 1906, p 104 (Turkish analogue).

Kümmell K, Drei italienische Prosalegenden, Halle a Salle 1906, pp 5, 20, 46 (König im Bade).

Herbert, 3.447.

Bolte J and G Polívka, Anmerkungen zu den Kinder- und Hausmärchen der Brüder Grimm, Leipzig 1913–30, 3.218n3.

Morin P, Les sources de l'oeuvre de Henry Wadsworth Longfellow, Paris 1913, pp 199, 204, 206.

Gerould G H, Saints Legends, Boston and N Y 1916, pp 253, 369n.

Günter H, Buddha in der abendländischen Legende, Leipzig 1922, p 158.

Anderson W, Kaiser und Abt, FFC 42, Helsinki 1923, [O] pp 207, 211, 281.

Hibbard Med Rom, pp 58, 62n8, 55n8 (Valentin und Namelos).

Wesselski A, Märchen des Mittelalters, Berlin 1925, Das Magnificat, p 137, no 49, p 237 notes.

Arne A, The Types of the Folktale: A Classification and Bibliography, trans and ed S Thompson, FFC, no 74 (Helsinki 1928), Type 757 (the King's haughtiness punished), Type 836 (pride is punished), and cross references.

Krappe A H, Solomon and Ashmodai, AJP 54.260.

Kapp R, Heilige und Heiligenlegenden im Eng, Halle 1934, 1.247.

Brotanek, edn, pp 39 (other versions), 43 (Robert the Devil, Sir Isumbras).

Noy [Neuman] D, Motif-Index to the Talmudic-Midrashic Literature, Microfilm Service, Ann Arbor, Michigan 1954, publ no 8792.

Hornstein L H, King Robert of Sicily: Analogues and Origins, PMLA 79.13.

Relations with the Gesta Romanorum. Oesterley H, ed, Gesta Romanorum, Berlin 1872, p 360, no 29, trans by C Swan, rvsd W Hooper, London 1912, p 100, no 59 and p 374n.

Dick W, Die Gesta Romanorum nach der Innsbrucher Handschrift, EBEP, 1890, 7.100, 148.

Herbert, 3.202, 214 (Anglo-Latin Gesta Romanorum, no 29).

Madden F, OE Version of the Gesta Romanorum, Roxb 55, London 1838, no 29.

Herrtage S J H, Early English Versions of the Gesta Romanorum, EETSES 33.75, no 23, p 462 and note (Jovinianus).

Dramatic Versions. Collier J P, History of English Dramatic Poetry, London 1831, 1.113, 2.128, 2.415.

Ward Hist, London 1875, 1.93; London 1899, 1.170.

Hazlitt Rem, 1.270.

Leach A F, An English Miscellany Presented to Dr. Furnivall 1901, p 223.

Chambers E K, The Medieval Stage, Oxf 1903, 2.151, 356, 378; OHEL, 2.65 (at Lincoln 1453, at Chester in days of Henry VII, and in 1529).

Schelling F E, Elizabethan Drama 1558–1642, Boston and N Y 1908, 1.50, 71, 406; 2.398.

Other Problems. Janson H W, Apes and Ape Lore in the Middle Ages and Renaissance, Studies of the Warburg Institute, London 1952, 200, 211, 231n59.

Smalley B, The Study of the Bible in the Middle Ages, Oxford 1952, p 350.

Thomas P G, English Literature before Chaucer, London 1924, p 117.

Schlauch M, English Medieval Literature and Its Social Foundations, Warsaw 1956, p 190.

Gröber, 2¹.843; Brandl, § 40; Ward, 1.763; Schofield, p 314; Kane, p 19 (crit A I Doyle, RES ns 4.70).

Herbert, 3.202, 214, 447; Hibbard Med Rom, pp 60, 63, new edn 1960, p 350; Renwick-Orton, p 388; CBEL, 1.157(j), 5.116(j).

INDEX

A bold-face number indicates the main reference in the Commentary: a number preceded by B indicates the reference in the Bibliography. Both English and Romance titles are indexed under the first word following an article. Indexed are all literary works and their authors, names of early printers, and main subject-divisions. No attempt has been made to index the names of characters and places in the literary works nor the names of scholars.